DESTROYER

D1463874

Praise for the hardback edition

DESTROYER

An anthology of first-hand accounts of
the war at sea
1939-1945

Edited by
Ian Hawkins

Foreword by
Len Deighton

Introduction by
Rear Admiral John Hervey, CB, OBE, RN, Retd.

CONWAY

ABOUT THE ANTHOLOGIST

Ian Hawkins became interested in the history of the Second World War as a boy growing up in East Anglia; his father, a Royal Navy destroyer commander, and an uncle, a Royal Air Force squadron leader, were both killed in action. A former civil engineer, he sustained severe head injuries in an attack in Saudi Arabia in 1976 and was left paralysed down one side of his body. He is now confined to a wheelchair as a result of his paralysis. This is his fifth book.

First published in Great Britain in 2003 by
Conway
A division of the Anova Books Company Limited
10 Southcombe Street, London W14 0RA

This paperback edition first published in Great Britain in 2005
Reprinted 2006, 2007

ISBN 10: 1 84486 008 6
ISBN 13: 9781 844 860081

Original design and layout by Steve Dent
Edited by Stuart Robertson
Printed by CPD, Ebbw Vale, Wales

To receive regular email updates on forthcoming Conway titles, email conway@anovabooks.com with Conway Update in the subject field.

Contents

Contents

1941

1942

Contents

Contents

Foreword

It is unnecessary to introduce the work of Ian Hawkins to those readers interested in Second World War aviation. Ian has long had an international reputation as an historian with extensive knowledge of the Eighth US Army Air Force and the strategic bombing of the European continent. The reason so many other historians turn to Ian for guidance is that he has known many of the veterans who flew these astounding raids and known them on a personal basis. Together with a few other English writers he has gained a reputation for fairness and accuracy. How else would he have been able to write such a fine book as the one about the US raid on Munster? In it his skilful technique incorporated the memories of the people under attack with those of the airmen in the planes above.

Now, just as we all thought we knew about Ian and his lifetime of historical research, he has surprised us all with this superb book about the grim and relentless destroyer war at sea. And it's a rewarding surprise.

It is typical of him that he is able to tackle this subject, without gimmicks or twisted ideas, and make it so thought-provoking. This account of the men who took their small ships into the deepest and cruellest waters is clearly the result of years of research and hard work. These crews endured the most terrible conditions imaginable even when not facing enemy fire. Not many fighting men – even those in tanks, the trenches or the planes – envied those for whom Ian Hawkins has produced this memorable book. I say memorable because I think I shall never forget some of the stories in this work. Here is a book that matches and complements that bestseller of the postwar years, *The Cruel Sea*.

Surely no one will read this book without being deeply moved and inspired by the ungrudging sacrifice and all-pervading cheerfulness of its protagonists. Some were professional sailors, some were peacetime naval men but most of them were civilians who never truly adapted to a cold, wet, cramped life in a bouncing tin can but did their duty nevertheless. If you want to know what that generation of matchless heroes were like, Ian's book will show you.

Len Deighton

Preface

From the earliest days of my life my family has been strongly attached to another family, that of the Royal Navy. My father, while serving on the 'B' class destroyer HMS *Boadicea*, was killed in action during the invasion of Normandy in June 1944, and an uncle, on the cruiser HMS *Aurora*, fortunately survived the Second World War.

I was 11 years old in 1950 when I joined my elder brother John at the Royal Hospital School, Holbrook, Suffolk, known locally as 'The Naval School', which until 1933 had been located for over two centuries at the Royal Naval establishment, Greenwich, London. A boarding school with impressive buildings to accommodate 660 pupils, aged between 11 and 18, all sons and grandsons of Royal Navy/Royal Marines personnel, it became co-educational in 1992, thereby allowing both my daughter and son admittance. The fact that the RHS maintains its proud traditions of RN uniform, seamanship, strict discipline, marching, Sunday parade, School Band, Guard of Honour, etc., in addition to providing a sound academic education and equally good sporting facilities, probably explains why there is a lengthening waiting list for entry to the school.

Looking back, it was indeed a privilege to attend the RHS although the intial year or so was occasionally tough and difficult, with the inevitable homesickness and strict naval discipline. But it was exactly the same for every 'New-Jack'. Firm and lasting friendships were formed during those six years.

In 1968, our family became aware of a recently-formed association for the 1939-1945 crews of three destroyers, HM Ships *Beagle*, *Boadicea* and *Bulldog*. We (my mother, sister, two brothers and I) immediately applied to the Honorary Secretary, the late Michael Back, for Associate Membership, were accepted and made most welcome. So began many subsequent years of enjoyable and occasionally very moving meetings; annual reunions in London on board HMS *President*; at HMS *Nelson*, HM Naval Base Portsmouth; and annual memorial services each June at the Royal Naval War Memorial overlooking the Historic Naval Dockyard, Chatham. The association was finally terminated after its 33rd annual reunion in May 2000 at HMS *Nelson*.

In 1972, a graphic aerial photograph of the 1944-built destroyer HMS *Cavalier* winning the annual North Sea Race to become the fastest ship in the British Fleet appeared in the national press and caught my attention. It was several years later that I became aware of the existence of the HMS *Cavalier* Association via the then Committee's Chairman, Mr Sidney Anning. Britain's last Second World War destroyer had been decommissioned and was then at Newcastle. As urgent restoration work was needed, the Association desperately searched for a new and permanent home. The destroyer was in danger of being sold to a Malaysian theme park, or scrapped.

An ultimately successful nationwide campaign to 'Save Our Ship' was launched by *Cavalier*'s committee, supported by various naval associations and countless individuals, including an ex-Minister of the Crown who, in 1997, wrote to the committee: 'The neglect of our Maritime Heritage is scandalous – and WWII in particular.'

Bearing in mind the distressing hardships faced almost daily by those comparatively small ships, and the 30,000 young Royal Naval and Commonwealth men who went down with their 153 destroyers during the Second World War, all royalties accruing from the sale of the hardback edition of this book of wartime experiences will be donated towards the renovation and ongoing maintenance of the unique HMS *Cavalier* at Chatham's Historic Dockyard.

Ian Hawkins

Editorial Note: The first-hand experiences of the destroyer men are the basis of the book, and background information is included only where it is indispensable to the stories being recounted. Thus, previously published sources are used as sparingly as possible, and primary accounts from veterans remain the essence of this book.

The typescript originals of the first-hand accounts which appear in this book have been transcribed literally, although British spelling has been standardized, and words supplied by the anthologist for clarity of meaning appear within square brackets. Misspelled or inconsistently spelled names, geographical place names, dates, points of the compass, ranks, colloquialistic terms and abbreviations have also been standardized for the sake of consistency and ease of reference. American English has been left in its original form.

Where necessary, footnotes explain all code names and technical abbreviations, such as those of operations and technical equipment, when first mentioned. Weapons, aircraft, devices, etc., are also explained in footnotes when first referred to unless already explained in the text of the account.

Acknowledgements

In addition to the veterans and correspondents whose names appear in the text of this book and who have kindly contributed their wartime memories, there are many other people who have also played a major role in helping to ensure the finished product is as interesting and informative to the reader as possible. I am deeply grateful for their assistance and encouragement over the past several years:

The late Michael Back, Honorary Secretary of HM Ships *Beagle*, *Boadicea* and *Bulldog* 1939-1945 Crews' Association since its founding in 1968; Julie Denyer, RN Research Department, Gosport Library, Hampshire; Elizabeth Dracoulis and Mary Pollard, Research Centre, Australian War Memorial, Canberra, Australia; Allison Duffield, Department of Printed Books, and David Parry, Department of Photographic Archives, Imperial War Museum, London; staff at the Library & Archives, National Maritime Museum, Greenwich, London; Paul McCue, Assistant Director of Leisure and Amenity Services, Wandsworth Borough Council, London; Lieutenant Colonel Angus Farrie, Retd., Regimental HQ, The Highlanders, Cameron Barracks, Inverness; Lieutenant Colonel Alastair Rose of Earlsmiln, Retd., 51st Highland Division, Army Headquarters, Edinburgh; Douglas Radcliffe MBE, Secretary, RAF Bomber Command Association, RAF Museum, London; and Norman Feltwell for producing the outstanding map for this book.

The following veterans and individuals also provided much relevant information and assistance: Richard Hallett and Don Loveridge, HMS *Beagle*; Albert Halls, HMS *Boreas*; Merlyn Noble, HMS *Boadicea*; Denys G. P. Strike, HMS *Brilliant*; Charles Price, HMS *Walker*; J. G. Greenhough, HMS *Ambuscade*; W. H. 'Dilly' Thomas, HMS *Lapwing*; Sidney Anning and David Thompson, HMS *Cavalier*; Michael Keir of Friends of HMS *Cavalier* Trust, and Stephen Dyer of the HMS *Cavalier* (Chatham) Trust Ltd.; Mrs Corinne Abel, Captain Brent Abel, USN, Ret'd, Mrs Eleanor Kahn, the late E. J. Kahn, Jr.; Jack Adams, Ed Davidson, Fred Kennie, Tommy Loftin and Captain R. J. 'Dick' Schlaff, USN, Ret'd, the late Jack Bozung and the late Jeffrey Ethell in the United States; the late Arno

Abendroth and Hans Hoehler in Germany; Gerald Ayres, Neville Edwards, Trevor Lewing, Andrew Pope and Peter Thompson of the RHS Association; Mike Bailey, Vivian Bennett, Larry Buckeridge, Bob Collis, Ray Crampin, Christopher Elliott, John Fleming, Peter Gipson, George Hall, Sidney Harvey, John Hawkins, Tom Heron, Graham Hunt, Mrs Noel Kent, Guy Miller, Fred Morgan, Mrs Lou Noble, John Randall, Jr., David Ruffley MP, Damian Green MP, Gerald Kaufman MP, Peter Sadler and Bill Stonestreet. My very grateful thanks also go to Len Deighton and to Rear Admiral John Hervey, CB, OBE, RN, Retd., for their valuable, experienced advice, and to John Lee and Stuart Robertson of Conway Maritime Press, for their helpful guidance along the way to publication.

Last, but by no means least, my wife Mary, daughter Alice, and son James for their constant help and support.

Ian Hawkins

Introduction

Rear Admiral John B. Hervey, CB, OBE, RN, Retd.

President of the HMS *Cavalier* Association

On 17 February 1998, the House of Commons Culture, Media and Sport Select Committee, under the chairmanship of Gerald Kaufman MP, took time out from their busy schedule to conduct an Inquiry into the future of one rather ancient Royal Navy destroyer, HMS *Cavalier*, which, it was feared, was about to be exported to Malaysia – or scrapped.

The Kaufman Committee took this step because, as they put it in their report, *Cavalier* was not only the last Second World War Royal Navy destroyer but also the last remaining vessel from the category of Minor Warship/Escort Vessel from that vital period in our national history. And they thought, rightly, that it would be regrettable if future generations were to be deprived forever of the opportunity to learn, through first-hand experience, about conditions on board such ships.

During the taking of oral evidence from those of us who had campaigned to save *Cavalier*, much time had to be spent shooting down the suggestion that we did not really need another ship from the 1939-1945 war era, when we already had HMS *Belfast* in the national core collection of historic ships.

Happily, the Select Committee agreed with us that going to war in a comfortable 11,000-ton cruiser – such as *Belfast* – with armoured turrets – could not possibly be equated with manning an open gun mounting in a barely 2,000-ton destroyer on a rough day, indeed on any day. The Kaufman Committee, therefore, very helpfully reported that *Cavalier* 'can and should be saved'. They also used their influence to persuade Ministers and the Heritage Lottery Fund to take a more positive approach to saving the ship. As a result, she is now an important part of the Historic Dockyard at Chatham.

So the story had a happy ending. But it would have been very much easier to convince everyone attending the Inquiry that we had a strong case if they had read the stirring stories in this excellent anthology of the war at sea, so well put together by Ian Hawkins. Because, although his book ranges widely, the backbone is provided by the frank and very personal recollections of, then, young men who went to war in British destroyers.

Throughout their accounts of their war, there is a vivid immediacy not to be found in official histories. They apportion praise and blame – as seen by themselves – and pull no punches. They give one the feeling of being there with the writer, experiencing events at first-hand, be it going through the extremely tough breaking-in process of a Boys' Training Establishment as a young lad, away from home for the first time; or later, in a destroyer, reeling from a dive-bombing attack, praying that something – anything – will prevent the aircraft from returning.

Ian Hawkins has done a wonderful job in getting these vivid stories together. They represent war at sea at its very rawest. But he has also managed to capture the great resilience and sense of humour of the British sailor, who can always be relied upon to find something to laugh at in the grimmest of situations. And any reader who, like me, thinks that Admiral Sir James Somerville was one of the great naval heroes of the Second World War, will enjoy Iain Nethercott's description of his salutation to a somewhat underdressed submarine stoker in the cramped after ends of HMS *Tactician*.

I promise, you will really enjoy this book. I certainly did. It is a marvellous tribute to the young people who served us so well in the war, to let them tell their stories in their own words. And we should never forget that many of their friends and shipmates were barely seventeen years old when they gave their lives for their country. This was the other reason why we wanted to save *Cavalier*. She is a memorial to some very brave, very young people.

John Hervey
Rear Admiral, RN, Retd.

Map of the North Atlantic, showing the principal ports and naval bases of the Battle of the Atlantic. *(Norman Feltwell)*

Starboard view line drawing of 'B' class destroyer (showing 1942 modifications – removal of A and Y guns and after torpedo tubes, addition of 'Hedgehog', extra depth charges, AA guns, radar and electronics). *(Conway Maritime Press)*

1939

PROLOGUE TO 1939

by

Rear Admiral John B. Hervey, RN, Retd.

THE ROYAL NAVY of 1937-1939 is accurately described by Iain Nethercott, who introduces himself well in 'Early Days'. An ex-grammar schoolboy on an accelerated advancement scheme, he had a tough time at HMS *Ganges*, the Boys' Training Establishment. But the prize was a draft from there to an 'H' class destroyer, HMS *Hotspur*, rather than to a battleship or cruiser, which he wanted to avoid.

The pre-war Navy was absolutely obsessed with its biggest ships, with gunnery, and with ceremony. A huge gulf, social and professional, often existed between wardroom and lower deck in such ships, whereas destroyer officers tended to be well in tune with their men, and gave them more responsibility. Nethercott's preference is very understandable. And he made good use of his time in *Hotspur*. Thus, when he joined HMS *Keith*, 'B' class leader, to go to war, he was already an Able Seaman at 18 with two years' sea time behind him, some of it spent under fire whilst his ship intervened to rescue refugees in the Spanish Civil War. Later, he made Leading Seaman at 19 and Petty Officer at 20 – good going. He appears frequently in this book, always with a wry, thought-provoking, sometimes sad, but more often amusing comment.

The period from September 1939 until Germany invaded Norway in April 1940 was called the 'Phoney War', because nothing was happening on land. By contrast, it was all too busy at sea. By the end of 1939 we had already lost three destroyers, HMS *Duchess* in a collision and HMS *Blanche* and *Gipsy* due to magnetic mines. Signalman Noel Thorne, who tells of the loss of *Blanche*, was sent next to HMS *Ivanhoe*, only to be mined again a year later. *Keith* was next astern of *Gipsy* when she was lost, and Nethercott was distressed by not being able to do more for her men visibly trapped below. Many merchant ships were also casualties of magnetic mines, especially in the entrance to the Thames. The overall impact of these mines and reaction to their appearance by Winston Churchill, as First Lord of the Admiralty, are well covered by an extract from *The Battle of the East Coast* by Julian Foynes.

The Navy was also very busy, right from the start of the war, trying to contain the activities of German warships and armed merchant raiders already at sea. These included the pocket battleship *Admiral Graf Spee*, one of whose victims was the SS *Huntsman*. Norman Watson, a retired post-war merchant seaman, gives a good description of events from the time of the *Huntsman's* interception, until the rescue of her crew from the German raider support ship *Altmark* by Captain Vian in HMS *Cossack*. Hans Langsdorf, Captain of *Graf Spee*, comes out of the story with considerable honour.

The remainder of the 1939 section is taken up with accounts by two members of HMS *Boadicea's* wardroom. Derek House was a young Sub-Lieutenant. He tells an amusing reminiscence about travelling to France and back with the War Cabinet embarked, during which Winston Churchill clearly enjoyed his sea time! The letters of Lieutenant Commander Hubert C. Fox, RN, the then-First Lieutenant of *Boadicea*, also mention this trip, but their main value is to describe the rush to settle down a new ship's company, followed by spending a boring 100 of the first 129 days of war at sea, cold and longing for it all to be over.

EARLY DAYS

Iain Nethercott, DSM, Gunner, HMS *Keith*

When I was a young lad at the Royal Naval Shore Training Establishment, HMS *Ganges*, in the village of Shotley, Suffolk, qualifying in navigation, a crusty old Jutland Commander wanted a three-point fix for some remote area off the Pentland Skerries, and nearly failed me because I was about two degrees out on a lighthouse bearing. One of my shipmates, a fellow Scot, failed in anchor work. The antediluvian Lieutenant Commander asked him: "You are a battleship, anchored at Scapa Flow on two bower anchors with a swivel-piece, and a gale blows up from the north. What would you do?"

"Drop the second bower anchor and send the cutter away to lay out a kedge to the north."

The next question: "The gale backs to the east and she starts dragging. What now?"

"Send out the pinnace and lay a second bower cable to the east, surge on it, using the bight of the cable as a spring."

"Now, without any warning whatsoever, the wind blows up to hurricane force from the south and SSE. What now?"

"Bring the kedge aft and send the pinnace away again and lay out a kedge anchor to the SSE to hold her."

That miserable old sod of a failed Lieutenant Commander then asked: "Where are you getting all these kedge anchors from?"

"I'm getting them from the same place as you're getting all these bloody gales..."

He failed, of course. Life was hard as a Second Class boy in the 1930s.

One bewildered lad from Suffolk, an ex-farm worker, was asked during the Lights and Signals test: "What signal does a ship not under control exhibit at night?"

The correct answer was two red lights on the forestay. By day they showed two black balls in the same position. But he was so anxious and confused that he blurted out: "Two black lights on the forestay..."

He failed too.

Mind you, in those days, you weren't allowed at sea as a First Class Boy, on five shillings and threepence per week (5/3d – about 26 new pence per week), on board any man-o'-war. With a grammar school education and on Accelerated Promotion, we were expected to attain 90 per cent before we were actually allowed on board destroyers. The 'other mob' went to battle-ships and cruisers, which were just an extension of boys' messes in HMS[1] *Ganges*.

In late 1937, at the tender age of 16, HMS *Ganges* itself was hell on earth for us Accelerated Promotion lads. In my opinion, it was run mainly by sadists who broke the spirit of many boys with extremely harsh punishments and ensuring blind obedience to all sorts of archaic rules drawn up in Victorian times. Many 14-year-old boys at *Ganges*, with a secondary school education, were accustomed to this, having been dumped on the front steps of an orphanage by desperate young mothers.

At the age of about seven they left the delights of the orphanage and were sent to one of the large number of training hulks, moored in Britain's major

---

[1] His Majesty's Ship (also used for shore establishments, as in this case).

rivers, which were run on a shoe-string by various societies where the boys were brought up on a diet of porridge and prayers.

Those I knew, on the River Thames and the River Clyde, were visited every Sunday afternoon by parsimonious women in Sunday black, clutching prayer books. In those days they were presumably strong on original sin, so if you were born out of wedlock, being illegitimate you were practically doomed from the start.

Consequently, in the journey through life, you were already two strikes behind. However, these lads who had been in sailor suits scrubbing the wooden decks of Nelson's old cast-offs, were eventually drafted into the Royal Navy, their legal guardians gaily signing them up for years of hard labour.

Perhaps the food at *Ganges* was better, but here the punishments were real and they were hard. Doubling around the huge parade ground, humping a heavy .303 Lee-Enfield rifle and wearing a back-pack full of sand was a lot for a 14-year-old to cope with.

I and a few others being ex-grammar schoolboys on the Accelerated Promotion Scheme, were under the watchful eye of a Lieutenant Commander, but we still had to fight our way with the rest of the lads. The greatest thing for us was that all boys drafted to sea were usually sent to bat-tleships and cruisers. The first group of *Ganges* boys on my scheme were sent to the new 'Tribal' class destroyers, while we were sent to the 8th Destroyer Flotilla, the 'H' class destroyers, in the Mediterranean Fleet.

Hooray! I was rated Ordinary Seaman after six months and a full AB[2] at 17-years-old. I made Leading Rate at 19 and Petty Officer at 20.

A song, to the tune of 'A Little Bit of Heaven', describes the food at HMS *Ganges*:

'Shotley Stew'

There's half a pound of bully beef left from the month before
And half a string of sausages found on the canteen floor
One or two old ham bones that were minus of their meat
And two old tins of meat and veg the dog refused to eat
They took it to the galley and they let it boil all day

---

[2] Able Bodied Seaman.

And topped it up with 'Number Nines' to pass the time away
And when they finished boiling, it tasted just like glue
And gave it to Ganges Boys and called it 'Shotley Stew'

The destroyer, HMS *Keith*, was on Neutrality Patrol off Spain in 1939 while I was out there on HMS *Hotspur*, but I didn't see her.

We were pressed into the Spanish Civil War after one of our flotilla, HMS *Hunter*, was torpedoed and damaged by an Italian submarine when on Neutrality Patrol off Cartagena. *Hotspur* used to pick up refugees from Malaga, often under savage attack from German Air Force Stukas (Ju 87 dive-bombers). We picked up many small, shell-shocked children and even pregnant women to take to Gibraltar.

Keith was the original Flotilla Leader of the eight other 'B' class destroyers. They were all ships of the 1928 Programme, launched and completed in 1930-31. They all had a displacement of 1,360 tons except the *Keith*, of 1,400 tons, and were fitted with Brown-Curtis all-geared turbines and Parsons LP Yarrow boilers with 34,000 SHP giving a speed of 35 and a half knots, and a little faster if you sat on the safety valves. HMS *Keith* differed from the others, by providing a little more accommodation space for the Captain (D)'s staff.

Up until the 'G' and 'H' classes of destroyers, all Flotilla Leaders had Scottish names, which, if in the case of *Keith*, coincided with a famous British Admiral, so much the better. Other examples of this were *Wallace*, *Bruce*, *Campbell*, *Douglas*, *Mackay*, *Malcolm*, etc. These older ships had an extra 4-inch or 4.7-inch gun mounted amidships between the two funnels. *Keith* was identical to its sister 'B' ships with four 4.7-inch guns, two 2-pounder pom-poms, five machine guns and fitted with two sets of quadruple torpedo tubes for 21-inch torpedoes.

When I was drafted in July 1939 from HMS *Hotspur*, a crack destroyer from the Mediterranean Fleet, which later fought in the First Battle of Narvik, I was a young AB, 18-years-old with two years of destroyer experience. The Reserve Fleet was mobilising and ships on Reserve in the dockyard were being hastily commissioned as men arrived from 'Civvy Street'.

I first saw HMS *Keith* when she was lying under the coal tips in No. 2 Basin of Chatham Dockyard. Our new coxswain, who was always a bit of a comedian, marched us past the ship to a point further on, near this huge mountain of coal, halted us, told us to equip ourselves with coal shovels and to start digging, saying, "Somewhere under this coal is a destroyer, so get digging. When you find it, it will be all yours and you can keep it!"

The gigantic mountain of steaming coal took up the whole of the southwest corner of No. 2 Basin and actually overflowed out into the water. According to the dockyard mateys, the coal had been ordered and delivered during the First World War when the British Fleet was coal-burning. Some inoffensive Admiralty clerk had mistakenly added an extra zero to their order, thus taking delivery of 100,000 tons of Welsh steaming coal instead of 10,000 tons. Purple faces all round at the Admiralty, but nobody would own up to it so the Supply Department somehow covered it up in their record books, assuming that the Fleet would gradually burn its way through the surplus. Unfortunately for them, the Fleet was converting to oil-burning, so, apart from loading a few tons on the odd trawler and minesweeper, the mountain of coal remained there under the tips.

We were not really amused by the antics of our new coxswain as we'd already had a tiresome day in the barracks. It was about that time when our distraught First Lieutenant arrived to find his lost flock. He'd been riding around the dockyard on an old Admiralty-issue bike for three or four hours, asking various people if they'd seen us. We were only too glad to see him and dutifully followed him, like Moses leading the Children of Israel, as we hauled our handcarts with our kitbags and hammocks to our new floating home.

We eventually 'fell in' in the Drill Shed at Chatham, then marched to No. 2 Basin to inspect what sort of 'gift horse' we'd got. She was filthy, paintwork peeling, her rigging a mass of Irish pennants and her guns covered in heavy grease.

When I eventually got aboard HMS *Keith*, humping my gear down to the forward mess deck, I was so slow that I had to grab the last kit locker in my mess which was next to the cable locker and practically impossible to get at. The only place left for me to sleep was on the wooden cover of the cable engine which permanently leaked steam and was known as 'The Fish & Chip Shop'.

Our decking was covered with greasy bootmarks from dockyard mateys, our mess table looked as though someone had been mixing paint on it and our kit lockers were full of ancient remains from past meals.

However, as this rubbish tip was to be my future home, like most of the other youngsters I cleaned out my locker, unpacked my kitbag and changed into old overalls. Encouraged by our elders, we found buckets and deck-cloths, discovered the caustic soda and soft soap, cadged some hot water from the galley and soon began to make our 'wigwam' more habitable.

After we'd made a big stew of tea, stored our gear in our lockers and piled our hammocks in the nettings, we fell in to be assigned our Watch and Quarter Cards and to find out where we'd drawn in the lottery. I discovered I was the second part of the Port Watch and an Iron Deckman. I was also Relief Quartermaster and No. 2 on the port pom-pom anti-aircraft gun at Action Stations. I'd been a 0.5-inch AA machine gunner on my previous ship.

The next day we were still a few missing, mostly elderly Reservists, who hadn't yet answered the call-up to Chatham Barracks and were probably lying prostrate on the benches at Waterloo Station in a drunken stupor, enjoying their last few hours of civilian life before rejoining the 'Andrew'.[3]

But one, a certain Cyril Arkroyd, a son of Lancashire, turned up in the forenoon, marching through Chatham Dockyard like a Japanese Admiral. He was wearing a magnificent Commissionaire's uniform, the property of Gaumont Cinemas. He'd never kept his naval uniform and kit up to date, not ever expecting another call-up, so when it came he embarked on an almighty 'bender'. Still wearing his maroon uniform complete with shoulder epaulettes, and wearing a wonderful peaked cap trimmed with gold braid, he arrived at Chatham Barracks where the two sentries on duty at the main gate, thinking it better to be safe than sorry, gave him an immaculate 'Present Arms'. Cyril responded with an unsteady salute of his own. The Master at Arms there, having never experienced a similar situation, sent Cyril straight down to report to the First Lieutenant on board *Keith*.

From all accounts, Cyril's was almost a Royal Progress through the dock-yard. Groups of curious sailors smartly saluted him, as did the Dockyard Police. I was polishing my new pom-pom gun when he appeared alongside us and was about to march up the gangway. The Officer of the Watch, a ner-vous young Sub-Lieutenant, quickly called the Quartermaster and Bosun's Mate to 'Pipe the Side'.

---

[3] See Appendix V for origin of this slang term, meaning the Royal Navy.

So our own Cyril came aboard HMS *Keith* for the first time to a Captain's salute and the trilling of Bosun's pipes. Hearing all the extraordinary kerfuffle, our First Lieutenant flew out of his cabin to discover Cyril on the quarterdeck with his draft chit in his hand. It was one of the big moments of my life to see our 'Jimmy's' face when all was revealed. It resulted in poor old Cyril being marched up to the Clothing Store to be completely kitted out and debited with the full costs on the Ledger, while at Captain's Defaulters the Skipper lashed him up to seven days' Number 11s for being 24 hours adrift.

Cyril also had to parcel up his magnificent uniform and return it to the mandarins of British Gaumont. He never did get to wear it again as he was blown to bits at Dunkirk less than a year later. This is only one of the *many* untold stories of the Second World War.

The elderly Reservists dragged from their comfortable homes and settled occupations as postmen, park-keepers, etc., just sat around commenting darkly on the faults of this younger generation of sailors. But retribution arrived in the form of a very rude gentleman, namely the Chief 'Buffer'. The Chief Bosun's Mate descended on them from a great height and chased them, like a flock of terrified hens, on to the upper deck, handed out chipping hammers and scrapers and put them to work, getting the rust off the iron deck.

Suffice to say that when we sailed for Portland we continued scrubbing and polishing until the various surfaces shone and sparkled.

We then went to sea with our new Flotilla, which consisted of old 'V & W' class destroyers in the same state as we were. We fired the guns, both under Director Control at a towed target, narrowly missing the civilian crew of the target-towing tug who frantically informed us to that effect in explicit and graphic terms via a loudhailer.

We fired a real torpedo with a blowing head, and recovered it: the Skipper exercised both his own Yeoman of Signals and ours, with a dozen flag hoists to our ships belting along astern, their own signalmen going mad and clipping on the wrong pennants.

I'd been made trainer on the port pom-pom anti-aircraft gun with my killick of the mess as gunlayer. I'd never seen these four-barrelled pom-pom guns before. Each barrel spewed out a continuous stream of 2-pounder shells into the flight path of a diving bomber. That was the theory anyway, but in practice the gun very often jammed after firing a few rounds. At this point the No. 3 who was one of the Loading Numbers would give the back-end of the offending breech an almighty clout with a giant mallet, and hope it cleared the blockage. If this failed, we'd all gather round, strip the breech, and throw the rejected shell over the side. To reassemble the gun was frustrating; there always seemed to be one piece left over where we'd placed it on top of the ammunition lockers.

On the 'Big Day' when we were actually going to fire our cannon, we cleaned, greased and polished the gun and had the first belt of shells loaded and ready to open fire. The lads down by the depth charge racks got the signal from the Gunner (T), and tipped a big wooden brewery barrel into the sea. Our Commanding Officer, Captain Simson, who had been in destroyers since the First World War and had a famous record from that time, then brought *Keith* round in a wide arc, about 500 yards away from our beer barrel target.

Up on the bridge, the Skipper told the First Lieutenant to open fire. He informed the Gunnery Officer on the Flag Deck, who, in turn, passed it on to the Chief Gunner's Mate. He was galvanised into action and screamed "OPEN FIRE!" in his special Gunner's Mate voice and stood, gesticulating frantically, at the rear of the Signal Deck.

Bob, my gunlayer, got the general drift of what was required of us, and swung the gun round until his ring-sight was on the bobbing barrel, while I sweated to keep my sight centred on the target. Then Bob kicked his firing pedal and a stream of 2-pounder cannon shells streaked towards the target. Then the gun jammed.

"HIT THE BLOODY THING!" Bob immediately yelled, and No. 3 nearly shattered his left arm with belting the breech with the mallet. Then, before I realised it, the Gunner's Mate, the Ordnance Artificer, and several gentlemen were dissembling the gun before our eyes.

Up on the bridge, the Skipper was getting really angry, shouting at the Gunnery Officer who was attempting, unsuccessfully, to hide behind the range finder. The Skipper eventually passed the message down that he would use the starboard pom-pom on the floating target.

He brought *Keith* round and passed slowly on a straight course, about two hundred yards from the floating barrel off the starboard side, and shouted "OPEN FIRE!"

Tragedy now occurred. With the gun on target, their gunlayer, 'Soapy' Hudson, a man of nervous disposition, kicked his foot-pedal to open fire. Nothing happened. He slammed his foot down again. Again nothing happened. By that time, everyone else on the gun deck was hammering at the breech, but to no avail.

Then our young Midshipman arrived on the gun deck. He breathlessly informed us that the Captain ordered us to secure the guns, and requested the immediate presence of the Chief Gunner's Master and Ordnance Artificer on the bridge.

We locked the guns in their fore and aft positions, put the tampions in, covered them up and then watched our two hapless Chiefs reluctantly pulling themselves up the bridge ladders, like doomed men going to the gallows.

A short time previously I had the orders to "Prepare for battle" for my gun deck. Amongst many other meaningful items were two that remain etched in my memory. One was 'one large bucket of carbolic and water' – to neutralise the smell of blood. The other: 'one large bucket of sand' – to prevent slipping in the blood.

After that day's fiasco, I had the distinctly uncomfortable feeling that the blood would be mine. Back in harbour, men in white overalls with big spanners worked furiously on these relics of another war, but we were never satisfied that all was well with our 2-pounder cannon.

But more important things were afoot. My new Skipper, Captain Pawsey, was a Captain (Destroyers) who drove us pretty hard to begin with. He was worried about the King's Reserve Fleet Review, off Portland in August 1939, and got the First Lieutenant to keep us painting and polishing, even during the dog watches.

The Review was an exercise to show Herr Hitler that he would stand no chance against the overwhelming power of Britain's Royal Navy. To grace the occasion they had dragged out ancient battleships of First World War vintage, two of which were actually targets for the Home Fleet to lob 16-inch shells at. Other rustbuckets had been given a lick of paint over the patches of rust, while the poor old destroyers and 'C' class cruisers were anchored in lines across Weymouth Bay. These were the veterans of the North Sea from 1914 to 1918. They'd been moored-up in deserted creeks and inlets for many years with a few ship-keepers on board.

In the dim light of early dawn and the late evening, the serried ranks of grey ships looked quite impressive. But to the Active Service men in this tattered old armada, it was all too obvious that after a few months of heavy sea duty, the elderly ships would need extensive docking and repairs.

Our ship's company on board *Keith*, mixed pensioners with RFR[4] men, RNR[5] fishermen and keen young RNVR[6] sailors, had settled down and the mess deck became a more peaceful place to exist while the 'old grousers' turned their wrath on the Chiefs and Petty Officers.

King George VI arrived in the morning, conveyed to Weymouth Pier, embarked in the Admiral's Barge and was taken across to the Royal Yacht, a relic of Victorian times. A quick hand shake, gin and bitter lemons with the Admiral, embarked again in the Admiral's Barge and then sailed up and down the lines of moored ships.

After the review, each ship's company always complied with an extra cheer following the Skipper's order for "Three Cheers", to ensure that the King, before leaving, would give the order for the Fleet to "Splice the Mainbrace."

Being only a 'sprog', this liquid bonanza didn't apply to me unless I felt like an extra dollop of limejuice, but it kept the troops happy.

Life aboard a pre-war destroyer was highly interesting, full of fun and good humour as most destroyer officers were younger and keener than those of the Battle Fleets, with their everlasting paint scrubbing and bugle calls. It seemed that socialite Dartmouth officers were trained to look upon common sailors as so many slaves to be kicked around and to be given frightening amounts of punishment. Most of these types of officers had been terrified by the ratings mutiny at Invergordon in 1931.[7] If they'd cared to analyse its prime causes, the mutiny was purely on the question of pay and its reduction by almost one third, down to 25 shillings a week, without any warning to the ratings. In addition, the pound sterling was devalued by 30 per cent, whereby the married men could barely manage on starvation pay. The deplorable situation wasn't helped when the Admiral met a deputation from the Lower Deck who attempted to explain they could barely pay the rent for

---

[4] Royal Fleet Reserve.

[5] Royal Naval Reserve.

[6] Royal Naval Volunteer Reserve.

[7] See Appendix X, Lieutenant 'Ginger' Le Breton.

their little terraced homes in the dockyard ports. The Admiral's response, which was recorded, was to tell the men to put their wives on the streets. A more wicked and unfeeling remark is impossible to imagine.

The whole sorry affair highlighted the schisms within the Fleet. The destroyer men, bolstered by their sixpence-a-day Hard-Lying Allowance, in addition to the close contacts of destroyer captains and officers with their men, kept the destroyers out of trouble. But the mass mutiny of Britain's Home Fleet sent shock waves around the world and took Britain off the Gold Standard.

Fortunately, the vast influx of RNVR Officers and Hostilities Only men completely changed the Royal Navy. Large numbers of these men held important positions in Civvy Street and their wives had access to their MPs. Consequently, many outrages against sailors were brought to the attention of Mr. Alexander, the Labour MP and First Lord of the Admiralty who ruled the Navy under Churchill. He put his support behind the Atlantic Escort Groups, the Submarine Service and the Fleet Air Arm.

However, the hopes of our mixed band of pensioners, etc., sank lower day by day as the threat of war approached. Their hopes of returning to their cushy civilian occupations receded daily as Hitler's venomous threats against Poland became steadily more aggressive. It made little difference to me, with many more years to serve in the 'Andrew' and the prospect of fighting the Germans. Well, that's what I joined for – and the sooner the better.

I first had words with *Keith*'s First Lieutenant when we were anchored off a salubrious south coast resort. One sunny morning I was dangling over *Keith*'s bow on a stage and painting a patch of the ship's side in a tasteful shade of grey.

It was a beautiful summer's morning. It brought out shoals of pleasure boats to watch the assembled ships of the Royal Navy and the silly sailors who manned them. There were many absolutely gorgeous girls on board the pleasure boats, many of them calling out and waving at me. Secure in the knowledge that no one 'up top' could see me under the flare of the fo'c's'le, I waved back and was really enjoying myself with all the special attention, when I accidentally dropped my paintbrush into the water. It surfaced almost immediately and started to drift away from the ship on the tide.

I was only in overalls so jumped into the drink and caught up with the brush as it bobbed close to our quarterdeck and after gangway. I looked up, and there was the Captain, in all his glory, pacing the deck with his telescope under his arm.

I crawled up the gangway leaving a wet trail behind me to be immediately confronted with a furious Officer of the Watch and his minions. They shoved me into the 'rattle' for breaking out of ship.

Next morning I fell in as a Defaulter at the 'First Lieutenant's Defaulters' where I attempted to explain why I'd taken an early bath. Apparently, this crime was so heinous that it had to be dealt with by my Captain. So next morning, I fell in at 10 a.m., cleaned up, and wearing my No. 1 uniform I was marched up to the Captain's table on the quarterdeck and asked if I had anything to say.

I explained to the Skipper about the possible loss of King George's paint-brush and the fact that I would have been charged for it, which at the current rate would have amounted to about ten shillings, which I could ill afford on my 14 shillings-per-week. Whereas if I got over the side, and although technically breaking ship, I'd salvaged the paintbrush and saved the cost of it being set against me in the ledger. I might even be commended for my prompt action!

However, the Skipper was not all that impressed. He explained, quite succinctly as I recall, that he had no intention of letting his sailors go leaping over the side. And "anyone but a cack-handed idiot would not have lost the paintbrush over the side in the first place", and adding a sarcastic remark about me probably making great sheep's eyes at all the extremely attractive 'skirt' sailing past.

"I think seven days' Number 12s should do it," was his verdict.

"SEVEN DAYS' NUMBER 12 PUNISHMENT!" roared the coxswain to the assembled congregation. "ON CAP!... ABOUT TURN!... DOUBLE AWAY!..."

I put on a look of injured innocence and slowed to a walk when I got off the quarter-deck. Seven days' stoppage of leave. All shore leave was stopped anyway so I was no worse off. I could do that on my head. At least I was spared the moralising by the Captain of: "I didn't get where I am today by leaping over the side after every errant paintbrush which came floating past", etc., etc.

But Commander Pawsey caught up with me again while *Keith* was anchored off Weymouth. I'd been polishing the tampions on the 4.7-inch forward guns and was leaning against the gun shield of 'A' gun, having a quiet 'burn' (cigarette), lost in deep thought when I nearly jumped out of my skin. A deafening voice, about three inches from my left ear, boomed:

"IT'S ALL RIGHT NETHERCOTT, YOU CAN RELAX – I'VE GOT THE WEIGHT NOW!..."

And there was the Skipper, also leaning up against the gun shield!

I rapidly resumed my polishing, at the same time dumping my fag end over the side. The Captain wandered off to see who else he could catch.[8]

[Long after the war, in 1997, I took a trip on the ancient paddle steamer *Waverley* from Southend Pier to Chatham Historical Dockyard. A keen gentleman in a blazer, apparently a guide, pressed me into going into the Ropewalk. I thought this was some sort of dance, but discovered it was a long building wherein they used to lay-up the hemp hawsers of Nelson's days.

My mind went back, thinking of appropriate crime and punishment and the errant paintbrush, and to the days when, as a stroppy AB resplendent in white belt, gaiters and NP armband, I was Cells Sentry down at Chatham Main Gate. Here resided the Royal Navy's villains, each in his wooden cell with a large chunk of HMS *Hood*'s chopped up old 4-inch hawsers that he had to pick into oakum to fill a large sack.

As they moodily reduced the thick strands to fluff it gave them plenty of time to meditate on why they'd "bloody well joined the Navy".

Before I rejoined the *Waverley* at the pier, I noticed that the old Dockyard Lavatories and Toilet Blocks had disappeared from the landscape. Surely, these buildings were an important historical feature of Chatham Dockyard, if only for the amazing and quite extraordinary quality of the poems and graffiti on the walls?]

---

[8] Anthologist's Note: A similar deafening admonishment befell a Sub-Lieutenant who, exhausted by watchkeeping in HMAS *Shropshire* (while operating with the US 7th Fleet in the south-west Pacific, 1942-1944), was seen to be 'nodding off' during Action Stations by the distinguished and fearless Royal Australian Navy destroyer and cruiser skipper Commander Warwick Bracegirdle, DSC and Two Bars, RAN. 'Braces' switched on the loudspeaker, turned the volume control up to full blast and then bellowed: "GOD IS WATCHING YOU, GRIFFITHS!" Sub-Lieutenant Griffiths later became an Admiral. Commander Bracegirdle retired to Gislingham, Suffolk in 1957.

Two days after the Review in August 1939, we sailed for Plymouth, taking with us several of our new 17th Destroyer Flotilla. These were HM Ships *Venemous, Vesper* and *Vanessa*. We berthed alongside Plymouth Dockyard and began landing all extraneous and flammable gear, such as wardroom curtains and carpets. Ready-use ammunition was brought up from the magazines and placed in the shell-holders round our four big guns, while on the pom-pom deck we dumped the faulty ammunition and filled the ready-use lockers with fresh belts from the magazines. We checked our gas masks and placed gas screens over all the open entrances to the mess decks, while steel helmets were issued to all gunners and torpedo ratings.

A select band of torpedomen, under the command of the Torpedo Gunner who held Warrant Rank, removed the dummy heads from their 'fish' and fitted warheads to our 21-inch Whitehead torpedoes. Primers, detonators, etc., were screwed home and the contact pistols fitted to the warheads, and they were ready for action.

Unlike the Westcountry ships, Chatham ships reverted to two straight watches at sea, Port and Starboard. Plymouth ships consisted of Red, White and Blue Watches. This, during a 24-hour cycle, gave all seamen four hours on watch and eight hours rest and sleep, except for the two dog watches of two hours each.

Our system of watchkeeping became unbearable after about a week at sea. During the night you were on watch from 8.00 p.m. until 12 midnight, and 4.00 a.m. until 8.00 a.m. The next night you had the last dog watch from 6.00 p.m. until 8.00 p.m., the middle watch from 12 midnight until 4.00 a.m., and then went on the morning watch from 8.00 a.m. until 12 noon, and so on.

Considering that the Night Alarm rattlers went off at intervals during the night, when everyone had to rush through huge seas along the upper deck to their Action Station, and often be closed up there for over an hour, the complete loss of sleep began to tell after a day or two during really bad weather.

On 3 September 1939, the 'Pipe Clear Lower Deck' summoned the whole ship's company to our tiny quarterdeck. Standing on the depth charge racks, Commander Pawsey read out the Admiralty signal that we were to commence war against Germany. He then read out the Articles of War that threatened us with execution for many crimes, from sabotage to mutiny, and even 'kipping' (sleeping) on watch. It all seemed rather severe to men who, after all, were volunteers.

We had painted all our brightwork black, put light excluders in every scuttle on the mess decks, put warheads in our eight torpedoes and fitted pistols. We then supplied a mix of live ammunition to the four 4.7-inch guns, armour piercing, semi-armour piercing, high explosive and star shell. My gun, the port 2-pounder pom-pom, was supplied with ready-use ammunition. Sand and buckets of carbolic water were provided at all gun positions. Dozens of other procedures were carried out to prepare for battle.

War was declared at 11.00 a.m. At 11.25 a.m. we cast off from Devonport, and leading our mix of old 'B' and 'V & W' destroyers, we sailed down past Devil's Point and Drake's Island, towards the harbour mouth.

Off Plymouth Hoe, we suddenly heard the wailing air raid sirens ashore. As we fell out from Harbour Stations to rush to Action Stations, we saw thousands of people running for their lives across Plymouth Hoe to the air raid shelters. But it eventually turned out to be a false alarm right across Britain caused by some innocent commercial aircraft arriving from Holland which had been detected by the top-secret radar masts at Bawdsey, just north of Felixstowe, on the Suffolk coast.

And so we went to war...

Heading out into the North Atlantic, at economical speed and with our Division in our wake, we went into the 'Two Watch' system with the order that we could no longer sling hammocks at sea and to sleep with our gear on.

Shortly after I'd gone to my gun at midnight, we altered course and increased speed to about 25 knots. A transatlantic passenger liner, the *Athenia*, bound for America with women and children, had been torpedoed without warning off the north-west coast of Scotland. She was sinking fast, but had launched lifeboats.

The U-boat must have been lying in wait long before any declaration of war. An attack on an unarmed passenger ship, without ensuring the passengers were safe, contravened all the agreements and covenants which Hitler had signed since coming to power with his thugs in 1933.

Two 'E' class destroyers were already on the scene with a Swedish liner that had lowered her lifeboats to pick up the shocked survivors from the water. Other destroyers from Liverpool were on their way, so our Skipper took our ships to seaward of the sinking *Athenia*, formed up in line abreast and carried out an Asdic[9] sweep on what the Skipper reckoned was the U-boat's line of retreat. We searched unsuccessfully for many hours, eventually closing to the coast, hoping the German was sheltering in some bay or inlet. We then received orders to patrol another area of the Western Approaches where a home-bound merchantman had been attacked with torpedoes, had out-run the U-boat and was steaming eastward at a phenomenal rate of knots which would have astounded her builders.

With various defects emerging in *Keith* and in other ships, we got orders to run into Milford Haven and effect our repairs, *Keith* to proceed to Devonport for a docking.

This then, was the pattern of our lives for nearly four months in the Western Approaches. Long periods at sea, meeting inward-bound convoys, bringing them into the English Channel, handing over to the Channel Escorts while we oiled and stored off the oiler up at Hamoaze. No shore leave was given as we were always at short notice for steam and there always seemed to be a solitary cargo ship, far out in the North Atlantic, torpedoed and sinking.

Sometimes we found a few pitiful survivors of those sunken ships, often oil-covered and grievously injured. Occasionally the foul weather had driven their little boats or life rafts into the vast wastes of open sea where they had either died of wounds, thirst, starvation, exposure, or a combination of all four.

Once or twice we escorted troopships of the British Expeditionary Force to Cherbourg, and on one very important trip, together with four other destroyers we brought the battered cruiser *Exeter* in from the Bay of Biscay on her homeward voyage to Plymouth after the Battle of the River Plate, off Montevideo Harbour, Uruguay where the German pocket battleship, *Admiral Graf Spee*, had been scuttled on 17 December 1939, after being chased and trapped by the cruisers *Ajax*, *Achilles* and *Exeter*.

Another memorable incident was when we took the *Bulldog* with us, and sailed out into the North Atlantic to tow in a large cargo ship that had lost its propeller. We eventually found the ship, about 8,000 tons, drifting before the wind. We passed a light rope across by means of a Coston Gun. Now came the interesting part.

[9] An early form of sonar; from (A)nti-(S)ubmarine (D)etection (I)nvestigation (C)ommittee.

We carried two long towing hawsers. Our Skipper decided to use about 20 fathoms of our starboard anchor cable, inserted as a spring between the hawsers. Our end of the anchor cable was brought up over *Keith*'s stern, clear of the depth charge racks and with a mass of padding on the ship's side to stop the chafing, as the sudden strain of 8,000 tons of cargo ship, compared to our 1,400 tons, should the tow wire suddenly become taut, would practically rip our stern off. The bight of the towrope would be passed to chains and slings round our after 4.7-inch gun mounting on the quarterdeck.

Naturally, being a merchant ship she carried no proper towing wires. 'Merchant jacks' usually tied up and moored their ships with some spare clothes lines or similar!

We put a Bosun's party aboard the drifting merchantman to secure the tow by passing wires and shackles round her capstans and mooring bollards. Very cautiously *Keith* took up the strain, working from one knot to bring the merchantman's head round on course, gradually increasing power until we were actually making all of five knots in comparatively calm seas.

Bulldog took up escort, keeping an all-round Asdic watch, as we were a dream target for a wandering U-boat. Night and day, the cable crew on the quarterdeck watched the towrope and reported the hempen heart of the steel cable being gradually forced out between the steel strands.

At long last, with most of us near exhaustion, we passed Land's End and were eventually met by two huge salvage tugs out of Falmouth. They passed their own hawsers, took over and towed the merchantman into Falmouth, while *Keith* went into Devonport for repairs.

At the end of October 1939, *Keith* was transferred temporarily to the 22nd Destroyer Flotilla, Nore Command, based at Harwich. We took over as Flotilla Leader of a motley group of destroyers; the three Polish destroyers that had escaped from the Germans, the *Grom*, *Burza*, and *Blyskawiza*, and HM Ships *Gipsy*, *Gallant*, *Worcester*, *Vimy* and *Boadicea*.

The old Submarine Depot ship *Titania* was also based at Harwich at that time, together with an assortment of our old 'H' class and 'S' class submarines that were carrying out patrols off the German coast. Three or four of these had already been sunk, together with the loss of all their crews, as the Germans had protected their coast and offshore islands with vast numbers of minefields.

For our part, we went on North Sea sweeps hoping to trap some of the German mine-laying destroyers that made forays down the east coast, laying magnetic mines. From early November 1939, German aircraft also began dropping magnetic mines off the east coast. Resting on the seabed in comparatively shallow water, the mines exploded when a steel-hulled ship passed in the near vicinity. At that time there was no method of sweeping these mines and de-gaussing had not yet been invented, so we just had to take our chances.

The whole of the Thames Estuary and way up the east coast was soon littered with the protruding masts and funnels of ships sunk by this new weapon. Off Harwich lay the wrecks of two large liners, the *Terekuni Maru* (Japanese) and the *Simon Bolivar* (Dutch) which had had their bottoms blown out by these new magnetic mines, and lay exposed at low tide on the sandbanks offshore. On 13 November, *Blanche*, one of our original Flotilla, was sunk by a magnetic mine in the Estuary while escorting a convoy.

At midnight on 21 November 1939, we received orders at Harwich, where we were tied up at Parkestone Quay, to proceed to sea forthwith on some panic or other. *Gipsy* was tied up to the oiler in midstream and should have waited for us to cast off and lead the whole line of destroyers down the narrow, winding deep-water channel out of Harwich Harbour, instead of which she slipped out ahead of us and led the way past Landguard Fort to the open sea. We couldn't take our proper place ahead as Flotilla Leader as the channel was too narrow.

Gipsy was steaming about five cables ahead when suddenly there was a huge explosion. She literally broke in half, folding at the break of the fo'c's'le with the forward mess decks protruding just above water, but the alleyways leading to the mess decks were deep underwater. The men in the mess decks, seamen and stokers, were completely trapped and, with the rising tide, were drowned. The destroyer's portholes were too small for a man to squeeze through, and the magazine gun-handups were jammed solid by the explosion. *Gipsy*'s captain had been catapulted from the bridge on to the breech of 'B' gun and broke his neck. Most of the officers and men on her upper deck had broken legs or concussion and there were many men in the water being carried away by the powerful current.

We got the boats lowered and pulled over to the wreck, illuminated by our searchlights and those of *Boadicea*, which was also rescuing survivors.

The trapped men were drowning behind the open portholes, with no means of escape. I was Bowman on No. 1 Whaler and it was terribly distressing to watch them die and be absolutely powerless to do anything to assist them.

We picked up as many of *Gipsy's* survivors as possible from the sea and passed them to the Harwich lifeboat and a tug that had also appeared from the harbour. We were then recalled by *Keith*, pulled back to our ship and were hoisted inboard. We then re-formed the flotilla in line ahead and sailed north to our assigned patrol area.

The Captain and the many dead of *Gipsy* were given a military funeral following a church service. The boys from my former Naval Training School, HMS *Ganges*, across the water from Harwich Harbour, marched with the coffins to Shotley Churchyard.

Following our North Sea patrol, *Keith* then had the honour of being degaussed in Chatham Dockyard. This procedure involved wrapping miles of cab-tyre cable round our guard rails and the installation of a new generator to ionise it in the tiller flat. Having been assured by the boffins that our magnetic flux had been neutralised, we sailed confidently away.

We went into Devonport in mid-December 1939, to let the 'Guz' dockyard mateys mend our battered ship. We had to endure the aggravation of the non-stop card schools on our mess decks, the deafening racket of riveting hammers and the unholy mess that these 'Sons of Devon' made of our home. But just before Christmas the repairs were complete and we were towed out into the stream and tied up to the oiler.

We were at one hour for steam and at about midnight the Signal Tower began flashing: "*Keith* to proceed to sea to aid a ship in distress about 200 miles due west".

Donning our Lammy coats and seaboots, we cast off, took up our Harbour Stations in a blinding snowstorm and steamed out toward Devil's Point to negotiate Drake's Island. I was on the bridge as Starboard Lookout when *Keith* suddenly started bucking up and down like a fairground horse. We had touched rocks off Devil's Point with the port propeller, instantly shearing off two of the four blades which heaved the ship up and down in the water every revolution the two remaining blades made.

Orders from the bridge were passed briskly and urgently: "Shut all watertight doors" – "Standby the Seaboat" – "Stop port engine" – "Hard a-starboard" – "Signalman! Pass the message to the Signal Tower 'We are out of control'" – "Hoist two red lights at the masthead."

We eventually limped back on one screw to the dockyard with the assistance of a tug that took us into the outer basin. *Keith*'s crew then had to wait until someone on a bicycle roused the dockyard mateys to get us into the dry dock. This was the period of the 'Phoney War' and the dockyard closed down at 5.00 p.m. For the Royal Dockyards the war finished at 'knocking-off time' and, of course, anything untoward like this required overtime. It was a very different story for naval sailors at sea. Working watches in foul weather with little sleep, living on hard tack when the galley was flooded, frozen to the bone most of the time and being buffeted about on reeling, flooded decks. At that time, we had very little weatherproof clothing, no heating on the mess decks that were often awash with sea water, buckets of gash food and often with foul-smelling oil fuel leaking up from the tanks through the manhole lids.

It would not be until the fall of France in mid-June 1940, and the real threat of an imminent invasion of Britain, that most British workers began to take the war seriously. The first bombs falling on British cities had the salutary effect in frightening the civilian workforce, but by then thousands of Royal Navy and Merchant Navy sailors had been killed and many of our ships lay on the sea bed with their dead sailors entombed inside.

The repairs to our damaged propeller took about two weeks to complete and in mid-January 1940 we resumed anti-submarine patrols in home waters in freezing weather. January 1940 was one of the coldest on record with frequent sub-zero temperatures accompanied by blinding snowstorms.

The following are the words of a song called 'The *Keith*'s Lament'. They describe the actual conditions we had to endure in the North Sea and North Atlantic in the early months of the war. We were always on two straight watches at sea and only came into harbour to refuel and take aboard food and water, and then we were back out to sea again:

'The *Keith*'s Lament'
Christmas 1939

There's steam in the capstan,
Smoke in the stack.

The lads on the fo'c's'le are hauling in slack.
We're slipping the buoy now the oceans to plough,
I wonder, my darling, who's loving you now?

We're cold, hard and hungry, little to eat,
No winter clothing, wet boots on our feet.
Our hammocks are soaking, the mess decks awash,
We're living on potmess and biscuits with hash.
They sent us a signal, "U-boat in sight."
Twenty-four knots lads, all through the night.
But no bloody U-boat came into sight,
Although we kept steaming until it was light.

We've had no bloody mail dear, no leave and no pay.
We're going ashore dear, one bloody day.
We're praying the boilers will soon crack up tight,
And give us the leave dear, we pray for each night.

And so into harbour, not before time,
With twenty more sea days, and a gut full of brine.
We'll get down the mess deck and gulp down our tots,
We're sailing at seven and I'm on First Watch.

Anon
(via Iain Nethercott)

THE SINKING OF THE SS *HUNTSMAN* AND THE DEMISE OF THE *ADMIRAL GRAF SPEE*

Norman Watson

On 18 August 1939, the last of the Harrison Shipping Line's illustrious breed of four-masted cargo ships, the 9,250-ton SS *Huntsman*, set sail from Colombo, Sri Lanka, homeward bound for London. Three days later the German pocket-battleship, *Admiral Graf Spee*, set sail from Wilhelmshaven, north-west Germany, into the North Sea bound for the South Atlantic. The formidable warship was supported by the 12,000-ton tanker/supply ship *Altmark*, flying a Norwegian flag and with the name *Sogne* painted on her bow and stern.

Seven weeks later, 10 October 1939, in a position several hundred miles east of Ascension Island in the South Atlantic, the two ships converged. *Admiral Graf Spee*, flying French Navy colours, approached what would be her fourth victim. After putting a 'Prize Crew' aboard *Huntsman*, the two ships parted company.

The German boarding party showed much interest in the *Huntsman*'s cargo, especially the chests of tea, cases of Indian butter, bales of carpets, burlap and cases of rubber shoes. A few days later, large quantities of these coveted goods appeared all over the available deck space of the proud old merchant ship.

Five days later, *Graf Spee* reappeared with *Altmark* to claim her booty. After a further two days of transferring the looted goods to the two German raiders, the officers and crewmen of the *Huntsman* were transported to the *Altmark*. On 17 October, after handing Captain Albert 'Yankee' Brown a receipt for his ship, *Graf Spee*'s Commanding Officer, Captain Hans Langsdorff, ordered the sinking of *Huntsman* by explosive charges.

The *Graf Spee* continued her voyage of destruction in the endless expanse of the South Atlantic, sinking another five merchant ships before encountering Force 'G', a Royal Navy Cruiser Squadron consisting of HM Ships *Ajax*, *Achilles* (both 6-inch gun cruisers) and *Exeter* (8-inch gun cruiser), at 6.08 in the morning of 13 December 1939. The 'Battle of the River Plate' had begun.[10]

During the ensuing battle, the *Graf Spee* was relentlessly attacked and pursued by the three cruisers. Under constant assault, the badly damaged *Graf Spee* ran for cover in the port of Montevideo at the mouth of the River Plate, in the neutral country of Uruguay. During the running battle 73 British seamen aboard the three cruisers were killed while the *Graf Spee* lost 37 crewmen.

After negotiations with the German ambassador and the Uruguayan

---

[10] See Appendix X for further details of Captain Ralph Medley, RN, of HMS *Ajax*.

authorities concerning the length of stay for vital repairs, Captain Langsdorff had the sad duty of attending the funerals of the 37 dead German sailors. Standing in front of each coffin in turn, Captain Langsdorff saluted each one for a full minute before moving on to the next. He used the traditional German Naval salute in contrast to most people around him, including the officiating clergy, who used the straight-armed Nazi Party salute.

Captain Langsdorff had gained the respect of all who came into contact with him, including the Captains, the officers and the crews of the nine ships he'd sunk. After he had secured the future welfare of *Graf Spee*'s remaining crew he made the decision to scuttle the great ship. Explosive charges were placed in the bowels of the crippled warship off Montevideo Harbour and the blazing hulk sank to the seabed at 1956 hours, 17 December 1939.

Within a few days of *Graf Spee*'s demise, and after having said farewell to his officers, he wrote three letters, one of them was to his wife, thousands of miles away in Germany. Early the following morning, Flag Lieutenant Dietrich found him in his apartment, in his bloodstained full dress uniform, lying on *Graf Spee*'s ensign which he'd removed from his ship a few days previously.

In a letter to the German Ambassador in Buenos Aires, Captain Langsdorff had written: "Now I can only prove by my death that the fighting services of the Third Reich are ready to die for the honour of their flag".

Two months later, during the night of 17/18 February 1940, the *Altmark* was returning to Germany with her prisoners. She was off the south-western coast of Norway, about 15 miles south of Bergen, when she was forced by the Royal Navy to run for shelter in a small fjord. It was here that Captain Philip Vian, Commanding Officer of the destroyer HMS *Cossack*, successfully rescued all 299 Allied merchant seamen, including the crew of the SS *Huntsman*.

A PERSONAL REMINISCENCE

Lieutenant Commander Derek House, RN, Retd., HMS *Boadicea*

In August 1939 I was a 19-year-old Acting Sub-Lieutenant doing technical courses at Portsmouth. Having completed the torpedo course at *Vernon* and navigation at Navigation House in the dockyard, I was in the middle of the Signals course in RN Barracks when, on 21 August, the news of the impending Russo-German Pact broke. All courses stopped forthwith – no gunnery at Whale Island for me! – and the students were dispersed to their war stations.

On 22 August, my term-mate Dudley Davenport and I drove from Portsmouth to join *Blanche* and *Boadicea* respectively, between-the-wars fleet destroyers designed to re-fight the Battle of Jutland, with four 4.7-inch guns and eight torpedo tubes, serving as emergency destroyers at Chatham with half complements.

On 3 September, when the War Telegram 'Total Germany' reached us, I had to decipher it (and have since often wondered why it was ever necessary for it to be sent in cipher). All 'B' class destroyers had reached Dover to form the 19th Destroyer Flotilla under Captain D. J. R. 'Ginger' Simson, the nucleus of the new Dover Patrol under the control of Vice Admiral Bertram Ramsay, who had commanded the *Broke* at Dover in the First World War. One of our first tasks was to cover the laying of the Dover Mine Barrage over the next fortnight.

The following is a description by Winston Churchill, then First Sea Lord, of an incident when he and the British War Cabinet were returning from France to Dover on board *Boadicea*:

"In early February [1940] when the Prime Minister [Neville Chamberlain] was going to the Supreme War Council in Paris, he invited me for the first time to go with him. I suggested that we should go by sea, which I could arrange: so we all sailed from Dover in a destroyer, and reached Paris in time for a meeting in the evening...

"The main subject of discussion on 5 February was 'Aid to Finland'...

"The next day, when we came to re-cross the Channel, an amusing incident occurred. We sighted a floating mine. So I said to the captain, 'Let's blow it up by gunfire.' It burst with a good bang, and a large piece of wreckage sailed over towards us and seemed for an instant as if it were going to settle on the bridge, where all the politicians and some of the other swells were clustered. However, it landed on the fo'c's'le, which happily was bare, and no one was hurt. Thus everything passed off pleasantly. From this time onwards I was invited by the Prime Minister to accompany him, with others, to the meetings of the Supreme War Council. But I could not provide an equal entertainment each time."

A good description? Well, nearly! For the outward passage the War Cabinet had crossed the Channel in the flotilla leader *Codrington*, but she was not available for the homeward passage, so *Boadicea*, with Captain (DO) embarked, entered harbour early on 6 February 1940, securing alongside a railway jetty.

As Officer of the Day, I was at the head of the gangway to watch all Winston's 'politicians and swells' arrive. The tall Prime Minister Neville Chamberlain, the even taller Foreign Secretary Lord Halifax, the diminutive Secretary of State for Air Sir Kingsley Wood, the First Sea Lord Admiral Pound, followed after a small gap by the very large Chief of the Imperial General Staff General Ironside, and a cigar-smoking and hatless – sacrilege for coming over the side! – First Lord of the Admiralty Winston Churchill, exactly like the cartoonists' portrayal of him. I was amazed and impressed. All our visitors except the last two were conducted to the bridge, but Winston and Ironside made their way aft to the wardroom.

Soon after we had left harbour, I was given a signal in cipher, so made my way aft to my cabin in the wardroom flat. Peeping into the wardroom, I saw Winston and Ironside quaffing wardroom port (somewhat to my surprise as it was only 8.30 in the morning), reading *Blighty* and yesterday's *Times*. The smell of cigar smoke filled my cabin while I was doing my subtraction to decipher the signal:

"*Boadicea* for First Lord, from Admiralty – B-O-R-D-E is out of bed again."

This meant nothing to me at the time but was, in fact, a reference to the mine destructor ship *Borde*. The very real threat of the magnetic mine had not been fully appreciated before war broke out; in November 1939, for example, no less than 27 merchant ships, as well as our flotilla-mate *Blanche*, had been sunk in the Thames Estuary. The mine destructor ship, of which *Borde* was the first, was one of the few mine-sweeping measures then available, though they proved very vulnerable to damage from the mines they exploded.

By the time I had finished the cipher, our visitors had left the wardroom. Sighting a floating mine was an everyday occurrence in the Straits of Dover at that time, mostly moored mines which had broken adrift from the Dover Barrage, but there were also a few First World War mines, both German and British.

Early in the war, we realized that trying to sink a 'floater' by rifle fire was an inefficient way of doing things. So we developed a better method, using the sub-calibre, a miniature gun loaded into the breech mechanism of a 4.7-inch gun, firing a solid 2-pounder shell and provided for practice purposes.

When the mine sighting described by Churchill occurred, I was on watch on the bridge. The weather was overcast and the sea calm. My recollection of events is not exactly the same as Churchill's. Certainly the anecdote I have dined out on for some years says that when the mine was sighted permission to sink it was requested through the usual channels. The captain (an aviator called Bodley-Kingdon) asked Captain (D) whether we should stop and sink it. Captain (D) referred it to Pound who conferred with Churchill. Approval then passed back down the line, the order to ship sub-calibre was shouted over the front of the bridge to 'B' gun, and way was taken off the ship.

In my innocence, I remember wondering at the time whether this was really wise in view of our valuable cargo; we certainly had no air cover and surface cover. With the mine some 50 yards on the starboard bow and the ship stopped, the order was given to open fire with sub-calibre. 'B' gun's gunlayer hit the mine first shot.

The main charge did not explode but the upper hemisphere blew off, going high, high, high into the air, looking indeed as though it might land on the bridge. In fact, it landed in the sea about five yards off the starboard bow, not on the fo'c's'le as Churchill said. But with the applause on the bridge, one could sense sighs of relief.

The following day, at our buoy in Dover Harbour, a signal arrived from Admiralty:

"From First Lord. My hearty congratulations to the gunlayer of 'B' gun for his superb marksmanship."

HMS *BOADICEA* – THE EARLY DAYS

By Lieutenant Commander H. C. Fox, RN, Retd., First Lieutenant, HMS *Boadicea*

On 25 August 1939, the British Government proclaimed a formal treaty with Poland guaranteeing that country's frontiers against aggression. On 1 September the Nazis invaded Poland. On 3 September Great Britain declared war.

I had been appointed First Lieutenant of HMS *Boadicea*. Excerpts from my letters to my family at home describe life in the early months of the war, mostly in the English Channel:

Chatham, 25 August 1939
I got here at 0200 hours yesterday morning and have since been hectically trying to make out action organizations – in fact, general organization of the ship, as everything was pretty chaotic with innumerable recent changes of personnel, and nothing like up to complement at that. We were embarking torpedoes all last night and have been busy embarking stores of one sort and another tonight. Quite untrained though as yet... I think we are for it this time, and it is going to be no easy job. The thing is, I suppose, for each of us to try and be adequate.

Just been ordered to sea.

27 August 1939
We were suddenly shot off to Portland in the middle of my last letter, creeping round the coast, darkened completely and hoping we wouldn't be expected to fire anything, as we are nothing like ready yet. The ship's company are mostly Reservists, but I think we'll manage. There is so much to be done.

31 August 1939
I may not tell you where we are. All I can say is that we are as near ready for war as can be expected after a week's commission. Most of the ship's company are oldish men called up from the Reserve and look like the sort of people you wouldn't like to meet in a dark street near the docks, but they work hard and will fight all right. We are just off to sea again.

4 September 1939

It is a curious feeling of unreality actually being at war at last, and already, after a couple of days, I feel more or less used to it. I should so like to tell you where we are, but I can't. We are more or less continually at sea and have already had several air alarms and submarine alarms – in fact we have, we like to think, sunk one submarine... Of course one gets very little regular sleep and the nerves get a bit raw, which is a pity but it can't be helped. It's a nice lot of officers, nine of them, including one elderly retired gunner who went all through the last war. He is a bit regretful at being launched on another. The Captain is helpful and pleasant. I suppose I ought to make some sort of will, but can't be gloomy enough to do so...

It is all a bit grim, I suppose, but it doesn't seem as if anything much can be done about it. Unless something very surprising happens it will probably go on for years and years. For goodness sake don't worry. It will all be the same in 50 years' time!

7 September 1939

What cynical, ruthless, unprincipled people these German-Russian politicians are.[11] It is unbelievable that the inhabitants of their countries should allow themselves to be played shuttlecock with in such a manner. I shouldn't be surprised to see them tearing at poor old Poland in a week or two.

12 September 1939

I am getting quite acclimatised to the routine now and don't really miss the sleep much. In a way life is quite fun, although not unlike prison. It is so interesting trying to get the best out of these men. They are such a curious mixture of Hebridean Reservists and old sailors who've been out of the RN for years and years. I'm trying to arrive at the right pitch of discipline with as little hustling as possible, but there must be some. It's not always easy, but it's always interesting... I'm for bed as we start early tomorrow morning, and all tomorrow night in my clothes on the end of a voice pipe when not actually on watch.

18 September 1939

I have just been ashore for a two-hour walk over the hills, the first visit to dry

---

[11] A reference to the Russo-German Pact of 1939.

land since a week before the war! It was very pleasant indeed, wind blowing and sun shining. Walking through the town, though, was a revelation. It was the first sight I had had of England under the pall of war, and it was gloomy, to say the least. Apart from that I have nothing much to say. We have been doing routine patrols at sea and nothing untoward has come our way. The weather hasn't been too good, but most of us are acclimatised to that now.

As I stand on the bridge watching the sad sea waves lashing the fo'c's'le I comfort myself with thoughts of turnips and cabbages, and the gunner and I discuss these things as he also has a small farm of his own. He is over 50 and was blown up in the last war.

20 October 1939

In the last week we have been almost continually at sea, and the last day or two has been unspeakable. Roll upon roll of heavy rain cloud in endless succession, each drop of rain beating against your face like crystal. Ship rolling and pitching. I wore my Siwash sweater, a great coat, an oilskin and a towel, but still after each 4-hour bout I was just about wet through. It was hell.

3 November 1939

We are in for a couple of days I hope and then out again for two or three, to be lashed again by spray and storm. However, I am getting accustomed to it and in many ways enjoy it. I wouldn't be anywhere else in a war for worlds...

5 November 1939

I called on a Polish destroyer the other day. They were quite pleasing people, some like the French and some a bit Teuton. Everything was normal and we joked, but there was an extraordinary undercurrent of sadness. Today we are at short notice for steam...

14 November 1939

If people wonder why we are losing ships the answer to that is we are bound to, using the seas as we do while the Germans stay in harbour. They should be grateful for the food and trade that they are enjoying. It's no joke convoying a fleet of merchant vessels, all darkened, in pilotage waters on a pitch dark night, particularly if you run up against another similar party. There are some pretty ghoulish situations from time to time. Last time I wrote I said we were at short notice and liable to be ordered to sea at any moment. I said I hoped we wouldn't be. Well, I was called at 0200 hours.

"Signal, Sir: 'Proceed to sea with all dispatch.'"

THE SINKING OF HMS *BLANCHE*

Signalman Noel Thorne, HMS *Blanche*

I served in HMS *Blanche* as a Signalman from September 1939 until she was sunk two months later. HM Ships *Basilisk* and *Blanche*, based at Harwich, sailed from the Humber on the morning of 12 November 1939, as anti-submarine escorts for the cruiser/mine-layer HMS *Adventure* on passage to Portsmouth. At about 0500 hours the following morning, whilst we were off Ramsgate, Kent, *Adventure* was mined under the bridge. *Basilisk* took off the wounded from *Adventure*, while *Blanche* carried out an anti-submarine sweep.

At about 0810 hours, *Blanche* struck a mine, under the port side abreast 'Y' gun. All steam to the main engines was lost, the ship's back was broken just abaft the engine room, and initial flooding below the lower deck aft quickly spread to the cabin flat and engine room.

By now *Adventure* had managed to get under way, and a tug had come out from Ramsgate and took *Blanche* in tow. But the ship's list to port increased, and she finally capsized at about 0950 hours. All the survivors were picked up safely by the tug and one or two other small craft in the vicinity. It was most fortunate that the damage was right aft, away from the crew's living quarters, as only two crew members were killed and 15 injured.

Within a few days it was established that the two incidents were caused by magnetic mines, and these caused immense damage to shipping until an effective countermeasure, de-gaussing, was introduced.

After *Blanche* I went to another destroyer, HMS *Ivanhoe*. She lasted only until the night of 30 August/1 September 1940, when along with two other destroyers, HM Ships *Express* and *Esk*, she was mined off the Dutch coast. *Express* was subsequently towed home and repaired, but *Ivanhoe* and *Esk* went down, both with heavy casualties.

I was selected for a commission, and then, very fortunately, saw the remaining five years of the war out safely, mainly on North Atlantic convoys.

MAGNETIC MINE MENACE

Excerpt from *The Battle of the East Coast 1939-1945* by Julian P. Foynes

(Reproduced by kind permission of Mr J. P. Foynes)

On the morning of 13 November 1939, the Harwich-based destroyers *Blanche* and *Basilisk* were escorting the large mine-laying cruiser *Adventure* from Grimsby down to Portsmouth. The three ships lay stopped near the Tongue Light Vessel, about ten miles north of Margate, Kent, owing to fog and problems *Blanche* was having with her paravanes (a form of anti-mine gear).

As they began to edge out of the misty dawn gloom at 0514 hours an explosion was heard and seen in the sea well ahead and to starboard. Eleven minutes later there was a blast right under *Adventure*, and no fewer than 62 of her crew were injured, at least three fatally, by being hurled down hatchways or against bulkheads. The ships stopped and waited for the Ramsgate tug *Fabia*, which took *Adventure* in tow while *Basilisk* conveyed her casualties to Sheerness and *Blanche* stood guard against possible U-boats.

No sooner had everyone got under way just after 0800 hours than *Blanche* was blasted aft, splitting her deck, buckling a bulkhead, and letting the sea into her engine room. The bridge was wrecked by the shock, which hurled the wheel and instruments about, stunned Lieutenant Commander Aubrey and all his officers, knocked out the radio and internal telephones and turned on the sirens at full blast so that shouted orders were drowned out. One crewman was killed and ten injured.

It seemed that *Blanche* might be towed in by another of the Ramsgate tugs, but as she waited she began to heel over dangerously, so it was decided to abandon her, soon after which she sank.

While warnings were radioed to other shipping, the Harwich patrol destroyer *Glowworm* stationed herself east of the Tongue Light Vessel to redirect Thames-bound shipping, and the trawler *Myrtle* did likewise for vessels coming out of the river. But meanwhile, a merchantman, *Ponzano*, had also gone down only a few miles to the south-east. A third ship, the large *Matra*, was lost that evening in the same area, in spite of a thorough search for mines and U-boats.

Over the next month, 14 vessels of various types were to be sunk around the Tongue Lightship, including a second warship – the Sheerness trawler *Mastiff*, while scouring the seabed for mines with nets on 20 November – and the 8,000-ton Dutch liner *Spaardom* on 27 November.

Of course, mines were suspected, but none were at first swept or even seen. None had actually come into direct contact with any ship. This came on top of 12 unexplained sinkings in September and October, starting with that of *Magdapur* near the Aldeburgh Napes on 10 September.

Were the mines being triggered at a distance, by, for instance, the hull magnetism of the ships?

At about 1900 hours, on the evening of 21 November 1939, as the First Destroyer Flotilla prepared to leave Harwich Harbour on a U-boat sweep around the Cork Lightship, two German float-planes, variously identified as Heinkel 59s or 115s, came in over the harbour entrance at less than 150 feet. They dropped what Landguard Fort, Felixstowe, reported as "Objects apparently attached to parachutes", machine-gunned the fort's observation post, and made off.

The defences cannot be described as having been ready. The crews of the examination boat and pilot boat had merely waved at the approaching planes, under the impression that they were seaplanes from RAF[12] Felixstowe. The intruders were too low for the heavy AA guns, while the light AA crews were apparently too stunned at seeing their first raiders to respond; and perhaps it seemed wrong to fire on planes from which parachutes were coming.

The Navy sent out light craft to search all round the Landguard Peninsula, and they reported nothing to the Operations Room. Accordingly, as planned, the Polish destroyer *Burza* slipped from Parkeston Quay, Harwich, followed in turn by *Griffin*, *Gipsy*, *Grom*, the leader *Keith*, and *Boadicea*.

---

[12] Royal Air Force.

At 2123 hours, *Gipsy*, just inside the boom gate and level with the fort, was rent by a terrific explosion. The 1,340-ton ship broke in half just astern of the bridge, her boilers torn out and one funnel crumpled over the side like a flimsy cardboard tube.

Fifty three years later her last surviving officer, Lieutenant R. D. Franks, recalled how *Gipsy* had only been back at Parkeston for two hours after rescuing three German airmen. The three were survivors from a reconnaissance plane that had been shot down the previous day by an RAF fighter aircraft.

When ordered to sea, Lieutenant Franks and the Captain, Lieutenant Commander Crosley, were on the bridge, talking about the mine threat, when they were thrown onto 'B' gun deck by the explosion. At least 50 of her complement of 150 were lost.

Other destroyers, the Army launch *Viking* (which was moored close to the fort jetty) and numerous harbour launches came to the rescue and landed survivors at both Harwich and Felixstowe. Lieutenant Franks found Lieutenant Commander Crosley lying injured on the foredeck, but he died later in Shotley Hospital (at HMS *Ganges*, the Royal Naval Shore Training Establishment at Shotley, Suffolk). His grave, along with those of eight other *Gipsy* dead, can still be seen in the Royal Naval Cemetery, beside St. Mary's Church, Shotley.

Daybreak revealed *Gipsy* awash up to the bridge, but with her bows jutting out of the water at a sharp angle from the stern, which was entirely underwater. Felixstowe police records show that floating corpses continued to be washed ashore for the next four months.

At 1330 hours on 22 November, the enemy discovered his success when a Heinkel 115 reconnoitred the harbour from 20,000 feet. Winston Churchill, then First Lord of the Admiralty, was baffled and furious at the loss of a ship inside a defended harbour. That day he came to Parkeston personally and interviewed Rear Admiral Harris.

Churchill wanted to know why the anti-aircraft guns had not fired, and why so many destroyers had navigated a channel just overflown by enemy minelayers. Someone's head had to roll – in this case that of the Garrison Commander (in charge of Harbour Forts and AA Defences), Lieutenant Colonel Ward. Within days he had resigned his command.

Churchill's descent on Harwich was not entirely negative, for it was Admiralty pressure which led the RAF, on 23 November, to raise the first barrage balloons for the protection of the harbour. And on 3 December 1939, a larger floating, i.e. shipborne, barrage was raised on the mouth of the River Thames between Sheerness, Kent, and Southend, Essex.

22 November 1939 was a day of crisis at the Admiralty. In addition to the two Harwich destroyers a dozen merchantmen had been lost, all without the exact cause being determined. All traffic in and out of the Thames was temporarily stopped; FN convoys were held at Southend and FS diverted to the Downs anchorage. All navigation lights in the Thames Estuary were extinguished. To by-pass the two danger areas a new channel, QZS 137, was buoyed via the Edinburgh Channels and Knock Deep, and had to be used for the next eight months.

1940

PROLOGUE TO 1940

by

Rear Admiral John B. Hervey, RN, Retd.

DURING 1940 Britain lost 37 more destroyers. Another seven were mined, but twice this number were sunk by enemy aircraft, against which they had a very inadequate anti-aircraft armament. Furthermore, they were operating in areas over which friendly aircraft never had air superiority. Added to five sunk by submarines, six in surface actions and six by sundry disasters, these were heavy losses. But the Navy had much to show for them. Whilst taking the Army to and from Norway in April/May they sank ten German destroyers at Narvik and either sank or temporarily disabled many larger German warships which might have assisted an invasion of Britain after the fall of France. They also played the key role in extracting 338,000 British and Allied men from Dunkirk and another 200,000 people from French ports right round to the Spanish frontier.

The article 'A Trip to Sea' describes well the later stages of the Norwegian campaign because HMS *Beagle* escorted reinforcements to Norway, supported our army at the Third Battle of Narvik – then helped re-embark them for the return to Britain. Throughout, they were under air attacks – often heavy. Roland Butler, *Beagle*'s senior Engine Room Artificer, who tells the story, was continuously at the throttles for eight hours during one particularly fierce battle. AB Stanley Robinson's account of surviving the loss of HM Ships *Hardy* and *Hunter*, and the destruction of all ten German destroyers at Narvik, paints in the earlier part of the Norway story. Len Deighton's *Blood, Tears and Folly* covers the gallant defence of aircraft carrier HMS *Glorious* by *Ardent* and *Acasta*, whose torpedoing of *Scharnhorst* prevented a much worse disaster – a subsequent interception of the returning troopships by two enemy battlecruisers.

The recovery of important Dutch and Belgian assets; the heroic evacuation of our own army from France, from port after port; and attempts to destroy other assets, which could help our enemy, are well covered in a kaleidoscopic series of articles. Iain Nethercott, in HMS *Keith*, and Captain Sam Lombard-Hobson, RN, then First Lieutenant of HMS *Whitshed*, paint a particularly vivid picture of rescuing the Irish Guards from Boulogne. Even Lord Nelson might have recognised this as warm work – with both commanding officers being killed by snipers. Able Seaman 'Phil' Merryweather, swept out of his training class at HMS *Vernon* to join HMS *Basilisk*, gives a good account of her short life, including the Second Battle of Narvik and ending at Dunkirk. Then three of HMS *Keith*'s ship's company: Telegraphist John Beeley, Stoker John Cranston, and Iain Nethercott give a moving account of her loss at Dunkirk, and their adventures whilst getting back to Britain.

HMS *Bulldog* and *Boadicea* did some difficult work rescuing men of the 51st Highland Division from the beaches near St. Valery, and only survived the subsequent dive-bombing attacks thanks to excellent damage control, the almost providential arrival of a bank of fog – and the bombs being released too low to fuse properly. Lieutenant Hewitt, 'Jimmy' of *Bulldog*, and Lieutenant Hubert Fox in *Boadicea* help tell the story in 'A Prayer Answered' – the latter by now anything but bored.

This section also includes descriptions of being evacuated from St. Nazaire by Sergeant Sidney Gaze of the 125th Yeomanry – who pays a fine tribute to the captain and officers of SS *Oronsay* – and the general scene at St. Nazaire by PO ERA Roland Butler, whose ship HMS *Beagle* went straight on to France, almost as soon as they got back from Norway. The story of *Beagle*'s 'Mission to the River Gironde', to destroy port facilities at Bordeaux – put together from accounts by other members of her ship's company – gives a good feel for the situation immediately after the fall of France: order, counter-order and near disorder.

As the Germans turned their attention to Britain in July, HMS *Beagle* was quite badly damaged off Dover and HMS *Brazen* sunk, events covered by Peter Smith in *Hold the Narrow Sea*. The *Daily Telegraph*, on 23 July, tried to reassure its readership that, despite grievous losses, we now had more destroyers than in September 1939. Maybe so. But the number needed was escalating much faster, as U-boats started to whittle away our under-protected Merchant Navy resources.

The article 'A View from the German Side' makes it plain that there never was any real possibility of their making a sea invasion of Britain – certainly not after their losses in Norway and Goering's misdirection of the

Luftwaffe. But there was every chance of them winning the war on shipping. So remaining articles in this chapter are devoted to giving readers a first feel for the demanding nature of our trade protection task. 'On Patrol with *Boreas* and *Brilliant*' gives a good idea of the mixed hazards of East Coast convoy escorting, and 'A View from the Merchant Navy', first of three articles by Merchant Navy seaman Sidney Davies, paints the grim reality of being a target in a slow moving Halifax-UK convoy – as do excerpts from Len Deighton's *Blood, Tears and Folly*, and accounts by survivors from SS *Arandora Star*, including Sergeant Sidney Gaze.

CHANNEL PATROL

Lieutenant Commander Hubert C. Fox, RN, Retd., HMS *Boadicea*

23 November 1939

One thing about the war. There is no difficulty in practising economy. Although Income Tax is pretty terrific, I feel I am gradually settling my overdraft and may be flush by the time the great peace arrives.

25 December 1939

I know what your Christmas has been like and I am sorry not to have shared it with you. Mine has been on somewhat different lines.

We were keeping our "ceaseless vigil", as I believe our King described it in his broadcast. At that time five officers were stretched out in front of our little electric stove and sleeping the sleep of the righteous. The Chief was the only one awake and was struck by the apt description.

9 January 1940

Since my leave we have been almost continuously at sea and it has been incredibly boring and monotonous. I have blessed you each night for your sleeping bag, in which I have wallowed in the short intervals between night watches.

The weather has been calm, for which we can be very thankful. Since the outbreak of war we have done close on a 100 days at sea. How I look forward to peace!

An Able Seaman requested leave to get married at 3 o'clock this afternoon, this at eight this morning. I refused it as I thought we'd be at sea, but
I sent him ashore then and there, to do what he could about it and be back
by 11. He was back at 11, duly married!

17 January 1940

I have been ashore for a short time today in the interval between spells at sea,
and walked through a snow-mantled town. Everything looked so beautiful,
rosy-cheeked children with snow-balls, snow-mantled towers, and all. It
wasn't too cold ashore, but it is icy on deck onboard. Everything seems to be
frozen. The decks are thick with snow. Tomorrow we'll be ploughing the sea
again.

21 January 1940

It has been cold, but I don't mind it. One's toes and fingers just give up feeling for nights at a time, but it is infinitely better than being tossed round the
ship like a pea in a pod. It's very picturesque having the ship garlanded with
icicles. By the way, we have been at sea since the war started as much as any
ship in the Navy.

7 February 1940

Yes. This time it was us. We had the whole outfit (the War Cabinet) on the
way back [from a meeting of the Supreme War Council], scenes very similar
to those in this morning's *Times*. It was most interesting. We lay at the quay
at Boulogne waiting to take them back. Presently the neat figure of Neville
Chamberlain approached, surrounded by his retinue like a popular master at
a preparatory school conducting the Sunday walk. One or two of the boys
preferred to trudge along by themselves. Among these was Winston
Churchill. They came on board, most of them going up to the bridge, where
they watched all that happened with great animation. There was one satis-
factory incident. A mine was sighted and we blew it sky high first shot, bits
of it very nearly descending on the Big Noises. Everyone was very gratified
at the good marksmanship. Winston soon disappeared off the bridge and
went to the wardroom. The Prime Minister got cold so we had some soup
brought up for him. Warm in the wardroom, Churchill growled, "Tell the

Prime Minister to have some gin". Churchill sat in the wardroom at the long polished table drinking port and sucking a cigar. He was flicking over the pages of *Blighty*, a popular magazine containing pictures of ladies without clothes. Later we lost him altogether for a time and eventually found him in the stokers' mess deck sitting on a mess table swapping yarns. The others mostly stayed on the bridge, where the press was indescribable. The PM was most gracious.

After seeing the *Times* we feel under no obligation to observe secrecy.

25 February 1940

There is nothing to tell you about from here. We are, as usual, at sea most of the time, but that is all right. We are starting a new watch-keeping scheme which will be much kinder to the First Lieutenant. I don't think I could have gone on another year with the old one, 8 or 10 hours a night at sea as well as most of the work by day, but not too much maudlin self-pity. The other officers are more experienced now so it can be done.

10 March 1940

I went ashore yesterday afternoon and got into a handy bus, was asked where I was bound, said "I don't know", was told that "That will be 1d", and went on until I was nicely in the country, where I got out, climbed over the hedge and walked. Every time I saw a roof I put the wheel over.

After about half an hour I found myself singing and having a nice chat with sheep lying happily beside their lambs. In other words, the walk did me good.

The Captain has flu and is in 'Sandhurst', so life has been eventful lately.

27 March 1940

While the Captain, Bodley Kingdon, was sick I took over command. We continued our patrols in the English Channel. During a brief visit to Dover the King came aboard to walk around. It was my privilege to escort him.

19 April 1940

There is really nothing much to say. You will have heard by now not to expect me when I said. I am very pleased at the lack of resentment and disappointment on board at the continued postponement of the refit. It is awfully interesting being on the pulse of 150 men, as the First Lieutenant is. I always know in lots of little ways exactly what the feeling is in the ship.

26 April 1940

It was fortunate that your flowers were posted when they were as I got them after only about two days in the post, and they were so well packed that they have mostly freshened out. Nearly every officer in the ship has some in his tooth-mug now, so if they all get pyorrhoea by not cleaning their teeth you will be responsible. They are lovely and very much appreciated.

27 April 1940

I estimate the time I shall see you as just about two weeks from now. It's all 'buzz', but there it is for what it is worth. 'Official date' is a great joke onboard now, and I saw this morning on a notice board a date (of the eating variety) pinned up with 'OFFICIAL' written on it!...

INVASION OF THE LOW COUNTRIES

Lt Commander Fox: On 10 May 1940 the Germans invaded Holland and Belgium, and their armour carried all before them. The British fought their way back to Dunkirk. Boadicea was refitting at Chatham at the time and I remember battle-scarred destroyers putting in for quick repairs. Meanwhile, thousands of men were being carried from the beaches at Dunkirk in small craft manned by RN personnel to the destroyers offshore while under fierce attack from the air.

By the beginning of June the evacuation was completed. However, we still had three British divisions in France holding, with the 10th French Army, the line of the River Somme. They now received the full fury of the German assault. The 51st Highland Division fell back on St. Valery, where they were eventually forced to surrender.

A TRIP TO SEA

Petty Officer Roland Butler, Engine Room Artificer, HMS *Beagle*

The ship you are about to take a trip in was ten years old, built at John Brown's, Glasgow, with a tonnage of 1,350 and a horse power of 34,000, from which we could manage to get 38 knots; with a crew of 150, mostly rookies, and commanded by Lieutenant Commander R. H. Wright.

At 0800 hours on 10 May 1940 we left ———— Docks, where we'd had our boilers cleaned after having steamed 12,000 miles since they were last cleaned. This distance was done in 63 days, 57 being sea time, the last 28 continuously with a convoy of merchant ships comprising Admiralty transports, oil tankers, colliers and a few Norwegian supply ships. We arrived at 'B' in company with the merchant ships at 1900 hours, and, after taking in a few hundred tons of oil, we proceeded to an anchorage for the night. Further up the river we could see French and English ships at anchor, amongst them being the ————.

We had been with her on our last trip only a week or so before, using our 'asdic' gear with other destroyers to screen her and the other ships from submarines. Then, while steaming about 45 miles from ———— at about three in the afternoon on a beautiful day, bombs began to fall and the guns began to fire. One of the bombers, having received a hit, came down, circling our stern from port to starboard, dropping his last bomb about 50 to 100 feet astern from a height of 100 feet. The bomber crashed into the sea right abreast of the ship, and those on deck were cheering frantically. We didn't stop to pick up survivors because of the importance of the ships having their screening all the time. The airmen were just unfortunate.

At 0830 hours next day, 12 May, we left ———— in company with our convoy, and, soon reaching the open sea, we headed north, picking up another tanker the next day. After having been with the carriers where high speeds were required, it seemed slow work doing only six knots, as indeed it was.

Leaving the Orkneys, the last land to be sighted, a couple of destroyers brought us some more ships, and took two tankers under escort to Scapa Flow. We steamed north-east, and then changed convoys, the 'W' and *Firedrake* taking the faster ships and leaving us with the slower, while for outside patrol we had two trawlers.

By now we were in a position 60°N 06°W, and, pushing ahead at eight knots, we were, by 18 May, in a position of 70°19'N 08°40'E. We picked up our first convoy of oilers, this being a good piece of work by a lookout spotting a puff of smoke 25 miles away. We could still see the sun on the southern horizon at midnight.

It was now very cold, and the wind very keen. Extra blankets and over-coats were needed to sleep on the mess decks, for there was no heating system installed. The trawlers, which were doing the escorting with us, were short of bread and meat, so we acted as 'baker and butcher' and supplied each of them with 30lbs of each. The bread had just been baked, so it would have been very welcome.

We were now getting short of oil for the boilers, and we decided to carry out an evolution of oiling at sea. In peacetime this is done from battleships or cruisers to destroyers, but now it was tanker to destroyer, and the *Oleander* was the tanker. The necessary springs were got aboard, and without much difficulty the hose was connected up and oil pumped into our tanks. As it was only a small hose, the job of taking in 100 tons was likely to take about three hours. Then one of the springs broke, but a new one was soon across with an additional one for safety. There was quite a heavy swell running, and, after taking in about 38 tons, the connection joining the hose about half way between the ships became loose, the hose parted and oiling ceased. We had, however, taken in another day's supply, and, as we were likely to be at sea some time, this additional fuel was valuable.

We were now in a position of 72°03'N, which is about 1,100 miles from the North Pole, and on the whole it had been a remarkable day's work. In peacetime the job of oiling at sea calls for shoals of signals and days of prepa-ration.

Next morning the trawlers, being short of coal, pushed on for harbour, taking with them a ship that was also short. On the morning of 21 May we had orders to look out for further destroyers, but our position was not very accurately known owing to the lack of getting a good shot at the sun, moon or stars. We eventually picked the destroyers up in the forenoon watch, the *Echo* and *Delight* and an escort vessel, the *Fleetwood*. The latter took over part of the convoy, and, we, together with the *Echo* and *Delight*, took the tankers, store ships, etc., on towards our destination. In the afternoon we sighted the carrier *Ark Royal* on the horizon.

We were now steaming south-east, and at noon our position was 69°14'N, 10°25'E, and land should have been sighted in the last dog watch, but visibility was poor. We arrived at the entrance to the fjord at 0400 hours, but having to take a tow slowed down our rate of travel, and we arrived at a place called Harstad at 1030 hours.

The coloured houses showed up well, with the snow-covered hills and mountains as a background. We learned that the bombers had been paying a great deal of attention to this place. In Harstad on the morning of 22 May we saw the results of twelve raids in five days. There was damage to houses as well as oil tanks near the beach. We proceeded to take in oil from the *British Governor*, and then went to anchor.

Although it was not our first view of Norway, we enjoyed the keen air, and the snow was rapidly melting in the hot sunshine. Not far away there was an Admiralty troopship disembarking men and stores. A signal told us that 13 enemy planes were in the vicinity, and not long after they came, and then again and again.

We were thankful to leave at 1500 hours, though we did not know our destination. This proved to be one of the entrances to the fjord which had to be patrolled. Another ship patrolled the second entrance and a third ship the third entrance. We patrolled all day on the 23rd, stopping a small boat for examination, a girl and a man being the sole occupants. It was a gloriously fine day, and we kept circling around the fjord at 13 knots. We had an air raid, but it looked as if they were after something bigger.

The next forenoon we left the patrol to escort the Admiralty trooper *Ulster Prince* to a position as ordered. The day was less bright, but I was able to see the midnight sun for the first time.

On returning to Harstad, we soon saw what the bombers had been after the previous day, for the Admiralty trooper was beached. Just as we were going to the oiler the bombers came over again, and dropped four bombs ahead and one astern. The raid kept us from oiling until 2030 hours, and afterwards we again cruised about. Mail came aboard at 2300 hours, so there was not much sleep that night. The next day started with an air raid at 0600 hours, another at 0900 hours, and three more before midday. We went alongside the quay at 1600 hours, taking in stores and embarking 150 troops, one a Barry man, from 50 Glamur Crescent.

We arrived at our destination at 0330 hours on the 26th, a place called Bodo. What a glorious morning! We disembarked the troops as hurriedly as possible since we were the last boat, the *Face* and the *Firedrake* having done a similar job and, being senior boats, they had to come first. We then had to return via the open sea, as we had come, but went back a much shorter way through the fjord. As we went alongside the oiler on our return the bombs started falling. The raid lasted two hours, and, after a lull of nearly an hour, the raiders came again but did not drop any bombs.

Later the alarm sounded again, and we cruised in the fjord until a signal was received ordering us to go to the help of the *Curlew*. We raced through the fjord, but could see no signs of her. Then, by a good bit of navigation, we turned and went back. The *Curlew* had gone, but we picked up the survivors with the exception of about a dozen who were missing. She was an anti-aircraft light cruiser. We returned to Harstad, and, having disembarked them, we went alongside an oiler. As a result of the air raids earlier in the day, the oiler *Oleander* was beached, together with a store ship. Several ships had holes in their hulls. Quite an eventful day, ending with the welcome news that 18 RAF Spitfires had arrived and that three Ju 88s had been brought down.

On the morning of 27 May we cruised near the harbour, everything being very quiet until an air raid at 0700 hours. While cruising we saw *Eskimo* whose bows had been blown off at Narvik. She had been towed here for temporary repairs before steaming home under her own power.

At 1200 hours we moved off up a fjord towards Narvik, but were ordered to return to Harstad for orders. We then sailed again in the direction of Narvik. The lower deck was cleared, and the Captain told us we were about to take part in 'The Third Battle of Narvik'. The attacking force would consist of three cruisers and five destroyers, together with the French Foreign Legion and Norwegian troops ashore. Air cover would be provided by two flights of RAF Hurricanes. The battle was due to commence at 2345 hours. At that time our planes were to attack the airfield from which the German planes had been mounting their attacks.

We reached the position of our proposed bombardment at about 2330 hours. The objective was a railway station and, opening fire with tracers, we soon found the range. No more season or excursion tickets would be issued from that place... Our firing at a second objective was just as accurate before the bombardment was due to conclude at 0045 hours and then the land forces were due to move in. It turned out that some of the planning had not been too successful.

At 0430 hours, enemy bombers came over. At 0450 hours a bomb fell close enough to shower bomb splinters on the deck while the bridge was machine-gunned. The *Beagle* was, in fact, exceedingly well handled on the bridge. This is high praise as it comes from a man who spent eight hours at the throttles of the *Beagle*'s engines for the whole duration of the air raids. The other ERA (Engine Room Artificer) was from Cornwall and was a 'rookie'. What the Navy would do without them I don't know.

Being below from 0425 hours, I didn't witness the events which immediately followed, but this account can be taken as accurate. There were air raids on and off all morning and, although we were due to be relieved by another destroyer at 1200 hours, things did not turn out as expected. We continued patrolling and endured several more air raids, but these stopped when fighters appeared.

The land forces evidently now expected that, in the course of 'mopping up', machine gun nests would be encountered and that our guns, and those of the other destroyers, would blow the emplacements to pieces.

In the meantime, the French Foreign Legionnaires were attacking the Narvik defences from the north, and the Polish troops from the south. In the north, naval bombardments lasting 35 minutes were carried out in support of the troops, and then more troops were landed by boat. In the south, the Poles and Alpine Chasseurs became held up by German forces, and then had to retreat under heavy machine gun fire.

The *Beagle* then returned to Rombaksfjord, where a signal was sent from shore giving positions of targets. After our successful bombardment of these positions, the troops rallied and counter-attacked, and eventually gained possession of the hill overlooking their objective.

After an air raid at 0030 hours on the morning of 29 May, we were left in peace from the bombers. At 0910 hours, a few rounds of 4.7-inch were fired into a position from where German troops were known to be escaping. Details were given through a naval unit ashore, under Lieutenant D. R.

Duff, which provided a link between us, the French Headquarters and troops on the other side of Rombaksfjord.

Later, we sailed for Harstad, and, feeling our way through fog, sighted a strange ship. We cleared for action, but the ship turned out to be from one of our convoys. We arrived at Harstad at 0700 hours on the 30th and refuelled from the oiler. We also took on ammunition and coal for the galley, and then steamed around the harbour. Later, the Captain went ashore to receive orders, as a result of which we sailed at 1230 hours, at high speed, down the coast.

While we were capturing Narvik, in northern Norway, our troops further south were now being evacuated. It was pretty rough, but a steady 26 knots was maintained. We learned that most of the other ships which had taken part in the 'Third Battle of Narvik' had been hit or damaged by shrapnel or concussion.

The *Beagle*'s 'A' gun was out of action due to a part breaking when bombs fell close by. We reached our destination in company with the Fame and the Firedrake at 2300 hours, and began the evacuation of 500 or 600 Allied soldiers in each ship, the Fame going in first, followed by the Firedrake, while we were the last ship away. Luckily, the clouds were low overhead, although the sun broke through at times.

The once quiet and peaceful town was now a shambles. In 95 per cent of the houses and shops the only things that remained standing were the fireplaces and the chimneys. We learned that 12 German bombers had attacked the town continuously, and when people ran for shelter the planes machinegunned them in the streets. Fires were still burning in many places.

The Allied troops appeared to be coming from all directions, and we took aboard 550 officers and men, leaving behind some 150 troops to be evacuated next day. The troops had many vivid stories to tell. And how they welcomed the Royal Navy...

The failure of this operation, and not by any means the only one, was lack of aircraft for support. We landed the troops safely, and afterwards returned to Harstad for oil and to await further orders. We welcomed this since we had several minor defects to make good.

I was just about 'all in'. I had my first food for 20 hours and my first rest for 48. We also took in stores from the store ship, whose hull was quite battered and holed above the waterline from the bombing of a few days previously. Then going alongside the *Havelock* for orders from Captain (D) we hit her stern with our port quarter, and as I was in charge of the engine room I had to be present at the Inquiry into the cause.

During all of 1 June and the morning of the 2nd, we were patrolling, stopping and examining small local craft. Then at 1400 hours on 2 June, orders came to proceed to Oersted to take in oil. On our way there, six bombs fell around us. We then went alongside the tanker to take in oil, emptying the water tanks to make room for another 30 tons of oil. But then we found that instead of oil we had been given 30 tons of water, which only added to our troubles.

3 June opened cold but fine, with *Southampton, Walker* and *Havelock* in company, and during the morning the water was pumped overboard and oil taken from the tanker instead. Rumours were rife in Harstad. At 1445 hours we left there, steaming south at 25 knots. We cruised around for some hours to put the pro-German element off the track, and then called into a landing-place 12 miles from Harstad, where we picked up 450 troops.

The embarkation completed, we raced them to the *Monarch of Bermuda*, which was one of several troopships waiting at the mouth of the fjord. There was a heavy swell and our ship's side suffered badly. We continued to repeat this operation over the next three days, taking more British and French troops and Royal Air Force personnel to the *Monarch of Bermuda*, as well as to the *Batory* and *Sobieski*.

Between these ferrying trips we continued to be engaged in anti-submarine patrolling. At 1830 hours on 7 June, after taking on oil, we left Harstad for Narvik. Reports that a squadron of bombers had been over Narvik during the day did nothing for our enjoyment of the move, and we were somewhat glad that this was to be the final evacuation trip. But the clouds stayed very low, and although enemy planes were reported we did not see any. In addition, our own planes from the carriers were prominent, so we felt well satisfied.

From 'puffer' fishing boats[13] at Narvik, besides a few British troops, naval ratings and Chasseurs-Alpins, we took aboard the French Foreign Legion.

---

[13] During the Norwegian campaign 'puffers' were British-manned fishing boats which operated with trawlers in the fjords, supplying General Sir Colin Gubbins's independent companies (forerunners of the Royal Marines Commandos) with stores, personnel and ammunition. General Gubbins was head of the Special Operations Executive (SOE) with orders from Prime Minister Churchill to "set Europe ablaze".

The Legionnaires looked tough and, from what we were told, they certainly were. To be 23 days on the march without a wash or even a cigarette takes some doing, and they were glad to be on board. The planes mentioned earlier had, in fact, been bombing them and they'd had a few killed; their wounded were treated by *Beagle*'s doctor. Souvenirs were plentiful. One sailor was given the German flag that had been flying over Narvik when the Legionnaires took it. They even had an Iron Cross!

The return trip was uneventful. At 0630 hours on 8 June, we disembarked all the troops on to the troopship *Duchess of York*. The disembarkation complete, the whole convoy, consisting of five troopships, two cruisers and nine destroyers, moved off. By 1030 hours we were in the open sea, sailing at 15 knots, despite a very heavy swell. At about 1330 hours we slowed down to allow three more troopships, which had left a day earlier, to join the convoy, and then on we went.

The sea wasn't so bad on 9 June, and as the day wore on the sun came out, although it was very cold. Blackburn Skuas from an aircraft carrier in the vicinity flew round us during the day. Later, a battleship with four destroyers appeared on the scene. Not long afterwards a German plane came swooping out of the low clouds, but soon returned there after a few bursts of fire from the ships.

The next morning a signal from *Ark Royal* confirmed that one Heinkel had been shot down and several Heinkels and Dorniers damaged by her fighters. Later in the day we were saddened to hear that the aircraft carrier *Glorious*, the destroyers *Acasta* and *Ardent*, the tanker *Oil Pioneer* and a troopship had been lost.[14] We had been in close contact with the *Glorious*

---

[14] Following the 'Third Battle of Narvik' and subsequent evacuation, the aircraft carrier HMS *Glorious*, her decks crammed with RAF Gladiators and Hurricanes and screened by the destroyers *Ardent* and *Acasta*, steamed south for Scotland. But on 8 June, the three ships were located by the German battlecruisers *Scharnhorst* and the *Gneisenau*. The heavily armed German ships opened fire at 1600 hours. The one-sided battle was over within two hours; the giant carrier rolled over and sank at 1740 hours. The gallant crews of the *Ardent* and *Acasta*, after laying a smokescreen in a vain attempt to protect the *Glorious*, turned towards the two battlecruisers at high speed and fired all their torpedoes before being sunk by ovewhelming firepower. However, the last torpedo launched towards *Scharnhorst* by the *Acasta* struck its target and caused sufficient damage to put the German ship out of action for the next six months. There were only 46 survivors from the three British ships. The Germans made no rescue attempts.

and *Oil Pioneer*, and we felt it badly. We also heard of Italy declaring war.

Later, a battlecruiser appeared on the horizon to join the battleship *Valiant*, and a flying boat circled us at intervals. As we were passing the Hebrides on a beautiful morning on 12 June, the *Valiant*, *Southampton* and the battlecruiser left us, presumably to go to Scapa Flow. We then reached the entrance to the Clyde at 1800 hours, and arrived off Greenock with the troopships at 2300 hours.

A RATING'S EXPERIENCE OF NARVIK

Anthologist's Note: One of the naval ratings who had been rescued earlier, and had participated in the First Battle of Narvik (two German destroyers sunk, three more damaged in addition to six merchant ships sunk), was AB Stanley Robinson of the destroyer HMS *Hardy*. Here is his brief account:

'We had steamed north to Norway from Scapa Flow. At 2300 on 9 April, 1940, entered Ofotfjord with other destroyers from our Flotilla, the *Havock*, *Hotspur*, *Hostile* and *Hunter*, and opened fire on several German destroyers off Narvik harbour at 0345 on 10th April. At about 0650 I suddenly found myself in the freezing water of the fjord swimming for my life. The *Hunter* had been sunk, the *Hardy* badly damaged and, having sustained heavy casualties, was beached. Exhausted, I laid by the water's edge with other survivors. Then a big Norwegian civilian picked me up and carried me to his house where I stayed for a few hours until the Germans came searching for us. We immediately left. We walked and ran, with virtually no clothes on, for about 15 exhausting miles through the snow, eventually arriving at a settlement called Ballangen. We stayed there, hiding in the nearby phosphate mine during the daytime and emerging at night for food and drink. The supportive Norwegians gave us bread, milk and fish during the next few days. Early on the 13th April, the battleship HMS *Warspite*, with her 15-inch guns, supported by a strong force of destroyers, entered the fjord, thereby trapping the eight remaining German destroyers. They were sunk, one after the other, by the battleship. This was known as the 'Second Battle of Narvik'. The few survivors from the *Hardy* were picked up by another destroyer which came right alongside Ballangen's pier at midnight and we filed aboard. When we got out of the fjord we transferred to the *Hero*, one of our flotilla, and eventually got home to Greenock, Scotland, with the other destroyers. An article in our national press dated 25 July 1940 describes in some detail what happened to the German destroyers on that fateful 13 April:

GERMAN LOSSES AT NARVIK
2,000 SAILORS DEAD

"It was disclosed by the Admiralty last night, that at least 2,000 sailors were killed when seven large German destroyers were sunk in the second battle of Narvik on 13 April. The destroyers were the *Diether von Roder, Hans Ludemann, Ewolfgang Zenker, Bernd von Arnim, Erich Koellner, Hermann Kunne,* and the *Erich Giese.*

The *Erich Giese* had on board 300 soldiers with full equipment, in addition to her normal complement of 300 officers and men. When the British warships attacked they got the range almost at once. The *Erich Giese* was struck again and again by shells. Guns, engine-room, funnels and wireless cabin were all hit.

The *Erich Giese* was the only German destroyer left, and her Captain could not keep steerage way on the ship. Wounded and dying men were lying everywhere and not one gun remained in action. No order could reach the engine room.

Finally, the Captain gave orders to abandon ship. Fifty or sixty wounded men were left to die in the burning vessel. The end came when one of the magazines blew up.'"

Excerpt from *Blood, Tears and Folly* by Len Deighton

(Reproduced by kind permission of The Random House Group & Jonathan Clowes Ltd.)

The German flotilla had already sunk a tanker and an empty troopship. HMS *Glorious* was spotted at 28 miles by a young midshipman in the foretop of *Scharnhorst*. At this time the German 'Seetakt' radar provided more accurate range measurement than optical range-finders, and was of course unaffected by fog, smoke or darkness.

The German ship opened fire at 28,000 yards and *Glorious* was hit. Set afire, she capsized and sank complete with most of her crew and two squadrons of battle-trained fighter pilots. Many of the ship's boats were holed by gunfire and others capsized in the heavy sea.

In a letter home, dated 26 June 1940, Squadron Leader Kenneth 'Bing' Cross wrote:

"When we were in the raft the Germans came up, had a look and then went straight away. I have a real hatred for the Germans now."

On his raft were 29 men, of whom only seven were left when finally they were picked up after three nights and two days at sea, and of these two died later. Of the ship's complement of 1,400 men, only 39 survived.

At the time of the action, two destroyers, *Acasta* and *Ardent*, which were the carrier's only escort, made smoke and retaliated with fearless torpedo attacks, but they too were sunk. One of *Acasta*'s torpedoes, fired while she was almost in her death throes, hit *Scharnhorst*, putting two of three engine rooms out of action, so that the flotilla had to limp back to Trondheim.

Of the crews of the British destroyers only three men survived, but this gallant action no doubt saved the weakly escorted troop convoys to which the Germans had got so close.

RAMIFICATIONS OF DEFEAT

Anthologist's Note: The Allies retreated from Norway, but from that defeat a vital fact emerged. The German Navy had been damaged to such an extent that any immediate plans for the invasion of Britain had to be ruled out. Allied losses were one aircraft carrier, two cruisers, one sloop, and nine destroyers. Six cruisers, two sloops, and eight destroyers were severely damaged, but were repairable. Apart from their repairable surface ships, the German Navy, after their costly encounters with the Royal Navy during the first eight months of war, consisted of one heavy cruiser, two light cruisers, and four destroyers.

EVACUATION FROM FRANCE

Anthologist's Note: During the night of 9-10 May 1940, the Germans launched a series of devastating air and ground attack against airfields, communications centres and fortifications in Holland, Belgium and Luxembourg on a front 150 miles wide. They then swung south towards northern France. By late May and early June, the exhausted survivors of the defeated British Expeditionary Force and Allied armies had retreated to the north-western coast of France. The majority reached the sandy beaches near Dunkirk, in the hope of being rescued by the Royal Navy, Merchant Navy, the Allied navies and numerous smaller craft, the 'Little Ships', manned by RN and MN seamen. The miracle that became known as Operation 'Dynamo' was only made possible by a combination of very fine weather and countless acts of extraordinary gallantry while under shellfire and fierce air attack from German forces.

On 4 June 1940, the Admiralty announced that Operation 'Dynamo' had been completed. More than 338,000 British and Allied troops had been landed safely in England. In that critical time-span countless acts of bravery had made the seemingly impossible a stunning reality, up and down the continental coasts.

'AN INCREDIBLE ACHIEVEMENT'

From *Hold The Narrow Sea* by Peter C. Smith

HMS *Brilliant* (Lieutenant Commander F. C. Brodrick) lived up to her name at Antwerp as the fighting moved down the coast. She arrived at that port on the evening of 10 May and succeeded in getting to safety a huge fleet that would otherwise have fallen into German hands. By 12 May, twenty-six merchantmen and fifty invaluable tugs, followed two days later by no less than six hundred barges, dredgers and floating cranes were evacuated: an incredible achievement.

At the Hook of Holland meanwhile, the demolition party was obstructed by the Dutch, but managed to carry out its work by 13 May. To protect these demolition parties Royal Marines were dispatched on the night of 11/12 May and troops of the Irish and Welsh Guards followed. The whole operation was controlled by Captain D. E. Halsey, Captain (D16) aboard the flotilla leader *Malcolm* with eight destroyers from Dover under his orders.

When the Dutch Army capitulated, as many troops and refugees as possible were brought out on 14 May, despite delays caused by fog. The Dutch still refused to co-operate in demolitions and also turned down offers to take off their troops. Many of their lesser warships sailed for England, however, under heavy air bombardment. This day saw the loss of the passenger vessel *Ville de Bruges* (13,869 tons), but other Dutch warships reached Portsmouth including the minelayers *Jan Van Brakel* and *Nautilus*, the tug *Amsterdam*, armed yacht *De Mok*, torpedo boats G13, G15, Z5 and Z8, and the armed trawlers BV42 and BV45. A second group consisting of the minelayers *Medusa* and *Dowe Aukes* and torpedo boats Z6 and Z7 also got away to England, as did the light cruiser *Jacob van Heemskerck*, destroyers G13 and G15, and seven submarines.

EVENTS LEADING TO THE EVACUATION OF BOULOGNE

Iain Nethercott, Gunner, HMS *Keith,*
Captain Sam Lombard-Hobson, RN, Retd., HMS *Whitshed*

Iain Nethercott: During February 1940, *Keith* relieved HMS *Codrington* as Leader of the 19th Destroyer Flotilla at Dover. There we found some of our original Flotilla. I vaguely recall *Basilisk, Boreas* and *Wakeful,* with *Vimy* tied up to a buoy in the middle of Dover Harbour. The indomitable *Whitshed,* under Commander Conder our Divisional Leader, was at sea in the Straits of Dover.

Every other night during the spring of 1940, we steamed into the Downs, near the East Goodwin Lightship, off Kingsdown, Kent, to act as Anti-Aircraft Guard to all the merchant ships anchored there, awaiting the Neutrality Control Inspectors, who inspected the cargoes and papers of ships bound for Holland and Belgium. Both countries preferred to remain strictly neutral at that time. However, as things developed they were in for an extremely unpleasant surprise in the very near future.

As the warmer weather of April arrived we took advantage of long evenings and nights spent at anchor in the spring sunshine, with little to do except keep the ship clean and ship-shape, and stroll the decks in the dog watches.

At the beginning of May, we sailed round to Sheerness and moored off Bullsnose. We were joined by a large number of 'V & W' class destroyers and the cruisers *Arethusa* and *Galatea* (to escort two merchant ships carrying gold bullion from IJmuiden to the United Kingdom). We carried out Fire Drills continuously, exercised the guns repeatedly until we were blue in the face and turned in at night completely exhausted. Captain Simson, our Commanding Officer, was obviously not prepared to take his ship into action with an untrained and ill-disciplined crew.

On 10 May 1940, things really blew up. Hitler's legions invaded neutral Holland and Belgium and an almighty panic was on... We immediately got steam up and sailed with *Boreas,* accompanying the two 5,000-ton cruisers at 30 knots to the Dutch coast. That was the first time in my career that I saw Battle Ensigns hoisted at all yardarms. The decks were strewn with fire-hoses and the wardroom had been turned into an operating theatre, with our resident 'quack' (Ship's Surgeon) and his Sick Berth Attendant busily laying out stainless steel scalpels, saws, knives, etc., ready to amputate shattered limbs and parts of our anatomies if we were injured in action.

We saw the two cruisers swing their main armament of 6-inch guns towards several small black dots in the sky ahead. *Arethusa* and *Galatea* then opened rapid fire, the shells bursting all around the German bombers, for that's what they were. But within a very short time they'd all disappeared back towards the east.

Leaving the cruisers outside the entrance to the Hook of Holland, we crept into the estuary. We saw a couple of German Air Force floatplanes tied up to a navigation buoy out in the stream. Our 'A' and 'B' 4.7-inch guns opened up and blew them to pieces as we passed slowly up the River Waal. HMS *Broke*, of another Flotilla, was alongside a deserted jetty. After a rapid exchange of signals, she cast off and, making a turn in her own length in the harbour, she steamed slowly down river and left us on our own, tied up to the empty pier.

There was a sound of rifle fire in the distance and a large warehouse on the jetty was well on fire, with no one to extinguish it. Apart from those inter-mittent rifle shots, it was eerily lonely. Our orders were to wait alongside at the Hook of Holland to pick up a party of Royal Marines who had gone to Rotterdam and Antwerp to collect industrial diamonds and any VIP Dutch officials who wanted passage to Britain.

We waited for several hours and, at last, a slow trickle of refugees began to arrive as darkness descended. The strangest party we took aboard *Keith* was a complete Dutch Army Military Band, complete with large, green bicy-cles. They were very lucky because when we had first spotted them riding along the pier, we first mistook them for German troops as they were wear-ing the same 'coal-scuttle'-shaped helmets worn by the German Army.

Just as it was getting dark, a German Air Force seaplane came in low over the harbour and dropped a parachute mine right under *Keith*'s stern. It came and went so quickly that only one Lewis gunner on our bridge had a shot at it.

We then began to come under sporadic fire from behind the warehouses, but there were still no visible targets. Having a considerable number of civilians with an assortment of suitcases and bundles, together with most of the Royal Marines who had also arrived, our Skipper decided it was time to shove off as it was getting less healthy by the minute.

We dropped astern, and from where I was on the pom-pom deck, I saw the parachute mine pass underneath our ship. Thank God for our earlier degaussing...

Coming down the River Waal, we came under fire from light German artillery from beyond the starboard bank. Our main armament returned fire. We reached the open sea, saw several other destroyers offshore, and set course for Dover at full speed with our precious cargo. We overtook dozens of ships of all sizes; tugs, fishing boats, canal barges and merchant ships, all making for England, but the strangest was a half-completed Dutch warship, about the size of a cruiser, being towed westwards by two large tugs.

We landed our passengers at Dover, went to the oiler and sailed back to Holland with the *Vimeira*[15] within the hour. Off the Dutch coast, *Keith* took over as leader of a mixed bag of 'V' and 'W' destroyers.

After about a week off the coast, assisting refugee ships streaming towards the English east coast ports, we returned to Dover for fuel and ammunition, and with most of our Flotilla, awaited orders. All was chaos at the Admiralty as the German Armies poured into northern France and advanced rapidly towards the coast.

On 19 May, our line of destroyers, patrolling off the south-western Belgian coast near Nieuport, was heavily attacked by Ju 87 dive-bombers. They hit *Whitley* on 'X' gun, killing all the gun's crew and setting fire to the ammunition. The bombers swept along the line and were met by a storm of pom-pom and twin Lewis gunfire. One Stuka came in from abeam, aiming at the *Burza*, a Polish destroyer which, among its armament, was equipped with twin Breda anti-aircraft guns. The bomber was practically torn in half and cartwheeled into the water off the port side. Another Stuka, coming in to attack *Keith*, released his bombs prematurely, which exploded ahead on the starboard bow. As the pilot banked low over our ship, the bomber flew through a curtain of our pom-pom fire and must have received about a

---

[15] See Appendix X: Captain Roger Hicks, DSO, RN.

dozen 2-pounder shells in its belly because it limped away towards the coast, trailing smoke. We then took the crew of the *Whitley* off and, as she was burning and full of exploding ammunition, she was beached. We finished her off to prevent her being used by the Germans.

I also recall that we sailed along the shoreline towards the Zuider Zee. There, in line ahead, we steamed in and, making a complete turn fired all eight of our torpedoes at a specific point along the high sea defence embankment. We were followed in by the other destroyers, firing torpedoes at the same target. All that could be seen of the target area were vast clouds of mud and seawater but we had no idea if it was successful or not.

We were sent to Dunkirk twice from Dover to collect 'special' people and some Army top brass, but the evacuation of Dunkirk hadn't yet been decided on as the BEF fought a rearguard action towards the port of Calais.

Then came the news that Calais was surrounded and the Rifle Brigade in the town was completely cut off. We expected to go in there and evacuate them, although we knew it would be a bloody fight. But at least we had no German Navy to contend with. Most of their destroyer force was pulverized in the First and Second Battles of Narvik and only a small E-boat force could be mustered in the North Sea. However, the German Air Force was a constant threat as it was now operating from captured airfields in France.

At that time Prime Minister Churchill had decided that the Calais Garrison should be sacrificed in order to allow the Army to form a perimeter round Dunkirk, which could be maintained while the bulk of the British and French Armies could be brought off by sea to fight again.

On 22 May 1940, the German Panzers reached Boulogne and attacked the port's defences. On 23 May, we sailed from Dover with *Venemous*, *Vimeira*, *Venetia*, *Whitshed* and *Vimy* to evacuate our troops from Boulogne. The previous day, a Battalion of the Welsh Guards and a Battalion of the Irish Guards had been sent over to hold the town while a Naval Demolition Team from Chatham, commanded by a naval captain, had been landed to blow up the sluice-gates of the docks.

Lieutenant Lombard-Hobson: As *Whitshed* approached the French coast we realized it was a very different Boulogne from the one we had just left. Four destroyers were bombarding the heights beyond the suburbs of the town, while, to the north, in the area of La Portel which was occupied by the enemy, there was the incessant sound of gunfire.

This time, the tide was high and we had no difficulty in berthing. Directly we got alongside, *Whitshed* was rushed by a wild rabble of panic-stricken Auxiliary Military Pioneer Corps (AMPC) troops, carrying bottles and other loot. Sailors had to be hastily assembled to repulse them. All round the quay there were Belgian, French and, regrettably, some British troops, lying about in heaps, dead drunk.

It appeared the French Army had completely left the port. Opposite the seaward end of Quai Chanzy the Welsh Guards were holding a small wood; while an Irish Guards battalion (about 1,000 men) was defending the approaches to the harbour.

Whitshed gathered up the many stretcher cases lying about on the jetty, before many of them were trampled to death by the drunken mob. In all, 72 badly wounded men were collected, and we only stopped when there was no more space on deck. We came under heavy machine gun fire from the direction of the Customs House. Captain (D) ordered us to cast off from the jetty, and proceed forthwith to Dover with the stretcher and some 150 walking wounded cases.

As we were backing out into the harbour we saw a section of Irish Guards engaging with rifle fire an enemy machine gun post established in a warehouse, as coolly and methodically as if they had been on the practise range. Captain Conder shouted at me to demolish the warehouse. The after 4.7-inch guns swung round and put two high explosive shells into the building at less than 100 yards' range, and blew it to pieces. A roar of cheering went up from the guardsmen. "Cease firing; don't waste ammunition," ordered Conder. I saw through my glasses other machine gun posts further on, and asked permission to engage. "Fire at anything you like," replied the Captain irritably, "I'm busy." Again and again the guns fired: three or four enemy positions were at once put out of action.

With our tails right up we looked around for more trouble spots. The search was answered for us. Some flashes from Fort de la Créche to the northward were followed almost instantly by projectiles plunging into the water all round the ship. One 'brick' smashed into the whaler, and another whistled between the funnel and the mainmast. "Open fire on that bloody

fort!" roared Conder; but before he had time to embellish his order, a broad-
side from our main armament was sent crashing into it. An ammunition
dump must have been hit because there was a terrific explosion. We then saw
a long train of enemy tanks and motor transport moving down towards the
quays. At very close range we couldn't miss; and we didn't. One huge tank
disintegrated completely from a direct hit.

There then followed a strange lull. All firing ceased on both sides, and we
returned to reality. I, for one, thought I had been through an incredible
dream. I had sensed nothing, and was only conscious of a tremendous feeling of exhilaration. It had been a most dramatic half-hour for all of us. The
moment of reckoning, however, was not so pleasant. Throughout the battle,
many of the badly wounded men on board had been dispatched by rifle or
machine gun fire from the shore. What those wretched men must have felt,
strapped helplessly in their stretchers on deck, was beyond imagination.
Sadly for us, our Torpedo Gunner, a splendid man, and the life-and-soul of
the wardroom, was killed while manning a Lewis gun. Conder, standing
conspicuously on the bridge, and recklessly not wearing a steel helmet, was
untouched; but many seamen on deck had become casualties.

Whitshed was now heading out to sea through the breakwater. As we
passed the destroyers outside the harbour, which had been bombarding the
heights, Conder ordered *Vimy* to enter harbour and take our place alongside
the jetty astern of *Keith*. When clear of Boulogne, he sent for me and said
that we would not be thanked if we took dead men back to England for
burial. It would have to be done at sea, in the traditional way. The dead men
were laid out on the quarterdeck, and each one stitched up in a weighted
hammock. Because there was a doctor on board we were able to dispense
with the naval practise of putting the last stitch through the dead man's nose.
In a ship without a qualified Medical Officer, this crude means of certifying
death is used to watch for any reaction in the toes as the needle goes in at the
other end. The ship was stopped and the White Ensign half-masted, while
the Captain read the burial service and each body was gently lowered over
the side.

Having disembarked the wounded at Dover, *Whitshed* hastened back to
Boulogne, without waiting to replace casualties amongst the crew. Conder
was convinced that Boulogne could be held, provided the Guards brigade

could get anti-tank reinforcements from Calais, and the Royal Air Force could give a modicum of air cover. He considered that the Royal Navy was there in adequate strength.

Imagine our disappointment when, only eight miles from the port, we intercepted the signal ordering the evacuation of Boulogne. Off the breakwater we found *Venemous*, *Vimiera*, *Venetia* and a French destroyer waiting to go in; *Keith* and *Vimy* were already alongside. Captain (D) had arranged for destroyers to come in in pairs, as soon as two ships were laden with troops and ready to leave. Overhead, two enemy reconnaissance aircraft continuously circled the port.

Iain Nethercott: On *Keith*'s arrival off the port entrance, we found five French destroyers bombarding the wooded slopes north of Boulogne where German armour was massing for an attack.

As Boulogne is a confined harbour, Commander Simson decided to order our six destroyers into harbour in pairs. Instructing *Vimy* to follow astern, we sailed slowly up the harbour, coming under rifle and machine gun fire from both banks as we moved alongside the Quai Chanzy.

We had no idea what troops were ashore in late May 1940, and had no orders to evacuate until the Senior Army Officer gave the order. Our primary job was to take off the Naval Demolition Party. They had not achieved their task, and their Captain had been shot dead. We subsequently recovered his body.

The British troops we were most concerned with were a battalion of the Welsh Guards and a battalion of the Irish Guards who had been transported over to France a day or so previously. Both battalions were fighting like fury, one battalion being isolated in a wood on the other side of the harbour entrance and being hotly engaged by German tanks.

As we came alongside the quay we saw a scene of complete confusion. A great mob of British soldiers, Pioneers, many of whom were drunk, were milling aimlessly around, some trampling over wounded men laying on stretchers on the quayside. On the far side of the quay were warehouses and lines of railway waggons. Behind these were lines of Guardsmen, crouching down and firing at targets behind the warehouses.

However, the Pioneers, some of whom had been released from jail to join the Army, had no intention of fighting anyone. As soon as we went along-side the jetty, there was a rush of drunken, panic-stricken soldiers who did-n't appear to have a rifle between them. They jumped down on our upper decks and rushed forward to get down to our mess decks. They'd obviously had a good time looting the town.

Captain Simson, looking down from *Keith*'s bridge, was appalled at the sight of all the drunken soldiers, and quickly issued appropriate orders. Our Damage Control Parties and Torpedomen were immediately issued with rifles and bayonets and got to work, driving the horde of cowardly drunks off the ship and back on the jetty. Small groups of them hung around, beg-ging us to take them on board. They were also driven off *Vimy* at bayonet point on the orders of their Skipper when they attempted to rush the ship.

Our Captain had no orders to evacuate anyone but the wounded and the Naval Demolition Team. He'd been instructed to liaise with a local Army Brigadier, as at that time there was a possibility of defending the port with fresh Army reinforcements.

A Guardsman from the Irish Guards swam across the harbour to us and asked to give a message to the Brigadier who had set up his HQ in *Keith*'s wardroom. Apparently, his battalion had been cut off in a wood on the left-hand side of the harbour entrance and requested permission to make a fight-ing withdrawal on the town.

Suddenly a German Storch plane flew low across the harbour which gave us a target to shoot at. The plane dropped a single white flare. Almost imme-diately artillery fire opened up on us from the hills surrounding the port. A number of Stukas then dived down straight at us from about 10,000 feet. All hell erupted as their bombs exploded on the jetty only yards from us, hurl-ing large chunks of timber and concrete over the gun decks. I felt a heavy blow on my left shoulder, but kept the training wheel going on one plane after the other as Bob, my gunlayer, followed them across the sky. The *Vimy*, lying astern, was also in furious action, although she was half-hidden in the smoke and the dust.

Almost immediately after the air attack, I saw hundreds of German troops pouring down the wooded slopes of the hills to the north, supported by tanks and trucks. On the port side, the jetty seemed to be clear of the drunken troops, and the Guardsmen were still engaging targets from their positions. We were receiving quite heavy rifle and machine gun fire across the gun deck and, glancing back behind our gun, I saw Sullivan and MacNair were down, both groaning and bleeding badly.

A new element made its ominous appearance. Mortar shells arched over and exploded on the jetty to our left. They seemed to be coming from behind the railway waggons on the sidings. Some of the waggons were hit by 4.7-inch shells from our 'A' and 'B' guns firing over open sights.

Bob, my gunlayer, shouted out across the top of the gun, pointing towards some buildings, like hotels, on the opposite side of the harbour. Following his directions, I saw the windows spouting flashes and drifting smoke, obviously German machine gun positions. We quickly swung our quadruple pom-pom gun round and swept whole belts of 2-pounder shells up and down then across the window openings, bringing down great swathes of masonry. Then the lads on our 4.7-inch 'X' and 'Y' guns commenced the speedy demolition of the complete fronts of several buildings.

Behind me I hadn't noticed the methodical march towards us of the exploding mortar shells, aimed by a hidden artillery observer, but suddenly there was a huge explosion below the gun deck on the port side. I was still trained on my targets on the far side of the harbour when I realised the gun had ceased firing.

When I looked towards Bob, he was slumped forward in his seat. I was horrified to see that his head had been lopped off by a large shell splinter, completely decapitated. Bob had been No. 1 on our gun. I was No. 2. Gun Drill, as rigorously and religiously practised in the gun sheds of Chatham Gunnery School, meant that I moved up to No. 1, while No. 3, a Loading Number, took my place as No. 2.

But first I had to get Bob's body off the seat. With the help of the loading numbers and the Warrant Gunner, we pulled him off his seat and dragged him to the rear of the gun. I got a huge handful of cotton waste and wiped down the laying and tracking wheels on Bob's side and got most of the blood off his seat. After testing the firing pedal, we recommenced firing at the remaining buildings opposite which provided diminishing cover for the German troops. The starboard pom-pom had also taken casualties. The First Aid Party was carrying them down the steel ladder, laying them on stretchers then taking them down below.

Lieutenant Lombard-Hobson: After a short while, *Whitshed* and *Venetia* were ordered to enter. As we were about to pass the breakwater someone shouted: "Aircraft!" Suddenly, hitherto unobserved, a mass of Stuka dive-bombers and Messerschmitts appeared from different directions, and delivered a concerted attack on the destroyers in and outside the harbour. Conder, with no room to manoeuvre, put the engines at full speed astern, to avoid *Whitshed* blocking the harbour entrance if sunk. There must have been sixty aircraft, with some twenty of them concentrating on *Keith* and *Vimy*. This was the moment for which the Germans had been waiting, to make their final assault on the town, and, as the first bombs dropped, troops in field grey uniform came pouring over the northern heights and *Keith* came under heavy mortar fire. Their attack was co-ordinated superbly.

The bombing could not have lasted more than a few minutes; but it was vicious, and the noise deafening. Every ship opened fire as the Stukas screamed down, with their angry hornet-like noise, to drop their bombs which sent up huge mountains of mud and water alongside the destroyers, drenching everyone on deck. To add to the bedlam, a splinter cut the wire to our fog siren which wailed continuously, and must have sounded to others like the final death-throe.

To avoid taking anybody off a gun, I climbed the funnel myself, and cut off the steam supply. It was a rather ungainly ascent which thereafter earned me the nickname onboard of 'Jimmy Steeplejack'.

Miraculously, *Whitshed* was not damaged. Looking round, I could see the French destroyer had received a direct hit, and was sinking. Bombs had fallen on to the quay within yards of *Keith*, and caused considerable damage. Captain (D) had been killed on the bridge by a rifle bullet fired from the top of a nearby building, his First Lieutenant wounded. *Vimy* had escaped major damage, but her captain was lying fatally wounded on the bridge. Both of these ships moved away from the quay as the relief pair approached.

Iain Nethercott: It was about that time when our Captain, up in the bridge, directing the fire of 'A' and 'B' guns, was shot through the head and killed by a sniper, positioned up in a dockyard crane. Others of our ship's company had been killed in the wheelhouse at the same time by a burst of machine gun fire. I watched the dead and the wounded carried aft.

Meanwhile a number of sailors from the Demolition Party brought the body of their Captain back from where he'd been killed in a vain attempt to blow the lock gates. The bodies of both Captains were placed in the officer's bathroom.

We began embarking our disciplined Guardsmen who brought their wounded aboard first. They then took up positions on board, by the timber racks and the searchlight platform to give them a better view, and recommenced firing at opportune targets as more Guardsmen arrived and embarked on *Keith* and *Vimy* until we could hardly take any more troops.

Our Captain had been killed, our First Lieutenant had been injured, although not seriously, and as we waited for orders, HMS *Whitshed*, under her redoubtable commander, Captain 'Crazy' Conder, came storming into Boulogne Harbour like Christ coming to cleanse the Temple.

Lieutenant Lombard-Hobson: *Whitshed* then re-entered the harbour. With Captain (D) dead, Conder was now senior naval officer present. The first thing he did was to send an emergency signal to the Admiral at Dover, reporting the situation, and saying that he was not going to order any more destroyers in until adequate air cover was provided. *Whitshed* and *Vimiera* in the meantime remained under way in the harbour, thus enabling their guns the better opportunity to cover any movement of enemy tanks and troops along the northern heights of the town. Within an impressively short time, nine RAF fighters appeared overhead, making short shrift of the two enemy reconnaissance aircraft, one of which crashed in flames close to the *Wild Swan* which had just arrived from Dover to reinforce the destroyers.

Iain Nethercott: *Whitshed*, with all guns blazing, engaged targets to left and right, hitting German tanks and silencing many of their gun batteries. Now that our Captain (D) was dead, Captain Conder was in charge and, followed by *Vimiera*, he steamed round Boulogne Harbour blazing away at anything that moved.

He then ordered us to proceed to Dover, together with *Vimy*, whose young Captain had also been killed on her bridge.

As we couldn't get anyone to cast off our mooring lines, we went full astern and snapped them. Our navigator[16] took us, stern first, out of the harbour, no easy task as the tide was low and it was a difficult deep-water channel to negotiate. *Vimy* followed us, with several mortar shell-holes visible on her upper decks.

On the way out both our ships continued firing at anything that looked aggressive while *Whitshed* and *Vimiera* covered our withdrawal. I saw the 4.7-inch guns of *Vimiera* register a direct hit on a large German tank which emerged from a side-street. The tank reared upwards, then pom-pom fire ignited the petrol tanks and incinerated its crew. Eventually, *Keith* and *Vimy* formed a line ahead outside Boulogne harbour and made for Dover.

Once we were well out to sea, I got our Sick Bay Tiffy to look at my shoulder. He took me down to the wardroom which was full of badly wounded soldiers and seamen who'd been made as comfortable as possible. Having pulled off my bloodstained protective gear, he found a small chunk of shrapnel embedded in the fleshy part of my shoulder. Our Ship's Surgeon removed the shrapnel with some special surgical pliers and the wound was bound up with a special type of shell dressing. I was instructed to report to the Chief 'Quack' aboard our Depot Ship, HMS *Sandhurst*, at Dover.

On our way back to Dover in mid-Channel, both *Keith* and *Vimy* hove-to, and with White Ensigns lowered, we buried our dead, all naval personnel, near the Varne Lightship. Our wounded First Lieutenant read the Burial at Sea Service, then, with the final note on the Bosun's pipes, we slid the individual hammocks containing the bodies of our Captain and many of my messmates over the side. The *Vimy* did the same for her dead Captain and Ratings.

It was sunset, both ships had stopped engines, as we lowered them into the sea. The 'Flowers of the Forest', played on the pipes by a Scots Guards piper, echoed and re-echoed across the calm, sun-lit sea between the two destroyers. We all stood there, heads bowed, with tears streaming unashamedly down our cheeks.

Only a short distance across the water, the men on the Varne Lightship had lowered their ensign and lined the upper deck, bare heads also bowed.

---

[16] See Appendix X: Captain Graham Lumsden, RN.

The dead Guardsmen were then moved to the quarterdeck for military funerals in England. The ensigns were raised and we continued on our way to Dover.

We entered Dover Harbour late in the evening. Tugs took us to a buoy until morning. It had been a long and bloody fight and I was completely exhausted, just laid on the mess lockers all night. I didn't wake until 9.00 a.m. the next morning when, like my surviving shipmates, I washed myself down then ate a huge breakfast.

It's a tale worth telling, especially for that little band of ancient, under-gunned and leaky old destroyers which had to meet the full force of Hitler's Panzers that hot and quite hellish afternoon in Boulogne harbour.[17]

From the *Cambridge Evening News*, Tuesday, 28 May 1940

(Reproduced with kind permission from the *Cambridge Evening News*)

BOULOGNE: FIRST FULL STORY OF EVACUATION

How Destroyers Fought Tanks as Troops Went Aboard

A vivid account by a naval eyewitness of the evacuation from Boulogne of British troops who, with the enemy closing in on the town, got away in destroyers, was told in London today.

The naval eyewitness, who had been sent to the port on an independent mission, described in glowing words the truly wonderful behaviour of the troops in the face of an attack by greatly superior forces assisted by aircraft, tanks and field guns and the no less admirable courage of the Royal Navy,

---

[17] HMS *Vimiera*, commanded by Lieutenant Commander Roger Hicks, RN, made an additional and successful voyage to Boulogne harbour under cover of darkness. During the early morning hours of 24 May 1940 she crept into Boulogne and surreptitiously rescued 1,400 thankful and exhausted guardsman. Although dangerously overloaded, *Vimiera* returned safely to Dover later that day. See Appendix X for further details.

particularly of the destroyers who evacuated the troops in circumstances of great difficulty and peril.

Rushed Across

Where so much happened in less than 24 hours, and event followed event in rapid succession, it is impossible to tell the story in chronological sequence. Indeed, when the naval eyewitness was asked what time such-and-such a thing happened, he could give no definite reply. "Things were so hectic," he said, "and there was so much going on that we had no time to look at our watches."

Anyhow, a demolition party was detailed to be ready to move at two hours' notice. It consisted of seamen, Royal Marines, and a small detachment of Royal Engineers. All the explosives and other demolition gear had to be provided. Embarking in lorries, the combined party was taken by road to another port, where they embarked in a destroyer and were rushed across the English Channel, reaching the main jetty at Boulogne in the forenoon.

On the way into the harbour they had seen some French and British destroyers shelling the high land to the north, over which enemy tanks and mechanised troops were advancing on the town. Inside the harbour, however, there was comparative peace for the time being, though not for very long.

The naval party was landed to hold the railway station, to place the demolition charges, and to earmark all the bridges, cranes, lock-gates, and so on, to be destroyed when the time came.

Some troops were in the railway station when it came under high-explosive shellfire from enemy field guns. The seamen were there, too, fitting the detonators to their explosive charges.

Baptism of Fire

"Some of them were quite young men who had never been under fire," the eyewitness said. "They just carried calmly on with their jobs with bits of the station roof flying around and casualties occurring. They never turned a hair."

The Officer in Charge went off to Military Headquarters to report his arrival to the Brigadier. He found all the roads barricaded with lorries and protected by machine guns. The Germans were gradually closing in on the town with light mechanised vehicles, followed by tanks and motorised field guns. Their aircraft were also busy using bombs and machine guns. Their attacks were intermittent throughout the day, and at one time there were 60 German aircraft overhead. On one occasion a greatly superior number made themselves scarce after an attack by Royal Air Force fighters.

Owing to the position of the Germans all round the town it had been impossible to send field guns or other aid, consequently the troops could not hold out indefinitely against the German armoured vehicles. Small parties of German troops soon began coming down the streets in the outskirts of Boulogne.

Accordingly, it was decided to shorten the defended perimeter by a slight British withdrawal. This would avoid the flank being turned, and would accelerate the evacuation when the time came, as come it must.

Could Not be Held

The destroyer bringing the naval demolition party had already left under orders. She was relieved by another, and the second was relieved by a third. The naval and military officers conferred, and soon came to the conclusion that the town could not be held. The Germans already held the higher ground commanding the town and the harbour, and were massing more troops and guns. Already our troops had been in action, and had sustained casualties.

Demolition of all the bridges and important points was decided upon, and small parties of seamen went out with their parcels of explosives. The enemy was closing in. Already the swing bridges giving access to the inner part of the harbour were under the fire of machine guns at a range of a few hundred yards. The explosives were placed beside the bridges, though they couldn't be destroyed until the last of our troops had withdrawn.

Meanwhile, in another part of the harbour was a large crane, with a wet dock beside it containing a naval trawler. Both might be captured by the enemy, so the Officer in Charge decided to destroy them, with the power-house and pumping station for the dock, without waiting for further orders.

Snipers at Work

He did so, though the crane did not collapse as was expected. It was eventually brought crashing down by a few rounds from the destroyer alongside the jetty. While all this was going on the Germans were all round the docks at a range of about 400 yards, and snipers were within 50 yards of the crane.

Another small naval party was searching the docks for any ships that might assist in the final evacuation. They found one small vessel of the drifter type in which some stokers raised steam in record time by using bits of packing cases and anything combustible they could lay their hands on.

The fire from field and machine guns continued. So did the bombing. Then came the long-expected orders: "Complete demolition."

The floating dock was sunk, and machinery, power houses and the like blown up. The hinges of some dock-gates were demolished, and so were another trawler, another crane – anything and everything that might be of some use to the enemy. The work was necessarily hurried, and in the midst of it the demolition parties were harassed by dive-bombing and machine gun attack by 15 enemy aircraft. They were the ones put to flight by RAF fighters.

Further charges were placed to make certain of the sluice gates and bridge. The Germans were very close and coming nearer all the time. At this time – the time cannot be stated – a considerable number of our troops were sheltering in the sheds round the railway station, and more were arriving every minute.

Evacuation having been decided upon, two destroyers came into the harbour and alongside, and then steamed stern first out of the narrow entrance with all the troops they could cram on board.

Tornado of Fire

Then three more destroyers came in and alongside, to be fired upon furiously by enemy field-guns concealed on a wooded hill to the north, overlooking the harbour, and by a number of machine guns in the second-storey windows of a hotel. The range was no more than 500 yards.

Then several German heavy tanks came down the hill and on to the foreshore. The troops, meanwhile, were on the jetty and embarking in the destroyer alongside. Their courage and bearing were magnificent, even

under the tornado of fire with casualties occurring every second. They were
as steady as though on parade.

But the destroyers had not been idle. Their 4.7-inch, 3-inch, 2-pounder
pom-poms and .303 machine guns were in hot action, plastering the hill-
sides and the German field guns on them at point-blank range; and blasting
the hotels opposite until the machine guns were silenced in showers of
hurtling masonry and shell fragments.

Tank's 'Cart-Wheel'

The first shot fired at the tanks missed. The second was a direct hit which
caused one of them to capsize and turn "over and over like a child doing a
cart-wheel," as an onlooker said. A third was knocked out with a direct hit.
The others swiftly retired.

If it had not been for the rapid and accurate fire of those destroyers, and
the bravery of the men manning their guns in the open, the retiring troops
must have sustained far heavier casualties. Indeed, the evacuation might
never have been possible.

"By God!" said one of the more senior military officers, voicing his admiration, "they were absolutely magnificent."

What the Army thought of the Navy, the sailors also thought of the
soldiers: "They stood out there like rocks and without giving a damn for anything," said one naval officer.

Those three destroyers cast off with full loads of soldiers onboard and
went stern-first out to sea through the narrow entrance. All of them were listing over heavily with the number of men on board, getting them safely away
and out to sea in such conditions involved a fine display of seamanship, particularly as the tide had fallen and there was a danger of grounding.

The Last Man

It was now evening, and there were still many troops ashore, and more were
still coming over the bridges under heavy fire. Still more were under the
doubtful cover of the station buildings. The shelling and the bombing continued.

The troops seemed never to end and the enemy was still advancing. Most
of the naval demolition party had gone in the destroyers, leaving the Officer

in Charge, a Sub-Lieutenant, a Petty Officer and one Rating. They blew up the bridge when the last soldier had passed over it.

Darkness came, and at ten o'clock the railway station was still crammed with men, with the Germans very close, and advancing. But word had gone forth to the Navy that the evacuation was not complete, and at about eleven o'clock another destroyer nosed into the darkened harbour and alongside, being bombed and fired on as she came.

'A Miracle'

She was also in danger of grounding; but moved stern-first out to sea with her quota and a list of fifteen degrees. Then two more destroyers arrived and evacuated the troops that remained, with many wounded. It was a miracle that all of these destroyers were not sunk.

"If the withdrawal was a misfortune," said the eyewitness, "the story of it is one of truly magnificent discipline, and of courage, determination and devotion to duty on the part of comparatively small forces of the Army, the Navy and the Royal Marines, which should be remembered long after we have passed into oblivion."

MESSAGE TO ALL COMMANDING OFFICERS OF ROYAL NAVY DESTROYERS

Admiral Bertram Ramsay, RN

The following message from Admiral Ramsay to all Commanding Officers of RN Destroyers was transmitted in early June 1940:

From: The Flag Officer Commanding Dover
Date: 8 June 1940 No. G.I. /3487/40
To: Commanding Officers.............

The following letter from the Colonel commanding the 2nd Battalion Irish Guards is promulgated for the information of Officers and Ships' Companies.

"Once again, within the space of a few days, I am writing to you on behalf of the Battalion to thank you and your destroyers for all you did for us at Boulogne.

As you well know, the situation was really far more difficult and critical than it had been at the Hook. We are all of us agreed that those of us who saw the actions fought by the destroyers while we were waiting to embark, and while we were actually embarking at Boulogne, are very unlikely ever to see anything more inspiring, gallant or magnificent.

We all felt that the destroyers would have been completely justified in leaving harbour and returning for us after dark. Had they done so we should not have had the very smallest complaint for we should have understood and appreciated the position they were in.

However, never for one second did there appear to be a thought of such a move, and the ships continued to embark the wounded and unwounded and to continue their fight with the shore batteries as if the whole affair was perfectly normal and hum-drum.

I cannot tell you the depth of the impression which has been made upon us all, but I can assure that there is no doubt of it. The whole of the Battalion is filled with an affection and admiration for the sailors who have on two occasions done so much for them.

I wish you could sense the feeling that exists here. I believe it would make you more proud than ever of the men and the ships you command.

Would it be possible to let the Captains and crews know how clearly we realise the dangers they ran for us and how clearly we realise too that it is due to their courage and conduct that we are here now."

To Admiral Ramsay
From Colonel, 2nd Battalion Irish Guards

HMS *KEITH* AT DUNKIRK

Iain Nethercott, HMS *Keith*

After leaving Dover we sailed for Chatham Dockyard for urgent repairs. On the way up the coast of Kent, we cleaned *Keith* up as much as possible. We also painted white circles around the dozens of bullet holes and splinter holes for the 'Dockyard Mateys' to patch up.

After two days, during which they replaced one set of torpedo tubes with a 3-inch high-angle anti-aircraft gun, our two quadruple pom-poms were replaced by new ones with articulated belts, which hopefully wouldn't jam in the heat of action. Splinter mats were fitted to the front of the bridge and our gun decks, while seamen from Chatham Barracks were drafted in to replace the seriously injured. New boats (whalers) were also slung from the davits to replace our original boats, which, after Boulogne, looked like colanders.

Among the replacements was a gun crew for the new 3-inch gun. I was temporarily kept as Captain of the port pom-pom, but I missed Bob, as killick of my mess, now 20 fathoms down in mid-Channel.

Keith's new commander, Captain Berthon, RN, was appointed Captain (D). We resumed as Flotilla Leader and, being ready for sea, proceeded down the River Medway to Sheerness where we anchored, oiled and ammunitioned.

On Tuesday, 28 May, Captain Berthon cleared the Lower Deck and read out the Articles of War to the crew. He then made a short speech, the gist of which was that we would be sailing immediately for Dunkirk, northwestern France, to assist in the evacuation of the British Expeditionary Force.

Captain Berthon went on to say, somewhat ominously, there was very little chance of our returning because, at that time, a titanic battle was in progress over there. But, he felt confident that we, as Chatham men, had always done our duty in the past. Being a Scot, together with at least 30 per cent of the ship's company, I didn't know what was so special about Chatham men.

Anyway, about noon we steamed for the French coast, closed up at Action Stations and found ourselves escorting a gaggle of Thames tugs, various motor launches and motor lighters with long tows of yachts, each with an unhappy Royal Naval sailor sitting apprehensively at the helm.

By the early afternoon it was quite obvious where Dunkirk was. Huge clouds of black smoke obscured the coast and the rolling thunder of gunfire easily drowned out the throbbing sound of our engines and the whistling wind cutting through our superstructure, masts and radio aerials. At frequent intervals we passed other destroyers and sloops belting back towards British ports, through moderately choppy seas, heavily laden with masses of soldiers crammed in and on every conceivable space.

Closing in toward the beaches, our smaller friends left us to proceed shorewards while we steamed along the coast and approached the pier-heads of Dunkirk Harbour. The new Quarters Officer, a young Lieutenant, gave us orders to open fire at will at any German aircraft approaching *Keith*, an order which 'Soapy' Hudson, the gunlayer on the starboard pom-pom, obeyed with alacrity when a fast and low-flying Heinkel 111 approached us. The new 3-inch high-angle gun crew got away a couple of wild shots, but 'Soapy' was close enough to the German's nose section to make the twin-engined bomber bank steeply and roar away to seek an easier target.

Keith then entered Dunkirk Harbour. The quays were an utter shambles. The troops were marched along the mole (breakwater or causeway), itself under sporadic long-range German Army artillery fire from both sides of the port. Every few minutes the unnerving and increasing scream of an approaching large calibre artillery shell was heard... then it would explode somewhere in the harbour with an almighty crash.

The British Army's Military Police appeared to be in charge on the mole, encouraging the over-loaded and weary troops, humping their packs, rifles and the occasional Bren gun, to hurry along the mole to the embarkation points onto waiting destroyers and sloops. We had normal gangplanks over to the mole, but had to station our sailors on the planks to prevent the exhausted soldiers from overbalancing and toppling into the sea below.

Our ship's cook worked minor miracles in the galley – large mess kettles full of piping hot soup and huge wads of corned-beef sandwiches. Once on board, lots of men, after days and nights retreating towards the coast, while under constant artillery fire and air attack, without proper sleep, were too tired to eat. They just rolled over and fell asleep where they were, having absolute confidence that the Navy would do its best to look after them, and get them home, away from this Hell on earth.

As soon as we had taken on board as many troops as possible, we were waved away from the mole. With a heavy list to port, we steamed for Dover with about 1,200 sleeping soldiers packed into our mess decks and laying everywhere along the upper deck.

For two days we ran this ferry service as the Panzers closed in on Dunkirk. The artillery bombardment and the bombing and strafing attacks by Stukas and Me 109 fighters intensified. Time and time again we were attacked from the air; fighters swooped in low to machine-gun us, but were met and driven off by a wall of defensive gunfire from our pom-poms.

Back in Dover Admiral Ramsay was running the show, while ashore at Dunkirk Captain Tennant, RN, was the Beachmaster. For a short period the Admiralty dispatched some of the modern Home Fleet destroyers to assist us 'Old Fogeys' – the 'V' and 'W' and 'S' boats of First World War vintage, backed up by a few old 'B' class and the odd 'G' and 'H' class. However, Prime Minister Churchill had apparently decided we were dispensable and held back the modern destroyers. Any troops saved were a bonus on top of the estimated 50,000 already evacuated. In the event, about 335,000 British, French and Belgian servicemen were actually brought home, and the myth of the 'Little Ships' was born.

While back in Dover Harbour for ammunitioning and storing, *Keith* took aboard Admiral Wake-Walker to take control of the ships off the beaches at Dunkirk and to maintain radio contact with Admiral Ramsay at Dover.

We hoisted his flag at the peak and arrived off Dunkirk on 31 May. We had several shoots with our 4.7-inch guns on German columns moving along the coast towards the Dunkirk defensive perimeter. We came under heavy return fire and had to steer a zigzag course at 35 knots to avoid the artillery salvoes and dive-bombing attacks.

Inevitably, we were all getting very tired as we could only 'cat-nap' beside our guns at night because of the very real danger of German E-boats which would creep into the area at night. During the early hours of 29 May, one

E-boat had already sunk the destroyer HMS *Wakeful*.[18] She was packed with soldiers at that time. Her sinking was a terrible tragedy with all those soldiers drowned below decks. There were a few groups of corpses still floating around in that area when *Keith* passed through, and while attempting to rescue the pitifully few survivors from *Wakeful*, including the severely injured, another destroyer, HMS *Grafton*, was itself sunk by a German submarine.

So much for Hitler's 'Chivalrous Legions'.

We had a bad night on 31 May, with one alarm after another. Little did we know what the immediate future held.

EVENTS LEADING TO THE SINKING OF HMS BASILISK

G. P. 'Phil' Merryweather

I was on the destroyer HMS *Basilisk* from 25 August 1939 until 1 June 1940. She was in the Reserve Fleet with a skeleton crew until the latter part of August 1939, when she was brought up to war complement with RN Reservists and from those at the Gunnery, Torpedo and Asdic Schools. I joined her as an AB LTO from the Torpedo School, HMS *Defiance*.

In late August 1939, *Basilisk* sailed from Devonport to Dover where the whole Flotilla of 'B' class destroyers became part of the Channel Force based at Dover and in the Nore Command based at Harwich. On 13 November 1939 we were escorting the minelayer HMS *Adventure* down the east coast when she struck a magnetic mine. At the time we were looking for a suspected U-boat in the vicinity of the Thames Estuary. We took off *Adventure*'s dead and wounded and rushed them to Sheerness for specialist

---

[18] In March 2001, nearly 61 years after she had gone down off the Belgian coast on 29 May 1940, the 'W' class destroyer HMS *Wakeful* was found only 57 feet below the surface, the final resting place of an estimated 690 British soldiers and sailors. The destroyer, from which only 25 sailors and soldiers survived, had been cut in two. The wreck had become a hazard to the-increasingly large size of the container ships using the Belgian ports of Antwerp, Ostend and Zeebrugge, and the top ten feet of her superstructure have recently been cut and secured to her side, allowing shipping to pass over the site.

medical attention. It was the first time I'd seen the results of a large explosion, blast injuries, burns and oil fuel on sailors. It was a considerable shock.

While at Dover we occasionally took VIPs across to France, one I recall was Jan Smuts, from South Africa. We spent Christmas Day on patrol in the English Channel and had our Christmas Dinner the following day in Dover Harbour.

During our time at Dover I passed for Leading Seaman. Early on in the bitterly cold winter months of 1940 *Basilisk* had a spell in East India Docks, London, for a boiler clean and minor refit – a very welcome break ashore.

In early April, *Basilisk* left Dover and sailed north to Scapa Flow on temporary detachment to the Home Fleet. We then sailed north to Narvik escorting a battleship with several other destroyers. On reaching Norwegian waters we patrolled and participated in the Second Battle of Narvik, when the battleship HMS *Warspite* accompanied by nine destroyers cornered eight German destroyers inside Narvik fjord. With a combination of torpedoes from the British destroyers and 15-inch gunfire from *Warspite*, all eight enemy ships were sunk.

We had our first air attack in a Norwegian fjord on the way to Narvik. Our Skipper, Commander Maxwell Richmond, watched the bombs leave the German aircraft and begin their descent, then tersely ordered 90-degree changes in our course, either to port or starboard. The bombs appeared to be heading straight for us, then seemed to veer away during the final few seconds to explode harmlessly in the sea, but they were still too close!

After Norway we headed for Devonport about mid-May where we were due for a boiler clean and a short break. However, it was cut short and we headed for Dover. We then did several trips to the Mole at Dunkirk and returned with exhausted Army personnel.

On 1 June, we were ordered further east to bombard the coastal road at La Panne leading to Dunkirk and thus became a primary target for the Luftwaffe. At 0800 hours that morning, one of several Ju 87 Stuka dive-bombers put a bomb between the boilers and the engine room thereby cutting the steam supply. We immediately slowed to a stop. All engine room and boiler room personnel were killed. One young torpedoman was badly burnt by steam and blown into the sea.

During the forenoon we ditched our depth charges and torpedoes.

German fighter aircraft strafed the ship twice and we were again bombed about noon. After another destroyer had tried unsuccessfully to take us in tow, Commander Richmond finally gave the order to abandon ship. I stepped into the sea which, by that time, was only about a foot below *Basilisk*'s deck.

Other survivors were also swimming away from our sinking ship, when we were picked up by a Belgian fishing boat. The badly burned torpedoman was also rescued and the last I saw of him his head was covered in bandages. I saw him again months later. Fortunately, he had no scars on his face, evidently from being immersed in the sea so quickly.

On arriving back at Dover we were kitted out in khaki and Commander Richmond arranged with Admiral Ramsay for us to be taken to Devonport in a 'W' class destroyer which sailed that same evening. One of *Basilisk*'s whalers eventually made its way back to Dover from Dunkirk. Our ship's surviving Officers and Ratings totalled 131.

THE LOSS OF HMS *KEITH*

Telegraphist John Beeley, Stoker John Cranston, DSM and Gunner Iain Nethercott

John Beeley: I served in destroyers throughout the war as a Telegraphist, and was 21-years-old at the outbreak of war in September 1939. Most of wartime service at sea comprised of routine, discomfort in bad weather, and sometimes even boredom, but this was punctuated occasionally by moments of high activity in action.

I joined HMS *Keith* in Chatham Dockyard when she commissioned out of the Reserve Fleet on 1 August 1939. She was a destroyer of some 1,400 tons, mounting four 4.7-inch guns, and eight torpedo tubes in quadruple mountings on deck. There were two 2-pounder single pom-poms between the funnels and two .303 Lewis guns on the searchlight platform as anti-aircraft armament. She was capable of 36 knots.

Destroyers were pretty basic in those days as regards accommodation. At sea, in rough weather, the mess decks were frequently swilling with sea water which had leaked in through the scuttles, and living conditions were pretty cramped.

There was no refrigeration so fresh meat, kept in the beef screen on the upper deck, lasted for only a few days; thereafter we lived on M & V rations, corned beef or other tinned food. If the weather was reasonable, the cook could bake fresh bread, otherwise we had ship's biscuits. Fresh water was in short supply after the first few days at sea, and we were dependent thereafter on what the Engine Room 'vaps' (evaporators) could produce. This was sufficient for cooking and drinking, but not much to spare for personal hygiene; but we were all in the same state so it didn't matter much.

Washing clothes ('dhobeying') was normally done in a bucket. The Bathroom was equipped with six or seven tie-up enamel bowels for washing and shaving, or a bucket of water could be placed in one of those bowls to provide more water for a standing wash-down which was the only bathing facility. At sea, when water was scarce, a change of underwear frequently took the place of a bath!

My duties were principally in the Wireless Telegraphy (W/T) Office. Being also trained in Visual Signalling (V/S), I frequently helped out on the Flag Deck, especially when we were with a convoy of Merchant Navy ships out in the Atlantic, because they were often quite busy up there, and it was a pleasant change from the cramped conditions below.

After a short work-up at Portland, we were sent to Plymouth where we became part of the force in the Western Approaches. Here some of the time was spent on Asdic sweeps trying to locate U-boats which had been reported. Our principal task was convoy escort duties. These were quite arduous in the early days of the war, largely due to the inexperience among Merchant Navy Captains and crews of close-quarter operating, and the interminable chasing and rounding-up of stragglers, not always an easy task in the North Atlantic in winter. We were usually at sea for 10 or 12 days at a time.

Communications were fairly basic in those days. We had not got the Very High Frequency Radio Transmitting (VHF R/T) sets which came along later, so all communication between escorts and Convoy Commodore, or individual ships in the convoy, were all carried out by V/S, i.e. light, flags or semaphore. This put a heavy load on the Yeoman of Signals and the flag deck staff. I often used to help out reading or transmitting messages by light or hoisting flags. It was often quite enjoyable to be up in the fresh sea air after the stuffiness of the W/T office or below decks. All instructions or messages for escorts or Convoy Commodores were broadcast at fixed times by Admiralty or Rugby Radio, and it was part of my job to read these broadcasts and help to decode them. Most traffic was, of course, encoded.

This continued right through the winter months of 1939/40, until on 1 March 1940, *Keith* was transferred to Dover as Flotilla Leader of the 19th Destroyer Flotilla. Commander Pawsey, our Commanding Officer, was relieved by Captain (D) Simson who had been appointed Captain (D) 19.

The period of the 'Phoney War' continued for a little longer. Our duties consisted mainly of patrols off the French and Dutch coasts at night during which we were frequently attacked by enemy aircraft, but their bombs always missed, and little notice was taken of it. I remember some considerable excitement one morning when returning from patrol. Someone discovered a jagged hole in the forward funnel, caused by a bomb splinter. During this time we were inspected by King George VI on the East Jetty in Dover Harbour. He looked a rather frail man.

By mid-May 1940 however, things began to 'hot up'. Although we didn't know it at that time, this was the prelude to the evacuation of the British Expeditionary Force (BEF) from France. The whole Flotilla became increasingly involved in the evacuation of personnel, the bombardment of coastal targets, escorting ships carrying reinforcements to Calais, etc.

On 15 May, *Keith* was dispatched at full speed, 36 knots, to the Hook of Holland with orders to embark the Dutch Royal Family and bring them back to Dover, but on arrival we found that they'd already left in one of their own warships. The Dutch government had surrendered to the Germans a few hours before our arrival. The scene on the jetty was a sad one of abandoned vehicles and general disorganized chaos.

There weren't many people to be seen, but we embarked about six or seven Dutch soldiers. As we were preparing to leave, a German aircraft flew down the estuary laying mines. *Keith* had been fitted with de-gaussing gear, but had never tried it in earnest before, so lower decks were cleared while we felt our way out of harbour, and happily got away without incident.

By 23 May 1940, Boulogne was surrounded by German troops. *Keith* and several other destroyers were sent over to evacuate the wounded Allied troops and any other personnel we could. We secured alongside the jetty in Boulogne Harbour, and began embarking wounded soldiers and some civilians. *Keith*'s doctor set up a casualty station on the forward mess deck where people were made as comfortable as possible. About six women, some with babies, were put in the communications mess deck where they were cared for as best we could. They were very calm in the circumstances. We gave them tea, but had no baby food, but I recall diluting some Ideal evaporated milk with water for them to try. I'm unaware if this was successful or not!

We had been alongside the jetty for over an hour when a formation of German aircraft dropped several salvoes of bombs on the harbour. Under cover of this bombardment we came under a hail of automatic fire from vantage points in the buildings and houses surrounding Boulogne Harbour which had been infiltrated by spearheads of the German Army.

Captain Simson was in his sea cabin just below the bridge at that time, and went straight up to the bridge, but he was immediately killed at the top of the bridge ladder by a sniper's bullet in the forehead. No one could have possibly survived on the fo'c's'le to let go our mooring wires so our First Lieutenant, Lieutenant Commander Miller, RNR, who assumed command, went full astern with both engines to part the wires, got *Keith* clear of the jetty and out of Boulogne Harbour while under heavy fire.

Our flag deck on the starboard side was full of dead soldiers who apparently had been blown aboard from the jetty by the bombing. These soldiers, together with our casualties and Captain Simson, were all buried at sea on passage back to Dover.

We had suffered damage to *Keith*'s upperworks and to some of the electrical wiring. After disembarking our wounded and our passengers, we were sent round to Chatham Dockyard for repairs.

It should be pointed out that Captain Simson was an excellent Commanding Officer. His enthusiasm was infectious and he showed considerable concern for the well-being of his ship's company. Whenever we went on an operation, Captain Simson went to great trouble to keep the whole ship's company informed as fully as possible, with details of the operation and what we might expect. This certainly produced high morale among us and a good spirit of co-operation between departments which resulted in a friendly atmosphere on board.

The loss of our Captain at Boulogne was keenly felt by us all.

After our arrival at Chatham, Captain Berthon was appointed Captain D19 to replace Captain Simson. Several ratings joined *Keith* to replace those lost killed and wounded at Boulogne. Speedy repairs were carried out at Chatham and three days later we returned to Dover.

By this time the evacuation from Dunkirk had begun, although Calais was still being reinforced by the Brigade of Guards, more, I feel, to play for time than to drive the German forces back.

Keith was sent over to Dunkirk immediately. Long before we arrived we could clearly see the smoke from the oil storage tanks in the port. Great black clouds of smoke rose thousands of feet high into the air and were visible for many miles.

Soon after arrival we secured alongside the mole, which was packed with exhausted troops, many in a pretty low state. As our fo'c's'le was more or less level with the mole, a gangway was put across and we commenced loading. I was among others on the gangway, assisting to hurry up these exhausted men, getting them down the fo'c's'le ladder at the bottom of which there were more sailors shepherding them along to the lower mess decks first, then the upper messes, and finally the torpedo deck and quarter deck until we were full to capacity. I don't know how many we embarked; probably about 700. Our normal freeboard was halved as we headed back to Dover. Mercifully, the sea was flat calm.

About 31 May, *Keith* embarked Admiral Wake-Walker who was to be in charge of the local RN operations at Dunkirk. He was joined by a number of Army 'brass hats', mainly General Gort's staff. We were to remain off the beach at Dunkirk as Control Ship for the operation and to provide a wireless link to the Operational Headquarters, under Admiral Ramsay, at Dover. As I recall, we arrived off the beach at Dunkirk before dawn, on 1 June.

Early in the morning, about 0600 hours, a few sporadic air attacks began to develop, but nothing particularly close. The only damage was due to our own gunfire, as our Lewis guns on the searchlight platform were apt to shoot away our W/T aerials which were strung between our two masts.

I was at the top of the foremast completing one such repair, when I heard the increasing drone of many approaching aircraft engines. I looked up and saw an enormous fleet of German aircraft – there must have been hundreds of them...

Hastily finishing the aerial repair, I quickly climbed down the foremast just as we opened fire with our H/A guns. I returned to the wireless office where I relieved the operator on the W/T link with Dover.

There was an enormous pile of messages awaiting transmission, all O-U (highest priority), and far more than we could possibly cope with as they all had to be transmitted by hand.

I had not taken over for very long when I heard the noise of a heavy air attack, the constant booming of our H/A guns and 2-pounder pom-poms, the characteristic ear-splitting howling scream of Stuka dive-bombers, one after another, and bombs exploding all around us.

Iain Nethercott: Just before 8.00 a.m., we saw through our binoculars, beyond the black smoke clouds of the burning oil tanks, wave upon wave of German aircraft. They were all heading ominously and menacingly towards us.

Keith was off Dunkirk; *Basilisk*, with only one functional propeller which reduced her speed to 15 knots, was to the west of us. HM Ships *Skipjack*, a minesweeper, and *Salamander* were off the pier-heads with *Ivanhoe*. Another destroyer, the *Havant*, was closing with us when the first wave of Stukas, which had formed up directly overhead, started their screaming dives.

The dive-bombers were met by a curtain of fire from every available anti-aircraft gun from the desperately weaving ships in the immediate area. *Basilisk* was the first destroyer to be targeted and immediately surrounded by numerous towering white plumes of water from near misses. It was impossible to keep an accurate sequence of events. I recall the *Havant* being heavily attacked and within minutes she sank under a salvo of bombs. *Skipjack* went the same way, bombed and gone within a minute with about 300 troops. A smaller ship – it could have been a small oil tanker full of soldiers near *Skipjack* – also went straight to the bottom when hit squarely by what looked like a 1,000lb bomb, taking all her soldiers with her.

I was blazing away at the Stukas diving on us from three different directions, coming in from ahead, the port beam and from astern. Captain Berthon, on the *Keith*'s bridge, had worked up to about 30 knots and was throwing the ship around to dodge the bombs. Unfortunately, at that time we were in the deep-water channel with sandbanks either side and there was little room for manoeuvre.

After almost continuous firing, our 3-inch high-angle gun ran out of ammunition. Our main armament of four 4.7-inch guns couldn't be elevated more than about 65 degrees so was completely useless against aircraft. That left us with our two quadruple pom-pom guns, both of which were rapidly running out of ammunition. The continuous noise of battle, the screaming dives of the Stukas, every available anti-aircraft gun of several destroyers firing almost without pause, was deafening.

The violent swinging from side to side made it very difficult to keep my gun lined up on the diving Stukas, so I just fired fused shells at 2,000 feet and hoped that would divert them. I then tracked a Ju 87 right across the ship. A large bomb then exploded about 25 feet from our starboard side, half drowning us in seawater. More dive-bombers were on their way down and it became increasingly obvious that the unequal battle could only have one outcome.

Suddenly, during another violent turn to starboard, two large bombs exploded close off *Keith*'s port side, blowing in a section of the steel plates. Then I actually saw a 1,000lb bomb as it hurtled straight down the aft funnel and exploded in the engine room, killing practically everyone down there and wrecking both engines. We slowed gradually to a stop.

The after part of the ship had huge clouds of smoke and escaping steam covering it. We listed gradually to port as tons of seawater flooded through shattered plates.

John Cranston: One bomb hit the after end of the ship as all the tremendous noise and at about 8.15 a.m. another bomb went straight down the after end funnel, exploding in No. 2 Boiler Room and the Engine Room, killing or seriously wounding everyone there. I was incredibly lucky, having come off watch from No. 1 Boiler Room at 7.50 a.m.

It soon became clear that *Keith* was mortally wounded as she listed dangerously to port. So over the side we went. As we were swimming away from our sinking ship, the German planes machine-gunned us survivors in the water.

I and a few other shipmates from *Keith* were eventually picked up, after about three hours in the water, by a Thames tug, the *Vincia*, itself packed with exhausted British soldiers, and landed at Margate, Kent later that day.

John Beeley: As the final bomb struck home the whole ship suddenly seemed to lift. I knew immediately we'd been hit very hard. All the lights went out, our W/T transmitters went off, and I heard the hiss of escaping steam. I couldn't do any more where I was, so switched everything off and went out on to the upper deck. There were clouds of steam everywhere, escaping through boiler relief valves.

One or two wounded stokers had been brought up from the boiler rooms and were lying on the steel deck. *Keith* was down by the stern with the quarterdeck almost awash, but we were still afloat forward and the torpedo deck was dry. Apparently, we had settled on the bottom aft, in comparatively shallow water.

Someone said the order to abandon ship had been given, but it seemed to me that there was no particular rush to get off. I went back to the W/T office to destroy the pile of messages awaiting transmission which I'd left on the desk. I switched on the 20-volt emergency lighting, cleared the desk, but on the way out I noticed that the bag of Confidential Books (RN codebooks) was still on the deck just inside the office door. There were no other members of the W/T staff to be seen, so I carried the bag of books and the unsent messages round to the starboard side, where there was an access hatch to an oil fuel tank. I dropped them all in there.

By that time, an MTB, 102, had taken off the Admiral and the Army Staff from the gradually sinking *Keith*. Some of our crew had abandoned ship and were swimming towards the beach when another air attack developed. The bombs missed the helpless and immobile *Keith*, but exploded in the water nearby, killing most of those who were swimming.

I was told later that this tragic incident affected Captain Berthon very deeply as he was on *Keith*'s bridge at that time and saw it all.

Iain Nethercott: Meanwhile, an Admiralty tug, the *St. Abbs*, came alongside our fo'c's'le and started to take off our wounded and crew plus a number of high-ranking Army officers we had on board. The starboard pom-pom had been put out of action as McLeod, the gunlayer, had been badly wounded by the German plane's machine gun fire as they raked our gun deck during the attack. He, with the wounded trainer, had been dragged clear, but as the Bosun had piped 'Abandon Ship' the remainder of the starboard gun crew had gone to the fo'c's'le to be picked up by the *St. Abbs*.

Owing to the heavy list, my gun couldn't elevate very high so, with Fred Osprey, we switched to the starboard gun and brought it into action at the enemy planes still diving on *Keith*, firing their machine guns at our crew and at *St. Abbs*. It was during this time that I registered my first 'kill' of the war. An Me 109 fighter swept down firing all his guns at almost masthead level when he ran straight into a wall of my shells which almost blew the entire nose section off. He careered crazily across the listing *Keith* and cartwheeled into the sea on the port side.

Our ship was listing increasingly to port and consequently this made the guns useless. I looked around and saw *Basilisk* over to port, a blazing wreck, *Ivanhoe* looked as though she was sinking. *Skipjack* and *Havant* had already gone.

John Beeley: After that air attack, things quietened down. I went below to the mess, and managed to retrieve my 'Number One Suit' and my camera from my locker in complete darkness.

While I was on my way up again, another air attack began which resulted in a 'near miss' aft, but no more hits. The near miss had, however, wounded the Gunner's Mate. He'd been down on the quarterdeck at the time and had collected a few bomb splinters in his back. Though groggy, he was still on his feet so Lieutenant Hughes and I got either side of him and helped him along to the comparative shelter of the fo'c's'le. There were now only a few of us left onboard.

I then saw the tug *St. Abbs* coming alongside again. She had already taken off our wounded and some of the ship's company, so we got the Gunner's Mate aboard, and the remaining six or seven of us followed, including the last of *Keith*'s officers and Captain Berthon.

On board *St. Abbs* the below-decks accommodation was very limited and already full to capacity, but there was plenty of room on deck, so I stayed there, talking to Leading Seaman Joplin from *Keith*.

The *St. Abbs* then tried to get as near to the beach as it could, but couldn't approach near enough to pick up any troops, but we had several ships' boats floating around nearby, among which was a whaler which the tug brought alongside. Joplin and I volunteered to take the whaler where there were long queues of 'Pongoes' (British soldiers) waiting to be picked up. Many had waded out into the water. The sea was flat calm.

I believe we made two trips to the beach and while returning to *St. Abbs* a second time we saw a man in the water supported by his lifebelt. He called over to us and we made over to him. He was a stoker from the minesweeper HMS *Skipjack*, whose sinking we had witnessed earlier, at about 0900 hours. She had taken a stick of bombs right down the centreline, from aft to forward, which must have split her in two. She sank like a stone. We had not expected any survivors. I later learned that nearly 300 soldiers went down with her.

As we got closer to the survivor, we could see that the poor man had lost both of his arms above the elbow, but assisted by some of the soldiers we got him into the boat and laid him down on the stern sheets. We then returned to *St. Abbs*, got our passengers onboard, and the wounded stoker was gently carried below where *Keith*'s doctor was tending the wounded.

By this time there were signs of impending air attacks, and we were told to secure the whaler astern and to get aboard ourselves. Fairly soon, *St. Abbs* herself came under concentrated attack, during which I noticed she'd been fitted with two Lewis machine guns, each of which was mounted on either side of the wheelhouse. It seemed absurd that they were not being used to defend the tug.

Joplin and I went to the port gun, and I had a go at the next diving Stuka as it came in. It is most unlikely that I hit it, but its bombs overshot. Anyway, it was much more preferable to doing nothing. It was unfortunate that the Lewis gun was supplied only with ball ammunition and no tracer bullets, spaced, I believe, at every fifth round. Consequently, there was nothing to indicate where my shots were going.

We were now about a mile offshore, and during the lull which followed, we kept a lookout for aircraft. I had a pair of binoculars that I'd picked up as I left *Keith*; they'd been left lying on the torpedo tubes and now proved to be extremely useful.

Joplin and I stayed by the Lewis gun and had found another circular pan of ammunition when, very suddenly, I had the sensation of being unable to stand up and a peculiar feeling of falling over and over, almost as if in a strange dream.

Iain Nethercott: The *St. Abbs* steamed away from our bow with most of our survivors on board. As I watched her go I realised we would have to attempt to get away on our solitary Carley raft. With the help of my loading number, a stoker, we got down to the starboard iron deck near the searchlight and lowered the raft into the sea, securing its mooring line to the guard rail.

We then made three or four journeys to bring down the wounded gunners, passing them down with a line around them, to McCleod and Jimmy Callan in the raft. Three badly burned stokers from aft joined us and we put them into the raft. One of them was screaming in agony with severe steam burns.

The German dive-bombers and fighters were still flying low and strafing the ship, but we were shielded by the overhang of the listing ship's side. We had to shove off as it was increasingly apparent that *Keith* would sink and take us with her. Wearing my oversized cork life jacket, I jumped into the sea as there was no room left in the raft. McCleod jumped in beside me and we hung on to the lifelines round the sides of the raft, and then attempted to push it clear of *Keith*.

We were now fully exposed to the low-flying German aircraft intent on finishing us off. It was then that I got hit in the knee by a machine gun bullet as I attempted to dive underwater, wearing a life jacket, as a plane swooped down. That merely exposed my legs and I suddenly felt a hammer blow on my left leg and a terrible pain. My first thought was that my leg had been shot off, but after cautiously feeling underwater I felt a small hole near my kneecap and a lot of my blood clouded the water around me.

When I pulled myself up to look into the raft I was stunned to see all its occupants lying in the bottom, lifeless, lolling gently to and fro with the raft's motion.

I shouted to McCleod that they were all dead. There was no answer from the other side of the raft. McCleod had disappeared and I never saw him again. I was too weak by that time to climb into the raft so decided to stay hanging on to its lifeline.

John Beeley: When I'd recovered my senses, I found myself in the sea, about 30 yards or so from *St. Abbs*, of which only the upperworks and funnel were visible above the water; the remainder of the tug, together with its many occupants, had already disappeared.

There were pieces of debris of various sizes from *St. Abbs* splashing down in the sea all around me, and I recall putting both hands on the top of my head as bits and pieces rained down. The binoculars, which had been around my neck, had gone, but my half-inflated lifebelt seemed undamaged and was keeping me afloat. There must have been very heavy loss of life on the tug, including our stoker from *Skipjack* and the two boatloads of soldiers we had brought off the beach.

I didn't know what had hit us, but can only assume it was a direct hit from a high-level German bomber as there was no low-level attack at that time. I hadn't even heard the explosion.

The remaining upperworks of *St. Abbs* suddenly disappeared in a mass of bubbles. I saw very few other survivors, about eight or ten, floating in the surrounding area. Somewhat miraculously, I appeared to be uninjured. I blew more air into my lifebelt, and swam over to the other survivors. We kept together, feeling this would improve our chances of being picked up.

After a while, we saw a ship's motor launch to seaward of us and hailed it, but it passed us by. This produced a torrent of very strong language from us. Shortly after this we were strafed by a low-flying German fighter aircraft, an Me 109. This was a very unpleasant experience which brought forth another abusive torrent. I vividly recall trying to dive under the surface of the water as the Me 109 came in with guns twinkling, but couldn't submerge because of my lifebelt.

After that, we decided to split up and go our various ways. Some, I think, tried to swim back to the beach, and I soon found myself alone.

I could see a ship some distance away to the eastward, towards which the tide was carrying me, so I made up my mind to try and keep myself in line in the hope of getting aboard if nothing else came along. After quite a long time in the water, the ship gradually got closer. I could see a rope ladder hanging over the port side of the fo'c's'le. And, as the tide carried me along, I made this my target.

I didn't realise at that time that the ship had been heavily bombed, the stern was awash and I could have got aboard there with comparative ease.

I grasped the rope ladder as the tide carried me along the port side, and started to climb, but found this to be a slow and difficult process as there was now little strength in my arms and legs. I took me a considerable time to reach the bulwarks about 25 feet above the surface of the sea. The ship was the *Clan MacAlister*.

After scrambling over the bulwarks on to the fo'c's'le deck, I was quite exhausted and lay on the deck to recover from the climb. I was also quite cold although it was summer. After a short rest in the warm sun, I got up and went to look for some dry clothes, and hopefully, something to eat.

The forward half of the vessel, including the bridge structure, was above water. I found what had probably been the Engineer's cabin, and there discovered a good supply of clothes and even a towel. I stripped off my wet things, dried myself, and then 'borrowed' some clothes, which fitted me quite well, from the chest of drawers. I also found an excellent torch and some lifeboat matches.

As I hadn't seen anyone else around me in the sea, I thought I was alone on board the bombed and abandoned *Clan MacAlister*. I lay down on the engineer's bunk for a rest and to think about what to do next. Before very long, however, I heard an aircraft diving towards the ship and a stick of bombs exploded nearby. I then realised that my refuge was not as secure as I'd thought. The pilot of the aircraft had obviously not realised that the ship was already sunk.

After the attack, I decided to explore, look for food and fresh water, and see what I could do about getting back to England. I soon found the saloon where I discovered some biscuits, which I ate.

I then went out on to the upper deck on the starboard side where I found a lifeboat had been lowered into the water, but was still attached to the falls (ropes for hoisting tackle). There were also two or three fishing boats, or schuyts, anchored about two cables (one cable = 200 yards) to seaward on our starboard side.

About that time, it became apparent that I was not alone on board *Clan*

MacAlister. There were a few additional survivors from *St. Abbs* and from *Keith*. I remember walking aft on the starboard side and seeing a man dressed in a white shirt and white drill trousers as worn by Royal Naval cooks. He was standing in a doorway of what I took to be the galley. His face was vaguely familiar so I knew he was from *Keith*, and was probably one of the new replacements who had joined us at Chatham Dockyard.

Just for something to say I then said to him:

"It's a f——— good job we've got a cook with us!"

But this only produced a scowl and certainly no reply. I thought, "Miserable so-and-so!" and continued on my way.

Shortly afterwards I came across Lieutenant Adams and Lieutenant Hughes, both from *Keith*. I took them over to the ship's side and showed them the lifeboat on the starboard falls. I said I'd try and find some more food, but Lieutenant Adams said I'd better come below with them to discuss our chances of escape.

I followed them down to the main deck, and to my surprise saw the cook sitting in a chair. It was an even greater surprise when I heard Lieutenant Adams addressing him as "Sir". I then realised that the vaguely familiar face was none other than Captain Berthon, who was an extremely religious man, and would definitely not have appreciated my bad language at all.

Iain Nethercott: I must have passed out because when I recovered consciousness I was all alone, the Carley raft had apparently drifted away with its grim cargo of bodies, and I was being carried along the coast by the tide, supported by my trusty cork life jacket.

It was a beautiful morning, but the sea was very cold. From sea level everything seemed very quiet and peaceful. I thought I was going to die. Gazing up into the cloudless blue sky, I had a word with my God and passed out again.

It was about noon when I awoke again. I was being carried by the current towards a large stranded cargo ship, the *Clan MacAlister*, grounded on an offshore sandbank.

As I floated nearer the ship I tried to shout, but my thirst and general exhaustion prevented any sound coming from my throat. I waved frantically with one arm and with a tremendous effort I paddled and thrust myself towards the ship's side which rose up vertically, about 50 feet, above the surface of the sea.

Someone on the upper deck spotted me. After a lot of paddling with my arms and one good leg, I reached the steel side. A long Jacob's Ladder then came snaking down from a great height and actually struck me. It was quickly followed by more rope ladders and heaving lines, down which slid three or four of my old messmates, survivors from *Keith*.

After passing a bowline round my chest, having about six men hauling from up on the ship's deck, and assisted by a messmate on either side of me on their rope ladders, my waterlogged body was swiftly pulled up the ladder, complete with steel helmet, cork life jacket, lammy coat, three sweaters, two pairs of bell-bottom trousers, thick socks and seaboots. Wringing wet, I must have weighed about 25 stone.

Captain Berthon, who had also luckily survived *Keith*'s sinking, then congratulated me on my swimming prowess, while my messmates humped me into the deckhouse, cleaned and bandaged my leg. The ship's galley appeared to contain only tinned pears. I gorged myself until I fell asleep.

John Beeley: It became apparent that there were seven survivors from *St. Abbs* on board *Clan MacAlister*, two with broken legs, one of whom was Leading Seaman Joplin. After some discussion, it was decided that we should stay where we were until dusk, and then try to row or sail the lowered ship's lifeboat back to the Kent coast.

Meanwhile, we foraged for food, water, blankets and anything else which might be useful for the passage. The French coast was only about two miles away on the port side. We felt fairly sure that the Germans had occupied it during that day, so there was no point in going there as we would, at best, become prisoners of war for the duration of hostilities.

There were no engine-room people among us and without them we felt that the fishing boats would be of little use as we would probably be unable to start the engine and keep it going. Meanwhile, we should get what rest we could, and as far as possible keep away from the port side of the upper deck and bridge, so as not to advertise our presence on board to the Germans.

Not very long after that – it was by now early evening – we heard the sound of an engine and saw a barge-like vessel heading east, and about a cable to seaward of us. We hailed her and she came alongside our starboard side. She turned out to be a yard craft from Sheerness Dockyard – *YC 73*, I think. She had an elderly Skipper who took us onboard.

We put our two casualties on the hatch covers, which was as comfortable as we could make them. The hold was already full with about 50 soldiers. Captain Berthon went below into the forepeak accompanied by Lieutenant Adams. We then cast off from *Clan MacAlister*.

I sat down on the hatch covers just behind the wheelhouse, but we had not gone very far when the Skipper called and asked if I'd take the wheel as he wanted to go below to get some rest. Apparently he and his Mate had been up since the previous day and were totally exhausted, so I took over. Signalman Walker, who was also in the vicinity, came up to the wheelhouse as a 'lookout'.

We hadn't been under way very long before the barge ran on to one of the many sandbanks off the coast. When that happened, I expected a rush of people on deck to see what was going on, but nobody appeared. So I sent Walker down to tell the soldiers to go to the after end of the hold, and by going astern on the engine we slid off the sandbank quite easily. After this I steered closer to the coast before feeling our way out to seaward again, and this time we were successful.

Before very long we fell in with another barge similar to ours. He was ahead of us, so we followed astern at a distance of two or three cables. I had no navigational knowledge, neither did Walker, but we decided that if we found ourselves on our own, we would steer north-west by compass and hope for the best.

Shortly before sunset, a Heinkel 111 twin-engined bomber appeared from astern at low level and dropped a stick of bombs. Fortunately, these missed both our barges and caused no damage.

Night fell, and on we went without much idea of time or where we were, but with all the traffic in the area at that time, we decided to take a calculated risk to turn on our navigation lights, as we could have easily been run down. Our slow speed didn't give us much chance to avoid a collision.

Later, I saw a ship to the southward, and flashed a Morse code message to him with my torch, asking for our position. He didn't answer but came over to us, and turned out to be a tug. He offered to take both barges in tow which we gladly accepted.

We secured to the tug and the other barge secured to us, and off we went again. However, despite the almost flat calm surface, the tow parted after about half an hour and the tug's Skipper said he'd have to leave us. We thanked him and continued under our own power on a north-westerly heading. It wasn't long before we also lost contact with the other barge in the darkness.

It must have been about 0100 hours, 3 June, when Walker reported two ships on our starboard side, both darkened. They were not far forward of the beam, and were approaching at high speed. It looked as though we were about to be run down, despite our lights, but there was nothing we could do about it.

In the event, they both passed ahead of us by no more than half a cable, much too close for comfort. I turned to starboard into their bow waves to try to avoid being swamped. They were two of our destroyers, in line ahead steaming at full speed, almost 40 knots, towards Dunkirk.

A little later, I saw another ship on our port side from which I again tried to get our present position. He replied, but his answer made little sense when we tried to relate it to the chart we'd found in the wheelhouse, but this was probably due to our ignorance of the subject. We continued steering north-west throughout the night.

As dawn gradually lightened the eastern horizon, we could hardly believe our eyes. We recognised the white cliffs of the Dover coastline and, as the light improved, we could see the breakwater of Dover Harbour in the distance. I sent Walker down to tell Lieutenant Adams where we were. I could see the Examination Vessel to the east of the entrance to Dover Harbour so altered course towards it.

Captain Berthon, Lieutenant Adams and Lieutenant Hughes came up from the forepeak. Lieutenant Adams asked me where I was steering, I said that I thought we should call at the Examination vessel. At this, Captain Berthon became very angry:

"I'm Captain of D19 and we are certainly *not* going to stop at any bloody examination vessel! Beeley, steer straight for Dover Harbour."

I altered course as ordered, but it wasn't long before the Breakwater Signal

Station called by light, telling us to go to the Examination Vessel. I conveyed the message to Captain Berthon, but he told me to ignore it and continue to the harbour. By then, we were about two miles off the harbour entrance and it wasn't long before I saw the big naval guns on the breakwater training ominously on to us...

I stopped the engine and reported the threatening guns to the three officers. While they were discussing, quite heatedly, what we should do I took the opportunity to contact the signal station and flashed:

"Captain D19, survivors from HMS *Keith* and some 50 military personnel. Request permission to enter harbour."

I told Lieutenant Adams what I'd done. He and Lieutenant Hughes had managed to calm Captain Berthon who, having personally witnessed the loss of his ship and several of his crew in quite horrifying circumstances, was severely stressed.

Permission to enter harbour was given in due course, so I asked Walker to go down to get the Skipper to take his barge into Dover. This was accomplished about 30 minutes later.

We secured alongside the jetty, and our two wounded men were quickly taken to hospital in an ambulance. We said goodbye to the Skipper and his Mate and went ashore ourselves. There were several double-decker buses on the jetty and we were taken in one to Claridge's Hotel, in Dover, which had been hurriedly transformed into a reception centre. There were lines of armchairs in the foyer in which we thankfully sat down. There were quite a number of people, mainly ladies, who came round with large mugs of tea, and equally large sandwiches – probably corned beef! Then another lady came round, noting our names, service numbers, ships, units etc.

When we'd eaten our sandwiches and drunk our tea we were taken upstairs to an enormous bathroom where there was a team of nurses, Wrens,[19] and other ladies busily cleaning us up. Most of us who'd been in the sea off Dunkirk were quite oily and dirty. I soon found myself being undressed and put into a hot bath by two of these girls who did their best to get the oil out of my hair, off my neck and shoulders.

When this was over, we were taken down to the ballroom, which had been

[19] Members of the Women's Royal Naval Service.

filled with two-tier bunk beds. Here we were given a large label on which our name and other personal details were written, which was tied to the end of the bed. We were told to lie down and sleep until called.

I dozed, but couldn't sleep. About noon, my name was called and told there was a bus waiting to take me up to Chatham. I boarded the bus and off we went. We must have looked a motley crew! When the bus stopped at traffic lights while passing through towns, I remember the civilians passing bars of chocolate and packets of cigarettes to us through the open windows.

We arrived at Chatham at about 1500 hours. Here we were checked by the doctor, issued with the bare essentials of a survivor's kit, a new Pay Book with some money, and sent home on leave. I arrived home that evening and by this time was beginning to feel very tired because I had hardly slept for about three days. I went off to bed after supper and slept soundly right through until the following evening.

Evidently, three officers and 33 ratings went down with HMS *Keith* off Dunkirk, 1 June 1940. With one exception, I didn't see any of my *Keith* shipmates again, and have little knowledge of what became of them. I did see Leading Seaman Joplin some three months later in Chatham Depot where I'd been sent from the old destroyer HMS *Campbell* to do a pistol course at the Shanghai Range in the Gunnery School. His broken leg had healed, and he was expecting to join another ship. Captain Berthon went to hospital for a much-needed rest. He subsequently recovered, but in about January 1942 I read that he'd been killed in action at sea. My brother met Lieutenant Hughes during the Normandy Landings in June 1944. He'd inquired about me at that time, but apart from that I heard nothing more from anyone.

In retrospect, it seems strange that Walker and I were allowed to bring barge YC73 across the English Channel, almost from Dunkirk to Dover, without the supervision of one of *Keith*'s three officers or YC73's Skipper and his Mate. I can only surmise that the officers assumed the Skipper was in charge, or they were so exhausted that they slept throughout the passage despite the occasional disturbances. I also wonder sometimes why we didn't go below to seek advice. We were obviously very lucky, as we could easily have run into serious trouble.

On 16 August 1940, I was notified that I had been Mentioned in Dispatches for my part in Operation 'Dynamo'.

John Cranston: After we'd been kitted out at Margate we were taken back to Chatham Barracks where I'd first joined *Keith* in 1939.

On my return to Chatham after two weeks Survivor's Leave, I was drafted to another destroyer, HMS *Duncan*, in the Mediterranean with Force 'H' under Admiral 'Slim' Somerville, escorting supply convoys through to Malta and witnessing various skirmishes with the Italian Fleet.

On leaving *Duncan* in 1942, I joined HMS *Savage*, a destroyer on the Russian convoy run to Murmansk, and on 26 December 1943 participated in the sinking of the German battlecruiser *Scharnhorst* off northern Norway, under Admiral Sir Bruce Fraser in his flagship *Duke of York*. Incidentally, I was awarded a DSM following the Battle of the North Cape.

The strain of the Arctic convoys, extreme temperatures, appalling weather, semi-darkness, constant threat of U-boat 'wolf packs' and air attacks, was severe, but we were fortunate and survived.

Iain Nethercott: After a short spell in hospital and 14 days Survivor's Leave, I was kitted out in Chatham Barracks and by Mr. Goldberg, my Naval Tailor.

Incidentally, as a survivor, I claimed for the watch I'd bought from H. Samuel in Chatham for 30/- and which was guaranteed to be water-tight. Like every other survivor claiming for watches, we all got £5 for our cheek.

As the threat of the German Army following the last British ship back from Dunkirk was high, we were all supplied with a metal cosh, an 18-inch length of gas piping with a large 5-inch nut from the Dockyard welded onto one end. With this deadly weapon, we were supposed to defend Chatham Dockyard against the Huns.

What our Teutonic friends were supposed to be doing while being struck repeatedly on their 'coal-scuttle' helmets was never divulged. Probably the same reaction as the stuffed dummies, hanging down from a cross bar, which were speared by inoffensive sailors learning the fundamentals of the art of bayonetting accompanied by the loud, bloodthirsty advice from Gunners' Mates.

I was then sent on a short torpedo course at HMS *St. Vincent*, Gosport, and then I spent more time with my trusty Ross rifle, 200 rounds of ammunition and full fighting kit guarding a Royal Air Force Fighter Command aerodrome near Southampton.

The Army bussed us there every evening, to occupy slit trenches and do battle with German paratroopers had they attempted to land. This was abruptly ended when a large force of German bombers, escorted by fighters, came over on a low-level daylight raid from their newly-occupied bases in north-west France, during late July or early August 1940, and completely wrecked the place and half its Hurricane fighters.

It was at about that time I was trained as a part-time diver in the RN. We wore a diver's helmet on our right sleeve which brought the princely sum of three-pence a day extra. I was trained at Gillingham in the hard-hat diving suits. An airline fed from a manual pump in the diving boat, while one chap held your lifeline for signals. We also had a throat telephone which never seemed to work.

All ships carried a diver who could be of any Branch of the ship's company, but were mostly from the Seaman Branch. We were often used to saw off wires wrapped around the propeller shaft or to recover lost anchors and cable. Occasionally we recovered the dead body of some drunken matelot who had accidentally fallen off a jetty and banged his head on the way down.

From Chatham Dockyard, together with three destroyer crews, I soon found myself back on an old troopship, crossing the North Atlantic, to man the first three ex-United States Navy four-stacker destroyers in Halifax, Nova Scotia under the American Government's 'Lend-Lease' agreement. I've since learnt that the 1940 scrap value of each of these 50 First World War destroyers was between $4,000 and $5,000.

I was, at that time, a Leading Seaman at 19, with a conscript crew, many of whom had never seen the sea before. They were of all ages and various occupations, from solicitors to burglars and who had only been in the Royal Navy for about six weeks after very basic training at the hastily adapted Butlins Holiday Camp, Skegness.

But that's another story, about how I got so fed up with escorting the slow North Atlantic convoys that I volunteered for submarines and found myself in the thick of it with the 10th Submarine Flotilla based at Malta and Beirut.

Postscript by Iain Nethercott: The only leave we had from September 1939 until we were sunk on 1 June 1940, was 48 hours' boiler-cleaning leave at Plymouth. There was a bitter song at the time to the tune of 'The Little Boy that Santa Clean Forgot':

> We're the little ships that Churchill clean forgot,
> And goodness knows we didn't ask a lot.
> A few more whacks of leave would do us all the world of good,
> We haven't got the comforts of the *Rodney* or the *Hood*.
> When it comes to weekend leave, there's none for us,
> We're always shoving off to do our stuff.
> Now the bigger ships get swing time,
> All we get is bloody sea time.
> We're the little ships that Churchill clean forgot.

Tribute to those lost in HMS *Keith*, sunk off Dunkirk, 1 June 1940:

> Now *Keith* lies sunk, many still trapped inside
> Their bones in the seaweed still rock with the tide
> But in Hell's nether regions we're not tending the fires,
> No, we're all up above in the Heavenly Choirs.

Iain Nethercott

A PRAYER ANSWERED

Able Seaman Ron Blacker, HMS *Boadicea*; **Lieutenant Hubert Fox, RN,** HMS *Boadicea*;
Lieutenant F. J. G. Hewitt, RN, HMS *Bulldog*

AB Blacker, HMS *Boadicea*: I joined the Royal Navy on 23 January 1940, and after basic training at Skegness and then HMS *Collingwood* at Pembroke Barracks I was drafted to HMS *Boadicea* at Chatham in late May 1940.

The *Boadicea* was my first sight of a seagoing ship. She was in the dockyard, having just undergone a refit, repair to damage caused by a collision, and last-minute enlargement of her portholes. The refit prevented us from participating in Operation 'Dynamo', the incredible evacuation of thousands of British, French and Belgian troops from the beaches of Dunkirk. Underlined by some of the destroyers sunk during the Dunkirk evacuation, it had become increasingly evident that the portholes were too small to allow a man to exit from a sinking ship. Consequently many lives had been lost.

By early June, the greater part of the BEF had already been evacuated from Dunkirk and the adjacent areas. On the afternoon of 8 June we left Chatham and sailed for Sheerness where we took on ammunition the next day. That evening we received orders to sail to assist in the evacuation of British troops from Le Havre. We joined other ships under the command of Admiral Sir William James and were to evacuate the 51st Highlanders, a famous Scottish regiment. Their soldiers had been cut off from Dunkirk and were making their way down to the beaches at Le Havre.

However, the main part of the 51st, under French command, had been cut off from Le Havre by the rapid advances of the German Panzer units. The only escape routes left were the beaches near St. Valery.

Bulldog and *Boadicea* were given orders to sail for St. Valery, hoping to evacuate the remaining troops. *Bulldog* had passed the earlier months of the war away from the flotilla, acting as 'chaser' to the aircraft carrier *Glorious*, hunting raiders in the Indian Ocean. *Bulldog* had returned to home waters in March 1940, and worked independently from Scapa Flow, Rosyth and the River Tyne for several weeks, culminating in her famous part in saving the *Kelly*. The damage she'd sustained at that time from an E-boat put her in the hands of the dockyard again, like the *Boadicea*, to be operational in time to sail to St. Valery.

Lieutenant Hewitt, HMS *Bulldog*: Dunkirk was just finished and our newspapers were full of the idea that our soldiers were going back to hammer again at the Germans. Nobody seemed to bother that all of the Army's stores, transport and guns had been left behind in Flanders.

We received orders to proceed at once to Le Havre. When *Bulldog* arrived at the mouth of the River Seine, the atmosphere was desolate. Oil tanks were burning on shore with huge black clouds of smoke rising further inland;

there were a few small ships anchored, mostly coasters. We began to suspect that this was not the prelude to another invasion but more likely another evacuation.

Another 'B' class destroyer arrived, HMS *Boadicea*, and she anchored close by. Nobody from shore seemed to take much notice of our arrival and the only information we gleaned was that the Army had lost touch with its forward units.

Things brightened up when, from the distant horizon across the Channel, appeared a fast-moving motor gunboat flying not only the White Ensign but the Admiral's flag of the Commander-in-Chief, Portsmouth. Admiral James had come across to find out for himself what was happening.

The next thing was that the destroyers were ordered to steam along the French coast on reconnaissance. So we set off, keeping about three miles off-shore. We were off St. Valery when we saw, some way ahead, a German air-craft carrying out shallow dives towards the water. We fired a couple of shells from 'B' gun, just to show our displeasure, and the plane made off.

AB Blacker, HMS *Boadicea*: We arrived off St. Valery during the early after-noon of 10 June. The weather was beautiful, sunny and warm, not a cloud in the sky, not a breath of wind and the sea was calm. We were at our 'Defence Stations' and things seemed ominously quiet.

Lieutenant Hewitt, HMS *Bulldog*: When we got to the German aircraft's div-ing position we came across a small rowing boat and in it we saw half-a-dozen khaki figures. When we got them aboard we found they were from the 51st Highland Division. In broad Scots accents they told us that they had become separated from their unit so they had 'borrowed' a boat on the beach and were intending to row to England!

Boadicea had meanwhile seen some soldiers on the beach and went inshore to pick them up. *Bulldog* carried on until opposite Dieppe and was about to turn into the approach channel when grave doubts smote us. A lucky thing because German tanks were already in the town.

Lieutenant Fox, HMS *Boadicea*: It was shimmering June weather, and I remember the electric atmosphere. We had no communication with the shore and it was tragic to contemplate the opportunities lost. On the after-noon of the 10th, while cruising along the coast, we saw a body of men on the beach and I was sent ashore to investigate.

AB Blacker, HMS *Boadicea*: My defence station was as a loader on 'X' gun. I was looking along the French coast from about one mile offshore and saw many people waving to us. It quickly became apparent that these were the troops we were looking for. The Captain ordered our motorboat to tow our whaler to the beach and the rescue mission began.

Lieutenant Fox, HMS *Boadicea*: It was about 3.30 p.m., on a hazy after-noon; the sea was calm. I stood with a group of soldiers on a shingle beach under the cliffs, a mile to the westward of Veulette. We were waiting for *Boadicea*'s motor boat and whaler to return from the ship, nearly a mile to the seaward, for another load of men.

AB Blacker, HMS *Boadicea*: Both boats had returned and came alongside *Boadicea* full of soldiers. They were exhausted, but greatly relieved to be aboard. Taken below, they were given food and drink. Our rescue boats returned to the beach for another load. Further along, about two miles away, the *Bulldog* had also picked up a boatload of soldiers.

As the boats were being reloaded with troops on the shore, we saw, from the turret of 'X' gun, what appeared to be many black shapes moving across the fields, raising clouds of dust, and approaching the cliff-tops above the beach. Our first impression was that they were either horses or cattle stam-peding out of control. However, when we looked through 'X' gun's tele-scopic sight we could clearly see that they were tanks, German Army Panzer tanks and they were approaching the beach fast.

Lieutenant Fox, HMS *Boadicea*: On the coast road above us the advanced units of the German Army were making their way to the west. French soldiers had thrown away their rifles and machine guns and dressed as peas-ants – they were greeted with friendly waves as the German soldiers went by; all the British troops had retreated to the beaches.

Exactly how near the Germans were we didn't know until I was returning to *Boadicea* with the last load at about 4.45 p.m., when the ship and boats came under fire. We had embarked about 80, mostly British soldiers, but there was also a woman, four children and two dogs.

AB Blacker, HMS *Boadicea*: We opened fire on the tanks as they lined up on the edge of the cliff. They promptly returned fire, but fortunately didn't hit us. They were also machine-gunning our small rescue boats. Some of our 4.7-inch shells began to score hits on several tanks which immediately caught fire and burned, sending up long plumes of black smoke.

The rescue boats hastily returned to *Boadicea* and the soldiers were taken below.

Lieutenant Fox, HMS *Boadicea*: The boats were quickly hoisted as shells burst in the water all around us, and the ship shaped course to the north-west. However, the Germans didn't intend to let us off as lightly as that; at about 5.30 p.m., nine Junkers Ju 87 dive-bombers were sighted emerging from wispy clouds at a height of about 8,000 feet, almost directly overhead.

AB Blacker, HMS *Boadicea*: I was then ordered to my action station, 'X' gun's magazine, passing up shells for the gun via the hoist, as German aircraft, Ju 87s, were approaching. Down in the magazine I could hear our anti-aircraft guns opening up in addition to our main armament, still heavily engaged with the German tanks.

Lieutenant Hewitt, HMS *Bulldog*: On our way back we saw *Boadicea* was having a spot of bother with some guns on shore and she was hurriedly hoisting her whaler. It was just then that we saw the enemy planes. Three Junkers dive-bombers were circling above *Boadicea* and then we saw another six above us. They attacked almost immediately in threes, three from each side. They penetrated very low before releasing their bombs, because, of course, we had nothing effective to deter them.

Lieutenant Fox, HMS *Boadicea*: Three aircraft dived on us and released their bombs at a height of 300 feet; three bombs from the first dive-bomber missed – 90 feet to starboard; all the bombs from the second Stuka penetrated the engine room and the after boiler room; the bombs from the third machine missed – 60 feet to port.

AB Blacker, HMS *Boadicea*: Then I heard the dull thuds of what I now know to be 'near misses' of bombs. My next sensation was of two loud explosions, causing very profound shuddering in 'X' magazine, then another much louder explosion and everything collapsed.

The lights went out as the ammunition racks collapsed and the shells tumbled out all around me. As my eyes adjusted to the sudden darkness, I could dimly see my two shipmates, by the daylight coming through the open hatch above, who had been sending up shells from the other side of the magazine. One of them called out, "Is everyone all right?"

Then someone's head and shoulders suddenly appeared in the hatch opening and shouted down: "HANDS TO ABANDON SHIP STATIONS!..."

I managed to free myself from under the racks and shells and clambered hastily up the ladder, suddenly realising that apart from a few bruises, aches and pains, I was uninjured.

Lieutenant Hewitt, HMS *Bulldog*: There were many near misses on either side of *Bulldog*. One large bomb penetrated the deck on our port side, just abaft the after funnel; this glanced off a chunk of machinery in the Engine Room and passed out through the side of the ship just on the waterline. Our sailors were very nippy about rigging a collision mat over the hole.

As the bomb entered the port boiler in No. 1 Boiler Room it blew out the side casing of that boiler and the explosion vented up the fore funnel with a huge flame. As First Lieutenant, I was going round the deck looking for damage when I came across a hole in the deck on the starboard side just forward of the fore funnel. This could not be accounted for, until it became suddenly apparent that another large bomb was still very much with us!

Lieutenant Fox, HMS *Boadicea*: Escaping steam clouded over *Boadicea*, the haze thickened into fog almost at once, and the enemy aircraft were not seen again. That night, Berlin wireless reported to the world that HMS *Boadicea* had been sunk.

Boadicea shuddered to a stop. I slid down the bridge ladders and carried out a rapid survey. The engine room and after boiler room were flooded, but otherwise the ship's structure seemed to be fairly sound. The Engineer Officer and engine room crew were still in the flooded engine room except one or two who had escaped and were now lying mortally wounded on deck.

AB Blacker, HMS *Boadicea*: When we emerged from the fog into bright sunlight we could see *Boadicea* had sustained severe damage and was gradually sinking. The steel deck was just above sea level. The ship's damage control party, however, evidently had other ideas. It became clear that the watertight doors and hatches, adjacent to the flooded compartments below, were holding firm and the ship had sufficient buoyancy to stay afloat.

In the meantime, during the same attack, the *Bulldog*, then about two miles away, had been singled out by a further six Stukas and had also sustained three bomb strikes, one boiler being blown up and a second put out of action by an unexploded bomb, while a third unexploded bomb lodged between decks, fortunately with only minor casualties.

Then I noticed our passengers who had been rescued from the beach, now assembled on the upper deck: British and French soldiers, French civilians and their children.

I was told by one of the crew that we'd been attacked by 18 dive-bombers, which by then had returned to their base to refuel and to rearm. Three bombs had already hit *Boadicea* causing casualties and severe damage in the engine room and boiler room. We no longer had steam power to get under way nor electrical power to transmit our desperate position.

The forward guns were firing off shells, previously passed up, at the tanks still arrayed on the cliff top. One of our officers and a PO were busily organizing the soldiers to man the pumps to get rid of some of the water intake. The Captain ordered the cooks to provide, if possible, the ship's company and our passengers with food and drink.

The weather remained beautiful and, fortunately for us, the sea was dead calm, the only disturbance of its surface coming from the regular splashes as various items of equipment were dumped over the side in an effort to lighten ship.

Lieutenant Fox, HMS *Boadicea*: All Wireless Transmitting/Receiving was out of action, I reported to the Captain on the bridge. We jettisoned heavy gear, torpedoes, depth charges, ammunition, cables, etc., emptied the fresh water tanks, started the pumps, and placed shores and collision mats as we prepared to be taken in tow. We applied first-aid to the many men who had been badly burnt. We turned out the boats and Carley floats in readiness to abandon ship. All the worst 'lags' rose magnificently to the occasion.

Broken down and in danger of sinking off the enemy coast, *Boadicea* was in a desperate situation.

AB Blacker, HMS *Boadicea*: Being my first time at sea and my first ship, I felt deep despair at our seemingly hopeless situation: *Boadicea* was alone, without power, just off the French coast and within short range of many German aircraft – not to mention U-boats and E-boats. It only seemed a matter of time before the bombers returned to finish us off.

I then did what I had never done much of before. I prayed for some sort of miracle to help us. Barely two minutes later I could not believe my eyes – a large bank of dense white fog appeared and slowly rolled its way towards the crippled *Boadicea*...

Very soon the whole ship was enveloped in the cool mist which, of course, effectively and miraculously blanketed out everything. We could no longer see the coastline... or the sky.

A little later we could hear the distinctive drone of numerous German aircraft overhead as they flew back and forth trying to locate us, but to no avail.

Lieutenant Hewitt, HMS *Bulldog*: Both destroyers had lost steam power but in *Bulldog* the engineers got enough power back on the engines to enable us to crawl across the Channel in the direction of the Isle of Wight.

Lieutenant Fox, HMS *Boadicea*: Evidently, *Boadicea*'s codebooks had been thrown overboard in weighted canvas containers. The Fleet Signal Book and Conduct of the Fleet were both ditched separately in leaded containers. As the destruction of all signal books was being reported to our Captain, the Leading Telegraphist arrived on the bridge to report that, thanks to a tray of lead batteries, the wireless transmitter/receiver had power and was serviceable.

The Captain was thus in a terrible quandary. Should he report *Boadicea*'s desperate situation in plain language?

AB Blacker, HMS *Boadicea*: While the ship's company were busily engaged in continued damage control, shoring up, manning the pumps, making our rescued passengers as comfortable as possible, passing food around, etc., three of us were ordered to ring the ship's bell every fifteen seconds.

In the meantime, we were told that our position had been logged and we would be put under tow when *Ambuscade* arrived, assuming she could locate us in the impenetrable fog. A little later, the most cheering, familiar and immensely reassuring sound was heard – a destroyer's siren blasting inter-mittently. We answered each blast with vigorous ringing of *Boadicea*'s brass bell.

How the *Ambuscade* ever found us in that dense fog, a real pea-souper, I'll never know, because at that time there was no radar equipment fitted to ships. Once under tow and heading westward, Lieutenant Commander Meyrick ordered 'Splice the Mainbrace' and I had my first tot of rum in the Royal Navy. Even our rescued passengers enjoyed that part of their ordeal!

The 51st Highlanders did a wonderful job manning the pumps all the way across the English Channel. The fog persisted for the rest of that day and all night. Conditions on board during that memorable and tense return voy-age were very cramped, but I cannot recall anyone complaining.

Lieutenant Fox, HMS *Boadicea*: Throughout that night I watched the threatened bulkheads of the engine room and the boiler room, hardly daring to breathe. Lieutenant Commander Meyrick stayed on the bridge, peering into the fog. No one but the damage control crews was allowed below decks; everyone had to remain silent.

AB Blacker, HMS *Boadicea*: As if it had all been prearranged by an unseen and guiding hand, the fog lifted the next morning as we were slowly being towed across the Channel, then into Portsmouth Harbour, and then into dry-dock. It was an emotional moment as crowds of people, crews of other ships in harbour, and dockyard workers lining the quayside watched in silence as *Boadicea* was towed slowly into harbour at approximately 3.15 p.m., 11 June.

Lieutenant Hewitt, HMS *Bulldog*: Our berth in Portsmouth Dockyard was to be the Middle Slip Jetty, so called because the jetty was in two halves with a slip in between. Across this slip was a footbridge and the rail of this was lined with dockyard men watching us being pushed alongside. They were quite used to seeing damaged ships brought in after Dunkirk and the actions of the previous weeks.

While *Bulldog* was still a few yards off the jetty, a Lieutenant Commander, a Bomb and Mine Disposal Officer from HMS *Vernon*, walked on to the jetty and called up to the bridge, asking what the trouble was. As First Lieutenant, I was in the wing of the bridge watching the berthing wires going ashore and I called back: "We have an unexploded bomb in the boiler." This was something of a guess at the time, but it is worth mentioning because I don't think I've ever seen a crowd disperse so quickly!

That officer was a very brave man and I regret I cannot remember his name. I understand he was killed later on doing this sort of work. He traced our bomb and, sure enough, he found it nestling among the tubes of the starboard water-tube boiler. It was disposed of eventually.

The explanation for our miraculous escape was that those Stukas had flown too low when they released their bombs, and the fuses had been burred over as they passed through our steel plating. The timing devices were for the safety of the aircraft and had not had time to work off. Our ineffectual anti-aircraft fire, which had allowed and encouraged the dive-bombers to press in so close, had therefore been a blessing in disguise.

Lieutenant Fox, HMS *Boadicea*: We eventually reached Portsmouth Dockyard; Butlin's Fun Fair was swinging and turning on Southsea Common, the kiddy cars painted in the colours of our Allies. Then, at last, we reached the dockyard and secured alongside. First on board were two Customs and Excise Officers, one of whom, seemingly oblivious to the surrounding devastation, asked me:

"What quarantine measures do you propose for the two dogs?"

AB Blacker, HMS *Boadicea*: I discovered that the bombs which had exploded in the engine room and boiler room, in addition to tragically ending the lives of several of my shipmates, had blown the bottom out of the ship. There was a large, cavernous hole, big enough to drive a bus through. I then went to 'X' Magazine, where I'd been during the bombing attack, and was horrified to see the shattered state of that compartment. It made us realise that we were very fortunate to emerge from the wreckage without serious injury.

Boadicea had been towed in to Portsmouth Harbour on 11 June. We tidied up the ship and on 12 June we assisted to get the 'old dear' into dry dock, then spent the rest of the day clearing out ammunition, etc., before going on leave.

The bomb damage was so severe that *Boadicea* remained under repair at Portsmouth Dockyard for the next two months. *Bulldog* also had a lengthy stay in the dockyard, during which Lieutenant Commander Wisdom was tragically killed in an air raid.

Lieutenant Fox, HMS *Boadicea*: An officer of the 51st Highland Division called Richard Seddon was one of those whom we brought home from France. He wrote of his experiences in *Boadicea* in a book called *A Hand Uplifted*:

'As trained soldiers we were deeply impressed on board *Boadicea* by the conversational tone in which the Royal Navy restored order from brief chaos. Within an hour of the explosion, without any voice being raised above drawing room pitch, the ship had collision mats over holes, the list had been reduced to a more or less even keel, the wounded had received first-aid, the ship lightened, and the bulkheads shored up.

'The show which the Royal Navy put on was under-played to the point of casualness. They were courteous, hospitable, and friendly. It made our stampings, shoutings and square-bashings in the Army ashore seem a little uncouth. As a show of casual ability to cope, it impressed us to the point where speech failed.'

DISASTER AT ST. NAZAIRE: SS *LANCASTRIA*

Anthologist's Note: During the next few days in June 1940, at ports further down the French coast, HMS *Beagle* was one of the Royal Navy destroyers which successfully evacuated British and Allied soldiers in another Dunkirk-type operation from St. Nazaire on the Atlantic coast. Larger British troopships and passenger liners were able to enter harbour and, in total, a further 156,000 British and Allied troops were rescued while under constant shellfire and air attack from Luftwaffe dive-bombers. Casualties were relatively light, apart from the disastrous sinking of the 20,000-ton passenger liner *Lancastria*, the greatest single loss in British maritime history. An eyewitness, Corporal Sidney Gaze, serving with the 125th Yeomanry, had been involved in the heavy fighting in north-western France as part of the British Expeditionary Force. His unit had fought its way, against overwhelming odds, to the western coast of France:

Corporal Sidney Gaze: In the early sunlight of the morning of 17 June 1940 (as events were to prove, an ominous day for France), I was ordered to join a long line of British soldiers resting by the side of the road and told to move when the man in front moved. The line of 'squaddies' followed the road and the contours of the surrounding countryside until, in the far distance, the road entered a built-up area at a low point, then curved upwards to rising ground, rounded a bend and was then lost to sight.

The situation was very confused at that time. None of us knew where we were or what we were there for. Our unit had arrived at this location in stages: by marching, by rail and finally by truck from the port of Dieppe, about 250 miles to the north.

During that hot, sunny and dusty day, our line of squaddies shuffled slowly forward. Then word came down the line that we were at St. Nazaire, a French port at the mouth of the Loire river which flows into the Bay of Biscay. We also heard that we were to be evacuated and were going home.

The German attacks had slackened noticeably and almost ceased. However, we were totally unaware that 17 June was the day the French Army was told to stop fighting and capitulate. So the lack of German action against us was possibly a gesture by the German High Command.

I eventually arrived on high ground and saw the port of St. Nazaire below me: a truly beautiful sight, especially the two large British passenger liners, proudly and defiantly riding at anchor offshore. There was also a tremendous amount of activity as smaller craft, including tugs, fishing smacks and small boats, were busily ferrying troops from the quayside out to the larger ships.

Our turn to embark came eventually after another long wait. We were packed on to a small fishing boat which was already low in the water, and headed out across the calm waters for the first ship. As we approached the liner, which towered above us, an officer came down the temporary gangway. He shouted down to us that his ship was leaving very shortly, that it was full to capacity, and told us to head for the other large ship, the *Oronsay*. The name of that officer's ship was the ill-fated *Lancastria*...

As we came alongside the *Oronsay*, we suddenly heard the roar of rapidly approaching aircraft engines. German Air Force bombers had arrived unseen, by gliding stealthily down out of the dazzling sun. The first stick of bombs straddled the *Oronsay*, wrecking the bridge, wireless room, chart room (destroying all the ship's charts), broke the de-gaussing gear (anti-magnetic mine equipment), and sprang several steel plates as a result of some near misses. It was a decidedly desperate situation.

Being so low in the water, it quickly became apparent that we couldn't reach the exterior gangway to board the ship and there didn't seem to be any scrambling nets or rope ladders available. We were wondering what to do when the French skipper of the fishing boat motioned to us that he had a plank of wood on board which was about 12-feet long and looked thick enough to bear a soldier's weight.

In the meantime someone on board the troopship had very helpfully opened some luggage-loading doors on the side of the *Oronsay*. One end of the plank was placed on one of the highest sides of our boat, near the bows, and the other end laid into one of the luggage-loading openings, so forming a precarious, 12-inch-wide bridge.

Crossing the short distance was difficult, with bombs exploding, numerous ships hurling up anti-aircraft fire, and shrapnel falling all around the harbour, causing turbulence on the otherwise calm surface. With a man at each end of the board, steadying the narrow upward-sloping 'bridge' from the fishing boat to the *Oronsay*, each man had to judge his opportunity to stride rapidly across the gap.

Almost all of the troops had got across safely and on board the ship when a nervous-looking young soldier said to me: "I don't think I can make it – I'm scared of heights!"

In view of our desperate plight this struck me as absolutely ludicrous. Before I could reply, a Jock (Scottish soldier) who was next in line said to him: "If you don't want to be a guest in a German prison camp for the rest of the war, you'd better get f——— moving!" or words to that effect. This was sufficiently encouraging and we got him safely aboard.

Suddenly there was a tremendous explosion. The *Lancastria*, just getting underway, had been hit by several bombs and was already sinking rapidly. It was an absolutely catastrophic scene. In addition to the thousands of troops, many refugees, nurses and medical staff went down with the ship. To this day, nobody knows how many were lost in the *Lancastria*, but it was at least 5,000, possibly as many as 6,500.

We managed to pick up considerable numbers of survivors before leaving St. Nazaire and heading for home. All the survivors, about 2,500, were ordered not to mention the catastrophe to anyone on their return to Southampton.

The captain and crew of the *Oronsay*, by an outstanding display of seamanship, steering manually through dangerous minefields and navigating from a school atlas, brought their overcrowded ship into Southampton the following morning. A heavy air raid was in progress at that time.

One of my most outstanding memories of that voyage across the English Channel was of an Army Chaplain conducting a Burial at Sea service from one of the lifeboats, as calmly and as unhurriedly as if he was in a quiet and peaceful English countryside churchyard.

Someone suddenly shouted impatiently from the over-crowded deck of the *Oronsay*:

"Come on! Come on! Let's take care of the living – we cannot help the dead..."

Much has been written about the miraculous Dunkirk Evacuation, and quite rightly so as it was a truly tremendous achievement against great odds. But it was also a disastrous defeat, with a loss of about 185,000 British troops captured who would spend the next five years in German prison camps.

However, comparatively little has appeared about the other evacuations from France which also took place – St. Nazaire for example, where British soldiers had literally to walk the plank at sea in order to escape.

'THE BATTLE OF FRANCE IS OVER'

Anthologist's Note: On 18 June 1940, Prime Minister Churchill concluded an inspiring speech to the House of Commons thus:

'What General Weygand called the Battle of France is over. I expect that the Battle of Britain is about to begin. Upon this battle depends the survival of Christian civilisation. Upon it depends our own British way of life, and the long continuations of our institutions and our Empire. The whole fury and might of the enemy must be very soon turned upon us. Hitler knows that he will have to break us in this island or lose the war. If we can stand up to him, all Europe may be free and the life of the world may move forward into broad, sunlit uplands. But if we fail, then the whole world, including the United States, including all that we have known and cared for, will sink into the abyss of a new Dark Age, made more sinister, and perhaps more protracted, by the lights of perverted science.

Let us therefore brace ourselves to our duties, and so bear ourselves that if the British Empire and its Commonwealth last for a thousand years men will still say: "This was their finest hour".'

HMS *BEAGLE* ON THE WEST COAST OF FRANCE

Petty Officer R. V. Butler, Engine Room Artificer, HMS *Beagle*

Reaching the Clyde at 2300 hours on 12 June 1940, after playing a part in the capture of Narvik and the later evacuations from Norway, HMS *Beagle*, commanded by Lieutenant Commander R. H. Wright, stayed only long enough to refuel before sailing for the war-torn shores of northern France.

We left the Clyde at 0400 hours on 13 June, with four troopships bound for Brest with French troops from Norway, together with the destroyers *Wren*, *Havelock* and *Hambledon*.

The day passed without incident, and we arrived in Brest at around 1500 hours on the 14th. We did not go right in, as we had orders to proceed to Plymouth for boiler cleaning and, at last, some leave. But we were wrong. For when we were only an hour from Plymouth we were ordered to return to Brest, arriving there again at 0800 hours on 15 June. Plenty of French naval craft and other shipping were in the harbour. We then left in convoy for St. Nazaire, arriving at 0800 hours on the 16th. We then started fetching troops. The *Georgic*, *Sobieski*, *Duchess of York*, and *Batory* were all there. More air raids started. We left St. Nazaire at 2230 hours with troopships bound for England.

When at sea the next day, the 17th, we received a signal to return to St. Nazaire, the *Whirlwind* carrying on with the troopers. On the approach to the channel to St. Nazaire we passed ships which looked as though they were abandoned and sinking, as well as some twenty lifeboats, Carley floats and hundreds of life jackets. Proceeding further up the channel we were greeted by the enemy bombers. At around midnight we started taking in about 500 troops.

We now heard that France had capitulated, and from the lights on cars and in houses it certainly looked as though the war was finished as far as the French were concerned. Then there were more air attacks, and, as the minesweepers swept a channel for our evacuation convoy, the *Lancastria* was sunk with heavy loss.

We left St. Nazaire at 1500 hours, and were clear of the channel and in position with the convoy by 0700 hours. We maintained a steady 13 knots. It was a beautiful day and a good job too, with soldiers everywhere. We arrived in Plymouth at about 1000 hours on 19 June, and, after discharging troops, having a defective 'A' gun repaired and gyro compasses checked, we took aboard a Rear Admiral, special parties of naval ratings and soldiers, and tons of demolition gear. We then sailed at 25 knots for Bordeaux.

In company with HMS *Arethusa*, we arrived at the mouth of the River Gironde at about 1000 hours, and tied up alongside. At 1115 hours we began sailing up the river to Bordeaux. The tide was low and the channel shallow. Magnetic mines had been sown, and one had sunk a French liner. There was a thunderstorm during the afternoon, and then the green parks of Bordeaux appeared. A fine sight.

We tied up alongside at Bordeaux at about 1500 hours on 20 June. There was gold braid in abundance, together with Embassy officials and people seeking passage. Parachutists had been arrested and bombs dropped nearby, and we saw fighter aircraft overhead. There were many comings and goings during the rest of a scorchingly hot day. The quay remained crowded with naval, military and air force personnel, together with many refugees needing passage.

At about 0130 hours on 23 June we sailed some miles down the river to do the job for which we had been sent – to blow up a huge oil refinery. But after the demolition party had landed and placed all their charges, they were suddenly recalled and the whole project abandoned. Having taken on oil, at 0900 hours we left and returned to Bordeaux.

We then learnt that the French/German armistice had already been signed, and we were in a dangerous position 60 miles up the river at Bordeaux. An immediate return was then ordered, and, after taking aboard many refugees, we left Bordeaux at 1715 hours and reached the mouth of the Gironde at 2130 hours. The expected fire from the forts was not forthcoming, and we proceeded to St. Jean-de-Luz.

At 0630 hours on 24 June a signal was received to return to Devonport. On arrival we anchored inside the bar at Plymouth and discharged the demolition squads and the refugees. We then left for the quayside to discharge stores and ammunition and take in oil and water. Then, after we had been paid some official compliments and been told that on the previous

Sunday special prayers had been said for us in the Dockyard Church, we were at last free to get away on that much anticipated leave.

MISSION TO THE RIVER GIRONDE, 22-23 JUNE 1940

Michael Back, Able Seaman, HMS *Boadicea*

It was to the crossroads of history that the *Beagle*, under the command of Lieutenant Commander R. V. Wright, sailed from Devonport on Wednesday 19 June 1940, after embarking a large demolition and Royal Marine Commando party under the command of Rear Admiral F. Burges-Watson.

In piecing the subsequent events together, I wish to thank Mr. S. E. Keane, BEM, then a Leading Seaman in HMS *Beagle*, who has given me a full record of diary notes which have survived, and others who were in the *Beagle* at the time, including Mr. E. M. G. Evans and Mr. H. H. Piper, with whom I have spoken and corresponded. I apologise for any inadvertent inaccuracies or omissions.

HMS *Beagle* had returned home to Devonport on the morning of 19 June after some hectic and dangerous days evacuating many hundreds of British troops from St. Nazaire. But hopes of a richly earned leave soon faded as a squad of workmen rushed aboard directly she was alongside to strip a defective gun.

Shortly afterwards, Lieutenant Commander Wright received orders to sail that same afternoon after embarking a mixed demolition party of sailors and soldiers under the command of Rear Admiral F. Burges-Watson.

Once at sea, the Captain revealed to his ship's company that they were proceeding at high speed to Bordeaux where the demolition party was to blow up oil tanks and port installations. They were due to arrive at the mouth of the River Gironde the following morning, and at Bordeaux, 60 miles up-river, during the afternoon. But Admiral Burges-Watson and Commander Wright were probably the only ones aboard who would have had sufficient knowledge of the speed of the German advance, and the imminence of an Armistice, to appreciate the great risks involved. Supposing the Germans should reach the river mouth and seize the fortifications and mine the estuary while the *Beagle* was 60 miles up-river? In addition, there was the ever-present threat of German air attack.

Arriving at Le Verdon, the anchorage at the mouth of the River Gironde, during the forenoon of 20 June, *Beagle* briefly secured alongside the light cruiser HMS *Arethusa*, where they received further instructions and advice for their up-river sortie. This was uneventful.

On arriving at the huge port of Bordeaux in the late afternoon, the Admiral and Lieutenant Commander Wright immediately went ashore to seek advice and co-operation from the French authorities for their demolition work, and immediately found themselves in direct discussion with the Commander-in-Chief of the French Navy, Admiral Darlan.

With the news they had achieved direct access to Darlan, new top-secret instructions arrived from London. For the moment, demolition plans were to be put aside, and a further attempt was to be made to persuade the all-powerful Admiral Darlan to sail the French Fleet to North African ports and continue the common fight. It is likely that there would have been further reason for the postponement of the demolition when Admiral Darlan reasoned that if the French government did decide to continue the fight from North Africa, demolition would prevent the large number of French naval and merchant ships from escaping from Bordeaux.

Despite rumours of the imminent arrival of the invading Germans, the full force of the disaster did not yet seem to have come home to the French people ashore. At night, lights were blazing from all the shops along the quay, and the scene was almost one of peacetime normality. But aboard the *Beagle* the possibility of air attack was well appreciated, and the ship's company remained at Defence Watches.

The talks ashore occupied all 21 June, and a second night was passed in Bordeaux. The talks continued on the 22nd, when there were disturbing rumours that the Germans were approaching Royan, at the mouth of the Gironde.

Leading Seaman Keane went ashore twice that day, once to help rig a

W/T station, and later that day to help remove a quantity of material from the British Consulate.

By the evening of Saturday, 22 June 1940, it was clear that the talks ashore had reached a complete stalemate, and finally the order was given to destroy the Bordeaux oil installations a few miles down-river at Blaye, whether the French approved or not. At 0130 hours in the early morning of 23 June, the *Beagle* quietly slipped downstream to Blaye, where the demolition party landed at a convenient jetty adjacent to the oil storage tanks.

Several bewildered French soldiers guarding the site hastily surrendered, apparently under the impression that the raiders were the first arrivals of the German Army. The task of laying the explosives was soon under way. But back aboard the *Beagle* a 'Most Urgent' signal had arrived. The previous order was cancelled. No demolition was to take place without official French approval. Messengers were rushed ashore and arrived just as the operation of laying the explosives was completed.

Watched by the now completely baffled French soldiers, the charges were dismantled and the demolition party returned to the *Beagle* carrying all the equipment with which they'd landed. Early that same morning the *Beagle* returned to Bordeaux to see if there was still a hope of obtaining French approval, only to learn that the French government had just signed an armistice with the Germans.

In her complete isolation, *Beagle* was now in great danger and was ordered to return home immediately. There was to be no demolition, as even at that stage there were still hopes in London that the French Fleet might decide to make for North Africa and continue the struggle against Germany.

Some staff from the British Consulate and some key Allied personnel were taken aboard, and HMS *Beagle* cleared the Gironde Estuary that evening and returned safely to Devonport.

ACTION AT ORAN

Anthologist's Note: In June 1940, Britain faced the prospect of having to oppose the combined fleets of Germany, Italy and France if the French

Navy was surrendered intact to Germany under vague and meaningless armistice terms. Most of the French fleet was based at Mediterranean ports and was kept from the Germans by prompt British action.

On 3 July, a final signal was dispatched by the Admiralty in London to Admiral Somerville at Oran, a major port on the Algerian coast, at 18.26: "French ships must comply with our terms or sink themselves or be sunk by you before dark."

But the action had already begun. The French had refused to surrender and had three battleships disabled by British gunfire from Admiral Somerville's Force 'H', the battleships HMS *Valiant*, and HMS *Resolution*, the battlecruiser HMS *Hood*, the aircraft carrier HMS *Ark Royal*, two cruisers and eleven destroyers. The French later scuttled most of their fleet at Toulon.

BRAZEN GOES DOWN FIGHTING

From *Hold The Narrow Sea*, by Peter C. Smith

On 19 July, things warmed up considerably at Dover. A heavy attack was mounted by Stukas with fighter cover. A squadron of RAF Boulton Paul Defiant fighters was sent up to meet them, but they lost six aircraft in as minutes over Folkestone to the fighter escort. They were not employed again. The Stukas were therefore able to inflict great damage.

At about 1215 hours the destroyer *Beagle*, on patrol off Dover, was attacked by a whole *Gruppen* of dive-bombers. It was estimated between 40 and 50 aircraft were engaged, including fighter escorts. *Beagle* fought back at this mass as best she could, but it was an uneven struggle. Although her high-speed evasion tactics ensured she was not actually hit, there were many near misses, which damaged her gyro and fan engines. Luckily there were no casualties at all. She returned to Dover for examination and had to be sent to Devonport for full repairs later.

Her gallant and lonely fight took some of the sting out of the dive-bomber attack, but a second wave came in at about 1550 hours. This time there were nine Dornier Do17s and they attacked the harbour itself and the ships therein in shallow dives. Twenty-two high explosive bombs fell in the area, the main casualty being the Admiralty oiler *War Sepoy* which received direct hits amidships, broke her back and sank in flames. The destroyer *Griffin* was 'near missed' forward and suffered damage which necessitated docking for repair, the drifter *Golden Gift* was near missed and badly damaged as was the tug *Simla*. Strangely, there were no casualties from this serious attack.

The increasing seriousness of the Stuka attacks on destroyer dispositions, especially those of the 1st Flotilla at Dover, was already causing concern. Three ships had been damaged in as many days. Losses could be made good, but in this war of attrition the limit was rapidly being approached.

On 20 July came another severe blow. Stukas with heavy fighter cover made a massive dive-bomber assault against convoy CW 7. The largest clashes of rival aircraft up to that time took place as the escorts and defenders fought overhead, but the dive-bombers again got through to do their worst. The main attack was preceded by a feint against Dover itself at 1330 hours, when a small formation of nine bombers attacked, but failed to inflict any damage at all. At 1800 hours, however, large formations of aircraft were sighted by the convoy, which was between Dover and Folkestone. The escort consisted of *Boreas* (Lieutenant Commander M. W. Tomkinson) and *Windsor* (Lieutenant Commander G. P. Huddart) along with the patrol destroyer *Brazen* (Lieutenant Commander Sir Michael Culme-Seymour) and the anti-sub trawler *Lady Philomena* (skipper J. Hodson, RNR). They estimated the attacking force to be some thirty Stukas escorted by many fighters.

Many of the dive-bombers concentrated on *Brazen* and she was soon surrounded by the spray of near misses. A bomb exploded under her hull in the vicinity of her engine room, splitting her frames and, ultimately, breaking her back. She quickly settled and began to sink. Her gunners fought to the last; no fewer than three Stukas fell to her gunfire as she sank, taking her last plunge at 2000 hours. Fortunately, casualties were light; one man was killed and four injured; but another valuable destroyer had been eliminated.

MORE BRITISH DESTROYERS

The *Daily Telegraph*, 23 July 1940 (Reproduced by kind permission of the *Daily Telegraph*)

TOTAL HIGHER IN SPITE OF LOSSES
By our Naval Correspondent

Although the sinking of HMS *Brazen*, 1,360 tons, announced yesterday by the Admiralty, brings Britain's total of destroyer losses since the outbreak of war to 27, the Navy's destroyer strength is considerably greater now than in September 1939.

When the war began there were 175 destroyers in service, a figure shortly afterwards increased to 183 by the completion of two ships of the 'Javelin' class, and the acquisition of six destroyers built for Brazil.

Under construction at that time were 24 more destroyers, many of which have been completed by now. A large number of other new ships will be completed by the end of the year.

The loss of the *Brazen* was announced yesterday in the following Admiralty communique: "HMS *Brazen* (Lieutenant Commander Sir Michael Culme-Seymour, RN) received damage during an attack by enemy aircraft and subsequently sank while being towed into port. There was no loss of life."

A second communique stated: "It is now known that HMS *Brazen* shot down three German aircraft during the engagement. One crashed alongside, the second received a direct hit in the nose section with a 3-inch shell, while the third received a direct hit abaft the port engine.

"In another engagement HMS *Beagle* (Lieutenant Commander H. R. Wright, RN) destroyed a Junkers 87 by pom-pom fire."

The *Brazen* was the destroyer which located the submarine *Thetis* when she sank during trials in Liverpool Bay in June last year. One of eight destroyers of the 'Beagle' class, she was launched at Jarrow in July 1930.

Excerpt from *British Destroyers* by E. J. March

The scale of air attack in Norway and France had far exceeded anything thought possible before the war. The German dive-bombers having struck terror on the Continent were now turning their attention to unarmed merchant ships and coasters. The call for some form of defence against Stukas and Junkers was overwhelming, but the cold fact was guns and ammunition simply were not available. Our Army had been forced to retreat to the Belgian and French coasts where tens of thousands of men were taken off open beaches by the Navy and auxiliary vessels at terrible cost, leaving behind guns, stores and all the impedimenta of a modern army.

After a few weeks' lull the full fury of the Luftwaffe was turned against England, now standing alone, well nigh defenceless, but the moat, the sea, prevented the panzers rolling across a frontier. Factories engaged on vital munition production were blitzed and priorities were difficult to arrange. To re-equip the Army was a first call, but if in the meantime the Navy ran short, we might well be starved into submission. Such was the grim situation in September 1940, when the armament and especially the close range weapons were being considered for the 'New Construction' ['Savage' or 'S' class (5th Emergency Flotilla)] destroyers.

A VIEW FROM THE GERMAN SIDE

Operation 'Sealion'

It was not until 2 July 1940 that the OKW[20] issued its first directive order-ing tentative preparation for a landing in England, the cover-name for which was 'Sealion'. At the Führer conference on 11 July 'Sealion' was only one of the items under discussion. Grand-Admiral Raeder was emphatic that this operation should only be launched as a last resort. Although Hitler agreed to this, Directive 16, issued to the three branches of the German armed forces on 16 July, ordered the preparations to start in earnest. It was

[20] *Oberkommando der Wehrmacht*: 'High Command of the German Armed Forces'.

soon apparent that these could not be completed by 15 August, as originally intended, and that it would be impossible to transfer the 40 divisions, as planned by the Army.

After lengthy discussions the Army agreed to reduce the number to thirteen, and to confine the main landing line to a line extending from Beachy Head, East Sussex, to Folkestone, Kent, with another landing between Selsey Bill, West Sussex, and Brighton, East Sussex. The total width of the front would thus be ninety miles, as compared with the original plan for a landing between Lyme Bay and North Foreland, which represented a total width of about 175 miles. But the three services never reached complete agreement as to the form of the Channel crossing. During July the Luftwaffe operated with success against enemy shipping, but Directive 17, issued on 1 August, ordered its efforts to be switched to attacks on England, and it was while doing so that the Luftwaffe developed its own independent form of total air warfare.

By great exertions the Navy was on time in bringing the coastal shipping and the barges from the inland waterways to the assembly ports between Antwerp and Le Havre. The following craft were requisitioned: 155 transport ships totalling 700,000 tons; 1,277 lighters and barges, mostly without means of propulsion; 471 tugs; and 1,161 motorboats.

The Navy also began the construction of heavy coastal batteries at Cap Gris Nez. The first of these, Grosser Kurfürst, with four 28-centimetre guns, was ready for action by 1 August, to be followed within six weeks by Friedrich August with three 30.5-centimetre guns, and Siegfried with four 38-centimetre guns.

It was, however, impossible to gain supremacy at sea. It is true that the Norwegian campaign had succeeded without naval supremacy, since its operational concept was based entirely on surprise by small groups of vessels speeding across the wide spaces of the open sea. In the English Channel such tactics were out of the question, for here the enemy not only possessed a powerful air force, but had also managed to re-equip a considerable proportion of the 300,000 men whom Hitler had allowed to escape from Dunkirk. The British could concentrate their medium and heavy artillery in the threatened area, as well as the guns of older warships.

The majority of the German troops would have to be carried in towed barges, which were not fitted with ramps for beach landings. The steamships would have to lie at anchor off the beaches, and it would probably take about 36 hours to unload them – an impossible situation within striking range of a hostile air force that was still intact. The barge convoys were made up of units of 33 tugs, each towing two barges, which would make two to three knots, but the tidal currents running up and down the English Channel could reach anything up to four or five knots. These slow convoys would need to cover 40 or 50 miles, and it would take them at least 15 hours. The two flanks of the crossing were very poorly guarded. The flanking minefields would provide only partial protection because of the strong tides and the big rise and fall.

A few destroyers, torpedo boats and a number of minesweepers were all that could be mustered in the way of fighting ships. Once the British naval forces had broken into the German convoys, the German aircraft would have difficulty in distinguishing friend from foe, and would presumably be fully engaged by British aircraft.

The position would have been very different if immediately after the Polish campaign the planners at OKW had concentrated on the construction of landing craft of a type similar to the ferry-barges later used by the Navy. These carried about 100 tons of equipment, and had space for three trucks or small armoured vehicles, or the equivalent weight in troops. Being flat-bottomed, they could run up on a beach, lower their ramps, and quickly discharge their cargo. If several hundred of these landing-craft, supported by parachute and airborne divisions, had been sent across the Channel immediately after Dunkirk, they would have stood a better chance of success than the slow troop convoys which it was now proposed to send; for these were even slower than Caesar's legions which had crossed these same waters, under sail, 2,000 years earlier.

It is hardly surprising that the various authorities were very sceptical when it came to a closer examination of these details. Hermann Goering, Commander of the German Air Force, had shown very little interest from the beginning. Meanwhile, his own offensive against the Royal Air Force had not come up to expectations, and when he switched the Luftwaffe to London as the principal target, losses mounted out of all proportion to the results achieved. Here the advantages were all on the side of the British – a highly developed communications system, a complete radar network which gave protection against surprise, and massed fighter defences.

The Luftwaffe would have suffered far smaller losses if it had continued to attack the poorly armed merchant ships and the English ports – targets that were not easy to defend. But by the beginning of September the British were able to start a counter-offensive by bombing the German invasion fleet in its assembly ports, with the result that 21 transports, 214 barges and five tugs were sunk or damaged, representing 10 per cent of the shipping intended for the invasion.

Consequently, the shipping was partly dispersed during the second half of September. Its reassembly would have involved further delays in the event of an invasion being launched. On 12 October 1940, Operation 'Sealion' was definitely postponed until the following spring, and that was the end of it.

Had Hitler been able to dominate the English Channel – be it only for 24 hours – he might have succeeded. But like Napoleon before him, he was never in a position to do so.

[Excerpted from *Sea Warfare 1939-1945: A German Viewpoint*, by Vice Admiral Friedrich Ruge; translated by Commander M. G. Saunders, RN, by permission of Cassell & Co.]

ON PATROL WITH *BOREAS* AND *BRILLIANT*

Anthologist's Note: HMS *Boreas* became a member of the 19th Destroyer Flotilla, Nore Command, and spent the first months of the war on escort duties along the East Coast and in the English Channel.

On 4 January 1940, while rendering assistance to the damaged mine-sweeper *Sphinx*, bombed by German aircraft in the Moray Forth, *Boreas*'s stern was damaged at the waterline and she was under repair until early February 1940. In late March 1940, *Boreas* was attached to the 12th Destroyer Flotilla but on 15 May 1940 she was in collision with her sister-ship HMS *Brilliant* and sustained hull damage above the waterline which required repairs on the Thames until 19 June.

Boreas then joined the 1st Destroyer Flotilla at Dover but didn't remain long. On 25 July 1940, just before 1500 hours, a westbound convoy, C 8 (Southend to St. Helen's Roads), was attacked off Dover by two waves of Stuka dive-bombers. After a short respite the convoy was attacked again off Sandgate at 1620 hours. At 1645 hours German E-boats could be clearly seen from the cliffs of Dover and seemed likely to be proceeding to attack the convoy in the vicinity of Dungeness. Accordingly, HM Ships *Boreas* and *Brilliant*, the only two destroyers available, were ordered to proceed out of Dover harbour independently to engage the enemy; two Motor Torpedo Boats (MTBs) were also detailed to accompany the destroyers.

At 1726 hours HMS *Brilliant* reported that she had six E-boats in sight. At 1745 hours she reported that she was engaging the enemy. By then, both destroyers were getting dangerously close to the French coast and, in fact, the German shore batteries opened fire at a range of approximately 10,000 yards. As the six E-boats had turned eastwards under cover of a smoke screen, the destroyers were ordered to withdraw, without knowing whether any damage had been caused to the enemy. On the return journey, after about ten minutes, a heavy dive-bombing attack was made by a large number of Stukas dive-bombers, escorted by fighters.

There were no direct hits during the initial air attack but *Boreas* sustained damage from near misses by bombs to port and starboard abreast the after engine room, which affected her steering and caused her to stop temporarily. *Brilliant* remained standing by until *Boreas* got under way, whereupon both resumed steaming towards Dover at 17 knots, *Boreas* being steered erratically by hand.

When the destroyers were three miles off Dover, a second air attack was made with more serious results. *Boreas* received two direct hits on the wing of her bridge which was penetrated; an explosion in the galley flat caused severe structural damage and serious casualties: 21 killed and 29 injured. *Brilliant* also received two direct hits, both on the quarterdeck; the bombs passed right through the ship and exploded underwater, causing no casualties to personnel. Apart from obvious structural damage, *Boreas* sustained damage to all boiler room fans and main cooler castings, leaving her unable to raise steam. *Brilliant* had her steering gear put out of action, with the steering compartment, magazine, shell rooms and spirit room flooded.

After the second attack tugs were dispatched and both destroyers were successfully towed into Dover harbour.

Boreas was subsequently out of action for six months, from 30 July 1940 to 23 January 1941, under repair at Millwall Docks on the Thames. On the night of 18/19 January she received superficial damage from bomb splinters during one of the continuous 'Blitz' bombing raids on the nation's capital.

During the repairs *Boreas* was fitted with the equipment to fire a ten depth charge pattern. After working up at Scapa Flow during February 1941, she joined Western Approaches Command as an unallocated vessel. *Boreas* and *Brilliant* were then assigned as replacements for HM Ships *Duncan* and *Foxhound* with the 18th Destroyer Flotilla of the South Atlantic Command. *Boreas* left the Clyde as escort for the Armed Merchant Cruiser *Comorin* and rendezvoused with HMS *Glenartne* and Canadian leader HMCS[21] *Assiniboine*, the ships arriving at Gibraltar on 11 April 1941. After repairs to defects at Gibraltar, *Boreas* arrived at Freetown on 28 April and then operated in West African waters on escort duties until 10 August, when she arrived at Gibraltar to join convoy HG 70.

Boreas subsequently rescued five survivors from the British steamer *Alva* (sunk 19 August 1941), four survivors from the British tug *Empire Oak* (sunk 22 August), 24 survivors from the Norwegian freighter *Spind* (sunk 23 August), and four survivors from the British steamer *Aldergrove* (sunk 23 August). *Boreas* then returned to Gibraltar with these survivors on 25 August 1941.

She subsequently refitted at Middle Docks, South Shields, from 19 September 1941 to 4 January 1942. *Boreas* then undertook full power trials while on passage to Greenock on 6 January 1942, before leaving as escort for a convoy to Freetown on 10 January. She arrived at Freetown on 25 January and rejoined the 18th Destroyer Flotilla for the next nine months.

---

[21] His Majesty's Canadian Ship.

A VIEW FROM THE MERCHANT NAVY 1939-1940

Sidney Davies

I recall paying off the *British Viscount*, an oil tanker, in Falmouth after a nine-month trip in December 1939. I was 19 at the time, having been in the Merchant Navy for the previous four years. During that trip, war had been declared. I went to my home in Port Talbot, South Wales, for a few days' leave and then signed on the SS *Lissa*, a tramp steamer registered in Glasgow, with a cargo of coal bound for Lisbon.

I experienced my first Christmas of the war in a neutral country and it was here that the crew of a German merchant ship, tied up at a nearby wharf, shouted across to us: "ENGLAND IST KAPUT! ENGLAND IST KAPUT!..."

Little did we realise what the uncertain future held for our respective countries.

After discharging, we took a cargo of 'pit wood', pit props for coal mines, back to Britain. After a few days' leave I joined another collier, the Swansea-owned SS *Amiens*, which carried about 3,000 tons of coal from South Wales to the French ports of Le Havre and Dieppe, having about three days in France during the 'Phoney War' of late 1939 to early 1940.

It was during these days ashore in the French ports that we discovered what shameful payment our British Army 'Tommies' received when we spoke to them in the French cafes – twenty one shillings per week (the equivalent of one pound and five new pence per week in decimal currency). Evidently, an 'allotment' had to be deducted from their weekly pay for their next-of-kin at home.

The comparative quiet of the Phoney War suddenly came to a screeching halt in May 1940 with the 'Blitzkrieg' by the German Army and Air Force rapidly and mercilessly smashing their way across Holland, Belgium and northern France.

We were advised by our shipping agent to slip our moorings and return to England to await further orders from Le Havre. We sailed for London and while moored in the River Thames, officials from the Royal National Lifeboat Institution (RNLI) and from the Port of London Authority came aboard to requisition our ship's lifeboats. These were subsequently towed across the English Channel to be used at the beaches of Dunkirk.

After this miraculous withdrawal, now equipped with replacement lifeboats, we resumed our coal trade from the north-east coast to Bristol Gas Works before paying off the *Amiens* on 22 June 1940.

Barely a month later the *Amiens* was sunk. Her fate was briefly described to me by a shipmate from Swansea: during a daylight air attack by the German Air Force on a convoy in the English Channel, a large bomb exploded virtually alongside the *Amiens* creating a huge column of water and signalling the end of the ship. With the sea gushing in from several locations below the waterline, she slowed to a stop. The crew lowered the lifeboats and pulled clear. Slowly, the old *Amiens* filled up and slid gently beneath the waves.

My former shipmate from Swansea was later lost at sea while aboard a torpedoed British oil tanker. Incidentally, the day a merchant ship went down, the pay of the surviving crew immediately stopped.

After a few days' leave in early July 1940, I signed on on the SS *Mariston* of Glasgow. Our cargo was coal to Montreal, on the St. Lawrence River, eastern Canada, then down to Norfolk, Virginia, the big port and US naval base, for a load of steel rails.

Then, in September 1940, we steamed up to Halifax, Nova Scotia, to join a convoy of 20 to 25 merchantmen, escorted by only two or three corvettes, sailing to Britain. Fortunately, we never realised the dangers ahead. While ashore in Halifax I met an old schoolmate, Granville Jones. He was on the oil tanker *Gullpool*, owned by Ropners of West Hartlepool. They eventually lost 80 per cent of their ships by 1945. On departing Halifax the heavily laden convoy sailed north, running at about six knots. Eventually, we could see the coast of Greenland appearing on the northern horizon.

"The Commodore will now make for Iceland," said our Captain, whom we affectionately knew as the 'Old Man'. It was during an especially black night that the alarm bells suddenly sounded. Our Royal Navy corvette escorts began firing off star shells, which transformed night into day on the flanks of our convoy. I was on 'Lookout' and saw a tanker in the next line abeam blazing, the leaping flames very quickly spreading from fore to aft.

"THERE GOES THE IRON ORE SHIP!" shouted one of my equally

shocked shipmates, pointing to another sinking vessel, clearly illuminated by the raging fires and massive explosions from the torpedoed tanker, its volatile cargo now spewing out a rapidly spreading sea of flame from ruptured tanks.

"Dear God," I thought. "That's the *Gullpool...*"

Then it was gone – no survivors visible. But I hoped…

Just as dawn was breaking on the eastern horizon, a Norwegian freighter was the third merchantman to be torpedoed and abandoned before she, too, disappeared beneath the waves.

After our Chief Engineer had reported the latest loss, the Lascar firemen refused to return to the stokehole (boiler room). Our Captain immediately gave the Chief his revolver. It instantly signalled the end of the minor mutiny.

When I arrived home, old man Jones asked me if I'd seen or heard anything of his son Granville on my travels: I replied, "No, I'm very sorry, but I haven't…"

Granville had been on board the torpedoed *Gullpool*. I didn't want to break the old man's heart.

I then rejoined the SS *Mariston*, but before sailing we had a 4-inch Japanese field gun mounted on the poop. We steamed out to Swansea Bay to test fire our new defensive armament. However, on firing the first shell seawards, several things happened in rapid succession: the entire poop deck was immediately enveloped in thick white smoke and choking cordite fumes; the topmast rigging parted; all the lights throughout the ship failed; and a considerable volume of accumulated soot in the funnel showered down into the furnaces of the boiler room, causing the firemen to rush up on deck, covered from head to toe in clinging black soot, and head straight for the lifeboats.

I had trouble with my teeth thereafter so chose a few days ashore, but in late October 1940, I joined the SS *Merchant Royal* for the iron-ore run to Wabana, Newfoundland. While anchored off Wabana I caught the fishing 'bug'. We caught codfish by the dozen on a handline until the ship's cook had filled the icebox. At that time there were no refrigerators.

During the following winter months of 1940/1941 we subsequently joined several convoys, to and from Britain and Halifax, Nova Scotia, ploughing through the frequently storm-swept, mountainous and icy-cold seas of the North Atlantic ocean. It impressed upon all of us that man is totally helpless and impotent when confronted with the immense and incredible power of the sea. During one such stormy period, one complete wing of the *Merchant Royal*'s solidly-built bridge, and a securely lashed lifeboat, on outboard davits, were swept cleanly away, like chaff in the wind. The extensive damage was later repaired on Tyneside.

We were often soaking wet and our very basic accommodation brought little comfort. The constant threat of attack from submarines meant that we were often tense, on edge and trying to conceal our deepest fears. Most of us got very little sleep, despite often being thoroughly exhausted after each period of duty. However, we all felt sorry for the crews of our much smaller escorts, the destroyers, corvettes, sloops and anti-submarine trawlers, especially when we encountered rough weather. They had to work, eat and sleep in far more crowded, cramped and hellish conditions than any of us.

There was trouble on one particular night as we entered the Western Approaches in relatively calm weather. A merchantman was torpedoed and sank very quickly. Then the crew of a Greek-registered ship panicked. All hands abandoned ship and took to the lifeboats. A Royal Navy boarding party then took over the deserted vessel early the following morning as a 'Prize Crew'. This extraordinary episode was described to us a little later in Londonderry, Northern Ireland, by several of the escort vessel's ratings.

Excerpt from *Blood, Tears and Folly* by Len Deighton

(Reproduced by kind permission of The Random House Group & Jonathan Clowes Ltd.)

Up to early September 1940, i.e. the first full year of the Second World War, total British shipping losses – Royal Navy and Merchant Navy – amounted to 452 ships. The ships kept coming. The Atlantic campaign was the longest and most arduous battle of the war, much of it fought in sub-arctic conditions, in gales and heavy seas.

When considering the moral questions arising from the RAF/USAAF[22]

---

[22] United States Army Air Force.

'terror bombing' of cities, consider too the civilians who manned the merchant ships. Casualties of the air raids upon cities usually had immediate succour; the merchant seamen, and ships' passengers too, men, women and children, were mutilated, crippled and burned. There was no warning save for the crash of a torpedo tearing the hull open. Few men from the engine room got as far as the boat deck. The attacks usually came at night and, on the northerly routes the convoys favoured, it was seldom anything but very cold.

Many of the merchantmen's crews were not young. Survivors, many of them bleeding or half-drowned, were abandoned to drift in open boats upon the storm-racked ocean where they went mad or perhaps died slowly and agonizingly of thirst or exposure. Almost all Britain's oil and petroleum supplies came across the Atlantic by ship. So did about half its food, including most of its meat, cheese, butter and wheat, as well as steel and timber, wool, cotton, zinc, lead and nitrates. British farmers could not have produced homegrown crops without imported fertilizers; neither could farmers in neutral Ireland have survived. "Ships carried cargoes they were never built for, in seas they were never meant to sail," said one official publication.

During the war I remember that in London scarcely a day passed without someone in my hearing mentioning our debt to the merchant service. Anyone leaving a particle of food uneaten on a plate was risking a reprimand from any waiter or passer-by who saw it. No heroes of the war – not even the fighter pilots – excelled in valour and dogged determination the men of the Merchant Service and their naval escorts. The public knew it.

One merchant navy officer, Captain Gwilym D. Williams, said: "Armed with a free railway ticket issued by the Shipwrecked Mariners' Society to my home in Colchester, Essex, I proceeded on leave. My journey across London via the Underground from Euston to Liverpool Street Station clad in a salt (not to mention vomit!) stained uniform and still jealously clutching my orange-coloured life jacket was more of an ordeal than the whole western ocean, with the masses of people sheltering from the nightly blitz all wanting to crowd around me to slap my back or shake my hand."

The Battle of the Atlantic continued until Germany surrendered in May 1945.

THE LOSS OF THE *ARANDORA STAR*

Anthologist's Note: The total number of British, Allied and neutral merchant ships lost in action throughout the oceans of the world during the 12 months of 1940 was 1,059, totalling nearly four million tons.

Among those British merchant ships sunk during July 1940 was the *Arandora Star,* a 25,000 ton luxury liner hastily converted to a troopship, which had played a full and active part in the evacuations from France. During the previous month, she sailed from Liverpool bound for St. John's, Newfoundland.

Her complement on leaving England was 1,673, comprised of 174 officers and crew, 200 military guards, 479 German male internees, 86 German prisoners of war and 734 Italian male internees. At about 0615 hours on 2 July, when the ship was approximately 75 miles west of County Donegal, Ireland, she was torpedoed by a German U-boat. A little more than an hour later the *Arandora Star* rolled over, its bows rose vertically into the air and she slid rapidly to the bottom of the Atlantic Ocean, together with many of her passengers and crew.

In the unfamiliar surroundings of a sinking ship the military guard were reported to have behaved magnificently.

One of the military guards was Corporal Sidney Gaze, who had been rescued from St. Nazaire on the *Oronsay* the previous month [see above] and was due to take the second period of guard duty that day and had taken the opportunity to get some much-needed sleep: "I don't know how long I slept, but I was awakened by an awful shuddering of the vessel and found myself on the floor at the far end of the cabin. Thank God I'd listened to advice and slept with my life jacket on although it was uncomfortable. I made my way up to the main deck ensuring that each cabin's occupants were evacuated along the way."

Sergeant Norman Price, of the Worcestershire Regiment, was another of the guards assigned: "There were great fears at that time that the Germans were going to invade Britain and it was felt that the internees and prisoners of war should be got out of the country and taken to Canada.

"I was asleep in my cabin when the first torpedo ripped into the ship but I was instantly awakened. I went straight up on deck where panic was breaking out. There were not enough lifeboats or life jackets for everyone and a lot of the men couldn't swim, so the panic was quite understandable in the circumstances. We had to fire a few shots over the heads of the crowd and that calmed them down.

"Then we concentrated on getting people into the lifeboats and life jackets and then started ripping wooden doors off cabins, wooden tables from the dining rooms, and anything else that would float so that there would be something for the survivors to cling on to.

"The end of the *Arandora Star* came quite suddenly. I found myself in the water and I could see hundreds of men clinging to the ship. They were like ants and then the ship went up at one end and slid rapidly down, taking the men with her.

"Just previously, many men had broken their necks jumping or diving into the water. Others injured themselves by landing on drifting wreckage and debris floating near the sinking ship. It was a terrifying experience but the ironic thing was that less than three weeks before, our unit had been pulled off the beaches at Dunkirk without a single loss."

Corporal Sidney Gaze: "Before the ship eventually went down I'd thrown two tables into the water to hold on to but, terrifyingly, I was sucked into the vortex as the huge liner went to her grave. Somehow I managed to struggle up to the surface. I'd injured my back while leaving the ship and was in the sea for about eight hours before being picked up by a Canadian destroyer."

The Canadian destroyer, HMCS *St. Laurent*, came to the rescue at about 1300 hours that same day. She picked up a total of 868 survivors and landed them at Greenock, Scotland. A British destroyer, HMS *Walker*, also arrived at the location of the sinking much later, but failed to find any more survivors.

A total of 805 lives were lost as a result of the U-boat's attack – Captain E. W. Moulton, 12 of his officers together with 42 of the crew of the *Arandora Star,* 37 of the military guard; 470 Italians and 243 Germans.

WINTER DIARY OF HMS *BRILLIANT*

Stanley Jones

M y service record reveals I joined HMS *Brilliant* at Dover on 21 June 1940, firstly as an Ordinary Seaman, then Able-Bodied Seaman, and left her at Southampton on 7 May 1941, when I did a 'pier-head jump'. I eventually arrived at King Alfred via Chatham, and then on to be granted an RNVR commission, subsequently serving in 'Flower' class corvettes.

Many of *Brilliant*'s company were Regular RN, with some Reservists, but not many of us Hostilities Only (HO) men. Many times I heard them discussing the Spanish Civil War and their rescuing Spanish refugees and taking them into St. Jean de Luz.

I recently came across a small hand-written record (strictly forbidden!) from 20 September 1940 until 31 January 1941:

20 September 1940 – Left Chatham Dockyard (after bomb damage repairs) to Sheerness.

21 September – Ammunitioned ship at Sheerness, then proceeded to Portsmouth via Dover.

22 September – Lay at Spithead.

23 September – On patrol in English Channel with *Vanoc*, *Volunteer* and *Witch*.

24 September – Spithead.

25 September – Southampton.

From then until 30 September at Spithead on Channel Patrol (27th, beat *Beagle* 4-1 at soccer).

1 October – Left Portsmouth with *Beagle* and *Bulldog* for Rosyth, arrived 3rd and joined destroyers *Cossack*, *Sikh*, *Ashanti*, *Zulu*, *Maori*, *Fame* and *Electra*. Battleships *Nelson* (Flagship) and *Rodney* also there.

Until 16 October – in and out on exercises.

17 October – Met battleship *King George V* off the Tyne and escorted her to Rosyth.

20 October – Left early with *Fearless* and *Electra*, escorting *Repulse* (battlecruiser) to Scapa Flow. We returned to Rosyth.

Until 4 November – again in and out on exercises, destroyers *Wallace* and *Winchester* appeared.

4 November – All ships to immediate notice. *Naiad* and *Bonaventure* sailed at noon, all destroyers at 1600 hours with *Rodney* and *Nelson*, arrived Scapa. All ships at one-hour notice.

6 November – All ships sailed at 0530 hours. Rumoured *Admiral Scheer* is out. With *Rodney* and *Nelson* to cover Iceland, severely cold. *Rodney* left for Halifax, Nova Scotia.

10 November – Gale continues unabated.

11 November – Left *Nelson* and, with *Vimy*, arrived Faeroe Islands. *Vimy*'s No. 1 boiler defective.

12 November – Arrived Scapa. Boiler clean.

13 November – *Hood, Repulse* and *Nelson* in, also *Electra, Beagle* and *Eskimo* alongside.

17 November – Left with *Beagle* and *Bulldog* for Loch Alsh (Ross and Cromarty), arrived 1600 hours.

18 November – Sailed 0100 hours escorting five minelayers to position west of Cape Wrath.

19 November – Laid 64-mile minefield in five hours, turned for home, arrived 1730 hours.

20 November – Sailed 1400 hours with *Beagle* and *Bulldog* for point 17°W to meet *Rodney*. Met *Electra* off Cape Wrath and headed west.

22 November – Met *Rodney* and turned for home. Bad weather set in. Lost track of *Bulldog* and others.

23 November – Mast snapped at 0100 hours. Weather terrible and no Wireless Transmitter (W/T). At dawn found others except *Bulldog*. Arrived Scapa 1430 hours. *Bulldog* arrived 1600 hours minus mast and boats.

Until 3 December – lay in for repairs and new mast.

3 December – At sea in Pentland Firth with *King George V*, then exercises until 10 Dec. Then left for Greenock. After Greenock, escorted the battleship *Queen Elizabeth* to Rosyth then we went to Scapa Flow on the 14th. Hurricane fighter plane crashed in sea off May Island, picked up Polish Pilot Officer.

16 December – Out with *Hood, Nelson* and *Rodney*, five cruisers and ten destroyers on night exercises.

18 December – Arrived Scapa 1100 hours, oiled and sailed at 1530 hours with *Beagle* and *Bulldog*, escorting *Nelson* on a night shoot. Quiet over Christmas. In floating dock until 2 January 1941. *Bulldog* going for refit.

6 January – Sailed 0100 hours for Greenock, arrived 7th. *Kelly*, *Kipling*, *Phoebe*, *Naiad*, *Beagle*, *Lincoln*, *Churchill* and *Leopard* here. *Ramillies* arrived.

11 January – Convoy ready to sail. Seven Union Castle, three Cunard White Star and five Canadian Pacific, said to have 40,000 troops and 3,000 ATS going to Gibraltar.

12 January – Sailed 0100 hours, joined up with Liverpool Section, 21 in convoy. One battleship, three cruisers and ten destroyers escorting.

15 January – Six destroyers left convoy, 52ºN 22ºW, good weather. After anti-submarine patrol, arrived Scapa 22 January.

31 January – Alongside Submarine Depot Ship *Maidstone* in Scapa. Destroyer *Boreas* arrived.

1941

PROLOGUE TO 1941

by

Rear Admiral John B. Hervey, RN, Retd.

ALTHOUGH DANGER of invasion had receded, 1941 was a very bad time at sea for Britain, who started the year fighting alone, now against both Germany and Italy. Merchant ship losses escalated sharply, especially once French West Coast bases became available to U-boats. A successful foray by *Scharnhorst* and *Gneisenau* further aggravated them. Meanwhile, heavy losses of destroyers were incurred in the Mediterranean, whilst extracting our Army from Greece where it was the Dunkirk story all over again – ships overwhelmed by air strikes. Of the 23 destroyers lost in 1941, 16 were sunk in the Mediterranean, 11 by aircraft and seven – in seven days – off Crete

Far from being able to build up our escort numbers, therefore, by the end of 1941, we could still only allocate an average of two to each convoy – little more than a token presence. There was also a huge job to be done training up new escorts for the Battle of the Atlantic – the one battle, above all others, which we could not afford to lose. Iain Nethercott gives a light-hearted account of the work-up organisation run by 'Monkeybrand' Stephenson in 'The Admiral of Tobermory', but in truth it was a desperately serious and important activity. How serious is made plain in 'The Hunters' and 'A Brilliant Orange Flash', which describe successful U-boat captains at work – and the frustrations felt by escort force commanders when shadowing enemy aircraft reported their every move.

However, in 1941 three helpful events occurred. On 22 June, Hitler attacked the USSR. On 7 December, Japan attacked the USA. Strategically, waking these sleeping giants ensured eventual victory. But helping Russia increased the British burden at sea. The third event – recovery, by HMS *Bulldog* on 9 May, of an Enigma machine from *U-110*, plus all relevant documentation – almost immediately reduced our losses and gave us an edge at sea for the rest of the war. The story is told in a series of articles, starting with 'OB 318 – The Exploits of a World War Two Convoy', and includes personal accounts by Commander Baker-Cresswell, RN, *Bulldog*'s commanding officer, and the officer and men who boarded *U-110*. When pinning the DSO on Baker-Cresswell, King George VI told him that this was perhaps the most important event in the whole war at sea. There is no 'perhaps' about it.

Although the USA officially entered the war on 7 December, US Navy warships had by then been augmenting convoy escorts to the mid-Atlantic position for some months. Able Seaman Michael Back, of HMS *Boadicea*, in 'Before Pearl Harbour', pays tribute to those who lost their lives in USS *Kearney* and USS *Reuben James*, while taking part in a war which was not yet theirs. The final article in this section, 'A Tribute to HM Submarines', brings Iain Nethercott back on stage and explains how he came to join submarines. It is a good reminder too of just how important their contribution was to the war in the Mediterranean.

THE ADMIRAL OF TOBERMORY

Iain Nethercott, ex-HMS *Keith*

During the early part of the war the Admiralty decided that the new escort ships being built and manned by Reservist Officers and civilian crews needed a good shake-up before they were allowed to go to sea. They appointed a fierce and grizzled old Admiral called Stephenson, gave him the rank of Commodore and shoved him up to Tobermory, a small port on the north end of the Isle of Mull, off the west coast of Scotland.

Not exactly renowned for being especially handsome in his active Admiral days, he'd been nicknamed 'Monkeybrand' due to his uncanny resemblance to the monkey on the packets of Monkey Brand soap used by housewives for scrubbing front doorsteps. In fact he was probably the ugliest Admiral in the Navy, retired or not.

Admiral Stephenson would go to sea with a new ship and put the crew through every evolution known to man, including Gas Drill, Collision Stations, Fire in the Galley, Shoring up a Bulkhead, etc., etc. He would have a barrel thrown over the side and as it slowly drifted away he got the Stokers and the Signalmen to man the guns. That inevitably resulted in the ship itself being nearly blown apart in their efforts to hit their target.

One day Admiral Stephenson boarded an Arctic trawler with a crew of fishermen and RNR men, and was attempting to do dummy depth charge attacks, while simultaneously doing another demanding task. He eventually had everyone on board running to and fro, wondering what they were doing. Up on the bridge of the trawler the old fisherman on the wheel was imperturbable, as he continued to chew his cud of tobacco.

This upset old 'Monkeybrand' to the extent that he whipped off his peaked officer's cap, adorned with gold braid, slung it on the deck, looked up at the helmsman and shouted: "THAT'S A GERMAN INCENDIARY BOMB! THIS SHIP IS NOW ON FIRE!"

The elderly fisherman left the wheel, strolled over to the cap... and very deliberately kicked it over the side. Then he strolled back, took the helm and continued on course.

THE HUNTERS

Excerpt from *Blood, Tears and Folly* by Len Deighton (Reproduced by kind permission of The Random House Group & Jonathan Clowes Ltd.)

At first the convoys outward-bound from Britain had been given Royal Navy escorts on only the first stage of their journey, about 15 degrees west longitude. Then the escorts stayed as far as 25 degrees west and then – by July 1941 – convoys were given continuous escort. Relays of escorts operated from Britain, from Iceland and from Newfoundland. But warships were scarce, and even by the end of 1941 the average convoy had no more than two escort ships.

The escort ships were not immune to torpedoes either. I make no apologies for the extra length of this excerpt from one of the most graphic accounts the Atlantic battle provided:[23]

'The sky suddenly turned to flame and the ship gave a violent shudder... Looking ahead, I could see something floating and turning over in the water like a giant metallic whale. As I looked it rolled over further still and I could

---

[23] Commander D. A. Rayner, *Escort* (Wm. Kimber, London, 1955).

make out our pennant numbers painted on it.

I was dumbfounded. It seemed beyond reason. I ran to the after-side of the bridge and looked over. The ship ended just aft of the engine room – everything abaft that had gone. What I had seen ahead of us had really been our own stern. There were small fires all over the upper deck. The First Lieutenant was down there organizing the fire parties. He saw me and called, "Will you abandon ship, sir?"

"Not bloody likely, Number One... We'll not get out till we have to." But a ship with its stern blown away does not stay afloat for long.

The deck began to take on an angle – suddenly, so suddenly. She was almost on her side. I was slithering, grasping all kinds of unlikely things. My world had turned through ninety degrees. I jumped for the galley funnel which was now parallel with the water and about two feet clear, and flat-footed it to the end. I paused at the end of my small funnel to look at the faces. They were laughing as if this were part of some gigantic fun fair.

The men called to me, "Come on, sir. The water's lovely."

"I'm waiting for the Skylark," I shouted back. But the galley funnel dipped and I was swimming too – madly. We swam like hell. I turned once more, but now there were very, very few bobbing heads behind me. I swam on. The destroyer from my old group was passing through us – I could see her men at Action Stations. They were attacking. They were attacking the wreck of the *Warwick*! I screamed at them in my frenzy. Wherever else the U-boat might have been it could not have been there. The depth charges sailed up in the air. Funny how they wobbled from side to side, I'd never noticed that before. When, I wondered, would they explode? It was like being punched in the chest, not as bad as I expected. I swam on. Things were a bit hazy. I was not as interested in going places as I had been. I could only see waves and more waves, and I wished they would stop coming. I did not really care anymore. Then I felt hands grasp my shoulders and a voice say, "Christ, it's the skipper. Give me a hand to get the bastard in!" and I was dragged into a Carley float which was more than crowded to capacity.'

To make the most of the pitifully few escorts, the Royal Navy had started 'Escort Groups', which usually meant nothing more than RN captains getting together, under one of their number named as escort group commander, to exchange ideas about anti-submarine tactics.

It was the 5th Escort Group which in March 1941 was in the same area as the German Navy's three most famous U-boat captains: Gunther Prien, Joachim Schepke, the celebrated and colourful captain of *U-100*, and Otto Kretschmer of *U-99*. At their collars these men wore the Ritterkreuz [Knight's Cross], to which the insignia of the oak leaves had been added to celebrate 200,000 tons of ships sunk.

Kretschmer and Schepke were both determined to be the first to sink 300,000 tons of Allied shipping. Kretschmer had left his base at Lorient with 282,000 tons (although German figures were usually very much inflated).

It was Prien in *U-47* who sighted the outward-bound convoy OB 293 and summoned his colleagues: Kretschmer in *U-99*, Matz in *U-70* and Hans Eckermann in *U-A*.[24] Although a primitive seaborne radar set played its part, this encounter marked little change in the methods or technology of either side. But there was a change in the men: the Germans, solidly professional, were at the zenith of over-confidence, while the Royal Navy's landlubbers and weekend yachtsmen had discovered a new determination.

Kretschmer started the sinkings. Firing while surfaced, he hit a tanker which burst into flames, and a Norwegian whaling ship *Terge Viken* which remained afloat. Using the same tactics in *U-70*, Matz hit a British freighter and the *Mijdrecht*, a tanker, which with true Dutch resilience steered at him as *U-70* dived. The *U-A* was detected and dived, its course followed by Asdic. Depth charges damaged it enough to make the German set course for home.

Matz in *U-70* had submerged. He now came under coordinated attacks from two corvettes. Wallowing and unstable he went to 650 feet – far deeper than the submarine was designed to endure. The damage sustained from the Dutchman which rammed him, together with the depth-charging, started leaks and made the U-boat impossible to control. Despite the crew's efforts the *U-70* surfaced and was fired upon. The crew surrendered as the stricken U-boat reared, bow in the air, and slid under, taking 20 of her crew with it.

Even the stubborn Kretschmer dived deep and sat 'in the cellar'. He watched the rivets pop and the lights flicker as the explosions came and went. Carefully he withdrew, with half his torpedoes still unused. The convoy

---

[24] *U-A*: 'A' for *Ausland* – 'overseas' – because this U-boat had originally been built for Turkey in 1938 and designed as a minelayer.

sailed on, having lost two ships and two damaged.

Prien followed the convoy and tried again at dusk, his approach covered in fitful rainstorms. But in a clear patch he was spotted by a lookout on HMS *Wolverine* and his crash dive failed to save him from the depth charges that damaged his propeller shafts. Instead of turning for home, he surfaced after dark for another attack, perhaps not realizing how clearly the damaged propellers could be heard on the Asdic. This time *Wolverine*, which had tenaciously waited in the vicinity, made no mistake. As the U-boat crash-dived, an accurately placed depth charge caused the submarine to explode under water, making a strange and awful orange glow. "The hero of Scapa Flow has made his last patrol," said the obituary notice personally dictated by Admiral Dönitz when, after 76 days had passed, the German Navy finally told the German public of their hero's death. Even then stories about his having survived circulated for months afterwards.

A few days later on 15 March 1941, south of Iceland, Fritz-Julius Lemp, now promoted to Korvettenkapitän, signalled the approach of a convoy. It was an attractive target but the escort was formidable. The escort commander was Captain Macintyre, RN, who was to become the war's most successful U-boat hunter. He was in an old First World War destroyer, HMS *Walker*. There were four other old destroyers with him, and two corvettes. The homeward convoy HX 112 consisted of almost fifty ships, in ten columns half a mile apart. They were heavily-laden tankers and freighters, and even in this unusually calm sea they could make no more than ten knots.

Lemp's sighting signal was intercepted by direction-finding stations in Britain. Such plots could only be approximate, but Captain Macintyre was warned that U-boats were probably converging on HX 112. Without waiting for other U-boats, Lemp's *U-110* surfaced and used darkness to infiltrate the convoy. Two torpedoes from his bow tubes missed, but one from his stern hit *Erodond*, a tanker carrying petrol, and the sea around it became a lake of flames.

The next day other U-boats arrived. The uncertainties of U-boat operations are illustrated by the way in which *U-74* never found the rendezvous and *U-37*, having surfaced in the fog, was run down by a tanker and had to return to base for repairs. But Schepke (*U-100*), and Kretschmer (*U-99*) provided enough trouble for the resourceful Captain Macintyre. Having spotted Schepke's boat, the escorts started a systematic search which kept it submerged and allowed the convoy to steam away. At this stage of the war the escorts had not discovered that U-boats impudently infiltrated the convoys to fire at point-blank range. The search for attackers always took place outside the convoy area. So the chase after Schepke was Kretschmer's opportunity to penetrate the columns of the virtually unprotected convoy, and at 2200 hours there was a loud boom which marked the beginning of an hour during which Kretschmer hit six ships. Five of them sank. The hunt for Schepke's *U-100* was abandoned as the escorts closed upon their charges.

'A BRILLIANT ORANGE FLASH...'

Excerpt from *The Cruel Sea* by Nicholas Monsarrat

(Reproduced by kind permission of Cassell & Co.)

They all stared at it, every man on the bridge, bound together by the same feeling of anger and hatred. It was so unfair... U-boats they could deal with – or at least the odds were more level: with a bit of luck in the weather, and the normal skill of sailors, the convoy could feint and twist and turn and hope to escape their pursuit. But this predatory messenger from another sphere, destroying the tactical pattern, eating into any distance they contrived to put between themselves and the enemy – this betrayer could never be baulked. They felt, as they watched the aircraft, a helpless sense of nakedness, an ineffectual rage: clearly, it was going to happen again, in spite of their care and watchfulness, in spite of their best endeavours, and all because a handful of young men in an aircraft could span half an ocean in a few hours, and come plummeting down on their slower prey.

Swiftly the aircraft must have done its work, and the U-boats could not have been far away; within twelve hours, back they came, and that night cost the convoy two more ships out of the dwindling fleet. The hunt was up once more, the pack exultant, the savage rhythm returning and quickening... They did their best: the escorts counter-attacked, the convoy altered course and increased its speed: all to no purpose. The sixth day dawned, the sixth night came: punctually, at midnight the alarm bells sounded and the first distress rocket soared up into the night sky, telling of a ship mortally hit and calling for help. She burned for a long time, that ship, reddening the water, lifting sluggishly with the swell, becoming at last a flickering oily pyre which the convoy slowly left astern. Then there was a pause of more than two hours, while they remained alert at Action Stations and the convoy slid southwards under a black moonless sky; and then, far out on the seaward horizon, five miles away from them, there was a sudden return of violence. A brilliant orange flash split the darkness, died down, flared up again, and then guttered away to nothing. Clearly it was another ship hit – but this time, for them, it was much more than a ship; for this time, this time it was *Sorrel*.

They all knew it must be *Sorrel*, because at that distance it could not be any other ship, and also because of an earlier signal which they had had relayed to her from *Viperous*. "In case of an attack tonight," said the signal, "*Sorrel* will proceed five miles astern and to seaward of the convoy, and create a diversion by dropping depth charges, firing rockets, etc. This may draw the main attack away from the convoy." They had seen the rockets earlier that night, and disregarded them: they only meant that *Sorrel*, busy in a corner, was doing her stuff according to plan… Probably that plan had been effective, if the last two hours' lull were anything to go by: certainly it had, from one point of view, been the ideal exercise, diverting at least one attack from its proper mark. But in the process, someone had to suffer: it had not cancelled the stalking approach, it did not stop the torpedo from being fired: *Sorrel* became the mark, in default of a richer prize, meeting her lonely end in the outer ring of darkness beyond the convoy.

Poor *Sorrel*, poor sister-corvette… Up on the bridge of *Compass Rose*, the men who had known her best of all were now the mourners, standing separated from each other by the blackness of the night. But bound by the same shock, the same incredulous sorrow. How could it have happened to *Sorrel*, to an escort like themselves? Immediately he saw the explosion, Ericson had rung down to the wireless office. "'*Viperous* from *Compass Rose*'," he dictated. "'*Sorrel* torpedoed in her diversion position. May I leave and search for survivors?'" Then: "Code that up," he snapped to the telegraphist who was taking down the message, "Quick as you can. Send it by R/T." Then, the message sent, they waited, silent in the darkness of the bridge, eyeing the dim bulk of the nearest ship, occasionally turning back to where *Sorrel* had been struck. No one said a word: there were no words for this. There were only thoughts, and not many of those.

THE SINKING OF THE ARMED MERCHANT CRUISER HMS *COMORIN*

Iain Nethercott, HMS *Lincoln*; and **Tristan Jones**, HMS *Comorin*[25]

Iain Nethercott: Following the sinking of HMS *Keith* off Dunkirk in June 1940, I underwent further training. In late August 1940, I found myself on a troopship crossing the North Atlantic to Halifax, Nova Scotia together with three conscript destroyer crews to man the first three of fifty US Navy four-funnel destroyers, dating from the First World War, under President Roosevelt's 'Lend-Lease' agreement. Such was the desperate need for more escorts to protect the vital convoys that the conscripts, from every walk of life, had only received six weeks' training following the bare minimum basic instruction.

I was assigned to HMS *Lincoln*, formerly the USS *Yarnal*, and the return voyage under the command of a young Lieutenant was uneventful.

One of the most memorable events while serving on the *Lincoln* happened in early April 1941. We received orders to go to the rescue of an Armed Merchant Cruiser, HMS *Comorin*, in the middle of the North Atlantic. Evidently, the AMC had had a fire break out in her engine room which, by the time we got to her assistance during the afternoon of 6 April, was raging out of control.

There was a heavy sea running and *Comorin*, with no engines and the fire rapidly spreading, was drifting with the ever-increasing wind. Her crew of over 400 wanted to abandon ship but the weather conditions were very much against an orderly transfer.

The destroyer, HMS *Broke*, an old First World War Flotilla Leader, was

[25] Excerpted from Tristan Jones, *Heart of Oak* (Bodley Head; reprinted by Random House, London, 1997).

the nearest ship to us and she was ordered to leave her convoy to give us assistance and guidance, as her Skipper was a four-ring Captain while ours was a young Lieutenant.

We came up in *Comorin*'s lee as close as we dared. She was being driven by both wind and sea and would have crashed aboard, undoubtedly sinking us. We fired Coston Gun lines aboard her and attached grass lines to haul survivors over to *Lincoln* in Carley rafts. This was a very slow and dangerous operation. Two rafts overturned in the high seas and all the men floated away to leeward and drowned.

Comorin managed to get one of her lifeboats launched from her falls. The boat was full of men but they had no idea of handling the lifeboat under oars. She fell off in the trough of a big wave and the following crest tipped her over. All her men fell into the sea. We had to let them go as we were in the process of hauling over a raft full of survivors and bringing them alongside the waist where we could grab them out of the raft. Then *Comorin*'s men on her fo'c's'le hauled the raft back for another load. But with over 400 men to transfer and at about eight per raft, it would take far too long.

Comorin then signalled us to start taking men off from her stern and work up to windward as the fire was spreading to her fo'c's'le. We got more lines up on to her poop and another Carley raft came into the picture. Also we were getting more than the original eight men to a float by more survivors hanging on to the Carley raft's lifelines and being dragged across in the water. This way we were achieving about 12 to 14 men every trip.

We were sweating away at this when *Broke* arrived. Her Skipper was going to take a chance and lay his bow against the stern of the liner which was rising and falling about fifty feet in the big seas.

We then moved off to windward, paid our lines out and watched the *Broke* coming ahead and creeping up to *Comorin*'s stern. *Broke*'s crew had brought all their hammocks up and lashed them on the port side of her fo'c's'le. The danger was that the liner's stern was rising and yawing thereby exposing her screws and her huge rudder, so *Broke*'s Captain kept having to make very quick movements on his engines to avoid being hit and sunk. Several times he crashed *Broke*'s bows alongside *Comorin* enabling the crew who had mustered there to jump down onto *Broke*'s decks. But a number of men fell between the two ships and were crushed to death.

I lost all count of time as I was getting close to exhaustion hauling these rafts over, but what seemed hours later there didn't appear to be anyone left on the burning AMC. When we pulled clear and recovered our lines and Carley rafts, *Broke* was already standing off.

When I eventually got down on the mess deck I found the survivors, many suffering from hypothermia whom our coxswain was treating with liberal rations of rum. There were about 260 survivors aboard the two ancient destroyers from *Comorin*'s crew of 423.

Tristan Jones: When we got back on the upper deck I saw that the men were crowding into *Lincoln*'s Carley floats, six to eight men per raft, which were being pulled to the destroyer over mountainous seas. The destroyer, all the while, was plunging like a wild thing. As the men in the Carley floats reached the destroyer's stern, some of them jumped too fast and fell into the sea. Some were recovered but many were not. I'd just made up my mind to hang on to the Carley floats whatever happened, until I was dead sure of being able to grab hold of the destroyer's survivors' nets, when another destroyer appeared, grey and ghostly at first, out of the thick weather.

She was the destroyer we had passed earlier that day, HMS *Broke*.

By now things were breaking loose aboard *Comorin* and some were sliding over the side into the violent sea, pumps and ammunition lockers. I saw several men carried away over the side.

We were heaving open drums of oil over the side in the hopes that the oil might calm the sea between us and the *Lincoln*, but all it did was to blow it over the upper decks of the destroyer.

The *Broke* then started to pump thick, black, oozy oil into the sea between us and the *Lincoln*. In the heaving seas she almost got herself crushed between the two ships and only got away by the skin of her teeth. As she slid out from the deadly passage between the now even lower in the water *Comorin* and the bucking, tossing *Lincoln*, I noticed men on Carley rafts looking like insects on the huge grey slopes, waving to *Broke*.

In our ship now, there was no semblance of separation by Branches, all the seamen and stokers, the cooks and the stewards, the signalmen, everyone was mixed up in the 'Abandon Ship' parties. Only the wounded and the dead had been sorted out and separated.

The waves, it was agreed, were about sixty feet from trough to crest. We were all mustered aft. There was nothing we could do but wait to be rescued, if that was possible.

Broke then came up on our windward side and cast a Carley raft into the sea. It drifted up under our stern and AB 'Shiner' Wright jumped down into the raft. As he and four or five more clambered over the rail and dropped into the raft he shouted, "Any more for the Skylark?" The raft was pulled right under the *Comorin*'s pounding stern as the heaving line had got entangled with her screws. The destroyer men pulled on the line, but then we saw that the heaving line was around our propeller shaft just as our ship, with an almighty crash, had descended. We never saw 'Shiner' and his mates again.

Broke steamed right up under our stern and after several near misses she managed to fire a Coston Gun line aboard us which was rapidly attached to a thick grass line and secured aboard us. They then lowered a Carley raft into the sea and signalled us to pull it over. As it surged alongside, many of our men jumped down into it but as it was being hauled back aboard *Broke*, it suddenly capsized throwing them all into the foaming sea. They were never seen again.

Then probably in reply to our own Captain's semaphore signal, as he was aft with his Chief Yeoman of Signal by his side, *Broke* started to head for our ship's side, so that we might jump directly on to her decks.

I remember many things, all in a rush, with extreme vividness. I could try to set down in words the rush of the sea between ships, the grinding rumble and screech as *Broke* crunched her hull alongside *Comorin*. I recall the shouts of our crew, some jocular now, some crying in their despair and fright, and one sickening lurch as the ships crash one against the other... they come to me like frames in a fast moving film. It is only thus that I can write what followed *Broke*'s sacrificial gesture; a complicated series of menacing events that could be seen in the glimpses of an eye. But there was something else besides: something invisible, a directing spirit of comradely essence; a willingness to lay lives down for the sake of friends.

The facts are plain. The *Lincoln* exhibited all her seamanship and cunning to maintain the Carley raft lifeline at terrible risk to herself, while the *Broke* ground and smashed in that raging sea alongside *Comorin* for about three hours.

It is difficult to give an impression of the risk of jumping from a ship's deck in a screaming wind and a mountainous sea. One second forty feet above the upper-works of a destroyer, able to look down her funnels, and the next second fifteen feet or so below her upper decks. The slightest misjudgement in the moment to jump, the slightest hesitation when the moment came, the slightest weakness in grabbing on to the destroyer, and you would be like so many other dead.

I remember clearly the first group to jump, nine seamen from the Quarterdeck Division. When they jumped as *Broke* rose on the swell, four landed on her fo'c's'le. Three got to their feet and stumbled down aft, but one had broken his legs and was quickly carried away by the destroyer's crew mustered on the fo'c's'le. The other five from *Comorin* missed their jump and fell between the two ships as they crashed together. Their broken bodies floated away down aft.

The second lot to jump were six men. Of them, only three landed safely on the piled up hammocks on *Broke*'s fo'c's'le. The other three were injured when they landed on the deck and carried aft by the destroyer's crew.

Then the destroyer pulled away from our side and we thought she was going to abandon us to take our chances with the *Lincoln*. But no, she crashed back, took off another 'flight' of men with its ensuing deaths, and pulled away again.

This she did again and again about two dozen times. By the time I jumped it was almost full night. I recall watching one man fall between the ships even as the destroyer crashed alongside, and me gauging the *Broke*'s rise, and Nobby by my side holding me steady.

I recall Nobby shouting above the roar and the cries, "All right, here she comes… two… six… Here she comes… JUMP!" And then I crashed down on the gun deck of the destroyer, a deck above her fo'c's'le, and landed splayed out on the deck. I banged my head against a steel ladder, but felt I was unhurt.

One of *Broke*'s crew pulled me up: "Nip down aft lad and get a drop of rum from the Coxswain," he told me. The rolling of the destroyer was much more violent than the old *Comorin* and it took me a few minutes to get accustomed to it as I staggered along her steel decks.

As I looked back I could see that the destroyer had rigged up floodlights to aid in jumping the gap between the ships. It looked like some ghastly horror film set – all the action and men on the foredeck, as if it was going on in a different world – with few left on *Comorin*, dying under her blood-red pall of smoke and fire, looking as though they were far away in time and space.

Soon the men injured during the transfer were being brought aft. Aboard *Broke* some of the injuries were grim. One man was completely impaled when he crashed on to a guard rail stanchion. There were many broken legs, arms and ribs.

The destroyer *Lincoln* was still getting men off by Carley rafts and was burning her searchlight to aid the rescue effort. As the night drew on, the wind and sea worsened, until by the time the last men were jumping, it was a roaring, boiling inferno, and as we stared aghast at the spray, the last three of all were lost over the side between the grinding hulls of the destroyer and dying armed merchant cruiser.

Broke and *Lincoln* stood by *Comorin* all night and watched her red glare a mile or so away in the gale. By about midnight the fire reached *Comorin*'s bridge where the rockets were set off in a huge display of fireworks. Great red and white blossoms lit up the sky. Then the ammunition began to explode with bullets and cannon shells whizzing overhead. She finally sank with a great hiss just before dawn and took hundreds of dead and dying men, the exact number will never be known, to her resting place on the sea bed.

The destroyer was overcrowded with twice as many men as her wartime complement. I slept in a borrowed blanket under the mess table wearing an old lammy coat.

We eventually sailed into Liverpool and were welcomed like heroes at Gladstone Dock. The dockyard mateys crowded the sea wall to cheer us in, and then again in the march from the docks to Lime Street Station, civilians lined the street to cheer us home. They too didn't know why they were cheering. News of the sinking was kept secret. I certainly didn't feel a hero at all, we were just lucky. But we all grinned as we marched along in the oil-skins of the *Broke*'s crew, because none of us had anything decent to wear.

The train journey to London took all night – about ten hours. We were transported across London in grey double-decker buses with white-painted windows so we couldn't see out and civilians couldn't see in. After another train journey we entered that awful place, Chatham Barracks, where we were kitted out and sent on fourteen days' 'Survivors Leave', but only after a very Senior Officer addressed us in the infamous Drill Shed, telling us to mention the sinking to no one, as it was important to keep this information from the enemy.

OB 318 – THE EXPLOITS OF A SECOND WORLD WAR CONVOY

F. T. Grover

During both the First and Second World Wars Great Britain's lifeline was the Merchant Navy, and in those desperate years a very large proportion of the country's food together with vital war equipment was imported by merchant ships. At the beginning of the First World War, British merchantmen were routed independently, as they had been in peacetime, but with the increasing number of German U-boats coming into service, losses mounted rapidly, and by the early part of 1917 the situation had become critical. In order to provide greater protection to the valuable ships and their vital cargoes, the convoy system was introduced. Although U-boats still accounted for many ships, losses decreased considerably.

In 1939, the convoy system was reintroduced. This is the story of one of hundreds of convoys which sailed the great oceans between 1939 and 1945, one which unexpectedly gave Britain its biggest intelligence coup of the whole war.

During the late evening of 4 May 1941, 38 merchant ships of six nationalities which had passed through the narrow waters of the Minches between the west coast of Scotland and the Hebrides, in two loosely formed columns, rounded the Butt of Lewis, the northern tip of the Outer Hebrides and, steering a north westerly course, formed up into nine columns, proceeding at about eight knots into the North Atlantic. This was convoy OB 318.

Of the 38 merchantmen, totalling 204,811 tons, 28 were British, four Dutch, three Norwegian, one Belgian, one Greek and one Swedish. Sixteen were in ballast, but the others carried a wide variety of goods including military stores for West Africa and the Middle East, and general cargoes, with a large amount of Scotch whisky for the United States of America, the latter earning much needed dollars for Britain.

When the convoy finally dispersed, destinations were to be almost world-wide – the West Indies, the eastern seaboard of the United States and Canada, West Africa and South Africa, South America, and through the Panama Canal to ports in the Pacific.

The heavily-laden merchantmen were escorted on the first part of their ocean passage by the Royal Navy's 7th Destroyer Escort Group, HM Ships *Westcott* (Commander Bocket-Pugh, Senior Officer), *Newmarket* (ex-USS *Robinson*), and *Campbeltown* (ex-USS *Buchanan*, later to achieve fame at St. Nazaire), the sloop HMS *Rochester* and the corvettes HM Ships *Marigold*, *Nasturtium*, *Dianthus* and *Auricula*. The anti-submarine trawler *Angle*, en route to join the 3rd Destroyer Escort Group, was also in company.

The convoy was made up of four contingents originating from various ports on the west coast of Britain. Ships of the 7th Escort Group had been dispersed among some of these ports, but as they were not numerous enough to adequately protect each separate section they were complemented by local escorts. The main contingent consisted of 17 ships, one of which was the British-owned *Colonial* carrying Rear Admiral W. B. Mackenzie, RN, Retd., a veteran of the Battle of Jutland in 1916, who had been appointed Commodore of OB 318. They sailed from Liverpool at 1300 hours on 2 May escorted by *Rochester*, *Primrose*, *Marigold* and *Nasturtium*. The Milford Haven contingent consisted of four ships escorted to their rendezvous with the main contingent by the destroyer *Vanity*, two anti-submarine trawlers and an anti-submarine yacht. Five ships from the Clyde were escorted by *Campbeltown* and *Angle* and the 12 ships from Loch Ewe, which had already been convoyed round the north of Scotland, were accompanied by *Newmarket* for the short distance they had to steam before joining the main convoy.

The other destroyers were able to top up with fuel at Loch Ewe to give maximum endurance for the westward passage. During their journey through coastal waters the ships were given continuous air cover throughout the hours of daylight by aircraft of Coastal Command.

Commander Bocket-Pugh in *Westcott*, with *Dianthus* and *Auricula*, had sailed from Liverpool about 24 hours after the main contingent and joined up with the convoy off Cape Wrath in time to deploy his force for the first night in open waters. Being the only vessel fitted with radar, *Westcott* kept no fixed station but remained free to sweep in any direction from which danger was most likely to come. The night passed peacefully and at dawn the next morning, when aircraft of Coastal Command arrived, all ships were in their assigned stations.

As with most convoys of the Second World War, merchant ships' names were not used at sea. Vessels were identified by two digits: the first being the number of the column to which the vessel was assigned, reading from left to right, and the second digit was its position in the column reading from the front. Thus '43' would be the third ship in column four.

Normally, the ships would keep station in columns at two cables distance, with columns five cables apart. This was considered to be the best formation in case of attack by U-boats, but distances could be shortened when threatened from the air, so that vessels could render more effective mutual support. In April 1941 the practice of zigzagging in formation had been discontinued for slow convoys, and a system of evasive steering introduced. When a convoy was considered to be heading into danger the Commodore could, at a given signal, turn the convoy 40 degrees at a time in either direction. This manoeuvre temporarily altered the relative positions, but when the normal course was resumed, ships were again in their allocated stations.

All the ships, apart from the neutral Swede, were defensively armed. Twenty-eight ships carried an elderly 4-inch naval gun mounted at the stern, while the other nine were equipped with dual-purpose guns. Each ship carried a nucleus of fully-trained RN gunnery ratings drawn from the Defensively Equipped Merchant Ships (DEMS) organization and, with members of the ship's companies who had received some initial training, these made up the gun crews. Ten of the vessels also carried single 40mm Bofors guns, which were manned by British Army personnel of the Maritime Anti-Aircraft Regiment. These would go with the ships to the nearest convenient port out of enemy aircraft range, where the Bofors would be unshipped and together with their crews would transfer to homeward-bound vessels. Except the Swede, all the ships in the convoy also carried light machine guns.

Throughout the hours of daylight on 5 May, Coastal Command aircraft continued to give air cover and Commodore Mackenzie exercised 40 degree emergency turns in formation. At 1600 hours, after receiving reports from the Admiralty that U-boats were lurking to the northward, the course was altered to due west. The following night passed quietly and after dark two evasive turns were made with the object of shaking off any pursuers.

At dawn on 6 May, a Coastal Command Whitley was patrolling overhead, but left soon after to cover two homeward-bound convoys in the vicinity. The day was uneventful apart from a sighting by the *Rochester* of a floating enemy torpedo which was recovered by a boat from *Westcott* with the intention of sending it to the Technical Intelligence Department of the Admiralty.

Steady progress westward continued throughout the next night and by the morning of 7 May the convoy was beyond the range of Scottish-based aircraft, but for part of the forenoon they were accompanied by a Sunderland flying boat from Iceland, until the threat of fog at its base caused it to be recalled. Earlier, at 0830 hours three vessels, *Iron Baron*, *Atlantic Coast* and the Dutch ocean-going tug *Zwarte Zee* bound for Iceland, left the convoy unescorted but reached Reykjavik safely.

In the forenoon an empty lifeboat was sighted by *Westcott*, and the escorts sank several floating mines which had probably broken adrift from the minefield which British mine-layers had laid between Iceland and the Faeroes. (The minefield had been laid to trap the U-boats breaking out into the Atlantic by the northern route, but proved to be ineffective as it accounted for only one U-boat).

Several Asdic contacts were made and a number of depth charges dropped with no result, which led Senior Officers to believe they'd been attacking whales or pockets of cold water.

At 1504 hours, a signal from the Admiralty stated that the U-boat Tracking Station had intercepted a message from a U-boat reporting the position of the convoy. Consequently, the Commodore ordered an evasive turn to starboard, bringing their heading to approximately north-west.

Meanwhile, the 3rd Escort Group, consisting of the destroyer *Bulldog* (Commander A. J. Baker-Cresswell, Senior Officer), *Amazon* and *Broadway* (ex-USS *Hunt*), the corvettes *Aubretia*, *Nigella* and *Hollyhock* and the trawlers *St. Apollo* and *Daneman*, which had recently been relieved from a previous outward-bound convoy, were refuelling in Iceland and preparing to sail in time to take over OB 318 from the 7th Escort Group in the early evening of 7 May.

Four merchantmen, *Cardium* (British tanker), *Bradglen* (British freighter), *Borgfred* (Norwegian) and *Gunvor Maersk* (Danish), which had been waiting in Iceland to join the convoy, left Reykjavik on the evening of 6 May, escorted by *Aubretia, Nigella, Hollyhock* and *St. Apollo*.

Commander Baker-Cresswell in *Bulldog*, together with *Amazon* and *Broadway*, sailed from Reykjavik at 0215 hours the next morning, accompanied by the Armed Merchant Cruiser *Ranpura* (Captain H. T. W. Pawsey) which was returning to Halifax, Nova Scotia. They met OB 318 still heading in a north-westerly direction approximately 160 miles south of Iceland at 1745 hours, 15 minutes ahead of schedule, and the two senior officers brought their ships close together.

Signals were exchanged, and because Admiralty Intelligence had reported U-boat 'wolf packs' in the area, Commander Bocket-Pugh agreed to leave *Rochester, Nasturtium, Auricula, Dianthus, Primrose* and *Marigold* to continue for another 24 hours, after which they would have to leave to meet HX 123, a fast homeward-bound convoy. His destroyers could not remain because their endurance was much less than the sloops and corvettes, and they were getting low on fuel. So, at 1945 hours, they departed for Iceland.

Ranpura was not fitted with Asdic and consequently was of little use for detecting submarines. It was therefore decided, by opening up columns five and six, to station her in the centre of the convoy. She was by far the largest ship in company and, according to Commander Baker-Cresswell, "She stood out like a sore thumb".

The first sign of trouble came at about 2100 hours when *Bulldog*, sweeping ahead of the starboard wing of the convoy, made a close Asdic contact, but lost it before any action could be taken. Fifteen minutes later, *Eastern Star* and *Ixion* were torpedoed almost simultaneously on the starboard side. Commodore Mackenzie immediately ordered the convoy to make a 40 degree emergency turn to port. The survivors of *Eastern Star* were picked up by *Daneman* which had recently arrived after being delayed in Iceland with engine trouble. The survivors of *Ixion* were taken on board *Marigold*.

The torpedoes appeared to have come from a position close to the point where *Bulldog's* recent contact had been made. Depth charges were immediately dropped in the area. *Bulldog, Amazon* and *Rochester* continued to search the area throughout the night, but Asdic conditions were poor and although they gained several contacts, each of which was attacked, there were no apparent results. At 0930 hours the following morning, 8 May, they abandoned the search and set off to rejoin the convoy.

About an hour after *Ixion* and *Eastern Star* had been torpedoed, the outward-bound contingent from Iceland had joined the convoy. Lieutenant Commander Taylor in *Broadway*, who had taken command of the escorts during *Bulldog's* absence, deployed the extra escorts around the convoy. At 2335 hours, in accordance with instructions from the Admiralty, the course was altered to due west. There were no further incidents during that night.

At 0830 hours on 8 May, a Sunderland flying boat of 206 Squadron Coastal Command arrived from Iceland, giving cover until early afternoon, when fog reappearing at its base caused it to be recalled.

On rejoining the convoy at about 1600 hours, Commander Baker-Cresswell released the ships of the 7th Escort Group who were due to rendezvous with convoy HX 123. This left him with three destroyers, three corvettes and three trawlers; not very many to look after 39 merchantmen.

The night of 8 May was clear with a bright moon, ideal conditions for two U-boats shadowing the convoy. One of the shadowers was *U-110*, commanded by Kapitänleutnant Fritz-Julius Lemp, who had achieved notoriety by sinking the Donaldson transatlantic passenger liner *Athenia* 250 miles north-west of Ireland while in command of *U-30* on the first day of the war, 3 September 1939, with the loss of 112 passengers and crew members, including 28 Americans.

No attacks were made during the night, and at dawn on 9 May the convoy was steering a south-westerly course. This was to be the escorts' last day with the convoy as they were now getting low on fuel. It was considered that by 1600 hours they would be clear of the area in which U-boats were operating. To date no U-boat had made an attack so far to the west.

The forenoon was uneventful, and the ship's officers and men could well have been thinking that perhaps the worst was over.

At 1201 hours a tall column of water shot up from *Esmond's* starboard side. A few seconds later *Bengore Head* was also torpedoed. *Esmond* stayed afloat long enough for all her crew to abandon ship and be picked up by *Aubretia*. *Bengore Head*, a small ship of only 2,609 tons, had been hit amidships and her back was broken. The bow and stern rose and her two masts crossed as she went down. Incredibly, only one life was lost and her 44 survivors were taken aboard *St. Apollo* and the Norwegian *Borgfred*.

Aubretia, steaming on the starboard side of the convoy, had picked up the sound of running torpedoes, and as soon as *Esmond's* survivors were on board she turned towards the direction from which the sound had come. *Bulldog* and *Broadway*, who were now sweeping ahead of the convoy, turned to follow. A few minutes later *Aubretia* established a firm contact, and at the same time sighted a periscope, but just at that dramatic moment her Asdic failed. Lieutenant Commander Smith immediately fired a pattern of depth charges by eye.

Shortly after, *Aubretia* regained the use of her Asdic and contact re-established at about 1,700 yards. The target was now moving towards the convoy, and at 1223 hours *Aubretia* made another attack with a full pattern of depth charges. Both *Bulldog* and *Broadway* had also now established contact and were preparing to attack when a large patch of foaming water suddenly appeared on the sea's surface. Guns were trained... At about 1235 hours the *U-110* broke the surface. Several of her crew immediately poured out of the conning tower and clustered around their 10.5cm (4.2-inch) gun.

Commander Baker-Cresswell, thinking that the slowly-circling U-boat intended to fight it out, gave the order to open fire and turned *Bulldog* onto a ramming course. Several shots found their target before it became evident that the Germans were abandoning ship.

GOTT MIT WHOM?

The Capture of *U-110*

By the spring of 1941, heavy shipping losses in the North Atlantic gravely imperiled the British war effort. But all that changed in early May, after a young Royal Navy officer boarded a crippled German U-boat and made a discovery that would shorten the course of the Second World War.

Sub-Lieutenant David Balme, RN: Life in HMS *Bulldog* was the happiest time of the war for me. We had a fine Captain, a good crew and just a handful of delightful and efficient officers. In May 1941, not only were we short of ships but also desperately short of officers and men. In the wardroom we had for watchkeeping on this convoy a Lieutenant aged 22, myself, aged 20, and an RNVR Sub-Lieutenant. So it was a very tiring life. Four hours on watch, eight hours off, but during those eight hours we had to do other duties. For instance, in May 1941, I was the navigator in charge of the ship's office and as we were one officer short, I was also doing gunnery control.

The most tiring of all was at night, because during the winter months in those northern latitudes, night was 16 hours out of 24. We had 40 to 50 merchant ships and eight to ten escort vessels. We would zigzag all night and day at a speed of only eight knots. On the bridge was an Officer of the Watch, a Signalman and two Lookouts.

On the 9th May 1941 we were attacked at noon. I'd been on watch from 0400 to 0800 hours and after a bath and breakfast, I was on the bridge. It was a sunny day, moderate wind but the usual big Atlantic swell. Suddenly, at noon, two ships were hit by torpedoes. We immediately went to Action Stations. We turned the convoy 45 degrees away from the attack and *Bulldog* headed for the position from which the torpedoes must have been fired, as did *Broadway*. *Aubretia*, a corvette that had joined us, made an Asdic run and dropped a pattern of depth charges. Lieutenant Commander Smith, commanding *Aubretia*, thought he had missed, and dropped another pattern. It didn't miss. The U-boat surfaced 400 yards from us and we opened fire with every gun.

In those days we didn't have sophisticated control systems. My job as Gunnery Control Officer was to call up the three 4.7-inch guns on my telephone headset, give the gun crew a bearing and range and tell them to open fire independently.

The noise was deafening, especially from our Lewis machine guns which were being fired from the bridge over our heads by anyone who could pick them up. However, it was undoubtedly the noise of all the shells and bullets hitting the U-boat which panicked the German crew, who all jumped overboard as fast as they could without successfully scuttling it.

F. T. Grover: Realising that there could be a chance of a capture, Commander Baker-Cresswell ordered: "Stop both engines. Full speed astern." *Bulldog* stopped about 100 yards from the stationary U-boat. The next order from *Bulldog*'s bridge was: "Away armed boarding boat's crew."

Broadway was still closing rapidly, and despite Commander Baker-Cresswell's shouted order through a loud hailer, "DO NOT RAM! – DO NOT RAM!" – as also flashed by Aldis lamp in Morse code – *Broadway* caught the U-boat a glancing blow, tearing her own bow below the water-line and losing her port propeller.

Lieutenant Commander Taylor, *Broadway*'s Commanding Officer, later explained that he'd intended to drop two shallow-set depth charges close to the submarine in an effort to prevent her diving; a difficult manoeuvre as she was still circling slowly.

While Sub-Lieutenant David Balme, with a boarding party consisting of six seamen, a signalman and a stoker, was closing the U-boat, *Aubretia* was picking up German survivors via her scrambling nets and hurrying them immediately below, preventing them seeing what was going on. Kapitänleutnant Lemp wasn't among the 34 survivors.[26]

Sub-Lieutenant Balme entered the U-boat cautiously. He found no one on board, the interior in relatively good order with the lights still on. Confidential books were intact, with charts showing all the searched channels leading to U-boat bases. The boarding party busied themselves removing as much equipment as possible, passing it from man-to-man up through the hatch to be loaded into the whaler, which made several trips between *U-110* and *Bulldog*. The whaler was later aided by *Broadway*'s American-type motor boat.

David Balme: I learned later that Smith [in *Aubretia*]'s [depth charge] pat-

---

[26] The fate of the Commander of *U-110*, KL Lemp, is somewhat obscure. One story says that after leaving the boat he swam back when he realised that the scuttling charges were not going to work and that he was shot and killed by a member of the boarding party. Another, more likely one is that Lemp, realising the catastrophic consequences which would follow the capture of *U-110* and her secret equipment, committed suicide by allowing himself to drown. His body was not recovered. Lemp was in command of *U-30* when he made the first sinking by a U-boat in the Second World War, the SS *Athenia* on 3 September 1939.

terns had broken vital guages in *U-110*, ruptured fuel tanks, damaged the electrical system, and ripped out the stopcock of the buoyancy tanks. Out of control, she shot to the surface, broaching not far off our starboard bow. We opened fire and turned to ram, as did *Broadway*. From intuition, and from inspiration based on experience, Captain Baker-Cresswell abruptly swerved and also ordered *Broadway* off her collision course.

Why not board her and, if possible, take her in tow back to base? Under our fire, the *U-110* crewmen could not man their deck-gun. Pouring out of the hatch, they leapt or fell, wounded or dead, into the sea, Lemp, her notorious captain, among them.

Then Captain Baker-Cresswell ordered: "CEASE FIRE! CEASE FIRE! AWAY THE BOARDING PARTY!"

That meant me. One of my duties was to command that boarding party, although we had never had time to drill. *Bulldog* lay to, about 100 yards to windward of *U-110*. The sea was calm for the North Atlantic, only the usual long swells.

The First Lieutenant ordered: "LOWER AWAY!" and then "SLIP!" and our five-oared whaler, clinker-built, was under way. "Under way for what?" I wondered. My orders were to recover all codebooks and papers I could find.

At the whaler's tiller, my thoughts of the scuttling charges the Germans must have set before we could even get to our prize would not go away; therefore I steered for the windward side of the boat, as faster than to more seaman-like leeward. That meant we had an unpleasant time of it, working ourselves up the slippery side of the boat and finally securing the whaler.

All that was busy preliminaries, but I now had starkly to face the fact that, alone as never before in my life, I, David Balme, was duty-bound to climb that conning tower and descend into – what? Remains of the German crew to greet me? Or scuttling charges rigged to explode as I opened the hatch? My previous seven years of training couldn't dull the vividness of such mental images. "Stop thinking... Do it!" I told myself. I climbed the conning tower, and at the top I took my Webley revolver out of its holster. I'd never fired it in my life.

I'm still haunted by my climb down that last vertical ladder, 15 feet into the bowels of *U-110*, now with the revolver holstered. I felt there must be someone below trying to open the seacocks, or setting the detonating charges, but no-one was there. There must have been complete panic in *U-110*, and she was left to us as the greatest prize of the war. But I still wake up at night 56 years later to find myself going down that ladder.

I made a preliminary reconnoitre in the blue emergency lighting. Not a German to be seen, but I could hear an ominous interior hissing between the rumble of depth charges not far off. Depth charges could detonate any scuttling charges. I called my men down, to learn that the whaler had been dashed to driftwood against the hull of the U-boat.

I signalled to *Bulldog* that the U-boat looked seaworthy and could be towed. Captain Baker-Cresswell sent the motor boat to remove any booty, and booty there was. Everything was lying about just as if one had arrived at someone's house after breakfast, before they had time to make up the beds. Books and gear were strewn about. My men formed a chain to pass up all books and charts except leisure reading.

Meanwhile the telegraphist found the W/T office in perfect condition: no one had so much as tried to destroy books and apparatus. Codebooks, signal logs, pay books and general correspondence were all intact. A coding machine, too, was plugged in as though it had been in use when abandoned. It resembled a typewriter, hence the telegraphist pressed the keys, and reported to me that the results were peculiar. The machine was secured by four ordinary screws, soon unscrewed and sent up the hatch to the motor boat alongside.

At about 1430 hours, when we had been aboard for two hours, I was sitting at the captain's desk eating a sandwich sent over from *Bulldog* and going through all the papers when I came on a sealed envelope. It turned out to be the June settings of the coding machine, the Enigma. The May settings were probably in Lemp's pocket when he perished. Later, the July settings were captured from the German trawler *Lauenberg*.

Now *Bulldog* closed *U-110* and we tried to secure a towing wire. It parted just as *Bulldog* steamed off to investigate a reported U-boat contact. This was a desolate and forlorn moment. There was I with my boarding party, aboard *U-110* in the middle of the Atlantic, alone with no ship in sight, and with wind and sea gradually rising. With no more movable gear to collect, I battened down hatches, and we waited.

Happily, *Bulldog* returned in an hour, and we set about securing another tow, with the great help of the Chief Bosun's mate, who arrived by motor boat. The tow held, and at about 1830 hours we returned to *Bulldog*, having spent some six hours in *U-110*. Now *Bulldog* set course for Iceland with our unique prize, but our hopes turned black when *U-110*, labouring in a heavy sea, sank at about 1100 hours the next day.

We could not have known then that the loss of *U-110* was the best possible outcome to the entire episode. Assuming that *U-110* had been destroyed, the Germans not only failed to realise that *U-110* had been captured; they also failed to realise that their precious Enigma machine with its codes had fallen into the hands of British Intelligence. And because the survivors of *U-110* had been rushed below decks of ships in the area, as late as 1981 Admiral Dönitz refused to believe that Enigma had been fatally compromised. It is also worth noting that some 400 men in the convoy and escorts knew of the U-boat's capture, but not one revealed the fact until the end of the war.

F. T. Grover: The Senior Officer was mindful of the danger from other U-boats, and had set up an anti-submarine patrol around the area. Several doubtful Asdic contacts were made, and while *Bulldog* kept a watchful eye on the surface operations, the other two escorts carried out depth charge attacks for about an hour before the echoes faded.

By 1600 hours, all the moveable material had been taken, and although *U-110* was down by the stern and listing slightly with her rudder jammed, there seemed to be a good chance of getting her to Iceland. She was battened down and after considerable difficulty a towline was passed, and most of the personnel taken off. As *Bulldog* took the strain the tow sheered off to port. More line was paid out, and just as *U-110* was coming under control a lookout reported: "Periscope off the starboard bow!"

Commander Baker-Cresswell couldn't afford to take any chances and reluctantly gave the order for the tow to be slipped. A careful search of the area was made with no positive result and after about half an hour the task of resuming the tow commenced. By 1850 hours they were once more heading for Iceland, and gradually worked up to seven and a half knots.

During the evening, in accordance with previous orders, *Aubretia* was detached to join up with a homeward bound convoy, HX 124, which was to be the responsibility of the 3rd Escort Group. This left only the damaged *Broadway* in company with *Bulldog*. At dusk the prize was slightly further down by the stern, but riding the seas satisfactorily. Then the wind and the sea began to rise, gradually increasing throughout an anxious night, and by dawn the following morning, *U-110* was yawing badly and had settled lower in the water.

At 0700 hours, 9 May, it became necessary to heave to, and at 1050 hours *U-110*'s bow rose high into the air and she slid slowly and gracefully beneath the waves. After so much effort there was great disappointment in *Bulldog*, no one except the Commanding Officer realising that the material they were now carrying was far more important that the U-boat. There was now no possibility of catching up with the convoy, and so a course was set for Iceland where *Broadway* could make temporary repairs. After refuelling, *Bulldog* sailed at full speed for Greenock with her priceless cargo.

Lieutenant A. M. Seymour, Anti-Submarine Officer, HMS *Nigella*: I was assisting with the deciphering of the signals, and, in the afternoon following the midday attack by *U-110*, a signal (I don't remember whether from C-in-C Western Approaches or Admiralty) arrived to say that this incident was to be known as Operation 'Primrose' and that no ships having any knowledge of Operation 'Primrose' were to enter harbour until further orders!

We had visions of a permanent life on the ocean wave!

With some escorts taking merchant ship survivors to Iceland, and destroyers going for oil, etc., only two of the 3rd Escort Group remained free to go on, when OB 318 was sent on its way, to meet the homeward-bound convoy of 108 ships (two convoys having been combined)! The two of us (*Nigella* and another 'Flower' class corvette) jogged on, and then sighted a ship.

At full-speed and with 'Long-Tom' 4-inch waving, we belted towards what we hoped was a blockade runner. She turned out to be the Armed Merchant Cruiser HMS *Salopian*, which was to be torpedoed and sunk less than 48 hours later as we met a new convoy.

It was during this spell, working from Iceland, that the 3rd Escort Group was painted pink all over instead of the usual camouflage. According to the particular shade of mixed-on-board pink paints, so particular ships 'disappeared' in the prevailing light, especially at sunrise and sunset.

It was early in March or April when the 3rd Escort Group adopted the blue and yellow chequered funnel markings – three rows, just like the then 'Flag 3'. Much later, in 1943, I joined a new 3rd Escort Group, a Support Group based in Belfast, where once again we wore 'Flag 3' blue and yellow squares round our funnels.

F. T. Grover: With the departure of *Bulldog, Broadway* and *Aubretia* from the convoy, Lieutenant Commander Roper in *Amazon* had taken charge of the remaining escorts, now reduced to four. *Angle* had been detached to Iceland because of fuel shortage and *St. Apollo* was still rescuing survivors from *Bengore Head.*

At 1228 hours *Empire Cloud* and *Gregalia* were torpedoed from the starboard side. Both crews abandoned ship and were picked up by *Nigella* and two of the merchantmen. All 52 of *Gregalia*'s company were saved, but five of *Empire Cloud*'s crew of 50 perished.

Lieutenant Commander Roper had another serious problem. Quite apart from the deficiency in numbers, all the escorts were running short of depth charges. A number of Asdic contacts were made, but full patterns could not always be dropped. Several evasive turns were made and by the end of the afternoon the echoes had faded and the convoy settled down on course.

During the early evening two more evasive turns were made in the hope of eluding any shadowers, and at 0200 hours, 10 May, the course was southwest. But at 0242 hours, *Aelybryn* was struck on the starboard side. *Daneman* immediately headed over towards the sinking ship and was successful in saving her entire crew of 45.

The convoy was due to disperse at daybreak, but after another emergency turn to port Commodore Mackenzie gave the order to disperse at 0325 hours.

Seven ships had been attacked while in convoy OB 318. Five of them went to the bottom of the North Atlantic ocean, but *Empire Cloud* and *Aelybryn* were reboarded and towed into port. After being unloaded and repaired in dry-dock, they sailed in other convoys. With a combination of good weather and the superb seamanship of the Merchant Service and the

Royal Navy, only six lives had been lost.

After the end of hostilities in 1945, when the German naval records of the Second World War became available, it was established that *Ixion* and *Eastern Star* had been attacked by Kapitänleutnant Kuppisch in *U-94*, Esmond and *Bengore Head* by Kapitänleutnant Lemp in *U-110*, *Empire Cloud* and *Gregalia* by Korvettenkapitän Schnee in *U-201* and *Aelybryn* by Korvettenkapitän Wohlfarth in *U-556*.

Unfortunately, four more ships from the convoy were sunk after dispersal: *Empire Caribou, Gand, Colonial,* and *Berhala. Colonial* was torpedoed when only 100 miles from Freetown, West Africa and Commodore Mackenzie was later rescued from a life raft.

Materially, OB 318 had suffered badly with nine ships lost and two damaged, but on balance there is no doubt that it was a worthwhile sacrifice. With the captured material, British Intelligence was able to decipher German naval signals until the end of the war. Although a great disappointment at the time, the sinking of *U-110* was fortunate for the British. The Germans assumed that she had been lost in the usual way, but had Commander Baker-Cresswell managed to tow his prize to Iceland it is doubtful whether the secret of *U-110*'s capture could have been kept.

Several members of the 3rd Escort Group received decorations in recognition of their services in this operation. Commander Baker-Cresswell was awarded the DSO. At the investiture, King George VI, who had himself been a naval officer, told him that this was perhaps the most important event in the whole war at sea.

Commander Baker-Cresswell's Official Report to Greenock, Scotland

(Public Records Office, London. Ref: ADM 1/11133 77151)

MOST SECRET

From: The Senior Officer, 3rd Escort Group, HMS *Bulldog*
Date: 10 May 1941
To: The Captain (D), Greenock

Adolf Hitler and Grand Admiral Raeder view the German Fleet (possibly at Hamburg). With Britain still undefeated, Raeder's warnings to Hitler of the dangers of waging war on two fronts were ignored in June 1941 with the invasion of Russia. *(Hans Hoehler)*

Some of 'A' gun's crew of HMS *Keith*, 'B' class leader. Four of these men were later killed at Dunkirk when HMS *Keith* was sunk on 1 June 1940. *(Iain Nethercott)*

Some of HMS *Keith*'s crew busy at their 'dhobeying' (washing of kit). *(Iain Nethercott)*

HMS *Keith* encounters rough seas in the North Atlantic in October 1939. *(Iain Nethercott)*

HMS *Bulldog*. (*Conway Picture Library*)

Junkers 87 Stuka dive-bombers spearheaded the *blitzkrieg* ('lightning war') of Poland, Norway, Holland, Belgium and France during the first year of the war and were a constant threat to shipping off the coasts of France. (*Conway Picture Library*)

A torpedoed cargo ship goes down off the east coast of England. A destroyer stands by to pick up survivors. (*William Vandivert*)

HMS *Beagle* at speed. (*Michael Back*)

The gun crew of HMS *Brazen* still mans the 3-inch high-angle AA gun. No fewer than three Stukas were shot down by *Brazen* during her final action on 20 July 1940. *(Commander Sir Michael Culme-Seymour, RN)*

HMS *Glowworm*, a mine-laying destroyer, encountered a force of enemy destroyers and cruisers off Norway and was sunk on 8 April 1940 after a gallant fight. This photograph was taken from the bridge of the German heavy cruiser *Admiral Hipper*, which was shortly after rammed by *Glowworm*, whose captain, Lieutenant Commander Roope, RN, was posthumously awarded the Victoria Cross. *(Hans Hoehler)*

The Second Battle of Narvik, Norway, as seen from the deck of HMS *Basilisk*. The German navy lost eight destroyers and one U-boat on 13 April 1940. The Germans' heavy losses during their Norwegian campaign were to prove significant when the German High Command planned the proposed invasion of Britain, Operation 'Sealion'. *(Phil Merryweather)*

Two marksmen using .303 Lee Enfield rifles near 'A' gun of HMS *Keith*, firing at floating mines. Spring 1940. *(Iain Nethercott)*

Late May 1940: HMS *Keith* returns to Dover from Dunkirk during one of her rescue missions, with exhausted British and French troops. *(Iain Nethercott)*

8 April 1940: Oil-soaked survivors from HMS *Glowworm*, the first loss of the Norwegian campaign, are rescued by a German ship.

HMS *Keith* leading in the cruisers *Arethusa* and *Galatea* to the Dutch coast. 10/11 May 1940. *(Iain Nethercott)*

HMS *Keith*, looking aft from the Signal Deck. Able Seaman Iain Nethercott (with cap) is on the port pom-pom anti-aircraft gun. *(Iain Nethercott)*

A graphic drawing by war artist Richard Seddon depicts HMS *Boadicea* exchanging fire with German panzers on the cliff tops north of St. Valery, 10 June 1940. *(Michael Back)*

Ship's stokers of HMS *Brilliant* in 1940. *(Frank Burton, HMS* Brilliant*)*

9 May 1941: HMS *Bulldog* lowering the ship's whaler prior to the boarding of the abandoned *U-110*. *(Sir Barry Sheen, First Lieutenant of HMS* Aubretia *in May 1941)*

The boarding party from HMS *Bulldog* on the deck of *U-110* prepare to get their captured prize under tow. The circling submarine's port engine was still running at that time. *(Graham Hunt)*

Subject: Capture of *U-110*

Submitted:-

1. At 1202 GMT on 9 May, two ships of convoy OB 318, which was being escorted by the 3rd Escort Group, were torpedoed in position 60°20'N, 33°40'W. Escorts were disposed as in the diagram attached. It was evident to me that the attack had come from a position between *Broadway* and *Aubretia*. Both ships were in contact almost immediately and attacked, *Broadway* at 1208 hours, *Aubretia* shortly afterwards. *Bulldog* was also in contact and I could see that *Aubretia*'s attack was a good one. *Bulldog* had moved over to join in the hunt.

    At 1235 hours a conning tower was sighted at about 800 yards' range on the port beam. Fire was immediately opened by 4.7-inch, 3-inch, 2-pounder pom-pom and stripped .303 Lewis guns. One 3-inch shell struck the conning tower and men were seen abandoning the submarine. Fire was ceased by the heavier guns but the men were speeded on their way by small arms fire. HMS *Broadway* was then seen to be about to ram. The submarine turned stern on to her and *Broadway* only grazed the submarine and in doing so had her port forward fuel tank holed. She dropped a depth charge close to the submarine's bow. Oil covered the water.

2. HMS *Bulldog* stopped within 100 yards of the submarine and sent away an armed whaler's crew. No sign of a white flag was seen and two men appeared to be manning the submarine's forward gun. Fire was again opened by the Lewis gun and two or three men were hit. My object was to keep the crew rattled. They already appeared dazed and uncertain what to do. By the time the whaler was alongside the submarine, the whole crew appeared to have jumped into the water. There was a moderate sea running and waves were breaking over the U-boat's deck. The officer in charge of the whaler, appreciating the need for speed, ran his boat hard on board the submarine and a wave carried it on to the deck where it was smashed. The crew found the conning tower hatch closed. They opened it and went below without delay. (Their orders were to seize all books and anything that looked important.) Shortly afterwards they signalled that the U-boat had been abandoned, and appeared to be sound and in no danger of sinking. I therefore decided to take her in tow

and passed her a 3" wire. (See report of Sub-Lieutenant Balme).

3. I had ordered *Aubretia* to pick up all German survivors.

4. The submarine was trimmed slightly by the stern and had a slight list to port. She was making little headway down wind.

5. Meanwhile another submarine had torpedoed two more ships of the convoy and was being counter-attacked by HMS *Amazon* and other corvettes and trawlers of the 3rd Escort Group. HMS *Broadway* and HMS *Aubretia* had obtained further contact and were dropping depth charges. They eventually reported having lost contact. *Aubretia* reported that it had been doubtful. I therefore ordered *Broadway* to close and lower a boat.

6. A periscope was reported from two lookouts in *Bulldog*. The tow was slipped and a search made. Nothing more was seen and no contact obtained, but a plank was passed near the position reported.

7. Tow was again passed to the U-boat. I ordered *Aubretia* to search round me. I sent my Engineer Officer and two ERAs to the U-boat, but unfortunately had no one on board with sufficient submarine experience to attempt to blow the after tanks, as no one could understand technical German. The Engineer Officer found that the port motor was running slow ahead with all switches put to the same position on the port side as on the starboard side, the engine still would not stop and the gauge showed 10 amps. The Engineer Officer reported that the bilges were dry and the pressure hull watertight, but that there was a bubbling noise of an air leak or an open vent somewhere aft.

8. *Broadway*'s boat made two journeys to bring back books, charts and documents. The wind and sea were rising all this time and the visibility had shut down to four miles. The convoy had turned away from the U-boat after the first attack and was very soon out of sight. Consequently, no ship in the convoy had witnessed the capture of the U-boat. From the amount of gunfire they must have heard, it may be supposed that they imagined the submarine to have been sunk.

9. It was now considered most important to get clear of the area as it was thought that other submarines may be near. As I had nobody who could work the U-boat in any way I considered it best to withdraw all men from on board her. She seemed to have some starboard wheel on and it

was only with difficulty that she could be made to turn to port on the homeward course. This was eventually done however, and she rode quite easily slightly on the starboard quarter and heading slightly to starboard on my course. When she was towing nicely at four knots I ordered all watertight doors and hatches to be closed and the crew to rejoin *Bulldog* in *Broadway*'s boat.

10. Everyone was back on board by 1830 hours, speed increased to six knots and the U-boat, although it had settled slightly more aft, seemed perfectly seaworthy.

11. I had ordered *Broadway* to escort me, carrying out a broad zigzag astern, and had told *Aubretia* to rejoin the convoy. *Bulldog* set course 045 degrees.

12. There were no incidents that night and the submarine seemed to be quite comfortable at the speed of tow.

13. The wind had risen slightly and was south-west Force Four at 0400 hours. By 0700 hours it had veered to west by south and increased to Force Six with a nasty lumpy sea. It was now impossible to hold the course and it was decided to let the submarine head down wind, as she seemed comfortable in this position, and to keep the wire just taut.

14. Suddenly, at 1100 hours, the U-boat began to sink by the stern. Very shortly her bow was standing vertically out of the water. She slowly sank and the wire was cut. The prize must have been working slightly in the heavy sea and this may have aggravated any damage caused by the depth charges or contact with *Broadway*. Her loss was a bitter blow as it was felt that having survived so many shocks, particularly *Broadway*'s depth charge close to her bow, she should be able to stand the 400 mile tow to Iceland.

15. I consider that she was forced to the surface in the first place by *Aubretia*'s well-executed attack. Great credit is therefore due to her Commanding Officer, Lieutenant Commander V. F. Smith, RNR, for contributing directly towards the destruction of *U-110*.

Signed: **A. J. Baker-Cresswell**
Commander D.

Sub Lieutenant D. E. Balme's Official Report.

(Public Records Office, London. Ref: ADM/I/I1133 77151)

SECRET

From: Sub-Lieutenant D. E. Balme, RN

Date: 11 May 1941

To: The Commanding Officer, HMS *Bulldog*.

Subject: Boarding 'Primrose'.

Submitted:

At 1245 hours, 9 May, I left *Bulldog* in charge of a boarding party to board an enemy submarine which had surfaced. The crew consisted of six able seamen, one telegraphist and one stoker. *Bulldog* was lying to windward of the U-boat and there was a heavy swell running so to save valuable time I made for the weather side (Port). There were numerous holes in the conning tower casing caused by *Bulldog*'s 3-inch and pom-pom.

As no small arms fire was opened up at the whaler from the U-boat, I was fairly confident that there was no one in the conning tower. This proved correct after having entered the conning tower through the opening on starboard side. The hatch down was closed tight. This hatch was 18" to 24" in diameter, spherical surface with wheel for screwing down; on unscrewing this, the hatch sprung open as soon as a clip was released.

I went down the ladder to the lower conning tower where there was a similar closed hatch. On opening this hatch I found the control room deserted, hatches leading forward and aft were open and all lighting was on. On the deck there was a large splinter from the conning tower. There was a slight escape of air in the control room but no sign of chlorine so gas masks which had been taken were now discarded. So also were the revolvers which now seemed more of a danger than an asset.

The U-boat had obviously been abandoned in great haste as books and gear were strewn about the place. A chain of men was formed to pass up all books, charts, etc. As speed was essential owing to the possibility of the U-boat sinking (although dry throughout), I gave orders to send up ALL books, except obviously reading books, so consequently a number of comparatively useless navigational books etc. were recovered. All charts were in drawers under the chart table in the control room; there were also some signal books, log books, etc. here. The metal sheet diagrams were secured overhead.

Meanwhile the telegraphist went to the Wireless Transmitting (W/T) office, just forward of the control room on the starboard side. This was in perfect condition, apparently no attempt having been made to destroy any books or apparatus. Here were found Codebooks, Signal Logs, Pay Books and general correspondence, looking as if this room had been used as the ship's office. Also, the coding machine was found here, plugged in as though it was in actual use when abandoned. The general appearance of this machine being that of a typewriter, the telegraphist pressed the keys and finding the results peculiar sent it up the hatch. This W/T Office seemed far less complicated than our own. Sets were more compact and did not seem to have the usual excess of switches, plug holes, knobs, 'tallys', etc. on the outside.

Forward of the W/T office was the Hydrophone Office. This was about the same size as the W/T office and about twice as large as the Anti-Submarine (A/S) Cabinet in *Sealion*, the only submarine I have been out in.

The hydrophone set was still running and the sensitivity could be increased or decreased by a control knob and the bearing on the gyro dial could be altered.

The first quick look around below took about five minutes after which I went up the conning tower and signalled to *Bulldog* that the U-boat seemed seaworthy and towable, and requested that an Engine Room Artificer (ERA) might be sent over to see if any machinery would work. Meanwhile our whaler had been carried on to the U-boat by the swell and was now firmly lodged between the conning tower and the steel guard rails; it was eventually a total loss.

During this time I had two hands (Able Seamen) on the fo'c's'le who located the towing bollards which were hollow steel 6" diameter flush with the deck but could be pulled up to a height of about 18" and clipped in position. They also located wires and hawsers in a porous locker. The only wire was an old and rusty 2" wire.

Bulldog now came up my port side and stopped with her stern just off the U-boat's bows and the end of the 2" wire was thrown over to her. I had hoped that this would hold while we got the proper tow secured but as soon as any tension came on it the wire parted. The heavy swell and the wind made it impossible for *Bulldog* to remain very close for long as she was drifting to leeward faster than the U-boat. By the time we got the end of the 3" wire from *Bulldog* she had been carried some way off which made the 3" wire heavy to man-handle. Two turns were taken around the bollard but we did not have a shackle to secure the thimble of the wire back to its own part. The end of the 2" wire was used as a temporary seizing.

Meanwhile *Broadway*'s boat had brought over the Chief Engine Room Artificer and party from *Bulldog*. Having inspected the engine rooms etc., he reported that the port engine was running slow ahead and he thought that it was best not to touch any switches for fear of causing damage. I agreed with this and reported the situation to *Bulldog*. All watertight doors were now closed except for the two hatches down and the first one forward.

Some equipment from the Hydrophone Office was now unscrewed but on trying to pass it up the hatch by heaving line it was found to be too large to go through. All officers' gear was now searched and several slips of paper, wallets, cameras, etc., were found and sent up. A cine-camera was found in the W/T office and with this I took a few shots of W/T and H/D offices at point blank range but as I afterwards discovered, the range on the camera was set for 25 feet and aperture to f2.5. I doubt if they will come out at all.

Another boatload had arrived by this time, with the Engineering Officer, Gunner and party. They were sent to see if they could stop the port motor, but having turned all the switches they found they could neither do that nor start the starboard motor. They did however collect some further important documents.

The wire had now got under the U-boat's bows and was being severely chafed on the sharp edge of the U-boat's casing. If this had continued it would certainly have parted so I decided to slip the wire. This was probably just as well as *Bulldog* now sighted a periscope and went off on an anti-submarine sweep.

I had now been on board for about five hours; during this time the U-boat was going down very slowly by the stern and taken on a list to port as if the port after ballast tank was slowly flooding. It seemed as if all possible material had been recovered so it was decided to batten down and wait for *Bulldog*'s return.

On *Bulldog*'s return she again came up the port side and with the extra hands and shackle having been previously supplied by boat, the tow was again successfully secured. All hands then returned to *Bulldog*.

Here are some of my impressions of the U-boat: she was new and a fine ship, both in strength of the hull, in the fittings and instruments and in the general interior construction. Absolutely nothing 'Ersatz' about her. Excellent anti-aircraft armament abaft the conning tower, consisting of a Bofors and Oerlikon-type gun. Deck around the forward gun was wood. Spotlessly clean throughout. The wardroom was finished off in light varnished woodwork and all cupboards were numbered with corresponding keys to fit. There were no signs of a safe and there was only one cupboard for which I could not find the key; this cupboard was over the Captain's desk so I broke into it and it revealed a medicine chest. In the Ward Room there were several sets of writing paper and envelopes, well printed and illustrated reading books, cards, dice, and the usual art studies. Bunks were one on top of another both in the officers' and the crew's spaces. A very compact receiver was in the W/T office with the names of about 200 stations printed on its dial.

Plenty of tinned ham, corned beef and three sacks of potatoes in the control room; also luxuries such as beer, cigars, Player's cigarettes (German printing on the packets), and a plate of shrimps were all found in the wireless room. A magnificent galley was forward of the wireless room.

There were no signs of voice-pipes, but I think loudspeakers and telephones were used – definitely a telephone in the conning tower.

One Tommy-gun was found in officers' clothes drawer; another was found in the lower control tower with an anti-tank type of rifle. Officer gear consisted of very good clothing, including anti-weather garments.

In the engine room I noticed a plate of mashed potatoes as if 'Action Stations' had been sounded suddenly while dinner was being taken from the galley to the after crew's space. The escape chamber was in the control room just abaft the upper hatch.

My original whaler's crew worked splendidly throughout the time.[27] They comprised of:-

---

[27] According to S. W. Roskill, *The Secret Capture* (London, 1959): 'Except for Allen Long, who was a short-service rating, they were long-service men; all came from the Portsmouth Manning Depot. Long was awarded the DSM "for obtaining valuable information from *U-110*." All the others were Mentioned in Dispatches for "good work in salving documents under conditions of danger and difficulty."'

S. Pearce, AB	A. Hargreaves, Ordinary Seaman
C. Dolley, AB	J. Trotter, Ordinary Seaman
R. Roe, AB	A. Long, Telegraphist
K. Wileman, AB	C. Lee, Stoker

I submit that service revolvers are far too cumbersome and dangerous for boarding and that small Police model automatics should be supplied to all boarding officers.

Possibly, in addition to ransacking the wardroom, the crew's quarters should have been thoroughly searched, but owing to frequent depth charge attacks continuing in the vicinity, I considered it safer to keep these water-tight doors closed.

The reason why no attempt to destroy any books or material was made is obviously because they thought the U-boat was certain to sink at once. The necessary demolition switches or other devices had been set; this was corroborated by statements from prisoners who had no idea that their U-boat had been boarded. But then again: why were both control tower hatches closed?

I have, Sir, the Honour to be your obedient servant,

Signed: **D. E. Balme**
Sub-Lieutenant, RN

Excerpt from *Ultra Goes to War* by Ronald Lewin

When *Bulldog* reached Scotland (having sent to the Admiralty a cautiously non-committal signal about her success) she was joined by Lieutenant Allan Bacon, RNVR, who worked in special liaison between the Naval Section at Bletchley and the Operational Intelligence Centre. (On 25 June he would take part in the 'pinch' of Lauenberg.) Bacon spent many hours examining the captured papers in the captain's cabin of *Bulldog*. His verdict:

"This is what we have been looking for."

Every page was photographed, the risk of losing the originals in air-transit to London being too great. And then, finally, the intact treasure-trove arrived at Bletchley.

Here was the breakthrough. When a U-boat sailed on operations it carried the daily settings for its Enigma to cover the period of its cruise – normally about three months. The settings acquired from *U-110* were valid up to the end of June. With the complementary material from Krebs, Munchen and Lauenberg, an actual U-boat Enigma and the current settings for seven or eight weeks, the Naval Section at Bletchley was in clover.

With great speed the cryptanalysts in Hut 8 now penetrated 'Hydra', which in 1941 was the general-purpose cipher used for ships in the North Sea and the Baltic; for minesweepers, patrol craft, etc. off the French and Norwegian coasts; and at that time, for all U-boats. At last the sieve was leaking. Nor did the benefits of the 'pinch' run out at the end of June.

Experience gained during those two months of working with known settings enabled Bletchley to continue to read Hydra, with occasional gaps, until the end of the war, as well as to penetrate in due course the 'big-ship' cipher 'Neptune' and the two naval ciphers employed for the Mediterranean, 'Sud' and 'Medusa'. History is written in terms of Trafalgars and Jutlands, but by any standard the seizure of *U-110* should rate as a major victory at sea.

Its consequences were instantaneous. To support what was intended to be the marauding cruise of *Bismarck* and her consort *Prinz Eugen*, and to replenish U-boats, a small swarm of tankers and supply ships had been stationed strategically over the vast area from the North Atlantic down to the divide between West Africa and South America. 'Ultra' derived from Hydra now made their elimination possible.

By 23 June hunting groups of the Royal Navy had sunk all the six tankers and the one supply ship assigned to *Bismarck*, as well as two more supply ships intended to sustain armed merchant raiders. Raiders themselves were sunk and harried along with their suppliers, the whole operation being so successful that Admiral Dönitz reached a distasteful conclusion. His Atlantic U-boats could no longer be maintained by surface ships: they would have to rely on underwater supply craft – the 'milchcow' U-boats.

Compared with the *Bismarck* episode, and coming so soon afterwards, these quick and positive operations illustrate exactly the practical value of the Ultra system when it was functioning at its best.

John McCormick, *Military History Magazine* **(28 May 2000):** The full significance of *Bulldog*'s coup was not lost on Bletchley Park, British code-breaking headquarters. Complacent about the security of Enigma, the Germans under Dönitz had directed all U-boat activity by radio signal, organizing their *Graue Woelfe* ('wolf packs') or directing individual U-boats with extraordinary efficiency. But when the Allies possessed the necessary rotor codes, Allied shipping losses dropped hearteningly, and in the months when they did not, losses rose.

In the summing up, however, one British analyst could say that the Germans had "radioed themselves to death"; while Jurgen Rohwer, a leading German naval historian, has written that "there were many factors which influenced the outcome of the decisive Battle of the Atlantic, but I would put the Enigma at the top of the list..." That German slogan from earlier wars, 'Gott mit Uns' ('God is with us'), was put in question by the apparent coincidences of 9 May 1941. If God was with anyone that day, He was with the British.

For "courage and initiative", Captain Baker-Cresswell was awarded the DSO (Distinguished Service Order), Balme the DSC (Distinguished Service Cross). King George VI assured David Balme after the ceremony of 1941 that were it not for the risk of tipping off the enemy, the two officers would have received honours more appropriate to their deed, but that this would be put right after the war. No such outcome could occur however, owing to the continuing security required during the next 45 years of the Cold War. It is only today that the whole story can be told. Now, in their old age, both men may rest content in the knowledge that their actions of May 1941 shortened a war, an achievement given to few men, ever.

NO MEAN ACCOMPLISHMENT
By John Baker, Telegraphist, HMS *Bulldog*

Weigh anchor, hear the chains thus groan!
As capstan turns so steadily;
The anchor there, all neatly stowed,
By cheerful hands the watch so chose.
So silently, the destroyer slips berth;
All ship-shape now, she heads for sea;
The bridge now bustling, quite all agog,
As Captain A. J. Baker-Cresswell, DSO, RN,
Of the 3rd Convoy Escort Group,
His initial briefing orders,
Commands both his officers and his men.
Through seas all heaving mightily,
To a rendezvous with merchants true:
Each, by some ingenious device, allotted station take,
For the long tedious journey of the ocean thus to make,
All in zigzag fashion, the foe to so bemuse.

The wireless cabin, all ears and eyes,
Filch intelligence from out the skies!
So vital for the Senior Officer to know,
His strategy and tactics intuitively to form,
To foil the ever lurking foe,
Forever onward still the convoy must go.
All ominous at dusk, hear the boisterous cry,
Of "Periscope sighted!" from crow's-nest on high;
Then throughout the convoy, all activity reigns,
As Captain's orders, so calm and clear,
Are instantly conformed with by every ship there;
The nearest escort ship to the foe, the corvette *Aubretia*,
Thus detailed, instantly gives chase, all speed to go;
As mysteriously subterranean the foe's periscope dives;
The 'pings' and 'pongs' are all in motion set,

As the echoes rebound from out the deep,
To fairly position, now lurking deep, the U-boat there
With all engines now stopped, all silent hope!
In patterns planned the depth charges flow;
Ingeniously set at certain depth, thus to explode;
See, rising to the surface of the sea,
Float oil and debris all clear to see; Is this a ruse? Could be so,
The wiles of the enemy thus we know;
A few more depth charges thus let fly,
To comfort of all, and onward, ever onward ply.
Now to zigzag more: to alter course so;
All precaution taken, an absolute must;
For much later still may the U-boat arise;
To enemy transmit our position, thus the convoy jeopardise.

Signals flow from shore to ship;
"Alter course, enemy shadowing still";
All through the night the convoy zigzags on;
Heralded at dawn by all hell let loose,
As torpedoed merchant, now all ablaze,
The whole convoy lights up in a reddened haze;
Action stations; all crews alert;
Another ship torpedoed, amidships hurt;
Thus in halves we watch the merchant float;
As suddenly, victim the sea claims,
And so to some untimely watery grave remains.

To port, to starboard, fore and aft,
Heave mightily each escort ship;
All as is fair, the 'pings' and 'pongs' repeat;
From Captain calm, his orders stern,
"More depth charges drop on suspected spot!"
Then out suddenly, the now lightening sea,
Burst forth so stark, like bolt out of blue,
The *U-110*, such a sight to see, bows skyward thrust in agony!

The convoy's deadliest foe, like Devil from the outer deep:
"Do not ram!" thus the Captain of the Escort's order stood;
But what heartening joy to see the U-boat encaptured, floating harmlessly!
No need the warning shot to fire!
For stumbling ever faster still through conning-tower,
Into the sea as one, leaps the U-boat's crew,
To whalers, all awaiting in swelling sea;
By Captain's orders "the U-boat take",
All volunteers, both officers and men,
With one accord, this order did thus execute.
All souls picked up from out the sea;
All damage assessed; comes quickly,
The order "Convoy, all ships rejoin!"
Leader destroyer then heaves to;
So much the prize is coveted now!

All hands to towing gear, thus U-boat enfolds,
As Captain to Admiralty his signals thus disposed;
In instance such, transmitting 'Silence' to break,
As ingenious words the message flows;
Concerning the whole exciting episode,
Of *U-110* under the unassuming name of 'Primrose';
Quick was the First Sea Lord's reply, made in all sincerity,
"Hearty congratulations, the petals on your flower are of rare beauty!"
So vital and immediate was the intelligence thus gained,
That Admiralty, hastily another message so made;
Ordering HMS *Bulldog*, thus the destroyer's name,
"With full speed to Greenock make",
Thus with *U-110*'s captured German crew aboard,
Plus enemy secrets and codes galore!

Traditionally, in the very merry month of May,
This singular naval incident early in the year 1941,
Did cause good King George VI to say,
(No mean sailor himself, by the way),

At an investiture of some later date,
As "perhaps the most important accomplishment
Of the whole war at sea."

'BREATHING SPACE'

Anthologist's note: A fitting end to this saga is the following letter written by Commander Baker-Cresswell RN, Retd., to Lieutenant Commander David Balme, RN, Retd., dated Christmas 1988:

'The whole beauty of our exploit was the providential timing of it. The situation was just about desperate at the time and if losses in the Atlantic had gone on increasing at the same rate, as in the beginning of 1941, we would probably have had to sue for peace. Churchill says it was the only thing he was really worried about and I remember thinking at the time that we could not go on.

In fact, I think that my remark on the *Bulldog*'s bridge: 'By God! We'll do a *Magdeburg*!' was as epoch making as some of Churchill's sayings! Because, if we hadn't done a *Magdeburg* our losses would have been insupportable. Later it didn't matter so much because the Americans were in it and ships and aircraft were being turned out faster than they were being destroyed.

'Long after we are dead and gone, it will be written up again and the true lesson will be learnt. That breathing space we were given in 1941, when Rodger Winn in the Submarine Tracking Room was so clever with diverting the convoys that we never got near a U-boat, was absolutely vital in the war. It is nice to think of the hundreds of ships and lives we saved, let alone the country.'

BEFORE PEARL HARBOR

Able Seaman Michael Back, HMS *Boadicea*

It is often forgotten that one American destroyer was sunk and another severely damaged by torpedo attack on the North Atlantic convoy routes weeks before the Japanese attack on Pearl Harbor brought the United States into the Second World War in such dramatic fashion. HMS *Bulldog*, although not directly involved in the actions, was in the vicinity on both occasions, and several of our members, then serving in *Bulldog*, have recalled mention of the incidents which were circulating at that time.

It started with the American Government's decision in April 1941 to take over the defence of nominally Danish Greenland, which they considered to be part of the Western Hemisphere, and which, under no circumstances, should be allowed to fall into German hands. But, since to reach the ports on the east coast of Greenland, American ships would have to approach the U-boat-saturated Denmark Straits, it was decided to provide them with US Navy escorts.

With America now steadily moving closer to Britain, there was also an implicit understanding that this move would release much needed Royal Navy ships from patrolling the seas of the eastern American seaboard, as USN escort ships would now be providing HM Ships, in plain-language radio broadcasts, with valuable intelligence concerning U-boat movements.

The meeting, in August 1941, between Winston Churchill and Franklin Roosevelt aboard the new battleship HMS *Prince of Wales*, at Placentia Bay, Newfoundland, produced an even more important result. On 12 August 1941, as part of the 'Joint Declaration' by the British Prime Minister and the American President, it was decided that US Navy warships, in cooperation with the Royal Canadian Navy, would in future escort some Britain-bound convoys as far as a mid-ocean meeting-place south of Iceland.

Such direct American involvement in the Battle of the Atlantic soon provoked reaction from the Germans. On 4 September 1941, the USS *Greer*, an American destroyer, was twice attacked by a U-boat without being hit.

In mid-October, the USS *Kearney*, a powerful new fleet destroyer of the 'Livermoore' class, was one of a group of American warships escorting a large convoy from North American ports to Iceland. During the first watch on 16

October the convoy sailed straight into a waiting U-boat pack. After at least two merchant ships had already been sunk, a U-boat appeared between the *Kearney* and the convoy and fired three torpedoes at the destroyer. Two missed, but the third torpedo struck her in the forward boiler room, killing eleven men and wounding seven.

Although taking in much water, the *Kearney* was saved by the notably strong construction of her whole class. After an hour she managed to raise a speed of ten knots to make her own way to Iceland, escorted by the USS *Greer*.

On 17 October, HM Ships *Bulldog, Highlander, Amazon, Richmond* and *Georgetown* took over the *Kearney*'s convoy. Two weeks later, the American destroyer *Reuben James* was escorting another big convoy from American ports to the mid-ocean rendezvous, south of Iceland. Unlike the *Kearney*, she was an old ship, one of the First World War four-funnelled types, fifty of which the Royal Navy had recently taken over.

There had been no sight or sound of U-boats when, at 0530 hours on 31 October 1941, a torpedo struck the *Reuben James* amidships. She broke in half following a great explosion in one of her magazines, the forward section sinking immediately and the after section within 20 minutes. One hundred of *Reuben James*'s officers and men were lost, forty being rescued from the after section.

Pearl Harbor was still five weeks away...

A TRIBUTE TO HM SUBMARINES

Iain Nethercott, ex-HMS *Keith*

The following speech made in the House of Commons on 9 September 1941 by Prime Minister Winston Churchill played its part in my joining the Submarine Service in November 1941:

"I have, for some time, looked for an opportunity of paying tribute to our submarines. There is no branch of His Majesty's Forces which in this war has suffered the same proportion of fatal loss as our Submarine Service. It is the most dangerous of all the services. That is perhaps the reason why the first First Lord tells me that entry into it is keenly sought by Officers and Men.

"I feel the House would wish to testify its gratitude and admiration for our submarine crews, for their skill and devotion, which has proved of inestimable value to the life of our country.

"During 1941, British submarines have sunk or seriously damaged 17 enemy warships. Some of them were U-boats. Besides the warships, 105 supply ships have fallen to their torpedoes. This is an average of 15 ships a month, or one ship every two days. The ships which have been torpedoed varied between large liners of 20,000 tons, caiques and schooners loaded with troops and military stores. They also included a considerable number of laden troop transports and tankers, most of which were passing across the Mediterranean, through the British submarine attack, in order to keep alive the enemy's armies in Libya.

"Submarines of the Royal Netherlands Navy and the Free French Naval Forces have been operating in combination with our submarines, and have contributed in a most gallant manner to these results."

When I first joined the 'Boats' in late 1941, I dumped my hammock and kit bag in the old red-brick barrack block (since renamed 'Pactolus'), on the corner of the sea wall at HMS *Dolphin*, a shore establishment, at Portsmouth. This was where the lower ranks of submariners camped out. It was named 'The Stables' at that time because there was a long ramp up to the first floors for the artillery horses to climb up to their stalls. Prior to 1901 it was mixed-manned by the Royal Marine Coastal Artillery and the Royal Artillery.

I suppose that the extreme dislike of the old-fashioned Admirals towards the infant Submarine Boats made it simple to shove the sailors into some old stables. It was an amazing place to live. Nobody called "Hands" in the morning, very few men worried about getting out of their hammocks before 8.30 a.m. 'Crown & Anchor' schools were running round the clock. The rum and the beer were quite plentiful.

Being on a tiny peninsula at the entrance to Portsmouth Harbour, with Haslar Creek running up to Gosport at the back with HMS *Hornet*, the Motor Launch and Motor Torpedo Boat base, Haslar Royal Naval Hospital on the coast road to Lee-on-Solent, we were completely isolated from Portsmouth with the awful Naval Barracks, HMS *Victory*, and all the unpleasant, disagreeable Naval Shore Patrols, etc.

Submariners were virtually excused all duties except for odd occasions helping out the crews of a boat alongside with their torpedoes etc. Of course, we got two-shillings-a-day extra when not crewing a boat, as Spare Crew, four-shillings-a-day when Operational. So, on top of our normal pay, plus 'hard-lying money' and with civilian beer at 8d-a-pint, but only 2d-a-pint in our submarine canteens at Blyth and Dundee, we were reasonably well off.

The drawback, of course, was that in 1941 and 1942, the life expectancy in an Operational Submarine was about three months. Of 14 submarines operating from Malta in 1941, only three returned to Britain. In 1942, of the boats operating out of Algiers, Beirut and Malta 12 were lost within nine months.

HMS *Dolphin* was manned and run by a collection of pensioner General Servicemen, both Royal Navy and Royal Marines. The ancient Royal Marine pensioners were supposed to carry out Guard Duties and provide escorts for errant sailors while *Dolphin*'s butcher and baker came from the ranks of ex-tram drivers and postmen. They had taken their tickets after World War I. The butcher ran a flourishing and highly lucrative business, smuggling our meat ashore to the butchers' shops in Portsmouth. All these old crabs had allotments supplied by the local council to grow all their vegetables, rear rabbits and chickens. With the ability to buy duty-free pipe and cigarette tobacco from us at one shilling and sixpence for an eight-ounce tin, their smoking habits were well catered for.

There was only one of their band who was the odd-man-out. We had a 15-year-old Marine Bugle Boy who was adjudged to be too young to go to sea. He used to stand outside the Regulating Office, clock-watching, waiting for the next Bugle Call which everyone ignored. As most of His Majesty's 'Jollies' shot off to the flesh-pots of Portsmouth on the First Shore Boat at 4.00 p.m., the pimply-faced little Son-of-the-Sea led a lonely existence in the evenings; apart from the occasions when the Commander practised Fire Drill he had no calls until "Pipe Down" at 10.00 p.m. This idiotic call may have meant something in the real Navy, but was merely an interruption for submariners not ashore, fully occupied with their games of poker and 'Fraz', which, in some cases, was reckoned to have continued non-stop since September 1939.

When I'd arrived from Roedean with my kitbag and hammock, I had to wait for the next draft up at the Submarine School at Blyth, Northumberland. In the meantime I had to carry out my ascent in the Davis Submarine Escape Tank to prove that I didn't suffer from claustrophobia. Having surmounted this hurdle, I was issued with a couple of white submarine sweaters with three 'HM Submarines' cap tallies and went on to submariner's pay.

A short time later, I went on draft up to Blyth. The Submarine School was in an old Reformatory with no fences or main gate. We trainees came and went as we liked after 4.00 p.m. so Stoppage of Leave was a time-wasting exercise.

The whole of our class of seven qualified at Blyth: one Lieutenant, one Sub-Lieutenant, an Engine Room Artificer, one seaman killick Leading Torpedoman, a Senior Torpedoman, and two First Class Stokers. On qualifying, we were inmediatelty drafted to HMS *Cyclops*, the ancient Submarine Depot Ship nicknamed the 'Cyclebox', which had a gaggle of 7th Flotilla submarines based on her at Rothesay, Isle of Bute, Scotland.

As the *Cyclops* was a coal-burner, it was coaled from 'Puffers' out of Glasgow. They didn't draft me to a submarine initially. Instead, for two long days, I slaved down the holds of these little ships, shovelling mountains of steaming coal into 2-cwt bags, which were put into cargo nets, winched over to the upper deck of *Cyclops* where unlucky sailors loaded them onto two-wheel trolleys, trundled them over to the manholes leading down to the coal bunkers where more unfortunate sailors down below had to trim them. At the end of each day, we could have easily joined the cast of the musical 'Old Man River'. It was peculiar, but the General Service crew of *Cyclops* always found 'important business' ashore or dismantling and overhauling machinery, leaving this awful, back-breaking, dusty and dirty job to the submariners.

I was eventually drafted to a tiny little World War I submarine, the *H-43*. It had a crew of 22, one heads, one bunk (the Captain's), four torpedoes and a Lewis machine gun should the Luftwaffe dare try anything with us.

We didn't dare dive *H-43* below 200 feet as she groaned like a pregnant seal below that depth and she assumed strange and disconcerting banana-like shapes. We had a 22-year-old Scots Skipper – the Chieftan of the Clan Menzies – the Menzies of Menzies, but pronounced the Mingis of Mingis for some unknown reason. Our crew was half Scots, like me. I was just 20 and my mother clan was the Gunns of Caithness. As usual, we had our quota of McDonalds and McKenzies to cope with.

We were loosely based between three ports, Campbeltown and Londonderry in Northern Ireland, and Tobermory, on the west coast of Scotland. Some, like me, had girlfriends in every port. I was in charge of the Motor Room, all the boat's electrical systems, her four torpedoes, together with five Torpedomen. The worst chore for us was topping up all 224 giant cells of our main batteries, but we managed and it was good training for us before we became operational.

But three months of this pleasant existence was my lot and one sunny afternoon at Londonderry, in early 1942, my draft back to *Dolphin* appeared. I was crewed together with 60 other hopefuls there and sent to Barrow-in-Furness to crew *P-314* a brand-new Super 'T' class boat, then being built up there. In the meantime, we had to live in lodgings with the Barrow landladies.

Three weeks later we commissioned HM Submarine *Tactician*. Meanwhile the first of this class, *P-311* and unnamed, had been depth-charged to destruction off Palermo. The Admiralty belatedly named her *Tutankhamen*. *P-312*, named *Tantalus*, had just sailed for her shakedown patrol off Northern Norway. *P-313* was two weeks ahead of us, but her crew mutinied at the Pennant Number 313. After a lot of high-level discussion she was given the pennant number 339 and named *Taurus*.

Like us in *Tactician*, *Taurus* survived the war, both of us filling up our 'Jolly Roger' flags with sinkings. The *Taurus* sank the Japanese submarine *I-19* on her way off patrol and going into Penang. Blew her to pieces. We were all out to get those bastards. She'd sunk a Dutch passenger ship in the

Indian Ocean, ordered the crew out of their lifeboats on to the sub's casing, then the Japs hacked their prisoners to death, then they threw the bodies back into the lifeboats. This horrific fate included the women stewards who were brutally raped first.

Only one crewman survived to tell the story.

ON PATROL WITH HMS *BOREAS*

Able Seaman Albert Halls, Gunner

Having worked on the land in north Essex, I volunteered for service in the Royal Navy on my 18th birthday, 16 February 1941. I passed my medical examination in June and was called up on 11 September. After three months' training at HMS *Collingwood*, Gosport, near Portsmouth, I joined HMS *Boreas* in December 1941. At that time she was in dry dock in South Shields. After sea trials, *Boreas* was one of the destroyer escorts sailing from Greenock, on the west coast of Scotland, down to Freetown, West Africa, arriving there in late January 1942.

During my first voyage, *Boreas* ran into very rough weather: our mess deck was awash, broken crockery was everywhere and I began to wonder what I'd let myself in for. However, I was very fortunate in that I never experienced the dreaded nausea of seasickness. Our first stop for oil fuel was at the Azores. We then carried on to Freetown which became our base with the 18th Destroyer Flotilla for the next nine months during which we mostly did convoy work around the Cape of Good Hope.

One of the Petty Officers on board *Boreas*, PO Snell, taught the other ABs and myself a considerable amount of seamanship in a short time; knots, Morse code, signalling, etc. He also told us a lot about navigation, including finding the position of a ship from the stars. It made all of us realise how much there was to learn.

One of the more significant memories I have of that first tour of duty was a patrol up the River Congo, ostensibly to bring some people out, but what we did bring out was locked and sealed in small wooden boxes, each of which took two of us to carry. What those boxes contained was a mystery, but it's very possible that they held diamonds.

1942

PROLOGUE TO 1942

by

Rear Admiral John B. Hervey, RN, Retd.

O NE GERMAN ARMY GENERAL, giving a pep talk to his troops the day they invaded Russia, stood up in front of them and said: "Men. We're off to India!" It seems absurd now, but by mid-1942, German armies were near to capturing Leningrad, Moscow, and the Caucasus oil fields. The Japanese had taken what is now Indonesia, Malaysia and the Philippines, had attacked our fleet off Colombo and indeed were knocking at the door of India – and Australia. Meanwhile, Rommel's Afrika Korps were perilously close to Cairo. We were losing merchant ships at a frightening rate and destroyer losses rose to 48 – our worst war year. The location of these losses – 26 in the Mediterranean, eight in South East Asia, 10 in the North Atlantic and four in Home waters – speaks of the world-wide nature of the war we were now waging.

Throughout 1942, the gruelling business of convoying supplies across the Atlantic went on, often in appalling weather conditions. Thus, this section begins with 'Random Notes by an Anonymous Watchkeeper' in HMS *Boadicea*, to which AB Johnny Randall has added his own recollections of five dreadful days in January, during which their ship lost her mast and only just survived thanks to sound construction by Hawthorn Leslie. The year ends with another such epic, 'A Wartime Battle Against the Elements', in which Lieutenant Commander Eric Mackay, DSC, RNR, nurses a disabled HMS *Caldwell* through hurricane-force weather off Nova Scotia, to save his ship. Convoying to North Russia often added severe icing to other hazards, well described in an extract from *British Destroyers* in which HMS *Oribi* estimated that they were once carrying 80 to 100 tons of ice – rather dangerous top weight. And even when you got there, Russia was no fun, as Lieutenant Jack Keir makes plain in 'A Christmas Miracle'.

Three Russian convoys are described in some detail. The *Daily Express* account of QP 11 covers how HM Ships *Bulldog*, *Beagle*, *Amazon* and *Beverley* bravely beat off five attacks by a German destroyer force which should have been able to overwhelm them. The *British Destroyers* extract also describes the heroic defence of convoy JW 51B by HM Ships *Onslow*, *Obdurate*, *Orwell*, *Obedient* and *Achates*, who, with support from the 6-inch gun cruisers HMS *Sheffield* and *Jamaica*, drove off a pocket battleship, an 8-inch gun cruiser and six heavy destroyers.

Sadly, these fine actions are often overshadowed in public memory by one disastrous convoy, whose fate is the subject of three articles, starting with 'The Tragedy of PQ 17' by Dick Fearnside, Radio Operator in SS *Hartlebury*. As Fearnside rightly points out, the worst result of the catastrophic decision to scatter this convoy – taken personally by the First Sea Lord – was not the loss of ships, men or war material: it was the loss of confidence in the Royal Navy by the Merchant Navy. Traditionally, escorts successfully defend their charges – or go down with them. They do not abandon them.

Another Whitehall embarrassment in 1942 was the escape from Brest, back to Germany through the Dover Straits, of *Scharnhorst*, *Gneisenau* and *Prinz Eugen*. Due to a number of mishaps, warning that they were racing up the English Channel was received very late. Nevertheless, three gallant but unsuccessful attacks on them were mounted, by MTBs, Swordfish aircraft, and then by the destroyers *Campbell*, *Vivacious*, *Mackay*, *Whitshed* and *Worcester*. The exciting story of the destroyer attack, pressed home to 3,000 yards, is well told by John Beeley, who, after *Keith*, went to HMS *Campbell* and was by now an acting PO Telegraphist.

The article 'A View from a Signalman' by David Walker retells some of the story of HMS *Bulldog*, already covered. But it is mainly interesting for its description of the tragic end of the cruiser HMS *Curaçoa*, sunk in an instant when over-run by the great liner-troopship RMS *Queen Mary*. *Bulldog* was in company. Subsequently, in the House of Lords, blame was attached to both parties, but two thirds of it to the Admiralty. As Walker says, it was an accident "which some idiot caused", and one made more likely when the cruiser was stationed so close ahead of the liner. As anyone who has done plane-guard duty for an aircraft carrier knows, it is better if little ships are told to keep out of the way of big ones, rather than the other way round.

Much of 1942 was spent in a desperate effort to get supplies through to Malta. Ron Blacker, by now a Leading Seaman in the 'W' class destroyer

HMS *Westcott*, gives a very good idea of this work – and its importance – in the latter part of 'Home and Away' and also in 'Convoy Duty in the Med.'. *Westcott* was clearly a very good ship and she played an important part in Operation 'Torch', the Allied invasion of French North Africa, sinking an Italian submarine off Oran. However, the best description of 'Torch' is given by Signalman Don Gooch in 'Don's Diary'. His ship, HMS *Boadicea*, was in the thick of it.

Allied landings at Casablanca, Oran and Algiers on 8 November, coming as they did only three days after victory at El Alamein, marked an important turning point. We were starting our fourth year of the war on the front foot. As Winston Churchill said, it was not the end. It was not even the beginning of the end. But it was the end of the beginning. No doubt Iain Nethercott and his shipmates had this in mind when they went for their epic run ashore the month after – so graphically painted in 'A Sort-Out in Gib.'!

RANDOM NOTES BY AN ANONYMOUS WATCHKEEPER

On board HMS *Boadicea*

Saturday, 20 December 1941

Too rough today for anything except to feel 'bolo'. Nearly over the side due to a wave which swept me up against the depth charge thrower outside our flat.

Baxter [Lieutenant R. Baxter, RNVR] merely irritated because his fine blue yachting trousers got damp.

Monday, 22 December

Could not get ashore in Reykjavik as we were only there to land injured man. First glimpse close up of American warships in Hvålfjord. They look good ships and the 8-inch gun cruisers compare favourably with our 'County' class.

Thursday, 25 December

Christmas Day at sea and very dull too. 'Guns' and I were invited down to the PO's mess where we disposed of several tots each and consequently slept excellently p.m. A parcel for everyone from the citizens of Greenock containing shaving soap, soap, writing pad, bag of expensive looking sweets and one Penguin book. The latter an excellent idea as there is a complete new library on board now.

(From 31 December 1941, until 6 January 1942, HMS *Boadicea* was in Liverpool. References to Adelphi Hotel confirm.)

Wednesday, 7 January 1942
Got 4lb butter and some tinned cream from the bumboatman at Moville (Loch Foyle, Ireland). Their supplies are scantier than usual and it looks as though Moville's heyday as a farm produce base is over. Not worth buying any eggs as there are still plenty at home and I have a feeling this trip will be rude and rough.

Thursday, 8 January
Still calm tonight but an ominous halo round the moon. The barometer is dropping, but only slowly – at present.

Monday, 12 January
The gap in these entries is due to bad weather which has dogged us into Hvålfjord. Apparently we have been on the fringe of a hurricane, whose centre was about 200 miles to the westward.

Lost Able Seaman Bourne, one of the messengers, last night when the ship broached to. Weather too bad to look for him and visibility down to nothing anyway. The barograph reading has gone right off the bottom of the paper. The upper deck was closed all this morning owing to a heavy following sea on our starboard quarter. 'Guns' and I lunched in the PO's mess. No chance of landing as we are a day late but a night 'in' is something.

The reason for our unfortunate loss last night was a sudden meeting with five American destroyers shortly before midnight. *Boadicea* had to alter course to starboard to clear the leading ship and increase speed to 20 knots. One sea, larger than the rest, swung us beam on to wind and sea, and presumably swept Bourne overboard as it crashed over the iron deck. The roll we did was presumably about 55 to 60 degrees as the Gunner and the Signalman-of-the-Watch had to stand on the port screen of the forebridge in order to keep upright. We hesitated at that angle for a few seconds and then came back to the upright, the first time she has ever really 'hovered' before rolling back.

Saturday, 17 January
Have been separated from my diary by the worst storm I hope ever to encounter. Weather was bad from the 13 January onwards, but in the morning watch of Thursday the upper deck became impossible to use and remained so until noon yesterday. Not very long really, but it seemed a lifetime to us marooned in the after part of the ship – and particularly to Gunner (T) Mason who could not leave the forward cabin flat for 30 hours and had to live off two bars of chocolate and the information we shouted through the bulkhead.

At about half-past-five on Thursday afternoon the mast came down due to the heaviest bump I can remember. The shock of it threw the Chief up in the air, caused the wardroom table to break adrift and tore Dent's (Lieutenant Digby Dent, RNVR) desk bodily from the bulkhead. I had a similar feeling in my inside to a time when I was once thrown off my bicycle going fast downhill, to land on the back of my head – just like a road smash, in fact.

The pounding went on for three or four hours and each blow seemed as if it must break the ship up. I've never felt such blows and could not help remembering that our steel plates were only three-quarters of an inch thick.

Our one meal, consisting of tinned pilchards, Heinz baked beans and baked potatoes, was anxiously and indelicately eaten off the wardroom carpet.

I slept on the settee in the Captain's day cabin, or rather lay down and listened to the waves passing over the deck above. Many of them loitered and insinuated themselves through the so-called watertight skylight, thus one heard a loud roaring noise followed by a torrent of water in the cabin with every now and then a furtive slithering as a splinter-mat came adrift from the after steering position.

Average barometer reading was 986.5 – not very low – although the instrument was pumping too heavily for accurate readings. We (Number One, Baxter, the Midshipman and our guest Fluellen) kept two-hour watches on the barometer aided by a torpedoman whose dreary duty was to dispose of the water in the after lobby.

Keir [Sub-Lieutenant J. C. M. Keir, RNR] tells me the height of the waves seemed incredible from the bridge. The Captain [Commander Henderson, RN] hardly left the bridge for two days and remained, as usual, not only cheerful but good-tempered throughout. When he finally did fall asleep it took two of us to wake him by banging his head against the side of his cabin.

Apart from the mast, the whaler was stove in, the after steering position torn to shreds, a Carley float carried away and metal ammunition lockers on 'B' gun deck swept overboard. Stanchions all along the deck were bent up to 45 degrees out of upright. There was water everywhere and the mess decks were a frightful sight – as usual with no word of complaint from the men.

The PO Telegraphist had one hour's sleep out of 48 spent in the Wireless Transmitting (W/T) office but had the satisfaction of aiding our landfall with the remains of his Direction Finding (D/F) set.

It says a lot for the ship and Hawthorn Leslie that there is no structural damage to the hull – even the gyro only went off the board once.

Wednesday, 4 February
We have Major Simon Bolitho and six NCOs on board. After a very unhappy first two days they have all settled down peacefully to ship routine and one may now find a Guards sergeant doing any job from quartermaster to mast-head lookout.

Three days ago we dropped a wreath over the stern in memory of Arnold Bourne, AB, who was lost overboard last time out. Ship's company mustered on the quarterdeck for the ceremony. An insignificant affair but the best we could do for a shipmate. There was little formality as everyone was in working rig but nonetheless the scene was very effective. The small, withering wreath looked indescribably pathetic as it disappeared from sight into the distance.

Note by AB Johnny Randall:

The above section is part of the story of the very severe storm in January 1942 written from an officer's viewpoint. You can imagine the chaos in the forward seamen's mess decks with two or three inches of water slopping from side to side with sundry items of clothing that had fallen down, smashed plates, cups, etc., when two racks broke away from the bulkhead. There was no chance of clearing up – it was all you could do to maintain your balance in getting from one place to another – many people had varying cuts and bruises.

The 12 January incident occurred just as the watch was changing. Seven of us were attempting to climb the ladder to the pom-pom deck when the ship heeled violently over and we had to hang on tightly. I was next to last on the ladder and I was completely in the water.

When we eventually and slowly came back to the upright position the chap behind me was missing, but he'd apparently climbed over us and had made it safely to the pom-pom deck.

After we'd sorted ourselves out, we realised that we had four hours to do on watch despite most of us being soaked to the skin. As captain of the Gun Deck, I wouldn't let anyone go below to try and get some dry clothing, but one lad named Tonkington said he would like to go to the galley and make us all a 'Fanny of Kye'. I reluctantly agreed and off he went. He was gone a long while and I was about to contact the bridge when he arrived back with the 'kye'. I thought he'd been skiving and began to give him a piece of my mind when he said flatly: "I was washed over the side..."

Apparently as he'd reached the bottom of the ladder from the gun deck, a heavy sea came inboard and swept him over the side. However, somewhat miraculously, the next sea washed him back inboard and he'd managed to frantically grab hold of a lifeline. He was rather quiet for the rest of the watch.

The Guards officer and NCOs did one trip with us and when he arrived back in harbour the officer gave us a talk on his impressions of convoy duty on board *Boadicea*. He said when they'd arrived on board just before we sailed, he thought he'd joined a band of pirates. We were, of course, in our 'Going-to-Sea' gear which consisted of wearing everything we needed to keep as warm and as dry as possible.

The Guards officer also wondered about our discipline as everyone seemed to go about their tasks ignoring any comments and remarks coming from anyone. He'd soon realised, however, after we'd had two or three tense incidents during our convoy escort duties, that we were all very well-disciplined and that we could handle ourselves in a crisis and as a team. He left *Boadicea* much happier with the state of the Royal Navy than when he'd joined us.

HOME AND AWAY

Ron Blacker, ex-HMS *Boadicea*

After seven days' leave following the bomb-damaged *Boadicea*'s arrival at Portsmouth in June 1940, I returned to the Royal Naval Base at Chatham. My next draft was to a brand new 'Hunt' class destroyer, then being built at Newcastle, HMS *Eglinton*. Several weeks later, which included completion of construction and trials in the North Sea off the Yorkshire coast, we were sent to the RNB[28] at Harwich, Essex, from where we carried out night patrols against German E-boats and U-boats.

We were at 'Action Stations' all night and returned to Harwich each morning. Those were very tense and anxious times because the constant threat of a German invasion, anywhere on the south and south-east coasts of England, was very real during the summer months of 1940.

There were several notable incidents while on board *Eglinton*, one of which occurred on 4 November 1940. We had been at 'Action Stations' since 1600 hours the previous day, out in the North Sea on E-boat patrol. On arrival back at Harwich on the morning of the 4th, the *Eglinton*'s crew spent the remainder of the forenoon cleaning the ship, to be ready for sea again that night. At 1200 hours all hands were piped to lunch and then piped down, giving us the rest of the afternoon to rest and relax before resuming our nightly patrols. However, it was my turn for keeping an eye on the ship's safety that afternoon.

---

[28] Royal Naval Base.

At about 1500 hours, I was walking the upper deck when I heard the unmistakable sound of a twin-engined German aircraft approaching. Everyone in Britain immediately recognised the dreaded sound of un-synchronised engines in German aircraft.

I looked up among the clouds while running towards the port Lewis gun mounted alongside the wheelhouse, stopping only to hurriedly press the alarm bell to summon all and sundry to 'Action Stations'. On reaching the Lewis gun, I cocked it for firing, when out of the clouds and flying directly towards *Eglinton* was a Dornier twin-engined bomber. Opening fire with the Lewis gun I saw the tracer bullets snaking skywards. Suddenly the bomber turned away from the ship, and, losing height, it headed towards Shotley, Suffolk, about a mile across open water where the Royal Naval shore training base, HMS *Ganges*, was located. I then heard what sounded like the plane's machine guns firing as it disappeared from sight.

By that time the remainder of *Eglinton*'s crew were scurrying to Action Stations and the navigating officer appeared from the wheelhouse where he'd been working. He said I'd done well and would inform the Captain that I'd possibly diverted the enemy pilot from attacking the ship.

At about 1700 hours I was approached by the Coxswain and told to report on the quarterdeck. The Captain had been informed of my efforts against the German bomber and immediately promoted me to Able Seaman. I was delighted, not only at my promotion, but it meant a 50 per cent rise in pay, from 14 shillings a week to 21 shillings which was a lot of pocket money at that time.

It was in late May 1941 that the devastating news reached Harwich of the sinking of the battlecruiser HMS *Hood* by the German battleship *Bismarck*, between Greenland and Iceland. It could not have been worse if we'd heard that we'd surrendered to the Germans. In fact, it was the only time since Dunkirk that we felt we were losing the war. That was why it became so vital to sink *Bismarck*, which happened a few days later after a long chase and an epic battle.

It was about that time that radar was installed on *Eglinton* in great secrecy. It was then called RDF (Radio Direction Finding), and mounted in the Telegraphy cabin where only W/T operators and officers were allowed entry.

We could detect an object, ship or plane, but couldn't tell whether it was friend or foe. We could also only say that the object was on the port side or starboard, forward or aft. But not even that was definite, as port forward could also have been starboard aft, due to 180-degree error possibility. However, it at least gave us sufficient warning not to get caught out and surprised by aircraft sneaking out of the sun.

During the autumn of 1941, I was recommended for a Gunnery Course and returned to Chatham. I qualified on 9 October 1941 as an AA3 and was drafted to HMS *Westcott*, a 'W' class destroyer, at Liverpool to serve as gunlayer on the multiple 2-pounder pom-pom gun mounting with Leading Seaman (AA2) 'Lofty' Jervis as trainer of the pom-pom mounting, commonly known throughout the Navy as a 'Chicago Piano'.

After two or three escort duties bringing back convoys across the Atlantic, *Westcott* was sent to Greenock and had a Bofors gun fitted on the stern in lieu of the 4.7-inch gun mounting, and a 'Hedgehog' depth charge launcher installed forward, in place of 'A' gun.

Being the first ship in the Royal Navy to have a 'Hedgehog' fitted we spent several days with its inventor, a Sub-Lieutenant, on board during trials. This device propelled a number of depth charges about 300 yards in front of the destroyer which, immediately after launching the bombs at a suspected U-boat's position, changed course to port or starboard, so that we could steam well to one side or other of the bombs as they exploded at a specified depth beneath the surface.

The first time we fired the thing I was at 'Defence Stations' on 'B' gun. As the first cluster of depth charges hurtled skywards, reached the top of their arc at about 275 feet and, as if in slow motion, turned over and began their descent, I saw what appeared to be a glove fall away from one of the bombs.

On glancing over 'B' gun's flare, I saw AB Blowers staring down and holding the bloodied stump of his right wrist where his hand used to be. He then fainted with shock and was rushed below for immediate surgery. Our new 'toy' had claimed its first victim due to premature firing. Following that tragic incident, all bombs had to be lowered into launch position in the 'Hedgehog' by using a wooden staff to prevent a repetition.

On completion of the trials *Westcott* received orders to proceed to Gibraltar at the end of November 1941 to join Force 'H', as it was then known and commanded by Admiral John Cunningham, RN.

We subsequently participated in several eventful runs to Malta, escorting convoys from Gibraltar and, in November 1942, Operation 'Torch', the Allied invasion of North Africa. The first big job *Westcott* was sent on in early 1942 was to rescue the troopship SS *Llangibby Castle* which had been bombed and hunted by U-boats while en route to Gibraltar. The liner had sought refuge in Ponto del Garda, in the Azores, after a hit from a torpedo damaged her steering gear. At the Azores the *Westcott* caught and rammed a lurking U-boat *U-581*, causing the submarine to sink. After taking the survivors of *U-581* back to Gibraltar as trophies of war in late February 1942, HMS *Westcott* participated in numerous runs in the Mediterranean, escorting convoys to beleaguered Malta which delivered fighter aircraft and vital supplies, including food and fuel, often while under determined air attack from high- and low-level bombers, and submarine attack.

Malta, as a military base, was in a vital strategic position to control the supply lines throughout the entire Mediterranean. Only 90 miles due south of Sicily, the comparatively tiny island had been under siege since June 1940 when aircraft of the Italian Air Force, based in Sicily, dropped the first of 12,000 tons of Axis bombs on Malta. Its population of 300,000 was almost entirely dependent on imports for food and other vital supplies for the military garrison of 30,000. By the end of the war 3,000 Maltese had been killed by the bombing and the island was awarded the George Cross medal.

Among the vital convoys from Gibraltar to Malta in which *Westcott* participated, escorting 'Spitfire runs' with the aircraft carriers HMS *Eagle*, HMS *Argus* and one of the American carriers, USS *Wasp*, on eventful voyages which usually lasted for about ten days, were those which departed Gibraltar on 1 June, 29 July and 27 August 1942.

There were several notorious convoys, including 'Pedestal' in August 1942, when only three merchant ships, including a battered oil tanker, the famous *Ohio*, got through to Malta after being under constant air and submarine attack throughout the voyage.

In November 1942 we sailed from Gibraltar and picked up a large Allied convoy coming through the Straits of Gibraltar during darknesss. Once we had got out into the Mediterranean, a message came over *Westcott*'s tannoy to say that, together with American forces, we were invading North Africa.

Westcott and other Royal Navy destroyers were to escort the invasion force into Oran.

During the night-time operation, bright searchlight beams from the French Foreign Legion garrison overlooking Oran Harbour turned night into day. Heavy defensive gunfire from French ships met the invasion fleet. We returned fire with 4.7-in and Bofors, supported by the big guns of the cruisers lying further offshore, while our landing craft went ashore and achieved all their objectives. We received a message that HMS *Boadicea*, in the thick of the action off Oran, had been hit, but was able to carry out her duties.

Westcott sank an Italian submarine outside Oran Bay the following day while screening aircraft carriers that were flying off fighter aircraft to protect our troops ashore and moving inland.

We received orders to sail for home shortly before Christmas 1942. Our final 'bag' during 1942 consisted of three Axis submarines, one Italian torpedo-bomber and saving the cruiser, HMS *Liverpool*, from being sunk.

Westcott's exploits earned her crew the following medals and awards; one DSO, two DSCs, five DSMs and eleven Mentions in Dispatches plus a wealth of experience.

I'd been promoted to Leading Seaman on 24 November 1941 after 22 months in the Royal Navy, and qualified for Petty Officer after 30 months service, but due to an AFO which precluded the promotion to PO of those ratings with less than three years' service, I couldn't be promoted until December 1942, shortly before *Westcott* returned home.

I left HMS *Westcott* on 24 December 1942. After a period of leave in January 1943, I qualified AA2 at the RNB Chatham and was then drafted to HMS *Agamemnon*, originally a Blue Funnel liner which had been converted into a mine-layer, and based at Kyle of Lochalsh, on the Isle of Skye.

Agamemnon carried 600 mines (or 800 anti-submarine mines). We laid mines around Iceland and throughout the Arctic Ocean, accurately recording the location of the minefields. I was in charge of the anti-aircraft armament and the 'Buffer' on the after deck.

On 25 August 1943 I was recommended to qualify for Gunner's Mate and drafted back to Chatham. After a short period of studying trigonometry, logarithms and navigation at the RNB School I was put on a Gunner's

Mate course of instruction and spent the next ten months studying all aspects of gunnery.

At the end of May 1944, I completed the Gunnery Instructor's course and started exams, which lasted just over two weeks, qualifying as Gunner's Mate and was rated such on 21 June 1944, having been a Petty Officer since 1942.

HMS *Crane*, a modified 'Black Swan' class escort sloop, was my next ship. She was at Harwich, taking on ammunition before being sent to join up the US Navy's 6th Fleet in the Pacific Theatre of Operations against the Japanese.

THE HISTORY OF *U-581*

The following narrative was obtained via the HMS *Westcott* Association

U*-581* was an unhappy ship. Her real master was her Engineer-Officer, Helmut Krummel, who dominated an easy-going Captain. This officer, Kapitänleutnant Werner Pfeifer, was, on occasion, readier to obey the calls of nature than the calls of duty. A destroyer was sighted and the junior officers urged their Captain to attack it but he excused himself, saying: "I've got to go to the lavatory for a moment." The destroyer didn't wait for him.

His lack of enthusiasm and enterprise depressed his crew. They felt it keenly when they had to return to harbour without any pennants flying. In a career which lasted a little over seven months only one ship was sunk by *U-581* and that on her second and last cruise.

Pfeifer's career had been unusually varied. Born in 1912, he'd studied in Hanover with a view of going into business, but he suddenly gave up the idea and joined the German Navy. After some time he was transferred to the Luftwaffe but, finding that he preferred the Navy, he'd rejoined before the outbreak of war in 1939.

After a spell in minesweepers, he was attached to the 'Experimental Barrage Command.' He then joined the U-boat service and apparently obtained command of *U-56*. While he was Captain, *U-56* rammed a timber ship and sustained considerable damage. An action was begun in the High Court of Hamburg and Pfeifer had to appear there on several occasions to give evidence. As far as he knew, when captured in February 1942, the case was still proceeding. In one thing at least, though it didn't add to his popularity, Pfeifer was firm; he didn't allow alcohol on board his U-boat. Otherwise he seems to have left the maintenance of discipline to the Engineer-Officer, with whom he'd been on the friendliest terms before the war. Helmut Krummel was a Doctor of Engineering of Berlin University. He'd been employed by the German General Electric Company and said he'd been a motorman on the Berlin Underground. He became a Naval Reserve Officer in 1935, had been called up in 1939, and, in early 1940, though critical of the hasty training, he'd volunteered for the U-boat service.

His ideas of discipline were truly Prussian. Not a single man, petty officer or rating, was said to have escaped punishment at his hands. Before *U-581* left Germany for St. Nazaire, Krummel made a short speech to the engine room staff. He spoke of the need for hard work and demanded strict attention to duty: "If you don't like it," he concluded, "there are plenty of cells standing empty at St. Nazaire." The pettiest things were noticed by Krummel. He even gave orders forbidding the crew to listen to any music unless he'd given his permission.

The easy-going Pfeifer, presumably finding that this strict disciplinarian's methods saved him trouble, excused him by saying: "Krummel was a devil for work." When *U-581* came to the end of her career, men were heard calling out to each other that they hoped that Krummel at least would be drowned. However, there was one thing which did disturb the Captain; when *U-581* was sunk his Leutnant had swum to nearby Pico Island and would probably get back to Germany. Pfeifer didn't relish the opinion which the Admiral of U-boats, Admiral Karl Dönitz, might have of him when he received a report of *U-581*'s career and sinking.

Apart from the officers, only three of *U-581*'s crew had any U-boat experience at all. Of these three men, all petty officers, two had done 13 cruises in U-boats and the third was making his seventh cruise.

U-581, built by Blohm and Voss at Hamburg, was commissioned in late July 1941. After trials, prolonged by the inexperienced crew and the zeal of her Engineer-Officer, who insisted on the most rigorous tests and found the compressor and the exhaust system functioning unsatisfactorily, the U-boat sailed from Kiel on 13 December 1941. The only incident of her passage to St. Nazaire, which she reached on 24 December, was an unsuccessful attack on a merchant ship sailing independently. Three torpedoes were fired, but a heavy sea was running and they missed.

On 10 January 1942, *U-581* left St. Nazaire on her last cruise, which was expected to last six weeks. She was to proceed to a position off the coast of Newfoundland and patrol for two weeks; four weeks was allowed in going to and from the patrol area.

The cruise didn't start well. In a practise dive not far from St. Nazaire, the U-boat struck the seabed and damaged her rudder. Consequently, she would answer the helm when the starboard diesel engine was running alone, but not when the port diesel was used by itself.

Towards midnight on 19 January, *U-581* chanced upon a ship, thought to have been HMT *Rosemonde*. It was a very dark and rainy night. The U-boat approached to within about 600 yards of what was thought to be a corvette and fired three torpedoes. One of these struck the trawler amidships. A huge cloud of smoke arose and she seemed to break in two. It was *U-581*'s only success. HMT *Rosemonde* had sailed from Milford Haven on 13 January 1942, bound for Gibraltar, and is known to have been lost about 19-20 January 1942. There were no survivors.

Shortly after this, *U-581*'s original orders to patrol off Newfoundland were countermanded by Admiral Dönitz who had received news of an attack on convoy WS 15 near the Azores (a group of scattered islands in the Atlantic belonging to Portugal, about 1,000 miles west of the Portuguese mainland).

U-402, probably aiming at another ship, had hit the Union Castle liner *Llangibby Castle* in the stern at extreme range. The torpedo blew away her steering gear and rudder; some of the thousand troops on board the liner saw the torpedo come bounding through the waves towards them. Her main engines were undamaged and, leaving convoy WS 15, she made for the Azores by steering with her engines. Despite bad weather and attack by a long-range Focke-Wulf aircraft, *Llangibby Castle* reached Horta on 19 January.

Three destroyers, HM Ships *Westcott*, *Croome* and *Exmoor* were sent to the Azores to escort the *Llangibby Castle* to Gibraltar. On the afternoon of 1 February, HMS *Westcott* entered the Fayal Channel and had a discussion with the liner's Master and the Master of the Dutch tug *Thames*, which had also been sent to the liner's assistance.

Informed of the liner's arrival at Horta and having also received a report that the troops were to be transferred to another liner, which was to be escorted by a cruiser, an anti-submarine vessel and another large ship, Admiral Dönitz ordered *U-581* to go to the Azores and there join *U-402*, which had followed the rudderless liner.

U-581 hurried to the position and reached Horta about 24 hours before the arrival of HMS *Westcott*. Entering the harbour during the night of 31 January, she surfaced within 100 yards of the shore and saw *Llangibby Castle*. To the Germans' disgust, she was made fast on the other side of a stone pier and it was impossible to attack her.

Putting to sea, *U-581* kept well out of sight of land during the next day, 1 February, but that night, she returned to the island and at 0200 hours on the morning of 2 February met *U-402* in the southern entrance to the Fayal Channel. It was agreed that *U-581* should stay more or less where she was and block the southern entrance, while *U-402* passed through the Channel and took station at the other end.

While the two U-boats were thus engaged, HMS *Westcott*, having had a conference with HMS *Exmoor* at the northern end, was on her way round Fayal Island to join HMS *Croome* at the southern entrance to the Channel.

A few hours later, while it was still dark, although the moon was full, *U-581* became aware of the presence of the destroyers and, after firing a torpedo which went wide, submerged. At a depth of about 270 feet a rivet on the flange of her port after exhaust pipe gave way. Water began to enter the engine-room compartment and couldn't be checked. It became difficult to keep trim and there was danger that the electric motors would fail.

At 0745 hours on 2 February, HMS *Croome* obtained contact in a position five miles south-west of St. Mattheus Point on Pico Island. *Westcott* closed and both destroyers lay to. Eventually *Westcott* went ahead. Almost immediately she sighted the conning tower of a U-boat on the starboard bow. It appeared to be steaming away from her and making for Pico Island. *Westcott* increased to full speed to ram.

Coming rapidly up fine on the U-boat's quarter, she missed, but having the enemy about 30 feet on her starboard beam, she fired a pattern of ten depth charges, set to explode at a shallow depth, as she raced past.

Westcott went on, turned under full port wheel and renewed the attack.

The destroyer and the U-boat, steering on almost opposite courses, were closing at a combined speed of over 40 knots. The U-boat altered to port, *Westcott* to starboard, and then, putting on full port wheel, struck the U-boat just abaft the conning tower. A few seconds earlier *U-581*'s crew, who had been lined up on deck in readiness, jumped into the water. *Westcott* turned to port to ram again, if necessary, but while she was doing so the U-boat sank.

After he was rescued, Kapitänleutnant Werner Pfeifer did an unusual thing. He delivered to the Commanding Officer of HMS *Westcott*, Commander I. H. Bocket-Pugh, RN, a formal protest in writing against capture. It was written in English:

PROTEST AGAINST CAPTURE

1. When being followed up, boat got gradually water without influence of the enemy. The consequence was to rise to the surface as soon as possible. The boat was in distress at sea.
2. According to our navigation (controlled by taking bearings on the coast) boat was four miles off the coast, before the persecution; afterwards boat was steering east-course for some time, later on when coming to the conclusion to emerge about ten minutes seventy degrees. After emerging boat was steaming on seventy degrees. The steam was setting NNE.
3. The boat would have been ready with the lay down 24 hours in a neutral port.
4. In spite of the possibility to shoot boat, I did not launch torpedoes. I made no use of the gun because it was a neutral zone.
5. After having seen that the boat should be rammed by the destroyer or covered with depth charges I commanded: All men off the boat.
6. The depth charges did not disturb the boat hardly because it was on the surface. I myself gave the order to sink the boat. It was flooded by the Chief Engineer who left the sinking boat with me.
7. Of course of above we beg for delivering in a neutral country.

(Signed) **PFEIFER**, Kapitänleutnant.

While the survivors of *U-581*, more than 40, were being picked up, the Commanding Officer of HMS *Westcott*, Commander Bocket-Pugh, had taken the opportunity to fix the position. Having ascertained it was outside territorial waters, he rejected the protest.

With regard to the first item, unseaworthy U-boats, he considered, should stay in harbour and, if at sea, should show "I am not under control" lights.

The second item was very vague and proved nothing, and his comment on the third was:

"It would probably have been ready within one minute if the *Llangibby Castle* had been observed to sail."

As for the rest of the protest, it seemed to him that after the first attempt at ramming and the pattern of depth charges there was, justifiably enough, panic on board the U-boat. The enemy realised that the outline of *U-581* had not been lost against the background of Pico Island as had been hoped. The torpedo tubes were not ready and the gun was out of action; either through panic or because the U-boat was too damaged to be fought, they decided, before *Westcott* ran in for her second attack, to abandon ship.

The destroyers then went on with their patrol. At about 1400 hours *Llangibby Castle* was observed to be heading into the Fayal Channel. *Westcott* steamed into the channel and signalled for her to steer for the southern end, which had been satisfactorily cleared, but her tug, *Thames*, had already cast off and was heading north.

It was considered more than likely that, as there had been a U-boat at the southern end of the Fayal Channel, there would also be one at the northern end. *Westcott* therefore went ahead of the liner, telling her of the good news as she went past, and exhorting her to make for the open sea and to "Steam like hell!"

Out in the open sea, off the south-east end of Pico Island and steering on a course of 90 degrees, due east, *Llangibby Castle*, which had been steering by its engines, felt the full force of a south-easterly wind and the liner's Master decided to take a tow from the tug *Thames*, which had been following astern. The time was about 1945 hours and getting dark.

While the towline was being passed between the liner and the tug, HMS *Croome* sighted a U-boat about five miles away as it was coming out of the Fayal Channel. *Exmoor* and *Croome* closed and carried out attacks with depth charges and gunfire, which may or may not have discouraged it from continuing to follow.

On each of the following days, shadowing U-boats were sighted, but *Llangibby Castle* was not attacked, and all her passengers reached Gibraltar safely.

ENGAGING *SCHARNHORST, GNEISENAU* & *PRINZ EUGEN*

John Beeley, Telegraphist, ex-HMS *Keith.*

During the second half of June 1940, I returned from Survivors' Leave following the loss of the destroyer *Keith* and the tug *St. Abbs* at Dunkirk, and within a few days received a draft chit to join the destroyer HMS *Campbell.*

I was Leading Telegraphist, and during the few days I was at the Royal Naval Base Chatham I had been issued with new kit which contained the necessities. Complete with my new kit bag and hammock I was transferred down to Gillingham Pier where I embarked on the 'Trot Boat' for the passage down the River Medway to Sheerness.

HMS *Campbell* was an old 'Scott' class leader, laid down towards the end of the First World War and completed at Cammell Laird's towards the end of 1918. Her accommodation was as basic as her armament and equipment.

Within a couple of days we were steaming back up the Medway to Chatham Dockyard to boiler clean, and receive on board Captain C. T. M. Pizey, RN, who had been appointed to D21. *Campbell* was to be leader of the 21st Destroyer Flotilla based at Sheerness.

For the next year, our time was occupied with escort duties for east coast and Channel convoys. On one occasion we escorted the old monitor *Erebus* across to the Dutch coast where she carried out a bombardment with her 15-inch guns.

In mid-1941 I was rated Acting Petty Officer Telegraphist. Towards the end of that year I was sent down to Royal Marine Barracks, Eastney, for a week's course on the new Type 271 centimetric RDF (Radio Direction

Finding) equipment, as we called it then. It was being fitted onboard *Campbell* in Chatham Dockyard and was still top secret.

I was accommodated in the RM Sergeants' Mess at Eastney which was an absolute revelation to one who had just emerged from the PO's Mess in an old destroyer.

By the end of January 1942, it had become apparent that the German capital ships *Scharnhorst*, *Gneisenau* and *Prinz Eugen*, which had been bottled up in Brest harbour for some time, might try to make the passage back to Germany. While they could have taken the long north-about route, the short passage up-Channel was considered to be the most likely.

As part of the plans to stop them, *Campbell* and *Vivacious*, the only two 'torpedo boats' in 21st Flotilla, were deployed to Harwich, where we joined up with *Mackay* (D16), *Whitshed*, *Worcester* and *Walpole*, all of 16th Flotilla. Captain Pizey assumed command of this force, and we remained at short notice for steam in Harwich for about ten days.

By this time the buzz had got around as to why we there, but we were, of course, ignorant of what was going on elsewhere. On Friday 11 February orders were received for *Vivacious* and *Campbell* to return to Sheerness. However, it was not often that six torpedo boats were together, and Captain Pizey decided that it would be a good idea to carry out an exercise torpedo attack before dispersing, and this was approved.

Therefore, on the morning of Saturday 12 February, the six destroyers sailed for the exercise area to the north of Harwich, where we split into two divisions preparatory to an exercise based more or less on the three German capital ships we had been earmarked to attack.

Mackay, with *Whitshed* and *Walpole* comprising the Second Division, had proceeded ahead, when, at about 1100 hours, while I was on watch in the W/T office, the port wave operator received an enemy report from Nore W/T: "Two battlecruisers, one cruiser off Cap Gris Nez on an easterly course, speed 28 knots." This was the first intimation we had that the German ships were making a run for home and we were unaware that the Coastal Forces at Dover had already attacked without success, or that Lieutenant Commander Esmonde and his six Swordfish aircraft were probably at that moment making their gallant but ill-fated attack.

Captain Pizey now had to assemble his force as quickly as possible, and decide how best to intercept, for the enemy were then passing through Dover Strait, and their speed of 28 knots was the same as our maximum as a flotilla. He decided that our only chance of intercepting them lay in crossing the East Coast Mine Barrier, and, as we approached this, the lower deck was cleared until the mine barrier lay astern.

It was a murky day with poor visibility and soon after 1300 hours, *Walpole* signalled that she had run her main bearings and would have to return to harbour. Our force was reduced to five.

Shortly after this, I was standing on the iron deck when a Royal Air Force Hampden bomber came up from the westward. He didn't cause any concern as he flew overhead, but he then released a stick of bombs which fortunately fell clear to port, about half-way down the line.

A little later, a squadron of German Air Force Me 109s approached from eastward; they circled us two or three times, then flew off in the direction from which they'd approached. It was becoming increasingly apparent that the sense of confusion was not all one-sided.

At about 1430 hours, I went up to have a look at the plot and from there went up to the Type 271 on the bridge where the RDF operator was on watch, to make sure all was well, and to see if there was anything to report.

Looking at the cathode-ray tube, it looked as if the tuning might be a bit off, so I relieved the operator, peaked up the tuning, and scanned the starboard bow. I immediately got two small echoes at about 20,000 yards. I reported this contact by voice-pipe to the bridge.

Captain Pizey came to the voice-pipe, and told me to remain on the set, keeping him informed of range and bearing plus any other information regarding the make-up of the enemy as it became evident.

We gradually closed the range and the smaller echoes of the escorting destroyers began to appear, but still only two larger echoes from the capital ships. We didn't know, at that time, that *Scharnhorst* had struck a mine and had dropped astern of the main force.

Finally, at about 1530 hours the enemy was sighted through the murk and we opened fire while closing the range to fire our torpedoes.

My job on the RDF was now done, and I was able to go out onto the bridge to see what was going on. I think we must have achieved an element of surprise, as initially there was hardly any fire from the Germans. But this didn't last for very long – we were soon under very heavy fire from *Gneisenau* and *Prinz Eugen*.

I could clearly see the vivid flashes of their guns as they fired. Great columns of water erupted into the air off either bow and large projectiles roared close overhead, sounding just like a very fast express train, as we rapidly closed in.

By the time the range had closed to 3,500 yards, I think Captain Pizey decided that we'd better fire our torpedoes while there was still a platform from which to fire them. We turned to port, firing our 'fish' as we did so.

Immediately after we'd fired our torpedoes, a heavy rain squall came down like a curtain between ourselves and the German ships, completely blotting them from sight. The gunfire quickly ceased.

I have always felt that many of us owe our survival to that rain squall. Our luck could not possibly have held for very much longer.

However, we hadn't all escaped relatively unscathed. We shortly came upon *Worcester*. She lay stopped, on fire forward and with heavy damage at the base of her bridge structure. Some of her company had abandoned ship, so we set about trying to pick these men up.

Two Beaufighter torpedo aircraft came in on the port bow and dropped torpedoes which meant an immediate abandonment of the rescue and full astern both engines to avoid the path of the torpedoes which were approaching. By the time we were able to continue picking people up, I'm sure some had succumbed to the bitterly cold sea.

After a time, *Worcester* signalled that she was able to raise steam and shortly afterwards got under way, indicating that she could proceed independently. The remaining four of us destroyers proceeded back to Harwich at maximum speed to reload with torpedoes. This was carried out overnight. The next day was crystal clear, and we sailed again at about 0600 hours but found nothing.

By this time, the dramatic escape of the German capital ships was on the BBC wireless news. I feel sure there must have been some red faces in high places.

Elaborate plans had been laid to prevent the escape. A submarine had been stationed off Brest, but had had to retire at a crucial time to recharge her batteries. A Hudson aircraft, equipped with ASV [air-to-surface vessel radar], patrolling the western approaches to the English Channel, experienced a technical failure and had to return to base. For some reason this aircraft was not replaced with another patrol. Coastal RDF suffered severe jamming, but nothing in particular was deduced from this. An early morning patrol by RAF fighter aircraft originally spotted the heavy ships steaming up the Channel, but their orders were not to break radio silence, so the presence of the German battlecruisers was not known anywhere until these aircraft landed back at their aerodrome and they made a verbal report.

For some reason, there was a further delay in getting the report through so that it was about 1030 hours before the presence of these ships was known at the Admiralty in London, by which time they were approaching the Dover Straits.

There was so little time to launch an attack that it is not surprising that there was so much confusion. The basic flaw in our plans lay in the assumption that the Germans would not pass through the Dover Straits in daylight, and that we should have due warning of their approach, to enable us to launch Coastal Forces, the Swordfish and to mount the destroyer attack under cover of darkness. None of these things came about, and we were left to salvage what we could from the 'wreckage'.

I remained in *Campbell* until after D-Day, 6 June 1944, in which we participated. Most of the intervening period was spent on east coast and Channel convoys, chasing off German E-boats.

After D-Day, I joined HMS *Cowdray*, L52, a 'Hunt' class destroyer, destined for the Pacific. We got as far as Australia, but by then, August 1945, VJ Day had arrived, and we returned to Colombo. Here I embarked in an LST[29] for Singapore where, due to a chronic shortage of drivers, I spent nearly six months as a driver with a Royal Marine Transport Unit, driving ambulances, trucks and a 500cc BSA motorcycle on which I travelled quite widely. I then returned to Trincomalee, and then back to Colombo, where I spent nearly a year in charge of a watch at Colombo Radio, before returning to the UK. By that time, I was approaching the end of my engagement. I had about three months as Petty Officer Telegraphist of the destroyer

---

[29] Landing Ship Tank.

Savage after my Foreign Service leave, and then left the Navy for a civilian job.

DESTROYER ACTION IN DEFENCE OF RUSSIAN CONVOY QP 11

(Reproduced by kind permission of the *Daily Express*)

Note by Michael Back: Although this brave and successful action against German Fleet destroyers was fought on 1 May 1942, the news was not released until 31 July 1942, when it received front page headlines. The following article is from the London *Daily Express* of that date. Security forbade the national press reports to mention that the ships, *Bulldog*, *Beagle*, *Amazon* and *Beverley*, had had half their main armament removed for the installation of anti-submarine weapons, and, against the ten 5.9-inch and five 5-inch guns of the German destroyers, mustered only six 4.7-inch and one 4-inch gun between them:

Daily Express
Friday, July 31 1942
Black-out 10.54 p.m. to 5.38 a.m.

BULLDOG AND CO. BEAT GERMANS
Four old ships get convoy through

When three big brand-new German destroyers swooped on one of our Russian convoys on May Day, every one of the five attacks they made was beaten off by four little British escorting ships between 11 and 23 years old. These were the destroyers *Bulldog*, *Beagle*, *Amazon*, and *Beverley*. *Beverley*, an ex-USN vessel, is only 1,190 tons. The others are 1,360-tonners. The German destroyers were of the *Hans Lody* or *Narvik* class, 1,625 tons, faster and more heavily armed. How the battle went was described for the first time in an Admiralty communique last night.

Close to ice

It began in the early afternoon, in bitter cold. The convoy was skirting a great patch of drift ice when the enemy was sighted. *Bulldog* at once led round to attack, and fire was opened at a range of about 10,000 yards from the British 4.7-inch guns, while snow squalls swept the sea. The Germans, with their 5.9-inch armament, concentrated on *Amazon*. She was hit, and suffered some casualties. But she was kept in action and remained in the line. The enemy was prevented from reaching a position to attack the convoy, and forced to retire.

Half an hour later they were sighted again. Once more the British destroyers were led in, and opened fire. They altered course directly towards the Germans, who turned away. By this time the convoy was well within the ice pack, and it was difficult for the escorts to keep touch. But when the enemy made a third attempt to reach the merchantmen about an hour later, our destroyers immediately engaged them again. They retired after a brief exchange of shots.

When the Germans made their fourth attack, after another hour, it was noticed that their fire was far less accurate and intense, indicating that they had received some damage. Only one of their ships continued to fire full salvos. And, as before, they retired after a brief exchange.

Last attack

The last attack followed half an hour later. But when the British destroyers tried to engage at close range the Germans immediately broke off the action, and in less than ten minutes had disappeared. Further damage is thought to have been inflicted on them in their final encounter. The Admiralty concludes the story in these words:

"Throughout this series of actions the behaviour of the ships in convoy was exemplary, all keeping station perfectly, while the smaller escort vessels maintained station close to the convoy in spite of the difficulties imposed on them by the weather and the heavy drift ice."

DSOs are awarded to Commanders Maxwell Richmond (*Bulldog*), Ralph Medley (*Beagle*), and Lieutenant Commanders Nigel Roper (*Amazon*) and John Grant (*Beverley*). Another sidelight is flashed on the perils of the Murmansk route by an Admiralty description of the last hours of the cruiser *Edinburgh*.

She was sunk by our own forces after she had been twice torpedoed while escorting a convoy. She was first hit by a U-boat on 30 April, and her steering gear disabled. Two Russian and two British destroyers – *Foresight* and *Forester* – went to her aid. *Forester* took her in tow, but heavy seas were running and the hawser parted. So to help *Edinburgh* to steer, *Foresight* was taken in tow by the cruiser. This went on for 16 hours. Then *Foresight* had to cast off, as U-boats were lurking. The convoy and the crippled cruiser were in danger. The following morning, in snow squalls, *Harrier* and *Hussar* sighted three large German destroyers about four miles off and immediately engaged them. *Foresight* and *Forester* joined in, and there was a running fight. It was so cold that sea spray froze as it fell.

Forester was hit in the boiler-room and stopped. Her commanding officer, while leaning from the bridge and encouraging a gun's crew, was killed. One of the enemy destroyers was hit and stopped.

Then the German destroyers fired a salvo of torpedoes. *Edinburgh* made an uncontrollable swing into the path of one, which struck her. *Foresight* scored a hit on the stopped enemy destroyer, and caused a tremendous explosion.

When the smoke had cleared, only two of the three German destroyers could be seen, and soon afterwards there was another heavy explosion in one of them. When it was found impractical to continue the attempt to tow *Edinburgh* into harbour, the surviving members of her crew were taken off, and she was sunk.[30]

For "seamanship and courage" in this action Commander Eric Hinton (*Harrier*) received a bar to his DSO. The DSO also goes to Commander J. S. C. Salter (*Foresight*), Lieutenant Commander T. C. Crease (*Gossamer*); and to Lieutenant R. C. Briggs (*Hussar*), the DSC. Lieutenant Commander G. P. Huddart (*Forester*), is posthumously Mentioned in Dispatches.

[30] The cruiser HMS *Edinburgh* was carrying five tons of gold bullion from Russia in her ammunition magazines, destined for the US Treasury in part payment for war supplies being shipped from America. Officially designated a war grave for the 57 British officers and ratings entombed in her, *Edinburgh* was left untouched until 1982 when divers were allowed to salvage the gold.

THE TRAGEDY OF PQ 17

R. F. 'Dick' Fearnside, Chief Radio Officer, SS *Hartlebury*

I sailed on various ships during the Second World War after leaving my home town of Ipswich, Suffolk, joining the Merchant Navy as Third Radio Officer on 17 August 1939. My first ship was the *Antonia*, of the Cunard Line, on the Liverpool/Montreal run. We sailed from Liverpool on 25 August and on the way down the St. Lawrence River, just after leaving Quebec City, on 3 September war was declared. After three more trips to Canada I joined the tanker *Dorcasia* in Avonmouth in January 1940 as Radio Officer, and sailed to Singapore via the Suez Canal, returning to the UK in July 1940.

Following more experience and sea time during the next two years, on board four more merchant ships, *Kainalu*, *Empire Snipe*, *Empire Penguin* and the *Empire Eagle*, I was posted to the freighter *Hartlebury* as Chief Radio Officer in May 1942.

We sailed from Sunderland up to Reykjavik, Iceland in May 1942, loaded with war supplies for Russia. This ship was part of the Arctic convoy PQ 17 with 34 other Allied merchantmen, taking war supplies via Iceland to ports in northern Russia. We spent several weeks waiting for the other ships to arrive and form up, leaving Reykjavik on 27 June. The *Hartlebury* was appointed Vice Commodore with the *River Afton* as Commodore.

Thirty five ships started out, but due to heavy ice floes in the Denmark Straits an American freighter was forced to return to Iceland.

We were sighted by a long range German Air Force Condor, based in northern Norway, on 1 July. Several reported U-boats were detected and harried by the escorts, and on 2 July the first air attacks were launched by torpedo-bombers, but they were beaten off by the concentrated anti-aircraft fire from our escorts. At least one bomber was shot down, crashing into the sea, and several others were damaged. The next day we had several U-boat sightings.

Following the brief Arctic twilight of the summer night, dawn on 4 July began with a heavy air attack by at least 25 torpedo-bombers, their sole success being the American Liberty ship *Christopher Newport*. The convoy's anti-aircraft fire shot down the bomber that had torpedoed the freighter. In fact, the aircraft flew so low between the next column of ships to *Hartlebury*, and the AA fire was so low, that my aerial was damaged by the American ship next to us.

The most concentrated air attack against PQ 17 came from both sides of the convoy at about 1000 hours. The aircraft on the port side were first sighted by the USS *Wainwright*, an American destroyer, and with all its AA guns blazing, together with the convoy's concentrated fire, the attack was beaten off. Their torpedoes were released well out of range and did no damage. However, the attack on the starboard side was more successful; three ships were hit including the Russian tanker *Azerbaidjan* which was holed but managed to eventually rejoin the convoy.

All day long the convoy was harried by U-boats and aircraft, but carried on towards Russia without further loss and reached the Barents Sea. Late on 4 July, at about 2230 hours, a message was received from the Senior Officer of the Escort, Commander Jack Broome in the destroyer HMS *Keppel*. He'd received orders from the Admiralty in London that the convoy was to scatter and proceed independently to the Russian ports of Archangel and Murmansk. Apparently, the German battleship *Tirpitz*, with other German capital ships, had gone from their well-defended anchorages in occupied Norway and elsewhere.

The submarines and aircraft redoubled their attacks against the scattered and virtually defenceless merchant ships. However, the rumoured German Navy capital ships failed to appear.

The *Hartlebury* headed north-east towards Novaya Zemlya and the ice-cap. We managed a speed of over 12 knots and within two hours there were no other ships in sight. I was on the 1600-2400 hours watch when we were ordered to scatter. I kept on watch during the next few hours. All was quiet until about 0600 hours on 5 July. Anti-aircraft fire issued from an American ship under attack by German bombers, followed later that morning by reports from ships under attack by either U-boats or enemy aircraft. The number of reports increased during the next few hours and 12 ships had reported attacks of one sort or another by the end of the night.

Things quietened down during 6 July – only two ships reported attacks late in the day. We soon sighted the ice-cap and were steaming along the edge which provided cover. Fog screened us from aircraft which we heard though no bombs were dropped. The fog was undoubtedly a blessing in disguise.

On 7 July, further attacks were reported over the radio, mostly aircraft. We sailed on past the ice floes heading for Novaya Zemlya, an island running north to south in the Barents Sea, which we sighted during the evening. We started to sail south along the west coast of Novaya Zemlya, keeping very close inshore. We picked up several signals from three ships which were being attacked by aircraft and U-boats.

At about 2000 hours, I had just come on watch when we were hit by two torpedoes on the starboard side. I was struck on the head by a falling piece of radio equipment that fell from the roof of the Radio Cabin. If it hadn't been for my Second Radio Operator, George Storey, who got me down to the well deck, I would probably have gone down with the ship. I managed to step up onto a raft which was alongside. I didn't even get my feet wet, even though the *Hartlebury* was listing at an angle of forty-five degrees.

Many years later I learned that we had been sunk by *U-335* and it turned out that we were its only success. It was lost with all hands in April 1944. The *Hartlebury* sank quite quickly. She went down with all three sections, the bow, midships and the stern together. The Skipper managed to get off the stern and was picked up by the only lifeboat which had managed to get away undamaged.

The U-boat circled around us and one of the crew told us they had been waiting three days for us. We thought, "What a pity you bothered to wait..." They told us that we were quite near the coastline of an island, gave us the direction to head for, wished us good luck and were away. We were able to manoeuvre our raft, with thirteen survivors, over to another two rafts floating nearby. Although the sea was quite choppy, we managed to transfer nine survivors on to the other two rafts. Unfortunately, six from the thirteen didn't make it and died of exposure within the next 24 hours.

We drifted and paddled around the bay for the next two and a half days, with a canvas screen to shield ourselves from the bitterly cold Arctic wind. We were eventually sighted by a lookout on the American freighter *Winston Salem* which had run aground close inshore. They sent a boat out and we were taken aboard, given hot food, coffee, fresh clothing and had a good sleep. The *Winston Salem*, which already had over 100 survivors from other sunken ships, was our saviour and I'm forever grateful.

As the only Radio Officer of the survivors from other sunken ships on board, apart from the *Winston Salem*'s own radioman, I went on watch to enable 24-hour wireless cover. We were there for the next five days. On 15 July a Russian Catalina flying boat turned up with a message to inform us that several ships and escorts had assembled in the Matochkin Strait and that all survivors, numbering about 100, would eventually be taken off the *Winston Salem* and taken down to the Matochkin Strait. In fact, I was taken down in a Russian survey ship; then we were split up amongst the various ships. I eventually finished up on HMS *Poppy*, a corvette of the original PQ 17 escort.

A few days later we formed up in a convoy to head south for Archangel, picking up the *Empire Tide* en route, a transport ship which was in Moller Bay. The trip into Archangel was very, very rough and two anti-aircraft ships came out from Archangel to provide extra cover.

On our arrival we were billeted in the Intourist Hotel which was very comfortable. As I recall, and owing to the increasing food shortage, we had only two meals a day. We considered ourselves fortunate, but over the next two months of our stay in Archangel food supplies became very short indeed. I also recall that there was one voyage made by some fast cruisers and destroyers which brought food and medical supplies and which improved the situation somewhat.

We eventually left Archangel on 13 September for home. I was on the Rescue Ship *Zamelak*. We arrived back in Glasgow and were bussed up to a civic reception where someone from the Ministry of Defence addressed us. Convoy PQ 17 had cost 24 ships together with 153 merchant seamen. He attempted to give a long speech, but was frequently and loudly interrupted by prolonged booing and furious shouts of "WHERE WAS THE NAVY?!"

The deeply-felt resentment was very real at that reception.

According to the records of those hazardous Arctic convoys, just over four million tons of war supplies got through to the Russian forces fighting on the Eastern Front, including 5,000 tanks and 7,000 aircraft. But three thousand Royal Navy, Merchant Navy, American Maritime Marine and Auxiliary Servicemen went down with their ships in those freezing waters while making it all possible.

Without doubt, anyone who experienced those convoys went through one of the very toughest assignments of the whole war, simply because of the harshest weather conditions imaginable which are prevalent in those extreme northern latitudes.

Was it worth the tremendous cost in young lives? Could there have been a less dangerous way to get the supplies through?

[**Anthologist's Note:** Total Allied losses in ships and personnel during the Russian convoys between 1941-1945 were: the Royal Navy and United States Navy lost 21 warships with 1,944 Allied sailors; and 98 merchant ships went down with their 829 crewmen.]

Convoy PQ 17 departed Reykjavik, Iceland on 27 June 1942 and dispersed in the evening of 4 July in the Barents Sea [Excerpt from *Convoys to Russia 1941-1945* by Bob Ruegg and Arnold Hague].

Vessel	Crew	Tons	Fate
Alcoa Ranger	53 Amer	5116	Sunk
Aldersdale	74 Brit	8402	Sunk
Azerbaidjan	64 Russ	6114	
Bellingham	43 Amer	5345	
Benjamin Harrison	72 Amer	7191	
Bolton Castle	23 Brit	5203	Sunk
Carlton	92 Amer	5127	Sunk
Christopher Newport	81 Amer	7191	Sunk
Daniel Morgan	93 Amer	7177	Sunk
Donbass	34 Russ	7925	
Earlston	62 Brit	7195	Sunk
El Capitan	22 Pan	5255	Sunk
Empire Byron	71 Brit	6645	Sunk
Empire Tide	63 Brit	6978	
Fairfield City	82 Amer	5686	Sunk
Gray Ranger	52 Brit	3313	

Hartleybury	31 Brit	5082	Sunk
Honomu	83 Amer	6977	Sunk
Hoosier	12 Amer	5060	Sunk
Ironclad	13 Amer	5685	
John Witherspoon	84 Amer	7191	Sunk
Navarino	42 Brit	4841	Sunk
Ocean Freedom	73 Brit	7173	
Olapana	33 Amer	6069	Sunk
Pan Atlantic	41 Amer	5411	Sunk
Pankraft	32 Amer	5644	Sunk
Paulus Potter	11 Du	7168	Sunk
Peter Kerr	61 Amer	5644	Sunk
Rathlin	35 Brit	1600	
River Afton	51 Brit	5479	Sunk
Samuel Chase	91 Amer	7191	
Silver Sword	44 Amer	4937	
Troubador	24 Pan	6428	
Washington	21 Amer	5564	Sunk
West Gotomska	?? Amer	5728	
William Hooper	14 Amer	7177	Sunk
Winston-Salem	54 Amer	6223	
Zaafaran	55 Brit	1559	Sunk
Zamalek	94 Brit	1567	

[Key: Brit=British;   Amer=American;   Russ=Russian;   Du=Dutch;
Pan=Panamanian]

Commodore was in *River Afton*, Vice Commodore in *Hartlebury*, Rear Commodore in *Empire Byron*. The position of *West Gotomska* in the convoy is unknown, probably as she returned to Iceland early in the convoy's passage, leaving there 27 July for the Clyde for repairs. The ocean escort from 27 June to 4 July comprised the minesweepers *Britomart*, *Halcyon* and *Salamander*, trawlers *Ayrshire*, *Lord Austin*, *Lord Middleton* and *Northern Gem*, destroyer *Middleton* and auxiliary AA ships *Pozarica* and *Palomares*. On 30 June the destroyers *Fury*, *Keppel* (Senior Officer Escort), *Leamington*,

Ledbury, Offa and *Wilton* and corvettes *Dianella, La Malouine, Lotus* and *Poppy* also joined. The destroyer *Douglas* also sailed, detaching on 2 July with the escort oiler *Gray Ranger*. The submarines *P614* and *P615* also accompanied the convoy as escorts from 30 and 27 June respectively until dispersal.

'SHEER BLOODY MURDER'

Excerpt from *Arctic Convoys* by Richard Woodman (Reproduced by kind permission of John Murray (Publishers) Ltd.)

The losses sustained by the Allies were enormous, amounting to 24 merchant ships, two thirds of the convoy; eight totalling 48,218 tons sunk by U-boats, eight of 40,376 tons sunk by aircraft, and eight of 54,093 tons damaged by aircraft and finished off by U-boats. In terms of lost *matériel*, 210 bombers, 430 tanks, 3,350 vehicles and a little under 100,000 tons of munitions, explosives and raw materials lay on the bed of the Barents Sea – all for half a dozen German aircraft.

In London Ambassador Maisky pressed Anthony Eden for news of the next convoy and was angry when told the Admiralty would not send any more until the nights closed in again. All Eden and Churchill would do was promise a meeting at which Maisky and the head of the Soviet Military Mission, Admiral Harlamov, could put their case. At the meeting, which included Eden, the First Lord, A. V. Alexander, and the First Sea Lord Admiral Pound, Maisky reiterated his request to know the scheduled departure of PQ 18. Pound said nothing could be done until better Russian air cover was arranged, whereupon Harlamov criticized the order to withdraw the cruisers from PQ 17. Pound was furious, deeply resenting the Russian attitude and angrily admitting PQ 17 was scattered by his personal order. Alexander attempted to smooth things over and Maisky purred, 'Even British admirals make mistakes.'

In the House of Commons the next day Emmanuel Shinwell MP asked the Financial Secretary to the Admiralty, George Hall, if he "was aware that a recent convoy proceeding in a very important direction was denuded by

the Admiralty of protection… and that a large number of vessels were lost?"
Hall remained seated and tight-lipped.

These were the first of a long series of inquests into what was, after all,
nothing less than a huge and awesome blunder. In the unwise official British
silence which followed, a silence which the reporter Godfrey Winn accurately warned the First Lord of the Admiralty would create mistrust on the
part of the Americans and much mischief elsewhere, rumours circulated
which sought to taint several officers, including poor Hamilton, with a whiff
of reprehensible conduct. They were as unworthy as their origin was uncertain. Admiral Tovey was so concerned that he boarded the USS *Wichita* after
her arrival at Scapa Flow and addressed her company, apologizing for the circumstances which had led to so many losses among American merchant seamen.

It was at least a manly act, to be expected of such a man, but no such con-
sideration was afforded British merchant seafarers. When the majority of the
PQ 17 survivors arrived home in QP 14 they were not allowed to disperse
on arrival in Glasgow but were marched to St. Andrew's Hall and addressed
by Philip Noel-Baker, Under Secretary of State to the Ministry of War
Transport. As a damage-limitation exercise this was an insult to the intelligence of weary men. "We know what the convoy cost us. But I want to tell
you that whatever the cost, it was well worth it." Unsurprisingly, the Under-
Secretary was howled down.

It has been suggested that the cost of PQ 17 has been exaggerated, that
the German offensive was in any case contained at Stalingrad (though at
enormous cost). It has also been claimed that the loss of 153 Allied merchant
seamen from 22 merchantmen was light compared to losses of 4,000 sustained in the preceding months by the Royal Navy from an equal number of
warships. Such comparisons are as invidious as they are unworthy. Like can
only be compared with like and this bald figure takes no account of the physical and mental scars of many others. Apart from the highly material fact that
to have destroyed the contents of those humble freighters in combat would
have cost the Germans dear, tragically, the reverberative effect on morale of
the loss of those 153 men, augmented by the tales of the survivors, was more
significant than the loss of 4,000. War is full of such savage inequities.

"Looks like a bloody business," Captain Jack Broome had shouted across to Dowding and Charlton. The rebounding irony was far greater than intended by Broome's well-meant, self-deprecating remark. Broome had anticipated a battle within a matter of hours, but the surviving merchant seamen remembered not that 'only' 153 of their comrades died in the catastrophe that followed the scattering of PQ 17, but that not one naval sailor died in their defence.

It was this that fuelled the ensuing bad feeling that spread like a viral infection and lasted long after the guns had fallen silent. American mercantile faith in the British Navy was shaken and the ulcerous wound was opened in the morale of the British Merchant Navy. The events of PQ 17 were a catalyst, a culmination of the bitterness resulting from social divisions, injustices, real and imagined, of misunderstanding, mistrust and mutual ignorance.

Sir Dudley Pound's fateful and wrong decision, compounded in its effect by an injudicious amendment, was contrary to what every thinking sailor knew in his bones: that a convoy *always* stuck together. The threat of surface warships had been met by scattering in the early days when only Armed Merchant Cruisers (AMCs) like the *Jervis Bay* guarded them and they had the wide Atlantic to lose themselves in. PQ 17 was a different operation; PQ 17 was ostensibly covered not only by the First Cruiser Squadron, but also by the Home Fleet in the offing, the battleship *Duke of York*, the aircraft carrier *Victorious* and all the might, domination and power of the King's ships.[31]

---

[31] Anthologist's Note: Belatedly, during 2002, an appeal for funds (with a target of £28,000) was launched for a memorial statue to be built at Harwich Harbour, Essex, honouring all Merchant Navy seamen who gave their lives during the Second World War. All donations can be made payable to: 'Forgotten Heroes' (sort code 40-18-51; Acct. No. 01236660) and can be sent to HSBC, North Station Road, Colchester, Essex.

CONVOY DUTY IN THE MED.

Ron Blacker, ex-HMS *Boadicea*; article from *The Gibraltar Chronicle*, 9 July 1942

During the summer of 1942 I was on board HMS *Westcott* which at that time was escorting convoys from Gibraltar to Malta. The following three press reports describe some of the action:

The Gibraltar Chronicle

Thursday, 9 July 1942

First Full Story of the Malta Convoy Battle

CARRIERS EVADED TORPEDOES AS RAIDERS CRASHED INTO THE SEA

From a Special Correspondent on board a British warship in the Western Mediterranean:

From a gun director 100 feet above the sea I watched the tremendous battle for supremacy between Axis (German and Italian) bombers and British warships escorting convoy merchant ships crammed with supplies bound for Malta.

It was a grim, merciless, day-long battle in which every form of aerial attack was launched against the ships. We were dive-bombed, bombed by high-level planes and attacked by torpedo-carriers. Six furious onslaughts cost the enemy 15 bombers – nine shot down by Fleet Air Arm Hurricane fighters and six by the ships' guns. Many more were badly damaged.

Submarines, too, attacked us as we steamed between the jaws of Italian air bases in Sardinia and Sicily. One of them was probably destroyed.

4 minutes – 4 down

The first air alarm sounded south of Sardinia when four Axis aircraft flying at 1,000 feet fled after dropping two sticks of bombs which burst in the sea well wide of an aircraft carrier and a cruiser. Then eight Axis torpedo-bombers swept in swiftly just above the water. A storm of shells met them, and in as many minutes four of the planes crashed into the sea. Several others pierced our smoke barrage and made for an aircraft carrier and a merchant-man, but these in turn encountered a hail of shells. One made a perfect attack on a carrier, dropping a torpedo 500 yards from her, but with a swift turn the carrier avoided danger and the attacker, hit by a shell, crashed into the sea in flames.

Dive-bombers chased off

A second wave of planes immediately attacked from the starboard, but a wall of bursting shells from six-inch and four-inch guns forced them to turn away and split up. Nine Heinkels then flew high over the ships, and when half the ships' armament was directed skywards torpedo-bombers drove in again flying barely 50 feet above the sea. After this attack had been beaten off the ships were left in peace for six and half hours. Then a dozen Junkers 87s made an unsuccessful dive-bombing attack on the merchant ships, an aircraft carrier and a cruiser. Fighters chased the raiders as they fled, and one bomber, diving frantically in an attempt to escape, crashed into the water.

The last attack of the day was made by 20 torpedo-bombers, five of which launched torpedoes at one of the carriers, but her bows swung round and the torpedoes slipped harmlessly by.

MALTA CONVOY MEN GET DECORATIONS

Naval men who got an important convoy through to Malta have been decorated. The awards announced last night form "a first short list in recognition of those whose gallantry and good services have so far been brought to notice." Such further awards as may be approved will shortly be published, last night's *London Gazette* added. First of the decorations are given "for bravery and resolution" in 14 warships. The ships mentioned are the aircraft carrier *Eagle* and the anti-aircraft cruiser *Cairo* – both lost in the big convoy battle last month – the cruiser *Liverpool*, the destroyers *Antelope*, *Badsworth*, *Bedouin* – sunk in early August – *Blankney*, *Matchless*, *Middleton*, *Partridge*, *Westcott*, *Hebe*, *Ithuriel* and *Marne*.

Two officers received bars to the DSO, six get the DSO, and two the DSC. There are three DSMs – for Chief Air Artificer F. E. Merwood and Leading Air Mechanics J. H. Humphries and W. J. Souter. Nine officers are mentioned in dispatches. One of the DSOs, Commander B. G. Scurfield, of the *Bedouin*, is now a prisoner of war.

A VIEW FROM A SIGNALMAN

David Walker, Signalman, HMS *Bulldog*

On joining the Royal Navy in February 1940, aged 19, I did my initial training in Signals at HMS *Royal Arthur*, Skegness, on the Lincolnshire coast. On completion and being posted to Portsmouth Division, my first Draft Chit was to Scapa Flow to join the battleship HMS *Nelson*, which, at that time, flew the flag of the Commander-in-Chief, Home Fleet. It was at this time that I first saw HMS *Bulldog*, one of the many Fleet destroyers based at Scapa Flow at that time. Little did I know that, in just over a year, HMS *Bulldog* would play a big part in my life.

The following nine months were quite mundane, with the occasional trip to sea, watchkeeping in harbour, then, for me, it was back to Portsmouth. My next draft was to one of the 50 old ex-United States Navy lend-lease destroyers, HMS *Georgetown*.

We were based at Greenock, Scotland, and our duties were North Atlantic convoys. However, the First World War American destroyers, although a generous gesture and appreciated, did not appear to be reliable and seemed to be always breaking down. This was before the absolute flood of modern armaments, aircraft, tanks, guns, etc., came across the North Atlantic for Britain, Russia, North Africa and the Pacific theatre of operations, when the rapidly expanding industrial might of America got under way from 1942 onwards.

It was no surprise when I left the *Georgetown* in June 1941 and was drafted to HM Signal School, Portsmouth for the next two months. I was then drafted as one of a new ship's company sent to recommission HMS *Bulldog* after an extensive refit on the Clyde. This followed *Bulldog*'s brilliant capture of the Enigma coding machine from *U-110* off Iceland.

After the usual working-up trials, *Bulldog* was ready for sea, under the command of Commander Maxwell Richmond, RN, along with her Flotilla consisting of *Beagle, Boadicea, Amazon* and *Ambuscade.*

(As I recall some of the highlights of the following fifteen months, I have to say that they will not necessarily be in the correct sequence.)

We were based in Greenock, and, after a couple of trips escorting Atlantic convoys, relatively uneventful apart from the usual anti-submarine activity, we received orders to proceed to Iceland. We arrived at a small place called Akureyri on the north of the island in late April 1942, and, after refuelling and topping up with provisions etc., we were on our way to Murmansk to rendezvous with HMS *Edinburgh*, a 'City' class cruiser, and pick up our first Russian convoy from Murmansk.

It was not possible to top up with provisions, and consequently we quickly exhausted supplies. For the remainder of the voyage back to Iceland we were reduced to a daily diet of boiled rice and corned beef.

The convoy was a large one, already formed up and under way with its escorting bevy of corvettes when we arrived. *Edinburgh* stationed herself in the middle of the convoy, and *Bulldog*, being Captain D, was in position ahead of the convoy with the other destroyers forming a screen around the perimeter.

It was not long before the first U-boats were sighted, two of them, surfaced on the horizon, and I am proud to say that I am the one who spotted them first. From that time on, it seemed *Bulldog* was at permanent 'Action Stations', defending the convoy against seemingly endless attacks by U-boats and destroyers. We were joined by a large four-engined Focke-Wulf Condor aircraft which flew round the convoy, keeping us under constant surveillance, and ensuring that our exact position, speed and course was known to the packs of U-boats in the immediate area of the Barents Sea.

On 2 May, *Edinburgh* went down in the Barents Sea after being torpedoed by a U-boat and then by a German destroyer. *Bulldog*, along with other destroyers, fought off a determined attack on the convoy by German 'Narvik' class destroyers. They were finally driven off, but the Flotilla suffered a few hits and sustained a few casualties.

Another outstanding memory of 1942 was a tragic collision. *Bulldog* was based in Greenock during the latter half of 1942, as part of the Greenock Special Escort Division. At the beginning of October, we were ordered to go out into the North Atlantic to meet the 81,237-ton transatlantic liner RMS *Queen Mary*, which was on her way back from America full of US Army troops, off the north-west coast of Ireland and escort her back to Greenock. In the vastness of the North Atlantic, a ship of her size and speed did not need an escort, but on approaching land she had to reduce speed. It was our duty to ensure that she had a safe passage into port while at this vulnerable pace. We were joined by the anti-aircraft cruiser HMS *Curaçoa*, which then became the Senior Officer present

When we met the huge liner, she was doing a high rate of knots, and the destroyers quickly formed an anti-submarine screen around her. She was doing a numbered 'Timed Zigzag' either side of the mean course, and, for some reason which to this day I find very hard to understand, *Curaçoa* stationed herself just off the starboard bow of the *Queen Mary*. To my mind, *Curaçoa* was much too close.

Tragically, at about 1300 hours, on a lovely sunny day, 2 October 1942, when the time came to alter course on the zigzag, *Queen Mary* altered course to starboard, and the cruiser *Curaçoa* altered course to port...

All 81,000 tons of the mighty *Queen Mary*, travelling at high speed, hit the *Curaçoa* and literally crushed her to death under her towering bows. In a matter of less than two minutes all that was left of the 4,200-ton cruiser, and her ship's company of 400, were a few floating bits of debris and a few very lucky survivors, bobbing in the wake of the huge liner.

Bulldog, as Captain D, ordered two destroyers to pick up the survivors, about 70, while the rest of the escort carried on with the *Queen Mary*. She never slowed one knot despite having a large hole in the bow, but as we approached the coast of Scotland she gradually reduced speed and we swept the *Queen Mary* safely into Greenock.

As one who witnessed this incident, as I remember it, I find it very strange that since the end of the war I haven't seen or heard any reference to it, either on television, radio or in the newspapers. It was a very tragic accident that should never have happened, but one that some idiot caused.

Bulldog, Beagle, Boadicea and *Brilliant*, among many other destroyer escorts, were then assigned to participate in the North African landings. Thus, after topping up with fuel, provisions and armaments *Bulldog* set course for Gibraltar.

Operation 'Torch', which took place on 8 November 1942, was a huge combined operation with American forces, with the Allied armies landing at three different locations; Casablanca, Oran and Algiers. *Bulldog* was assigned to Algiers. When the initial skirmish of the actual landing was over things soon settled down. We heard later that several French Navy ships, in the three harbours, were sunk or severely damaged by Royal Navy and United States Navy cruisers and battleships when they chose to oppose the Allied landings.

On our return to Greenock, our next duty was escorting a convoy to Murmansk from Loch Ewe, Scotland, departing on 22 December. However, we encountered extremely severe weather conditions with mountainous seas, and we had to return to Greenock for urgent repairs.

Bulldog's next duty, between January and March 1943, was to patrol to the north of the convoy routes between Iceland, Murmansk, and Scotland. This was carried out at high speed when weather conditions allowed. Even so, the destroyers took a pounding, but at least we were able to spend more time on the mess deck when not on watch, either reading, playing cards or other hobbies to pass the time. While up in those extreme latitudes of the high Arctic, that 'frozen hell' virtually on the roof of the world, we experienced almost 24-hours' darkness in mid-winter and 24-hours' daylight during the summer months, a strange and uncanny experience for us all.

In April 1943, *Bulldog* returned to Greenock for a refit at Clydebank and the ship's company enjoyed a well-earned leave. I was then sent to HM Signal School, Portsmouth, promoted to Leading Signalman and rejoined *Bulldog* with a new captain in command, our very senior Commander having been replaced by a Lieutenant.

HMS *Beagle* took over as Senior Officer of the Flotilla, and I was then transferred to *Beagle* due to this, but shortly afterwards *Beagle* went into dock for a refit and the ship's company paid off. So ended my association with the 'B' class destroyers for the remainder of the war.

After leaving 'B' class destroyers, it was back to Signal School at Petersfield, and eventually a Draft Chit to America, via (would you believe it) RMS *Queen Mary*, to pick up a new 'Captain' class frigate, HMS *Burges*, that had just been built in the Boston Navy Yard, Massachusetts.

After six weeks' sea trials off Bermuda, we picked up our first Atlantic convoy. On arrival in the UK we were informed that our base would be Belfast, Northern Ireland. One of our main duties was escorting fast troop convoys en route to the Far East as far as Malta, then rendezvous with an incoming convoy and escort it back to the UK.

During the early summer of 1944, *Burges* supported the invasion of Occupied Europe, 6 June 1944. Afterwards we were engaged on anti-sub-marine patrol in the English Channel for quite some time.

While I was on *Burges*, I passed the examination for Yeoman of Signals and was promoted to the rank of Petty Officer. I never experienced any problems with Signalling/Receiving. I thought the 14" Shutter Lamp, Aldis Lamp, and even the small Heather Lamp, which fitted on binoculars and was used at night, were all excellent and reliable items of equipment.

But, as the saying goes, all things must come to an end, and so it was with me. My relief Yeoman of Signals arrived onboard and I was on my way back to Signal School at Petersfield. My next and final draft was to the staff of Flag Officer Submarines at Gosport, and I was eventually 'demobbed' from there.

Despite some of the most trying circumstances imaginable, the hidden dangers, the tensions and the numerous discomforts which we tend to for-get, it was a thoroughly enjoyable and memorable association while it lasted. The comradeship was outstanding.

THE QUEEN MARY

Anthologist's Note: The three-funnelled *Queen Mary* was a remarkable ship. Launched in 1934, she was one of the premier liners in the world. She was 1,019 feet long, about one-fifth of a mile. Four sets of single-reduction geared turbines powered the great ship. Each developed 160,000 shaft-horsepower, driving four 18-foot diameter propellers. Normal cruising speed was 27 knots, consuming fuel at a rate of about 1,000 tons every 24 hours.

In wartime, items of luxury such as six miles of carpeting and 220 pack-ing cases of china, crystal and silver were removed and stored away in a Southampton warehouse.

The *Queen Mary* entered service for the war effort on 17 April 1940 and was refitted to bring Canadian troops to England as soon as possible. Normally, 1,904 passengers sailed with a crew of 1,285. As a troopship she would normally carry between 14,000 and 16,000 troops with a crew of 200. As the war progressed, the return trip to America would have fewer than 3,000 passengers, mostly wounded, several hundred USAAF and RCAF[32] personnel, ground troops returning home on leave, and a contingent of pregnant WACS[33], WAVES[34] and nurses.

In total, she made 89 wartime crossings. One of her most memorable logbook entries was the following:

'New York to Gourock (River Clyde, Scotland), 16,683 souls aboard. New York, 25 July 1943 – Gourock, 30 July 1943. 3,353 miles, 4 days, 20 hours, 42 minutes – 28.173 knots average speed of passage. The greatest number of human beings ever embarked on one vessel.'

To carry these huge numbers of troops, 'standee' bunks were developed. These were a 'tree' of metal tubes supporting six canvas stretchers to accommodate six sleeping soldiers. The Observation Lounge deck was converted into a maze of five-tiered bunks. Each normal cabin, instead of accommodating one couple, was fitted with 18 triple-tiered units for 54 men. When 16,000 soldiers were being transported across the North Atlantic, three men rotated shifts in each bunk over a 24-hour period.

Meals were served to 2,000 men at a time, commencing at 6.30 a.m. 30,000 eggs were boiled every morning, to give some idea of the catering scale.

The *Queen Mary* was armed with about 40 guns of various calibres, including several anti-aircraft guns. Apart from practice gunnery, they were never used in action.

ANTI-SUBMARINE PATROLS
OVER THE GULF OF MEXICO

Tommy Loftin, Pilot, USAAC/USAAF

Following the sneak attack by the Japanese on the US Navy's Pacific Fleet at Pearl Harbor in December 1941, we found ourselves desperately short of modern aircraft and trained aircrew. Like many other young Americans, I volunteered and was fortunate to graduate and be commissioned as a Second Lieutenant in the US Army Air Corps on 5 August, 1942. I was then assigned as an Instructor at Brook's Field, San Antonio, Texas, but shortly thereafter I was re-assigned and sent to the 124th Observation Squadron, equipped with single-engined North American O-47A aircraft, flying anti-submarine patrols over the Gulf of Mexico from an airbase near New Orleans, on the southeast coast of Louisiana near the mouth of the Mississippi river delta.

The O-47A aircraft had a 450hp engine and carried a crew of three: pilot, observer and a gunner. We carried two 300lb depth charges, one .30 caliber machine gun firing through the propeller, and another .30 caliber swivel-mounted machine gun in the rear cockpit operated by the gunner. Flying lengthy patrol patterns with the single-engined O-47A over the Gulf, about 200 miles from land was, to say the least, nerve-wracking. We challenged ships not displaying the Flag Signals of the Day, and any unreported ships and boats in our patrol area. The duties of the Observer were to relay the information gathered to A/S Headquarters in Miami, Florida. This was all done by CW (Morse Code) on our radio transmitter/receiver. The improved O-47Bs had a larger radial engine, the 1,060hp Wright R-1820, a cruising speed of 200mph, a range of about 800 miles and better radio equipment.

In May 1943, I was transferred from the 124th Observer Squadron to the 21st Anti-Submarine Squadron. We moved about 60 miles northeast from New Orleans AFB to Gulfport AFB, on the south coast of Mississippi. The 21st AS Squadron was equipped with twin-engine B-25 Mitchell medium bombers. The B-25 had two powerful Wright R-2600 engines (the five crewmen felt much more confident with two engines over the Gulf!), it carried six 325lb depth charges, five .50 caliber heavy machine guns, cruised at around 230mph and had a range of about 1,200 miles.

Our patrols were consequently extended by quite a distance, lasting about six or seven hours. We had several sightings of German U-boats in the Gulf, usually as they hurriedly dived after their lookouts had seen us approaching. We released our depth charges as we passed over the submarine's estimated position, and although we saw the patterns explode beneath the surface we had no confirmed sinkings.

It was always a distressing sight to witness the final death throes of American and Allied freighters and oil tankers on fire and sinking in the Gulf after attacks by German U-boats. My elder brother, Able Seaman N. M. Loftin, was aboard the oil tanker *Gulfpin* when it was torpedoed by a U-boat off Grand Island, Lousiana, on 10 July, 1942. Luckily, he was one of the 13 survivors from the crew of about 40. As the tanker was quite old, she had larger portholes than more modern ships. Although trapped below, he managed to squeeze through a porthole and escape before the burning *Gulfpin* went down.

The losses of Allied merchant ships following U-boat attacks during a seven month period between March and September 1942 in the Gulf of Mexico off Port Arthur, southeastern Texas and Gulfport, southwestern Mississipi, a distance of about 300 miles, were about 57 freighters and tankers.

In September 1943, the US Navy took over all A/S work and the 21st A/S Squadron was disbanded. There were 72 pilots involved, all B-25 qualified. We were all transferred up to Ephrata AFB, Washington State, to the 483rd Bombardment Group (H), a B-17 Fortress-equipped outfit, at that time staging for overseas shipment to Italy. We were at Ephrata for six weeks and re-assigned to Lockborne AFB, Columbus, Ohio to become Instructors on the four-engined B-17. We completed the Instructor's Course and transferred to MacDill Field, Tampa, Florida.

Instructing in the B-17s was enjoyable, but occasionally nerve-wracking. I'd been promoted Captain by then. Most of the student pilots had been through B-17 transition and were proficient, ten-man crews which fitted together as close-knit teams. After completing their phase training they were ready for combat assignment overseas.

In December 1944, I completed my phase training for combat. My crew and I were then ordered to the New York docks. When we saw the name of the ship we were loading on, *Queen Mary*, we immediately knew we were going to the European Theater of Operations.

The *Queen Mary* was a huge trans-Atlantic liner and had over 16,000 troops aboard when we departed the Zone of the Interior. We had escorts of aircraft, dirigible 'blimps', and smaller escorting ships during the first day at sea. The second day we awoke to find ourselves all alone travelling at speed on a vast expanse of the North Atlantic without escorts. On the fifth day we awoke to find we again had the same type of escorts we'd had on our departure from New York. On the sixth day we docked at Gourock, Scotland.

My crew was eventually assigned to the 95th Bombardment Group, based at Horham Airfield, Near Eye, Suffolk. After flying one combat mission to Berlin and five mercy missions dropping food supplies to the starving people of Holland in April/May 1945, Operation 'Manna/Chow-hound', we flew home in a B-17 named 'Better Duck' after V-E Day in mid-May, 1945.

After 30 days' furlough at our respective homes throughout the US we reported to Sioux Falls AFB, South Dakota to stage for combat missions against Japan, but in mid-August 1945, V-J Day was declared while we were at Sioux Falls and all activity ceased apart from a few local flights.

In February 1946, I was transferred to Randolph Field, San Antonio, Texas and was released from active duty. The wheel had turned full circle.

HMS *PETARD* AND *U-559*

The events of 30 October 1942, and their significance
Mark Baldwin

From the start of the war, the British were able to read many of Germany's military wireless communications, because we had developed techniques for breaking the codes then in use. The codebreaking was done at Bletchley Park, a country house some 50 miles north-west of London. Most of Germany's military messages were enciphered using an ingenious portable machine – the Enigma – which had been adopted before the war by all branches of the German armed forces, and many civil agencies such as the Post Office, railways and secret police. The Enigma had at its heart three rotors containing wiring of different patterns, which effected the enciphering by switching one letter into another. Such was the sophistication of its design that the machine could be set up to work in many millions of different ways.

Our ability to read enormous numbers of enciphered wireless messages was of particular value in the conduct of the Battle of the Atlantic, because Dönitz was using wireless to order U-boats at sea to proceed to specific locations to lie in wait for, or to intercept, our convoys. From our deciphering of these messages, and from other sources such as sighting reports, Western Approaches Command was able to advise our convoys on routes which would minimise the chance of U-boat attack. Intelligence alone does not, of course, provide total immunity, but by such means we were keeping our merchant shipping losses to an acceptable, though uncomfortable, level of around 100,000 tons per month during the second half of 1941.

On 1 February 1942, by an amazing piece of planning, the U-boat service alone modified all its Enigma machines, both afloat and ashore; into each machine was introduced a fourth rotor – an extra element which made the codes even more complicated. This move made it impossible for the British to interpret the messages being sent to the U-boats. Partly as a direct result, our monthly losses of merchant shipping in the North Atlantic climbed from an acceptable level of around 100,000 tons to five or six times that figure. Dönitz had said that if his U-boats could sink 800,000 tons of Allied shipping per month, worldwide, then Germany would win the war.

His monthly target figure was exceeded three times in 1942, and there were few who doubted that Germany was at this time winning the war. After the war, Churchill said that during the war many things had worried him, but the only thing which had frightened him was the 'the U-boat peril'. In 1942, he had every reason to be frightened.

Although the entry of the USA into the war after the Japanese attack on Pearl Harbor in December 1941 had improved our prospects, this was a desperate time for Britain. The rate of loss of merchant vessels, crews and cargoes was unsustainable, making it impossible to import into Britain raw materials and foodstuffs on a scale sufficient to keep ourselves fed and keep our factories working, while still waging war on an appropriate scale. Plans were even laid for the evacuation to Canada of the central war planning units, the Royal Family and others.

The Admiralty was pressing Bletchley Park to provide details of U-boat communications as had been done so successfully in 1941, but the code-breakers could neither provide these details nor estimate when they might be able to do so. The outlook was grim, and nobody could foresee how we might escape disaster. In the event, the breakthrough was achieved by the Royal Navy's good seamanship and outstanding bravery, rather than by code-breaking skills.

In the early morning of 30 October 1942, Lieutenant Commander Mark Thornton, Commanding Officer of the destroyer HMS *Petard*, at Port Said, Egypt was ordered to proceed to a point where a U-boat had been sighted. Five destroyers then engaged in a coordinated hunt for the submerged vessel, but many hours of Asdic-location and depth-charging failed to produce any positive result. However, Lieutenant Commander Thornton continued the attack after nightfall and his dogged perseverance was eventually rewarded by a great foaming on the surface of the water, and the strong, pungent smell of diesel fuel oil, and then the dark, ominous shape of a German submarine, *U-559*, suddenly broke the surface.

The U-boat's Commanding Officer, Kapitänleutnant Hans Heidtmann, had realised that his vessel had been so damaged by the depth charges that the lives of his crew would be needlessly endangered if he didn't surface immediately. Aware of the potential harm the U-boat's gun could inflict, Lieutenant Commander Thornton took no chances and *Petard*'s guns were brought to bear on the surfaced U-boat, causing further damage, one 4-inch shell passing right through the conning tower. Gunfire was only halted when it was clear that the U-boat's crew were abandoning ship.

Lieutenant Commander Thornton had prepared his crew for just such an event, and was keen to send a boarding party over to the U-boat as soon as possible, even while the German crew were still in the water. *Petard*'s First Lieutenant Anthony Fasson and Able Seaman Colin Grazier stripped off, dived into the sea and swam across to the U-boat, and made their way into the damaged submarine. They were soon joined by Tommy Brown, a 16-year-old NAAFI[35] assistant, who had lied about his age in order to serve his country.

Fasson and Grazier cleared all the available documents from the Wireless

---

[35] Navy, Army and Air Force Institutes: an organization providing canteens, shops, etc. for British military personnel home or abroad.

Operator's desk and the Captain's cabin. They passed these to Brown who, in turn, passed them down to his shipmates who had come across to the wallowing U-boat in one of *Petard*'s whalers. Despite rough seas, the priceless documents were taken across safely to *Petard*. Meanwhile, Fasson and Grazier again descended the steel ladders into the U-boat in an attempt to collect more material, and were struggling with a piece of equipment, possibly a radar set or an Enigma machine, when it became clear to those on the surface that the U-boat was sinking fast. Tommy Brown called down the conning tower to his colleagues, urging them to come out, but the submarine sank so fast that they were unable to escape. He, and all other members of the boarding party, were picked up by the whaler. The U-boat's engineer later confirmed that he'd opened *U-559*'s seacocks, thus ensuring that it would sink very rapidly. Seven of its crew were also lost.

The documents seized by Lieutenant Fasson and AB Grazier were sent to Bletchley Park where they proved of immense value. By mid-December 1942, the code-breakers had used this new information to devise an effective technique for breaking the 4-rotor codes – a goal which had eluded them for over ten months. This proved to be a vital factor in turning the tide of the Battle of the Atlantic, because from then onwards we never again for long lost the ability to read the U-boat messages.

Although there were to be some bitter and damaging convoy battles in the spring of 1943, never again would we suffer the frightful losses that we did in 1942 – a year in which the Allies lost over 1,000 merchant vessels in the North Atlantic alone, with a total tonnage of 5.5 million tons. Lieutenant Fasson and AB Grazier had undoubtedly played a leading role in this change of fortune. Their brave and prompt action led to the war's most significant capture of Enigma material, although few appreciated this at the time.

Thirty years passed before the immense value of the work of Bletchley Park was revealed, and yet another thirty years before a fitting memorial to Anthony Fasson, Colin Grazier and Tommy Brown was raised in Grazier's home town of Tamworth, Staffordshire. The memorial was dedicated on 27 October 2002, a date chosen to coincide as closely as possible with the 60th anniversary of the boarding of *U-559*.

DON'S DIARY

J. D. 'Don' Gooch, Signalman, HMS *Boadicea*

I served on *Boadicea* as a signalman for about two years and apart from Atlantic convoys, I had one trip to Russia in convoy PQ 15, departing Reykjavik, Iceland for Murmansk, north-western Russia in late April 1942, returning on QP 12 during early May. I was also at Oran during the North African landings in November 1942, during which I made the following diary entries:

Sunday 18 October 1942

Left Gourock with *Beagle* and, after passing through boom, proceeded at 23 knots towards Moville. *Bulldog* caught up with us about halfway and we started to do high-speed manouevres for exercise.

On arrival at Moville, we went alongside the oiler and in tying up, we got a wire hawser round our starboard screw. We sent a signal to Commodore, Londonderry, for a diver who, we were told, would arrive next morning.

Monday 19 October

Bulldog and *Beagle* shoved off at 0700 hours and we were to await the diver. Diver arrived at 1030 and he managed to cut the hawser away by 1200. Proceeded to sea at 1230 at 14 knots and caught up the convoy at 1800 hours.

Had the first watch – weather was good – beautiful moon. Thought of a nice walk I could have had if I'd been at home.

Tuesday 20 October

Weather dull and wet. Sea – heavy swell with 15 foot troughs. Ship rolling heavily. New chaps in our Mess not very happy about the weather. Old salts quite happy (including me), although roll makes everything inconvenient. Everything has to be lashed down.

Convoy having heavy weather – reduced speed to 7 knots to allow stragglers to catch up.

Wednesday 21 October

Weather still bad – looks like keeping up. Ship still rolling. New hands still sick – old hands still cursing the roll. Cups and plates still being smashed. *Bulldog* dropped astern to round up stragglers.

Told by signal to expect escort from Sunderlands but weather too bad to see them!

Thursday 22 October

Weather shows no sign of abating. Roll still bad – new hands *still* sick – old hands *still* cursing. Officers fed up as well. Told we are altering course south tomorrow. Hopes rise for better weather.

Friday 23 October

Weather clearing. Roll not so heavy. New hands cheer up – old hands stop cursing! *Bulldog* reports enemy aircraft on horizon. Gun crews close up. Aircraft disappears. Revert to normal.

Escort of B-24 Liberators turns up and relieves the monotony. Weather fine with hot sun. Let's hope it keeps up! Action stations are being exercised tonight at 1800 hours. Beautiful sunset tonight. Weather turns chilly later but weather dry with full moon.

Saturday 24 October

Weather remains fine with hot sun although ship still tends to roll. Turned in this afternoon to make up for sleep lost during the Morning watch. On watch during first Dog, kept very busy with flag signals. Signal from Liberator escorting us says, "Estimate two hits on U-boat." Turning in now ready for the Middle.

Sunday 25 October

'Jimmy' orders us to repeat all flag signals – result was we tore four flags and I had to climb up the mast and release one of them. With the ship rolling this was no joke!

Weather still quite fine with occasional heavy showers. Still trundling along at 8 knots.

Monday 26 October

Same as any other day, only sun a bit hotter. One ship straggled a long way behind – trawler detailed off to look after it. Two ships with escort of two trawlers left convoy this evening to go to Lisbon. We altered course. Only four hundred miles from Gibraltar now – expect to arrive within two days.

Tuesday 27 October

Poured with rain during the Morning watch but weather cleared during the day. Cook this morning. I made a 'Manchester Lovely' and an awning for the pie.

1230 hours – Lookouts spotted smoke on the horizon so we went out to investigate. Increased speed to 23 knots. We found it was one of the trawlers who had gone to Lisbon last night, rejoining the convoy.

Wednesday 28 October

Weather still good only sea a bit heavier. More plates and cups broken. Altered course towards Gib. – ETA 2200 hours. Arrived off Gib. but weather too bad to enter in the dark. Hung around outside all night. Very wet night – got soaked!

Thursday 29 October

Entered Gibraltar after ten days at sea. What a spectacular sight 'The Rock' is! *Rodney* is here, with about four destroyers.

Stayed on board tonight to let other Buntings go ashore. Four of our Mess came back flat out and we had to put them to bed.

Friday 30 October

Got browned off for an exercise of oiling at sea. We oiled a cruiser and then came back at about 1800 hours. *Charybdis* and *Aurora* came into Gib. *Furious* was flying off aircraft for exercise and then she came in with eight more destroyers. *Bermuda* arrived yesterday with escort of four destroyers.

Went ashore for an hour and bought some grapes and pomegranates. Plenty of bananas, oranges and lemons about.

Saturday 31 October
Nothing much doing. Weather still good. Bought some more grapes. *Scylla* came in with two more destroyers.

Sunday 1 November
Weather roasting – had Divisions and Church on board. Had a gramophone request programme on board which I arranged and announced. One of our chaps got hit with a bottle ashore.

Monday 2 November
Lord Roberts came in today. Went ashore to see if I could get any records – no luck.

1600 hours – left Gib. with nine other destroyers.

Tuesday 3 November
At sea with the others in 'Arrowhead' formation – 16 knots. Going to meet Force 'H' – weather wet.

Wednesday 4 November
0800 hours – Met Force 'H' with escort of 11 destroyers and cruiser *Argonaut*. Took over escort and previous escort shoved off. Force 'H' consists of *Renown, Duke of York, Nelson, Victorious* and *Formidable*. Tons of flag signals. Practised firing at target towed by aircraft. *Bermuda* joined us at 1700 hours.

Thursday 5 November
Cruised around with Force 'H'. Met large convoy of troopships. Went alongside *Duke of York* to get a letter and then transferred it to the *Victorious*, collecting stores for the *Biter* at the same time.

Friday 6 November
Went into Gib. and left Force 'H' to carry on with four destroyers. Left Gib. at 2030 hours and as soon as we got out the Captain broadcast over our SRE and told us what we were going to do. It seemed we were launching an attack on Algiers, Oran and Casablanca. Over 500 ships had passed through the

Straits of Gibraltar the night before. We are going to attack Oran with *Rodney*, *Aurora* and *Jamaica* and 12 destroyers. Two ex-American cutters (*Hartland* and *Walney*) were going to go into the harbour at Oran to land 600 US Rangers. We were going to patrol three miles off the town to see that no destroyer or submarine attempted to leave the harbour. The *Aurora* was going to stand off about six miles to bombard if necessary – we hoped to take Oran peacefully if possible, but if not, we are ready for them. The carriers *Furious*, *Biter* and *Dasher* are with us to give us air support. Met large convoy of troops and supplies during the night.

Saturday 7 November
Very quiet day. Still with convoy. Everybody keyed up for attack Sunday morning.

Sunday 8 November
0100 – Zero hour. We are at Action Stations. Our ship is lying off Oran. Town is lit up as they evidently don't expect any trouble. Four Motor Launches have just passed us to take up their position just outside the breakwater. All is quiet.

0300 hours – First sign of action? Cutters are evidently in the harbour – firing is going on and we can see tracer shells going through the air. MLs are firing back at shore installations. Both cutters on fire. Searchlight being trained on cutters and motor launches – the cruiser *Aurora* opens fire on the searchlight and it goes out. We are trained on it as well in case it spots us. Light comes on several times but each time *Aurora* lets fly and it goes out.

For the rest of the night firing goes on in the town and the cutters are still blazing. Their ammunition starts exploding. These ships are the same class as the *Lulworth* who rammed a submarine four times a little while ago. Reports reach us that troops have landed successfully either side of the town and one aerodrome is captured.

Daylight comes and we see *Aurora* and some of our destroyers around. We give them the unknown call sign in case they are not ours. Quite all right, they are friendly. See another destroyer almost invisible against the cliffs. Challenge it with unknown call sign – no reply. Challenge it with secret call sign – still no reply! Skipper gives order to open fire. Keep on challenging to make sure and No. 1 tells me to stop. Enemy returns fire and we find we have taken on three of them! Skipper tells me to ask *Aurora* to help and I do so. It seems she will never open up. Eventually we withdraw and *Aurora* finishes them off. Action on our part took 19 minutes and we fired about 140 shells at them. At that rate we had between 2-300 fired at us and only one scored a hit. We were being straddled and we could see purple and red splashes all around us. We were hit in the Stoker's Mess deck and shell exploded in shell room. We were lucky – only one man killed and one other seriously wounded. We are making water fast and we have to keep pumping to keep water down. After the action we hover around six miles from the town. *Aurora* has been fired at about six times with torpedoes and we start chasing submarines. Something I've missed.

During the night *Aurora* opens fire on an enemy destroyer and sets it on fire. Firing ceases and then the fire goes out suddenly so I presume it was sunk!

0900 hours – Suddenly we are fired on again and we find that a 9.4-inch battery has opened fire on us! Our guns are only 4.7-inch so we cannot return the fire. Skipper increases speed to 30 knots and zigzags. He ordered smoke floats to be dropped and the engine room to make smoke. Lieutenant Commander Brodrick, the Skipper, deserves a VC. He stood up on the bridge watching the splashes and judging where the next shell was going to drop and altered course immediately. Not one shell hit us and after a hectic quarter of an hour, we were out of range. We started cruising around out of range – keeping on chasing submarines. An RAF Walrus dropped depth charges on one but don't know if he scored a hit.

1300 hours – stopped to fix collision mat over hole in our side – MLs protecting us from submarines. One ML had picked up a survivor from aircraft from *Dasher*. Another had hit the boom in the harbour and made a mess of her bows. *Rodney* has opened fire on the 9.4-inch guns with her 16-inch guns – won't know what results. All our meat had to be thrown over the side because of the sea water and carbon dioxide which had polluted it – from now on we are on Corned Dog. Buried the seamen killed in action at sea – Lieutenant Commander Brodrick read a short service. At night we resumed our patrol outside Oran harbour at increased range.

Monday 9 November

Firing continued ashore but no action at sea. Have had signal to say that *Brilliant* has sunk a destroyer and a sloop. We now take over Air/Sea patrol with *MS 13* at 'Z ' Beach – all our Troop Carriers are anchored there.

1200 hours – go alongside oiler to top up. Take the opportunity of plugging hole in our side: heavy swell; we snap three hawsers. During afternoon we see two Spitfires open fire on something ashore. Immediately everyone opens fire on them so we presume they are two that the French have captured and are using them against us? Army are landing tanks all day – we can see them ashore.

Received signal that two enemy destroyers have attempted to escape from Oran – *Jamaica* intercepts and so badly damages one that she has to be beached – the other is damaged and she nips back into harbour. *Jamaica* pursues, but has to retire on being straddled by 9.4-inch battery.

1530 hours – Leave oiler and resume A/S patrol. At night, ourselves and two other destroyers carry out sweep at 15 knots in case of attack by surface craft.

Tuesday 10 November

0630 hours – *Rodney* commences to bombard the 9.4-inch battery – dive-bombers from Force 'H' attack as well. Will quote two signals from spotting aircraft:-

1st Aircraft – "No ship has opened fire yet."

2nd Aircraft – "Well, *someone* is knocking hell out of the batteries!"

Sounds good – keep it up!

Farndale and *Calp* stand by to enter the harbour at first available opportunity. Report received stated that one tank column is in the centre of Oran – Americans are launching a big attack there today.

1400 hours – Received signal saying General Oliver negotiating with the French for an armistice – further signal says French Fleet have given in and also French Army; not confirmed yet. *Rodney* has just been ordered to cease fire.

We have just increased speed to intercept any enemy merchant ships that attempt to leave harbour at Nostaganem. Missed something again. On patrol outside Nostaganem – merchant ships don't attempt to leave.

Wednesday 11/11/42

0430 hours – Received signal from *Viceroy of India* to say she has been torpedoed.

0500 hours – Received signal ordering us to proceed to give assistance.

0630 hours – Arrive at ship which has heavy list. If possible, we are going to tow her to Oran or beach her. Master of *Viceroy* wants crew taken off first. They lower boats and we take on 424 survivors – 350 Lascars – the rest are British. Only 5 were killed when the torpedo hit. Master is last to leave and he goes round to see what chances there are to save her. He comes on board and says: "It is hopeless..."

So we just stand by until she sinks, which isn't long. It's tragic to see such a lovely ship go under. She goes under stern first and her funnels snap off as she disappears. When she is under her boilers burst.

Captain decides that as we have so many survivors we will go straight to Gibraltar. We increase to 28 knots and arrive at 1700 hours. We land the survivors on the *Llangibby Castle* and then go into the harbour.

Thursday 12 November

Commodore D comes on board to see the damage. Compliments Chief Engineer on excellent emergency patching – Captain says docking unnecessary. There's a buzz that we are going back to UK tonight; buzz is correct.

Left Gibraltar at 1630 hours with 11 Troopers and 2 Carriers. As soon as we got through the Straits it started to blow.

Friday 13 November

Weather very rough – sea breaking over the bridge. One ship lost convoy during the night – one destroyer went back to look for it.

0930 hours – ship torpedoed, two destroyers stay behind to pick up survivors and keep the U-boat at bay; convoy carries on.

Saturday 14 November

Nothing new – weather very rough. There's a leak in our mess, water all over the deck. Mess traps go sliding backwards and forwards, buckets of water get tipped over and forms join in. A box of dried peas falls off shelf, cups and plates get broken, knife drawer comes out and everything, including the chaps, joins in the mad surge backwards and forwards across the deck.

Sunday 15 November

Weather even worse. Ensign halliard gets snapped down aft, so 'Muggins' goes down to put a new one up; while I'm down there a wave breaks right over me and I get soaked to the skin!

A destroyer joins us today who had been picking up survivors. Her mast had been carried away by the sea.

The First Lieutenant closes the upper deck at night and when the watches change over, he reduces speed to eight knots and they go down in convoy.

Monday 16 November

Weather much calmer. Have run out of meat, spuds and bread! Our fridge got blown to bits when the shell exploded, so we can't keep any meat or yeast on board. We had been keeping the meat on the upper deck, but the sea got at it and the spuds and turned it all bad, so it had to be ditched. So, for the rest of the trip, we go without.

Tuesday 17 November

Weather still calm but cold. *Cleveland* leaves us and *Escapade* takes over as SO.[36] We change screen and take over position at head of convoy. The day quite eventful.

Wednesday 18 November

Straggler has caught up with us and rejoins the convoy. We receive orders to go in search of crew of a Catalina reported down in the sea. We search all day off the Irish coast but unfortunately can't find them – they may have already been picked up.

Rejoin convoy at about 1700 hours. We are out in the Irish Sea on the last lap of our journey.

Thursday 19 November

0400 hours – Came up to take over morning watch to find we are sailing up

---

[36] Senior Officer.

the Clyde past good old Ailsa Craig. Its been a month and a day since we saw her and I think it's been the most hectic month I have ever spent.

Drop anchor off Gourock at 0530 hours and everyone relaxes except the Signalman of the Watch who still has to look out for signals!

0800 hours – A pilot comes on board and we up anchor and proceed upriver to Glasgow.

2300 hours – Move into dry dock.

Friday 20 November
Repair experts come on board and estimate that repairs will take three weeks. 1600 hours – Proceed on leave for nine days – well earned I think! Look forward to a real night's sleep – the first since I left England on October 18th.

A 'SORT-OUT' IN GIB.

Iain Nethercott, ex-HMS *Keith*

The wartime Royal Navy produced so many marvellous characters, especially in submarines, the smaller escort ships, and patrol craft, whose crews always considered that they belonged to separate navies to the 'Big Ships' with all their terrible bullshit.

The problems arose when these cheerful brigands went ashore in a 'Pusser' naval port, infested with Naval Patrols and sometimes even a Warrant 'Jaunty' (Warrant Officer).

I remember Gibraltar in late 1942: I was on HM Submarine *Tactician* when some of the lads from our crew, together with several more from HM Submarine *Turbulent* (sunk with all hands during her next patrol on 27 February 1943), went ashore. We all ended up at the 'Universal Bar' which was crammed to the rafters with matelots from dozens of small ships from Canada, America, Norway, Greece, France, etc.

The bar had the only women in Gibraltar, a ladies' band set up on a platform, surrounded with what looked like barbed wire to foil amorous sailors. All the other women and children had been evacuated to England in 1939.

One drunken 'Canuck' (Canadian) sailor was up on a rickety table singing 'This Old Hat of Mine' and gradually stripping off as he completed each verse, to deafening roars of approval from the inebriated crowd.

Then in marched a Warrant 'Jaunty' at the head of about twenty or so quite burly RN patrolmen carrying stout wooden staves. The W/J strode through the crowd and attempted to arrest the disbelieving Colonial. Unfortunately, we had other ideas. The patrolmen were given a good beating-up and fled, while the little popinjay was grabbed unceremoniously, and a large mob marched him kicking and screaming with fright out into the cool night air, with the apparent determined intention of hanging him from the nearest lamp-post.

The Canadians were fighting mad as usual, the other foreign nationalities were only too eager to see blood, and it was only the British contingent who realised that things had gone far enough. So it was us who had to fight it out with all these foreigners for the possession of, of all things, a bloody Warrant 'Jaunty'.

It was a good scrap. Being a veteran of numerous pub fights I had armed myself with a heavy chair leg. About 200 of us eventually formed a 'Flying Wedge', and beating the living daylights out of the 'Jaunty's' captors, had just grabbed the terrified individual when we were suddenly confronted by dozens of Royal Marines with fixed bayonets who had arrived, as if by magic, to quell the riot.

Very fortunately, we Petty Officers managed to convey to the Captain of Marines that we were actually the 'Relief Party', and his men were pointed in the direction of the Canucks, etc.

We then faded into the nearest 'Boiled Oil Shop' to lick our wounds, and to count our blessings.

We lived life to the full in those uncertain days...

A CHRISTMAS MIRACLE

Lieutenant Jack Keir, RN, HMS *Boadicea*

The motor boat was adrift. We felt helpless as it disappeared into the blizzard with its precious load of fresh provisions intended for our

Christmas dinner. It was the eve of Christmas 1942. My ship, HMS *Boadicea*, a fleet destroyer, was anchored in Kola Inlet, the waterway that leads to Murmansk, North Russia.

World War Two was three years old. 1942 had been a particularly bad year at sea – the U-boats had sunk over six million tons of Allied shipping and, on the 'Russian Run', the Royal Navy had escorted 13 convoys round the North Cape with the loss of 63 ships.

The prospect of spending Christmas in the bleak wastes of Kola was not cheering. However, we had taken the precaution of stocking up with turkeys, plum puddings, decorations and festive trimmings before leaving our base at Greenock, Scotland.

On the 2,000-mile voyage north we had run out of fresh provisions. The Russians had nothing to offer other than yak meats and black bread. That meat was as tough as old boots and the bread went sour in two days.

Somebody suggested that we should put two cases of whisky in the motor boat and do a round of the merchant ships we had just brought from the United Kingdom – bartering scotch for vegetables. The idea was a great success and the boat returned to our stern boom loaded down with 'goodies'.

The duty part of the watch was piped to muster on the quarterdeck to unload. The Arctic in winter is no place to have a boat in the water so the sooner it was cleared of the provisions and hoisted the better. The men took hold of the painter (a stout rope in the bows of the boat) to haul the boat alongside. As she came clear of the ship's stern, a sudden squall and flurry of snow struck her. The rope, encrusted with ice, slipped, the men couldn't hold it and the end of the rope splashed into the sea. We watched as the boat-keeper tried to start the engine but, in a matter of seconds, the boat vanished. The blizzard pulled a blanket of snow over the whole scene.

What to do next? What a situation to be faced with at Christmas... We felt powerless. Hope of ever seeing the boat again seemed slight. As for the boatkeeper, his chances of survival were nil.

Alerted by the commotion, the Captain came on deck. Although he had an unbroken record of destroyer command since the war began, he had never been confronted with a situation like this before.

A hurried conversation took place. It was suggested that a volunteer party should set off in the ship's only other boat, a whaler which had no power –

only oars and sails – in a bid to find the missing craft.

The 'Old Man' turned the suggestion down flat.

"I've already lost one man. I am not prepared to lose another five," he snapped and went below.

Nothing more could be done. We had to wait another day – or rather the brief lightening of the southern sky at midday which served for an Arctic day. This would provide a brief opportunity to make a search.

At first light, about 1100 hours, the whaler was prepared and, with a crew of five volunteers and the First Lieutenant in charge, set sail. The sea was calm, but the crew found itself sitting in a film of ice particles which lay, like a misty mantle, over the surface of the water to a height of about three feet. The men all looked alike, huddled in sheepskin coats, balaclava helmets and scarves against the bitter cold. The air temperature was about 10 degrees below freezing and the sea only slightly warmer. The First Lieutenant had hand-picked his crew. They each had a special skill – seamanship, handling of small boats, navigation or signalling. 'Jimmy' had the impossible task of searching a gulf about 30 miles long and two miles wide in two hours of twilight.

To add zest to the venture, there were frequent air raids – the nearest German base was at Petsamo, only about 70 miles away. The whaler sailed the most likely course of the drifting motor boat. Beaches were examined through binoculars. Nothing was seen.

The coastline was in the grip of winter – a truly Christmassy scene. There was no apparent life. Nothing moved. Nothing grew.

Then the wind dropped. The whaler was left in icy stillness. The light began to fail, so 'Jimmy' decided to call off the search. The crew turned the boat and made for *Boadicea* under oars. The long pull back kept them warm but 'Jimmy', who was at the helm, had to be hoisted from his seat in the stern sheets when the whaler arrived alongside the ship. He was frozen stiff and incapable of movement.

By tradition, Christmas Day in the Royal Navy is a great event. The messes are decorated and the galley staff make a special effort. After a short church service, the Captain does rounds led by the youngest man in the ship dressed in the Skipper's uniform. Routine, just for a moment, becomes topsey-turvey.

We went through it all and, after rounds, the Captain invited the Chiefs and the Petty Officers to the wardroom for a beer – an unknown departure from discipline in those days. It could only have happened in a small ship. There is no room to dance and skylark in a destroyer so we organized an inter-mess tug-of-war and the Red Navy Choir, a group of tip-top singers, came to entertain us. But the loss of our shipmate placed a dampener on the celebrations. We could not capture the true Christmas spirit.

When the festivities were over a Russian naval launch was sighted approaching the ship. Out of it jumped the lost boatkeeper looking none the worse for wear! He told us that after finding himself adrift, he tried several times to get the boat's engine started, but failed. He realised that his chances of survival were slim and there was little he could do but wait for the end.

After drifting for a long time the boat struck some rocks. He was thrown out, but managed to scramble ashore wet and shivering. He ran along the beach knowing that if he stayed still he would freeze. Sighting a light, he made for it and burst into a small dwelling. Here a group of Russians gave him dry clothing, hot food and arranged for his return to his ship.

The boatkeeper's arrival made our Christmas complete. What an unexpected present! We sailed for home without our boat. It was returned on our next trip to Kola. Although damaged and stripped of its valuables, we were glad to see it again. Repairs were made and it continued to do us good service. As for all the provisions – spuds, onions, cabbages and fruit – they were all lost when the boat hit the rocks.

ARCTIC CONVOYS

Excerpt from *British Destroyers* by E. J. March

On 22 December 1942 a convoy of 14 ships (JW 51B) sailed for Murmansk escorted by two cruisers, six destroyers and five smaller vessels. A week later a U-boat reported their position and *Hipper*, *Lützow* and six powerful destroyers put to sea. In heavy weather the British destroyer *Oribi* lost touch with the other ships off Bear Island and proceeded independently.

About 8.30 a.m. on 31 December, in the almost total darkness of an Arctic day, contact was made with the enemy, but as Russian destroyers were expected it was difficult to identify the German ships until fire was opened on *Obdurate*. The convoy altered course under cover of a smoke screen while *Onslow* and *Orwell* made for *Hipper* approaching from the north; the Leader was soon badly hit and Captain Sherbrooke severely wounded. The Commanding Officer of *Obedient* now took command; then *Lützow* was sighted on the south flank of the convoy where *Achates* lay disabled. *Obdurate*, *Obedient* and *Orwell* closed to attack and held the cruiser off until the German forces retired to the westward. Meanwhile, *Onslow* had retaken station on her convoy.

The Battle of the Barents Sea had far-reaching consequences. When Hitler was told that five destroyers and two 6-inch gun cruisers had, for four hours, prevented a pocket battleship, an 8-inch gun cruiser and six destroyers from sinking a valuable convoy, he flew into one of his ungovernable rages. Grand Admiral Raeder thereupon resigned and Admiral Dönitz, a ruthless exponent of U-boat warfare, became Commander-in-Chief of the German Navy.

Oribi, proceeding independently to Kola Inlet, encountered severe cold, high wind and sea which steadily reduced her sea-worthiness and fighting efficiency. Freezing spray covered everything with heavy masses of ice, driving snow collected in every crevice on the windward side and packed tight by the bitter wind soon made mast and rigging almost solid ice. During the night of 29/30 December, rolling increased and the ship was sluggish in recovering. De-icing was attempted by the watch on deck but was ineffectual owing to the lack of suitable tools and the dangerous conditions.

Soon after midnight when "the after whaler had been rolled under and severely damaged, it was decided to flood Nos. 1 and 2 oil fuel tanks for ballast – about 100 tons. This improved stability... During the morning watch course was 090 degrees, speed 16 knots, wind NW force 7, sea 57, air temperature 18 degrees, sea temperature 29 degrees."

The Commanding Officer estimated the weight of ice at from 80 to 100 tons, anchors and windward side of 'A' gun being covered a foot thick, bridge six inches, the thickness of the masts and rigging was almost doubled, aerials three inches diameter solid ice, side and decks had up to a foot.

A WARTIME BATTLE AGAINST THE ELEMENTS

Alfred Carpenter, HMS *Caldwell*

From *Warship World* magazine, Winter 1986 (Reproduced by kind permission of *Warship World* magazine/Maritime Books)

This is the story of an old destroyer's epic fight against appalling weather conditions during the Atlantic winter of 1942-1943. The hero of the story was Lieutenant Commander Eric Mackay, DSC, RNR. The ship, an ex-American 'four stacker' dating from 1918, had the task of escorting Allied merchant ships which were Great Britain's lifeline.

On 12 December 1942, HMS *Caldwell*, with two others of her class, was with a convoy 700 miles north-east of Newfoundland. The barometer was dropping ominously, the seas had been building up and a rough time was clearly in store for the columns of slow moving ships. That night they were in a full gale when suddenly, out of the darkness, *Caldwell*'s Officer of the Watch saw high up to port a white crested, towering sea surging towards him. He stared wide-eyed. There was nothing he could do. Then it crashed onto the ship with a thunderous roar, making her stagger and tremble. The Captain, seated in his cabin in the bridge structure, was pitched to his feet and almost catapulted through the door. He dashed down the passage towards the bridge ladder, followed by a green flood that was pouring in from somewhere. From the top rung of the ladder he saw the last of the toppling wall, still suspended over his ship; then he felt the icy water trying to tear him loose and carry him away. Drenched and winded he forced his way to the bridge and took command.

The great wave had spilled away but left ample evidence of its immense power. The port side of the bridge was smashed and the rum locker, with its precious contents, completely demolished. The forward bulkhead of the Captain's cabin was stove in and the scuttle breached.

When *Caldwell*'s damage was reported to higher authority she was ordered to return to St. John's, Newfoundland and when a suitable opportunity offered, course was set. Repair parties were put to work, plugging breaches with wood and blankets and shoring bulkheads, particularly in the area of two other cabins where scuttles, close to the water line, had been demolished and were taking in sea. Water sloshed in mess decks and cabins while strong rum fumes percolated everywhere. Progress was made but then it started to blow even harder and at 0200 hours on 16 December an entry in the log read "Running into hurricane."

Shortly, a strange hush fell over the sea. The little ship found herself in an oasis of eerie silence and calmer water. The Captain murmured, "We're passing through the centre of the depression." Then from afar came the first low whisper of a great turbulence, of the forces of nature gone mad as suddenly the hurricane tore into the area with a howling that struck the watchers dumb with awe. The sky was black, against which ghostly patches of grey rushed past; the wind screamed though the rigging and through the holes in the damaged bridge, tugging at the men on watch who held on for all they were worth. *Caldwell* pitched wildly in the seas that now rose and yawed in all directions. This continued without abatement with the small destroyer still hove to.

At about 1400 hours on 18 December, after 36 hours of the hurricane, it was the turn of Lieutenant Commander Mackay, who was in the charthouse just aft of the bridge, to look up and see a colossal green mountain of sea staring him in the face. He made a leap for the door but was hurled back as the sea struck, making the whole ship quiver and shake. It literally forced *Caldwell* under, ton upon ton of water engulfing her, pouring into the wardroom, cabins and mess deck. This time scuttles on the starboard side were smashed and seas poured directly in. The ship's plates strained and groaned under the impact as the men listened and waited with bated breath.

Once again the Captain dashed to the helmsman's side through an avalanche of salt water. The bridge was in chaos. Men lay on their backs bruised and bleeding. "Steering has broken down, Sir!" reported the Quartermaster, and while the tiller flat was being manned for emergency steering aft, the Captain pushed the ship's bows back into the teeth of the hurricane with her engines and fought to hold her there. Eventually the tiller flat reported ready to take over and *Caldwell* had survived the second attempt at her destruction.

The starboard wing of the bridge was now folded up. The ship's starboard side from bow to stern had been swept clear of minor fittings, including the whaler and its davits. It was found that scuttles in more cabins were stove in and the Captain's cabin utterly demolished; even his safe was forced open. He realised that the ship could not survive another blow like the last two and must now run before the storm. But the problem was to turn in the wild seas without being pushed over. There was only one solution; precious oil fuel would have to be jettisoned to form a temporary calm. This was done, "Hard a-starboard!" ordered, and after some nasty moments when she seemed to take ages to answer, the ship was successfully brought round.

Keeping the hurricane on the starboard quarter, a course roughly due east was steered, away from St. John's. It was so cold on the wrecked bridge that two-hour watches were stood. Seamen's duties were arranged so that there was no traffic along the deck, those working forward and those aft likewise. In the tiller flat four men were required to steer by hand, an exhausting task.

It was not possible to move about anywhere below without holding on as the ship rolled savagely in the mountainous seas. On the morning of 19 December, the Duty Stoker reported that the Chief Stoker could not be found. He never was. He had busied himself during all hours with little rest, shoring, repairing, and generally attending to the safety of the ship. He had presumably been washed overboard. In the howling winds and commotion that prevailed, no cry for help would have been heard, nor could anything have been done if it had.

Later on, during 19 December, the weather moderated enough to try and head for St. John's, but the little ship slammed so badly that it was necessary to 'tack' first to the south and then to the north of the course, which anyway was approximate as no sights had been possible for days.

The sun at last appeared on 21 December and the resulting fix indicated the grim fact that *Caldwell* had made no headway. There was still 400 miles to go and fuel would run out if this weather persisted.

Following a Situation Report by Flag Officer, Newfoundland, a naval ocean-going tug was dispatched to stand by *Caldwell*, now doing ten knots, in case she came to a standstill. That night the destroyer HMS *Wanderer* appeared; she couldn't spare any oil but homed HMCS *Skeena* and the tug to their positions. All had ceased to worry about U-boats, though *Wanderer* gave such anti-submarine protection as she could.

Out of the darkness a lamp suddenly flashed, "We have heard of you from afar and here we cometh". It was the *Skeena*.

"Her Captain must be a bible-thumper," said Mackay.

"Hope he's a prophet as well and brought some oil," muttered a rating.

Yes, she had fuel to spare but the weather worsened again and it was not possible to transfer it. *Wanderer* then left for St. Johns before she herself ran out.

Caldwell was now in a desperate state. Her oil tanks were almost empty, the last dregs being transferred by hand. All movable woodwork was broken up to feed the boilers. The Defaulter's Table brought a cheer from tired men and grins to the faces of the Captain and his haggard officers. But to no avail. At 2000 hours the Engine Room reported "Fires out. No steam." A black-out descended, except where auxiliary batteries were available. There was no heat. On deck the temperature was below freezing with ice everywhere and the ship soon became equally cold below. Moreover fresh water and food were beginning to run out. There was still 125 miles to go. The Captain had last seen his bed five nights ago; with his cabin destroyed he took what rest he could in the Wardroom. All below were literally blue with cold.

Help came at last in the form of a tug that took *Caldwell* in tow and on Christmas Eve, 24 December 1942, the little destroyer, without heat and light and with huge icicles adorning her battered superstructure, was secured to a harbour wall in St. Johns. A shore-based official, coming aboard to see what he could do to help, stood silently watching a group of heavily clothed, bearded men, looking more like Arctic explorers than naval officers, standing round a little fire they had going on the ice-covered deck. While one fed the meagre flames with the last of the wardroom furniture the others grilled sausages from pointed sticks which they watched with eyes red with fatigue and strain.

However, a good Christmas was had by all ashore. But what they had endured proved to be by no means the end of it. The *Caldwell*'s turbine bearings were found to be badly damaged, necessitating removal of the two screws. She would have to go Boston, Massachusetts for this, 885 miles away. On 18 January 1943 the tug *Foundation Franklin* took her in tow with the minesweeper *Wasaga* as escort.

Almost immediately the weather changed for the worse, the barometer continued to fall and another gale was upon them. The escort had to part company but the tug battled on until suddenly her towing winch broke.

Reluctantly she signalled *Caldwell*, "Suggest you request new assistance. We cannot hold you." Then the tow parted and more than 400 fathoms of 6" manilla lay suspended from the helpless destroyer's bows. As if this was not enough, heavy ice began forming all over her again. Determined not to leave without exhausting every possibility, the tug passed a line to the destroyer's stern to try to tow that way, but *Caldwell* yawed dangerously. Lieutenant Commander Mackay decided that a drogue, or sea anchor, must be contrived to steady his ship.

The quarterdeck, swept continuously by waves, was a very dangerous place but the effort had to be made. *Caldwell's* First Lieutenant, along with a few specialists, began to construct a drogue out of Carley floats, a kedge anchor, canvas and spars. In the middle of this task all members of the work party were suddenly engulfed by a particularly large wave. When it had passed, the battered quarterdeck revealed a scene of twisted railings, bent posts and injured men who'd been hurled in all directions. Though mercifully none were lost overboard all were casualties, ranging from fractured skulls to broken legs and ribs. The work had to be abandoned. Then the tow parted again.

Oil was again pumped over the side to becalm the waves. It gave a brief respite. However, the weather didn't improve and on 19 January the tug, badly in need of repair herself, had to leave for Louisbourg, Nova Scotia. As the ship's company of *Caldwell* watched her disappear their morale reached a new low. For three days and nights they held on physically as well as mentally. They couldn't sit, they couldn't sleep and the injured in the sick bay suffered dreadfully. The only occupation, and a vitally important one, was the continuous hacking away of ice, particularly on the bridge to prevent the ship becoming top heavy and capsizing. The howling wind continued to blow at over 70 miles an hour, carrying *Caldwell* further and further out into the Atlantic.

On 20 January 1943 the tug *St. Anne* had put to sea to assist the drifting destroyer but had become so dangerously caked with ice that she had to return to St. Johns. A sister destroyer, HMS *Salisbury*, was diverted to *Caldwell* but she had to turn back with similar problems. But on the morning of 22 January a flash of light shone through the gloom. It was HMS *Columbia*.

"Signalman, make 'Hail Columbia!'" said the Captain, not one to lose his sense of humour. The seas were at last subsiding and the wind moderating. Then another ship was sighted heading towards them. She proved to be *Caldwell*'s original escort, the *Wasaga*, who had remained hove-to, waiting for a let-up in the appalling winter weather so that she could return to look for *Caldwell*. *Columbia* decided to attempt to tow immediately – it was 420 miles to Halifax, Nova Scotia – making use of the 400 fathoms of wire and manilla that still hung from *Caldwell*'s bows. An attempt was made, now that the destroyer's pitching and yawing were less pronounced, to heave the wire and manilla line in by capstan but the weight proved too much. *Columbia* closed, passed a line to which her own rope and wire was attached, but the wire was paid out too quickly and the rope broke. The wire then sprang back and wrapped itself round *Columbia*'s propeller. Her value as an immediate help vanished. *Wasaga* then took a turn and with 150 men slithering and sliding on *Caldwell*'s icy decks, a wire was at last secured to her starboard cable and the tow began.

All seemed well when at 1500 hours that afternoon the tow parted and *Caldwell* was adrift yet again. *Columbia* had now returned to the fray. When a line had been got across to *Columbia*, Lieutenant Commander Mackay decided to utilise part of the original tug's towing wire that was still hanging from *Caldwell*'s fo'c's'le. After an hour's hard work *Columbia*'s cable-eye was finally attached to the wire pendant of the hanging tow line and the shackle allowed to run down the wire until it brought up against the 14" towing hawser. By this method 90 fathoms of the 6" wire were brought into service and the remaining 330 fathoms and the 14" manilla served to hold the tow down, thus acting as a spring and taking up the tension. There were no further traumas, though the length of the tow had to be carefully suited to the wave intervals in order to obviate the jerks which previously had been so damaging.

At noon on 24 January 1943 a shout went up: "LAND IN SIGHT!" and *Caldwell*, still covered in ice, came to rest in Halifax Harbour. But their destination was Boston and three days later *Caldwell* was under tow again, this time by the tug *Black Chief*. The elements had yet another go at the luckless destroyer as a fresh gale, with heavy falls of snow, fell on the destroyer. Efforts to shelter at Shelburne, southern Nova Scotia failed as the tug could not locate the entrance, but visibility improved next day and after six hours of trying, *Caldwell* was manoeuvred alongside a pier in Shelburne Harbour until the weather moderated.

Flurries of snow were still encountered when the voyage was resumed, so that those on *Caldwell*'s bridge could only occasionally see the tug. There was only one consolation in all this: no U-boat had come upon them in their helpless state. Finally, during the night of 31 January HMS *Caldwell*'s Officer of the Watch saw the white flashes of the Whistle Buoy at the entrance to the North Channel and soon they were secure in Boston Harbour.

Fifty-one days and nights crowded with quite extraordinary hardships and tension were finally at an end. Lieutenant Commander Mackay, whose outstanding seamanship and dogged determination had saved his ship, was given a temporary shore job and, to end on a happy note, was very soon to find the future Mrs Mackay.

1943

PROLOGUE TO 1943

by

Rear Admiral John B. Hervey, RN, Retd.

MEDITERRANEAN ACTION dominated the news for most of 1943 – understandably, as the British were doing well there. By 13 May, all Axis resistance in North Africa had ended. On 10 July, we put two Allied armies into Sicily. On 9 September, we landed at Salerno and Italy stopped fighting. By December, we had also landed at Anzio. Naturally, naval support for all this land force activity involved casualties, ten destroyers being lost in the Mediterranean out of a total for the year of 17. But this was also the first war year in which destroyer losses due to air attack – three – were overtaken by those sunk by submarines – eight. In short, growing air power was providing better cover for our ships.

The North Atlantic situation also improved enormously this year. Indeed, arguably, May 1943 was the decisive month of the whole war at sea. Although the enemy continued to sink our ships, it was at an unacceptable cost to themselves. Dönitz lost 41 U-boats in May and had to withdraw the rest to quieter areas. Success hinged on knowing enemy patrol areas – thanks to 'Ultra' information – and having five well-worked-up Support Groups to bolster the escort of convoys nearing a U-boat pack. Also, escort carriers were beginning to have an effect, and long range maritime patrol aircraft could almost cover the whole Atlantic. Above all, in July, Allied, mostly American, merchant ship production tonnage overtook loss tonnage, and never went below it again.

The importance of the air element of anti-submarine warfare (ASW) is emphasised by Jack Adams in 'Closing the Gap Over the North Atlantic'. Adams flew for both the US Navy and US Army Air Force, and was navigator in a twin-engined B-25 Mitchell bomber – later in four-engined B-24 Liberators – both adapted for ASW. His unit played a very important role in the Battle of the Atlantic from May 1942 until October 1943, and his own Liberator carried out roughly 100 ten-hour patrols. His admiration for the competence and man-management skills of their pilot, Lieutenant 'Cookie' Bowman, makes attractive reading. Personal relationships are so important when your life is on the line.

We could have used a lot more Liberator patrols in 1942, and the arguments for a greater and earlier allocation of US Navy assets to the Atlantic – and greater allocation of RAF assets to Coastal Command – are well rehearsed in excerpts from *Convoy* by Martin Middlebrook. Sir Arthur 'Bomber' Harris always maintained that the place to destroy the U-boats was on their building slips. The argument has some merit. But if the convoys did not get through, the RAF would have no aviation spirit – to go anywhere!

Even when the higher management of affairs is at its best, however, everything still depends on the performance of individual people, as much in the engine room as on the bridge. Stoker Len Perry, in 'A Learning Process', is very conscious of his increasing responsibilities as he advances from cleaning bilge pumps in HMS *Beagle* to the day he proudly joins the elite on the throttles, with control of her 34,000 horsepower in his hands. And Angus Currie, who was a young Engine Room Artificer in HMS *Brilliant*, paints a wonderful picture of his wise old Chief ERA in the first of his four 'Views From the Engine Room'. He also gives an amusing account of their New Zealand Captain, in his 36-knot destroyer, trying unsuccessfully to coax more than four knots out of a bowler-hatted merchant ship skipper!

Sidney Davies in his second 'View From the Merchant Navy' makes plain how much better the situation was in the Atlantic by the latter half of 1943. But he also gives a good description of the mayhem which could still be unleashed on an East Coast convoy, where German E-boats would secure to buoys marking the swept channel – which prevented them from being separately identified on radar – and then spring into action as the convoy got to them. And an excerpt from Nicholas Monsarrat's classic *The Cruel Sea*, entitled 'The Burning Tanker', is a sobering reminder of the desperate situation faced by merchant seamen in a torpedoed, blazing tanker.

On a lighter note, it might be mentioned that at a party in Malta in 1955, a large lady with an unmistakably North American voice was heard to say: "Gee! There's that dear lil darkter Mack-darnald who cured me of that haar-ruble de-sease." Everyone in the room immediately swung round to see which Doctor McDonald she was looking at. Ronald McDonald was the GU specialist at RN Hospital Bighi... and a very good one too, for whose professional competence – and discretion – many an unwise mariner had cause to be grateful. But 12 years earlier he had been a newly qualified, newly joined MO in HMS *Beagle*. In the first of two articles entitled 'Doctor at Sea' he tells how he quickly found that there was more to the job than just seeing patients.

There is a graphic description of 'Crossing The Line' in HMS *Boadicea*; one marvels at how much they managed to pack into a one and three-quarter hour visit by King Neptune. The article 'A Royal Salute', in which Iain Nethercott describes the participation of his submarine HMS *Tactician* in King George's visit to Malta after the Italian surrender – and then later a visit to it by Admiral Sir James Somerville in Trincomalee – is also light-hearted. The crew were somewhat under-dressed on both occasions. This article also gives an excellent, very serious, description of the unpleasantness of being depth-charged, and pays a sincere, well-deserved tribute to the quality of our submarine commanding officers in South East Asia.

A VIEW FROM THE ENGINE ROOM (Part I)

Angus Currie, Engine Room Artificer, HMS *Brilliant*

B eing one of a small band of young ERAs I was very proud and conscious of the serious responsibilities expected of us. Three of us carried out all the watchkeeping and the associated duties. But to begin at the beginning: I served my engineering apprenticeship with Cowans Sheldon & Company Ltd. in Carlisle. For a long time previous to that I'd intended to go to sea as an Engineer in the Merchant Service. A grand uncle had been a Chief Engineer and Superintendent in his time and he supplied me with engineering books etc. Then war broke out, but I couldn't leave before I'd completed my apprenticeship. However, I was released, along with five or six other apprentices who wanted to become Engine Room Artificers.

My ERA's engine room and boiler room Certificate were received after some 18 months' service on HMS *Alecto*, which was a submarine escort, supply and depot ship based in Chatham. Built in 1909, *Alecto* had a beautiful engine room, with much highly polished brass and mahogany all round.

Watchkeeping was a pleasure, but the coal-fired stoke-holds were filthy and a death-trap. I was the original 'green as grass' ERA and spent some months in the stokehold of this coal-burning ship, shovelling coal out of the bunkers – a 'Trimmer'. Upon earning my Boiler Room ticket and my Engine Room Certificate, I was thereby rated as Chief Petty Officer ERA. *Alecto* was eventually broken up in South Wales after the war.

I reported back to Chatham and after some delay I was drafted to HMS *Brilliant* in March 1943 at Portsmouth where she'd just completed a lengthy refit, during which she was fitted with forward-firing 'Hedgehog', a device for hurling depth charges at suspected U-boat contacts. After several months in *Brilliant*, I received my Charge Certificate and in July 1946, my service in her ended. The intervening period was most interesting, and at times, terrifying.

My experience had been with coal-fired triple expansion engines, and it was all hard work. The maintenance work was routine because most of my time in Carlisle had been spent on building steam-engine cranes. I was very proud of my capabilities as a good fitter/engineer.

Three of us (ERAs) who carried out all the engine room watch-keeping and associated duties were always very conscious of our responsibilities. We had to carry out routine maintenance work to a very high standard and, in the main, were answerable to the often austere individual who was our Chief ERA – Jack Wheeler. He'd been a young ERA in *Brilliant*'s first commission back in 1931.

The Chief used to patrol round the engine room, listening and checking auxiliary machinery. He had the knack of gripping his 12-inch steel rule between his teeth and thereby he could find the precise location of even the slightest 'knock' in an engine or auxiliary machinery. A chalked 'X' marked the spot, it was also noted in his little black book, and we could be sure of the jobs to be completed as soon as we returned to harbour.

We dug in and helped each other. For example, the time taken to loosen or remove a rusted nut was recorded, as was the time taken for various routine engineering tasks in order to ascertain the time elapsed. There was no relaxing or reading a novel when our own particular task was completed. All assistance was welcome and was reciprocated.

In the 'B' class destroyers the three lubrication oil steam pumps each took their oil from the port and starboard oil tanks, and the middle pump drew oil from both oil tanks. However, it was quite common for the port pump in *Brilliant* to stop on the bottom stroke, but it could be restarted with certain manipulations. First, and as soon as possible, it was essential that the other two pumps be isolated otherwise the port lubrication oil tank would be drained and the port turbine starved of oil with very severe consequences.

The white metal bearings would be stripped and the turbine shafts would come down on the brass bearings. The turbine blades would, in turn, be stripped and the rotor totally wrecked.

It was necessary for the ERA of the Watch to go down aft between the port and starboard turbines to see the 'killick' stoker on watch down there. When *Brilliant* was at high speed the noise in the engine room was such that communication between engine room personnel was quite a big problem. For example, you couldn't be heard at all from the manoeuvring platform. Certain signals were made by rattling on the deck plates with the wheel spanner, which were understood by the Leading Stoker.

The Chief ERA in small ships, such as sloops, frigates, corvettes and trawlers, was always an ERA who had been given an outstanding reference and had passed a stiff oral and written examination called a Charge Certificate. Being on one particular ship for three years and five months the reader should be forgiven for thinking that most of the work was boring and repetitious. Destroyer life was never like that! Watch keeping itself, when at sea for extended periods, can seem to be boring, but there are always occasions and incidents when something extraordinary and unexpected suddenly changes the routine of everyday life. Personalities make all the difference in a small ship. I never served on a big ship so I don't know what life was like, but I'm sure it would have been strict, but fair.

I recall a particular occasion when *Brilliant* was in harbour for an unexpected few days, and the opportunity was taken to attend to a few adjustments, leaking steam joints and valves. We had super-heated steam so any leaks were quite difficult to trace.

Our three ERAs and Chief were ever watchful for the slightest leaks when at sea. Our Chief ERA took notes of the offending 'knocks' in our Paxman-Ricardo four-cylinder diesel generator. When in harbour we changed over from steam to this generator for lights, heat, etc., in the mess decks.

My part of the ship at that time was Boiler Room Maintenance and all that that entailed. I was therefore responsible for the efficient running and the maintenance of the diesel generator. The 'knock' was in the after block so I proceeded to undo the bolts after checking to see that we had a cylinder head gasket, as a new one was usually necessary. I was getting on with this task with the help of my Stoker assistant when who should come down the steel ladder into the Boiler Room but our Engineering Officer, in his spotless white boiler suit, gloves in one hand and a big gleaming torch in the other.

Our small band of 'Tiffies' had little faith in this chap, a Lieutenant and a downright snob with a strong dislike of wartime Hostilities Only men (HOs) in his branch of the Service. He was clever enough up top, a BSc I believe, but mechanically he was absolutely useless. He had no idea of using tools, or the lathe, etc., but was very quick to find fault and criticize. Regrettably, he had no rapport with us ERAs and we all felt that we could have managed all the engineering problems quite easily without him.

He stood and watched me with loud disdainful sighs as I used grinding-in paste while doing the valve seats: "Let me see those before you replace the valves, Currie."

He didn't appear to trust me to let me get on with the job, which was straightforward enough. Then he took over the replacement of the cylinder head which was quite heavy. However, despite my pointing out the potential dangers of serious damage, he insisted on having the minimal amount of cooling water discharging overboard. I was instructed to go up and look over the side once we had started the diesel to let him know the amount of flow. The end result was that after he'd closed the cooling water valve, the cylinder head became very hot to the touch. Suddenly, there was a loud crack in the cylinder head itself. Immediate consternation – what had 'we' done?

"Get the head off and then report to me, I'll be having lunch."

The head had split in two – a brand new head.

When the stoker took the report to the Engineering Officer he said: "Oh dear... what has Currie been doing now?"

When he eventually arrived in the Boiler Room to see what I was doing about the situation, I responded: "Well, you've made a right balls-up of this, haven't you, Sir? If you recall, I did say that you had insufficient cooling water!"

I'd made a real enemy. He then told our Chief ERA that he wasn't too pleased with my work in general. But Jack Wheeler was a very straight and good man. He told the Lieutenant that I was a very competent ERA in every respect, that he'd every faith in me and that I could be thoroughly relied upon in any emergency.

After two or three more incidents in which the Lieutenant got himself into all kinds of scrapes with the ERAs and the Chief Stoker, which was to prove fatal, our Chief requested to see the ship's Captain. Consequently, it wasn't too long before the Lieutenant was on his way. I vaguely recall standing on the upper deck, silently clapping my hands and waving goodbye.

We then got a practical man, Lieutenant Carson from Portrush, Coleraine on the north-east coast of Ireland. What an entirely different atmosphere! Lieutenant Carson was a great chap, larger than life, very knowledgeable, fully experienced in every aspect, approachable, friendly and he told the most outrageous jokes, even one or two Irish stories! He certainly got the work done quickly and efficiently, and it was a pleasure to work with him. Personalities make all the difference in a small ship.

Between ships at Chatham in early 1943 I worked for a few weeks on the cruiser *Shropshire*, going over from Chatham Barracks every day. Even though there were some unpleasant and dirty jobs to do, Chief Petty Officers and Petty Officers had to march over to the *Shropshire* in double ranks, dressed in No. 3s, with white shirt, collar and black tie. Fortunately, Chiefs and POs could march across the parade ground, other ranks had to run or trot.

Brilliant eventually left Portsmouth in June 1943 and made for Scapa Flow, for running up, training, etc. After several weeks, we left Scapa along with the battleship *Resolution*, the aircraft carrier *Stalker*, and several other destroyers with a convoy bound for the Mediterranean, Casablanca, etc. Our base was to be Gibraltar with the 13th Flotilla, Gibraltar Defence Force.

All kinds of ships left from there – up and down the Mediterranean, Atlantic, home ports and back to Gibraltar. One convoy was with the French battleship *Richelieu*. On another occasion, *Brilliant* intercepted a big white Spanish cargo ship which was ordered to head for Gibraltar. She was reported as laden with wolframite (important ore of tungsten) from South America for Germany, via neutral Spain. She was later anchored in Rosia Bay under arrest.

There were occasions during my time in *Brilliant* that things sometimes got quite 'hairy'. Our work was usually convoy escort, to and from Gibraltar, halfway across the Atlantic, down as far as Freetown, West Africa, up to Plymouth (Devonport), and then back to Gibraltar. The hidden threat from a lurking U-boat or a surprise attack from the air were always possibilities while in those dangerous waters.

To counteract the tensions and to relieve the monotony while at sea, the officers and ratings organized interviews of crew members, spelling contests, and some of the lads with good singing voices got together and entertained us with popular songs of the day. There were several jolly good singers amongst them. I particularly remember one of the stokers, a 'Geordie' from the north-east, who had a very fine voice, singing such popular songs as 'Begin the Beguine', 'Trees', 'Annie Laurie', 'Down Mexico Way', and others. And when the microphone was brought to the engine room we answered all the technical questions asked.

A trip to the Azores came our way and we tied up at Hortha in the island of Fayal, but for no longer than 24 hours. The area outside was well scanned before we left as an escort for an unladen and ancient looking cargo ship, the SS *Nancy* of London.

Our Commanding Officer at that time was a New Zealander, Captain Smallwood. When he shouted across to the merchantman through a loud hailer about his slow speed, the reply came from a distinguished looking bowler-hatted gentleman on the bridge:

"Aye-aye... Just four knots, Captain."

Our Captain retorted, somewhat impatiently, "BLOODY HELL! I BET YOU WOULD GO A DAMN SIGHT FASTER THAN THAT WITH A TIN-FISH UP YOUR ARSE!..."

"No Captain – Just four knots..."

Brilliant echoed to cheers all round!

We subsequently circled round the old tub all the way to Lisbon, where she disappeared up the River Tagus.

About six months later, we set off from Gibraltar with our 13th Flotilla,

Anthony, Antelope, Active, Vanity, Vanoc and *Wishert*, and there were others. We peeled off to go north. Our independent turn was immediately followed by a signal from HMS *Active*: "And where are you off to, my pretty maid?"

All the rest of the ships were going on a concerted hunt, together with Allied aircraft and US Navy dirigibles, for suspected U-boats in the approaches to the Straits of Gibraltar, one of the several 'Swamp' operations. I can't remember the response, but I can almost guarantee that it was something very caustic, endowed with one or two vivid expletives by our Captain up on the bridge from 'Down Under'.

We eventually arrived and steamed off the Portuguese coast, near Lisbon. An old ship appeared in the distance. Would you believe it was the SS *Nancy* again? Its superstructure painted a shining white, the remainder black, its propeller blades visible, threshing round, tips well out of the water. Having recognised our old friend with the bowler hat from the Azores, our Captain, using the loud hailer again, called across: "AND WHAT SPEED CAN YOU DO NOW?"

"Four knots, Captain – just four knots..."

Captain Smallwood then asked him if they couldn't do any better than that.

Bowler Hat: "Aye, well, *maybe* four and *a half* knots, Captain..."

We steamed round and round her, like an old mother hen, until we reached Rosia Bay, Gibraltar. We never saw her again. (Long after the war, I wrote to *Sea Breezes* magazine and it was confirmed that *Nancy* had survived the war.)

Ships were unaccountably being sunk in Gibraltar Harbour until it was discovered that skin divers from a false-bottomed ship at Algeçiras, southern Spain, were swimming across and leaving small limpet mines stuck to the ships' keels. It was very shortly after that we discovered that a few depth charges at the mouth of the harbour stopped all that nonsense.

Patrolling the Gibraltar Straits was really monotonous, backward and forward. Two destroyers on patrol to intercept U-boats as they attempted to slip through with the powerful tide. These patrols would extend to about ten days or so; then we had to return for fuel. US Navy dirigibles would hover and spot for us. The echoes from our Asdic equipment – 'Pinnng-Ga... Pinnng-Ga... Pinnng-Ga...' – were very plain to hear. We would then run in and drop a pattern of depth charges. After the tall columns of sea-water hurled up by the underwater explosions had slowly and gracefully subsided back to the surface, very occasionally there were no longer any echoes from our Asdic.

It used to make me feel sick at times, but it was either them or us.

We escorted several battleships. One was HMS *Queen Elizabeth* when Winston Churchill was on board. We had been with her several days when, taking our turn to pass down the 'Battler's' starboard side prior to being relieved, there was the shrill sound of Bosun's pipes.

The familiar figure of Prime Minister Winston Churchill then appeared on the flying bridge, complete with a large cigar, waving like mad at us and shouting through a loud hailer:

"THANK YOU!... SHPLISHE THE MAINBRAISHE!... BON VOY-AGE!..."

Brilliant returned home in early October 1944 and after a refit in Portsmouth Dockyard we rejoined the 1st Destroyer Flotilla, escorting convoys in home waters after our eventful period in the Mediterranean area.

A 'HAPPY THREESOME' GO OUT HUNTING TOGETHER

From the *Evening Standard*, Friday, 12 March 1943

BEAGLE, BOADICEA AND *BULLDOG*
A 'Happy Threesome' Go Out Hunting Together

From Gordon Holman, *Evening Standard* Naval Reporter – Atlantic Base, Friday

Destroyers are often found in pairs, but here I have met a happy threesome. *Beagle, Boadicea* and *Bulldog*, three ships of a class of nine, have been out hunting together. The Atlantic might be called their 'home' ocean, but German aircraft have fallen to them in the Arctic, and U-boats have respected their presence on the North African convoy routes. *Bulldog*, on a recent run to Russia, shot down two out of three German torpedo-bombers which came out to attack the convoy.

Boadicea had an extended stay in Russia – 23 days. "We had a tug-o'-war every day, just to keep fit," one of the crew told me. "The Russians used to come and watch and cheer the winners. We wanted to pull against them, but they were rather shy of the idea. We had just about persuaded them when we had to leave."

There are many ways in which our Russian allies show their appreciation of the Royal Navy. One small ship was presented with a large husky dog. Possibly thinking of their limited living space, the British sailors tactfully suggested that feeding the dog might be a difficult problem if they took it on the long voyage to England.

The next morning they found that the Russians had met this difficulty at once. A large consignment of yak meat had been sent to the ship.

When *Beagle* went north, her stay was extremely short. She did a turn round in the remarkably quick time of 36 hours. A ship that pays an in-and-out visit of that description becomes a sort of 'Rich Uncle' to all and sundry who have duties to perform in the far north.

All supplies that she will not need on the homeward journey are distributed among the British units remaining behind. If there is time, the 'Great Share-out', I'm told, is marked by some degree of celebration. In the wardroom of *Bulldog* they have a ship's mascot. It is an almost life-size model of a namesake of the ship. It can be made to growl and show its teeth. Above its head is the motto of the 'Fighting Bs': "We shall not flag or fail. We shall go on to the end."

[By kind permission of the *Evening Standard*]

CLOSING THE GAP OVER THE NORTH ATLANTIC

Jack Adams, B-25 & B-24 Navigator, USN/USAAF

When the Japanese carriers launched their planes at Pearl Harbor and crippled the US Navy's Pacific Fleet on 7 December 1941, I was inducted into the Army Air Corps and was sent to Navigation Training School. After completing my training in May 1942 I was assigned to the 41st Squadron, 13th Bombardment Group (Medium), one of the few squadrons flying anti-submarine patrols over the North Atlantic from the east coast of the United States. Our squadron continued this duty until October 1943 after assignments at Westover Field, Massachusetts, Gander Air Base, Newfoundland and finally at Dunkeswell Airfield, about 20 miles north-east of Exeter, Devonshire, England from where we flew patrols over the Bay of Biscay together with Royal Air Force Coastal Command.

We were equipped with twin-engine B-25 Mitchell bombers for the first seven months, May-December 1942, then from mid-December 1942 we were re-equipped with long-range, four-engine B-24 Liberator bombers for the remainder of this anti-submarine work before the RAF Coastal Command took it over entirely.

It was around late August 1942 that I first met our replacement pilot and aircraft Commander, Lieutenant John Poole 'Cookie' Bowman. With the exception of members of my family, I can think of only a few who have left the impressions which are as clear, or even as indelible, as those that 'Cookie' left upon me. I'd just arrived at Langley Field, located at the mouth of Chesapeake Bay, with a group of airmen from Westover Field, an Army Air Base near Springfield, Massachusetts. We had been flying anti-submarine patrols, trying to protect shipping from German submarines operating in the Gulf of Maine, located on the north-east coast of the United States.

At that time we had been flying patrols in twin-engine B-25 Mitchell aircraft, and as the need became greater to significantly increase the patrol coverage, there was a call for a four-engine patrol aircraft. We were to train at Langley Field for operations in modified B-24 Liberator bombers. Large capacity gasoline tanks were installed in one half of the bomb bay area originally designed for bomb racks. Depth charges were carried in the other half of the bomb bay.

In order to man aircraft of that size we were assigned to ten-man crews. Under the command of the pilot we had a co-pilot, a navigator (myself) and a bombardier, all Commissioned Officers. The rest of our crew consisted of six highly trained enlisted men; a flight engineer/top-turret gunner, radio operator/gunner, who were Technical Sergeants, two waist gunners, a ball-turret gunner and a tail gunner, all Staff Sergeants. Each B-24 carried a defensive armament of eleven 50-caliber heavy machine guns, each capable of firing 800 rounds-per-minute with an effective range of 600 yards.

While the personnel making up such a crew had been determined by the basic requirements for offensive and defensive bombardment duty, the effectiveness of patrol work, depended to a great extent on our ability to observe surface activity of enemy submarines in our designated patrol area, and thus it was quite appropriate to have extra crew members. Furthermore, it was anticipated that these crews, who had worked together, could be transferred to bombardment duties when the need became greater in the European or the Pacific Theater of Operations.

When the orders were posted for our new training assignment at Langley Field we found that while nine of us would continue to work together, as we had for several months, Lieutenant Wilson Moore, who was our pilot, had been replaced by Lieutenant John P. Bowman. It transpired that Lieutenant Moore was significantly more experienced than Lieutenant Bowman, and Moore went on to a more demanding assignment. Lieutenant Nick Robson, co-pilot with our original crew, was not quite experienced enough to take over as first pilot and aircraft commander.

The disappointment and even apprehension that accompanied the announcement of the new replacement crew member was inevitable as we felt so secure after so many patrols together. Taking on new, unknown leadership had often been regarded as somewhat chancy. But sooner than anyone expected, we discovered that we'd 'lucked out' with our new pilot.

'Cookie', as he preferred to be known by the other three officers of our crew, was of medium height, slender but well built. He turned out to be a 'man's man', not in the sense of a jut-jawed macho, but one who had a sincere and thoughtful respect for those with whom he worked. He had interests and feelings that were compatible with a masculine world, enjoyed sports, loved his three-year-old Buick convertible and had an abiding, cheerful disposition reflected in his large brown eyes when he smiled. He had a unique, personal style; quiet, somewhat reserved, but confident. He was highly intelligent without trying to appear as though he 'knew it all'.

Probably the most important feature 'Cookie' brought to our crew was his outstanding talent in flying the B-24 Liberator. During the nine months we were together, we were credited with just short of 800 hours of anti-submarine patrol, equivalent to one hundred patrols averaging eight hours each. Many more than one hundred takeoffs and landings were made in all kinds of weather conditions with never a serious incident. Nick Robson, our co-pilot, certainly deserves much credit, but 'Cookie' provided the glue that undoubtedly made us stick together.

As we neared the end of our training at Langley Field, our travels took us to Bermuda and Cuba for brief periods when submarine sightings were reported in those areas. In early 1943, we were transferred north to Gander Field, Newfoundland. From patrolling over the Gulf of Mexico, while based in the relative warmth of Cuba, up to Canada with a temperature of 24 degrees below zero Centigrade, flying 8 to 12-hour long anti-submarine missions, was quite a change. On three or four occasions, during the following months, especially when faced with strong head-winds, I recall we had to land in Reykjavik, Iceland to refuel in order to get back to our base at Gander Field.

Our long range patrols over the seemingly endless North Atlantic ocean gave us all a vivid, lasting impression and a frightening insight into the perils and the horrors endured by the men at sea with the Atlantic convoys. Although the German submarine attacks, by the summer of 1943, had lost some of their deadly effectiveness that they'd enjoyed earlier in the war, occasional sightings of U-boats cruising on the surface were made. They wasted no time in immediately diving, frantically changing course as they disappeared beneath the waves. And I recall, very clearly, at least two occasions when we silently observed the frightful, final agonies of torpedoed ships beneath towering clouds of black smoke.

In early October 1943, our B-24 squadron was transferred from Dunkeswell, Devon up to Wendling, Norfolk to join the 392nd

Bombardment Group, that had arrived in England a few months earlier, one of the B-24 Groups of the 2nd Air Division, 8th USAAF. 'Cookie' Bowman, our pilot, was assigned to the 44th Bombardment Group, Shipdham, Norfolk. His pilot's seat in the cockpit was taken by Lieutenant Ralph Lamma.

We lasted for only four daylight missions over Germany and were shot down on Friday, 13 November 1943, near Oldenburg, 25 miles west of Bremen, northern Germany. Sadly, five crewmen, including Lieutenant Lamma, went down with the plane, trapped in the spinning B-24. Three other 392nd Bomb Group Liberators went down during that mission.

Five of us (who were very fortunate in being able to bale out or be thrown out) were arrested almost immediately on landing and sent under armed escort to the Interrogation Centre at Frankfurt-am-Main. Here I was put in solitary confinement in a small cell for seven days. I was then taken across to a large administration building and interrogated.

It was absolutely incredible what then transpired. At Wendling, we had been instructed to give no information to the enemy apart from our names, rank and serial number should we be unfortunate enough to be shot down and taken prisoner. The interrogator, a German Officer who spoke English perfectly, was seated behind a small wooden desk. There was a single electric light in the sparsely furnished room. After about twenty minutes of verbal sparring back and forth, he suddenly got up, strode across to another desk and took out a brown folder. He returned to his desk, took several sheets of typewritten paper from the folder and said:

"Lieutenant Adams, I'm getting *very* angry with you and your reluctance to answer my specific questions. Of course, you fully realise that you could be treated as a spy.

"Now, let's see… Your home is in Hampton, Connecticut. You have an elder sister and a younger brother. You went to Yale and majored in English. You ran with the Track Team and won an award. You were trained in navigation. You were transferred to Norfolk, England last month…"

It was amazingly accurate information. I was stunned and could only ask:

"Where are you getting all of this?"

"We have many, many friends in the United States and they keep us fully informed," he replied.

It later transpired that he had equally accurate information in that desk concerning every American officer whom he'd interrogated. I met a few of them at our assigned Prisoner of War camp, Stalag I, Barth, northern Germany, on the Baltic Sea coast. We were eventually liberated by the advancing Russian Army in April 1945.

It wasn't until 1994 that I finally managed to trace the records concerning the fate of Captain John Poole 'Cookie' Bowman. Sadly, he'd been shot down and killed en route to Bremen on 17 November 1943, just four days after we had gone down.

2,000 MILE LIBERATORS HELP BEAT U-BOATS IN MID-ATLANTIC

From the US Armed Forces newspaper *Stars and Stripes*, 10 June 1943:

A merican Liberators with a range of more than 2,000 miles are the Coastal Command weapons defeating Nazi submarine packs in the Battle of the Atlantic, the Air Ministry disclosed yesterday. The announcement revealed the identity of the aircraft which Prime Minister Winston Churchill referred to as VLRs – Very Long Range planes.

Speaking before the House of Commons earlier this week, in a review of his Washington conferences with President Roosevelt, the Prime Minister declared that the Lib's flights were closing the mid-Atlantic gap in which U-boats used to be able to operate without fear of air attack. Equipped with especially large fuel tanks enabling them to carry depth charges great distances, squadrons of Liberators are patrolling the sea lanes from bases in the United States, Newfoundland, Iceland and Northern Ireland.

One recent Liberator attack occurred 1,100 miles from the plane's base. It is not unusual, the Ministry stated, for a Liberator to be on patrol for 18 hours.

Referring to their activities, Mr. Churchill said: "No longer has the U-boat a section of the Atlantic in which it can operate without fear of air attack – and there is reason to believe that attack is becoming more deadly."

Excerpts from *Convoy* by Martin Middlebrook

In the first twenty days of March 1943, the Germans sank ninety-seven Allied merchant ships totalling more than 500,000 tons. This was almost twice the rate of new tonnage being built at that time. During the same period the Germans lost seven U-boats, which was just half the number of new boats coming into service.

The Very Long Range version of the American-built B-24 Liberator was an aircraft that was in great demand in early 1943. This was an aircraft best suited for work at extreme ranges over the sea and their allocation was in theory decided upon by joint Allied decisions at the highest level. But the Americans, with their vast naval commitments in the Pacific and the Atlantic, received a greater share of each batch of newly-built VLR Liberators and these were allotted in turn between the Army Air Force and the US Navy, for there was not yet a unified US Air Force on the lines of the Royal Air Force. The US Navy had 112 VLR Liberators at this time but most of these were operating in the Pacific and not one was based in Canada, Newfoundland or Iceland where they could have given cover to the North Atlantic convoys. The Canadians, who had good bases in Newfoundland, had not been allocated a single Liberator.

The result of this disposition of the Liberator was very simple. The RAF was using its Liberators to give cover to that part of the North Atlantic convoy routes for which the Admiralty was responsible. The two US Army squadrons were working off Morocco. The western half of the North Atlantic, over which the US Navy had operational control, did not have a single VLR aircraft although that Navy possessed 112 of these aircraft. It is unfortunate that blame for this situation must lie in the office of one of

America's famous naval officers – the Commander-in-Chief, Fleet Admiral Ernest J. King. This officer, of such determined character, showed on many occasions two facets of his thinking – that he regarded the Pacific as the prime theatre of operations for the United States, despite the joint Allied decision that victory over Germany should take priority over the Pacific war, and that, in fighting the U-boat, he was not willing to follow British experience hard-won in more than three years of war at the same time as he retained personal control over his navy's anti-submarine operations.

It would have been quite feasible to have based two squadrons of US Navy Liberators in Newfoundland many months earlier; they would still have remained under US Navy control, would have flown over an American operational area, and would have saved the lives of American as well as British sailors in the North Atlantic convoys. With the excellent intelligence available to the Submarine Tracking Rooms this modest diversion of effort would have been sufficient to close the 'Air Gap'.

At 0750 hours on 5 April 1943, Flying Officer Smith (120 Squadron, RAF) took off from Gander in Newfoundland and made his own small contribution to the history of the Second World War when he flew across the 'Air Gap' with a fully operational aircraft. Smith failed to meet convoy HX 231 but he did spot a surprised U-boat which dived before he could attack. The Liberator then landed safely at Reykjavik. Flying Officer Smith (even his initials are not recorded) and his crew had closed the 'Air Gap' in this somewhat makeshift manner. During the next few weeks 120 Squadron flew seven shuttle patrols, using Goose Bay in Labrador as the western landing ground, and sighted no less than ten U-boats. These crews had the worst of luck, however, for in every one of the attacks they made on these U-boats there were failures in their depth charge release mechanisms.

It was left to the US Army Air Force to close the gap in a more conventional manner. As a result of President Roosevelt's inquiries and the decisions of the Atlantic Convoy Conference, the Army's 6th (Anti-submarine) Squadron brought the first American-crewed Liberators to Newfoundland. The squadron became operational on 19 April 1943 and on that day Lieutenant E. J. Dubeck's crew made a very good attack which damaged a U-boat. At the same time the RAF Coastal Command decided to forgo their next allocation of Liberators, as long as these were given to Canadians who had crews already trained in anti-U-boat work and experienced in the weather and navigation problems of the North Atlantic. In this way, 10 Squadron RCAF obtained its first Liberators on 23 April and started operations from Gander on 19 May, the first flight being made by Flight Lieutenant F. J. Green. The first US Navy Liberators (PB4Ys) appeared at Argentia, Newfoundland with VB-103 Squadron from San Diego in the middle of May, and their first operational flight was made by Lieutenant H. K. Reese on 20 May.

The subject of provision of aircraft for distant convoy work generates strong international and inter-service feelings. The British blamed the Americans for being slow to close the 'Air Gap' from the west; the RAF blamed the Royal Navy for failing to provide aircraft carriers for convoy work; the Navy pointed at the large force of four-engined bombers being used to bomb Germany and asked why Coastal Command could not have more of these instead of relying on American production. It is a fact that that fine aircraft, the Lancaster, if modified, had the range to become a long-range anti-submarine aircraft; the RAF's standard post-war maritime reconnaissance aircraft, the Avro Shackleton, was a direct descendant of the Lancaster. Not one Lancaster ever went to Coastal Command; the "bomb Germany into defeat" lobby, backed by Churchill, got the lot.

The arguments on this general use of air power all have some validity and have been well thrashed out over the intervening years but, dealing with the specific situation in March 1943, Admiral King had let both his own people and his Allies down badly by insisting on hanging on to operational control of the western North Atlantic but failing to put his VLR Liberators into Newfoundland to plug the 'Air Gap'. Dönitz had been given eight months' grace, but the flights of Flight Lieutenant Smith, Lieutenant Dubeck, Flight Lieutenant Green and Lieutenant Reese and of the other Liberator crews who finally closed the 'Air Gap' settled the outcome of the Battle for Merchant Shipping. Other Allied advances took place in the spring of 1943 but none were as decisive as this one.

It is not possible to extract figures for merchant ships lost in North Atlantic convoys between August 1942 and May 1943, but many Allied merchant seamen paid the price of Admiral King's failure to see that the 'Air Gap' was closed earlier.

'WHO WAS RIGHT?'

Anthologist's Note: Excerpts from a speech made in 1977 to veterans of RAF Bomber Command at a reunion in London by Marshal of the Royal Air Force Sir Arthur 'Bomber' Harris, commander of RAF Bomber Command 1942-45, give a further insight:

'I have read an account by a so-called expert Naval Correspondent who said: "In the whole of the war, Bomber Command sank only one submarine."

What does Albert Speer say? He was directly responsible for the production of submarines and everything else... This simple sentence in one of his books: "We would have kept to our promised output of submarines for Admiral Dönitz's U-boat war if the bombers hadn't destroyed one third of them in our ports."

Well, who was right? The Royal Navy, who wanted to pinch all our Lancaster bombers to go looking for needles in haystacks all over the vast Atlantic Ocean, or we, who said the place to get the submarines was where they came from, and not where they were going to.

But that was only the *beginning* of the Naval war...

The German Admiral in charge of the training of U-boat crews in the Baltic Sea, off the northern coast of Germany, wrote a letter to Speer in which he said:

"Without trained U-boat crews you cannot have a U-boat offensive – and I can't train the crews if you cannot keep these air-laid mines away from my training grounds."

Well, they couldn't keep the air-laid mines away. The major expense of the German Navy was trying to counter the *30,000 tons* of mines that you fellows laid in waters approaching *every* major port that the Germans used, from the Baltic, the whole of Continental Europe's North Sea coast, and down to the Bay of Biscay...

And you can be quite certain that apart from the other wreckage they caused, those mines *certainly* accounted for quite a number of U-boats which disappeared – if my German pronunciation is correct – I'm not very good at it: *Virschwinden… Versenken* – Disappeared… Sunk without trace.'

U-BOAT BUNKER

Anthologist's Note: An extraordinary relic of the Second World War which, over the years, has become a popular tourist attraction is situated at Bremen, in north-western Germany, beside the River Weser less than 30 miles from the North Sea.

Bremen was a major industrial city during the war and consequently became a primary target for RAF Bomber Command and the 8th USAAF. The city was the target for no less than 173 bombing raids by the Allies; the last of which took place on 7 April 1945.

In addition to a large aircraft manufacturing plant and associated industries, the Germans were also in the process of constructing a massive steel-reinforced concrete bunker, designed to manufacture and repair U-boats for the German Navy. Construction of the gigantic U-boat bunker commenced in February 1943, but was never completed and utilized for its intended purpose.

Although the bunker itself took many direct hits it received little structural damage and its 18 feet-thick roof was never penetrated by bombs. The huge building is 82 feet high, 328 feet wide, and 1,396 feet long.

The reason for the bunker's failure to launch a single U-boat was the fact that the Allied bombing attacks continually destroyed the roads, railways and the canal systems which prevented the Germans transporting the prefabricated U-boat sections and relevant supplies to the site.

Had it been capable of production, the method of assembling the U-boats was in three successive stages, from right to left, towards the River Weser. When finally completed, each U-boat would be lowered into the water, then navigated down the river and out into the North Sea.

CROSSING THE LINE[37]

Saturday, 2 October 1943
HMS *Boadicea*
Foreword

Saturday, 2 October 1943, was a memorable day for the majority of the ship's company, marking as it did the first occasion of their Crossing the Line. Since we had but short notice of our journey through King Neptune's Domain, we were not able to make those necessary preparations for the elaborate ceremony which usually takes place on this auspicious occasion. None the less, an opinion is that the very impromptu nature of the ceremony lent charm to it: the whole ship must be congratulated upon rising to the occasion in such a splendid way.

Things could not have gone better had the most exhaustive plans been made. The dialogue and hastily improvised dresses of King Neptune's Court were indeed most excellent.

The Equator was actually crossed at 0145 hours on 2 October in position 8°00'E. His Majesty King Neptune, accompanied by His Queen and Court, arrived on board at 1000 hours, preparations already having been made for his greeting and subsequent levee. In place of the usual monotonous forenoon, our life took on a gayer aspect, everyone enjoying himself to the full.

It was with much regret that we bade farewell to King Neptune and his Court as, at 1145 hours, they departed for their Watery Domain leaving behind them happy memories and a few heel abrasions, to say nothing of many well-shaved faces and much doctored stomachs.

SEQUENCE OF EVENTS
Friday, 1 October 1943

At about 2000 hours three signals which had passed between King Neptune and the ship were promulgated, and as a result we expected a visit from him later that evening. However, it was learned that, owing to the fact that there

---

[37] Ceremony traditionally performed when a RN ship with uninitiated crew crosses the Equator.

were numerous ships in the convoy, all equally desirous of the honour of a Royal Visit, HM King Neptune was unable to come on board himself. We were fortunate, however, in receiving as his deputy the Court Herald who proceeded to serve the Royal Summonses.

NAVAL MESSAGE

To: *Boadicea*

From: The Equator W/T Station

His Oceanic Majesty King Neptune has received information from his Chief Sea Scout that you are shaping course which at your present speed will bring you within the Royal Domain this a.m. The laws of his watery Domain demand that permission be first asked.

(1900 hrs/1st) October 1943

To: King Neptune

From: *Boadicea*

Request permission for His Britannic Majesty's Ship *Boadicea* to proceed through the Royal Domain. Anticipated she will arrive at dusk Friday, 1st October. We should be honoured to see your Majesty hold levee onboard, as there are many who have not yet had the honour of being presented.

(1930/1)

To: *Boadicea*

From: King Neptune

King Neptune is pleased to welcome His Britannic Majesty's ship *Boadicea* to his Equatorial Kingdom, and will arrive onboard at 0900 hours on Saturday, 2nd October 1943. He hopes to renew friendship with any who may have already had the honour of being presented.

(2000/1)

Owing to a combination of war conditions and a somewhat heavy call on his services, it was not possible for King Neptune to arrive onboard with his Court before the ship entered his domain. His Herald had been instructed to pay a preliminary call at 1915 hours, bearing King Neptune's Greetings.

All went off well, not even the lookouts of gun's crews closed up having observed the secret arrivals of King's Herald and his Bears.

After a loud voice giving the shout "White Line Ahead, Sir," the following was heard:

"Ahoy there! At your peril, stop engines: What ship are you?"

Captain: "His Britannic Majesty's ship *Boadicea*."

Herald: "Pray! Your name, Sir?"

Captain: "Francis Cumberland Brodrick"

Herald: "Aha! A landlubber!" (Followed by loud growls from the bears).

"Thank you. You may proceed."

"Captain, Sir, of His Britannic Majesty's Ship *Boadicea*. I bear a message from my most excellent and salubrious Majesty, King Neptune, Ruler of the Deep, Keeper of Davy Jones's Locker, Most Honourable Holder of the Order of the Barnacle, Knight Grand Cross of the Jellyfish, Commander of all Deep Sea Animals, he, together with Queen Amphitrite, the Finest Lady of All Mermaids, Holder of the Order of Crabs, has commanded me, His Humble Herald, Holder of the Order of Herringbone, to bid you Greetings and welcome you, Sir, and your Honourable Ship's Company to His Royal Domain.

"He will be pleased to meet all initiated members and those who have not had the privilege and honour of Membership, further commands me to tender his apology that, owing to number of ships in convoy, he will be unable to pay you the honour of a ceremonial visit until 0930 hours Saturday, on the morrow.

"He further commands that Twelve Royal Summonses be issued to your Merry Band of Matelots to pay him special homage. At your peril of being condemned to a shark's fin or honourable whale's belly, you will command said transgressors to attend Court."

Captain: "Be pleased to inform His Majesty King Neptune that I shall be overjoyed to receive him and his Court tomorrow, and will undertake to present to him all those on board who have not previously had that privilege.

(After many growls from the bears in anticipation of their feed on the morrow, the Herald and they disappeared from view.)

Saturday, 2 October 1943

At 0900 hours hands were piped to 'Clean into Crossing the Line Rig'; then at 0930 hours the lower deck was cleared and all hands laid aft on the quarterdeck. Meanwhile, King Neptune and His Gracious Consort, Queen Amphitrite, together with their whole Court, were forming upon the fo'c's'le via the hawse pipe. The constitution of the Court was as follows:-

HM King Neptune	- PO C. Gogel
HM Queen Amphitrite	- AB E. Jackson
King's Herald	- PO A. V. King
King's Page Boy	- ERA R. J. Tonkin
Lady in Waiting	- AB D. Keeble
Clerk of the Court	- LS[38] J. McNichol
Clerk's Secretary	- AB Summerell
Chief Barber	- PO M. Turner
Assistant Barber	- Sub-Lieutenant K. Robinson, RNR
Surgeon	- PO R. Daynes
Assistant Surgeon	- AB C. Monkhouse
Chief of Police	- Lieutenant J. C. M. Kier, RNR
Chief Bear	- Mr. Howting, Gunner 'T', RN
Band	- LS J. Halliday
	LS A. Randall
Court Jester	- AB R. McMunn
Police	- Yeoman Spencelayh, PO Davis,
	LS Mawdsley, LS Taylor,
	AB Bright, AB Barratt
Bears	- SY[39] PO Pike, Stoker PO Coghlan,
	CPO White, AB Cain,
	AB Taylor, AB Rayment,
	AB Rogers, AB Leggett,
	Stoker Hinksman, AB Gibson,
	AB Henshaw.

[38] Leading Seaman.
[39] Signals Yeoman.

On the Quarterdeck

At 0945 hours the entire Court moved aft to the strains of 'Waltzing Matilda'. The costumes made a brave show in the tropical sunlight, that of His Majesty doing much to enhance his natural dignity, and his Queen's tasteful selection of apparel for the occasion made many a matelot's heart beat a little faster. When the assembly was complete, the Court faced the Captain and his ship's company, and the Herald made the following announcement:-

"Pray silence for King Neptune!

"Be it known that King Neptune, his Consort Queen Amphitrite and all his Court, including hungry bears and subtle policemen, have come on board to hold levee. There are many who have not yet had the honour of initiation into the laws and customs of our Watery Domain, and the King desires that these be brought before us at Court.

"PRAY SILENCE FOR KING NEPTUNE!"

King Neptune then read aloud from the scroll:

"Neptune! To Our Right Trusty and Loyal Subject Captain Francis Cumberland Brodrick – Greetings! It gives Queen Amphitrite and myself great pleasure to welcome the good ship *Boadicea* with her merry crew into our watery domain. It has been brought to our notice that there are many aboard this gallant ship who enter our domain for the first time. It is therefore our desire to hold court on board, and we charge you to produce before us such persons so that they may be dealt with according to our law. Before so doing, it is our desire to honour you, Sir. In recognition of many years' faithful service upon the Seven Seas, I therefore bestow upon you the 'Order of Ship Handler First Class Without Tugs.' May you wear and keep this for many years to come, and we look forward to you passing in the good ship Boadicea once more thro' our Domain steaming north."

The Captain was then invested by King Neptune with the 'Order of the Ship Handler First Class – Without Tugs and Pilot's Certificate', which read as follows:

THE ORDER OF SHIP HANDLER, FIRST CLASS

This order, issued to Lieutenant Commander F. C. Brodrick, RN, hereby certifies that he has fully qualified as a First Class Pilot on the troubled sea of Beverages, has a complete knowledge of Bars, knows all harbours where the biggest schooners can be unloaded and is willing to do his share in the emptying of such schooners, can steer a straight course for Watney's Brewery, can sail on an even keel when fully loaded, and furthermore, is entitled to rank as Chief Pilot of any vessel using Watney's Brown Ale, John Haig's Whisky and Booth's Gin or other beverages loaded at the brewery. He is also recommended as a skilful steerer of battered hulks looking for a snug harbour to lay up in whilst waiting for the storm to blow over at their own port.

In Witness Whereof we have hereunto set our hands and a Seal of the Pilot and Landlubbers Society this 2nd day of October 1943.

NEPTUNE REX

The First Lieutenant was then invested with the 'Order of the Flowers' (and was given a bunch), King Neptune then expressed his very great pleasure of conferring the very greatest of all honours on Lieutenant E. Hoyes, Royal Navy, 'The Grand Order of the Knight of Dakar', to be passed on to his future generations without reserve.

Following this the Engineer Officer, Mr. F. C. Schroder, was presented with the most noble 'Order of the Most Rusty Kipper', in recognition of his many years of loyal service and unending patience with Turbo Troubles and Fuel Oil Consumption, and having served in the *Boadicea*'s predecessor (1914–1918).

King Neptune then continued: "I have a further decoration to bestow. My Trusty Herald has been my friend and companion for many moons, and I decree that he be styled 'Knight Companion of the Daily Order'."

The Captain then replied: "Welcome, your Majesty, to HMS *Boadicea*, and accept my grateful thanks for the honour you have conferred on me.

"I didn't realise until last night that your faithful Herald was none other than Alvar Liddell of BBC fame. As the depths in these parts of your Domain is two thousand fathoms, I expected you to arrive somewhat bruised, battered and bewildered. Instead of which you look Bold, Bad and Busy.

And Queen Amphitrite, whom I thought fat and forty, is a flower from fairyland.

"I trust your sons, Triton and Proteus, are well, and I am surprised that I have not been charged other than that of being a landlubber, and, of course, as Commanding Officer of one of His Britannic Majesty's ships, it is my prerogative to refrain from being initiated into your mysteries due to the stress of war or diverse reasons.

"However, I prefer to plead guilty of being a landlubber, tho' I have travelled far to the North, East and West of your Majesty's Kingdom, and therefore expect leniency from your Court, also on account of my advanced age and delicate physique.

"Pray let us adjourn to your Court for the Ceremony, and I will undertake to present such others of my comrades besides myself who are desirous of being initiated as your faithful subjects. On conclusion of the Ceremony, I hope your Majesty and Court will partake of some refreshment on the quarterdeck."

The Court then proceeded to the Bath which was situated on the starboard side of the Torpedo Tubes, King Neptune and his Queen, his Herald and Clerk of Court taking up position on a raised platform. Assembled on the port side were discovered certain notorious characters whose misdoings were such as to be deemed worthy of a Special Summons; in each case a Summons had been issued in the following terms:

NEPTUNE, By the Grace of Mythology, Lord of the Waters, Sovereign of all Oceans, Governor and High Admiral of the Bath, etc.

WHEREAS it has pleased us to conceive a Court to beholden on board His Britannic Ship *Boadicea* on the upper deck thereof at the hour of 0945 hours on Saturday, 2 October 1943, and having satisfied ourselves that your prescription has not been found in our records by those present, we hereby summon you:

FRANCIS CUMBERLAND BRODRICK, BIG CHIEF No. 1, to appear at the said Court to render to us the usual homage, and to be initiated into the Mystic rites according to the Ancient usages of our

Kingdom. Hereof not you, nor any of you, may fail, as you will answer at your peril and to the delight of our Trusty Bears.

Given at our Court on the Equator: First day of October in the year One thousand nine hundred and forty three.

NEPTUNE REX

The culprits were now dealt with by the Court one by one and the Herald read out the following indictments and proclaimed the punishment decreed:

LIEUTENANT COMMANDER FRANCIS C. BRODRICK

Charge: Did wilfully lose his way in that he did arrive on the wrong station much to the chagrin of 180 matelots, namely the West African Station instead of Glasgow Central. "Was Your Journey Really Necessary?"

Judgement: Should be lashed to both screws: Heaved hard-a-port: topped both (gin and lime) and deprived of fish for breakfast: Cast to the Bears.

JIMMY THE ONE

Charge: Did befoul our Royal Domain by his evil presence in that he did cause great eyestrain to the Gunbusters and cause the troops to bestir themselves at an unearthly hour of the morning. Did disturb the peace and slumber of our Domain by shooting stars and other heavy objects into the sky and cause a Moonbox to be shone at a non-moon period.

Judgement: To be shaved, analysed, sterilized, tampion removed, bye-pass closed, telescope unshipped, target obscured and made to eat a bunch of flowers and hurled to the bears.

SURGEON-LIEUTENANT CLIFF

Charge: Did cause to be brought to the Bay of Sickness for vile potions and injections; was guilty of being the worst Chess player in the ship, and did spread 'Buzz'. Did display wicked instruments when loyal subjects reported for inoculation.

Judgement: To return his Pork Sword, have his scalpel removed, his Arkin-in-set to be abandoned; pulse removed, blood pressure revved up, scrotum painted with silver nitrate, and what is left to be thrown to the bears.

SUB-LIEUTENANT RENNIE

Charge: Sprog Officer in the ship! Did bring weird and mystic signs and formulas for spreading 'Buzzes' into the Royal Kingdom, thereby causing great distress amongst our subjects; was adrift at the PO's Tea Boat, causing the dish-up to be late.

Judgement: To be centralised, decentralised, lashed to the CBs and SPs; to be confined to the VCVF, and to be delivered of AFO's two pills and slung to the bears.

LIEUTENANT MACKAY, BOADICEA'S SOCIAL OFFICER

Charge: Did serve out bad and lousy scran through his henchman, Bill Sykes, such as bad butter, meat, and bread, causing same to be ditched in our Royal Waters thereby poisoning our Royal Deep Sea Monsters, and did wander aimlessly in my brother's domain 'The Arctic Wastes' to the peril of real good, true and lusty sailors.

Judgement: To eat his own scran, to be minced, served up as teawater, sliced and stuffed, curried and riced, toasted, and to be called henceforth 'Backbiting, Belly-crawling, Burgoo Twisting, Caber Tossing, Thistle Gnawing, Haggis Waffing, Bagpipe Busting, Heather Chewing Spalpeen', and to be thrown to the bears and diminished forever.

CHIEF GUNNER'S MATE

Charge: Did cause rifles to go pop and many flags to be waved, did cause the Mess to be used for a Gunnery School, too many overs, too many shorts, 'Up 500', and a miss. Did ditch a cordite charge in my Royal Domain causing my fish to be put to 'Latch to Dismantle'.

Judgement: To have his driving band removed, to be used as a pull through, to be fitted for and not with Night Tracer, Sponged out,

Ejector forced back, seat of obstruction obliterated, bashed with a Mushroom head, vent tube cleared, rimed, to be banished from the Royal Domain, repeating the Misfire drill. Two pills and cast to the bears.

CHIEF TIFFY, ALIAS SMILING BOY

Charge: Did fail to smile in my domain, did cause great labour amongst his messmates, did fail to repair the Refrigerator thereby causing nasty smells in my domain.

Judgement: To be tickled, pickled, placed in irons, his cap removed, locked in the Fridge, bashed, and turned about. Two pills and cast to the bears.

CHIEF STOKER SAMPSON

Charge: Did, for reasons quite unknown to anyone, misregulate the Stokers, did flood the Torpedomen's Mess deck with stinking oil, did fail to repair the Domestic pump. Did muck the galley up, pump bilges into drinking tanks, did sip too many Stokers' Tots.

Judgement: To forego his tot while in the Southern Hemisphere, to be Squeegeed down the sounding tube, dragged through the oil tank, wiped round the sprayer, red-leaded and cast to the bears.

CANTEEN MANAGER JACKSON

Charge: Did build a house with the huge profits he reaped from the honest and hardworking matelots. Did serve out sausage whose pedigree was an unknown quality thereupon causing many Bellyaches and Queues at the Local Headery. Did have all night in his 'Mick' much to the chagrin of the 'Gunbusters', his snores being taken for aircraft overhead.

Judgement: To have his sausages stuffed in his ears: to surge and veer same, to bring him to, flake him down, secure him up, mash his bollards. Two pills, a Glauber sluice, and wanged to the bears.

ERA TONKIN

Charge: Did work too much and too hard not allowing himself suffi-cient time to clean for football, did play spanking games and did with great malice and forethought smash the Circulator.

Judgement: To walk on top of a lit up boiler, reduced to a grease spot, fattened up, and the process repeated; eat oily wads, gargle with fuel oil, dragged through the bilges, up through the boiler tubes, slung down the funnel, two pills and cast to the bears.

ABLE SEAMAN NORMAN WYNNE

Charge: Did with malice and forethought allow the Court to nominate another Royal Subject to be known as the youngest member of the ship. Did paint wavy lines all round the Iron Deck, much to the Knight of Dakar's disgust.

Judgement: To paint all the wavy lines out with a toothbrush, not to fall asleep somewhere whilst putting up revs. To shave with a wicked razor. To be turned round Chadburn's Rod Gearing from Bridge to Tubes. To be put half ahead and stopped at 350 revs. Fed with Glauber salts. Two pills and thrown to the bears.

ORDINARY SEAMAN MOORES

Charge: Did fail to find a rivet of a particular kind, which was stowed in the Tiller Flat. Did fail to bring the messes issue of 'Cake' RN at 1615 hours on the afternoon of 16 August 1943. Did fail to fill the 'Fog Locker' when ordered to do so. Did fail to find 'The Sky Hook' which was stowed overhead.

Judgement: To grow a beard, shave it off, have a haircut. Two pills, a Glauber injection, and tossed to the bears.

The Bath

In each case, after the judgement had been promulgated the accused was forthwith dealt with by The Surgeon who administered Soap Pills or

Glauber Salts mixed with quinine as was requisite. In cases of difficulty, Soap Pills were helped down with salt water. The accused were then handed over to the Barber's Assistant, who gave him a generous supply of lather not forgetting ears, eyes and mouth. The Barber then took charge of his rusty razor and shaved the victim off.

The chair was then tipped and the criminal found himself seized ignominously by many pairs of willing hands of the hungry bears, and, after several duckings, was passed to the next bath where the process was repeated.

After this, the patient, who was not quite sure of what was happening from the time he sat in the chair, found himself again on his feet, none the worse for wear and the cause of great amusement to the onlookers.

After the special cases had been dealt with, the remainder of the novices entered the platform and a suitable treatment was meted out to them by the Doctors, Barbers and Bears. The Police were tireless in their rounding up of would-be truants and of those who had not made up their minds. Ably led by their Chief, they saw that there were no dodgers, and since 17 persons in all paid tribute to King Neptune, it proves that the Police knew all the hideouts.

On completion of the Ceremony which lasted until 1145 hours, the entire Court was seized by the newly initiated members and were well and truly ducked, after which the Court were entertained to refreshment on the Quarterdeck bringing the whole proceedings to a merry close.

A VIEW FROM THE MERCHANT NAVY 1941-1943 (cont'd)

Sidney Davies, Merchant Navy

After arriving home from another voyage on board the SS *Merchant Royal* from Wabana, Newfoundland with a cargo of iron ore in late 1940, I took a few days leave. We were allowed two days leave per month.

I then decided I'd try Home Trade – coasters – for a comparatively peaceful change. I joined the SS *Arthur Wright*, running coal from South Wales to

Portslade Power Station, Brighton, in convoy from Land's End to the Isle of Wight.

On dark nights the German E-boats, very similar to our Motor Torpedo Boats, used to tie up to the swept channel (i.e. mine-free) marker buoys. Once a convoy was abeam of the waiting E-boats all hell broke loose. On those frightening occasions, at the first sign of trouble, our escorts fired starshells, the targets became visible and battle commenced.

On one such night in July 1941, with tracer bullets and bigger calibre shells flying in all directions, a nearby explosion forced our propeller shaft out of line. We limped into harbour, then dry-dock for repairs.

In August 1941, I met an old shipmate at South Shields, Newcastle, paid off the coasters and signed on an ex-Vichy French ship, the *PLM13* with him on the Wabana, Newfoundland (iron-ore) run again.

At this stage of the war things were hotting up. We were part of a home-ward-bound convoy in fine weather one night when the alarm bells suddenly began clanging. Then we saw the incredible sight of a U-boat in the middle of our convoy, going at full speed *on the surface*, between the convoy's columns, picking off the oil tankers. We couldn't open fire on the U-boat for fear of hitting merchantmen abeam.

What little sleep we had during the next few nights had to be on deck because, having lost seven ships from the convoy, we didn't relish the night-mare of being trapped below deck in our bunks during the middle of the night, like so many of our fellow merchant seamen had been.

We had a good relationship with the Shipping Federation Officers who were responsible for manning the merchant ships with personnel. They also had the unenviable and terribly difficult duty of informing the close relatives and loved ones of the many merchant seamen lost at sea.

After many months on the North Atlantic run, a few of my shipmates yearned for a voyage to warmer climes. The 'Fed. Man' duly obliged and arranged for our transfer to an old tramp steamer that had recently dis-charged a cargo of wheat at Barry, and was then loading coal at Cardiff for a secret destination.

In June 1942, we signed on the *Masunda*, owned by McLay & McIntyre of Glasgow. The coal loaders told us the cargo was bound for the Egyptian State Railway. We headed south as there was no passage through the

Mediterranean at that time, and when we passed Gibraltar, on the southern tip of Spain, we became aware of a plague of rats. They had gnawed their way through the timber and canvas hold coverings, having lived off the remnants of the wheat from our previous cargo.

Our Captain gave us a rat trap each and offered a tot of rum for each rat dispatched. We entered Alexandria Harbour in a 'slightly drunken haze' in September 1942, after a trip lasting 75 days, having stopped at Freetown, Capetown and Lourenco Marques, South Africa.

Among my memories of that trip are: a Royal Navy destroyer getting its side blown out while clearing mines off Tobruk; putting the fear of God into the Arab street traders by whispering to them, "The Germans are due in town within five or six days," which, of course, enabled us to bargain very successfully for much cheaper goods; and meeting my brother Alfred, who was Second Mate on the MV *King Arthur*, then loading cotton for the UK.

However, he got torpedoed (for the third time) off Bermuda in late 1942. Alfred was eventually landed in New York to await passage home as a DBS (Distressed British Seaman), and as his pay ceased on the day his ship went down, it merely added to his tale of woe when he eventually arrived home.

Our next trip was across to Rio de Janeiro, Brazil, for a cargo of bauxite ore bound for Middlesbrough. It was a safe voyage and while on leave, in January 1943, Federation Officer Trevor Denbry did me a favour. I rejoined the SS *Arthur Wright* with Captain Ling who greeted me with, "You still around, Davies? I hope our luck holds."

After a good laugh and a few beers in the Dock Hotel, Port Talbot, we sailed for Shoreham, Sussex. It was a lovely Saturday afternoon, lying at anchor off nearby Brighton waiting for a pilot to take us into harbour. The air raid siren, warning of an imminent attack, sounded across the water from Brighton. Suddenly, three German aircraft came roaring past us at just above sea level. The SS *Ala*, at anchor about a hundred yards away, took a direct hit from a bomb and immediately blew up.

Our 12-pounder gun was manned by four merchant seamen and a Royal Navy Petty Officer gunner. We couldn't miss one aircraft as it turned and headed straight for us. It immediately crashed into the sea. A second plane was on us. We could clearly see the pilot in his leather flying helmet as a bomb left his plane. Time seemed to stand still, everything then appeared to happen in slow motion. The falling bomb narrowly missed as it plunged under our stern and exploded directly below our ship's propeller, causing severe damage. We were towed into Portslade and paid off. The *Arthur Wright* spent the next two months in dry dock being repaired.

In July 1943, I joined the *British Fortitude*, an oil tanker on the North Atlantic run. By that stage of the war (the second half of 1943), we had a large protective escort and although sinkings continued during the trips I did, compared to the earlier appalling losses, things were comparatively quiet.

In late 1943, I was at Blyth, Northumberland, on 'the pool' and having a retainer of eight pounds sterling per week I was able to 'live it up' a little and enjoy life. We had to inform the Federation Officer of our lodgings address where he could contact us for a 'Pierhead Jump'. If any ship was short of ABs or other specialist crewmen and ready to sail, we had to join immediately. My luck held for several weeks and then I signed on the *Freeman Hatch*, a smaller version of the American-built Liberty ships. We called them 'Jeeps'. Our all-British crew collected the newly built *Freeman Hatch* from an American shipyard on the Great Lakes. On arrival home we ran coal from Blyth and Newcastle to Woolwich Arsenal, London. The *Freeman Hatch* was a happy ship. Most of the trips were uneventful, apart from the occasional air raids on London. We never knew if it was safer to stay aboard or go ashore while in London.

A ROYAL SALUTE

Iain Nethercott, ex-HMS *Keith*

Throughout our commission the crew of the submarine *Tactician* were probably the scruffiest submarine crew in the Royal Navy. While operating out of Malta in 1943 and after the North African victory we were selected to represent the Submarine Service in Grand Harbour when King George VI visited the island on board the cruiser *Aurora* in 1943.

Why on earth Captain (Submarines) 'Shrimp' Simpson decided on us, we'll never know. We didn't even belong to the Tenth Flotilla. Our real home was in Beirut with the Eighth Flotilla with *Taurus* and *Trooper*.

Our boat had just come in from patrol off Bari where we had the jumping wire shot away and several new shell holes in the bridge and casing. *Tactician* had originally been painted dark blue while at Algiers. Most of the paint had rusted off and was now a mixture of rusty red and grey. Our uniforms were still aboard our depot ship *Maidstone* at Algiers, and we were mostly garbed in army khaki bush shorts, together with a mixture of captured German Army Afrika Korps uniforms and peaked caps. Others amongst us sported a variety of football shirts and funny hats. I favoured the black and white striped shirt of Newcastle United with black shorts. The outside 'Tiffy' always wore a trilby hat at sea, and so on.

However, orders were orders. We sailed from Lazaretto Creek round to Grand Harbour, and anchored near the entrance, ahead of all the beautiful destroyers and cruisers with their immaculate crews in their No. 1 uniforms. We looked more like a garbage scow than ever...

At about 11.00 a.m. the cruiser *Aurora* entered Grand Harbour to the roars of cheering and the ringing of gharry bells of the thousands of Maltese up on the battlements, the King saluting from his saluting point above the bridge. He was in the uniform of Admiral of the Fleet and had not yet spotted us, so he was looking very cheerful.

Suddenly, he glanced down at us and quite visibly flinched. Our Skipper, who had cleared the casing of those crew members in the more exotic garb, called on the rest of us for three cheers for His Majesty. Doffing his gold-braided Officers cap in the correct manner, as laid down in King's Regulations and AIs, "HIP-HIP!" he called, to be greeted by a ragged cheer from the motley band of vagrants on the fore-casing of *Tactician*. Twice more we responded as the King swept past in his wonderful cruiser with its gleaming, immaculate Royal Marine band belting out 'Rule Britannia' on the quarterdeck.

The King looked away, obviously not believing the evidence of his own eyes. *Aurora* swept serenely and smoothly on and reached the serried ranks of surface ships to be greeted by the roars of their cheering crews.

We, for our part, weighed anchor and crept back to our buoy at 'The Creek' to await the magic signal: 'Splice the mainbrace.'

Later on, in September 1943, *Tactician* found herself based at Colombo and Trincomalee, Ceylon, with the Far Eastern Fleet. When we'd first arrived at Colombo, reinforcing HM Submarines *Taurus*, *Tally Ho*, *Tantalus* and *Truculent*, all battle-hardened boats with magnificent reputations in the Mediterranean, we discovered that the Far East Fleet had run for their lives when a large Japanese fighting fleet had attacked Ceylon in early April 1942. The Japs sank the aircraft carrier *Hermes*, the two cruisers *Cornwall* and *Dorsetshire*, an armed merchant cruiser, two destroyers and a corvette.

We reckoned that there were two reasons why the Japanese fleet sailed back to Japan; primarily to resupply and secondly because a hard core of five British submarines had arrived, were patrolling the Malacca Straits and already taking a steady toll of enemy shipping. All five of us were fitted with eight forward-firing torpedo tubes, two external, and three aft-firing tubes, all external, and carried six spare torpedoes. Most of the Super 'T' class submarines out there had a surface range of about 11,000 miles which had been achieved by transforming some of the ballast tanks to carry additional fuel.

Initially, our submarines were constructed to operate in Home or Mediterranean waters, although the huge 'River' class boats, based on Singapore and Hong Kong, had a greater range. Each Super 'T' class submarine carried a fully experienced crew of about 65; all five of our Commanding Officers were double or triple DSCs and DSOs, were experts at their trade, and we were soon to be joined by a dozen more, plus the 'S' boats. The big American boats based at Fremantle, Western Australia, had enough fuel reserves to stay on patrol from Fremantle up through the Lombok Strait to the Sea of Japan and operate very successfully off the Japanese coast before making the long journey back to Fremantle.

When we were under prolonged and concentrated depth charge attack from surface ships it was, to say the least, very nerve-wracking and most unpleasant. The sheer unpredictability of the attacks was heightened by the fact that we had very little warning as to when the next packet was arriving. My first submarine Commander used to plane down to between 200 or 300 feet and many of the depth charges exploded way above our depth line. But on the occasions when we got the whole pattern at our approximate depth, many of our lights would go out and showers of cork from the deck-head would fall all over us.

A depth charge has a hydrostatic pistol which should activate at a predetermined depth. The inner tube containing the common explosive is encased in a large steel drum containing about 250lbs of amatol, a high explosive consisting of ammonium nitrate and trinitrotoluene. The pistol is inserted into this tube with a fulminate of mercury detonator at its tip which fits snugly into a cavity of the charge which is pushed in from the other end. Incidentally, the fulminate of mercury in even a small detonator is powerful enough to blow a man's hand off.

The face-plate of the pistol has a series of different sized holes marked off in their various depths. When setting the depth of a charge, a brass key is inserted in the face-plate and moved round to select the particular hole for which the charge is to explode.

In the hydrostatic pistol was a large steel striker pin held back by a strong spring. A hydrostatic diaphragm retained this spring until the water pressure inside the tube overcame the washer or diaphragm. At that point the water pressure overcame the valve's resistance, allowing the striker to plunge into the detonator and the whole contraption explodes. The settings were 50, 100, 150, 200, 300 and 400 feet, so that when the enemy ships dropped a pattern of say, six depth charges, they were set to various depths hoping to make a sandwich of us.

My small Motor Room crew and I have sat in our cramped compartment of *Tactician*, sweating with apprehension, silently wondering if we'd ever see daylight and breathe fresh air again, while about three enemy frigates methodically criss-crossed overhead on the surface, their Asdic sets 'pinging' on our metal hull and the increasing 'chuffling' beat of their propellers above. Then came the ominous silence when we all knew a cluster of depth charges were descending towards us, some so close we clearly heard the distinct sound of the strikers being triggered.

As the enemy ships' Asdic sets would be switched off during the actual explosions of the depth charges to save the operator's ears with his headphones on, the Skipper would then 'corkscrew' the boat at full speed. My crew and I would switch the Main Motors to Full Ahead Grouped Up (in parallel). Depending on the Skipper's experienced decisions, the Planesman in the Control Room would set the hydroplanes Hard to Dive or the opposite, Hard to Rise.

As we were at 'Silent Routine' when under attack, it always sounded much louder than it really was. I clearly recall the occasion when one of my LTOs (Leading Torpedomen) passed me a scrap of sweat-stained paper. On it he'd shakily scrawled the usual Royal Navy joke: "If you haven't got a sense of humour, you shouldn't have bloody well joined…"

Our Chief 'Tiffy', a phlegmatic old-timer who was known as 'Tug', always sat on a stool under his engine room hatch during depth charge attacks and always wore an old, much-battered trilby hat, but he reckoned it was lucky.

On one particular occasion, a whole basket-full of depth charges came down fairly close to his engine room hatch. The hatch imploded, lifting an inch or so and sheared all the dog clips. While the hatch was momentarily off its seating, about two tons of seawater descended on the Chief before the hatch slammed back on its seating again.

Poor old 'Tug' was thoroughly drenched, his saturated trilby was forced down over his ears like a gnome who'd lost his toadstool, but he was soon back to his old self again as he rapped out orders to his engine room crew to hurriedly place 'Strong-backs' across the inside of the hatch to brace it.

On another occasion, during a prolonged depth charge attack, the Stoker in charge of raising and lowering the periscope turned to the Commander and handed him a piece of paper. It was a written request for an immediate transfer back to General Service. That was only a joke on the Skipper. All RN submariners were highly trained and remained calm under most circumstances which was sometimes rather difficult to maintain especially when the boat was doing violent underwater manoeuvres.

I served aboard the last Barrow-built submarine constructed with rivets compared to the new boats which were welded together. This fact added extra spice to life when, being heavily depth-charged, one of the rivets in our hull 'blew' and a stream of sea water jetted into a compartment. To reduce the pressure we'd bring our boat up to a reasonable depth and, with brute strength, would quickly hammer home a tapered wooden bung into the hole, then shore it up with heavy wooden braces. To make a permanent repair our Submarine Depot ship in harbour would weld a patch over the hole. When we eventually sailed back to the UK after two years, our pressure hull had so many patches it looked like an elderly tramp's overcoat. In retrospect, I never knew anyone in submarines who made light of a heavy depth charge attack. In my case, it was probably the main cause of my Post Traumatic Stress back in the 1970s.

Because the Submarine Service was no pathway to promotion, the more snobbish and aristocratic avoided it. They sailed their serene ways on the spotless decks of ancient battleships under the kindly eye of Admiral uncles or Daddy's friends, while the sailors continued their endless rounds of painting, scrubbing and polishing huge guns which would never be fired.

Anyway, the Japanese Fleet never came that way again because, after the big carrier battles of the Coral Sea and Midway, fought over distances of hundreds of miles with the US Navy's Pacific Fleet, their back was broken.

Our Admiral out there, the redoubtable 'Slim' Somerville never worried what we wore. He used to come down and chat with the crew, walk through the boat and have a few words with us at Harbour Stations before we set off on a four or five-week patrol down the grisly Malacca Straits.

The Admiral found it difficult to fight his way through the boat which appeared to have hundreds of bunches of bananas and yams, all triced up in any vacant space, even behind Chiefy's beloved diesel engines, much to his dismay. Just aft of my Main Motor Room with its large switchboards and Starting Resistances, which was actually situated at the after end of the Engine Room so I could communicate with the ERAs on the engines by means of hand signals, there was a bulkhead door leading into what was popularly known as 'Hell's Kitchen'.

Here lived the stokers, crammed into an ever-decreasing space towards the pointed stern. The stokers shared their tiny mess with two huge compressors, all the internal mechanics of my No. 11 external torpedo tube in the tail, all the telemotor gear, shafts, and gearing for the after hydroplanes and rudder. All the remaining space was theirs to enjoy.

We had two gigantic killick stokers, one of whom, when in the tropics, chose to stroll around stark naked. We, being slightly more coy, would sport multi-coloured sarongs.

When Admiral Somerville came through the boat before we sailed to lay in wait in the Japanese minefields off Singapore, he chatted cordially with my lads and I in the motor room. He then dived through the door to the Stoker's Mess, with its dozens of bunches of bananas crammed into every spare space. Jack Coss, our resident nudist-cum-killick stoker, was casually sprawled out on an upper bunk, surrounded by fresh fruit, stark-bollock-naked as usual, and looking slightly bored.

The Admiral, Commander-in-Chief of the Far Eastern Fleet at that time, glanced up at Jack, but never turned a hair. He turned to me: "'Tarzan of The Bloody Apes', I presume?..."

Typical of good old 'Slim' Somerville.

UNDERNEATH THE SURFACE
(To the tune of 'Underneath the Arches')

Underneath the surface
We dream our dreams away
Underneath the surface
On battery boards we lay

Big ships we never cared for
Destroyers they can keep
There's one place that we know
That is deep down deep

Waiting for the daylight
Then we dive at dawn
There you'll always find us
Tired out and worn
'Til the Skipper wakes us
With the klaxon horn

And when the panic's over
We'll go down again

Underneath the surface
We'll dream our dreams away.

Anon
(via Iain Nethercott)

A LEARNING PROCESS

Len Perry, Stoker, HMS *Beagle*

In December 1943, I found myself at Gourock, a naval base and port on the River Clyde. It was a cold, dark evening and I was in the dreaded draft pool, waiting to be assigned to any ship bound for anywhere. I suddenly felt lonely and apprehensive as the motor drifter took me through the darkness, towards the outline of a black object at anchor in the distance. As I climbed aboard, my kit bag and hammock were thrown onto the iron deck of an old 1930s destroyer. Nobody took much notice of me in the gloom, the ship's crew were noisily and busily preparing to get under way.

The rating who I was relieving was one of several injured crewmen after a very rough passage returning from Kola Inlet, northern Russia. As the ship was about to sail, I was needed so straight on watch I had to go.

After hurriedly stowing my gear and changing into overalls I went below, opened the hatch to Number 2 Boiler Room and dropped into that steel box they called 'the air trap', closing the cover above me. I was then in pitch darkness, fumbling around to find the release handle, finally located it, the door flew open and there, before me, were the roaring fans and the noisy boilers, momentarily blinding me. After fumbling through the darkness, then looking down through the gratings, it was like Dante's Inferno.

Being a comparatively inexperienced newcomer to *Beagle*, I was given the basic duty of cleaning the bilge pumps. This involved cleaning the filters by plunging your arm into freezing, filthy bilge water. By this time, we were clear of the relatively calm waters of the river and heading out to sea, in rough seas with the inevitable pitching, tossing and rolling. Unfortunately, so was the bilge water and I caught a bucketful in the face. I have no idea what the mixture was, but I immediately felt like throwing up. But I survived.

Eventually, our Chief Stoker assigned me to look after the boiler control while *Beagle* was on escort duties. This assignment, I rapidly discovered, involved moving like a gazelle when the bridge called down for "Full Speed".

The following is a brief description of the sequence of events: the steam pressure dropped rapidly, the oil jet burners were opened, thereby transforming the boilers into howling monsters, sucking every vestige of oxygen from the boiler room. My lungs were close to bursting as I grabbed the wheel to increase the speed of the fans. I was then caught in the opposite extreme as a blast of freezing air filled the boiler room and left me gasping.

Then, just as I thought I had everything under control and balanced, taking care to avoid making smoke, a violent slew to port or starboard would take me completely by surprise and I'd go stumbling clumsily across the deck plates, clutching frantically for the hand rail. When the Telegraph rang down for "Slow" the whole process was reversed. The steam pressure indicator subsided as the oil supply was reduced which, of course, often left my ears splitting with the air pressure before the fans could be slowed.

This procedure was repetitive while on escort duty. We never knew if the people on the bridge of *Beagle* were having a bit of fun to relieve the boredom, or they were about to drop depth charges, launch torpedoes, or taking desperate avoiding action to dodge 'tin fish' or bombs. All these things flashed through our minds. We were certainly under no illusions that nobody would tell us that a large hole was about to be ripped in the side of *Beagle*.

Then came promotion to the engine room. I again started at the bottom, which meant the distilling plant, water for the boilers from seawater. The Distilling Unit was located fully aft and well below, where the drive shafts extend out to the actual propellers. This area was known as 'The Big Dipper'. It was advisable to lash yourself to a handrail during heavy weather. When the screws (port and starboard propellers) rose up clear of the water as *Beagle*'s bows crashed downwards in the troughs of huge waves, the shuddering vibrations were such that it was like a large dog shaking a small rabbit. You had two choices; either you wrapped yourself around a very hot steam pipe or you risked being thrown on to a spinning propeller shaft, revolving at a very high rate of knots.

I was in the engine room when I first saw the 'Throttle Party' at work. They moved like finely honed and superbly trained athletes, who moved as one team, instantly responding to every instruction from the bridge, like a modern-day motor racing Grand Prix pit-stop crew. The ship's continued existence, not to mention all our lives, depended on their efficiency.

The day came when I was given a trial in a 'Throttle Party'. Despite my apprehension and self-doubts, I was thrilled to be selected and assigned to the Starboard Watch Team. I'd joined the elite.

DOCTOR AT SEA

Surgeon Captain R. S. McDonald, RN, Retd., HMS *Beagle*

I was appointed to the Royal Naval Base, Devonport, on 19th November 1943, as an Acting Temporary Probationary Surgeon Lieutenant, RNVR, having qualified at medical school on 19 April 1943. I joined in company with some 40 other doctors, 20 dentists and about 12 padres.

We all paraded the next morning in a large drill shed and were taught how to salute, march and how to conduct ourselves in the barracks, on board HM Ships and ashore. Later, we were issued with Identity Cards and red plastic neck tags, imprinted on one side of the tag was our name and rank, on the other our religion and blood group.

We drilled for another day until they discovered that most of us had previous experience at school or at university in the OTC (Officer Training Corps) and the OCTU (Officer Cadet Training University). We then progressed to excellent fire-fighting and anti-gas training – this was to remove my fear and dread of fire. Then we moved on to medical matters, were vaccinated and inoculated. Next, we worked with a Surgeon Commander – we examined ratings, day after day, moving through the barracks, to and from various ships. We saw hundreds of sailors, we also diverted a lot of sailors for treatment – coughs, colds and nits.

Our evenings were our own and we left Barracks for the pleasures of

Devonport or Plymouth. Soon we were up-rated and I travelled by ambulance to visit those on-shore sick. My first ambulance driver had been a professional dirt track racing cyclist! We travelled fast and safely and it was an enjoyable job. Then influenza descended on the area. We visited a nearby camp of huts, which accommodated forty to sixty bed-bound ratings under the care of a Sick Berth Attendant (SBA). I visited the camp daily, gave advice and if necessary arranged for ratings to be sent to the RN hospital in Plymouth. We went to the camp in relays so that each Rating was seen by a doctor at least three times a day. The epidemic gradually subsided and we returned to the familiar routine. My ambulance driver now drove more slowly and parked a discrete distance from pubs.

On Wednesday and Saturday afternoons I managed to get a game of hockey in the Barracks team. It was like hospital days again. Most of the team consisted of doctors, and we'd played against each other on previous occasions. The goalkeeper, a senior RN Padre, was superb – we usually managed to win our matches but with so many university players that was only to be expected. Incidentally, I'd been captain and secretary of the hockey team at London Hospital.

Christmas 1943 arrived. We were not given leave because appointments were due. We went down to breakfast to find the Mess virtually in the possession of the doctors and dentists. We had a fine day... After a splendid lunch the port was passed round several times, the gift of many past mess members. We raised our glasses joyfully in remembrance and appreciation.

Dinner was a dull meal. Afterwards we gravitated to the billiards room or listened to the wireless near the Hall Porter's office – sitting comfortably near a roaring fire. On Boxing Day I was fortunate to get home to Dartmouth for a brief visit, then back to the routine at Devonport.

Quite unexpectedly, I was summoned to the Senior Medical Officer's department and 'asked' whether I would like to assist one of the doctors in a cruiser, HMS *Mauritius*, alongside. Off I went at the crack of dawn and became the medical officer on board *Mauritius*, filling in for the day on which two of her doctors, who both lived in Scotland, were on leave. I had a marvellous day, was shown all over the ship, given a pink ticket at the bar, held an evening surgery and was sorry to depart that night. But I was now a 'seasoned' medical officer!

A short time after that pleasurable day, I was called to the Commodore's office to find I'd been appointed to HMS *Beagle*, a destroyer. I was given an identity card, a naval pay book and a travel voucher by a Wren. Charming as she was, she would only tell me that *Beagle* would be somewhere on the west coast of Scotland and I was to enquire at the Rail Transport Office (RTO), Glasgow. I noted that the order was dated 27 December 1943, and it was now early January 1944...

After congratulations from others at the bar, I gathered that I could now get to know the west coast of Scotland and Scapa Flow if I missed *Beagle* at one port while I travelled from A to B. So I packed my kit, returned my hockey stick to the Hall Porter[40] and set off for Scotland in search of HMS *Beagle*.

I travelled overnight by train to Glasgow, via Crewe. On arrival in the very early hours, it was cold, dark and miserable. My fellow passengers vanished into the gloom. On enquiring at the RTO they'd never heard of HMS *Beagle* and suggested I come back later that morning after breakfast. I thought *Beagle* might be at Scapa Flow or Loch Ewe. I was lucky. A nearby taxi-driver had overheard our conversation. He offered to take me to *Beagle* and off we went to Govan Dock.

There she was – in dry-dock, clad in electrical leads, wires, cables, ropes and hoses hissing compressed air. Here and there a light glowed, struggling to illuminate running repairs.

A solitary sailor appeared at the prow and welcomed me aboard. He informed me that the Captain, Lieutenant Commander N. R. Murch, was on leave. I was shown to the Wardroom, dropped my bags and went to the First Lieutenant's cabin. He was asleep at the time and seemed upset by my reporting my presence: "See you after breakfast."

The Wardroom was the officer's mess. After a good breakfast and a rest in came No. 1, affable and tidy: "Well Doc, the Captain said you could go on leave as soon as you can manage the ciphering."

"But, Sir," I replied, "I am a non-combatant – Red Cross, Geneva Convention, and all that..."

---

[40] "The Hall Porter was a great character who worked all hours. On my return from late calls I'd find a hot drink waiting and hear the latest doings of 'ITMA', a popular radio comedy at that time."

"Doc – possibly you didn't hear me. You can go on leave when you can manage the ciphering."

So, mid-morning I was off to St. Enock's, Glasgow, and introduced myself to the WRNS officers who did the ciphering. They proved to be a very happy, hard-working group of young officers who were delighted to instruct. After a break for lunch, back to the tuition.

On my return to *Beagle* I located my cabin (which was also being altered), on the starboard side, above the break in the fo'c's'le, unpacked some gear and so to bed. My cabin was small, contained a bunk, washbasin, electric sterilizer (water), Dangerous Drugs Acts & Drugs cupboard, a small desk and two chairs. Under the bunk were drawers for clothing and cipher books.

The next morning, it was back to the ciphering and at the day's end the happy group said: "That's enough for now. Go on leave but come back to us on return."

Rushed back to *Beagle*, reported to No. 1, got travel warrant, packed after dinner and was off to London on the midnight train. I settled down in the compartment, got out a book to read and started on a glass of red wine. The wine had been 'liberated' in Algeria following the North African invasion in November 1942. *Beagle* was an escort on that operation and subsequently received praise for her work from an American Army Commander, General Mark Clarke.

The wine was in three large barrels or casks stowed in the tiller flat, cool and vibrating while we were under way. We bottled it ourselves, cost a penny a bottle – please return empties. The wine had body, was smooth and it had strength! In London, I stayed at the Prince of Wales Hospital, in my old room, assisted in the surgical division and did some firewatching on the roof.

On my return journey to Scotland, I shared a carriage with an elderly Surgeon Commander. At Crewe we walked the platform for exercise. He was approached by an agitated porter: "Please come and see a suicide in the lavatory." We were saved by the train guard's whistle and ran for our train. It was rumoured that it had been the third suicide in the previous two weeks.

When I arrived back at *Beagle* I found the Captain on board. The refit was finishing and the urgent haste was noticeable. After breakfast I had a short interview with the Captain: "Ciphers, Doc; no scrimshankers; stop VD;

keep the wine books in order, I see them on Mondays. Welcome aboard a good ship."

It was then that I met my Sick Berth Attendant, Hamer, and my valet, MacDonald. I was shown the medical stores, first-aid posts and secondary medical stores. Then I was taken round all the different departments and exhibited to them. The tour took the remainder of the forenoon.

The next day back to ciphering and I was told that I was welcome at any time I needed a break from the ship: "Good luck – all will be well."

As I was leaving I received a message to pick up the ship's company's pay! I looked around for an escort and tentatively asked about transport back to *Beagle*. I got two negatives. So, with the bag full of money, it looked like a doctor's bag, I went back to *Beagle* by bus and arrived quite safely.

The ship now hummed with activity. The next day the dry dock filled and all hell was let loose as a few errors and omissions became apparent – everything and everyone in sight moved like lightning. However, the hectic activity quickly subsided to quiet and efficient order.

The following day I was invited down to the boiler room where I discovered it was my privilege, and a good luck omen for the ship's company, to light the boiler. I lit a paraffin-soaked rag on the end of a long steel rod and poked it through an aperture into the boiler. This was followed by a distinct 'whoosh' – a tongue of red flame and a large puff of oily black smoke. The red glow confirmed the boiler was lit: "Next time, Sir, don't stand there... A bit to your left."

I felt extremely happy, realising this was the beginning of a happy association. (Fifty years on, at a reunion, I met that same stoker. He was my first patient on board *Beagle* – he'd sustained a head injury and I'd sewn the wound up.)

After tidying up, I went to the Wardroom where a small party was to be held to enable us to show our appreciation to all those who had helped in *Beagle*'s refit.

"Doc, we need some charming feminine company for our party. Go along to St. Enock's and invite some of your young ciphering friends to our party."

At St. Enock's: "Hello, Doctor. Have you come to invite us to a party?"

"Is it so obvious?"

"No, but very nice. How many?"

The party was a success; the girls lovely company. The following morning, we sailed down the Clyde to Gourock, passing fields and open countryside until we were close to Gourock. Greenock and Gourock were full of service people, ships stores and the dockyard labour force. Puffing steam trains arrived and departed constantly. No rest at any time, everything dull and grey beneath damp and threatening skies.

The bar in the Pier View Hotel was our meeting place ashore. Peggy and Tess were the hostesses and did a splendid job. Anyone unable to return to his ship at any time of day, because of bad weather or the lack of a boat, would always be given a blanket, a chair and an early call. There were no apparent opening or closing hours. When whisky was in short supply it was offered only to RN officers. (Personal note: a year later when they got to know I was off to London to propose to and marry Kay: "Double scotch for you… Report back to us on return.")

Beagle was tied outboard of another destroyer, HMS *Ambuscade*, affectionately known as 'Am-bust-again'. All of our ship's company tramped over her deck on our way to and from training and classes. My SBA and I checked our stores again and again. We also checked emergency posts and identified the areas they serviced. We then got down to correcting and updating the cipher books and continued to receive new cipher material to store in the sick bay.

I explored *Beagle* thoroughly, identified people's tasks with the relevant equipment, machinery or armament. There appeared to be no spare space on deck or within the hull. I was told that the ship was about 500 tons heavier in 1943-44 than in 1939. I also discovered that, as more medical or cipher stores arrived, so did my bunk rise toward the deckhead. I could touch the deckhead when lying on my bunk. I was now quite close to the machinery/joint of the engine-room telegraph which passed from the compass platform above, to pass below the deckhead the length of my bunk and disappear beyond my feet. The gearing above my head was noisy and occasionally sprayed water over me.

Then one day, all managers, supervisors and 'dockyard mateys' disappeared. We cast off fore and aft and spent the day at Tail O' Bank swinging the compass. Then back alongside at Gourock.

The NAAFI manager got his last stores aboard and the vegetable locker on the upper deck was filled. Then, as predicted by Peggy and Tess, we were off. We encountered rain at Dunoon, as always, then into rough seas, setting course for Loch Ewe on 20 February 1944, where convoy JW 57 awaited. I went ashore at Loch Ewe, to the services cinema and had a beer – one ticket issued for each. Back aboard a little later and we set off for Russia. Sitting in my cabin I noticed that, with the rolling and the pitching, I could see daylight between the deck and the bulkhead – and when the roll was to port, water came in.

"Oh yes, Sir," said Hamer, "and it will become ice very soon." And it did...

After passing the Minches we were joined by our heavier escorts; a light cruiser, an escort carrier, seventeen destroyers in all, and a Norwegian tanker, the *Norweg* of Oslo. We were on the outer screen, zigzagging constantly; the sound of the pinging from the Asdic set kept me company.

As I had few patients to attend to, my time was filled with working on the ciphers and moving about the ship, observing the cramped, cold and damp conditions in which the men had to work and sleep.

NADIR

Anthologist's Note: In late December 1943, the Admiralty recorded: "The Germans never came so near to disrupting communications between the New World and the Old as in the first 20 days of March 1943."

During those twenty days more than half a million tons of Allied shipping were sunk. Of the 67 ships lost, two thirds of them were sunk in the Atlantic.

Among the many Allied merchant ships sunk were numerous oil-tankers. Their fiery end, with thousands of gallons of blazing and rapidly spreading oil gushing from split tanks, often trapped and then engulfed the crews in their lifeboats or when frantically swimming away from their stricken vessels.

'THE BURNING TANKER'

Excerpt from *The Cruel Sea* by Nicholas Monsarrat

(Reproduced by kind permission of Cassell & Co.)

'There was the time that was worst of all, the time that seemed to synthesize the whole corpse-ridden ocean; the time of the Burning Tanker.'

Aboard *Compass Rose*, as in every escort that crossed the Atlantic, there had developed an unstinting admiration of the men who sailed in oil-tankers. They lived, for an entire voyage of three or four weeks, as a man living on top of a keg of gunpowder: the stuff they carried – the life-blood of the whole war – was the most treacherous cargo of all; a single torpedo, a single small bomb, even a stray shot from a machine gun, could transform their ship into a torch. Many times this had happened in *Compass Rose*'s convoys: many times they had to watch these men die, or pick up the tiny remnants of a tanker's crew – men who seemed to display not the slightest hesitation at the prospect of signing on again, for the same job, as soon as they reached harbour. It was these expendable seamen who were the real 'petrol-coupons' – the things one could wangle from the garage on the corner: and whenever sailors saw or read of petrol being wasted or stolen, they saw the cost in lives as well, peeping from behind the head-line or the music-hall joke, feeding their anger and disgust.

Appropriately, it was an oil tanker which gave the men in *Compass Rose*, as spectators, the most hideous hour of the whole war.

She was an oil-tanker they had grown rather fond of: she was the only tanker in a homeward-bound convoy of fifty ships which had run into trouble, and they had been cherishing her, as they sometimes cherished ships they recognized from former convoys, or ships with queer funnels, or ships that told lies about their capacity to keep up with the rest of the fleet. On this occasion, she had won their affection by being obviously the number one target of the attacking U-boats: on three successive nights they had sunk the ship ahead of her, the ship astern, and the corresponding ship in the next column; and as the shelter of land approached it became of supreme importance to see her through to the end of the voyage. But her luck did not hold: on their last day of the open sea, with the Scottish hills only just over the horizon, the attackers found their mark, and she was mortally struck.

She was torpedoed in broad daylight on a lovely sunny afternoon: there had been the usual scare, the usual waiting, the usual noise of an underwater explosion, and then, from this ship they had been trying to guard, a colossal pillar of smoke and flame came billowing out, and in a minute the long shapely hull was on fire almost from end to end.

The ships on either side of her, and the ships astern, fanned outwards, like men stepping past a hole in the road: *Compass Rose* cut in towards her, intent on bringing help. But no help had yet been devised that could be of any use to a ship so stricken. Already the oil that had been thrown skywards by the explosion had bathed the ship in flame: and now, as more and more oil came gushing out of the hull and spread over the water all round her, she became the centre-piece of a huge conflagration. There was still one gap in the solid wall of fire, near her bows, and above this, on the fo'c's'le, her crew began to collect – small figures, running and stumbling in furious haste towards the only chance they had for their lives. They could be seen waving, shouting, hesitating before they jumped; and *Compass Rose* crept in a little closer, as much as she dared, and called back to them to take the chance. It was dangerously, unbearably hot, even at this distance: and the shouting, and the men waving their arms, backed by the flaming roaring ship with her curtain of smoke and burning oil closing in around her, completed an authentic picture of hell.

There were about twenty men on the fo'c's'le: if they were going to jump, they would have to jump soon... And then, in ones and twos, hesitating, changing their minds, they did begin to jump: successive splashes showed suddenly against the dark grey of the hull, and soon all twenty of them were down, and on their way across. From the bridge of the *Compass Rose*, and from the men thronging her rail, came encouraging shouts as the gap of water between them narrowed.

Then they noticed that the oil, spreading over the surface of the water and catching fire as it spread, was moving faster than any of the men could swim. They noticed it before the swimmers, but soon the swimmers noticed it too. They began to scream as they swam, and to look back over their shoulders, and thrash and claw their way through the water as if suddenly insane.

But one by one they were caught. The older ones went first, and then the men who couldn't swim fast because of their life jackets, and then the strong swimmers, without life jackets, last of all. But perhaps it was better not to be a strong swimmer on that day, because none of them was strong enough: one by one they were overtaken, and licked by flame, and fried, and left behind.

Compass Rose could not lessen the gap, even for the last few who nearly made it. Black and filthy clouds of smoke were now coursing across the sky overhead, darkening the sun: the men on the upper deck were pouring with sweat. With their own load of fuel-oil and their ammunition, they could go no closer, even for these frying men whose faces were inhumanly ugly with fear and who screamed at them for help; soon, indeed, they had to give ground to the stifling heat, and back away, and desert the few that were left, defeated by the mortal risk to themselves.

Waiting a little way off, they were entirely helpless: they stood on the bridge, and did nothing, and said nothing. One of the lookouts, a young seaman of not more than seventeen, was crying as he looked towards the fire: he made no sound, but the tears were streaming down his face. It was not easy to say what sort of tears they were – of rage, of pity, of the bitterness of watching the men dying so cruelly, and not being able to do a thing about it.

Compass Rose stayed till they were all gone, and the area of sea with ship and the men inside it was burning steadily and remorselessly, and then she sailed on. Looking back, as they did quite often, they could see the pillar of smoke from nearly fifty miles away: at nightfall, there was still a glow and sometimes a flicker on the far horizon. But the men of course were not there anymore: only the monstrous funeral pyre remained.

AMERICAN GASOLINE TO THE GERMANS
Excerpt from *The Munster Raid: Before and After*, by Ian Hawkins

Anthologist's Note: In December 1943, Lieutenant Arthur 'Art' Horning, a navigator of a US Army Air Force B-17 Flying Fortress heavy bomber which had been shot down over eastern Holland three months previously, finally reached neutral Spain after an arduous and dangerous journey through southern Holland, Belgium and France, then over the forbidding Pyrenees

Mountains into Spain, aided by members of the resistance organizations in Occupied Europe.

'Art' Horning: On reaching north-western Spain, just north of San Sebastian, and after being fired on by Spanish guards, the 'Guardia Civil', we were marched to a small guard-house. Later that morning we were escorted about six miles to Irun, the most northern Spanish town on the border with France. We were then put in a temporary jail, two rooms in a house which had been taken over by the local authorities.

There was a mixture of nationalities among the 12 or 14 men in a large cell, including an Australian and a New Zealander. Both had bailed out of British night bombers and both acted as though life was a bowl of cherries. There was also a Dutchman, John Masin, who spoke several languages.

We didn't know if the US authorities were aware of our existence, but after a few days the young American Consul appeared and told us we'd soon be released.

After about a week we were all transferred to the Hotel Del Norte in Irun and given freedom to come and go, but were not allowed to leave town. Every morning, John Masin and I took an early-morning stroll. It wasn't long before we noticed German tanker trucks driving down to the railroad station and then going back over the border with their loads. When we inspected further, we discovered they were loading up with gasoline.

About a week later, the American Consul, with his beautiful Spanish señorita, came to see us. I asked him when we would be leaving because I had important information from my stay in Europe that was 'hot' and had to be taken to the US military soon.

He gave me a rather indefinite answer to which I replied that if he didn't start me on my way within the week he needn't come for me. He then asked me where I thought I was going. "Call me in Lisbon," I replied immediately.

I then asked him if he knew the gasoline being taken across the border was coming from the USA. He answered: "We know – don't worry about it."

I got hot with that reply as we were losing men and planes bombing refineries and oil storage tanks in Occupied Europe and in Germany. The Germans were having fuel shortages and here we were supplying them with gasoline through the back door, all seemingly supplied and approved by the USA...

It didn't make any sense. I lost all faith with the State Department in Washington.

By the latter part of that week, a few of us were transferred to Madrid in an automobile driven by a US Army Major. I sat in the front seat and told him about the gasoline affair and what had transpired between the Consul and me. He said nothing, but when we got to Madrid he dropped the other men off at a hotel and told me to stay with him.

We drove to another building where our Military Attaché had an office. The Major escorted me in, telling the Colonel I had some information for him. After telling him the story, the Colonel asked if I had confirmation and I told him about the Dutchman John Masin.

Without blinking an eyelash, he picked up the phone and called someone representing the State Department. Using very explicit 'Army language' he made it known that they'd been looking for this information for over two years and even though the State Department knew of this, and were told of it by me, they did nothing. He promised me an embargo on oil the next day.[41]

---

[41] See Appendix IX on the activities of I. G. Farben group.

1944

PROLOGUE TO 1944

by

Rear Admiral John B. Hervey, RN, Retd.

HALF OF 1944 was spent preparing, then launching and sustaining Allied armies, in their re-invasion of Europe via the Normandy beaches – the greatest amphibious operation of all time. During it, destroyers operated vulnerably close inshore. We were also supporting our armies in Italy, and still doing much convoy work. So total destroyer losses of 18 in 1944 seem modest – and indicate a weakening enemy. Of the 18, U-boats sank four, two of them in the Arctic. Aircraft sank three, two off Anzio and our old friend HMS *Boadicea* off Portland Bill. Most of the rest were sunk in Seine Bay, two by E-boats and three due to mines laid by E-boats.

Before tackling convoys and D-Day, however, we look at an important role performed by both destroyers and submarines: rescuing downed – sometimes also nearly drowned – Allied airmen. Lieutenant Deryk Wakem, who was an RN Writer in HMS *Verdun*, describes such a rescue in 'All In a Day's Work'. His destroyer saved the ten-man crew of a B-17 Flying Fortress 'Superstitious Aloysius' from icy water off Felixstowe in January, and sorted out a few details with them at a reunion at Duxford in 1986.

Conditions were much warmer in every sense when HMS *Tactician* surfaced in Sabang harbour to rescue the pilot of a US Navy Wildcat dive-bomber, shot down during an air strike on Japanese oil refineries by HMS *Illustrious* and USS *Saratoga*. The plane was already underwater, with shore batteries shooting at *Tactician*! Iain Nethercott and his shipmates did very well to recover the pilot. The story is told vividly and modestly in 'A Kiss from Betty Hutton'. After such incidents, our allies were effusive in their gratitude – as the title indicates.

The report by Desmond Tighe 'Big Convoy to Russia Gets Through' covering Convoy JW 47 in February 1944 sets the Arctic scene well. 250,000 tons of war materials were delivered, a massive escort provided and no merchant ships lost. Our own carrier-borne aircraft were buzzing around the force throughout – like wasps at a jam sandwich picnic – and whilst doing so drove off enemy planes, sank two U-boats and kept the others down. But sadly, destroyer HMS *Mahratta*, our one casualty, was survived by very few of her men and none of her officers. The later article 'Russian Convoy RA 59' by Michael Back paints a similar picture, with 44 out of 45 merchant ships getting home safely. Len Perry also covers convoying in 'Convoy JW 61A'. But this convoy is mainly significant, indeed notorious, because it was taking Russian dissidents back to certain death in Stalinist USSR – shabby political work.

An interesting article on ocean warfare is 'Annals of War and Peace' by E. J. Kahn, Jr., who describes an astonishing encounter between the USS *Buckley*, a destroyer under the command of Lieutenant Commander Brent Abel, USN, and *U-66* in which the *Buckley* rammed the U-boat – and both sides then resorted to hand-to-hand combat! Equally interesting is 'USS *Guadalcanal* Task Group and *U-505*', in which Captain Dick Schlaff, USN, Ret'd, describes how the Task Group captured a U-boat intact, just before D-Day. Her contents added invaluably to the Enigma information acquired earlier by HMS *Bulldog* – and at a very timely moment. *U-505* is now in the Museum of Science and Industry in Chicago.

Considering their losses, morale held up amazingly well in the U-boat Command. This could sometimes result in their commanding officers still seeming very arrogant, even following loss of their boats. Nicholas Monsarrat captured the nuance of this position well in *The Cruel Sea*, an extract of which is given under 'U-boat Germans'. More rewarding work was recovering our Russian seamen allies when they were in trouble, as Stoker Len Perry of HMS *Beagle* found. He was less enthusiastic at their reception from the mighty battleship HMS *Duke of York* upon return to harbour – as amusingly recounted in 'A Spelling Problem'.

Prior to D-Day it was essential that landing craft carry out practice landings. One of these, scheduled to take place on Slapton Sands in Start Bay, went terribly wrong. Exercising forces ran into real opposition – nine German E-boats – and were without the destroyer that should have been escorting them. Heavy loss of life and equipment ensued and the incident was put under a security blanket for many years. The story is well told by Arno Abendroth, German military historian, in 'Exercise 'Tiger' – A View from the German Side'.

'Destroyer Diary of D-Day' and 'Men Who Got Their Tanks Through', both by Reuters correspondent Desmond Tighe, give an excellent idea of the busy scene close inshore. He was embarked in HMS *Beagle*. The huge scale of operations during and soon after D-Day is well conveyed by excerpts from *Chronology of the War at Sea 1939-45* by J. Rohwer and G. Hummelchen. Viewing it all from a German perspective means that we also see what German forces were supposed to do – and actually did. The bottom line was that by D+6 (12 June 1944) 326,000 troops, 104,000 tons of supplies and 54,000 vehicles were ashore. By 2 July, the US had landed two Armoured and eleven Infantry Divisions; and UK/Canada three Armoured and four Infantry Divisions – a total of 929,000 troops, 177,000 vehicles and 586,000 tons of supplies, a truly staggering achievement.

Of course, not everything went smoothly. Two American LSTs approaching Normandy on D+2 were attacked by German E-boats. Their escort, HMS *Beagle*, did an outstanding job of picking up about 300 survivors. Stoker Len Perry sets the scene in 'A Vision of Hell' and Desmond Tighe speaks of their 'Courageous rescue' off Cherbourg. Surgeon Captain Ronald McDonald, in 'Channel Convoy', then describes very well the work he and his Sick Berth Attendant had to do that night. And his article is followed by two very heartwarming tributes from LST survivors: 'No Greater Heroism…' by William V. McDermott, USN (*LST 314*); and 'A Beam of Light…' by Albert E. Duncan, USN (*LST 376*). Ironically, *Beagle's* Captain got an administrative 'kick in the arse' for taking his ship into mined waters to effect the rescue. The Americans gave him a medal! Personal memories of this episode and the miseries of Arctic convoy work are vividly described by George Miller in 'Memories of HMS *Beagle*'.

'The Sinking of HMS *Boadicea*' was a lone Luftwaffe success during the Normandy landings. A Junkers 88 tagged onto the back of a stream of allied aircraft returning to UK – then peeled off and attacked *Boadicea*, which was escorting follow-up forces to France. She was hit with one of the new radio-controlled glider bombs – forerunners of modern guided weapons. The story is told by Leading Seaman John Randall and Lieutenant Harry Howting, *Boadicea's* gunnery officer. Other eyewitness accounts from HMS *Pearl* and Sidney Davies, who by now was at the helm of the Liberty ship *Freeman Hatch*, confirm that *Boadicea's* destruction was almost instantaneous. The article 'Glider Bomb is No "Toy"' gives some details of the German weapon programme.

The worst post D-Day incident was the sinking of SS *Leopoldville* by *U-486* on Christmas Eve. This troopship was close to Cherbourg and carrying 2,100 infantrymen of the US 66th Division, badly needed in the Battle of the Bulge. HMS *Brilliant*, escorting *Leopoldville*, managed to rescue about 700 men, and other vessels eventually picked up about another 600; but 802 were lost – about 500 of them quite unnecessarily. The tragedy was that poor communications, and perhaps the Christmas Eve-effect on both sides of the Channel, prevented *Brilliant* from tapping into help at Cherbourg much earlier. The story is told by ERA Angus Currie in 'A View From The Engine Room (Part II)' in his usual vivid way, supplemented by survivor accounts from two of the embarked infantrymen: Morton Wood, Jnr. and Richard L. Ducta. They give fair accounts of a bad business and do not blame *Brilliant*. The Admiralty, however, did. Readers must judge for themselves whether they agree with Angus Currie that his Captain was unfairly censured.

After a ship is lost, one of the extra agonies her commanding officer has to undergo is putting it all down on paper. A model for doing so is contained in 'The Sinking of HMS *Swift*' by Captain J. R. Gower, DSC, RN, who was a Lieutenant Commander when his ship was mined in Seine Bay. It is admirably short, factual and unemotional – and concentrates on the good arrangements he made for the survivors.

Before leaving 1944, we have to say goodbye to Iain Nethercott in 'Returning Home'. His submarine HMS *Tactician* was to have many years of peacetime service to add to her fine war record, but by this time she was badly in need of a refit. Iain describes very accurately the rigours of service in tropical waters without proper air conditioning, and coping with problems like numerous leaks on the high pressure air systems. Nevertheless, despite these infirmities, they managed to get back all the way from Fremantle in Western Australia to Britain – still in one piece – only to be very nearly hit by a German V-1 'Doodlebug' rocket as they came up the Medway!

ALL IN A DAY'S WORK

Lieutenant Deryk Wakem, RN Writer, HMS *Verdun*
(Excerpt from *B-17s Over Berlin* by Ian Hawkins)

Tuesday, 4 January 1944 saw me serving the destroyer HMS *Verdun* as a sort of 'supercargo'. I was a Royal Naval Writer, which meant that there were wasn't much to do apart from the times when we were called to 'Action Stations', to act as the Captain's secretary, to compile and complete Convoy Reports from the ship's and Captain's log, plus my own gleanings.

During January 1944, HMS *Verdun* was assigned to East Coast Convoy Escort Duty, north and southbound, through 'E-boat Alley' from the Thames Estuary up to Britain's north-east ports. Among the many problems facing us at that time – besides the bitterly cold winter weather with sleet and snow driven almost horizontally by icy easterly winds, together with the endless pitching and rolling in the cramped and claustrophobic living conditions of a wartime destroyer – was the ever-present menace of high-speed German E-boats.

When we were in action against them, I operated the ARL plotting machine[42], which was very crude by today's refined technology. Basically the equipment worked from the speed and direction of the E-boat's movements, and I drew in bearing and distances of targets that I received from two radar sets. This enabled me to calculate the enemy's course and speed and also to work out their angle of attack relative to our course.

Apart from our radar we often received reports from the RAF and the US air forces that the E-boats were leaving their pens at IJmuiden, the Netherlands, usually just before dusk, prior to a night operation against our convoys. Seated beside me were two radio listeners who both spoke fluent German. They listened-in on the E-boats' radio frequencies and reported the German Squadron Commanders' orders to their boats. The 'Confidential Book' on all this had a remarkably comprehensive listing of the German Codes of Orders to the E-boats, e.g. "Make Smoke", "Retreat To The North", "Re-Group", etc. The names of the E-boat Commanders were also well known, and we knew exactly who and what we were up against. We

---

[42] Admiralty Research Laboratory plot; see Appendix VI.

even knew how the German Commanders spent their time ashore in Holland, which was reported to us via the Dutch Resistance Movement. I suspect the German Intelligence had exactly the same sort of information on our chaps.

Some of our destroyers had quick-firing Bofors guns mounted on their bows. During one particularly vicious night action, I vividly recall seeing one destroyer's Bofors gun firing *downward*, at point-blank range, on an E-boat.

A trawler used to lie astern of the convoy in order to pick up survivors from sunken ships. Men couldn't be expected to live for any length of time in those freezing waters of the North Sea, especially during the winter months. Speed was absolutely essential in locating the very small dots that were sighted bobbing about in the floating wreckage. It was very much a case of looking for a needle in a haystack. This is where the High Speed Launches (HSLs) and Motor Torpedo Boats (MTBs) of the RAF Air-Sea Rescue did such sterling work throughout the length of the war. MTBs quite often went in right under the noses of the German defences to within a few miles of the enemy coast to rescue 'ditched' Allied aircrew.

On 4 January 1944, we were part of a northbound convoy of twenty merchant ships. The escorts were the destroyers HMS *Charleston* and HMS *Verdun*, and HM Tug *Attentif*. The weather was fine with good visibility, although extremely cold. The wind was Force 6, northerly and increasing. At 1510 hours a 'Mayday' call was received from a US Air Force B-17 Flying Fortress which was about to ditch in the vicinity of No. 41 Buoy, which was about five miles off Felixstowe, Suffolk. Speed was immediately increased as *Verdun* left the convoy and moved eastward. A signal was sent to the Commander-in-Chief of the Nore and the Flag Officer at Harwich: "Aircraft crashed in sea at Buoy 41. Investigating."

A twin-engined Supermarine Walrus flying boat appeared and passed low overhead, heading for the scene. Within a few minutes, the tall tail fin of the ditched Fortress, in a vertical attitude, was sighted. Drifting down to the south and away from the wallowing B-17 were two bright yellow circular inflatable life rafts containing all ten crew members.

The freshening wind was blowing foam from the near-freezing wave crests as *Verdun* manoeuvred to pick up the rafts. This took some minutes as they were drifting quite rapidly. Meanwhile the Walrus had returned and dropped a smoke-marker into a huge patch of green fluorescent-dyed water.

From *Verdun*'s bridge a Coston gun-line was fired from a .303 rifle, but the first two lines fired were carried away by the wind. On the third attempt, which also blew away, one of the B-17's crewmen jumped overboard and swam to retrieve it. He then struggled back with the line to the rafts, which were lashed together.

At 1535 hours both rafts were hauled alongside, and a scramble net lowered over the port side and, one by one, the ten American airmen were pulled up on deck. Both rafts were awash with the green dye, and some of the airmen were also coloured with it. They were all taken down to the wardroom, given hot rum, and survivor's kit clothing. I then collected their names, rank and serial number for entry into the Log and Convoy Report.

My report reads: "Rescue of American airmen from Fortress No. 26098, 'Superstitious Aloysius', 95th Bombardment Group, Horham, Suffolk, was effected in twenty-nine minutes from the time they hit the sea until they were aboard the *Verdun*. The B-17 sank after about thirty minutes in position; Latitude 52°13'N, Longitude 01° 37'E. The crew were Lieutenant P. V. Milward (Pilot), Lieutenant A. Farris (Co-pilot), Lieutenant W. J. Milton (Navigator), Lieutenant A. R. Scroggins (Bombardier), Technical Sergeant R. L. Spears (Top-Turret Gunner/Flight Engineer), Technical Sergeant E. S. Winstead (Radio Operator), Staff Sergeant C. R. McComber (Ball-Turret Gunner), Staff Sergeant W. L. Weekes (Right Waist Gunner), Staff Sergeant F. P. Miles (Left Waist Gunner), and Staff Sergeant J. L. Kolarik (Tail Gunner). One of the crew members was still dry beneath his flying clothes."

The two life rafts were also hauled aboard and stowed between the two funnels. They were eventually landed at Rosyth Dockyard, Scotland, for salvage. Souvenir hunters among *Verdun*'s crew came up with a pistol, lots of Horlicks-type tablets, morphia syrettes, paddles, and some interesting cans of drinking water, canned in the Midwest of the United States.

By 1650 hours we'd rejoined the convoy and an RAF High-Speed Launch arrived on the scene. Astride the gun turret an airman signalled with semaphore flags, which seemed odd, even in those comparatively primitive times.

The ten airmen were brought up on deck and transferred to the HSL, no mean task with the launch bouncing up and down some ten to twelve feet with each wave. They were taken to Felixstowe and then by truck back to their base at Horham Airfield that same night.

Most of their flying kit was left behind with us, and it very rapidly appeared on the *Verdun*'s crew. The leather helmets and sheepskin flying jackets were especially welcome during the winter months, as we were about to experience some of the roughest and worst weather imaginable. In fact, sadly we lost a man overboard from the after gundeck during one very stormy night.

In addition to the two postscripts to this story which happened during the summer of 1944, i.e. some of the *Verdun*'s crew met, by pure chance, two of the B-17's crew in Southend, of all places; and secondly, that the *Verdun* received a huge cardboard box of American cigarettes, enough for 120 men, from the crew of 'Superstitious Aloysius', the third postscript happened at Duxford Airfield, Cambridgeshire, on Sunday, 4 September 1986.

After being put in touch with the 95th Bomb Group Association in the United States, I managed to contact six out of the ten members of the B-17's crew, including the pilot, Peter Milward. The actual meeting, which of course made my day, answered several questions that had been on my mind, on and off, for those intervening forty years.

The weather in the North Sea on 4 January 1944 was bitterly cold, the tail end of a gale was still blowing, the seas were still quite high and there was more of a hint of the snow to come. The tops of the waves were being blown away into long columns of spume down to leeward. When the Coston gun-line was fired across to the drifting life rafts, the first three lines were blown away. In the end one of the American flyers jumped overboard and swam to pick up the floating line and then towed it back to the rafts. The gallant swimmer turned out to be Peter.

Only one of the ten men was totally dry beneath his flying clothes, I'd recorded at that time, but which one? And what were the circumstances?

It was Staff Sergeant McComber, the giant of the crew, and the unlikely Ball-Turret Gunner. How these two events came about I heard from Peter Milward at Duxford: the first life raft had inflated with no problems and eight of the crew took off in her. McComber volunteered to stay with Peter and attempt to inflate the second life raft. As they stood atop the B-17's fuselage, rolling in the sea, they struggled with the equipment, especially the lines that had become tightened by immersion. It was still possible, however, to walk along the top of the slowly sinking Fortress from one end to the other.

At last the second dinghy was inflated and, just before climbing aboard, Peter decided it was time to 'take a leak' from the stable platform afforded by the bomber's fuselage. This he duly did with some sage advice from McComber as to which direction was downwind! Then they both dropped into the circular dinghy, cast off, and drifted down to join the others.

Almost thirty minutes later an RAF Walrus arrived and dropped two large smoke floats. Peter said that it was a little unsettling to see them tumble out of the flying boat and land in the water nearby. Immediately afterwards the *Verdun* arrived and began the difficult task of catching the dinghies that were then drifting rapidly downwind to the south-east.

This was the moment when Peter got wet, and how McComber managed to stay dry in the lightly loaded dinghy. The other life raft with eight men aboard was full of water by that time, much of the gear having been washed away initially, while the rest was rolling about in the water-filled raft.

This had been their first and last flight in 'Superstitious Aloysius', which had lost three engines on the way back from Kiel, north-west Germany. They had dropped steadily back from the 95th Bomb Group's defensive formation until they were alone, when they were approached by two RAF Spitfires. This alone produced its own doubts and problems. The Spitfires were obviously reluctant to approach too closely, unaware that the Fortress crew had ditched their .50-calibre heavy machine guns, ammunition, Norden bombsight and all movable equipment in the North Sea to keep themselves airborne for as long as possible.

The Fortress crew were equally suspicious of the two fighter planes that were standing off at some distance. However, the Spitfires rolled to display their friendly markings and then, having been identified, approached more closely and remained with them for some time, until diminishing fuel levels forced them to leave.

As we drove away from Duxford on that autumn afternoon, a British Airways Concorde was flying across our path and the famous 'Red Arrows' were tightening up their formation preparatory to giving their last aerobatic flying display of the afternoon. Meeting Peter once again after our earlier, brief meeting on that winter's afternoon so many years ago was one of the high spots of my researches. I'd found a new friend: Peter Milward – a gentleman in all senses of the word.

BIG CONVOY TO RUSSIA GETS THROUGH

(Reproduced by kind permission of the *East Anglian Daily Times*)

East Anglian Daily Times
20 May 1944

Desmond Tighe, with the Home Fleet in Northern Waters (Delayed).

RUSSIAN ROUT – FEBRUARY 1944
U-boat Rout in Arctic Circle Battle: Two Sunk

BIG CONVOY TO RUSSIA GETS THROUGH
Largest Arctic Cargo Docked Without Loss

Fighting for twelve days amid snow and rainstorms and in high seas in the Arctic Circle, one of the biggest convoys sent to North Russia, on the outward and return journeys routed U-boat packs without the loss of a single merchant ship. At least two U-boats were sunk by destroyers and Swordfish aircraft of the Fleet Air Arm, stated an Admiralty communique last night. Several were damaged and one or two more were probably sunk.

The convoy delivered safely more than 250,000 tons of war material – tanks, guns, munitions and aircraft – after having been shadowed practically all the way by the enemy.

The operation was carried out under the command of Vice Admiral I. G. Glennie, CB, RN, flying his flag in the new cruiser, HMS *Black Prince*, which recently led destroyers that routed German destroyers off the French coast.

ONE WORD – SUBMARINE!
Signal for the Kill

U-boat packs hunting in the Arctic received one of their worst hammerings of the war when they tried to interfere with the passage of an Allied convoy bound for Russia. The great convoy went through in appalling weather conditions – snow, blinding rainstorms and high seas. Young destroyer men and pilots of the Fleet Air Arm 'blasted' their way through to Russia.

The U-boats that tried to attack the convoy were completely blasted in the Arctic Circle. Those counted as sunk left behind them a trail of twisted metal and floating lifebelts.

Honours for the first 'kill' were shared by the crew of a Fleet Air Arm Swordfish and a British destroyer, HMS *Onslaught* (Commander the Hon. A. Pleydell-Bouverie, RN).

The pilot of the Swordfish aircraft, 20-year-old Sub-Lieutenant Peter J. Beresford, RNVR, from Chorlton-cum-Hardy, Manchester, said: "I had with me as observer Sub-Lieutenant Bill Laing, RNVR, from Colnton, Edinburgh and tail gunner Leading Airman John Beech (20), of Clumber Avenue, Newcastle.

HIS FIRST SUBMARINE
Two Hits on Hull
"It was bitterly cold and cloudy, but reasonably clear low down. My gunner suddenly sighted a surfaced U-boat about nine miles away. The cloud was too high for protective cover, so we just went straight in 'hell for leather'.

"It was the first time I'd seen a sub. Flak started to come up at us, but we weren't hit. Then I let fly with my bombs and got two direct hits on the hull.

"We pulled out of the dive, with the Germans belting away at us with 40mm flak. Tracers were flashing all around."

Beresford then described how the U-boat was zigzagging and leaving a great trail of oil behind her, so he made a signal to the nearest destroyer, HMS *Onslaught*, to come and finish her off.

Commander Pleydell-Bouverie, RN, finished the story: "We were screening the convoy when we saw something firing at one of our Swordfish aircraft. There was a lot of black flak in the sky. We altered course and turned towards it at full speed.

"The aircraft signalled the one word 'Submarine'. I held my fire until we were within 8,000 yards, and then gave her 50 rounds with my 4.7-inch guns. The U-boat stopped, turned beam into wind and started to abandon ship.

"We were now within two miles, firing with our close-range weapons. It was by now quite clear that she was going to sink, but we gave her two more 4.7s from close range to make certain.

"The Germans were scrambling up the conning-tower and tumbling off the U-boat in rubber boats and life jackets. We picked up as many as we could. The last to leave was the captain, in a rubber boat of his own.

27 NAZIS SAVED
"Long-haired and ascetic"

"It was appallingly cold, and the survivors looked like sodden paper, frozen stiff. Altogether we saved 27 men, including the captain and one officer. I was surprised at their appearance. They were not tough-looking seamen, but long-haired, ascetic types, aged about 25.

"Another destroyer, HMS *Oribi* (Lieutenant Commander J. C. A. Ingram, DSC and Bar, RN), picked up the Engineering Officer and three more men." One of the survivors later died.

The second kill was made by a Swordfish aircraft piloted by Lieutenant E. B. Bennett, RNVR, 24, of Southbourne Grove, Westcliff-on-Sea, Essex, with Sub-Lieutenant Kenneth Horsfield, 22, of Genoa Street, Mexborough, Yorks., as observer, and Petty Officer Clifford A. Vines, 22, of Lincoln Road, Peterborough, as rear gunner.

Bennett said: "It was bitterly cold when we saw a U-boat on the surface about 12 miles away heading straight for the convoy. We quickly took a bearing and climbed into the clouds.

"We flew for five minutes, then dived through a gap and saw the submarine immediately below. I got her fixed in my bombsights and attacked with bombs. She was taken completely by surprise and I saw the bombs hit.

"As we climbed away to port, Vines gave her 500 rounds from the machine gun in her conning tower. The U-boat was by now zigzagging out of control. About two minutes later she turned hard a-starboard, her stern rose some 60 per cent and she sank.

"We dived low and saw about 15 survivors struggling in the water and masses of wreckage. We signalled a destroyer, HMS *Boadicea* (Lieutenant Commander F. W. Hawkins, RN)[43] who picked up those alive, numbering about three men. We had dropped a float-marker on the spot so that they could be found."

Observer Horsfield's story was very brief: "It was damn cold."

THE APPENDIX CASE
He Attacked Submarine

An attack was made by a Fleet Air Arm pilot suffering from acute appendix trouble. He attacked a U-boat in the morning and was lying on the operating theatre table the same evening, while the aircraft carrier was still in action. The hero of this action was Sub-Lieutenant J. F. Mason, 21, of South Road, Newton Abbot, Devon. He had been taken to hospital so he could tell the story himself.

But here it is told by his observer, Sub-Lieutenant Donald Street, RNVR, 21, of Mayfield Mount, Halifax, Yorkshire: "When we set off on our patrol there was plenty of snow about, and it was very cold. I had with me as air gunner Dennis Franklin, of Broomfield Place, Broomfield, Smethwick, Staffordshire.

"We hadn't been up long before we sighted a U-boat on our starboard bow. There was a slight haze, but we had the sun astern of us and got her rather by surprise. We went right into the attack, and hit her the first time with our bombs.

"Her stern settled, and two minutes later her bow came right up, and she sank in a cloud of bubbles. Some survivors were left on the surface. Nobody was rescued, so this attack will go down only as a 'probable' kill."

I met Able Seaman L. Hutchinson, of Cambridge Terrace, Station Road, Heacham, Kings Lynn, Norfolk. In peacetime he is a railwayman on the London & North Eastern Railway (LNER) and this was his sixth convoy trip to Russia: "My job is the 4.7-inch gun turret," he told me. "There seemed to be more U-boats than usual on this trip. We were narrowly missed by a torpedo once, but otherwise it was quite quiet. It's the cold that gets us down. We have to keep stamping our feet to keep warm."

---

[43] The anthologist's late father.

OBSERVED ALL THE WAY
Like Going Down High Street

Vice Admiral Irvine G. Glennie, CB, RN, flying his flag in one of Britain's latest cruisers, HMS *Black Prince* – which last month led the destroyers that routed four German destroyers off the north-west coast of France under shore guns – was responsible for getting the convoy through.

"The Russian convoy operation is always a very difficult problem," he said. "In the Atlantic you have sea space, but on the North Russian run we are under close observation the whole way. Imagine a little square of ships entirely self-contained wandering off on its own.

"We have got to fight it out. It's like going down the High Street. The Germans know which route we are taking, as we are under observation the entire time from the Norwegian coast.

"It's the destroyermen who get the really bad time on these runs. It's nothing for them but a hard slog all winter, in the most terrible weather conditions. I must give all these destroyermen, including Captain Campbell, of HMS *Milne*, who led the screen, full marks. They were magnificent."

Admiral Glennie paid the highest tribute to the young Fleet Air Arm pilots of HMS *Chaser*, who flew the Swordfish aircraft and the fighters off the escort aircraft carriers.

"They never let me down once," he said. "They were so frozen after their flights they had to be lifted out of their open cockpits when they had landed on the flight decks."

DESTROYER LOST
Officers and Men Go Down With Ship

One destroyer, HMS *Mahratta* (Lieutenant Commander E. A. F. Drought, DSO, RN), was torpedoed and lost. Loss of life was regrettably heavy in the *Mahratta* because of the appalling weather conditions.

The captain and all other officers went down with their ship, only 17 men were saved. It was a pitch-black night with high seas running, making rescue attempts practically impossible.

Fleet Air Arm fighter planes – American Wildcats – operating from carriers gave the Swordfish bombers constant cover.

Of 13 German aircraft (operating from bases in Norway), attacked by the

Wildcats, a Junkers 88 and an Fw 200 were damaged. Other Luftwaffe planes made for home. Neither our bombers or fighters sustained any damage.

'U-BOAT GERMANS'

Excerpt from *The Cruel Sea* by Nicholas Monsarrat

(Reproduced by kind permission of Cassell & Co.)

But there was still something about them, something which attacked the senses and spread discomfort and unease, like an infected limb in a sound body... They were strangers, and their presence on board was disgusting, like the appearance of the U-boat on the surface of the sea. They were people from another and infinitely abhorrent world – not just Germans, but U-boat Germans, doubly revolting. As quickly as possible, they were searched, and listed, and hidden below.

Ericson had ordered the German captain, who was among the prisoners, to be put in his own cabin, with a sentry on the door as a formal precaution; and later that morning, when they were within sight of the convoy and steaming up to report to *Viperous*, he went below to meet his opposite number. That was how he phrased it, in his mood of triumph and satisfaction: *Compass Rose* had done really very well, she had brought off something which had cost two years of hard effort, and he was ready to meet anyone half way, in the interests of good humour. But after the testing excitement of the morning, his mood was a matter of careful balance; he was not prepared for the sort of man he found in his cabin, and he experienced, during the interview, the swiftest change of feeling he had ever known.

The German captain was standing in the middle of the cabin, peering somewhat forlornly out of the porthole: he turned as Ericson came in, and seemed to collect himself into some accustomed pattern, the only one the world deserved to see... He was tall, dead-blond, and young – nearly young enough to be Ericson's son, but thank God he was not, thought Ericson suddenly, noting the pale and slightly mad eyes, the contempt that twitched his lips and nostrils, the sneer against life and the hatred of his capture by an inferior. He was young, but his face was old with some derivative disease of power. There's nothing we can do with these people thought Ericson with sombre insight; they are not curable. We can only shoot them and hope for a better crop next time.

"Heil Hitler!" began the German crisply. "I wish to...."

"No," said Ericson grimly, "I don't think we'll start like that. What's your name?"

The German glared. "Von Hellmuth. Kapitänleutnant von Hellmuth. You are also the captain? What is yours?"

"Ericson."

"Ah, a good German name!" exclaimed von Hellmuth, raising his yellow eyebrows, as to some evidence of gentility in a tramp.

"Certainly not!" snapped Ericson. "And stop throwing your weight about. You're a prisoner. You're confined here. Just behave yourself."

The German frowned at this breach of decorum; there was bitter hostility in his whole expression, even in the set of his shoulders. "You took my ship by surprise, Captain," he said sourly. "Otherwise..."

His tone hinted at treachery, unfair tactics, a course of conduct outrageous to German honour; suitable only for Englishmen, Poles, negroes. And what the hell have you been doing all these months, Ericson thought, except taking people by surprise, stalking them, giving them no chance. But that would not have registered. Instead he smiled ironically, and said:

"It is war. I am sorry if it is too hard for you."

Von Hellmuth gave him a furious glance, but he did not answer the remark; he saw too late, that by complaining of his method of defeat he had confessed to weakness. His glance went round the cabin, and changed to a sneer.

"This is a poor cabin," he said. "I am not accustomed ...."

Ericson stepped up to him, suddenly shaking with anger. In the back of his mind he thought: if I had a revolver I'd shoot you here and now. That was what these bloody people did to you: that was how the evil disease multiplied and bred in the heart... When he spoke his voice was clipped and violent.

"Be quiet!" he snapped out. "If you say another word, I shall have you put down in one of the provision lockers..." He turned suddenly towards the door. "Sentry!"

The leading seaman on duty, a revolver in his belt, appeared in the doorway. "Sir?"

"This prisoner is dangerous," Ericson said tautly. "If he makes any sort of move to leave the cabin, shoot him."

The man's face was expressionless: only his eyes, moving suddenly from the Captain to von Hellmuth, gave a startled flicker of interest. "Aye, aye, sir!" He disappeared again.

Von Hellmuth's expression hovered between contempt and anxiety. "I am an officer in the German Navy…" he began.

"You're a bastard in any language," Ericson interrupted curtly. He felt another violent surge of anger. I could do it, he thought, in amazement at his wild feeling: I could do it now, as easily as snapping my fingers… "I'm not particularly interested in getting you back to England," he said, slowly and carefully. "We could bury you this afternoon, if I felt like it… Just watch it, that's all – just watch it!"

He turned and strode from the cabin. Outside, he wondered why he was not ashamed of himself.

A SPELLING PROBLEM

Len Perry, Stoker, HMS *Beagle*

It was, to the best of my recollections, in early April 1944 and about *Beagle*'s last run to Russia prior to D-Day. We were assembling off Iceland, expecting to join up with the merchant ships, but we met up with five small boats, American submarine chasers, similar to our wooden five-ply Motor Torpedo Boats, but all-metal. We were to escort the Russian-crewed sub-chasers, with two other destroyers – I believe they were *Bulldog* and *Westcott* – to Kola Inlet.

The first day at sea there was a heavy swell running and the sub-chasers were pitching their bows in deep, so they had to slow down. The next day the weather moderated and good progress was made, but by the third evening, it was blowing and gusting, heralding a typical Arctic storm as we neared the North Cape. By the following morning visibility was limited, the

sub-chasers had been scattered, and re-assembling them was proving difficult. Then one of the destroyers reported that one had foundered but its
Russian crew had all been picked up in time.

Beagle then came across another sub-chaser that was hove to, its engine
swamped by sea water. We secured a tow line, took the crew off, but after a
short time it became very low in the water. The tow line was cut, and it was
scuttled by gunfire and we eventually made port with our somewhat battered
charges.

We were very surprised at the excellent winter clothing of the rescued
Russian seamen. Ours was very poor in comparison, apart from the thick
woollen knitwear sent up to us by the dear ladies of Newton Abbot, in distant Devon.

I'm not sure if it was that particular occasion, but *Beagle* had returned to
Scotland from a Russian port from a similarly rough escort duty, with its
inevitable losses, and tied up to a buoy near the battleship *Duke of York*
which, incidentally, hadn't participated in that extremely harrowing convoy.

An urgent signal was blinked across the anchorage to *Beagle* by Aldis
Lamp from the mighty battleship's bridge:

"WILL YOU KINDLY WEAR THE RIG OF THE DAY – STOP –
YOU LOOK LIKE A CROWD OF PIRATES – END."

Before responding, our Chief Yeoman of Signals, nearing exhaustion with
little sleep, was overheard to murmur to Number One: "Sir, how do you
spell 'BOLLOCKS'…?"

A KISS FROM BETTY HUTTON

Iain Nethercott, ex-HMS *Keith*

Around mid-1944, when on HM Submarine *Tactician*, and after over
three weeks on station, having landed various spies into Malaya and
sunk two Marus[44] and a few junks with gunfire, we were withdrawing from

---

[44] *Maru*: sailor's slang for any Japanese merchant vessel (many of whose names ended in
maru).

our patrol billet off the minefields of Singapore into the Malacca Straits. We were ordered to enter Sabang Harbour at 0530 hours on a stipulated date to coincide with a joint British and American air strike from the aircraft carriers HMS *Illustrious* and USS *Saratoga* on the refineries and oil storage tanks in the harbour area. Our assignment was to attempt to pluck any downed pilots from the sea as, in those days, like submariners these unfortunates were executed by lopping their heads off with a sword when captured by the Japanese.

Our Skipper, Sir Anthony Collett, got Frankie Mustard, a big, burly Leading Stoker and a champion water polo king, and myself, being the best underwater swimmer on the boat, to volunteer for the job of 'Diving Party' to attempt any rescues as appropriate. We both opted to take knives; Frankie a diver's knife while I took a jungle knife.

Come the morning, the boat went to diving stations and we crept into Sabang Harbour, avoiding the patrol boat at the entrance, and waited...

Almost spot-on schedule, the American planes appeared with the dawn, single-engine Hellcat and Wildcat dive-bombers. They came in high out of the rising sun while we surfaced and picked up an escort of circling USN fighters as we surfaced and established R/T communication with them.

The dive-bombers caught the Nips by surprise and by the time I'd climbed out on to the casing the oil refineries were "burning like buggery", to borrow an RAF expression. Every anti-aircraft gun around the harbour was firing as the British carrier planes came in.

Meanwhile, the harbour batteries had opened up on *Tactician* and we had to zigzag, trimmed down to dodge the salvoes. It was then that our escorting fighters homed us across the harbour where one of their dive-bombers had just 'gone in'. We steamed across amid a hail of shells and small-arms fire and saw the plane slowly disappearing under the surface. The Skipper took the way off the boat and, as we came alongside he went astern and told us to "have a go".

We both immediately dived in. I found the still-sinking plane about 10 feet down with the pilot still struggling under the cockpit canopy. Frankie then joined me and we both tried to slide the canopy back. He suddenly noticed a red-painted handle on his side of the plane's fuselage and yanked it back. We both heaved and tugged on the canopy and it gave.

Frankie left to surface for air while I hacked at the pilot's straps. He was now unconscious and I was practically out myself. Then Frankie appeared with the 2nd Coxswain who was wearing a DSEA set.[45] Together they cut the rest of the webbing and brought the half-drowned pilot to the surface, closely followed by me, blowing like a grampus.

The lads on the ballast tanks quickly grabbed the pilot and got him down the gun hatch. Frankie and the 2nd Coxswain hauled themselves out and were hurried down below while the Skipper got under way to dive. I was still hanging on to a Kingston Valve on the ballast tank, being all-in... totally exhausted. Fortunately, our First Lieutenant looked over the tower and saw me drowning. The Skipper stopped engines and I was dragged down below in a state of indignation, but felt decidedly better after a couple of his whiskies.

Our American friend had by now been pumped out. He'd found himself on board a British patrol submarine which was practically out of fresh water, with only weevily flour for bread, the boat alive with cockroaches and rats, an unwashed crew dressed in sweaty old sarongs and with four-week-old beards... He probably thought he'd be better to have his head lopped off...

A few days later we sailed into Trincomalee Harbour, Ceylon, the base for the Far Eastern Fleet under Admiral Somerville. We looked our usual disreputable selves – still unwashed as we only had drinking water aboard, the upper-deck crew attired in a mixture of khaki shorts and Afrika Korps uniforms.

Tactician had initially been painted blue in the Mediterranean, which had been over-painted deep green out in the Indian Ocean. What with depth-charging removing most of the paint, and the red rust biting its way through our skin, we resembled something out of an East End scrapyard.

Our ragged old 'Jolly Roger', newly emblazoned with a white lifebelt to record our latest saga, was flying from the after periscope, while our Yankee aviator, in a newly-pressed uniform, was perched up on the platform of the forward periscope so that as we passed the huge American carrier USS *Saratoga* they could get a good view of him.

The British ships ignored us as we came alongside our mother ship HMS

---

45 Davis Submarine Escape Apparatus.

Adamant, but as we'd passed *Saratoga* she was 'dressed overall' and all her ship's company were lining the side, waving and cheering. Most of *Saratoga's* motor boats were in the water. They followed us across the anchorage, loaded with American newsreel men, cases of Coca-Cola, cigars and candy bars.

It was a marvellous welcome, especially for us as we were always treated like Cinderellas by the Royal Navy with its snooty admirals and battleships. When the American newsmen came aboard they spent hours taking miles of film down below. All I wanted to do was to get my mail after four weeks, and get ashore for a bath and a hair trim before we were bussed up to the Rest Camp at Dyatalawa, in the hills of Ceylon.

But it was not to be. We were all cordially invited aboard *Saratoga* for a meal and a film up on her flight deck. She was truly massive, about 52,000 tons and had been built in the 1920s. At the top, we were met by her Commanding Officer and her Air Operations Officer who insisted on shaking hands with each of us before passing us to a 'minder' to look after us on board.

We all went down to *Saratoga's* gigantic mess hall and queued with her crew, each of us carrying a sort of aluminium tray, inset with various sized bowl shapes. When we got up to the serving bar, the American cooks slapped great dollops of your choice into the bowls of your tray. It would be no good coming the old 'Oliver Twist' on this ship. The cooks would give you another great dollop. And if your blueberry pie and ice cream landed on top of your two-inch thick beef steak with trimmings, it was very much in your own interest to hustle along the queue rather than hold up the whole of *Saratoga's* crew, all 3,000 of them...

Later we all congregated on the flight deck with our minders to watch the latest Betty Hutton film from Hollywood, so unlike our film shows on the *Adamant* where we were regaled with such films as *All Quiet on the Western Front,* etc. Before the film the *Saratoga's* captain led forth 'our' pilot (incidentally an Admiral's son) and gave a really glowing speech, with our skipper alongside him who was puce with embarrassment.

Betty Hutton, herself on tour, then came forward and poor old Frankie Mustard and I had to shake hands with and be kissed by Betty Hutton for the assembled American newsreel man.

She smiled sweetly at me and planted a lingering kiss, a big screen 'plonker', on my unwilling lips. I countered by remarking that I would never, ever, wash my lips again.

When I got back among my mates on the front row, the Coxswain hissed: "You've got more guts than me. I'll have you thoroughly checked out in the Sick Bay as soon as we get back on board…"

Why did he have to spoil my illusions? Just jealousy, of course. My Skipper got a big American medal, Commander of the United States Legion of Merit. I got a good meal and a lipsticky kiss.

Anyway, Sabang Harbour was practically knocked out by this dual effort. I was much impressed by the American Navy fliers who seemed to be better trained than ours.

EXERCISE 'TIGER' – A VIEW FROM THE GERMAN SIDE

Arno Abendroth, German military historian

Towards the end of 1943 the British Government assigned an area on the south Devon coast, near Torbay, as a Battle Training Ground for the US Army and the US Navy. Slapton Sands was one of the beaches chosen because it closely resembled the features of 'Utah' beach in Normandy.

On 26 April 1944 nearly 30,000 American GIs were assembled in the Plymouth area, and boarded several landing craft to participate in a rehearsal for the invasion of Occupied Europe. At the beginning of the exercise however, while assembling the LSTs and LCIs,[46] the British destroyer HMS *Scimitar* collided with an LCI and had to return to port, leaving eight US Navy LSTs without adequate escort for the remainder of the exercise.

Just before dawn on 28 April 1944, by pure chance, nine German S-boats[47] of Flotilla 5, based at Den Helder, Holland (occasionally at Cherbourg, France), and Flotilla 9, based at Den Hoofden, Holland, commanded by Korvettenkapitän Bernd Klug, were patrolling the South Devon

----

[46] Landing Craft Infantry.

[47] *Schnellboote*: 'fast boats'; 'E-boats' to the Allies.

coast looking for coastal shipping. They saw the unescorted LSTs, and Klug, previously decorated with the Oak Leaves for bravery, decided to go in close at high speed, at one stage within 200 metres of the Devon coast, torpedoing several LSTs, sinking *LST 507* and *LST 531* and severely damaging *LST 289*.

The young, comparatively inexperienced American GIs were unfamiliar with a new specially developed and bulky 'Mae West' life jacket, which was designed to be crossed and fastened over the chest. They'd received only limited and hasty instruction in the life jacket's design and proper use. Consequently, many GIs drowned because they'd tied the harness tapes around their abdomen. When they entered the sea after jumping from the sinking and burning LSTs, wearing their heavy equipment, they were dragged under the surface, immediately turned upside down, and were drowned.

At dawn, as it gradually grew lighter, Korvettenkapitän Klug after his surprise attack decided to withdraw at high speed in case a large Allied destroyer screen arrived on the chaotic scene of death and destruction.

Total casualties were 749 American servicemen, comprising 541 US Army and 208 US Navy personnel including eight officers. It was nothing less than a large-scale disaster. Furthermore, the US General Staff were aware that some of the US officers who had participated in the ill-fated exercise had already been informed that the primary areas selected for the forthcoming invasion of Europe were the beaches of Normandy and the Cherbourg Peninsula. This was priceless information to the German High Command in Berlin which, at that time, was successfully being led to believe that the primary invasion area would be the Pas de Calais, the shortest route across the English Channel. The US General Staff, fearing that one or more of the officers had been picked up by one of the German Navy MTBs, hastily organized a desperate and detailed search of the beaches. Eventually, all officers who had participated in Exercise 'Tiger' were all accounted for, either as survivors or as corpses on the beaches.

Many years were to pass before the true facts of what really happened were admitted by the Allied authorities in Washington and London. In 1984, Mr Ken Small, with the help of local divers, recovered a US Army Sherman tank, which had gone down on 28 April 1944 only 300 metres from the shoreline of Slapton Sands. The Sherman tank is now a permanent monument complete with an official memorial plaque, approved by the US Congress, in the village of Torcross, Devon, placed in memory of the American servicemen who died during Exercise 'Tiger'.

RUSSIAN CONVOY RA 59 – APRIL/MAY 1944

Michael Back, Able Seaman, HMS *Boadicea*

The last outward-bound convoy to Russia in the winter of 1943/1944 was JW 58, which sailed on 27 March 1944, with the return convoy RA 58 arriving back in UK ports in mid-April. The supply route to Russia was then switched to the Persian Gulf for the duration of the summer. However, there were still a number of empty ships in Russian ports waiting to return. In addition, there were some 2,300 Russian sailors waiting to be transported to the UK to take over HMS *Royal Sovereign* and a number of old destroyers and submarines, in addition to the American crew of the cruiser USS *Milwaukee*, which had been handed over to the Russians at a Kola Inlet base, who were also waiting to return.

A strong escort force was accordingly sent to Russia, under the command of Rear Admiral R. R. McGrigor. The force included the light cruiser HMS *Diadem*, the escort carriers HMS *Fencer* and HMS *Activity* and 16 destroyers, including HMS *Beagle* commanded by Lieutenant Commander N. R. Murch, RN, and HMS *Boadicea* commanded by Lieutenant Commander F. W. Hawkins, RN. As the German battleship *Tirpitz* was at this time known to be temporarily out of circulation, no covering force was considered necessary.

Arriving at Kola Inlet on 23 April 1944, they sailed on 28 April escorting the convoy RA 59 of 45 ships. They at once ran into atrocious weather, but despite this they were still detected by a German reconnaissance aircraft on 30 April, resulting in a U-boat pack being positioned across the Bear Island passage in the path of the convoy.

Despite the violent snowstorms and rough seas, the escort carriers still managed to fly off their aircraft. The Swordfish squadron of the *Fencer* had the magnificent record of sinking three U-boats (*U-277*, *U-674* and *U-959*) during the 1st and 2nd of May. Only one merchant ship was lost, and the remaining 44 ships of the convoy anchored safely in Loch Ewe on 6 May.

The achievements of the Swordfish of HMS *Fencer* in breaking up the U-boat pack was lost neither on the Russian Admiral who was taking passage aboard her, nor on Admiral Karl Dönitz, Commander-in-Chief of the German Navy. Consequently, Dönitz sought an urgent interview with Hitler to recount the failure against convoy RA 59, and to urge, successfully, that all available torpedo-bomber squadrons should be transferred from the Mediterranean to Northern Norway.

RA 59: ALLIED SUCCESS

Anthologist's Note: A more detailed factual account of the convoy is contained in the invaluable *Chronology of the War at Sea* by J. Rohwer and G. Hummelchen. (Reproduced by kind permission of Ian Allan Ltd.)

21 April–6 May 1944
Arctic:
An escort force (Rear Admiral McGrigor), comprising the cruiser *Diadem*, the escort carriers *Activity* and *Fencer*, the 3rd DD[48] Flotilla with *Milne*, *Meteor, Marne, Marne, Musketeer, Verulam, Ulysses* and *Virago*, the 6th SG[49] with the Canadian frigates *Waskesiu, Grou, Cape Breton* and *Outremont*, and the 8th SG with the destroyers *Keppel, Walker, Beagle, Westcott, Whitehall, Wrestler, Inconstant, Boadicea* and the corvette *Lotus*, goes to Kola Inlet to fetch convoy RA 59 where it arrives on 23 April. At the same time on 21 April, Vice Admiral Moore proceeds with the battleship *Anson*, the carriers *Victorious, Furious, Searcher, Striker, Emperor* and *Pursuer* and cruisers and destroyers to the northern Norwegian coast to carry out another raid on the *Tirpitz*. On 24 April and 25 April the weather prevents the aircraft from taking off. After refuelling the destroyers, the aircraft fly off on 26 April for an attack on shipping near Bodo. Here they find a southbound convoy and sink

---

[48] Destroyer.
[49] Support Group.

three German ships of 15,083 tons. Six aircraft are lost to the defending fighters and AA fire.

After a feeder convoy of 16 steamers from the White Sea, accompanied by the Soviet destroyers *Gremyashchi* and *Gromki*, the minesweeper *T-119* and five patrol ships, arrives in the Kola Inlet on 27 April, convoy RA 59 puts to sea on the following day with the escort force. Initially, it is reinforced by the Soviet destroyers *Razyarenny*, *Grozny* and *Kuibyshev*, the minesweepers *T-112*, *T-114*, *T-119*, and the submarine chasers *BO-201*, *BO-204*, *BO-205*, *BO-207*, *BO-209* and *BO-212*. The US crew of the cruiser *Milwaukee/Murmansk* are distributed among the ships, as are 2,300 Soviet sailors who are to man the British units (one battleship, nine destroyers and four submarines) which are to be taken over as a share of the Italian war booty in Britain. Admiral Levchenko is on board the *Fencer*. The convoy is located by German air reconnaissance towards midnight on 28-29 April.

The U-boats, which are waiting for an eastbound convoy, are deployed against RA 59 from 30 April as the 'Donner' group (*U-277*, *U-636*, *U-307*, *U-278*) and the 'Kiel' group (*U-711*, *U-739*, *U-674*, *U-354*, *U-315*, *U-959*, *U-313*). After a FAT[50] salvo miss from *U-307* (Lieutenant Herrle) on the convoy, *U-387* (Lieutenant Commander Buechler) and *U-711* (Lieutenant Lange) repeatedly attack destroyers and steamers with T-5s and FAT salvoes towards midnight on 30 April. *U-711* sinks the *William S. Thayer* (7,176 tons). In the course of 1 April *U-278* (Lieutenant Commander Franze), *U-307* and *U-959* (Lieutenant Weitz) each miss destroyers twice with T-5s. Aircraft of the *Fencer* sink *U-277* on 1 April and *U-959* and *U-674* on 2 May, while *U-307* and *U-711* again miss destroyers with T-5s. Early on 3 May *U-278* is attacked by two Swordfish and one Martlett, but shoots down the latter and escapes.

---

[50] The FAT (*Federapparat Torpedo*) ran an irregular course incorporating 180-degree turns.

ANNALS OF WAR AND PEACE (Part I)

E. J. Kahn, Jr. (via 'Jack' Adams, USN/USAAF, Ret'd), excerpt from *The New Yorker*, 8 February 1988. (Reproduced by kind permission of Mrs E. Kahn/*The New Yorker*)

B y alphabetical chance, Brent Maxwell Abel, a Harvard College classmate of mine who is also a fellow combat veteran of World War II and a long-time friend, always comes first in the autobiographical accounts that we 1937 graduates submit to an anniversary album every five years for poster-ity's sake and our own. Twenty-six of our classmates died in service during that war. Abel and I came out of it physically unimpaired but not, I hope, emotionally unchanged. I doubt, though, whether either of us shed any tears, between Pearl Harbor and VJ Day, for any of our German or Japanese armed opponents. Why should we have? They were trying to kill us, as we were trying to kill them.

If in 1962 I read through what Abel wrote for our twenty-fifth reunion report, his words didn't make a lasting impression. I have recently had reason to reread them. This past 29 September (1987), I was aboard a floating restaurant on the outskirts of Frankfurt-am-Main when Abel received a hero's ovation from eight onetime crewmen of a German U-boat whose lives he saved in 1944, following one of the most unlikely high-seas battles in modern history. What Abel had to say about that episode in 1962 was:

'I commanded a destroyer escort, USS *Buckley*, which achieved particular distinction on account of her successful ramming and sinking of the surfaced German submarine *U-66* in the central Atlantic, after a brief struggle which included hand-to-hand fighting. The *Buckley* had no casualties, although about half the submarine's crew were lost, and we took the others prisoner. The *Buckley* later received a Navy Unit Commendation, which still gives me a warm sense of accomplishment.'

Abel neglected to add that he himself had received, for "extraordinary heroism" in that engagement, the not-lightly-bestowed Navy Cross.

It was on 6 May 1944 (Abel's 28th birthday, which was something his 210 officers and men didn't know) that the *Buckley* sent *U-66* to the bottom. Over the next 42 years, Abel thought back to that day every now and then –

most notably when Rear Admiral Samuel Eliot Morrison, working on his history of American naval operations in World War II, phoned for details.

Abel was born in Washington, DC in 1916. His parents were divorced when he was five, and thereafter he never laid eyes on his German-born father, a retired Lieutenant Colonel in the US Army. After college, Abel moved to the Harvard Law School and spent a prewar year with a distinguished New York law firm. After the war he settled and practised law in San Francisco. As an undergraduate, Abel was one of 39 men in his class who enrolled in the Navy's ROTC[51] program and acquired seagoing experience. After being called up for Active Duty in March 1941, Abel spent a year ashore at Corpus Christi, Texas, as a Naval Air Station Instructor in Aerodynamics.

In July 1942, he put to sea. He wrote in that 1962 report:

'On account of the seniority acquired from taking naval science as an undergraduate, my sea duty included responsibilities which I found terrifying, challenging, or funny by turns, and sometimes all three at once. For example, my first hour afloat was spent in simultaneously assuming command of a sub-chaser, an escort unit of four other sub-chasers, and a 15-ship convoy of tankers, all sailing at night from the blacked-out port of Curaçao, to meet another convoy in the Caribbean. To this day I do not understand how this expedition came off without mishap.'

Later, from his Curaçao base, he set off in pursuit of a German submarine that had particularly vexed the Allied naval forces in the Caribbean by mining the harbour of St. Lucia. Abel never made contact with it, and he didn't know until he was shown a *U-66* logbook in Frankfurt 45 years later that the submarine he'd vainly chased on August 30 1942 was the one he caught up with and demolished in May 1944.

In the spring of 1943, Abel was transferred to the destroyer escort *Buckley* – DE 51, in cold Navy parlance – and that summer he assumed command over 15 subordinate officers and 196 enlisted men. 306 feet long, and displacing 1,850 tons, the *Buckley* had a top speed of 24 knots and an arsenal composed of 3-inch, 40mm and 20mm guns, depth bombs, and small arms.

---

[51] Reserve Officer Training Corps.

In the course of the war, Nazi Germany built approximately 1,100 U-boats, about 800 of which were destroyed, but not before they had sunk almost 23,000 Allied and neutral merchant ships. *U-66*, commissioned on 2 January 1941, was 252 feet long, displaced 1,120 tons and had a capacity for 22 torpedoes, with four firing tubes forward and two aft. It carried a crew of 60, all volunteers for that cramped and perilous service. By 6 May 1944, when its path crossed the *Buckley's*, *U-66* had, according to its record-keepers, spent 676 days at sea, sunk 36 ships with an aggregate of 240,000 tons, and racked up 80,787 surface sea miles and 9,334 submerged.

The *Buckley* was part of a Task Group of American naval vessels – three other destroyer escorts and a mother ship, the escort carrier *Block Island* – that sailed out of Norfolk, Virginia, on 22 April 1944. On 5 May, the group, whose mission was to hunt and kill U-boats, was some 500 miles west of the Cape Verde islands. The *Block Island* had Grumman Avengers aboard, single-engine fighter aircraft called 'Night Owls', that could operate in the dark. The planes had been stripped of all their ordnance to make room for extra fuel tanks and could stay aloft for 14 hours, longer than most nights lasted. On the night of 5/6 May, the sea was calm and a near-full moon was shining brightly.

At 9.22 p.m. Oberleutnant Gerhard Seehausen, Captain of the *U-66*, decided to surface to get some fresh air and recharge his batteries, unaware that the *Block Island* had been tracking him for four days by aerial observation and by radar. The carrier spotted the submarine when it surfaced and ordered the *Buckley* to take out the U-boat, which immediately dived.

When he resurfaced, he was 18 miles from the carrier, but his new position was quickly spotted by an Avenger piloted by Lieutenant Jimmy Sellars and at 2.16 a.m. on 6 May he began guiding the *Buckley* by VHF radio toward the submarine. Lieutenant Commander Abel ordered "General Quarters" and at 3.20 a.m., only 2,100 yards from the U-boat, he ordered his 3-inch guns to open fire. The very first salvo smashed into the submarine's conning tower. Then Abel opened fire with everything he had.

Sellars radioed the *Block Island*: "*Buckley* is cutting hell out of the conning tower!"

The two vessels zigzagged as they drew closer. By 3.25 a.m., the U-boat and the destroyer were parallel only 20 yards apart – so close that Avengers that had taken off from the carrier to reinforce Sellars couldn't bomb or strafe, lest they hit the *Buckley*.

At 3.29 a.m. Abel shouted, "Hard right rudder!" He had decided to ram. As the *Buckley*'s bow crunched into the *U-66*'s foredeck, Oberleutnant Seehausen – who was shot and killed minutes later – issued his last command: "Abandon ship."

Lieutenant Commander Abel completed his Action Report of the engagement 48 hours later:

'0329 hours: *Buckley*, alongside sub, gives hard right rudder. Rides up on fo'c's'le of sub and stays there. Men begin swarming out of submarine and up on *Buckley*'s fo'c's'le. Machine gun, Tommy gun and rifle fire knocked off several. Ammunition expended at this time included several general mess coffee cups which were on hand at ready gun station. Two of the enemy were hit on the head with these, empty shell cases were also used by crew of 3-inch gun No. 2 to repel boarders. 3-inch guns could not bear. *Buckley* suffers only casualty of engagement when one man bruises fist knocking one of the enemy over the side. Several men, apparently dead, could be seen hanging over side of the sub's bridge at this time. The Boatswain's Mate, in charge of the Forward Ammunition Party, kills a man, attempting to board, with a .45 pistol. Man falls back over the side. Midships Repair Party, equipped with rifles, mans lifelines on starboard side abaft light lock, and picks off several men on deck of submarine. Chief Fire Controlman uses Tommy gun from bridge with excellent results.

0330 hours: *Buckley* stops all engines and backs off, to avoid boarding by too many of enemy, some of whom came aboard armed. Sub draws ahead rapidly, maintaining speed of about 18 knots. Five prisoners are disarmed and taken aft.'

The surviving Germans aboard the *U-66* did not, as ordered, abandon ship. Enough of them remained at their stations to get their battered vessel underway, though at reduced speed. Lieutenant Commander Abel gave chase, caught up and was about to bombard it with depth charges when *U-66* swerved, possibly out of control, and struck the *Buckley*'s starboard side a glancing blow. While the two vessels were touching for the second time, one of Abel's men leaned over and dropped a hand grenade down the U-boat's hatch. The submarine veered away, now manifestly out of control. The few men still aboard jumped into the ocean – the very last was its Chief Engineer, Oberleutnant Georg Olschewski – and an instant later *U-66*, sheathed in flames, went to the bottom of the Atlantic, its end signalled by a muffled underwater explosion. It was 3.36 a.m.

The entire battle, later descried in a United States Government communique as "probably the closest naval combat of modern warfare," had, beginning with Abel's "Commence firing", lasted just sixteen minutes.

Years later one of the survivors, Oberleutnant Klaus Herbig, the U-boat's Executive Officer, set down his version of the mid-ocean boarding:

'As I came up onto the bridge, our Commander was again standing, but the destroyer was on our port side, with its crew preparing to board and capture our U-boat. Our Commander then ordered me to take all the men on the bridge and board the destroyer in order to prevent boarding by the Americans. Boarding by the Americans would have meant scuttling our boat with part of our crew still below decks, in order to prevent the Americans from getting their hands on important material.

I immediately jumped over with eight men to where we could hang on to the rail of the destroyer. The command was successful, because the destroyer immediately moved away from our sub. Our sub then rammed the destroyer in its starboard propeller. The pause in firing, which had been in effect, was suddenly over, and a rain of bullets pelted our sub. We stood on the destroyer and watched as we were guarded by whites and blacks with various guns and ammunition belts.

Our Chief Engineer, Georg Olschewski, who had experience on many missions, was the last person on board our sub, which was still floating despite the hail of bullets. All others had left the boat. Many must have been killed during the jump into the water or while waiting on the bridge. As far as it is possible to ascertain, no one went down with the boat. The engineer then sank the boat and left, with the waves which foamed over the bridge. Now the destroyer ceased firing. The chase, which had lasted over 30 minutes at a speed of 16-18 nautical m.p.h., was now over.

You can imagine how our crew was scattered over a large area. The destroyer first returned to the point where the first men had jumped overboard and began picking them up out of the water. This action by the American Commander was very commendable, a deed which we appreciated very much, because the men who had jumped overboard first of all were naturally more exhausted than those who had just jumped in.

The airplanes dropped flares, because the moon had set in the meantime. The destroyer searched and hoisted our men out of the water for a long period of time. The airplanes helped in the search, so that all human efforts were made to save the very last survivor. But we were badly shaken when we surveyed our small group of survivors and realized which of our comrades, with whom we had made many voyages and overcome many dangers, no longer lived.'

Seaman First Class Vinzenz Nosch, an Austrian in *U-66*, remembers:

'The destroyer *Buckley* continued on its course in trying to ram us and I heard our on-board guns shooting at the approaching destroyer. At this time we were on the surface, and suddenly I heard the sound of a grenade exploding in our boat. The lights went out, there was a smell of powder and a strong odor in the boat, and in the front area you could hear water pouring in the boat.

Suddenly we heard the command: "Everyone out of the boat." At this point there was a lot of chaos – everyone ran to the same mid-point, put life jackets on, then tried to get out of the tower and onto the bridge whenever there was a pause in the firing, and to get overboard.

As I entered the tower, Privates Jahn and Sundermann, badly injured and lying on the floor, asked to be taken along. Jahn had had his arm blown off, and you could see that there had been many hits in the tower area. My comrade Ronge and I climbed up on the bridge, and as we were hidden behind the periscope supports we saw how our dead comrades were lying around the bridge and near the 3.7-centimetre cannon.

During a pause in the firing, Ronge yelled I should jump overboard and swim with him to the destroyer. I saw Ronge jump and fall between the approaching destroyer and our boat. I jumped from the starboard side of the tower into the water. As I was swimming I saw the destroyer slowly approach, shooting at our boat which sank, stern first, at about 4.00 a.m.

My life jacket was ruined, and I'm not ashamed to say, I was exhausted by the 16-week voyage, and since I knew that there were no ships' routes in the area where we were sunk I wanted to give up. But through praying, I still had hopes that I would be saved. As the sun rose, I suddenly saw an airplane and a flare above me. After I'd been swimming in the Atlantic for three or four hours, I saw a mast on the horizon. I was picked up by the destroyer *Buckley*.'

The *Buckley* eventually transferred the survivors to the carrier *Block Island*, which ferried the German prisoners to Casablanca, north-west Africa, where they were placed in a guarded compound near the waterfront. Some of them were taking a stroll on 29 May 1944 when the carrier, en route to Casablanca from another sortie, was hit by three torpedoes from *U-549*. Six of the carrier's crew were lost, but 951 were rescued by the destroyer escorts *Ahrens* and *Robert I. Paine*.

Several weeks later, the survivors from *U-66* were put on another carrier and taken to Norfolk, Virginia. Many of them ended up at Camp McCain, Mississippi, where the enlisted men picked cotton and a couple of officers made, and profitably sold, cigars. Not until 1947 were most of the submariners repatriated to Germany.

The *Buckley*, damaged but navigable, made it back home and then underwent a month of repairs at Boston Navy Yard, Massachusetts. Brent Abel, soon to be promoted to Commander, was relieved of sea duty and sent to the University of Minnesota, to share his expertise with ROTC students.

He retired in January 1946, as a Captain – a promotion to which his Navy Cross automatically entitled him. As he embarked on his postwar law practice in San Francisco, it never occurred to him that he would have – or want to have – anything to do with that particular lot of Germans. And for the next 42 years he didn't.

USS *GUADALCANAL* TASK GROUP AND *U-505*: THE EVENTS OF 4 JUNE 1944 AND THEIR SIGNIFICANCE

Captain R. J. Schlaff, USN, Ret'd

Sunday, 4 June 1944. Lunch was being served aboard *U-505*. The German submarine was submerged in the Atlantic Ocean off the West African coast and she was heading home empty-handed after a lengthy patrol, having just completed an 84-mile detour to avoid a hunter-killer group believed to be hot on her trail.

Constructed in Hamburg and commissioned in 1941, *U-505* had sunk seven Allied ships during her first six months at sea. But in November 1942 the boat had been attacked by a British seaplane, and following six months of repairs in an increasingly hostile shipyard in Lorient, France, had returned to active service as the most heavily damaged submarine ever to do so. However, her second Commanding Officer committed suicide during a concentrated depth charge attack in late 1943 and there had been only one more sinking. The *U-505* was considered an unlucky boat.

American Task Group 22.3 included the escort aircraft carrier USS *Guadalcanal* (CVE 60), and five destroyer escorts: USS *Pillsbury* (DE 133), USS *Pope* (DE 134), USS *Flaherty* (DE 135), USS *Chatelain* (DE 149) and USS *Jenks* (DE 655). The task group had sailed from Norfolk, Virginia in mid-May and searched unsuccessfully in the vicinity of the Canary Islands, off Morocco, north-west Africa. With fuel running low on 4 June 1944 the task group headed for the Moroccan port of Casablanca.

Ten minutes after turning north, USS *Chatelain* reported a possible sound contact. Within minutes, aircraft from the *Guadalcanal* had spotted the still-submerged submarine. 'Hedgehogs' and depth charges from the escort destroyers soon forced her to the surface. Heavy gunfire then forced the submarine's crew to abandon ship.

Had the usual accepted doctrine been followed the U-boat would have been sunk, but the task group had left port with the specific intention of attempting to capture a submarine. It had earlier forced another submarine to the surface and watched it abandoned by its crew. Reviewing that event had led to the decision to attempt to capture instead of simply sinking a submarine should another opportunity arise. The decision had been approved at the highest level.

When the *U-505*'s crew began jumping overboard, the "Cease Fire" order was given. Then came "Away Boarding Parties". The *Chatelain*, *Jenks* and *Pillsbury* each lowered boats in the water. *Jenks* and *Chatelain* were ordered to pick up survivors. 58 prisoners were subsequently picked up; one German sailor was killed during the hectic and dramatic action.

The *Pillsbury*'s boarding party of eight men, led by Lieutenant A. L. David, was ordered to board the abandoned submarine. Lieutenant David was subsequently awarded the Congressional Medal of Honor, America's highest award for bravery against the enemy. The accompanying citation states:

> 'Fully aware that the U-boat might momentarily sink or be blown up by exploding demolition and scuttling charges, he braved the added danger of enemy gunfire to plunge through the conning tower hatch and, with his small party, exerted every effort to keep the ship afloat and to assist the succeeding and more fully equipped salvage parties in making the *U-505* seaworthy for the long tow across the Atlantic to a US port.'

Two sailors were awarded the Navy Cross and the entire Task Group received a Presidential Unit Citation. Established by Executive Order on 6 February 1942, this is the nation's highest unit award and it is issued in the name of the President of the United States as public evidence of deserved honor and distinction for outstanding performance in action. Not only had the group seized the only German U-boat captured by the United States Navy in World War II, it had also accomplished the unique and difficult feat of boarding and capturing an enemy warship on the high seas. This was something that the US Navy had not accomplished since the USS *Peabody* captured the British brig-cruiser *Nautilus* at the end of the war of 1812. With the help of the codebooks recovered from *U-505*, the Allies sank almost 300 U-boats during the next eleven months.

After remaining secreted in Bermuda after the 1939-1945 war, *U-505* was eventually brought to the Museum of Science and Industry in Chicago,

Illinois. The citizens had raised over $250,000 to preserve it as a permanent exhibit and memorial to the 55,000 Americans who lost their lives at sea during World War II. In 1989, as the only submarine of its class still in existence, *U-505* was designated a National Historic Landmark. It has remained in Chicago and intrigued over 24 million visitors. Two of those visitors in 1996 were two of the eight sailors from the USS *Pillsbury*'s boarding party who had found, and replaced, the vital cover of the 8-inch bilge strainer that had been flooding the U-boat.

The significance of the capture of *U-505*, and of other submarines such as *U-110*, *U-570*, and of *U-559*, took on new meaning for the general public in the years following the 1974 publication of F. W. Winterbotham's *The Ultra Secret*. The book revealed for the very first time at least some of the secrets of the code-breaking activities at Bletchley Park. That is when it was learned that German submarines carried coding typewriters called Enigma Machines and that capturing the machines and the manuals containing the various settings they used enabled the Allies to read the messages that were being sent to the submarines by their Commander, Admiral Karl Dönitz. *U-505* carried two Enigma machines, but the machines were not the biggest prizes.

The now de-classified Top Secret memorandum published by the US Navy noted that also obtained were U-boat cipher keys for the month of June 1944 and the then-current grid-chart, or geographic location cipher. These documents enabled the Allies to read every message sent to the U-boats as soon as the Germans could, and also to know precisely where coded locations actually were.

Also found in the haul from *U-505* was a complete description of a new German electronic-navigation system which was considered superior to the Allied systems then in use and was eventually adopted for use all over the world. The list goes on and surprises still appear. In September 2002, *The Chicago Tribune* reported that the US Navy had decided *U-505* could have its original periscope back. Shortly after *U-505*'s capture in 1944 its two periscopes were taken away by Intelligence officials eager to evaluate the German optics. One periscope ended up in a laboratory in San Diego, southern California in the 1950s and was installed at the bottom of a 250,000-gallon cold-water tank used to experiment with submarine technology and materials suitable for warfare beneath this planet's polar ice caps.

Inventions from the laboratory were installed on the world's first atomic submarine, the USS *Nautilus*, when she made the first 1,100-mile underwater passage into the Arctic Ocean in 1957. The laboratory was being demolished so the periscope was returned to the German submarine after more than 50 years.

Daring feats of skill and bravery notwithstanding, it should also be noted that secrecy is what made these efforts absolutely vital. Had the German High Command been aware of what had occurred it could have quite easily changed the codes and so denied the Allies of the advantage they had clearly gained. Many thousands had learnt the lesson: "Loose lips sinks ships."

'A THOUSAND MILES FROM SALT WATER...'

Anthologist's note: Rear Admiral D. V. Gallery, USN, Ret'd, former Commanding Officer of the escort aircraft carrier USS *Guadalcanal* (1944-1945), concludes his excellent book *We Captured a U-boat*, thus:

'The *U-505* will be alongside the Museum for many years to come, perhaps over a hundred years if it isn't blasted to atoms by a hydrogen bomb in the meantime. It should serve as a constant reminder to us Americans that seventy per cent of the earth's surface is salt water, and the United States owes a great deal to the sea which carried our ancestors to freedom and to a new way of life on a virgin continent, was the bulwark that protected us when the country was young and weak, and gave us access to the markets and resources of the world to make our industry thrive and grow.

In both World Wars, after bloody battles against submarines, the sea was the great military highway over which we deployed our military might to fight the enemy a long from our home shores. Now that America is the world's greatest industrial nation, the sea's highways bring in the strategic raw materials needed to keep the wheels of our mighty industry turning.

Fifty five thousand American soldiers, sailors, airmen and merchant seamen have gone down to unmarked graves defending the freedom of the sea. What more fitting memorial could they have, and what more appropriate symbol is there of our victory at sea than an enemy U-boat itself, beaten in a mid-ocean battle, towed across the Atlantic, and installed in the Midwest, a thousand miles from salt water?

Even in the atomic age, the submarine is still the greatest threat to our control of the seas. This captured submarine at the Museum of Science and Industry is a tribute to the heroism of our Navy men, a memorial to the dead, and a stern reminder to the living that control of the seas, so vital to our existence, has been purchased at great price.'

OVERLORD – ORDER OF BATTLE

Excerpt from *Chronology of the War At Sea 1939-1945* by J. Rohwer and G. Hummelchen (Reproduced by kind permission of Ian Allan Ltd.)

6 June 1944 – English Channel: Operation 'Neptune' (amphibious phase of the Operation 'Overlord'): the major Allied landing in Normandy. Overall command: Supreme Commander SHAEF[52], General Eisenhower; Land Forces 21st Army Group, General Montgomery; Naval Forces, Admiral Ramsay; co-ordinator of Air Forces, Air Chief Marshal Tedder.

After heavy air attacks (3,467 heavy bombers, 1,645 medium, light and torpedo-bombers, 5,409 fighters – and 2,316 transport aircraft are deployed) the 82nd and 101st US Airborne Divisions land on the southern part of the Cotentin Peninsula and the British 6th Airborne Division south-east of Caen by parachute.

In the morning, supported by strong naval forces, there follow by sea the 4th US Infantry Division on the east coast of the Cotentin Peninsula ('Utah'), the 1st Infantry Division near Vierville ('Omaha'), the 50th British Infantry Division near Arromanches ('Gold'), the 3rd Canadian Infantry Division near Courseulles ('Juno') and the 3rd British Division near Lyon-sur-Mer ('Sword').

---

[52] Supreme Headquarters Allied Expeditionary Force.

Forces deployed: 'Western Naval Task' (Rear Admiral Kirk on the USN cruiser *Augusta*) with the 1st US Army (Lieutenant General Bradley).

First, 102 US, British and Allied minesweepers clear the approaches with 16 buoy-layers.

In the night, Force 'U' (Rear Admiral Moon on the Headquarters ship *Bayfield*, VII US Corps, Lieutenant General Collins) with the 4th US Infantry Division (Major General Barton) on the convoys U 2A, U 2B, U 1, U 3, U 3C, U 4, U 5A and U 5B and Force 'O' (Rear Admiral Hall in the Headquarters ship *Ancon*, V US Corps, Lieutenant General Gerow) with the 29th Infantry Division (Major General Huebner) on the convoys O 2A, O 2B, O 1, O 3, O 3C, O 4A, O 4B and O 5 approach.

The convoys for 'Utah' and 'Omaha' consist of 16 attack transports, one LSD, 106 LSTs, one LSR, 15 LCCs, 93 LCIs, 350 LCTs, 34 LCSs, 94 LCAs, 189 LCVPs, 38 LCS(S)s, 54 LCPs and for fire support, nine LCGs, 11 LCFs, 14 LCT(R)S, two LCS(M)s and 36 LCS(S)s.

Support Force for 'Utah': Force 'A' (Rear Admiral Deyo), comprising the US battleship *Nevada*, the British monitor *Erebus*, the US cruisers *Tuscaloosa* and *Quincy*, the British cruisers *Hawkins*, *Black Prince* and *Enterprise*; the Dutch gunboat *Soemba*; the US destroyers *Hobson*, *Fitch*, *Forrest*, *Corry* (Destroyer Division 20); *Butler*, *Shubrick*, *Herndon*, *Gherardi* (Destroyer Division 34); and the destroyer escorts *Bates* and *Rich*.

Support Force for 'Omaha': Force 'C' (Rear Admiral Bryant), comprising the US battleships *Texas* and *Arkansas*, the British cruiser *Glasgow*, the French cruisers *Montcalm* and *Georges Leygues*, the US destroyers *McCook*, *Carmick*, *Doyle*, *Baldwin*, *Harding*, *Satterlee*, *Thompson* (Destroyer Squadron 18) and the British 'Hunt' class destroyers *Melbreak*, *Tanatside* and *Talybont*.

As escorts for the approaching 'U' and 'O' convoys, the US destroyers *Jeffers*, *Glennon* (Destroyer Squadron 17) *Barton*, *O'Brien*, *Walke*, *Laffey*, *Meredith* (Destroyer Squadron 60), the US destroyers *Frankford*, *Nelson*, *Murphy*, *Plunkett* (Destroyer Squadron 33), the French corvettes *Aconit* and *Renoncule*, the British destroyers *Vesper* and *Vidette*, the US destroyer escorts *Borum*, *Amesbury* and *Blessman* and the French frigates *L'Aventure* and *L'Escarmouche*.

The British battleship *Nelson*, the British cruiser *Bellona*, the US destroyers *Somers*, *Davis* and *Jouett* (Destroyer Division 18) and the French frigates *La Surprise* and *La Decouverte* available as a reserve for the Western Task Force.

On 6 June 23,250 troops are landed in the 'Utah' Sector, and 34,250 troops are landed in the 'Omaha' Sector.

Eastern Naval Task Force (Rear Admiral Vian on the British cruiser *Scylla*) with the 2nd British Army (Lieutenant General Dempsey).

First, 102 British and Canadian minesweepers with 27 buoy-layers clear the approaches.

In the night Force 'G' (Commodore Douglas-Pennant on the Headquarters ship *Bulolo*), British XXX Corps (Lieutenant General Bucknall) with the British 50th Division on the convoys G 1 to G 13; Force J (Commodiore Oliver on the Headquarters ship *Hilary*) with the 3rd Canadian Division on the convoys J 1 to J 13; and Force S (Rear Admiral Talbot on the Headquarters ship *Largs*), British I Corps (Lieutenant General Crocker) with the British 3rd Infantry Division on the convoys S 1 to S 8 approach.

The convoys for 'Gold', 'Juno' and 'Sword' consist of 37 LSIs, 130 LSTs, two LSRs, one LSD, 11 LCCs, 116 LCIs, 39 LCI(S)s, 487 LCTs, 66 LCSs, 408 LCAs, 73 LCS(S)s, 90 LCPs and 10 LCP(S)s. In addition, for fire support: 16 LCG(L)s, 22 LCT(R)s, 14 LCS(L)s, 24 LCS(M)s, 18 LCFs, 45 LCA(H)s and 103 LCTs with armament.

Support Force for 'Gold': Force 'K' (Captain Longley-Cook), comprising the British cruisers *Argonaut*, *Orion*, *Ajax* and *Emerald*, the Dutch gunboat *Flores*, the British destroyers (25th Flotilla) *Grenville*, *Ulster*, *Ulysses*, *Undaunted*, *Undine*, *Urania Urchin*, *Ursa* and *Jervis* and the British 'Hunt' class destroyers *Cattistock*, *Cottesmore* and *Pytchley*, and the Polish destroyer *Krakowiak*. Support Force for 'Juno': Force 'E '(Rear Admiral Dalrymple-Hamilton) comprising the British cruisers *Belfast* and *Diadem* and the British destroyers *Faulknor* (8th Flotilla), *Fury* and *Kempenfelt* (27th Flotilla), *Venus*, *Vigilant*, the Canadian destroyers *Algonquin* and *Sioux*, the Norwegian 'Hunt' class destroyers *Stevenstone*, *Bleasdale* and *Glaisdale*, and the French destroyer *La Combattante*.

Support Force for 'Sword': Force 'D' (Rear Admiral Patterson), comprising the British battleships *Warspite* and *Ramillies*, the monitor *Roberts*, the cruisers *Mauritius*, *Arethusa*, *Frobisher*, *Danae* and *Dragon* (Polish) and the destroyers *Saumarez* (23rd Flotilla), *Scorpion*, *Scourge*, *Serapis*, *Swift*, *Stord* (Norwegian), *Svenner* (Norwegian), *Verulam*, *Virago*, *Kelvin*, *Slazak* (Polish), *Middleton* and *Eglinton*.

Six destroyers, four sloops, eight frigates, 17 corvettes and 21 trawlers (British, Canadian, French and Norwegian) are deployed to escort the 'G', 'J' and 'S' convoys.

The British battleship *Rodney* and the cruiser *Sirius* are among the ships which form the reserve for the Eastern Task Force.

On 6 June 24,970 troops are landed in the 'Gold' Sector, 21,400 troops in the 'Juno' Sector and 28,845 troops in the 'Sword' Sector.

To escort the first follow-up wave Force 'B' (Commodore Edgar), consisting of the US destroyers *Rodman*, *Ellyson* and *Hambleton*, the British destroyers *Boadicea*, *Volunteer* and *Vimy*, the 'Hunt' class destroyers *Brissenden* and *Wensleydale*, and the corvettes *Azalea*, *Bluebell* and *Kitchener* (Canadian), is deployed in the west; and in the east, Force 'L' (Rear Admiral Parry) comprising the 'Hunt' class destroyer *Cotswold*, the escort destroyer *Vivacious*, the frigates *Chelmer* and *Halsted*, the corvettes *Clematis*, *Godetia*, *Mignonette*, *Narcissus* and *Oxlip* and three anti-submarine trawlers, 49 LSTs, 19 LCI(L)s and 53 LCTs.

The British 10th Destroyer Flotilla consisting of *Tartar*, *Ashanti*, *Haida* (Canadian), *Huron* (Canadian), *Blyskawica* (Polish), *Eskimo* and *Javelin*, a group of frigates and eight groups of coastal forces with MTBs and MGBs, form the covering force against attacks by surface craft in the western entrance of English Channel. In the east the same role is undertaken by the 17th Destroyer Flotilla, consisting of *Onslow*, *Onslaught*, *Offa*, *Oribi*, *Obedient*, *Orwell*, *Isis* and *Impulsive* and seven groups of coastal forces. In addition, the following belong to the escort forces:

Cruisers: *Dispatch*, *Ceres* and *Capetown*.

Destroyers: *Kimberley*, *Opportune*, *Pathfinder*, *Beagle*, *Bulldog*, *Icarus*, *Campbell*, *Mackay*, *Montrose*, *Walpole*, *Windsor*, *Whitshed*, *Vanquisher*, *Versatile*, *Wanderer*, *Walker*, *Westcott*, *Wrestler*, *Caldwell*, *Leeds*, *Lincoln*, *Ramsey*, *Skate*, *Saladin* and *Sardonyx*.

'Hunt' class destroyers: *Cattistock, Eglinton, Garth, Holderness, Meynell, Avon Vale, Belvoir, Goathland* and *Haldon.*

Sloops: *Scarborough, Rochester, Hart, Kite, Lapwing, Lark, Magpie* and *Pheasant.*

Frigates: *Deveron* and *Nene.*

Frigates (ex-USN destroyer escorts): *Cubitt, Dakins, Ekins, Holmes, Lawford, Retalick, Stayner* and *Thornborough.*

Corvettes: *Puffin*; British 'Flower' class: *Armeria, Balsam, Burdock, Buttercup, Campanula, Celendine, Dianthus, Gentian, Heather, Honeysuckle, Lavender, Nasturtium, Pennywort, Primrose, Starwort, Sunflower, Wallflower,* the French *Cdt Estienne D'Orves,* the Norwegian *Acanthus, Eglantine, Potentilla, Rose,* the Canadian *Alberni, Baddeck, Battleford, Calgary, Camrose, Drumheller, Lindsay, Louisburg, Lunenburg, Mimico, Moosejaw, Port Arthur, Prescott, Regina, Rimouski, Summerside, Trentonian* and *Woodstock.*

In all, seven battleships, two monitors, 23 cruisers, three gunboats, 105 destroyers and 1,073 smaller naval vessels are employed.

On 6 June the German Navy has in the English Channel area the following surface vessels: five torpedo boats, 34 motor torpedo boats (five others are non-operational), 163 minesweepers, 57 patrol boats and 42 gun-carriers. On the Atlantic coast five destroyers, one torpedo boat, 146 minesweepers and 59 patrol boats are available.

From 6 June to 30 June 1944, Allied warship losses off the Normandy coast: as a result of German air attacks, the US destroyer *Meredith II* and the British destroyer *Boadicea.* As a result of mines, the US destroyers *Corry, Glennon* and *Rich* and the British destroyers *Wrestler, Fury* and *Swift*; as a result of German coastal artillery the French destroyer *Mistral.* In addition, a number of smaller ships and transports sink as a result of mines and coastal artillery.

6-30 June English Channel/Bay of Biscay.

The following forces are deployed against the U-boat danger for the invasion: the reinforced No. 19 Group, RAF Coastal Command; and, under the Commander-in-Chief Western Approaches, the escort carriers *Tracker, Activity* and *Vindex* with Support Group 1 (the destroyer escorts *Affleck,*

Balfour, Bentley, Capel, Garlies and *Gore*), SG 2 (the sloops *Starling, Wild Goose* and *Wren*, the frigates *Loch Killin, Loch Fada, Dominic* and *Lochy*), SG 3 (the Destroyer Escorts *Duckworth, Essington, Rowley, Berry, Cooke* and *Dunnett*), SG 4 (the Destroyer Escorts *Bentinck, Byard, Calder, Bazely, Blackwood* and *Drury*), SG 5 (the Destroyer Escorts *Bickerton, Aylmer, Bligh, Kempthorne, Keats* and *Goodson*), SG 6 (the Canadian frigates *Waskesiu, Outremont, Cape Breton, Grou* and *Teme*) and SG 9 (the Canadian frigates *Matane, Swansea, Stormont, Port Colborne, St. John* and *Meon*). Under the Commander-in-Chief Plymouth, the destroyers of SG 11 (the Canadian *Ottawa, Kootenay, Chaudiere, St. Laurent* and *Gatineau*), SG 12 (the Canadian *Qu'Appelle, Saskatchewan, Skeena* and *Restigouche*) and SG 14 (the British *Hesperus, Havelock, Fame* and *Inconstant*).

Four to six Support Groups of the Commander-in-Chief Western Approaches operate in the operational areas 'CA' west of the English Channel and the Bay of Biscay, and two groups of destroyers in the entrance to the Channel.

On 6 June, 17 U-boats set out from Brest, 14 from St. Nazaire, four from La Pallice and one from Lorient from the 'Landwirt' group.

On 7 June aircraft from No. 19 Group sink the homeward-bound *U-955* and *U-970* in the Bay of Biscay. The Brest boats, *U-963, U-989, U-256* and *U-415*, return damaged.

On 8 June, a B-24 Liberator of No 224 Squadron, RAF (Flying Officer Moore) sinks *U-629* and *U-373* in turn and others damage *U-413*. On 9 June *U-740* is sunk. It proves impossible to enter the English Channel with the non-schnorkel U-boats.

U-766 from the Brest boats, *U-228, U-255, U-260, U-270, U-281, U-382, U-437, U-445, U-608, U-650, U-714, U-758, U-985* and *U-993* from the St. Nazaire boats, *U-262* and *U-333* from La Pallice and *U-981* from Lorient are stationed in the Bay of Biscay until 15 June. Of the nine schnorkel boats *U-212* has to return twice; the others try to reach the invasion area, followed by *U-767, U-1191, U-988, U-671* and *U-971* which come down from Norway.

On 7 June and 8 June *U-984* (Lieutenant Sieder) fires four T-5 torpedoes, *U-621* (Lieutenant Struckmann) fires two and *U-953* (Lieutenant Marbach) four T-5s against the four destroyers of the 12th SG, but they all explode prematurely or in the ships' wash. Early on 9 June, *U-764* (Lieutenant von Bremen) fires four T-5s during a destroyer engagement without securing a hit.

Up to 11 June, *U-621*, *U-269* (Lieutenant Uhl) and *U-275* (Lieutenant Bork) attack destroyer groups unsuccessfully in the western entrance to the English Channel. *U-821* (Lieutenant Knackfuss) is lost in an air attack.

From 14 June, the first U-boats reach the shipping routes simultaneously with the Support Groups, some of which are moved to the Channel.

On 14 June *U-984* misses a search group and on 15 June *U-621* sinks the Landing Ship *LST 280*, *U-767* (Lieutenant Dankleff) sinks the frigate *Mourne* operating with the 5th SG, and *U-764* the destroyer escort *Blackwood* of the 4th Support Group (taken in tow but a total loss).

On 18 June *U-621* misses two US battleships with a salvo. *U-767* is sunk by the 14th Support Group and *U-441* (Lieutenant Commander Hartmann) by a Wellington of No 304 Squadron (Polish).

Of the schnorkel U-boats arriving in the second half of June, *U-763* (Lieutenant Commander Cordes) misses a search group with two T-5s in the night of 22-23 June; *U-971* (Lieutenant Zeplin) is sunk in the western Channel by the destroyers *Eskimo* and *Haida* after an attempted attack fails because of faulty firing.

On 25 June the destroyer escorts *Affleck* and *Balfour* sink *U-1191*, the *Bickerton* (Commander Macintyre) *U-269*, while *U-984* from the same group torpedoes the *Goodson* and misses a destroyer escort.

On 27-29 June *U-988* (Lieutenant Dobberstein) torpedoes the corvette *Pink* (total loss) and sinks two ships of 9,444 tons before she is sunk on 29 June by the 3rd Support Group.

On 29 June *U-984* attacks the convoy EMC 17 and hits four ships of 28,790 tons of which only one ship is beached and can be salvaged, the other three becoming total losses. *U-671* (Lieutenant Commander Hegewald) misses a destroyer from a search group on 30 June.

After another unsuccessful attack on a search group on 2 July, the boat is damaged by depth charges and has to put in to Boulogne. The schnorkel mining U-boats *U-214* and *U-218* lay mines off Plymouth on 26 June and off Land's End on 1 July. One ship of 7,177 tons is damaged on 6 July on the latter barrage.

By 30 June, 570 Liberty ships, 788 coastal motor boats, 905 LSTs, 1,442 LCTs, 180 troop transports and 372 LCIs reach the assault area in supply convoys. The convoys are chiefly escorted by British and Canadian corvettes.

7 June-2 July, English Channel

Operation 'Neptune'. In the days after the first landing the following units are put ashore in Normandy from the follow-up convoys:

In the 'Utah' sector: the 90th US Infantry Division, 7-9 June; the 9th US Infantry Division, 10-13 June.

In the 'Omaha' sector; the 2nd US Infantry Division, 7-8 June; the 2nd US Armoured Division, 10-13 June.

In the 'Gold' sector: the 7th British Armoured Division, 8-10 June; the 49th Infantry Division, 11 –12 June.

In the 'Juno' and 'Sword' sectors; the 51st British Infantry Division 9-11 June.

By 12 June 326,000 troops, 104,000 tons of supplies and 54,000 vehicles are landed. By 2 July the figure is increased to four Corps of the 1st US Army with two Armoured and 11 Infantry Divisions and four Corps of the 2nd British Army with three Armoured and four Infantry Divisions, totalling 929,000 troops, 177,000 vehicles and 586,000 tons of supplies.

On 7 June General Eisenhower and Admiral Ramsay visit the assault area on board the fast minelayer Apollo.

On 12 June *PT71* brings Generals Marshall, Eisenhower, Arnold, Bradley and Hodges, and Admirals King, Stark, Kirk, Moon and Wilkes to Normandy.

10-11 June, English Channel

The British 58th Motor Torpedo Boat Flotilla, comprising *MTB 687*, *MTB 681*, *MTB 683*, *MTB 666*, *MTB 723*, and *MTB 684* attacks the German convoy 1253 off Den Helder and sinks the patrol boats *V 1314*, *V 2020* and *V 2021* for the loss of *MTB 681*.

On the following night (11-12 June) the Norwegian 54th Flotilla (Lieutenant Commander Monsen), comprising *MTB 712*, *MTB 715*, *MTB 618*, *MTB 623* and *MTB 688*, attacks off the Hook of Holland the German 11th Minesweeper Flotilla (Commander Seifert), which is being transferred from Borkum and which includes *M 348*, *M 307*, *M 347*, *M 264* and *M 131*. *MTB 712* is damaged.

DESTROYER DIARY OF D-DAY
'The Navies Do It Again', by Desmond Tighe

Reuters Special Correspondent for the Combined Press, Mr. Desmond Tighe, had already experienced much action reporting many of the previous major wartime operations. His memorable dispatches from HMS *Beagle* appeared in all the British national newspapers. The following is his first dispatch, dated 7 June 1944:

(Reuters Special Correspondent for the Combined Press aboard a British destroyer off Bernier-sur-Mer).

Guns are belching flame from more than 600 Allied warships. Thousands of bombers are roaring overhead, fighters are weaving in and out of the clouds as the invasion of Western Europe begins.

We are standing eight thousand yards off the beaches of Bernier-sur-Mer and from the bridge of this little destroyer I can see vast numbers of naval craft of all types.

The air is filled with the continuous thunder of broadsides and the crash of bombs. Great spurts of flame come up from the beaches in long snake-like ripples as shells ranging from 16-inch down to 4-inch find their mark.

In the last ten minutes alone more than 2,000 tons of high-explosive shells have gone down on the beachhead.

First On The Beach
It is now exactly 7.25 a.m., and through my binoculars I can see the first wave of assault troops touch down on the water's edge and fan up the beach.

Battleships and cruisers are steaming up and down, drenching the beaches ahead of the troops with withering broadsides. Great assault vessels are standing out to sea in their hundreds, the invasion craft are being lowered like beetles from the davits and head towards the shore in long lines. They are crammed with troops, tanks, guns and armoured vehicles of all types.

The tin-hatted British and Canadian forces in this sector are cheerful and smiling as they go in. A Tank Landing Craft has just passed, with the crew of one tank sitting on top of the turret. The tank is named 'Warspite'. The crew give the 'thumbs-up' sign and grin at us cheerfully.

Allied bombers are passing over us in their thousands.

Fighters keep up a constant patrol, protecting the great invasion fleet.

Just ahead of us lies the little town of Berniere-sur-Mer. We can see the spire of Berniere belfry rising out of the swirling smoke.

Some German shore batteries are opening up on us, but their fire is ineffective and ragged.

Gallant little fleet destroyers are steaming up and down, close inshore, protecting the landing troops and plugging shore batteries with 4-inch shells.

The whole planning of this great amphibious operation – the greatest in world history – has been done in the utmost secrecy and has taken nearly twelve months.

Hundreds of factors had to be taken into account before the assault could be launched, the most important being the question of weather. It is giving away no secret now to say that weather conditions for the landings were not perfect, but despite high-running seas and a strong north-westerly wind, a bold decision was taken to go ahead.

From the bridge of this destroyer, commanded by Lieutenant Commander Norman R. Murch, of Dawlish, South Devon, I have had a grandstand view of every phase of the operation.

Just after four o'clock we reached a position some 18 miles off the coast of France. The night bombing was in full swing.

Events then moved rapidly. Here is the diary kept on the bridge as, wrapped in duffle coats and thick mufflers, we watched the dawn and saw the invasion start.

05.07: Lying eight miles from the lowering position for invasion craft.

05.18: Spitfire with clipped wing-tips skims low over our deck.

05.20: Grey light of dawn. The great shapes of innumerable assault ships appear smudgily on our starboard beam. A little MTB follows in our wake –

obviously off his course. A young signalman stands on the bridge and flashes: "We are lost. Please direct us to ——— Beach." We put him on his way.

05.27: Night bombing has ceased and the great naval bombardment begins.

05.33: We move in slowly. Coastline becomes thin smudge of grey.

05.36: Cruisers open fire off our starboard bow. We can recognise *Belfast* and *Mauritius*. They are firing tracers.

05.45: The big assault ships start lowering their boats crowded with tin-hatted Tommies.

'What A Party!'

05.46: There are at least one thousand ships of all sizes in our sector alone. Big battleships join. On our port bow we see *Warspite*, the 'old lady' of Salerno fame, belching fire from her eight 15-inch guns. *Orion*, *Mauritius* and another cruiser, *Black Prince*, are belting away with all they've got.

Fleet destroyers are darting round us. Everybody seems to be there.

"What a party!" I hear the captain say, "I wouldn't miss this for all the tea in China!"

05.50: I see the first flash from a German shore battery. Above us we hear the sweet drone of our fighter cover. Sky cloudy, but fairly high ceiling. So far, not one enemy plane has shown up. It appears we have taken the enemy by surprise.

05.55: On our port beam I can see a thin line of stout tank-landing craft heading towards the shore.

06.00: The coast is now clearly visible. Enemy batteries are opening fire spasmodically. Cruisers continue to belt away.

06.50: The fleet destroyers now close to shore. Weather is worsening. Sky is turning grey and big clouds are coming up.

Covered With Smoke

07.00: First wave of B-17 Flying Fortresses come in. The roar of their engines coupled with the 'crump' of bombs and the noise of shells is terrific.

07.20: It is now quite light. I can see the spire of the Berniere belfry. We are 9,500 yards from the shore, still closing. The town is covered with smoke. Buildings appear to be smashed and crumpled.

07.25: The first wave of landing craft have reached the shore. I see them touch down. Red tracers from close-range enemy weapons are searing across the beach. Men leap out of the landing craft and move forward. Tanks follow.

07.35: We move out on patrol. It is too early to know how the initial landings have gone, but they were made to a split second according to timetable. The battle goes on.

MEN WHO GOT THEIR TANKS THROUGH

Heroic Efforts to Save Landing Craft from Sinking

From the *Yorkshire Post*, 8 June 1944

(Reproduced by kind permission of the *Yorkshire Post*, Leeds)

From Desmond Tighe, Reuters Correspondent aboard HMS *Beagle*, off Normandy Beaches – Tuesday evening, 6 June 1944:

D-Day has come to a close and the Royal Navy has put up one of the finest jobs of the war. In this tough little destroyer *Beagle* we have passed long lines of tank landing craft, motor launches and supply ships steadily streaming towards the beachhead. In the other direction similar groups of ships of all sizes have been streaming for home to bring up more and more reinforcements.

Conditions have not been easy, and the smaller ships of the Navy have had a very tough time.

S-O-S in Darkness

It was about midnight, just before zero hour on D-Day, that we found our first casualty. We were steaming for the coast of France, the wind was high, and seas were lashing over our bows.

A faint light signalled S-O-S out of the darkness. We turned towards it and found a small Assault Landing Craft, manned by a Royal Marine Second Lieutenant, three Marine privates and three naval ratings, tossing about in the sea. She was holed badly up forward.

We pulled the crew aboard; one of the Marine privates had been so seasick that it took the ship's doctor some time to pull him round.

They are not all big ships that have swarmed across on this invasion. Many motor launches, motor-torpedo boats and small assault landing craft crossed the sea under their own power.

A Tank Landing Craft, badly holed, limped into the anchorage off the beaches late today in a sinking condition. She was being towed by a small minesweeper.

As she passed the bows of the *Beagle* I could see the ratings and the 'Tommies' feverishly baling out the water with buckets, pans and anything they could lay their hands on. They were knee-deep in the swirling water. The shore was only a few hundred yards off, and they were determined to get those tanks through. I don't know who the young skipper of this LCT was, but if any man had done his job properly in the assault, he certainly had.

This evening, as we lie at anchor close into the invasion beaches, the waters of the Bale de la Seine present an even more amazing sight than they did at first light this morning.

Naval craft seem to have increased in number, and the whole area is packed with shipping. Cruisers, destroyers and lumbering Tank Landing Craft flying their barrage balloons from the stern, supply ships, motor launches, tugs, minesweepers – they are all there.

Beach Battle

The seas have now abated and the sun is shining, but the beach battle goes on. Away to the south-west British destroyers are bombarding. Through our binoculars we can see German tanks deploying on the beaches just below the sea wall. A stubborn battery on the cliff-tops just to the right keeps up intermittent fire, and the shells are sending up large plumes of water around the destroyers; but they fight on, darting in and hammering enemy gun positions.

Away inland, pillars of dull grey smoke show where stubborn artillery battles are being fought. We can see lines of Allied tanks and trucks moving slowly over the winding roads across the green fields and hills.

Air Cover

The Royal Air Force and the US Army Air Force continue to give air support to a degree never before known by an expeditionary force. Late this afternoon we watched Flying Fortresses high up in the blue sky flying over enemy positions in their hundreds. We watched as they unloaded their bombs, and we could see explosions as they found their objectives.

Not once during the whole course of D-Day have we seen or heard a Luftwaffe plane. British and American fighters are never absent. Flying at heights ranging from about 15,000 feet to 1,000 feet they have given constant cover.

The climax to the whole Allied air invasion plan came late this evening, when we watched the second wave of glider-borne troops soaring in over the area. They came in hundreds in one endless stream, flying at an incredibly low altitude. The whole sky was black with them. Great Halifaxes slipped these gliders, which landed gently away in the distance over the coastline.

A VISION OF HELL

Len Perry, Stoker, HMS *Beagle*

I was a stoker aboard *Beagle* from 1943 until 1945 so I have no recollections of the early, eventful and most interesting years of 1940, 1941 and 1942 at sea. That's not to say that the war was over, far from it…

My most harrowing memory must be the events which took place shortly after D-Day. Those nights in the crowded English Channel were, to put it mildly, hell. Not much has been written about the first few weeks of the build-up following the Allied landings in Normandy on 6 June 1944, but 'Jerry' knew what he was doing, and doing it very effectively and quite ruthlessly.

During the night of 8/9 June 1944, *Beagle* was escorting American LSTs (Landing Ship Tanks). The voyage towards the French coast was proceeding as scheduled when suddenly, off Cherbourg, two LSTs were hit simultaneously and immediately began burning furiously, rapidly turning night into day. Evidently, an unseen German E-boat had opened fire.

I've always felt that there was more than one enemy E-boat lying in wait, stationary, as *Beagle* was leading the convoy, and allowed the destroyer to pass by in order to ensure their 'kill'.

It was already like daylight as *Beagle* turned to go in for the rescue attempts. The first of the American GIs were in the sea. A lot of them were not going to see the dawn, as the whole terrible scene worsened with each passing minute.

The scrambling nets were lowered over *Beagle*'s sides and we began to haul the first of the GIs aboard. They were surprisingly young, as most of us were, their fixed, glazed expressions seemed to prevent them from talking or crying. They were very cold, covered in oil and shivering uncontrollably. They clung on to us so tightly with a vice-like grip which visibly bruised whatever part of our hands, arms or shoulders they were clinging to. Consequently, it was almost impossible to pull out two or three water-sodden human beings. They, in turn would not release their grip which resulted in several of *Beagle*'s crew themselves being pulled into the oil-covered sea.

The problem was partly overcome by launching the whaler and hauling them aboard into it, thereby enabling the survivors to be handed up one at a time from the whaler. Then some of us decided to move forward away from the nets. We hastily made up ropes with a float on the end and threw them out to the struggling GIs in their life jackets and hauled them in.

By that time of course, we were literally covered in oil, vomit, blood and excrement. Lieutenant McDonald, *Beagle*'s doctor, and his Sick Berth Attendant, were moving quickly around the decks, checking the rescued and exhausted GIs and showing us how to stop them choking. One young soldier, who we pulled out quite easily, was helping himself and was talking to us. Suddenly he went limp, and slumped to the deck, apparently unconscious.

I then said: "Come on! WAKE UP!…"

He looked so peaceful. He was dead.

That was my first experience of witnessing a death. His body was taken down to the Seamen's Mess Deck where some of the bodies of other American soldiers were laid out, as dignified as possible in the circumstances.

However, even the grimmest situations have their moments of farcical humour. We saw a US Army Sergeant almost cruising across *Beagle*'s bows. He appeared to us to be waist-high, out of the water. He held a five-gallon petrol can under each arm, the type you see on the back of a jeep. We didn't know if he was drunk or not, but when we threw him a line with a float, he refused our offer, yelling: "Get all these other bums in first… Get 'em in first!…"

Then the order came down from the bridge to clear all personal lockers for dry clothes as the soaked, cold and shivering survivors had already used all our blankets. One or two hours had passed since the initial attacks and some of the GI survivors had recovered sufficiently to play an active role in the rescue attempts, in fact some were in better shape than us, as we were nearing exhaustion ourselves.

By that time, one LST had gone down to the bottom of the Channel together with its precious cargo of Sherman tanks, trucks and jeeps. The other LST had somehow stopped burning and together with *Beagle*, had drifted into a known minefield.

Our Skipper, Lieutenant Commander Murch, in a calculated risk, then ordered our searchlights to be switched on, thereby again turning night into day, which we all thought was a bit 'hairy'. We suddenly became lit up like an illuminated Christmas tree and became an easy target for the E-boats, either still lurking in the surrounding darkness, or speeding back to their bases on the Dutch coast.

In retrospect, our Skipper was well aware of what he was doing. His action was three-fold; sweep the searchlight to locate more survivors; keep a look-out from all quarters of the ship for mines on the surface; and the E-boats were not likely to venture anywhere near the minefield.

Eventually, the eastern sky gradually lightened, heralding the grey dawn after a truly horrific night. There seemed to be no more survivors; the surviving LST was barely afloat, just a smoking, drifting hulk. It was decided, reluctantly, to sink her by gunfire, a decision which evidently didn't please some of the GIs. However, it was done and we gently moved off and set course for Portsmouth.

About halfway back, we were met by a US Navy ship which we would have liked to have gone alongside, but they lowered a boat with a medical team and took off the dead and some of the injured. We would have preferred to transfer all survivors, but too much time would have elapsed and *Beagle* was only two hours from Portsmouth. So we steamed direct for

Portsmouth and disembarked all survivors for the superior, well-equipped facilities at Haslar Royal Naval Hospital.

HMS *Beagle* was in an awful state. Most of the problems were caused by the black, slippery and foul-smelling oil. But we were given 24 hours to clean up and get some much-needed sleep, to be ready for sea and another convoy escort duty the next morning.

Desmond Tighe, in his dispatch for Reuters, wrote:

'It was the most courageous and cold-blooded rescue venture I have seen at sea... The bravery of the *Beagle*'s officers and ship's company was something I shall never forget.'

CHANNEL CONVOY

Captain Surgeon R. S. McDonald, RN, Retd., HMS *Beagle*

After the initial D-Day landings during the early hours of Tuesday 6 June 1944, in which we had escorted minesweepers and various types of landing craft, witnessed the bombing, the naval bombardment and the landings, we had two days patrolling off the beaches of Normandy. We then anchored in Weymouth Bay. At the end of a 'free day', 8 June, we volunteered to take over a convoy of five American LSTs[53] from our sister ship *Boadicea* to give her a rest.

We then proceeded to cross the Channel and subsequently had a very

---

[53] Landing Ships Tank (LSTs) had a crew of between 80 and 110. In addition to carrying tanks, trucks, DUKWs etc., they could carry from two to six smaller Landing Craft Vehicle Personnel (LCVPs). Landing Craft Tank (LCT) had a crew of three and could carry a tank or a large truck. The Landing Craft Infantry (LCI) had a crew of about ten. It had narrow ramps on both sides, lowered to discharge troops close to the beaches. The LCI was a much larger craft than the LCT, but smaller than the LST. The firepower on LSTs comprised several single 20mm and double 40mm guns. Early LSTs had both single and double 40mm mountings. Some LSTs, like the '314' class, had a 3-inch gun placed on the stern. These guns were installed in Londonderry, Northern Ireland, but were never fired after initial training as they caused cracks in the ship. Two .50 calibre heavy machine guns were installed on the LCVPs which could also carry a Jeep.

busy night, beating off some German E-boats, but not before they'd succeeded in sinking two LSTs.

I was called to the bridge by our Captain, Lieutenant Commander Murch, who said: "Doc – get over there to that burning LST and make sure that no one is trapped under the anchor chains or cables – you can amputate as necessary…"

I quickly collected my gear and was in one of *Beagle*'s two whalers, with the Sub-Lieutenant and his crew, within two or three minutes. We rowed towards the burning LST, only to see it sink when we were about halfway across. So we rowed on until we were in the midst of a group of struggling survivors. They were in a very poor state – badly burnt, covered in oil, already much weakened, coughing and vomiting. We managed to get them inboard the whaler until we were dangerously overloaded. We then rowed back to where we thought *Beagle* might be, but no sign of her.

Suddenly a searchlight pierced the surrounding blackness and almost blinded us. It was a very gallant act by *Beagle*'s Captain and extremely dangerous as we were then in a known minefield and only a few miles off Cherbourg. The searchlight turned the blackness of the night into day and enabled us to come smoothly alongside and transfer our load of survivors, with much help from the ship's crew, several of whom jumped down into the sea to help the wounded on board. Some of the survivors were so weakened and exhausted they could do no more than hang onto the lines and the scrambling netting hastily draped over the ship's side. When we had transferred all our survivors safely on board *Beagle* we immediately returned to collect more, passing our other whaler loaded with survivors on its way back to *Beagle*.

After two more rescue missions, I came back on board, feeling that I could be more useful in the ship, and started work on the wounded, to the obvious relief of my SBA (Sick Berth Attendant). Every available space on *Beagle* was occupied by injured American military personnel. Some were badly wounded, but all were in some degree of shock, burned, grazed or cut. All survivors had a coating of oil from the oil fuel on the surface of the sea, and a lot of them had respiratory distress.

It was during this time I injected one US sailor with morphine who, despite what must have been several painful fractures, appeared to be unduly happy. The reason for this apparent jollity became clear when I met a US Army Medical Officer in another area of *Beagle* who had also given the sailor an injection of morphine.

In the meantime, more Allied naval units had arrived to take over the escort of the remaining LSTs and to beat off the E-boats. We had rescued about 300 US military personnel. We went swiftly to Portsmouth, stopping only to give a short but moving 'Burial at Sea' service for those few who regrettably had died from their injuries after rescue while on board *Beagle*.

What a night it had been... By the time we had issued warm blankets to those survivors able to walk, their soaking wet, oil-covered uniforms, clothes and life jackets made a huge pile on *Beagle's* upper deck, reaching almost to the top of the torpedo tubes.

A large silent crowd of medical personnel and ambulances awaited our survivors at South Railway Jetty, Portsmouth Harbour, where they were landed. Before disembarking, each of our patients expressed their gratitude to the crew.

While having a 'wash-up' in the wardroom before lunch, the Captain came in and announced that he had been warned that he might be court-martialled for 'hazarding his ship' in a minefield. However, the US authorities sent a most pleasant and complimentary signal, accompanied by a Commendation, for Lieutenant Commander Murch. My SBA and I were also graciously thanked for our services. There was no subsequent court martial for our Captain.

Beagle left Portsmouth to resume our patrols off the Normandy beaches, supporting the build-up following the invasion of Occupied Europe.

'NO GREATER HEROISM...'

William V. McDermott, USN, *LST 314*

I enlisted in the United States Navy ten days before my 18th birthday. You were subject to the Draft at the age of 18, the choice was then the Government's, but I had no desire to go into the Army or the Marine Corps. I left for 'Boot Camp' on 15 February 1944 and spent four weeks at Sampson Training Center, New York State. The training there consisted mostly of marching, although we recruits spent a few hours on the rifle range target shooting.

After we'd received our basic training and a week's leave, we boarded trains for New York City, boarded the transatlantic liner *Queen Elizabeth* and sailed for Scotland. The trip over took only four days. We then boarded trains for southern England where most of us were assigned, in alphabetical order, to LSTs.

About thirty of us were assigned to our battle stations on board *LST 314*, based at Weymouth, the day we arrived in late April 1944. Twenty five had surnames beginning with Mc. There were two McDermotts, three McDonalds, etc. Our Commanding Officer, Captain Alvin Tutt, USN, was under the distinct impression we were all fully trained. Little did he know!

That same night the German Air Force dropped several bombs in the surrounding area. Captain Tutt sounded 'General Quarters' and we went dutifully to our respective battle stations. He ordered us not to open fire. I called back to our Gunnery Control Officer, asking him to send someone to show us what to do in case we were ordered to fire. From then on it was 'on the job training'. The next morning was spent learning how to load and fire our 20mm and 40mm guns.

Later that day, five LSTs sailed out of Weymouth Harbour for gunnery practice, firing at a target sleeve being towed about 120 yards behind a Royal Air Force aircraft. We were all instructed in the importance of 'leading' the target sleeve but to be quite certain we didn't fire close to the plane. As things turned out, that plane made only one pass and immediately headed back to its base, its pilot evidently deciding against being shot down by 'friendly fire'.

However, following a really intensive period of training during the next two weeks we became reasonably proficient and confident sailors and gunners.

The *314* participated in a pre-D-Day practice manoeuvre off the white cliffs of Dover. They were an absolutely beautiful sight in the bright, clear morning sunlight. I'd been sick in bed that morning with a high temperature, aches and pains, and I'd been ordered to stay below. But I wasn't about to miss such a truly memorable sight!

For the actual invasion on 6 June 1944, *LST 314* was assigned to 'Omaha' Beach, one of the two US beaches from the five beaches to be attacked. We had loaded 15 amphibian DUKWs[54] and sailed with a huge armada of ships for Normandy. The pre-invasion bombardment was awesome, with battleships, cruisers, destroyers, etc. all hurling high explosive shells of every calibre at the German fortifications. The skies above us were filled with Allied bombers and fighter aircraft going to and fro. We had many USAAF P-38 Lightning fighter-bombers constantly flying over us, ensuring no German aircraft had the chance to threaten us.

The sights and the sounds were incredible to behold.

We had no need to go ashore as our cargo was launched offshore. We began to discharge the DUKWs so they could make their run up to the beach. We got them all launched, but, as they circled, nine from the fifteen were swamped and sank to the bottom of the English Channel due to the choppy seas. We had our small boats out and managed to rescue some of the survivors. In retrospect, an additional factor was that the DUKWs were possibly overloaded with extra 105mm artillery ammunition. But the main thing was that the troops of the 1st Infantry Division, although suffering heavy casualties, had managed to get ashore and were holding on, supported by Allied naval gunnery and overwhelming air power.

On our return to England for more supplies, our tank deck had many American casualties, with their ID tags, killed in the first assaults on 'Omaha' Beach. We had very little sleep before leaving on the return trip to Normandy.

Our destination was the Cherbourg Peninsula and we left England close to midnight on Thursday 8 June. There were five LSTs in the convoy, with the destroyer HMS *Beagle* as escort, three on one side and two on the other. LSTs *314* and *376* were last in line.

We were nearing the French coast when out of the blackness of the night, at about 0200 hours, a German E-boat approached us from the rear. A torpedo struck *LST 314* on our port side, blew away much of the hull in a tremendous explosion and our ship went down barely 20 minutes later.

I was sleeping at the time of impact. I slept rear mid-deck, alongside a

---

[54] DUKW: D – the fourth year of the American wartime military standardisation; U – it is an amphibious vehicle; K – it has six-wheel drive; W – it has an inversely-sprung rear axle.

short downward sloping passageway that led into the screw drive compartment. The force of the explosion blew me out of my bunk, landing at the bottom of the passageway. I was dazed for a few moments and by the time I'd eventually managed to clamber my way up to the top deck there were very few people around.

On the way up, I'd tried to open the starboard side passageway hatch, but couldn't. I then ran to the port side passageway. This hatch was hanging sideways, partially in and out, but I was just able to squeeze through. I ran up the passageway, but couldn't open the port side top deck hatch. I then crossed over to the starboard side, along the galley way passage and thankfully up to the top deck.

All I had on was my underwear shorts, and as I was barefooted I became increasingly aware of the unbearable heat transferred to the iron deck from the uncontrollable fires raging below. It was obviously the end of the line for *LST 314*.

I then joined two other sailors and three soldiers hurriedly trying to release a life raft. Eventually, we succeeded, but the raft was still attached to the ship by its safety rope. One of the soldiers hastily hacked away at the rope with his small pocket knife, freeing the raft, which we immediately launched over the side and clambered in.

A short time later, we saw a German E-boat approach our rapidly sinking LST. I can only assume the Germans were looking for our LST's identification number.

Strange to relate, we found a drifting broom nearby and used it as a paddle, and desperately tried to propel our raft away from the blazing ship. But I was convinced we were gradually and relentlessly being sucked into the large gaping hole in the port side where the torpedo had exploded minutes earlier. My fears must have been shared because one of the three soldiers, who wasn't wearing a lifebelt, suddenly got up and jumped off the raft into the sea. I was later told the temperature of the water was around 13 degrees Centigrade and I thought the air temperature was not much better.

It was very shortly after that when I was convinced the Good Lord worked one of his miracles. When we reached the gaping hole in the port side, our raft was suddenly propelled rapidly and powerfully away from the sinking ship as if by an unseen hand.

We were about 100 yards behind the stern of *LCT 314* when she went down, stern first, twenty minutes after being torpedoed. We also saw *LCT 376* burning fiercely, but there was no sign of the other three LCTs, presumably they'd continued heading for Normandy. We then floated around the English Channel in the darkness, neither seeing nor hearing any other survivors, entirely at the mercy of the prevailing currents and wind, with no idea where we were heading or the direction of the nearest land. As we drifted aimlessly, we came across the soldier who'd earlier decided to jump off our raft, floating face up. Unfortunately, he was dead.

The raft's netting had broken away and this enabled us five survivors to stand chest-deep in the water while holding onto the raft. We moved about, sometimes almost submerged and sometimes sitting on the sides of the raft.

Eventually, the eastern sky gradually brightened as the grey dawn arrived, heralding Friday, 9 June 1944. The westerly wind was noticeably stronger which in turn made the seas distinctly choppier. I was very cold. We still couldn't see anyone and I could feel the first insidious stages of exhaustion and exposure.

At about 0800 hours a whaler manned by British sailors suddenly appeared on the crest of a large wave. The whaler was from HMS *Beagle*. The sailors quickly hauled all five of us aboard and took us back to their destroyer. The *Beagle* must have known where we were and kept us in sight while they were busily rescuing other shipwrecked soldiers and sailors, mostly covered in fuel oil, from the sea. We later learned that the destroyer had sailed into a German-laid minefield and had switched its searchlight on, looking for struggling survivors. The ship was also within the range of German batteries on the French coast.

The *Beagle*'s crew wrapped us up in warm blankets and gave us generous shots of rum from their own rum ration. I honestly thought I could never be warm again, but the combination of shelter, blankets, steaming hot drink and one or two generous swigs of strong rum changed my mind.

Tragically, a number of rescued Americans on board *Beagle* from both LSTs died from a combination of exposure and serious injuries, mostly extensive burns. During *Beagle*'s return to southern England, we met a US Navy ship. The more seriously wounded and those who had died after rescue were transferred to the American ship in mid-Channel.

I was later told the total of those lost from *LST 314* that fateful morning was 104. They comprised 54 sailors from our ship's crew of about 100, and 50 soldiers out of a complement of 58, all specialists in radar and harbour control. I also later learned that two Allied convoys were passing in opposite directions, within a few miles of each other. The German E-boat was picked up on radar but unfortunately it was mistaken for a British minesweeper which apparently was approximately the same size.

The fact that *Beagle*'s Captain and crew had deliberately sailed into a known minefield within range of enemy shore batteries, at great risk to everyone on board, on its mission of mercy to pick up about 250 struggling, mostly oil-covered survivors of our two LSTs, confirmed that no greater heroism was ever displayed than that of 9 June 1944.

———————

'A BEAM OF LIGHT...'

Albert E. Duncan, USN, *LST 376*

I joined the US Navy during WWII, was a crew member of the USS *LST 376* and participated in the Normandy Invasion on 6 June 1944. We crossed the English Channel, but couldn't get onto the beach to discharge our cargo because the Germans had blocked the beach with obstacles. We had towed a smaller motorized Rhino Ferry which went to the beach under its own power. We also sent in some small boats, LCVPs,[55] with troops.

After we had unloaded our cargo, we returned to the south coast of England and reloaded with about twelve Sherman tanks on our tank deck and about twenty 6x6 trucks on the main deck, along with the military personnel to operate and support them in Normandy.

We sailed on the return trip across to France during the late evening of June 8 in an unescorted convoy of five LSTs when the British destroyer HMS *Beagle* overtook us and asked for permission to join us. Of course, we were glad to oblige and the destroyer led us toward the coast of Normandy.

We were under what we called 'Condition 2' at that time, which meant

———

[55] Landing Craft Vehicle/Personnel.

that all Compartment Hatches were closed and watertight, with half of the ship's crew on duty and half off, in four-hour periods of duty.

I happened to be on duty in the Radio Shack early on June 9 when, at about 0220 hours, I heard a very loud explosion, the ship lurched violently and all lights were immediately extinguished. I didn't know what had happened, was partially stunned by the explosion and just sat in complete darkness, dazed for a few minutes.

Then the familiar voice of our Communications Officer called out from the ladder which led up to the radio shack, saying we had been ordered to abandon ship. I quickly began to recover and felt fully conscious again. I searched and felt around until I found a battery-powered lantern. Turning it on, I found my pneumatic life belt, put it on and squeezed the mechanism that punctured the inflating cartridges. Then, to this day I don't know why, I turned the lantern off and hung it back up on its hook.

I then went down the ladder and quickly walked out onto the main deck. I was shocked to see the military trucks were all well ablaze, with their gasoline tanks and their loads of ammunition exploding in what was literally a horrifying inferno.

The ship appeared to be listing to port and the main deck was only a few feet above the sea. I then heard and saw a life raft full of men from the ship, about a hundred feet away. They were calling for me to swim to them. Without a moment's hesitation, I plunged into the sea and found the water extremely cold. Swimming with an inflated life belt was rather difficult, but I managed to make it out to the raft eventually. However, I found there was no room for me to get onto the raft, so I just grabbed a rope that was attached to its side and hung on for dear life.

Soon after I'd reached the raft, a beam of light stabbed through the darkness. It was *Beagle*'s searchlight. Her crew quickly got a lifeboat, called a whaler, lowered it into the water and began pulling our men into it. At that point I was feeling relieved, convinced that we'd soon be picked up. Some of our survivors were able to make it across to *Beagle* and grab onto a cargo net that had been draped over the destroyer's side enabling them to clamber aboard the destroyer assisted by her crew.

It was a shock to us all to see *Beagle* suddenly turn off her searchlight and speed away. It was later learned that some men in the water near *Beagle* were pulled into her twin screws as she sped away to repel the German E-boats that were about to attack again.

By that time I was beginning to feel quite numb with cold and tried to get a better grip on the rope. I noticed that there were not as many men on and around the raft as there had been. It seemed like an eternity when the blackness of the night gradually gave way to dawn and *Beagle* returned. Her whaler had remained throughout and picked up all the men it could carry without itself being swamped by endless waves whipped up by a bitterly cold wind.

After the survivors in the whaler had been assisted aboard *Beagle*, the whaler then made its way over to our raft. Along with the other survivors, I thankfully felt my numb body being pulled from the water. We were then taken across to the *Beagle*, handed up to the strong and willing hands reaching down. Once safely aboard we had our soaking clothes ripped off, quickly covered with blankets, lined up on deck, taken below, given hot tea, shots of rum, cleaned up and given dry clothing.

By that time, *Beagle* had drifted miles from the mine-swept channel and into known mined and very dangerous waters. Regrettably, there were many lives lost from the crews of *314* and *376* in addition to the US Army personnel who were our passengers. One of the officers from the *Beagle*, who had been in her whaler during the rescue efforts, said they'd counted 270 dead soldiers floating in the sea.

It was a horrible experience, but that is war.

Several of our crew and a few soldiers passed away, either from their severe injuries, hypothermia or sheer exhaustion on the way back to England. They were buried at sea by *Beagle*'s crew in a brief but very moving ceremony.

Many years later, I began trying to find surviving crewmen of *LST 376*. By 1993 I'd located 42 and we held a reunion on 6 June 1994. It was then, and at seven subsequent annual reunions, that I learned of most of the events during that dramatic and tragic night.

Captain C. B. Stanley, Commanding Officer of *LST 376*, told me that the torpedo from the German E-boat had penetrated the hull of our ship on the starboard side, exploded in the engine room and had then blown a hole through the port side. Captain Stanley and a few of the crew were subsequently able to get one of the smaller boats, an LCVP, released from its davits and dropped into the water, but not without damaging some of its electrical wiring and its tiller. Fortunately, one of men was a Motor Machinist's Mate. He was able to 'short-wire' it, start the engine and rig an auxiliary tiller. They were then able to pick up some survivors, some wounded and some of the dead.

This LCVP held 40 men and was able to rescue a couple of full loads of survivors from the sea and get them aboard *Beagle*. Our life raft had been in quite rough water throughout the ordeal and I could see very little of what was going on because I was in the trough of the waves half the time.

In order to save our lives *Beagle*'s Captain, Lieutenant Commander Murch, had disobeyed orders and put his ship and his crew at risk by deliberately entering mined waters. All the American servicemen he saved in doing so owe him our lives. He was subsequently reprimanded by his superiors, but our country awarded him a medal.

HMS *BEAGLE*: COMMENDATION

Anthologist's Note: The following is a copy of an official USN letter.

26 June 1944

USS *LST 314*,

c/o   FLEET POST OFFICE, NEW YORK, N.Y.

From: Commanding Officer

To: Commander Task Force 124

Via: (1) Commander LST Group Thirty-four, Flotilla Twelve

         Commander Task Force 124.3

Subject: HMS *Beagle*: Commendation, Recommendation of

1. This command would like to express the deep gratitude and appreciation of my officers and men for the valorous and highly capable work performed by HMS *Beagle* on 9 June 1944, after this ship and LST 376 had been torpedoed and sunk in the operations of war concomitant with the Allied invasion of France.

2. Due to the extreme skill in the handling of his ship exercised by the commanding officer; and the countless acts of heroism of his officers

and men who in instances with no regard to personal safety, dove into the water and effected the rescue of men, who due to their weakened condition, were unable to reach the lines cast out by the ship, upwards of two hundred and fifty lives were saved.

3. This command would also like to extend its thanks to the medical officer and his assistants for their tireless efforts on behalf of the survivors.

4. It is recommended by this command that an award commensurate with the excellent performance of HMS *Beagle* be accorded her.

(Signed) **Alvin H. Tutt**

[A United States award was later made to Lieutenant Commander Murch]

MEMORIES OF HMS *BEAGLE*

George W. Miller, Gunner, HMS *Beagle*

After concealing my true age, I transferred from the Merchant Navy and joined the Royal Navy in 1940. After basic training, I was sent to Cardiff for anti-aircraft gunnery training in a large dome-shaped building. We had quite an advanced training system on an Oerlikon 30mm anti-aircraft gun without using live ammunition. A moving shadow of an aircraft on a wall provided the target and we used a 'Spider's Web' type gunsight to practise our gunnery. Later on in the war we were supplied with an excellent American sight for the Oerlikon which improved our accuracy.

I was eventually assigned to the 'B' class destroyer HMS *Beagle*, which was based at Plymouth. My position, as Oerlikon gunner, was on the port side amidships, Air Defence.

Beagle operated from the River Clyde, near Glasgow, while assigned to Russian convoy duty, which was hard and often very brutal. Quite apart from the freezing temperatures, bitterly cold winds and the permanent winter darkness and gloom of those northern latitudes, it always seemed as if the slow and ponderous convoys of merchantmen never had enough escorts for adequate cover.

It seemed we were constantly cold and wet. The only place where we could warm ourselves was in a small compact compartment that had a heater. We knew it as 'The Hut'. It wasn't a powerful heater, but at least we were out of the icy wind as we huddled round attempting to get warm and dry.

Despite the fact that we were supplied with thick woollen clothing, a large overcoat, thick gloves and bulky sea boots, we were still cold, even when wearing the full kit against the biting cold. It was estimated that if we were unlucky enough to be swept overboard, or otherwise find ourselves in the freezing sea up in those extreme northern latitudes, we could expect to survive no longer than three minutes.

Living and working in those extreme temperatures was both physically and mentally exhausting, and when, inevitably, we got absent-minded and happened to touch any metal parts of the ship when not wearing gloves we could expect trouble and lacerated fingers.

When the atmospheric conditions were such that layers of ice began to silently build up on the exterior surfaces of *Beagle*, all hands, when not on watch, were put to work chipping the ice off, especially the ship's superstructure. We needed no better incentive than the nightmare of the ship gradually becoming top-heavy with the accumulation of ice and eventually capsizing.

The Beaufort Scale, in my opinion, was barely adequate to measure the colossal strength of the wind-speed of some of the incredibly rough storms we encountered in Arctic waters and in the vastness of the North Atlantic. There were many times when I thought our ship was going to be torn in half. It was very easy to get washed off deck by the all-powerful seas. For hours on end *Beagle* would be tossed around like a cork in a hurricane, but she always seemed to plough her way through the towering waves. Others were not so fortunate.

When we arrived at our anchorage in northern Russia, the Russians were not very co-operative and regarded us with a certain amount of suspicion. But didn't they realise we were risking our lives and ships to bring them countless tanks, guns, aircraft, vast amounts of ammunition, and a multitude of other vital supplies, all of which sustained their war effort? Their attitude didn't make much sense. On one occasion they wouldn't supply us with fresh water so we had to get it from other ships in the harbour. Needless to say, it was always a relief to get under way again for the voyage home.

In April 1944, we sank a U-boat while escorting a convoy to Russia. The alarm was immediately sounded when the U-boat was located and damaged by one of our escort carrier's aircraft. We rapidly increased to full speed as we went tearing through the convoy towards the submarine's reported position. Very soon we picked up an echoing signal on our Asdic equipment.

After several accurate depth charge attacks, the U-boat partially surfaced and then sank out of sight. We didn't find any survivors despite a thorough search of the surrounding area, only odd bits of wreckage and the telltale patches of oil that bubbled to the surface. The Admiralty in London later confirmed that *U-355* had been sunk in that position and on that date, 1 April 1944. It was difficult to locate and hit submarines. They proved to be very elusive while we searched endlessly in set patterns above them.

I vividly recall some terrible sights. In my opinion, the worst part of convoy escort was during the hours of darkness. Seeing and hearing spectacular explosions at night, knowing they were our ships and having very little chance of locating the survivors, if any... The oil tankers, heavily loaded with aviation fuel, and the lumbering ammunition freighters, when torpedoed or sustaining hits from German bombers, would simply disappear in huge, towering explosions. Their crews, if surviving the initial blast, stood no chance in those icy waters.

We of the Royal Navy felt bonded to our fellow mariners in the Merchant Navy and we felt their losses just as keenly as our own.

At first light, which was only about two hours of Arctic half-light during the mid-winter months, we had a ritual of counting the merchantmen and escorts to see how many were left.

It wasn't always so. We took part in the D-Day landings in June 1944 during which I shot down a German fighter aircraft which flew low over *Beagle*, from bow to stern, and it crashed into the sea. Shortly afterwards, off Cherbourg, western France, *Beagle*'s crew again distinguished themselves by entering a known minefield and rescuing about 250 American Army troops whose two Tank Landing Craft had been sunk by enemy action.

One of several terrible and vivid images which remained fixed in my mind for all time was seeing the horrible burns suffered by some of those exhausted young American soldiers as we helped them aboard *Beagle*.

Looking back, it was the most eventful and dramatic period of my life and

I count myself among the very fortunate ones to have survived. *Beagle* was a good ship with a good crew, and she had an outstanding Captain.

THE SINKING OF HMS *BOADICEA*, 13 JUNE 1944

Excerpt from *Hold the Narrow Sea: Naval Warfare in the English Channel 1939-1945* by Peter C. Smith

The destroyer HMS *Boadicea*, commanded by Lieutenant Commander F. W. Hawkins, had sailed from Milford Haven on 12 June 1944, for Normandy with the corvette HMS *Bluebell* and four trawlers escorting a convoy of six merchant ships, with *Boadicea* as Senior Officer of the escort. The passage was quiet for most of the evening and night. Overhead, huge formations of Allied aircraft were passing in both directions; the radar screens were swamped with contacts. Then a Junkers 88 torpedo-bomber was able to tag onto the Allied bomber stream, avoid detection and then make a swift breakaway attack against a totally surprised ship.

One of the 12 survivors, Leading Seaman John Randall, recalls:

'I was on the morning watch with three others of the gun's crew on the after Oerlikon gun deck. Dawn was just breaking, and all seemed quiet and normal in the small convoy.

Our own aircraft were streaming back across the Channel, as they had been for some time. Suddenly, I saw one aircraft apparently peel off from the rest and flatten out towards the port side of the ship. I immediately recognised it as a Ju 88, shouted a warning to the other lads and turned to the starboard Oerlikon which was my station.

As I swivelled the gun I saw a torpedo running towards the stern, but not running correctly – it was bouncing out of the water. It blew up some fifty yards astern. At the same instant the ship gave a tremendous shudder and lurch. As I glanced forward I had an impression of just a skeleton of the bridge silhouetted against a sea of flame. Then a large tongue of flame shot towards me and I ducked, managing to get my hands over my face and head before it hit me with some force.

Whether it was blazing wreckage or burning oil I shall never know, but I was knocked from the Oerlikon gun deck and pinned under it on the main deck. I remember thinking quite detachedly, "Oh well – this is it – I can't get up," and then I was seized with what I can only describe as an insane rage at what was happening.

My only thought was to get back to the gun – I must have thrown off whatever was lying on top of me and started to climb back up the ladder to the gun deck. I must, however, have been blown along the deck quite a way. I realised that I was on the ladder leading to 'X' gun deck.

As I reached the top, what was left of the ship tilted straight up and I was thrown into the water accompanied by various items such as depth charges. Fortunately, these were set to 'safe' and didn't explode and, as I reached out, I touched a rolled up cork scrambling net.

I clung to this for a moment, then half a Carley raft floated by. I managed to scramble into it despite the oil fuel which by this time covered me and most of the surrounding area. As I looked round I saw the *Boadicea*, propellers still turning, slide beneath the surface.'

Another survivor, Lieutenant Harry Howting, *Boadicea*'s Gunnery Officer, remembers:

'At about 0440 hours a terrific explosion rocked *Boadicea*, which resulted in everything forward of the funnels disappearing. Eyewitnesses have stated that this was caused by the torpedo hitting the ship near the break of the fo'c's'le. The attack was so sudden that nothing could be done to defend the ship, nor was there any chance to open fire at the attacker. The rest of the ship remained afloat for two or three minutes.

I literally fell out of the HF/DF office, after having been shaken to the deck when the explosion occurred. The atmosphere was full of steam, dust and smoke. At the same time the deck started to tilt downwards.

I heard Leading Seaman Randall shout "WE'VE BEEN HIT!". He'd been thrown from the after Oerlikon gun deck to the main deck, sustaining burnt hands. It was obvious that the end of the *Boadicea* was near, so I jumped into the sea. When I surfaced for air I saw, above my head, the port propeller still turning. I decided to swim away and after a few seconds she was gone, taking with her most of the ship's company.

Whilst waiting to be picked up, a lashed hammock brushed against me. Remembering my instructor's advice in my youth that "a well lashed hammock will keep a person afloat for 24 hours", I also remembered that, due to the dilution of the service because of the war, some of those caught in the dilution had possibly not been instructed in the '24-hour survival duty'. Nevertheless, I'm certain that they were very well versed in many more important items. Anyway, I found a large piece of wood and clung to it.

We were eventually picked up by the American Liberty ship *Freeman Hatch*, contrary to Convoy Orders: "Not to stop and lower boats to pick up survivors." This duty was normally carried out by rescue ships, trawlers, etc. We numbered 12 survivors from a total crew of 188, some with injuries necessitating immediate hospital treatment, such as broken legs, broken wrists and burnt hands, and all of us sick with the taste of fuel oil.

Frantic loud-hailing conversation between the new Senior Officer of the escort and *Freeman Hatch* resulted in our eventually being transferred to HMS *Vanquisher*, which deposited us on the jetty at Portland dressed like characters from a child's fairy story book. We had on grey/white sweaters, tweedy drainpipe trousers, grey socks and brown gym shoes – the end result of some warmhearted Association, God bless them – but we were a strange looking bunch.

We finished up at Portland Prison, incidentally, the first visit to one of those places for us! There we were re-washed, re-kitted and re-fed in that order. The injured survivors had been taken straight to hospital from the jetty, while the rest eventually finished up in HMS *Osprey* (a shore base) where we stayed the night. Early next morning, after a certain amount of 'table-tapping' (I was not senior enough for table thumping!), we left for our homes and fourteen days' leave. Orders were given for us to report back after leave to attend the Inquiry.'

Telegraphist Jack Yeatman, HMS *Pearl*, one of the armed trawlers in the Escort Force, recalled:

'*Boadicea* was part of our Escort Group for the Normandy Landings and was Senior Officer on our second visit to the beachhead with convoy EBC 8 from

Milford Haven on 11 June. My diary entry for 13 June 1944 reads:

"0445 hours. Violent explosion on our starboard beam. By the time I got on deck a large cloud of smoke was drifting away, and what appeared to be small-arms ammunition was bursting on the water. Apparently, an enemy aircraft had dived out of a low cloud and dropped two bombs or torpedoes. A ship had been hit, but can't see which. R/T busy… *Cornelian* [sister ship to *Pearl*] called up *Boadicea* but got no reply and asked us to try. No result – wonder if it was her who went? Another plane flew over and was fired at. A lot of oil on the water. Nothing else was seen. Turned in at 0530 hours.

1200 hours: It was *Boadicea*. She blew up and sunk literally in seconds. Only 12 survivors. Everyone is a bit shaken."'

Another crewman, Lieutenant George Hattesley, RN, on board HMS *Pearl*:

'The *Pearl*, together with *Bluebell*, *Ellesmere* and *Boadicea* were on their second trip to the 'Omaha' Beachhead, when, just south of the Isle of Wight, at the end of the Middle Watch, of which I was Officer of the Watch, I had a call from the Radar Cabin to say that they had a couple of aircraft on the starboard side. Almost immediately, this was followed by a loud explosion and *Boadicea* disappeared. We closed up to Action Stations.

Our Close-up Escort Group for the D-Day Landings consisted of *Bluebell*, *Boadicea*, *Cornelian*, *Ellesmere* and *Pearl*. Of this group, only *Cornelian* and *Pearl* survived the war. *Bluebell* was sunk with all hands in Russian waters and *Ellesmere* was sunk with all hands in the Bay of Biscay.'

Sidney Davies, Merchant Navy:

'On 13 June 1944, I was at the wheel, enclosed in the wheelhouse on the bridge of the American Liberty ship *Freeman Hatch* with an all-British crew, bound for 'Omaha' Beach with supplies for the US Army. We were steaming across the English Channel, about an hour off the Isle of Wight. Dawn was breaking, the sea was calm, and about 400 yards ahead of us was one of escorts, the destroyer HMS *Boadicea*.

Suddenly, a bright flash of light, then a muffled explosion. *Boadicea* appeared to literally rise up from the sea, break in two distinct halves then, just as suddenly she disappeared beneath the waves.

There was a stunned silence – then panic stations. The 'Old Man' (Captain Thomas) rushed out of the Chartroom, where he usually slept, and instantly assessed the situation.

We were steaming straight towards the oil and assorted debris now floating among the pitifully few survivors from the *Boadicea*.

"Take the wheel, Mister Mate," ordered Captain Thomas. "Davies, get all the Abs and the Bosun into the lifeboat to search for survivors…"

After the order to "Stop engines" we lowered our lifeboat into the water and eventually picked up a total of 12 oil-soaked survivors, most of whom had various injuries.

There was very little freeboard on our ship as she was loaded down to the Plimsoll line,[56] so we had no problems in getting the survivors aboard the *Freeman Hatch*. They were taken to the saloon and given hot tea and rum. Their wounds were dressed and paraffin was used to clean off the fuel oil.

About an hour later, another destroyer, HMS *Vanquisher*, which had been summoned urgently from Portland, hailed us out of the morning mist:

"STAND BY TO TRANSFER SURVIVORS…"

The transfer was successfully completed. Then: "Thank you, Captain – carry on to the beachhead – you have escort vessels in the vicinity."

We then continued on towards 'Omaha' Beach. After we'd unloaded our cargo (small-arms ammunition, cigarettes and whisky for the troops ashore) from our offshore anchorage onto amphibious DUKWs driven by black GIs, we were given permission by a US Army officer to go ashore.

One of the amphibious DUKWs took us ashore and we walked round the small harbour town of Barfleur. Two outstanding memories of this visit were: seeing the local girls with their closely-shaved heads because of their fraternising with German troops who had occupied and subjugated France with occasional brutality, for the previous four years; and of the local French people joyfully giving us their treasured bottles of Calvados.'

---

[56] The markings on a ship's side showing the internationally-agreed limits of legal submersion under various conditions.

Excerpt from an article which appeared in the *Milwaukee Sentinel*, 24 January 1944:

GLIDER-BOMB IS NO "TOY"
US Amphibious Base, England

'It looks like a small fighter plane with its tail on fire, and lacks accuracy, but it's no plaything.' That's the description of Germany's new rocket glider bomb given by two US naval officers who saw the weapon in action. The bomb, apparently controlled by radio by the launching plane, can turn, bank and maneuver with amazing facility, according to Ensign Luvern H. Rusch, of Raymond, South Dakota.

Rusch saw a glider-bomb attack when he was returning to Britain from Italy with a convoy in mid-November 1943. Both Rusch and Ensign John K. Horan, of Staten Island, New York, who also witnessed one of the attacks, possibly on the same convoy, agreed that the bomb proved highly inaccurate, but might, with development, become a real menace.

'Enemy planes were diving through the overcast and attacking, then returning to the clouds,' Rusch said in describing the attack. 'Suddenly a plane came out of the clouds on our starboard quarter and out of range of the convoy's guns.

'It released the glider bomb, which dropped from the plane's belly. The glider did an inhuman, freakish loop over the top of the plane – then headed for the convoy.

'It did two or three turns and dived into the sea, just missing the stern of one vessel. Navy gunners cheered, thinking they had downed an enemy plane,' Rusch said.

Ensign Horan said the attack he witnessed was made entirely by rocket glider bombs released from eight or ten Heinkel He 111s, lasted several hours, and that one ship, a straggler, was sunk.

'Apparently the German planes carry at least two and probably more of the bombs,' Horan said, adding that he believed that the glider-bombs could be released and guided toward the convoy from any direction as long as the mother plane could keep it in sight.

———

FRITZ-X AND HS 293 MISSILES

Anthologist's note: Among the numerous exhibits at the Royal Air Force Cosford Aerospace Museum, Shropshire, are 'Fritz-X' and 'HS 293' air-to-surface missiles, part of a unique collection of German missiles dating from the Second World War, including the V-1 Flying Bomb and the V-2 rocket.

The following are excerpts from the museum's handbook of exhibits (1981 edition):

The Rocket Exhibition

The Fritz-X missile, also known as FX 1400 and SD 1400, was a high-angle glide bomb, radio-controlled from a parent aircraft and had no propulsion unit. It was designed for air-to-surface use, primarily against armoured shipping targets.

During the late 1930s, as a result of the Spanish Civil War, the German authorities were sympathetic to any proposals which increased the accuracy of free-falling bombs. The first practical design, in 1939 by Dr Mac Kramer, was that of using radio-controlled spoilers in the tail fins of a 500lb (250kg) bomb. In March 1942 the trials were moved to Foggia, Italy. These final trials were completed in four weeks.

The Fritz-X consisted of a standard amatol-filled 1400kg bomb modified to permit the addition of four wings and a tail unit containing a radio unit and stabilising gyroscopes and, attached to the after end, a set of four fins in a 12-sided framework. The fins were equipped with radio-controlled spoilers which were made to protrude at command into the slipstream, thus affecting a change of range or azimuth.

The missile had a span of 4' 5" (1.35m), a length of 10' 8" (3.25m), and a diameter of 1' 10" (0.56m). The launching weight was 3,454lb including the 595lb of amatol explosive and was capable of piercing 5.1" (130mm) of armour plate when dropped from 20,000ft. It was intended that this missile be dropped from the Heinkel He 177 but due to development problems of this aircraft, the Dornier Do K2 was modified to carry two missiles albeit with drastically reduced range and so normally only carried one, slung underneath the fuselage.

Major German success with the Fritz-X missile includes the sinking of the

Italian battleship *Roma* and severely damaging the *Italia* on 9 September 1943. The Italian fleet was at that time sailing to surrender to the Allies. HMS *Warspite* was severely damaged on 16 September 1943. Other notable successes were HMS *Janus*, a destroyer, HMS *Spartan*, a cruiser (both sunk), and the USS *Philadelphia*, a cruiser, badly damaged.

In January 1940, Dr Herbert Wagner left Junkers to take charge of the Henschel guided weapons development team and after some study of the proposal, submitted a design for a glider-bomb to be controlled by radio from a parent aircraft. The addition of a propulsion unit increased the speed of the missile and reduced the risk of it being shot down in flight after being released.

The air-launched radio-controlled HS 293 missile was a small midwing monoplane weighing 1,730lb, with a wingspan of 10ft 2in (3.1 metres) and a length of 10ft 6in (3.2 metres). Aerodynamic control was achieved by conventional aileron and elevator surfaces. Changes in direction were achieved by banking the missile.

The warhead had a total weight of 1,120lb, filled with approximately 600lb of an explosive known as Trialene 105, and was armed by a delayed action fuse. In case of a malfunction of the warhead, an impact-fused destructive charge was placed adjacent to the radio receiver.

The rocket propulsion unit was slung beneath the fuselage and weighed 320lb empty and 475lb with fuel. It developed a thrust of 14,500lb for ten seconds and accelerated the missile to about 375mph. During the transit flight to the target area the rocket propellants were kept warm by feeding hot air from the engines of the parent aircraft through hoses into the missile.

Due to the delay in the production of the Heinkel He 177 bomber, the Dornier Do 217 was modified to carry the missile. The second test flight, in December 1940, was extremely successful and the Luftwaffe formed a special squadron to assist in the development and trained a number of radio operators.

Notable German successes with the HS 293 missile include the British destroyers *Inglefield, Boadicea, Intrepid* and *Dulwich*.

In all, the German Luftwaffe claimed that, by using both the Fritz-X and the HS 293 missiles, a total of 79 naval units including 40 warships were either totally or partially put out of action with 500 missiles and for the loss of 48 aircraft, in a period of 13 months' operations.

THE SINKING OF HMS *SWIFT*

Official report by Captain J. R. Gower, DSC, RN, Retd.

<u>SECRET</u>
ROYAL NAVAL BARRACKS,
PORTSMOUTH.
27 JUNE 1944

Sir,

1. I regret to report the loss of HMS *Swift* under my command on 24 June 1944, in approximate position 5 miles to the northward of Ouistreham Light House, under the following circumstances:

2. The ship was returning from patrol which she had left at 0500 hours, and proceeding to 'Sword' area prior to going alongside HMS *Scourge* for ammunition. The speed at the time was 9 knots (80 revolutions), in accordance with Portsmouth General Order 1503 which was the latest information received.

3. At about 0710 hours a large explosion occurred, presumably from a mine, apparently under No. 1 Boiler Room, which immediately broke the ship's back. The ship took a slight list to port and started swinging to port, and looked as if she might collide with an LCP (Landing Craft Personnel) which was steaming on a parallel course on my port bow. To check the ship's way, I ordered the port anchor to be let go, and this brought the ship up. This mid-ship portion of the ship was soon under water to the height of the top of the funnel while the bow and the stern remained above water, at an angle of about 30 degrees, in which position she remained for some little time.

4. At the time of the explosion one watch of seamen were on deck standing by wires and fenders, the remaining hands were below at breakfast, having been called at 0700 hours. The lower deck hatches were closed and the men already dressed as the ship had been at 'Action Stations' throughout the night.

5. Some of the men on the upper deck and practically all the Bridge personnel were thrown into the sea, such was the force of the explosion. The ship's company quickly mustered on deck, the rafts and life saving appliances were cleared away and launched. It was obvious to me that the ship would remain in her present position some little time, and I ordered all men to remain on deck and not attempt to leave the ship in rafts, although some had already jumped into the sea as boats would soon be standing by. As it was, Motor Launch 197 and the same LCP, together with boats lowered from ships in the vicinity including HMS *Venus*, HMS *Belfast*, HMS *Roberts*, HMCS *Sioux* and HMS *Argonaut*, were soon on the scene. I was fortunate to land back on the bridge from whence I was able to control operations. The ship was then abandoned in good order, the calmness of the sea and the number of boats greatly facilitating this. Having satisfied myself that both ends of the ship were evacuated, I stepped into HMS *Venus*'s motor boat. Survivors were then taken to ships in the immediate vicinity, and I proceeded on board HMS *Venus* to report to Commander J. S. M. Richardson, DSO, RN, under whose orders I was operating.

6. While the bow and the stern of the ship were still above water I returned to the ship with a working party from HMS *Venus* and my Chief Boatswain's Mate, in order to satisfy myself that there were no living trapped on board, and that there were no Confidential Books left on the Bridge not finally disposed of. Having satisfied myself on these two points and as the ship was now gradually settling with the rising tide, I deemed it wise to finally leave the ship and returned to HMS *Venus*. The ship completely disappeared about an hour later in ten fathoms of water leaving only the top of the foremast visible.

7. During the forenoon I reported on board HMS *Largs*, and then visited each ship in turn to count the survivors, whose return to the United Kingdom I was anxious to arrange as soon as possible. This was arranged by Flag Officer, Force 'S', and all men fit to travel returned that evening in SS *Princess Margaret*. The Flag Officer, Force 'S', further arranged for the collection of the wounded from destroyers, and their return to the United Kingdom the following day.

8. As the Flag Officer, Force 'S', was ashore at the time I was accommodated in HMS *Largs* for the night to make my report to him, and returned to the United Kingdom the following day in HMS *Sirius*.

9. The ship's total complement was 231, and as far as can be ascertained, one officer and 13 ratings are missing, and four ratings are known dead and have been buried at sea. Of the numbers saved, one officer is seriously wounded, two officers slightly wounded which includes the Army Bombardment Liaison Officer. Ten ratings are seriously wounded and 21 other ratings wounded. Steps have been taken to inform the necessary authorities.

I have the honour to be,
Sir,
Your obedient Servant,

Signed: **J. R. Gower**

LIEUTENANT COMMANDER

The Naval Commander,
Eastern Task Force, HMS *Hilary* (eight copies)
The Vice Admiral Commanding Home Fleet Destroyer Flotillas,
HMS *Tyne* (One copy)
The Captain (D), 23rd Destroyer Flotilla, HMS *Saumarez*, (One copy)

[Captain Gower was awarded the DSC for the whole Normandy operation. On D-Day, 6 June, HMS *Swift* had picked up 70 survivors from the Norwegian ship *Svenner*.]

RETURNING HOME

Iain Nethercott, ex-HMS *Keith*

I remember coming home from Pacific operations, based at Fremantle, Australia, on board HM Submarine *Tactician* in September 1944. It had been a very tense and eventful period in comparatively appalling conditions. The terrible heat in a submarine operating near the Equator with no air-conditioning and no ventilating fans when under attack and at 'Silent Routine' was incredible. The temperature would climb to 130 and 140 degrees Fahrenheit. The added factors of a low percentage of oxygen and excessive amounts of carbon dioxide in the boat all made us dreadfully ill.

Our American Admiral at Fremantle could not believe our comparatively primitive living conditions. All the American Navy's submarines were bigger and faster, with air-conditioning, a bunk for every man, a big refrigerator and iced water for the crew.

We had no fridge, so any fresh food became mouldy within days, our butter was liquid, our fresh water was strictly rationed, we shared two bunks between three men and we were covered in prickly heat and sweat rash. We took salt tablets and Vitamin C which only seemed to make us worse!

Everything we ate had to come from tins and the flour from our store was full of weevils and cockroaches. I used to exist on tins of pineapple chunks and sliced peaches, thus losing at least 14lbs in weight during one steamy four-week patrol.

We were nearing the end of our commission having started in November 1942 with patrols off the North Cape, then to Algiers, Malta and Beirut doing patrols until late 1943, and then to patrols from Trincomalee in the Malacca Straits and then to Australia patrolling from Manus.

After D-Day in June 1944, both the crew and the boat were on our last knockings. Most of us were 'bomb-happy' and very jumpy. The boat was full of leaks, while the joints and couplings on the high-pressure air lines, which supplied air pressure at 3,500lbs per square inch, had dozens of tiny leaks which, when dived, raised the pressure in the boat until my ears were at bursting point.

Before surfacing at night to charge batteries, our Skipper had to run the two big air compressors to suck much air out of the boat and into the high-pressure groups of steel bottles. Otherwise, even with him lashed securely to the conning tower ladder with men hanging onto his legs, if he'd opened the conning tower hatch he would have been projected straight out of the boat like a bullet from a gun and smashed his skull against the periscope standards.

Wherever we were in the boat at 'Diving Stations', we immediately felt the pressure ease off, and many, including me, had bleeding noses and ears.

Having ensured that no enemy ships were lurking 'up top', the Skipper gave the order to start the diesel engines so that I could begin to get a strong charge on my batteries. When those two huge 16 cylinder diesel engines started up, they immediately sucked fresh air down into the boat. The Skipper would then give us permission to carry on smoking as it was strictly forbidden to smoke all day when dived.

We'd all light up and the combination of the foul air on our lungs with the tobacco smoke made us smokers immediately sick into the nearest bucket. Life was certainly no picnic in the old diesel-electric boats. No wonder they gave us an extra two shillings a day!

We took the long way home from Port Darwin, Australia: Trincomalee, Ceylon, Aden, Port Said, Malta, Gibraltar, up to Dunoon on the Isle of Bute, northern Scotland, and then going further north – about Cape Wrath. Then down the east coasts of Scotland and England, to arrive at Chatham Dockyard and to eventually pay off.

When we were off the Humber, near the Yorkshire-Lincolnshire border, under the protection of an old 'Smoky Joe' coal-fired trawler and an over-enthusiastic RN Motor Launch, we noticed hundreds of small silver shapes wheeling round above us at about 20,000 feet in a clear blue sky. They were American B-17 Flying Fortresses and B-24 Liberators, four-engined heavy bombers assembling into formation before setting course for Germany on a daylight raid.

They gradually disappeared to the east and we ploughed on, heading south towards the Thames Estuary. A little later we found ourselves directly under the flight paths of a steady stream of hundreds of DC-3 Dakotas towing gliders at about 10,000 feet, heading for the Arnhem and Nijmegen areas of eastern Holland in one of the largest airborne operations in history, 'Market Garden'.

To finally cap our eventful day, we sailed up the River Medway with a small escort and had to anchor off the entrance to No. 1 Basin to raise the level in the entrance lock. It was a beautiful evening in late summer and we had opened up the hatches and were sitting around on the casing. The silence was suddenly broken by loud volleys of anti-aircraft gunfire to the east. A V-1 'Doodle-bug' flying bomb came rocking and spluttering along in our direction at about 1,000 feet. Its motor suddenly cut out and it dived straight towards us from the other side of the Isle of Grain. Those who could, dived desperately for the hatches. I was literally frozen, as up to that moment I thought it was a crashing German fighter aircraft.

The V-1 plunged into the riverside mud, not far astern of *Tactician*, and threw up an eruption of foul-smelling black mud in a gigantic circular sheet which fortunately, didn't reach our boat. It would have been just our luck to be hit by that bloody awful contraption, especially after two years of hard fighting all over the world, then being blown up on our own doorstep.

The extraordinary sight of us being towed into Chatham Dockyard certainly raised a few eyebrows amongst the smart Home Fleet cruisers, corvettes and destroyers, immaculate as usual in their grey paint. We crept along, painted deep green with huge patches of red rust showing through, with several unpatched shell holes, flying our Black 'Jolly Roger' with all our sinkings and Royal Marine commando raids recorded in white paint on the side of our conning tower, our 200 foot long Paying-Off pennant flying from the after periscope, and with our crew in old Afrika Korps uniforms, or just bush shirts, shorts, and covered in grease.

They wasted no time at all in hiding us away in No. 5 Dry Dock.

The following day, our kit bags and assorted gear arrived from the Submarine Depot Ship HMS *Forth*, so we could change into 'blues'. We took up residence in the Submarine Building and those staying with the boat went ashore to arrange 'digs' with the Chatham landladies, as we were *persona non gratae* in Chatham Naval Barracks, having been adjudged to be a 'thoroughly bad influence' on the supposedly good little General Service Ratings.

The dockyard stripped out the boat and took my 'Defect List' from me. I then went on eight weeks' leave to see if the old shack was still standing amongst the hail of V-1s and V-2s, and found my poor Mum lurking down our brick-built air-raid shelter. I also found one of my brothers, a Lieutenant in the RNVR, was back home again on Survivor's Leave. He was Skipper of an LST and this had been the second LST he'd lost over on the French coast.

For my part, I was recalled off leave for a 'Pierhead Jump' to HMS *Upstart* operating out of Dundee, Scotland, on Norwegian patrols where the last of the German U-boats were based. They were operating close inshore in the English Channel.

I had a tremendous moan about all this and told the old Drafting Commander so. I said that based on this, if he had his way, I would be the very last matelot left fighting in the Second World War. Only to get his usual response: "If you haven't got a sense of humour, you shouldn't have bloody well joined the Royal Navy…"

Life can be very cruel sometimes…

RUSSIAN CONVOY JW 61A

Len Perry, Stoker, HMS *Beagle*

One night in late June 1944 we were patrolling off the Channel Islands, which had been occupied and fortified by the Germans since June 1940. We fired a star shell intending to have a look round, but the shell merely illuminated *Beagle* more than the enemy coast. A large-calibre shore battery immediately opened fire, which resulted in two near misses and some shell-splinter damage.

Another inadvertent error occurred when our anti-submarine Asdic set located a fairly large object on the bottom of the Channel, off Dunkirk, though there was no wreck on the charts. After a couple of dummy runs our Skipper decided to depth charge, using the 'big one', a very powerful depth charge especially designed to be launched from one of our 21-inch torpedo tubes. But I don't think our torpedomen were too sure how to use it. They were familiar with dropping depth charges over the stern at high speed, but the 'big one' had to be fired from a torpedo tube amidships

The 'big one' was duly fired and away it went. *Beagle* immediately slewed away from it at high speed but the depth charge didn't go far enough and splashed down, about 40 yards away, and quickly disappeared from sight. Then there was a tremendous explosion and our ship was lifted bodily upwards. Everybody was momentarily dazed as they watched the huge white water spout leap skywards and then slowly subside, then the incredible sight as the sea turned from dark green to silver, as far as the eye could see, with stunned and dead fish.

A few pieces of wreckage did eventually float to the surface. From this it was concluded that it was the wreck of the paddle steamer *Maid of Orleans* which went down off Dunkirk in 1940.

During that same period, we witnessed the very early launching of the V-1 flying bomb. It was no more than 100 feet high, flying very slowly and clumsily, with its tail apparently on fire. We were under the impression that it was a plane crashing and made ready for rescuing its pilot. But the 'plane' gradually gained more height and airspeed as it disappeared from sight towards southern England. During the next few days we saw more of them. We were then told they were pilotless aircraft but not to open fire at them. I don't know why, because I'm certain that our ships could have shot down a considerable number into the sea while they were such comparatively easy targets shortly after being launched.

About mid-July, we were lying off Sheerness waiting to go up the River Thames for dry-docking. *Beagle* and her crew were tired. Nobody had been ashore since well before D-Day in early June, and most of the time since the invasion we had been closed up at 'Action Stations'. In addition to partici-pating in the actual invasion, *Beagle* had rescued the survivors from the two American LSTs in a minefield off Cherbourg, and our gunners had shot down two German Air Force Junkers 88s into the Channel when they'd attacked us in late June.

We picked up one of the German airmen from the Channel. He was onboard with us for several days. Nobody was sent out to collect him, and we certainly didn't have time to drop him off at a port on the south coast. It was the first time we'd actually come face to face with the enemy. As we stared at him I don't quite know what we'd expected, but eventually we spoke. His English was good and he really believed he was on the winning side even though he knew, and we knew, that the German armed forces were now retreating on three fronts, east, west and south. He said: "Our armies have no need to fight you – we have secret weapons and you will have to surrender."

It was while we were entering Green & Silley Weir's shipyard at Blackwall that we saw the V-1s, or 'Doodle-bugs' as the Londoners called them, ending their flights from their launching sites near the German-occupied French coast. They came over at a speed considerably faster than when we'd first seen them, approaching 400 mph, no higher than 2,000 feet and sounding like a two-stroke motorbike. All eyes were glued to them, mesmerised. Then their engines would suddenly stop, then gravity took over in a variety of ways. Some V-1s dropped like a stone, some glided on while rapidly losing height. Some would bank sharply and turn back on themselves before plunging down and exploding among the densely populated areas of London.

Evidence of the Blitz during 1940-1941, huge areas of bomb-shattered buildings and wasteland, were a stark reminder of what Londoners had suffered and endured. Later the dreaded V-1 flying bombs and, from September 1944, the truly devastating V-2 rockets rapidly became a continual and indiscriminate threat, causing even more deaths, injuries and destruction on a very large scale.

The V-1s were absolutely terrifying. Everybody dived for cover when a V-1 headed down, seemingly straight for your location. It was while *Beagle* was in dry dock, having several large plates removed from either side of her hull, when a V-1 crashed and exploded in the river, close to the dry-dock. The resulting blast of the shock wave was tremendous, closely followed by a wall of river water which slammed against the outer caisson with great force which, although damaged and leaking, fortunately held firm. The dockyard workers later told us if there had been more modern lock gates, they would have collapsed, and the subsequent inrushing wall of water would have certainly crushed *Beagle* and caused her loss.

By the time we were in dry dock in Blackwall, the majority of *Beagle*'s crew had been paid off, were on leave and awaiting a draft to new ships. I was one of the few remaining ship's company to stay on board. Casualties among the 'dockyard mateys' would have been high if that caisson had collapsed. By a cruel stroke of ill fortune one of *Beagle*'s Petty Officers was killed while he was staying at a Salvation Army Hostel, which suffered a direct hit from a V-1 along the Mile End Road.

Being on board a ship in dry dock is unpleasant at the best of times; cables, ropes and assorted rubbish everywhere, together with constant hammering and other unfamiliar noises. We had to get our heads down where we could and the thought of being blown to bits at any time didn't improve the situation.

I got to my home by bus to south-east London. I eventually arrived to find all doors locked and the house deserted. A near neighbour then explained that my father was in hospital with stress due to overwork; and my mother, sister and her young baby were staying with an uncle at Mildenhall, Suffolk, because of the bombing.

Then she said: "Did you come home because your brother, Charles, has been killed in Italy?"

I was absolutely shattered at this terrible news. My elder brother, whom I adored, had been serving in the Army in North Africa and then in Italy as the Allies advanced. Still dazed, I refused her kind offer of tea and just wandered alone, completely oblivious to the outside world. Charles used to take me everywhere as a child, he would share everything with me during our childhood together. When war came we both joined up, we would write to each other, make plans to start up a small business of some sort together when peace returned. These, and a hundred other memories of him, crossed my mind as I wandered aimlessly. I don't know how long I strolled, but it must have been well past midnight when a London fire tender stopped, its crew offered me a lift and kindly took me back to their Fire Station for a hot meal and a night's rest.

Back on board *Beagle* I found comfort with my messmates. I was then given seven days' leave to visit my mother up at Mildenhall, which was even more comforting. It was at the nearby Royal Air Force Station that I saw the powerful four-engined Lancasters of RAF Bomber Command taking off on missions to bomb Germany. The continuous drone of heavy bombers seemed to last until midnight. That week passed very quickly and I returned to the ship.

Amidst the clutter on deck I spotted a piece of wood suitable for making a model of HMS *Beagle*. There was plenty of other scrap around for the guns, bridge, funnels, masts, etc., and it would be something to relieve the boredom. Having got the hull into some sort of shape, interest was shown by some of my messmates. Pithy advice and terse criticisms flowed forth, not least from the 'dock-yardies', a really friendly lot, being a comparatively small yard.

How I admired them, the way they turned up for work each morning, flying bombs or not, full of humour. They'd been doing that for the past four years – now they had to face a new threat in the silent and invisible approach of the V-2 rockets. But they all considered that we were the boys at the 'sharp end' of the action.

One day, Maisie, who was an electrician's mate and a lovely blonde girl, came to see how the model of *Beagle* was progressing. I can best describe Maisie as the girl who, while pulling on her boiler suit, had considerable difficulty in fastening the top three buttons.

At that time, I was working on the model's fo'c's'le. Maisie mentioned that she had a broken necklace at home which would be just right for the anchor chain. Sure enough, the next morning all the lads gathered round as Maisie delicately passed the chain around the capstan. From that time on, that anchor chain was known as 'Maisie's Chain'.

With repairs completed towards the end of October, the model put away in my locker, it was time to say farewell to our friends from the East End of London, but as *Beagle* moved out into the River Thames it was discovered that 'A' gun was missing! Sure enough, there it was on the dockside... A great cheer went up from the lads as we thought it would mean a bit more leave. No such luck! We pulled in alongside the jetty, a dockside crane soon had the gun aboard and within about eight hours it was fully installed, ready for action. Our new Skipper, Lieutenant Commander Williams, was very anxious to get away. That minor delay had put *Beagle* behind schedule as we were heading for the Clyde and a very special deployment of some kind.

We hit very rough weather the next day as *Beagle* ploughed her way up the Irish Sea at about 20 knots, hitting every large wave like a sledge hammer. Conditions on board were quite bad, and with about 70 per cent of the crew being new arrivals – *Beagle* was their first ship – a large proportion were ill.

We also had a problem below decks. During the refit, a new main bearing was fitted to the starboard propeller shaft and, during normal circumstances this would be 'run in' on trials, but in this hasty dash north the bearing was getting red hot and the lubricating oil was boiling.

The Chief ERA requested the Bridge to slow down. His request was refused, so we played two fire hoses of cold sea water on the bearing. But by doing so, we were filling up the bilge to a dangerous level when we discovered a bilge pump was out of commission. However, by judging a balance between the incoming and the outgoing sea water we eventually completed the voyage north. Incidentally, several months later when that bearing was dismantled during a routine inspection, it was found to be beautifully 'run-in', thereby proving that brute force sometimes pays off.

Refuelled and fully kitted out with stores and ammunition at Gourock, we put to sea and had a practice shoot off the Isle of Arran. We checked all systems for the things that refused to function, to be seen to later, and pressed on.

On 31 October 1944 we put to sea from Liverpool with the destroyer *Westcott*, the frigate *Nene* and the sloop *Cygnet*. We were to escort another convoy to Russia and after four hours being on watch below I came up on deck, curious as to why we were maintaining high speed for so long.

I looked around and there was the awesome sight of two very large liners steaming in line astern at a speed I estimated to be at least 20 knots, accompanied by four escorts, a sight rarely seen on the high seas. They were the Canadian-Pacific liner *Empress of Australia* and the Cunarder *Scythia*. The ship's notice board confirmed our orders were to escort convoy JW 61A up to Murmansk, northern Russia.

This merely deepened the mystery for us. Why make a fast run to Murmansk with large liners? We made several guesses, but we were never told the real reason why we were escorting these two fast ships to Russia.

Both the voyage up to Kola Inlet and the return were uneventful.

Survivors of *U-581* calling for help to the crew of the destroyer HMS *Westcott*, after their submarine was rammed and sunk by depth charges off the Azores, 3 February 1942. *(Ron Blacker)*

The torpedo launched from HMS *Brilliant* which sank the SS *Egerland*, German oiler and supply ship, 5 June 1941 *(F. H. Burton)*

Ken Radcliffe's oil painting, 'The Capture of *U-110*', shows the surviving German crew swimming across to the safety of the corvette HMS *Aubretia*, while the boarding party from HMS *Bulldog* approach the stricken U-boat in the ship's whaler. Convoy OB 318 departs over the horizon. *(Author's Collection)*

This photograph is believed to have been taken aboard *U-30* in 1940. Kapitänleutnant Fritz-Julius Lemp, later captain of *U-110*, is third from the right. *(Graham Hunt)*

Loch Ewe, Scotland, where merchant ships assembled for Arctic convoying. An inscribed granite memorial to the Royal Navy, Merchant Navy and Allied seamen lost on Arctic duties was dedicated in 2000 by the Russian Convoy Club.

Severe icing caused many serious problems to ships on the Arctic convoy runs to Russia, in this case the cruiser HMS *Nigeria* in 1942. *(Lieutenant F. W. Hawkins, RN)*

HMS *Boadicea* takes a heavy sea inboard while at sea north of Iceland on Arctic convoy duty. The stern of the motor boat referred to in the account 'A Christmas Miracle', 1942, by Jack Keir, is seen on the bottom left. The hut between the two funnels is the 'Spud Locker' which had been virtually emptied by Christmas time. *(Michael Back)*

'Crossing the Line', June 1942. King Neptune's Court survey proceedings from the starboard pom-pom deck of HMS *Brilliant*. (F. H. Burton)

10 July 1942: SS *Gulfpin*, an American Mercantile Marine oil tanker, on fire and sinking off Grand Island, Louisiana, after being torpedoed by a German U-boat. The photographer's brother was onboard the *Gulfpin*. (*Tommy Loftin*)

South Atlantic, June 1942. Neptune and his Court on HMS *Brilliant*. (F. H. Burton)

June 1942: Two low-level German bombers fly through intense anti-aircraft fire after releasing their bombs on a convoy to Malta. Photograph taken from HMS *Westcott*. *(Ron Blacker)*

June 1942: The destroyer HMS *Bedouin* going alongside the cruiser HMS *Liverpool* to take on oil on the outward voyage from Gibraltar during Operation 'Harpoon' to relieve Malta. On the 15th of this month, HMS *Bedouin* was sunk south of Sardinia after sustaining heavy damage from Italian torpedo bombers and 6-inch gunfire from two Italian cruisers. *(Ron Blacker)*

June 1942: The cruiser HMS *Liverpool* had been torpedoed by aircraft during a convoy to Malta. The destroyers HM Ships *Westcott* and *Antelope* were assigned the task of towing and escorting *Liverpool* back to Gibraltar. All three ships were subsequently attacked by high- and low-level bombers. Photograph shows a torpedo bomber launching a torpedo at *Westcott*. The torpedo missed and the bomber was itself shot down by *Westcott*'s anti-aircraft gunners. The pilot was rescued by the destroyer. *(Ron Blacker)*

9 June 1944: HMS *Beagle* rescues US Army troops and sailors picked up by an LCP in a minefield off Cherbourg, after their two LCTs had been sunk by German E-boats. *(Len Perry)*

German Navy *Schnellboote* – 'E-boats' to the Allies – were a constant threat to Allied shipping in the English Channel. *(Hans Hoehler)*

9 June 1944, 0300 hours: HMS *Beagle* steamed into an enemy minefield to save the lives of American sailors and soldiers from the Landing Ships (Tank) *LST 314* and *LST 376* which had been sunk off Cherbourg by E-boats. The destroyer braved mines and coastal batteries, and illuminated herself and her surroundings with a searchlight to aid the struggling survivors, at great risk. *(Author's collection)*

18 July, 1945; Battersea, London: The crew of HMS *Bulldog*, Battersea's adopted ship, march past the Town Hall. The salute was taken by the Mayor of Battersea, Councillor S. Fussey, JP, and Admiral Sir M. E. Dunbar-Nasmith, VC, KCB, RN. *(The* South Western Star*, Battersea, London)*

Ship's badges of the 'B' class destroyers. *(Artwork by D. Strike, HMS* Brilliant *1939-1941;* Keith *badge by Michael Keir)*

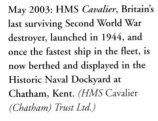

May 2003: HMS *Cavalier*, Britain's last surviving Second World War destroyer, launched in 1944, and once the fastest ship in the fleet, is now berthed and displayed in the Historic Naval Dockyard at Chatham, Kent. *(HMS* Cavalier *(Chatham) Trust Ltd.)*

Conditions were moderate. We may have been too fast for the U-boats, but why the Luftwaffe didn't attempt to attack us is another mystery because there were several occasions when we heard, and saw, the Focke-Wulf Condors droning and circling high above us, keeping out of range of our anti-aircraft guns.

Did the Germans know what the two liners were carrying?

It wasn't until many years later, during our post-war reunions of the ships' crews of the *Beagle*, *Boadicea* and *Bulldog* Association, that the brutal and squalid facts emerged.

Aboard those two liners, under armed guard, were 11,000 'Russian collaborators', mostly Ukrainians who had been captured by the German Army on the Russian Front, then forced into the German Army. They were then captured by our Allied forces on the Western Front at Normandy during the summer of 1944, and then transported back to England as Prisoners of War in accordance with the Geneva Convention.

However, Winston Churchill had agreed with Josef Stalin, the Russian leader, to return all Russian PoWs to Russia. The Ukrainians were well aware they were being returned to face almost certain execution as 'traitors' and 'collaborators'. Apparently, they were dressed in British Army uniforms, taken under heavy British armed guard to prevent escape and herded aboard those two liners. It must have been obvious to all involved, and equally distressing, that the PoWs knew what fate awaited them on return to Russia.

While discussing that tragic episode at post-war reunions, we all felt pangs of guilt and distress at having participated, although unknowingly, in that forcible repatriation.

In his excellent book *Arctic Convoys*, Richard Woodman refers to convoy JW 61A as "the least creditable convoy in a saga of otherwise honourable endeavour."

CONVOYS JW 62/RA 62, NOVEMBER/DECEMBER 1944

Michael Back

Although it is true that losses on the Russian convoys never again became as bad as they were during the dire year of 1942, the crews of our three ships can testify that these convoys remained constantly hazardous right up until the closing stages of the war. In fact, some of the very last convoys to Russia during the winter of 1944/1945 faced new dangers. There were fresh U-boat packs on the route equipped with the revolutionary new schnorkel breathing tubes, and these same U-boats were now carrying the dangerous new 'Gnat' acoustic homing torpedoes. In addition, new squadrons of Ju 88 bombers had been transferred from Germany to northern Norwegian airfields specifically for convoy attack.

These were the considerations when HM Ships *Beagle* and *Bulldog*, commanded by Lieutenant (later Lieutenant Commander) C. T. D. Williams, RN, and Lieutenant Commander A. Williams, DSC, RN, respectively, left Scotland to form part of the close escort for the Russian convoy operation JW 62/RA 62 of November/December 1944.

Captain S. W. Roskill, DSC, RN, in Volume 3 of his official history *The War at Sea*, wrote:

'It was rather paradoxical that the first pair of Arctic convoys after the destruction of the *Tirpitz*, JW 62 and RA 62 of 30 and 28 ships which sailed from Loch Ewe and Kola Inlet on the 29th November and 10th December respectively, should have encountered stronger opposition than their predecessors. But such was the case, for the Germans had managed, after an interval of two years, to send two 'Gruppen', each consisting of about 35 Ju 88 torpedo-bombers, back to northern Norway, and had also stationed nearly a score of U-boats in the Barents Sea.'

In fact, despite submarine and air attack, there were no merchant ship losses from either convoy, and against a torpedo hit on the new destroyer *Cassandra* (she was successfully towed to Kola Inlet but unfortunately suffered a number of killed and wounded), two U-boats, *U-387* and *U-365*, were destroyed.

A more detailed factual account of the two convoys is given in Volume 2 of *Chronology of the War at Sea 1939-1945*, by J. Rohwer and G. Hummelchen. (Reproduced by kind permission of Ian Allan Ltd.)

27 November–14 December 1944
Arctic:

Convoy operation JW 62/RA 62 in the Arctic. JW 62 has 30 merchant ships, escorted by the 8th and 20th EGs including the destroyers *Keppel, Beagle, Bulldog* and *Westcott*, the sloops *Cygnet, Lapwing* and *Lark* and the corvettes *Allington Castle* and *Bamborough Castle* and the Norwegian corvettes *Tunsberg Castle* and *Eglantine* which are being transferred to Murmansk. Covering force: the cruiser *Bellona*, the 1st Division of the 7th DD Flotilla comprising *Caesar, Cassandra, Caprice* and *Cambrian* and the 17th DD Flotilla comprising *Onslow, Orwell, Obedient, Offa, Onslaught* and *Oribi*. As Support Groups there were the escort carriers *Campania* and *Nairana* with the frigates *Tavy, Tortola, Bahamas* and *Somaliland* and the Canadian 9th EG with the frigates *St. John, Stormont, Monnow, Loch Alvie, Nene* and *Port Colborne*.

On 27 November the convoy is located by German air reconnaissance. A fighter from the *Nairana* shoots down the contact-keeper. The U-boat group 'Stock' (*U-313, U-315, U-293, U-363, U-299, U-365, U-286, U-318, U-995* and *U-992*) and 'Grube' (*U-295, U-1163, U-387, U-997, U-668, U-310* and *U-965*) are deployed west of Bear Island, off the Kola Coast. On 1 December the 'Stock' group is moved to the Kola Coast because it is assumed that the convoy has passed the Bear Island passage. The convoy makes a diversion whilst the support groups make sorties against the suspected U-boat concentration – without result.

On 4-5 December in attacks on a Soviet coastal convoy in the entrance to the White Sea *U-997* (Lieutenant Lehmann) misses steamers and sinks the ex-US submarine-chaser *BO 226* (ex-*SC 1485*); *U-295* (Lieutenant Wieboldt) misses the destroyers *Deyatelny* and *Zhivuchi* with T-5s near

Jokanga and is pursued by them. From 5 December to 7 December *U-293* (Lieutenant Commander Klingspor), *U-992, U-995, U-365* (Lieutenant Todenhagen), *U-318* (Lieutenant Will), *U-997* and *U-1163* (Lieutenant Balduhn) attack, sometimes repeatedly, Soviet A/S groups as well as escorts and ships of the incoming JW 62. But only on 7 December is the ex-US submarine-chaser *BO 229* (ex-*SC 1477*), belonging to a Soviet anti-submarine group (Captain Third Class Gritsyuk) comprising *BO 227, BO 228, BO 229* and *BO 150*, sunk by *U-997*. JW 62 comes into harbour without loss. Before the return convoy RA 62 sets out with 28 ships and escort of JW 62 on 9 February 1945, the Allied support groups and a Soviet destroyer force (Rear Admiral Fokin) composed of *Baku, Gremyashchi, Razumny, Derzki, Doblestny* and *Zhivuchi* try to drive off the U-boats from the entrance to Kola Inlet. In the process *U-997* misses the *Zhivuchi* and *Razumny* with T-5s on 9 December. *U-387* is sunk by depth charges from the corvette *Bamborough Castle* (according to Soviet claims by ramming from the *Zhivuchi*). Only *U-365* is able to establish contact with the convoy and to torpedo the destroyer *Cassandra* on 11 December after an unsuccessful attack on a tanker the day before. On 13 December the boat, while keeping contact with great determination, is sunk by an aircraft from the *Campania*.

An attempt by German torpedo aircraft of KG[57] 26 to attack the convoy south-west of Bear Island is unsuccessful and results in the loss of two Ju 88s. The Norwegian corvette *Tunsberg Castle* runs over a mine of the German flanking barrage near Makkaur on 12 December and sinks.

A VIEW FROM THE ENGINE ROOM (Part II)

Angus Currie, Engine Room Artificer, HMS *Brilliant*

There is one very important part of *Brilliant*'s history which should be told. This refers to Christmas Eve 1944: *Brilliant* was detailed to lie off the Isle of Wight, somewhere near Cowes as I recall. About 2,800 American soldiers had arrived at Southampton and required transport to Cherbourg to

---

[57] *Kampfgruppe* – 'battlegroup'.

reinforce General Omar Bradley's US Army in north-western France.

Brilliant was leader of the escorts, with *Anthony*, the frigate *Calpe* and two other escorts. We were to escort the troopships SS *Leopoldville* and SS *Cheshire*, loaded with American troops, to Cherbourg. Later, as we approached the French coast, the frigate *Croix De Lorraine* joined us. *Brilliant* had the starboard quarter, beside the *Leopoldville*, all the way across the English Channel.

Nearing France, *Cheshire* was ordered to go in and off-load. About five miles from Cherbourg and at about 1730 hours, there was a tremendous explosion.

I was ERA of the Watch at the time, and we had just turned off to sweep the area for U-boats. The stern of the *Leopoldville* was badly holed. One or two seconds sooner and *we* would have had the torpedo in the ship's ammunition magazine, with dire results. When I was relieved at about 1810 hours, I was able to get up top and see the damage.

I had wondered what all the many engine changes and movements ordered from our bridge were for and thought that they were having a difficult time in manoeuvring *Brilliant* alongside the gradually sinking *Leopoldville*. I saw that the fo'c's'le deck of *Brilliant* was lined with hammocks and all the movements were to keep our bows as close as possible to the *Leopoldville*.

The American soldiers were jumping, one after another, from the *Leopoldville* onto the hammocks laid out on *Brilliant*'s steel fo'c's'le deck, on a signal from someone on the upper deck of the trooper. Some didn't make it, jumping either too soon or too late, as *Brilliant* bumped and scraped alongside the *Leopoldville*.

It was later estimated that we rescued 700 troops. But because the young American soldiers would not leave the upper deck and go below (quite understandable in the circumstances – U-boats probably remained in the area), *Brilliant* couldn't take any more as we were top heavy and were in imminent danger of capsizing.

During the desperate manoeuvres, our ERA's Mess was stove in at the after porthole and the sea was rushing in, dirty sand-coloured sea water. Our damage-control party was busy trying to block the damage and the low-power room was leaking badly, but both damaged sections were quickly and efficiently plugged.

We then proceeded to Cherbourg, expecting other ships in the vicinity would be queuing up to get the other US troops off from the *Leopoldville*, but I never saw any other ships. On our arrival at Cherbourg, we found the port closed down and everyone apparently on leave for Christmas. We tied up and all the troops were dispersed to different Units.

Much later we were told that the American soldiers' letters home were all censored and they were told to "keep quiet". Apparently, a very considerable number of American troops were lost with the *Leopoldville*, estimated at 800 men, in the freezing waters of the English Channel. Their parents and relatives in America were told their sons had been killed in action, which, of course, was bad enough, but it was not the truth.

The *Brilliant* patrolled for five days after that, but found nothing. Two other ships were also torpedoed in the following days. The *U-486* had had a successful patrol, but she was herself caught a few months later steaming up a Norwegian fjord by one of our submarines.

I have seen the videotape of the *Leopoldville* sinking and Captain Pringle was definitely treated very unfairly.[58] If it had not been for the alert and active ERAs in *Brilliant*'s engine room and Captain Pringle issuing a stream of precise commands from the bridge to the engine room, we would never have saved so many men as we did.

A few days later, an official notice of gratitude from the US Army appeared on *Brilliant*'s notice board, thanking Captain Pringle, his officers and crew of HMS *Brilliant* for all their help in having saved so many men of the 10th Battalion, Black Panther Regiment.

I wish I could write to *someone* and tell them what I think of their so-called "enquiry" and their decision to condemn Captain Pringle. He was relieved of his command and sent to another ship. But he should have been congratulated and awarded a medal. He did his very best under the most extreme circumstances imaginable, and the lads on board *Brilliant* would do anything for him.

[58] Refers to the subsequent accusations and official reprimand made against Captain Pringle's conduct as officer responsible for the rescue efforts; recently, books and a film documentary have brought this complex disaster wide-reaching publicity.

A SURVIVOR'S STORY

By Morton Wood, Jr., 66th Infantry Division, US Army

I was Second Lieutenant, an Infantry Rifle Platoon Leader of about 40 infantrymen. I begin these recollections with our boarding of the converted troopship and end with our 3rd Platoon of Company 'I', 264th Regiment of the 66th Infantry Division, being safely deposited on dry land.

It is natural, I believe, in times of stress and danger for a person to limit his focus to what immediately concerns his own situation plus, hopefully, the situations of those for whom he may be responsible or have a special friendship with. The 'Big Picture' for most of us under those conditions seems to cover an area just big enough to swing a cat in.

It was Christmas Eve 1944. The general situation at the time was that what was later called the 'Battle of the Bulge' was in full swing. Since 16 December powerful German armored units had suddenly attacked US Army positions through the hilly, snow-swept forests of the Ardennes in southern Belgium and Luxembourg. It was assumed that the 66th was headed to France to help plug a hole in the line.

We boarded the *Leopoldville*, a converted Belgian passenger liner of 11,509 tons, under the supervision of the British, but commanded and crewed by Belgians and Belgian Colonials, at Southampton, bound for Cherbourg, a port on the north-western coast of France, during the early hours of 24 December 1944. We quickly discovered that the troop accommodations therein, compared to the *George Washington*, which brought us across the North Atlantic from New York to England a month earlier, were dismal. The compartment for 'I' Company was the lowest, several decks below the loading deck, down into the depths of the liner via a ladder which passed through circular openings of about three feet in diameter at each deck level.

I had First Duty with the Company in the hold and didn't get to my own bunk until I was relieved about two hours later. During my duty period the *Leopoldville* left Southampton and headed out into the English Channel into rough seas. At least half of our guys rushed for the 'heads' moments later.

During those two hours a meal was served. Infantry soldiers don't expect first-class service but this was last-class. A large bucket of green, smelly stew was lowered on a rope down through the ladder openings. It paused at each deck long enough for each soldier, if he had the stomach, to scoop out some of the green liquid with his mess kit. Most of it ended up clogging the latrines.

I didn't try the stew because I knew that Officers' Mess was later in the ship's dining room. Lunch, or dinner, or whatever it was, brought about a revelation as to the differences in the treatment of enlisted men and officers in the European maritime services. After seeing the Enlisted Mess, I couldn't quite believe the Officers' Mess: spotless white tablecloths, jacketed waiters, good food, and if I remember correctly, a glass of wine. I wasn't shocked enough to pass up the feast, but I remember hoping that none of the guys in the Platoon found out about it.

This memory is one of the clearest of my military service and helped to reverse any good opinions I may have had about "rank has its privileges". My thought at that time was that this sort of privilege may work in the Belgian Merchant Marine, but it would never work for more than a couple days in the United States Army.

Some time during that day we had Boat Drill. This involved sounding the alarm, everyone putting on his life jacket and then scrambling up on deck to his assigned position. We had been briefed on this and the boat drill was duly completed. I was off duty by then and after it was over I went down to my cabin. The cabins were not fancy, but were quite comfortable. There were six of us to a cabin and I had the top bunk of the two triple-decker bunks. One bunkmate was Lieutenant Corbie Truman, a nephew, we were told, of Harry Truman, who was shortly to become President of the United States following the death of President Franklin D. Roosevelt in April 1945.

I was in my bunk when the torpedo hit, around 1800 hours. I was thrown against the ceiling but not injured. The alarms sounded and we went through the boat drill again, but this time it was for real. Our designated assembly area was near the *Leopoldville*'s bow. We soon got word that a torpedo, or a mine, had hit near the ship's stern and that there may be some casualties.

It is difficult to remember how much time had elapsed, but as I stood there on the deck surrounded by men of the 3rd Platoon, an officer using a megaphone on a higher deck announced that the ship was not sinking and we would be towed to port. Cherbourg, as we discovered later, was only a few miles away.

After that announcement, however, some of the *Leopoldville*'s Belgian crew started lowering lifeboats. There was some cheering from the American troops who thought the crewmen were preparing the boats for us to use, but the cheering stopped abruptly when it became apparent that they were abandoning ship themselves...

In retrospect, it is difficult to criticize them too much. They had probably seen a lot more of the war at sea than we ever would, and many of them had probably experienced previous sinkings. Our feelings at that time, however, were not too kind.

The seas were quite heavy and the crewmen had a difficult time with the lifeboats. They kept getting the ropes snarled and had trouble lowering the boats to the deck level so they could get in. One boat, and probably others judging from the screams, tipped over and spilled the crewmen into the bitterly cold sea. There didn't appear to be any rescue attempts for them by the other crewmen.

The *Leopoldville* began to list, and there were rumors that we might have to abandon ship. We were unaware of what was happening at the stern of the ship where the torpedo had struck and exploded. Our 'Megaphone Man' was trying to keep us calm and warning us not to leave the ship. Apparently, it was still believed that we would be towed to Cherbourg.

It was about that time that a very special thing happened. The picture is still vivid in my mind: hundreds of infantry soldiers standing on the deck of a ship that was very probably going to sink; all lifeboats gone or hopelessly snarled; the ship's crew abandoning ship; several lights glowing on deck in the pitch-black night inviting further attack... Then a single soldier, close by, started to sing 'The Star Spangled Banner'. Other soldiers took it up until everyone around was singing the American national anthem.

It didn't matter that not every infantryman knew all the words. I didn't, but I could hardly sing anyway because I kept choking up with the emotion of the moment. To this day, I still choke up each time I think of it, even when we sing it at the Washington Redskins football games, 55 years later.

A British destroyer, HMS *Brilliant*, had at some point pulled alongside the *Leopoldville*. We were told by the 'Megaphone Man' that some troops would be allowed to jump over the side and onto the destroyer's deck, but only when and where directed. The seas were still very heavy and we could see the destroyer bobbing up and down as the two ships took the waves.

After a while the 'Megaphone Man', who was on the deck above us, pointed down at me and said something like: "Lieutenant... Line up your platoon and bring them up to this deck."

We didn't waste much time climbing the ladder and found ourselves in the line leading to the position where men were jumping down to the destroyer. There was an opening in the handrail where one man at a time could jump. Two men from Company 'K', 264th, Lieutenant Ben Thrailkill and Lieutenant George Washko, were directing the jumping. They stood on either side of the gap, and then by judging the considerable movements of the two ships, gave a signal, and sometimes a shove, to each soldier at the critical moment when they felt the two decks were close enough for a safe jump. That, of course, meant judging both the vertical and horizontal distances between the two ships, which were constantly changing – a truly massive responsibility.

I don't know how many men got off at that particular point, or whether there were other positions on the *Leopoldville* where the two ships were close enough for the same thing to happen. Fortunately, many men from my platoon completed the hazardous transfer safely from where I was positioned (sadly five didn't make it), along with a good proportion of the rest of 'I' Company.

My own leap down onto the destroyer was fairly easy, although I twisted my ankle on landing among some sort of depth charge devices on the *Brilliant*'s deck. My jump was made a little easier because I'd given my life jacket to a soldier who had left his on his bunk in the hold and said he couldn't swim. I remember being reprimanded by someone for not having mine on, but it was too late to do anything about it. I certainly wasn't about to go back down to the hold to look for a spare life jacket.

As we landed on the destroyer we were led in turn by British seamen to a cabin and given hot drinks and blankets. Relieved greetings awaited each man as he entered the cabin and was recognized. I was glad to see that many men from the 3rd Platoon were already there. I have never discovered what happened to the five infantrymen who didn't make it. They were later presumed drowned when the *Leopoldville* went down. My guess was that they didn't make it to our assigned position on deck because of being away from the Platoon for some reason or another when the torpedo hit. Another possibility, too terrible to think about, is that they were among those few who mis-timed their leap. They were instantly crushed between the ships as they slammed together in the heavy seas.

I have always very much regretted not making more of an effort to discover how they died. They were: Staff Sergeant James Doherty, our Platoon Guide; Private First Class John Worden; Private Gregorio Contreras; Private First Class Thomas English; and Private First Class Marvin Barton.

The *Brilliant* delivered us to a dock at Cherbourg. The authorities there had to scramble around to receive the survivors of approximately 2,100 troops on board. In addition to the survivors on board *Brilliant*, about 700, many men were rescued from the sea by smaller vessels from Cherbourg and other points along the French coast as word of the sinking rapidly spread.

The American Red Cross took over and put us up in a large tent, fed us and issued dry clothes. The story of the sinking ends there for the 3rd Platoon. We took on several replacements and within a few weeks were in combat against the Germans, but not in the 'Battle of the Bulge'.

The first real indication of the magnitude of the tragedy came to me several hours after our landing. We were standing on the dock as other survivors were coming into Cherbourg. A small rescue vessel arrived and five or six men got off, among them a Platoon Leader in the 262nd Infantry and a former classmate of mine at Officer Candidate School. He was apparently unharmed physically but was thoroughly shaken. He said:

"My God! This is all that's left of my Company – five men... "

His Company had been in the compartment near the stern where the torpedo hit.

I have tried to recall only my own observations and experiences. Books, documents, and other written records tell, in detail, the full story of the actual torpedo strike. They tell of the heroism of those who went down into the stricken hold to bring up the wounded, the stories of those who were rescued from the sea by the outstanding efforts of men from other craft after the *Leopoldville* went down. My own personal heroes were the individual with the megaphone, two guys named Ben Thrailkill and George Washko, some brave and efficient British seamen, and the infantryman who started singing 'The Star Spangled Banner'.

After the sinking, the survivors of our 66th Infantry Division assembled in Cherbourg and then relieved the US 94th Infantry Division which was surrounding the by-passed French ports of Lorient and St. Nazaire which had German submarine bases with fortified repair facilities. We had been scheduled to join the Allied forces engaged in the 'Battle of the Bulge' but the 94th took our place because of our somewhat disorganized situation.

Our job there was to contain the German forces in the two pockets. Our duties were mainly patrolling and counter-artillery fire against them; certainly an easier job than on the main western front, but with enough dangerous assignments to keep us on edge. We were spread thinly along the lines and operated generally on our own, but there were not too many memorable events during the final five months of the war.

We learned much later that the *Leopoldville* was torpedoed by the German submarine *U-486* which was itself sunk, with all hands off the Norwegian coast, under the command of a Captain Gerhard Meyer, by the British submarine HMS *Tapir* on 12 April 1945.

Many of us concluded our WWII service with the Occupation Forces in Austria. Our trip home from Europe was on the SS *Lehigh Victory*, one of the many Kaiser-built wartime 'troopers'. We took almost three weeks for the crossing, most of it during a monstrous storm in the North Atlantic which we couldn't get away from. The entire ship shuddered each time the screws came up out of the water and we could hear groans and loud snapping sounds from the ship's plates as they twisted with each lunge. We were happy to get home away from the ocean.

A VIEW FROM AN INFANTRYMAN

Richard L. Dutka, 66th Infantry Division, US Army

It was Christmas Eve 1944, when the SS *Leopoldville*, an Allied troopship registered in Belgium, was sunk by a German submarine off the French coast. It was not until 40 years later that the full story came to light, but those of us aboard her have never forgotten what we experienced. I was a member of the 66th Division, scheduled to replace the hard-pressed forces taking part in the 'Battle of the Bulge' and the siege of Bastogne.

I'd recently learned that my wife, Marion, had given birth to twin daughters, Lois and Diane, while I was crossing the Atlantic to Southampton where we arrived on 15 December 1944, aboard another troopship. Naturally, I was delighted, but very sorry I couldn't be with them. Our 66th Division was ordered to move out on 23 December.

We started boarding at Southampton at about 10.00 p.m. that night. Our unit, the 264th Regiment, was scheduled to be the first to board the troopship, but for some reason we were late to arrive, so the 263rd Regiment went aboard first. It was very ironic, because they all went down below to the hold and we stayed on an upper deck.

The 11,500-ton steamer, manned by a mixed crew of Belgians and Congolese, was in company with other merchantmen. The convoy was escorted by four naval vessels. The Channel crossing was uneventful until shortly before 6.00 p.m. on 24 December. Suddenly, without warning, a torpedo slammed into our troopship. It was almost an instantaneous knockout and everyone knew we'd been badly hit. You could almost hear the steel being ripped apart, all the lights immediately went out and we were left standing in the darkness of a cold, windy December night.

Despite the fact that our slowly sinking ship was only five miles from Cherbourg, the base for a small fleet of US tugboats, the rescue efforts, from start to finish, were very haphazard. The Congolese crew abandoned the ship in lifeboats with all their belongings and fled, leaving no one to show us how to lower the remaining lifeboats from their davits. Only the ship's commander, Captain Limbur, and four senior Belgian officers remained aboard.

Soon, a British destroyer, HMS *Brilliant*, one of the convoy's escorts, pulled alongside to take off the wounded. With great difficulty and some highly skilled manoeuvring by the destroyer, mooring lines were secured. The English Channel is not a very smooth body of water and the sea was quite choppy. Even though the two ships were almost together, their decks kept alternately rising up and down independently with the heaving seas, making the transfers very difficult, but not impossible as the *Brilliant*'s deck rose up.

When the vertical distance between the two ships' decks shortened considerably as the destroyer rose, the uninjured troops were transferred. The British sailors yelled up to us: "JUMP YANK! – JUMP!…" But there were troops who slightly mis-timed their leaps for safety, and ended up falling 30 or 40 feet onto the bobbing deck of the destroyer. They jumped, hit the deck and just lay there. They were the lucky ones… There were a few who tragically mis-timed their jumps, splashing down in the sea between the ships and were crushed when the two ships, weighing thousands of tons, crashed together. The steel sides of the *Leopoldville* and the *Brilliant* were crimson with blood from those crushed. A truly terrible but mercifully instantaneous death…

Before very long, the deck of the destroyer was covered with troops. I can't say enough good things about the heroic crew of the *Brilliant*.

After I'd assembled on the main deck of the *Leopoldville* with our outfit, our Platoon Sergeant, Louis Strossi, yelled to three of us to help him hold down a Sergeant whose unit was in the very area of the torpedo hit. Deeply distressed and anguished, the Sergeant implored us to let him go below to try and help his men. It would have been a futile effort and one which would have probably have added another good man to the many killed, some 300, by the exploding torpedo.

Leopoldville had started to list badly so that we could no longer stand up. I'd been handing out blankets to the men who were still being pulled up from below decks so that they could keep warm. Shortly before we went down, we had an American-crewed tugboat assisting us with a line on one of the starboard davits. They hit trouble when the line became taut as the *Leopoldville* began her slow and inevitable descent to the bottom. There was no way to relieve the tension of the hawser.

The tug's Captain shouted desperately across: "SOMEONE CUT THE LINE! CUT THE LINE – OR WE WILL GO DOWN WITH YOU!…"

Sergeant Lou Strossi, being left-handed, yelled to the soldier nearest the fire-axe to get it to him. With no time to spare, he hit that line with one mighty swing of the axe. The hawser snapped back with tremendous force against the pilot-house. Then I began to slide down the deck as the troop-ship slowly sank deeper. I grabbed a guy-wire and climbed towards the mast, but as the bow rose up I lost my hold and fell about 50 feet into the freezing sea.

I found myself swimming with other troops in almost total darkness. We struggled through the icy waves to an emergency life raft that suddenly appeared among the other floating debris. It was soon almost submerged with the weight of soldiers hanging on to its sides, or stacked on top, blue with cold – some already dead or dying.

Then the captain of one of the tugs that had come out from Cherbourg to rescue us, despite the threat of U-boats in the area, shone his spotlight on an American flag. You wouldn't believe the inspirational feeling that act gave to us.

After hanging onto the life raft, I was eventually picked up by a US Coast Guard patrol boat. Other soldiers were screaming and yelling to be picked up. We were all terrified, freezing cold, but as long as I live I'll never forget that boat's serial number – *USCG 15*.

I'm convinced most of us who survived made it because all the troops were dressed in their full uniforms, which gave them some protection from the freezing waters. I went down with a full canteen of drinking water on my cartridge belt. I could have sold that fresh water for a million dollars to the other men just to get the taste of sea water out of their mouths.

Despite further rescue efforts, more than 800 United States soldiers were lost. It was the worst troopship loss of the war involving American troops, and one whose consequences could have been less horrendous had there not been the confusion, indecision, lack of communication and a ship's crew that fled in lifeboats, leaving the troops to fend for themselves.

The *Leopoldville* did not sink until two-and-a-half hours after the torpedo hit, only five miles off Cherbourg. The lights of the French port could be seen twinkling on the horizon. There were enough tugs in the harbour to have towed the stricken troopship to shallow water, and enough boats to rescue all the surviving troops.

HMS *Brilliant* had no radio contact with Cherbourg and radioed Southampton but for some unknown reason contact could not be established with the port officials at Cherbourg. *Brilliant* then signalled to Cherbourg with her Aldis Lamp that help was urgently needed. About 1,500 troops were rescued.

Because of the tragedy, the 66th Division arrived in Cherbourg so under-strength that we never made it to the 'Battle of the Bulge' in the snow-covered, hilly forests of the Ardennes. Instead, the surviving troops were sent to contain the German fortress garrisons at St. Nazaire and Lorient, where the Germans had their U-boat pens. We relieved the 94th Division, which was assigned to the Ardennes in our place.

Despite the serious losses, our government kept secret the sinking of the *Leopoldville*. It wasn't until 1966 that the full details of the disaster were released from the National Archives, in Washington, DC. In 1984, the National Underwater and Marine Agency, a non-profit foundation based in Washington, announced the discovery of a sunken ship two miles off the French coast – the *Leopoldville*.

1945

PROLOGUE TO 1945

by

Rear Admiral John B. Hervey, RN, Retd.

WAR IN EUROPE finished on 8 May, and against Japan on 15 August. However, in January, there still seemed much to do. The Russians may have been entering Budapest, but our armies in Italy were bogged down and we had only just recovered from a dangerous German counter-attack in the Ardennes over Christmas. Above all, we were worried about new classes of German U-boats and still suffering casualties on big convoys to North Russia. We lost only two destroyers in 1945. But six smaller escorts were sunk, mostly near Murmansk, by U-boats.

These treacherous waters are well remembered by those in HMS *Cavalier* who went up to reinforce the escort of Convoy RA 64 from Murmansk to the Clyde in February – when the wind reached hurricane force for several days and was never less than Force 7 (28 to 33 knots or 51 to 61 km/h). Twelve of the RA 64 escorts had to go into dock for repairs. Richard Woodman, in an excerpt from *Arctic Convoys*, and Commander Ian Leitch in 'The Loss of HMS *Lapwing*', show how active U-boats still were in the Arctic, right up to VE Day – successful too, when bad weather grounded carrier- and shore-based air assets.

ERA Angus Currie of HMS *Brilliant* in the third of his 'Views From the Engine Room' gives a light-hearted account of a disastrous voyage he made in *LST 364*, whilst *Brilliant* was being repaired following a collision. LSTs were very busy ferrying military vehicles to Antwerp, in preparation for the crossing of the river Rhine in March 1945. But *LST 364* never got there. However, the end of the war in Europe was now close. And it is marked by several articles. Senior Telegraphist Dennis Abbott in 'Liberating a Part of Occupied Britain' tells how HMS *Bulldog* and *Beagle* took the surrender of the Germans in Guernsey and Jersey – not without an element of farce, as the enemy military tried to put a brave face on a bad moment. Abbott saw all the signals that were exchanged, which makes his account particularly interesting.

The announcement of VE Day by the Prime Minister – who above all wanted the occasion to be seen to be the King's – and the message sent to the Supreme Allied Commander, General Eisenhower, by the King, whose foremost thought is to thank the troops, are both moving. Even the words used by Grand Admiral Dönitz, the new Führer, in accepting unconditional surrender – whose hope was that Germany might remain as an undivided nation and, one day, be less hated than it was by all its neighbours in 1945 – have a surprising dignity.

For many ships, however, end of war in Europe was celebrated by visits to the towns which had adopted them before they went out to the Far East to complete the outstanding business with Japan. Thus, HMS *Cavalier* went to South Shields and fifty of HMS *Bulldog's* company were brought up from Plymouth and entertained in Battersea, as reported in an extract from the *South Western Star*. Important naval people were there to greet them, as one would have hoped.

Only one of our authors, Ron Blacker, had direct experience of working with the British Pacific Fleet. We last saw him in HMS *Westcott*. By now a Gunnery Instructor, he was sent to HMS *Crane* in June 1944, and was with her in the BPF when it joined the US Navy Sixth Fleet for a number of the toughest island-cracking operations of that war, including the two worst: Iwo Jima and Okinawa. He tells the story in 'Victory in the Pacific'. The Japanese got as far as they ever were to in the first six months of their campaigning, but it took three years for the Allies to get it all back – not surprising when one remembers that capturing Okinawa took 84 days of hard land fighting. In a fascinating Anthologist's Note we are with Commander Frederick J. Becton, USN, as he very ably defends his destroyer USS *Laffey* (supported by *LCS 51*) against a force of 50 kamikaze aircraft, and survives, albeit in bad shape by the end.

Finally, to mark the war's end, 'Counting the Cost', derived from E. J. March's *British Destroyers*, gives some overall statistics and a breakdown of how our destroyer losses occurred. Of course, totals vary depending on criteria used for inclusion. But the March figures are near those agreed by the HMS *Cavalier* (Chatham) Trust Memorial Steering Group and the Naval Historical Branch, who will name 142 destroyers individually on a Destroyer Memorial in Chatham Historic Dockyard. These ships were all Royal Navy-manned and either built in Britain or acquired from the USA, like HMS

Campbeltown, originally the four-stacker USS *Buchanan*. If one includes British-built destroyers manned by Commonwealth and Allied navies the total rises to 153. Their contribution will certainly be recognised on the Memorial.[59]

A VIEW FROM THE ENGINE ROOM (Part III)

Angus Currie, Engine Room Artificer, HMS *Brilliant*

An unfortunate accident occurred on 22 January 1945, when we were going down to Portland Bill from Portsmouth to escort another 'trooper' over to Cherbourg.

I was on watch in the engine room. It was about 6.00 a.m., still dark. Our Asdic had been acting up and eventually broke down completely. Suddenly the ship's telegraph ordered: "STOP!… FULL ASTERN!" I happened to be leaning on the throttle wheels at the time. I had the 'Ahead' control shut in no time and the 'Astern' fully open in five seconds flat. We waited, hearts suddenly beating wildly, not knowing what was going on up on the bridge.

Suddenly there was a most awful crash and we felt a tremendous jolt. We had collided heavily with a Canadian corvette, HMCS *Lindsay*, which also suffered very considerable damage. About 15 to 20 feet of *Brilliant*'s bows had been thoroughly smashed and mangled. The upper deck had been forced upwards and our bows had been forcibly twisted by the collision and were pointing in the wrong direction. While the specialist Damage Control Party put in timber posts and planks to reinforce the threatened bulkheads we had no alternative but to continue going astern, under escort, back to Portsmouth for emergency repairs. Mercifully, there were no crew casualties on *Brilliant*, but I believe there were several on *Lindsay*. A ship in their group took care of them.

On arrival at Portsmouth half of *Brilliant*'s crew were given eight days'

---

[59] The totals used in the yearly prologues are taken from *The War at Sea* by S. W. Roskill. They amount to 148 overall but include some Commonwealth and Allied-manned Royal Navy destroyers.

leave. Fortunately, I was in the first half. Our ship was then made seaworthy for the cross-Channel passage to Antwerp for completion of repairs.

While at home enjoying a rest, I received a telegram to report to the NOIC[60] at Tilbury where I met some of my shipmates. We were taken out to a docking area in the back of British Army trucks where *LST 364* was loading Army trucks, cars, Bren-Gun carriers, Sherman tanks and motor bikes for Antwerp in preparation for the crossing of the Rhine River, which eventually took place in late March. We went aboard, found our new billets and sailed down the Thames in the late evening. We dropped anchor off Margate and waited for the remainder of the convoy to arrive before setting off, at about dawn, for Hoboken on the River Scheldt, near Antwerp.

We were about halfway across, in the Goodwin Sands area, when *LST 364* was torpedoed. The huge stern sustained serious damage and, as there were no pumps and as the hand-operated fire extinguishers were quickly emptied, an uncontrollable fire was soon raging in the tank section. Eventually, and none too soon, we heard the 'Pipe' to clear the lower deck. CPO King, *Brilliant*'s Chief Yeoman of Signals, was with us and he calmly signalled an Admiralty trawler: "Get yourselves over here fast and take us off!" or words to that effect. The escape hatches were a tight fit; however we all made it up to the main deck.

The LST was sinking fast, but we all managed to jump down on to the trawler. About five minutes later *364* capsized and sank with a great crashing, grinding and rumbling as the trucks and tanks tumbled noisily out of control, amidst much hissing as the raging fires were gradually extinguished by the freezing seas.

After watching the sad sight of the ship going down, we were taken to Dover where those of us in uniform were allowed to proceed to London and then home on survivors' leave. After seven days, I received another telegram instructing me to report to NOIC at Tilbury. We were taken to the same dock where *LST 366* was loading more Army vehicles and tanks for Antwerp. We all chose the same bunks as in *LST 364*.

Several of us went for a pint in a nearby pub to cheer ourselves up. The

---

[60] Naval Officer in Charge. To control arrivals, discharge and departures of vessels from ports and places of (dis)embarkation.

pub was named 'The End of The World' and we hoped the pub's name was only a coincidence... While there, we toasted *LST 365* and wondered where she was! Our subsequent voyage over to Antwerp in *LST 366* was uneventful.

We rejoined *Brilliant* in Cockerill's Shipyard at Hoboken, near Antwerp, which at that time, was under almost constant attack from V-1 flying bombs and the even more devastating V-2 rockets. Those 'V'[61] weapons certainly made a terrible mess of most of the medieval buildings in Antwerp.

Brilliant was in a dry dock which was cut into the bank of the Scheldt. We had been back on board only one or two days when we heard the unmistakable engine sound of an approaching V-1 coming straight for us, and then an incredible and truly terrifying silence as the pulse-jet engine ran out of fuel directly overhead... My shipmate and I hurled ourselves down onto the steel deck, hoping and praying. The bomb plunged into the River Scheldt about 200 yards away with a mighty explosion. It was lucky that the caisson held firm as all our underwater valves had been removed for cleaning before being refitted.

We eventually made our way back to Portsmouth in *Brilliant*, her bows rebuilt, in late April 1945. By then, the war in Europe, which had lasted for six long years of madness, was almost over. In that time HMS *Brilliant* had experienced many narrow escapes but luckily she had survived.

Excerpt from *Arctic Convoys* by Richard Woodman

(Reproduced by kind permission of Richard Woodman and John Murray (Publishers) Ltd.)

Despite the fact that the Red Army were almost at the gates of Berlin, the Germans persisted in their attacks on the Arctic convoys to the bitter end, maintaining pressure on their defence which was, in turn, met by an equally relentless doggedness.

---

[61] 'V' for *Vergeltungswaffe*: 'vengeance weapons'.

The convoy (JW 65) itself proceeded unremarkably, the air patrols being divided between night flying from *Campania* and day flying from *Trumpeter*. Until 20 March 1945, the only thing of general interest had been a vast area of the curiously rounded floes known as 'pancake ice'. But on that morning, in dense snow showers and squalls which grounded the airborne patrols and halted the Russian fighter cover, the convoy was sighted by Oberleutnant Hess in *U-995*, who promptly torpedoed and sank the American Liberty ship *Horace Bushnell* before JW 65 cleared the first line of the redeployed wolfpack.

Three hours later, at about noon, the second line were in contact. Swordfish patrols were airborne but this did not deter the enemy. *U-716* fired at, and missed, an escort, but Westphalen once again made his sinister mark in *U-968*. Attacking with Kapitänleutnant Schweiger in *U-313*, he struck *Lapwing* and shortly afterwards a second American Liberty ship, the *Thomas Donaldson*, both of which sank. Only sixty officers and ratings were saved from the British sloop.

THE LOSS OF HMS *LAPWING*

Commander Ian Leitch, RN, Retd.

A mong the thousands of young Allied seamen who perished in the icy seas of northern waters were most of the crew of HMS *Lapwing*, a 'Black Swan' class sloop, during one of the last convoys to Russia in March 1945.

I hardly knew anyone in *Lapwing*. I'd spent the previous year on constant Arctic convoys in HMS *Cygnet* (another 'Black Swan' class sloop), as Staff Anti-Submarine Officer to the Senior Officer 7th & 8th Escort Groups. During that time we had lost *Kite*, *Lark*, *Tunsberg Castle*, *Denbigh Castle* and *Bluebell*, all in the same graveyard area off Kola Inlet, the entrance for Murmansk.

In February 1945, the homeward bound convoy suffered severely from hurricane-force weather and twelve escort vessels were damaged, including *Cygnet* which had to dock for repairs. My Commanding Officer decided to take a break too and handed the Group over to the ship next in seniority,

Commander Hulton in HMS *Lapwing*, and told me to transfer. I joined *Lapwing* the morning the convoy of twenty-six merchantmen sailed from the Clyde, on 11 March 1945.

Nine days later, during a snowstorm in the Kola graveyard, we were sunk by *U-968*, one of eleven U-boats concentrated in that fateful region.

I had two fellow 'Staffies' with me, young RNVR Sub-Lieutenants, specialists in Radar and HF/DF,[62] but sadly neither survived the icy sea. *Lapwing*'s captain, Commander Hulton, was knocked unconscious by the explosion but was picked up and recovered two days later in Vaenga Hospital – he remembered nothing.

I submitted the following report of my impressions on the sinking of HMS *Lapwing*:

'On the forenoon of 20 March 1945, in a position approximately five miles north of Kildin Light House, *Lapwing* and *Allington Castle* were on the extended screen six miles ahead of convoy JW 65. The screen had originally consisted of *Lapwing* and the five 'Castle' class corvettes, but at 0930 hours *Bamborough Castle* and *Lancaster Castle* had been detached to stand by one of the merchantmen in the convoy which had been torpedoed at 0917 hours, and shortly after 1000 hours *Alnwick Castle* and *Farnham Castle* had dropped out of the line to investigate an Asdic contact classified by *Alnwick Castle* as "probable submarine".

Allington Castle was stationed 4,000 yards on *Lapwing*'s port beam, course 270 degrees, speed 12 knots, Zigzag No. 45, *Lapwing* was weaving 40 degrees either side of the MLA. Radar was carrying out an 'all-round' sweep, Asdics sweeping 80-80 relative, and 'unifoxer' streamed and operating efficiently.[63] 'B' gun's crew had been ordered to keep a sharp lookout either side, in addition to normal lookouts, as a south-westerly wind was just strong enough to cause 'white horses' on wave tops, which considerably reduced the chances of sighting a U-boat's periscope.

Shortly after 1100 hours I went into the plotting room, on the after end of the bridge, to discuss something with Commander Binnie, RN (from HM Anti-Submarine Experimental Establishment at Fairlie, Ayrshire). He

---

[62] High-Frequency Direction-Finding.

[63] See Appendix VI for explanation of convoy terms.

was taking passage in *Lapwing* to observe the U-boat menace concentrated off Kola Inlet.

A few minutes later a heavy explosion occurred which knocked us off our feet, wrecked the ARL plot, PPI and Asdic instruments in the adjacent cabinet. The door of the compartment jammed and wouldn't open. It was several minutes before the attention of those on the bridge could be attracted. AB Birtwhistle then kicked the panels of the door in from outside and let us out.

I looked over the side and noticed the way was off the ship and she was beginning to settle – it appeared her back was broken and there was a large hole torn in the upper deck, starboard side, abreast the funnel. The whaler had disappeared and two empty Carley floats were visible some distance astern. Oil fuel covered a lot of the superstructure. I considered it unlikely that the ship would remain afloat for more than a few minutes.

I then saw Lieutenant Embleton-Smith, RNVR, Navigating Officer, organizing the slipping of the port forward Carley float with some ratings. Surgeon Lieutenant Wilson, RNVR, was on the bridge and I said, "Where's the Captain?"

"He's been knocked out, I'm just going to attend to him," he replied.

I then saw the Captain lying unconscious on the port side of the bridge under the chart table.

Sub-Lieutenant Baldwin, RNVR, Officer of the Watch, had apparently sustained a broken leg, so Commander Binnie and myself assisted him down to the wheelhouse and then lowered him on a line to the upper deck, starboard side. Here I noticed Petty Officer Doney efficiently organizing things for the care of the wounded. He had already got Sub-Lieutenant Worker, RNVR, Group Radar Officer, who seemed badly injured, in a Nail-Robertson stretcher. The starboard Carley float had apparently already been slipped and was about twenty yards away on the beam, so the problem of getting casualties off the ship appeared a serious one.

Some ratings on 'B' gun deck were cutting free a Flotanet from the starboard guard rails, but there appeared insufficient life-saving equipment for the large number of ratings, about one hundred, who had mustered on the fo'c's'le. I shouted to them to cut everything adrift that would float off, such as the whaler's gear, which was slung overhead on the Bofors gun platform support.

About fifteen minutes had now elapsed since the explosion, and loud breaking-up noises could be heard from the region of the boiler room.

On reaching the upper deck I saw that the ratings forward were starting to jump over the side, as the ship was now settling rapidly and listing heavily to starboard, so I assisted Sub-Lieutenant Baldwin through the guard rails into the water and then followed him.

A few seconds later the ship broke in half, the forward part capsized to starboard and the after part floated vertically, stern uppermost. As I swam clear to avoid being fouled by the mast and rigging, I saw the captain holding on to the port side of the bridge. As it turned over, he dropped clear into the water. A few minutes later I saw Surgeon Lieutenant Wilson in the water; he spoke to me and appeared extremely cheerful.

I found my inflatable lifebelt gave ample buoyancy. There was also a vast amount of floating wreckage such as wooden planks, danbuoys, floats and cork life jackets to help support one, although oil fuel made it difficult to grasp them. I clung to a wooden plank but later transferred to a Flotanet attached to a fully-manned Carley float, whose occupants were singing cheerfully and appeared admirably confident of being rescued.

Snow then began to fall, and about half an hour later I found myself drifting under *Allington Castle*'s starboard quarter, but cannot recall anything after this until I found myself being stripped and cleaned on board her in the seaman's bathroom.

I would like to pay tribute to the gallant rescue work of the officers and ratings of *Allington Castle*. I feel certain that had it not been for their untiring efforts our casualties must have been much higher.

Commander Hulton, captain of *Lapwing*, could remember nothing of the explosion and the sinking of his ship. When he came to in Vaenga Hospital (a converted school) I was by his bedside and he murmured: "We are approaching Kola so I must go up to the bridge." He later asked me to write a report of the sinking which I did, and which more or less tells the sad story.

From a ship's company of 220 there were 60 survivors.

LIBERATING A PIECE OF OCCUPIED BRITAIN

Dennis Abbott, Senior Telegraphist, HMS *Bulldog*

One minute to midnight on VE Day, 8 May 1945, *Bulldog* sailed into the harbour of St. Peter Port, Guernsey. Our sister ship HMS *Beagle* (Lieutenant Commander C. T. D. Williams, RN) sailed to nearby Jersey. I still keep the press reports about the surrender and the Guernsey news-sheet announcing "THE WAR IS OVER".

Before the midnight meeting, preliminary wireless discussions had taken place in the morning with the Germans on the Channel Islands. I was wireless operator for our captain, Lieutenant Commander D. B. G. Dumas, RN, several senior officers and the Germans.

Earlier that day *Bulldog* had sailed to a rendezvous four miles off the coast of Guernsey. An eyewitness account of that quite extraordinary rendezvous was a front-page story in the *Daily Herald*, a national newspaper:

'At 2 p.m. precisely we arrived at the meeting place. A naval guard with fixed bayonets was drawn up on the quarterdeck, the ship's crew was at Action Stations, soldiers of the first landing party stood stiffly to attention.

A few moments later, looking ahead, we saw the German surrender ship. She was a dirty, battered minesweeper, her sides red with rust, the paint on her superstructure chipped and discoloured.

It seemed crudely fantastic to see, but heaved over the side of the trawler, was a 3 foot by 6 foot rubber dinghy. Three Nazi sailors climbed into it, followed by a young Nazi naval officer carrying an attaché case. This youth, of not more than 23 or 24, was the German Emissary.

As the sailors clumsily applied their paddles, he sat in the stern of the dinghy, his seat a few inches from the water, the waves sweeping up and soaking him from the waist downwards.

And so, dripping and pale-faced, Kapitänleutnant Arnim Zimmerman, of the 46th Minesweeping Flotilla, came to the *Bulldog* to be received by the click of saluting rifles and the shrill of boatswain's whistles.

The eyes of the slim grey youth flashed nervously as his right arm shot out in the Nazi salute. From his attaché case he produced his credentials and then a young, immaculate Royal Navy Lieutenant from Birmingham escorted him below to the wardroom.

Facing the German was an imposing array of British officers, Brigadier A. E. Snow, the chief British Army emissary, Rear Admiral C. G. Stuart, representing the Royal Navy, a representative of the Royal Air Force, an interpreter, and several other staff officers.

Zimmerman's arm again shot out in an exaggerated Nazi salute. He again presented his credentials, which stated that he had the authority to receive armistice terms for conveyance to Vice Admiral Huffmeier, the German Commander-in-Chief of the Channel Islands.

The Brigadier turned to the interpreter: "Make it quite clear to him that this is an immediate surrender, and not an armistice," he said.

Zimmerman rapped back his reply. He hadn't the power to sign unconditional surrender, but had only come to receive the terms of the armistice, and that armistice, he added with a touch of hauteur, did not come into force until 0100 hours the next morning.

He was told to withdraw and later was again summoned to the wardroom to be informed that he would be sent back to his chief with a copy of the instrument of surrender in English and in German and with instructions that another rendezvous must be arranged forthwith.

Then came an astonishing touch of arrogance and stubbornness. With the sweat on his forehead, Zimmerman stood up. "I will do that," he said loudly, "but I am instructed to inform you that your ships must move away immediately from these shores. If they do not, Admiral Huffmeier will regard their presence as a breach of faith and a provocative act!"

The implied threat to the British destroyers, now within a few miles of a coast reputed to be one of the heaviest defended in the world, was obvious.

Sternly he was told to withdraw, and saluting again, he went. For nearly an hour he was kept kicking his heels while instructions on the rendezvous were prepared for him.

The old rusty minesweeper, flying her Swastika flag, rolled flatly between the two spick-and-span British destroyers, and there was a fantastic sight of three men paddling around in the rubber dinghy.

Zimmerman came out and shouted "Hoch!" as he saluted. His dignity broke as he scrambled into the leaping rubber boat but as he drew away he saluted Nazi-fashion, time and again.

The *Bulldog*, and its accompanying destroyer, the *Beagle*, withdrew and for six hours slowly patrolled out in the Channel. Then at midnight they returned, to a vastly different sight.

Out of the darkness came a German armed trawler. For the first time since 3 September 1939, our own ships were illuminated, and as we swept a searchlight over the German vessel there came into view a white, eight-oared cutter. In her stern sat the same naval officer, but with him was a resplendent figure in light blue army greatcoat with great red lapels. He was Major General Heine of the German Army. He came aboard and went to the ward-room.

Heine was immediately asked if he accepted unconditional surrender on behalf of his Commander-in-Chief. "Ja," he replied.

And so on the following morning, 22 British soldiers landed on the island. It was this tiny force which took over Guernsey from 10,000 Germans. The welcome they and the newspaper reporters received from the people of the island was overwhelming.

Thousands of cheering, laughing people, and people speechless with tears running down their cheeks, surrounded our little force, tearing at our clothes, embracing us, pumping our hands. They couldn't say much: "We've waited so long for this. We're so glad you've come."'

THE LIBERATION OF SARK

Lieutenant E. A. Cowell, RNVR, Retd., HMS *Beagle*

Forty years is a long time to stretch one's recollection, particularly if one is relying on memory, as I am. However, the most important events of life seem to be indelibly etched upon the mind even if time blurs them at the edges.

The relief of the Channel Islands in May 1945 embraces a whole group of such memories for me, and as I have been asked to put them in writing, I do so in the hope that they may offer something for posterity and equally that those who read them will do so in a forgiving frame of mind if they, in any way, run counter to their own most vivid recollections...

Nearing the island of Guernsey at dead of night was an unnerving affair. We had all become well-accustomed on convoy duty to the absolute need for a dark ship during night-time because the slightest chink of light could have betrayed the ship's position to a lurking enemy. On this occasion it was quite the reverse; our orders required fully-lit ships and the flying of illuminated battle ensigns at the masthead as we approached the sea rendezvous for the initial parley with the German representative.

All that light coming from ships at sea induced a kind of cringing embarrassment as we approached, slowed, and ultimately waited about for our contact. Even then it proved to be all in vain; the Germans, who came out in a tiny launch, had no power to sign or speak with authority, so it was 'lights-out' and thunder away at full speed into the darkness, imagining the German guns following us by radar into the distance...

The next day we approached the land in daylight, anchored safely off St. Peter Port and the surrender parley continued.

It was while we were at anchor on the forenoon of 10 May 1945 that Axel Mortensen, First Lieutenant of the *Beagle*, detailed me to join him with a party, under the command of Colonel Allen, which was to go to the island of Sark that afternoon, taking an Army Detachment of only 20 men to receive the official surrender there, and to ensure that the 280 German troops on the island gave no further trouble.

We were to commandeer a small German vessel from St. Peter Port for this purpose. That involved travelling by ship's launch into the heart of the port.

As we approached I can remember being struck by two thoughts. One was the enormous range of the tide in this area – about 30 feet – which was clearly shown by the great height of the jetty as we came alongside at low tide. The other was the uncomfortable reminder of our adversary who had visibly festooned that jetty with naval shells wired up for demolition.

If the Germans had changed their minds about surrender, the result hardly bore thinking about as we slid in to tie up.

The departure for Sark was inauspicious and even exhibited undertones of sabotage. The German launch was apparently ready as we went aboard with a minimal crew and the small British Army Detachment. As Technical Navigation Officer, I was relieved to welcome on board a Channel Islands pilot, whose name unfortunately I can no longer recall, but who did most of my work that day.

The German Engineer was hastily sent ashore and replaced by our own Engine Room Artificer after indicating the engine room controls. Almost immediately, Axel Mortensen gave the order to let go and get under way. Instead of moving forward, however, the boat went astern and the stern spring hawser at once started to cut its way noisily through the wheelhouse.

Hasty orders from Axel retrieved the position before any serious damage was done, but the corner of the wheelhouse looked much the worse for wear and had to be temporarily shored up for the trip.

I often wondered whether that German had deliberately misled our ERA about the engine controls as a last strike against his new masters.

The short eight-mile crossing to Sark was soon over, but as we passed round the northern tip of Bec-du-Nez and down the east coast of the island, I was amazed by the strength of the tide and the ferocity of the tide rips so close inshore.

Our pilot performed one final hair-raising fear by taking the launch through the Goulet, a very narrow passage inside the tiny Burons Islets. Here, the sea appeared to boil and the passage was like some wild rapid as the jagged rocks whisked by on either side.

Almost at once the helm was put hard over and we approached the smallest harbour I've ever seen. A single breast rope was thrown to those good islanders who'd watched our approach, and by this means we were warped round the edge of the jetty into the tiny haven of Creux Harbour. Here Mrs Hathaway, Dame of Sark, appropriately greeted the liberation party.

At that time, the only way inland from the harbour lay through a tunnel to the island's roads. As we walked slowly through the tunnel, I again noted the wired-up shells, ready for demolition, again prompting that uncomfortable feeling of nakedness.

On the cliffs surrounding the harbour the deadly festoons were also to be seen and I, for one, was quite relieved when we eventually emerged from the tunnel. There to meet us was 'La Dame's' famous horse-drawn carriage into which she got, accompanied by Colonel Allen.

The procession slowly wended its way up the hot and dusty island road, the carriage leading, Axel Mortensen and I walking at a discreet distance, followed by the Army Detachment in their crunching boots.

Eventually, we came to the Manoir, Headquarters of the German Kommandant. La Dame led the British Army force inside while Axel and I waited dutifully in the roadway with the carriage and its faithful driver, Charlie Perree.

I suppose I must have felt some lingering apprehension as we waited... What if the German Kommandant refused to acknowledge the authority of this tiny force? Supposing he had given the order to blow those threatening demolition charges!… We would then most certainly have been trapped on Sark, at least for a time, in the face of 275 German troops who remained on the island.

However, I needn't have worried. La Dame, more forceful than any Army officer and more than equal to any German Kommandant, interpreted for Colonel Allen in his confrontation with the German and the official surrender was accepted.

Thereafter the slow procession, now triumphant, moved on to The Seigneurie, home of La Dame, from which she had dominated the Germans by her sheer force of character during the occupation.

It was satisfying to see the Union Jack flying proudly from the tower of The Seigneurie as we approached, raised the very morning of 8 May on the orders of La Dame on hearing the radio news of the surrender of Admiral Dönitz.

We were invited inside for a short celebration of the historic event we had just witnessed. La Dame instructed her gardener to go and dig up the five bottles of champagne which she'd so thoughtfully hidden nearly five years previously, in anticipation of this very day of freedom from the German yoke.

As we waited, Colonel Allen asked La Dame if she would mind being left without any relieving force for a little longer as there was only a token force in Guernsey and no men could be spared permanently for Sark.

This request prompted a typical reply from the great lady to the effect that she had been left alone for almost five years and that she thought she could stand a few days more!

On this happy note the champagne arrived, Axel and I popped the corks (some appropriately hitting the ceiling), and toasts were drunk to His Majesty the King and to the 'Day of Freedom' which had dawned.

We eventually wended our way back across the island, through the tunnel, which I felt was now a less forbidding place, and so back on board the little launch. The return to St. Peter Port with Colonel Allen and his Detachment was uneventful and we duly disembarked at the dockside.

Before Axel and I went ashore we lowered the small White Ensign which had been flown all day at the stern of the launch, indicating the auspices of the Royal Navy, under which we had sailed to Sark and back.

Axel, with a typical gesture, handed the flag to me, remarking that I'd better keep it as a souvenir of that memorable day. I'm glad that that White Ensign, with other mementoes of 'our' *Beagle*, eventually found its way into the showcase on board the present HMS *Beagle*.

WAR'S END

The following four articles appeared on the front page of the *East Anglian Daily Times*, Ipswich, Suffolk, on 8 May 1945 (Reproduced by kind permission of the *East Anglian Daily Times*):

WAR IN EUROPE WILL END OFFICIALLY TODAY
BROADCASTS BY KING, PREMIER AND VICTORIOUS GENERALS
NAZIS FIRST TO ANNOUNCE THEIR DOWNFALL
ALLIES DELAY NEWS TO SECURE SYNCHRONISATION

Today is VE Day and at 3 p.m. Mr. Churchill will broadcast the news that the war in Europe is officially at an end.

But for Germany the war ended yesterday, when at 2.41 am (French time)

General Jodl, German Army Chief of Staff, signed his country's unconditional surrender in Rheims, which is General Eisenhower's headquarters.

It was the Nazis who undertook the final humiliation of announcing to the world a few hours afterwards that they had, after five and a half years, bowed the knee in final and utter defeat.

At 9 p.m. tonight the King will broadcast to the Empire and the world, and there are to be broadcasts by General Eisenhower and Field Marshals Montgomery and Alexander.

Mr. Churchill is anxious that VE-Day shall be first and foremost the King's occasion. For that reason Mr. Churchill will simply announce to the nation that the war in the West is over. It is constitutionally important that the responsibility for this actual declaration should be taken by the King's Ministers and not by the King.

In a sense, Mr Churchill started the victory celebrations before anybody. Yesterday he gave a special lunch at 10 Downing Street to the Chiefs of Staff. Some members of the Cabinet were also there. It was a very private party.

The principal guests were Admiral of the Fleet Sir Andrew Cunningham (Chief of the Naval Staff), Field Marshall Sir Alan Brooke (Chief of the Imperial General Staff), and Marshal of the Royal Air Force Sir Charles Portal (Chief of the Air Staff). All three, with their Services, were toasted with VE-Day enthusiasm.

Buckingham Palace became the focal point of the nation's rejoicing. The area outside the massive railings and the Royal parks around were thronged with waiting crowds. The Royal Standard fluttered in the breeze from the Palace roof indicating the presence of the King and Queen.

In Piccadilly Circus last night thousands of people formed into circles, waved flags, danced and sang. After nightfall hundreds of bonfires threw a lurid glow over London.

In Cambridge several thousand Servicemen, students and others held their own celebrations on the Market Square. Home made fireworks exploded all around and there was a big blaze when a paper salvage dump was set on fire.

MESSAGE TO ALLIED EXPEDITIONARY FORCE
"OUR UNBOUNDED ADMIRATION"

King George VI last night sent the following telegram to General Eisenhower, Supreme Commander, on the Allied victory:

"Eleven months ago you led the Allied Expeditionary Force across the English Channel carrying with you the hopes and prayers of millions of men and women of many nations.

To it was entrusted the task of annihilating the German Armies in Western Europe and of thus liberating the peoples whom they had enslaved.

All the world now knows that after fierce and continuous warfare, this force has accomplished its mission with a finality achieved by no other such expedition in history.

On behalf of all my peoples I ask that you, its Supreme Commander, will tell its members how deeply grateful we are to them and how unbounded is our admiration for the courage and determination which, under wise leadership, have brought them to their goal of complete and crushing victory.

I would also ask you to convey a special message of congratulation to my own Forces now under your command. Throughout the campaign they have acquitted themselves in all services with a valour and distinction for which their fellow countrymen will forever hold them in honour."

"DELIVERED INTO VICTORS' HANDS"
GERMAN GENERAL'S SURRENDER COMMENTS

"With this signature the German people and the German armed forces are, for better or worse, delivered into the victors' hands," said General Jodl, German Army Chief of Staff, after signing his country's unconditional surrender yesterday. The ceremony took place at 2.41 a.m. (French time) at the little red schoolhouse at Rheims, General Eisenhower's HQ in France.

General Bedell Smith, Eisenhower's Chief of Staff, signed for the Supreme Allied Command, according to an account of the ceremony broadcast by New York Radio. General Susiapatov signed for Russia and General Sevez for France.

Germany's unconditional surrender, announced in an order by Admiral Dönitz, the new German Führer, was broadcast by the German Flensburg Radio, and followed a Danish radio announcement that the German forces in Norway had capitulated.

Count von Krisigk, German Foreign Minister, who read the Order, said:-

"German men and women, the High Command of the armed forces has today at the order of Grand Admiral Dönitz declared the unconditional surrender of all German fighting troops.

As the leading Minister of the Reich Government which the Admiral of the Fleet has appointed for dealing with war tasks, I turn at this tragic moment of our history to the German nation. After a heroic fight of almost incomparable hardness Germany has succumbed to the overwhelming power of her enemies.

To continue the war would only mean senseless bloodshed and a futile disintegration. A government which has a feeling of responsibility for the future of its nation was compelled to act on the collapse of all physical and material forces and to demand of the enemy the cessation of hostilities.

It was the noblest task of the Admiral of the Fleet and of the Government supporting him, after the terrible sacrifices which the war demanded, to save in the last phase of the war the lives of the maximum number of fellow countrymen. That the war was not ended immediately, simultaneously in the West and in the East, is to be explained by this reason alone.

In the gravest hour of the German nation and its Reich we bow in deep reverence before the dead of the war. Their sacrifices place the highest obligations on us. Our sympathy goes out above all to the wounded, the bereaved, and to all on whom this struggle has inflicted blows.

No one must be under illusions about the severity of the terms to be imposed on the German people by our enemies. We must now face our fate squarely and unquestioningly. Nobody can be in any doubt that the future will be hard for each one of us and will exact sacrifices from us in every sphere of life.

We must accept this burden and stand loyally by the obligations we have undertaken. But we must not despair and fall into mute resignation. Once again we must set ourselves to stride along a path through the dark future.

From the collapse of the past, let us preserve and save one thing – unity, the ideas of the national community, which in the years of the war have found their highest expression in the spirit of comradeship at the front and readiness to help one another in all the distress which has afflicted the homeland. In our nation, justice shall be a supreme law and the guiding principle.

We must also recognise law as the basis of all relations between the nations. We must recognise it and recognise it from inner conviction.

Respect for treaties will be as sacred as the aim of our nation to belong to the European family of nations, as a member of which we want to mobilise all human, moral and material forces in order to heal the dreadful wounds which the war has caused.

Then we may hope that the atmosphere of hatred which today surrounds Germany all over the world will give place to a spirit of reconciliation among the nations, without which the world cannot recover."

South Western Star
London Borough of Battersea
20 July 1945

BULLDOG'S CREW IN BATTERSEA
Warm Welcome For Adopted Ship's Men

About 50 members of the crew of Battersea's adopted ship, HMS *Bulldog*, found a warm-hearted welcome in the borough that was much to their liking.

After their arrival from Dartmouth the Navy men marched through the borough, via Bolingbroke Grove, Northcote Road, St. John's Road and Lavender Hill, to the Town Hall where the Salute was taken by the Mayor, Councillor S. Fussey, JP, and Admiral Sir M. E. Dunbar-Nasmith, VC, KCB.

Headed by the band of the 2nd Middlesex Regiment, under Bandmaster C. Dennis, these young fellows appeared to thoroughly appreciate the applause and cheers that greeted them throughout their march. In command was Lieutenant Commander D. Dumas supported by Engineer Lieutenant L. A. Whitfield. With the party was the ex-Commander of the *Bulldog*, Commander A. H. Williams, DSO.

Traffic along Lavender Hill was completely held up while the Mayor and Admiral Dunbar-Nasmith inspected the contingent the Mayor having a cheery word of welcome for every man. Then the party filed round to the Grand Hall, where they found beer, tea and sandwiches awaiting them, together with welcome seats.

Included in the party at the saluting base were Commander R. M. R. Hoare, representing the Admiralty, the Town Clerk, Mr. R. G. Berry, members and officials of the Council and *Bulldog* Comforts Fund Committee.

(Reproduced by kind permission of Wandsworth Council, London)

THE USS *LAFFEY* OFF OKINAWA

Anthologist's Note: On 16 April 1945 the Japanese Navy and Air Force launched its third massed kamikaze attack on the radar picket ships protecting American land forces heavily engaged in battle on Okinawa.

The USS *Laffey*, a destroyer (Commander Frederick J. Becton, USN), some 50 miles to the west of Okinawa on Radar Picket Station I, was equipped with an armament of six 5-inch dual-purpose guns, twelve 40mm and eleven 20mm anti-aircraft guns. The destroyer was supported by *LCS 51* with six 40mm anti-aircraft guns stationed some 500 yards to port of the *Laffey* which was attacked by no less than 22 kamikaze aircraft from a total force of 50 suicide planes, during a time span of 80 very traumatic minutes.

The following is a chronological partial record of events as witnessed by surviving crewmen on board both ships (Reproduced by kind permission of H. Kwik/W. Keim, *Bulletin Airwar 1939-1945*, no. 245, p. 14):

0827 hours, 16 April 1945: While *Laffey* waited for the arrival of a Combat Air Patrol the kamikazes began their attack. The first was shot down by *Laffey*'s 5-inch gunfire at a range of 9,000 yards.

0830 hours: 'Val' shot down by *Laffey*'s 40mm anti-aircraft fire.

0830 hours: Another 'Val' shot down by *Laffey*'s 40mm anti-aircraft fire.

0830 hours: 'Val' shot down by *LCS 51*'s 40mm anti-aircraft fire.

0835 hours: 'Judy' shot down by *Laffey*'s 40mm and 20mm anti-aircraft fire.

0835 hours: 'Judy' shot down by *Laffey*'s 40mm and 20mm anti-aircraft fire close to port. Resultant explosion damaged destroyer's fire control radar.

0839 hours: Diving 'Val' glanced off *Laffey*'s stern hatch and crashed into the sea very close to the ship.

0843 hours: Kamikaze shot down by *Laffey*'s 40mm and 20mm anti-aircraft fire. Commander Becton manoeuvred his ship brilliantly and succeeded in taking most of the damage astern, so preserving full engine power throughout.

0845 hours: Kamikaze hit. 'Judy' crashed and exploded into 20mm/40mm anti-aircraft gun mountings aft, starting fires with burning fuel.

0847 hours: Kamikaze hit. 'Val' struck aft.

0847 hours: Kamikaze hit. Aircraft struck No. 3 5-inch gun mounting.

0848 hours: Bomb hit. Diving aircraft dropped a bomb which struck aft.

0849 hours: Kamikaze hit. Aircraft crashed into after deckhouse.

0850 hours: Kamikaze hit. After deckhouse struck a second time, fire and flooding aft. All remaining guns were now firing under local control.

0850 hours: *Laffey*'s new Combat Air Patrol arrived. With a USN Corsair fighter on its tail, an 'Oscar' collided with the destroyer's mast before crashing into the sea on the ship's starboard side. The Corsair, having followed the kamikaze through *Laffey*'s intense anti-aircraft barrage, was also shot down, but its pilot baled out.

[Unknown] hours: Bomb hit. A 'Judy' was shot down by the Combat Air Patrol close to the port bow after its bomb damaged No. 2 5-inch gun mounting. Commander Becton declared his intention "never to abandon ship as long as a gun will fire."

[Unknown] hours: 'Judy' shot down by 20mm and 40mm anti-aircraft fire at 800 yards.

[Unknown] hours: 'Oscar' shot down by 5-inch at 500 yards.

[Unknown] hours: 'Val' shot down by 5-inch at 600 yards.

[Unknown] hours: Kamikaze and bomb hit. A 'Val' flew over the ship and released a bomb which struck aft. The 'Val' then glanced off the starboard yardarm and was then shot down by the Combat Air Patrol.

[Unknown] hours: Bomb hit. Kamikaze flew across *Laffey*, released a bomb which struck the 20mm anti-aircraft gun mount. The kamikaze was then shot down by the Combat Air Patrol.

0947 hours: 'Judy' was shot down by combined anti-aircraft fire from *Laffey* and the Combat Air Patrol. The battered destroyer had only four 20mm anti-aircraft guns capable of firing when the attacks ended at 0950 hours.

USS *Laffey* had 31 men killed and 72 wounded. Her rudder was jammed, she was on fire and flooded aft. She was taken in tow to Hagushi, Okinawa for temporary repair and within six days was able to proceed to Guam under her own steam.

It is probably true to say that no ship has sustained such an intense attack – seven kamikaze hits and four bombs – and still survived.

————

During this same sustained attack on other Allied ships supporting the invasion of Okinawa, the destroyer USS *Pringle* was sunk with the loss of 65 crew, and the destroyer-minesweeper USS *Harding* was damaged beyond repair with the loss of 44 crew. In addition, a USN aircraft carrier and two USN destroyers were so severely damaged by kamikaze attacks that they had to return to the USA for repairs.

VICTORY IN THE PACIFIC

Ron Blacker, Chief Petty Officer, ex-HMS *Boadicea*

HMS *Westcott* was ordered home to the UK from the Mediterranean in December 1942, a month after the Allied invasion of North Africa. I didn't see *Boadicea* again, but hadn't forgotten her.

In June 1944, I qualified as Gunnery Instructor, was drafted to HMS *Crane* at Harwich as Gunner's Mate and was sent to the Pacific. *Crane*, launched in late 1942, was an anti-submarine and anti-aircraft sloop of 1,350 tons and capable of 20 knots. She was a modified 'Black Swan' class sloop, *Black Swan* itself having achieved fame for its successes against the U-boats during the Battle of the Atlantic.

The *Crane*'s main armament consisted of six 4-inch guns (dual high-angle and low-angle action) in twin turrets, two 20mm hydraulically-powered twin Oerlikons amidships, a single 20mm Oerlikon on each side of the bridge, plenty of depth charges and the latest sonar equipment of that era.

We joined the United States Navy's 6th Fleet and subsequently were in action during the costly invasions of the Philippines, Saipan, Tinian, Iwo Jima, Okinawa, etc., where Japanese defenders often fought to the last man. Their kamikaze planes, flown by dedicated and absolutely fanatical pilots, were the greatest threat to our operations. I believe we, the USN and the RN, lost a combined total of 27 ships of various kinds during the battle for Okinawa alone.

In early August 1945, we were on our way to bombard the Japanese mainland in preparation for invasion when it was announced over the tannoy that we'd received orders to steam slowly in large circles and await further orders.

Two atomic bombs had been dropped on two Japanese cities, Hiroshima and Nagasaki, and it was rumoured that the end of the war was imminent. This was confirmed a week later. Thankfully, the Japanese surrendered before the scheduled invasion. Their High Command had prepared an armed militia of over 35 million men, women and children to defend their homeland to the last.

How many millions of Japanese lives were undoubtedly saved by those two bombs will, of course, never be known.

We sailed with the American battleship USS *Missouri*, 'The Mighty Mo', into Tokyo Bay and on the upper deck of that great ship witnessed the signing of the surrender documents by the senior Japanese commanders to end six long and terrible years of global war.

"These proceedings are closed," announced General Douglas MacArthur, the American Army Commander.

We then had the task of sailing around the battle-scarred islands of the South Pacific for a few weeks getting the small groups of cut-off and isolated Jap troops to surrender their arms and return to their homeland. The beaches of each island were littered with half-sunken landing craft, every type of wrecked aircraft, and all the paraphernalia of a vicious, bloody war.

Of course, a few Jap survivors refused to believe the war was over and retreated deeper into the dense jungles. I believe the last one finally gave himself up in one of the swampy Solomon Islands, and went back to Japan as recently as the late 1990s.

Incidentally, while at anchor in Tokyo Bay, Petty Officer Batty and I were chatting over the guard rails when he asked me what ships I'd been on. I mentioned *Westcott* and he said that his brother had been on board, Able Seaman Len 'Ginger' Batty. I knew him well and, before I was rated PO, used to belong to the same Mess.

He then told me that after *Westcott* paid off, his brother was drafted to the *Boadicea* and was killed when she was sunk in June 1944, a week after D-Day.

It was a sad day for me as I hadn't heard this very sad news. PO Batty didn't know any details of the tragedy. It was especially tragic when I recall all that that gallant ship had come through.

A little later, the indescribable brutality of the Japanese was made clearly apparent in the pitiful appearance of Allied prisoners of war, often little more than living skeletons, who had miraculously managed to survive the slave labour camps in Thailand, Malaya, and mainland Japan for four years.

We finished up in Hong Kong as an anti-pirate patrol ship along the China coast and finally came home in 1946.

WENT THE DAY WELL?

Excerpt from *Blood, Tears and Folly* by Len Deighton

(Reproduced by kind permission of The Random House Group & Jonathan Clowes Ltd.)

The two atomic bombs dropped on Japanese cities did not bring the war to an end. The Japanese continued to execute captured American fly-ers, a policy they adopted when the heavy raids on Japan's towns began. It was 800 heavy bombers, B-29 Super-Fortresses, striking Tokyo a week after the dropping of the second atomic bomb that enabled the Japanese to over-come their pride and call for a cease-fire. By that time the American bomb-ing raids were virtually unopposed. Japan had no fuel to train pilots, aircraft engine production was down by 75 per cent, airframe production by 60 per cent and refined oil by 83 per cent.

The oil that Japan gained from its advance southwards was of little help. The US Navy's submarines sank Japanese transports so that of the oil extracted in 1942 only 42 per cent got to the homeland; in 1943 15 per cent; in 1944 5 per cent; in 1945 none. The way in which subsequent history overlooked the submariners' contribution to victory was not an accident. It was due to a wartime Navy Department directive. The US Navy prohibited all Press references to the submarines, whether or not there was any security aspect to the story. The Navy didn't want their story told that way. Several correspondents filed reports but all were stopped. It was probably feared that the true story would bring an end to the big ships and reduce the Navy's influence.

In 1941 Japan decided to grab oil sources rather than accede to inter-national demands to stop a pointless campaign in China. A long and costly war brought Japan to an even worse position. In that same year, Hitler followed an even more futile course of action. Instead of continuing to trade with Stalin, who was supplying him with ample oil and raw materials, he sent his tanks and bombers to conquer the Soviet Union, and never again had sufficient supplies. For nations of energetic, highly intelligent and well educated people, where engineering, art and product design were more highly esteemed than they were anywhere else in the world, trading could be cheaper and far more beneficial than making war. The history of the second half of the twentieth century clearly indicates that both Japan and West Germany learned that simple lesson.

But of course Hitler didn't fight a war to improve his adopted country's living standards. His invasions, like his totalitarian regime, were fundamentally a result of a pathological hatred of foreigners, especially those ill-defined foreigners that he liked to classify as Jews.

For the French, Dutch, Belgians, Norwegians, Greeks, Danes and everyone else suffering under German occupation, the Pearl Harbor attack in December 1941 brought a ray of hope. Soldiers, sailors and airmen already fighting the Axis were given a new purpose. Until now the casualties had cried:

Went the day well?

We died and never knew.

But, well or ill,

Freedom, we died for you.

After Pearl Harbor, men and women drowning in the Atlantic, crews in stricken planes, tank men bleeding into the desert sand and the soldiers and civilians alike expiring in horrifying prison camps, knew that eventually the incomparable resources of the Allies would bring victory.

COUNTING THE COST

From *British Destroyers* by E. J. March

The landings in Normandy called for intensive patrolling, but only six destroyers were lost in these operations out of the 16 casualties for the year. Of the 110 destroyers engaged on escort duties at the end of 1944 about 25 per cent were in Western Approach Command. Germany was making tremendous efforts to build submarines of an improved type and in the early months of 1945 U-boats were being launched faster than we were sinking them. New tactics and the Schnorkel tube were making it far more difficult for our forces to bring about the destruction of these pests of the sea. Had the new type of Walther turbines, fuelled by hydrogen peroxide and with a surface speed of 25 knots compared with the 17 knots of previous classes, become operational in any numbers, the Battle of the Atlantic would have flared up again to full intensity and might well have gone in favour of the enemy.

Germany surrendered unconditionally before these swarms of new boats became operational. Their potential menace can be judged by the fact that 156 submarines surrendered and 221 were scuttled. During the years of the war 1,162 U-boats were completed, 781 were destroyed, 632 were sunk at sea by warships and aircraft. 105 U-boats were sunk by destroyers, also 24 Italian and two Japanese submarines; we lost 35 destroyers to torpedoes.

Shipping losses had been appalling. From all forms of enemy action 5,150 vessels were sunk, a little over half being British. 2,232 went to the bottom in the North Atlantic, 1,431 in coastal and Arctic waters. In one month alone, March 1942, 273 ships were lost. In addition there some 1,600 casualties from ordinary marine hazards, i.e. foundering through stress of weather or collisions, groundings, fire, etc.

On VE Day, 8 May 1945, 108 fleet destroyers and 66 'Hunt' class destroyers were in service. 141 of the destroyers laid down during the war were complete, some after the cessation of hostilities; in addition 86 'Hunts' were built.

As in the 1914-18 war, destroyers suffered the heaviest casualties among warships, 127 and 12 leaders being lost, a total of 139, or 154 if Commonwealth vessels, ships lent to Allied Navies and Allied boats under

British control are included. Submarines, with 76 losses, came second.

The areas in which the losses occurred were: Mediterranean, 63; Home Waters, 50; North Atlantic, 21; Arctic, 10; Pacific, 7; and Indian Ocean 3. Total 154.

Aircraft accounted for 50, submarines 35, mines 23, surface craft 20, shore batteries 2, unknown enemy action 2, wrecked 2, collision 3, accident 1, used as a block ship 1. *Thracian* was captured at Hong Kong in December 1941. The fact that only two destroyers were wrecked and three lost in collision speaks volumes for the high standard of navigation and seamanship during the long years of total war, with the absence of shore lights, light vessels and the dim navigating lights adding to the hazards of steaming at night, often at high speed and in close company.

In September 1939, Germany had 22 destroyers and 30 powerful torpedo boats in service, with 16 and 10 under construction, many of the destroyers were heavily armed and comparable with our 'Tribal' class. At the end of June 1940, only four destroyers were effective with six under repair, ten having been lost during the Norwegian campaign.

The later ships of the 'Z' class running up to 410 feet overall length were practically light cruisers with deep displacement exceeding 3,650 tons and 5.9-inch guns, some in twin mountings, making them very formidable destroyers.

45 were lost during the war by surface craft, mine and aircraft, the latter including two 'Z' class bombed by the Luftwaffe.

Italy had 59 destroyers and 69 torpedo boats in commission with ten and four of each building. The modern vessels were extremely fast; many, credited with speeds in excess of 40 knots, could and did show their sterns to many of our warships in the Mediterranean.

Epilogue
by
Rear Admiral John B. Hervey, RN, Retd.

THE ARTICLES in the postwar Epilogue provide a follow-up to some of the stories in the book. Thus, in 'Annals of War and Peace (Part II)', survivors from *U-66* meet veterans from USS *Buckley* in an encouraging spirit of friendship. In 'A View from The Engine Room (Part IV)', Angus Currie visits HMS *Brilliant* one more time – and gets an enthusiastic reception from the US 66th Division veterans at a reunion in Omaha. In the last of his 'Views from the Merchant Navy', Sidney Davies rounds off his wartime career and says something about the sad rundown of our Merchant Navy since 1945. He also, quite rightly, deplores the length of time it took for the MN to get proper recognition for their contribution to the war. And Ron Blacker says a little more about HMS *Boadicea* and her links with both Accrington and the 51st Highlanders.

The article 'Bringing Forgotten Stories Back to Life' covers the restoration of SS *Lane Victory* as a splendid but also belated tribute to the US Merchant Marine. And some idea of the work of US amphibious vessels in the Pacific is given in 'An Extraordinary Reunion'. Especially notable is the very slow progress that such vessels could make across the vastness of that ocean. A recent Commandant of the US Marine Corps once termed it "the tyranny of distance" – they were also very vulnerable when they arrived at the beach!

In view of the importance the Arctic plays in this book, however, it is perhaps appropriate that almost the last article, 'Pilgrimage to Portland', should describe how 35 British Arctic convoy veterans attended the unveiling of an Arctic Memorial in Portland, Maine, from where so many merchant ships – the famous Liberty ships – started their hazardous journeys via Nova Scotia, Iceland and thence into the Barents Sea.

HMS *Cavalier*, last of Britain's Second World War destroyers, and holder of the Arctic 1945 Battle Honour, is today afloat in Chatham Historic

Dockyard, in a dock built on the site of the one from which HMS *Victory* was launched in 1765. The story of rescuing *Cavalier* is told in a number of articles under the general heading 'Save Our Ship'. Alongside her in Chatham soon will also be an appropriate memorial to the destroyers, and their men, who did not survive the Second World War.

ANNALS OF WAR AND PEACE (Part II)

E. J. Kahn, Jr. (Concluding excerpts from *The New Yorker*, February 1988; by kind permission of Mrs E. Kahn/*The New Yorker*)

Full Circle

On 7 January 1986, Captain Brent Abel, USN, Ret'd, received a letter from a stranger, Robert W. Bell, who had tracked him down through the Destroyer-Escort Sailor's Association of Orlando, Florida. Bell was among the 17 survivors (adrift on a life raft for 19 days before being rescued by British destroyer HMS *Vimy*) from the 56 crew and passengers of the freighter *West Lashawaya*, torpedoed by *U-66* in August 1942 in the South Atlantic.

In 1975 Bell established contact with a few of the survivors of the life raft. He then wondered about the U-boat's former crew, eventually establishing contact in 1978 with several of the German veterans who were aboard *U-66* in 1942 and in 1944. After Bell had assured Abel that the German survivors would be interested in contacting him, he received a letter:

'Dear Mr. Brent Abel,

You are certainly going to be surprised to receive a letter from Austria.

My name is Vinzenz Nosch. I am 65 years old.

While I was attending a reunion of the *U-66*, I made acquaintance of Bob Bell and his wife, Ruth, who had come to Europe on a visit. Because Bob took the initiative, forgot everything that had happened during the war and forgave us, we really gave him credit and have become very good friends since then.

Now to the heart of the matter. All of us survivors of *U-66* have

always had the desire to get to know our onetime adversaries in the war
on the sea and if the opportunity presented itself to say thank you for
the fair treatment on board the *Buckley* and for saving our lives.'

Another of Bell's correspondents who had survived from *U-66*, Karl Degener-
Boning, had been the submarine's chief radioman, joining the German Navy
at 19 in 1938 and serving on the *U-66* from its maiden voyage straight
through until its fiery demise. He later wrote to Brent Abel. On the back of a
snapshot of himself, his wife, their children and grandchildren, he wrote:

'I must tell you, the fact is: without your act of humanity, on May 6,
'44, these two happy families would not exist.'

The extraordinary reunion of three American veterans Brent Abel, Joe
Aucoin and Bob Burg (former shipmates on board *Buckley*), and the eight
survivors of the U-boat's sinking, together with their respective families,
took place on 29 September 1987, at a floating restaurant on the outskirts of
Frankfurt-am-Main. Abel received a hero's welcome from the eight survivors.

Karl Degener-Boning, after profusely thanking the three American veterans of that long-ago hand-to-hand fracas for travelling so far "to shake hands
with us", affixed to Abel's lapel a German Submarine Service pin. Not to be
outdone, Abel distributed a clutch of authentic orange-and-black San
Francisco Giants baseball caps. Degener-Boning, alluding to the reunion as
"a highlight of our lives", presented to Abel, Aucoin and Burg three serving
trays engraved with the dates '6 May 1944' and '29 September 1987' and the
words, in English, 'Enemies Become Friends'.

Brent Abel had sat through the proceedings quietly, reflectively and
inscrutably. He and his wife Corinne had visited the American Military
Cemetery at St. Avold in the district of Lorraine, north-east France the day
before, and had walked though the long, long rows of immaculate white
crosses, interspersed with some Stars of David, precisely aligned on carefully
tended turf. The Superintendent of the enclave had presented Corinne with
an armful of roses to lay at the foot of her brother's cross, Plot E, Row 22,
Grave 44. Now Abel rose up and delivered a short speech, first in German –

deliberate but resolute, like a ship with one disabled propeller – and then in measured English. He concluded:

> 'Many of us in America are direct descendants of you in Germany. My father was born in Mannheim. My wife is of German descent through both her mother and father. Yet her brother was killed in Germany in World War II while serving in the US Army. No doubt most of you lost relatives in the war. Old as we are, we must nevertheless do what we can to see that mankind forswears both the ideologies and the weapons which make such destruction possible. I am now 71 years old. In my entire life, there is no accomplishment of which I am as proud as that the USS *Buckley* under my direction took the risks and made the choices that enabled us to save the lives of you and your shipmates who survived. I wish we could have saved more. I know my shipmates, whether here or not, agree. Thank you.'

A VIEW FROM THE ENGINE ROOM (Part IV)

Angus Currie, Engine Room Artificer, HMS *Brilliant*

The last Chief Engine Room Artificer of *Brilliant* before she was finally decommissioned was CERA Jack Wheeler, from Norwich, Norfolk. Before she was taken to Troon for scrapping, she'd been laid up in Holy Loch, and was given a brief reprieve to go out into the North Atlantic and bring in surrendered U-boats. I was still a member of her crew when we escorted one or two U-boats up the River Foyle to Lisnehally, near Londonderry, Northern Ireland.

Some of the many boats lying there were sabotaged by their German crew members. The cylinder heads were taken off the diesel engines, bolts or nuts inserted, the cylinder head replaced and then the diesel engines started up again – with ruinous results.

The *Brilliant* was sent round to the River Forth where the U-boat Depot Ship *Huscaran* was tied up to a buoy. One of my jobs was to maintain the motor boats on *Brilliant*, but on one occasion at that time, our absent-minded coxswain had run the boat aground and twisted the propeller and the propeller shaft. I managed to straighten up the propeller, but the shaft was too long for our small lathe. This was rectified, however, on the U-boat Depot Ship when we got round to the Forth.

Before returning to Lisnehally, we collected a goodly supply of spare parts when on board *Huscaran*. I also obtained a very nice set of engineer's tools from my opposite number. As all the threads were Whitworth[64] they were all very useful. I have since learnt that the *Huscaran* was refitted as a cruising liner until she caught fire and was a total loss.

Brilliant was built in 1930 by Swan Hunter and Wigham Richardson at Wallsend-on-Tyne. It was the shipbuilder's custom to present the Engine Room Artificer of each new ship with a big brass clock, which, very thankfully, didn't chime! Our Chief ERA, Jack Wheeler, wound it up every Sunday night.

One day, after the war, a seaman complete with a large board and a list called at our Mess to compile an inventory of all the ship's equipment, and he had his eye on the big brass clock. He was about to add it to his list, but the Chief stopped him.

"Oh no you don't!" said Jack Wheeler. "That clock belongs to the ERAs of the Mess. I was in this ship's first Commission and I can well remember the presentation by the builders."

This information, of course, was always passed on to each successive Chief ERA. It was strange how Jack Wheeler was in *Brilliant*'s last commission as well as the first...

The decision as to who should have the brass clock was being discussed before *Brilliant* was eventually scrapped. It was unanimously decided that we should draw lots for it. Very fortunately, I won the draw and with it the clock. It is now on the wall of my conservatory, I wind it up every Sunday evening and it still keeps very good time. There was also a framed picture of HMS *Brilliant* on the bulkhead of our Mess. The lad also had his eye on that, but I told him it was mine, bought for the Mess in Portsmouth in 1943. I took the picture home and still have it.

---

[64] Common British screw thread devised by machine tool engineer Sir Joseph Whitworth (1803-1887).

HMS *Brilliant*, as recorded, was scrapped at Troon in 1947. Strange to relate, my aunt telephoned me from Rothesay to say that HMS *Brilliant* had been towed into Rothesay Bay one day in 1947. *Brilliant* had often spent time in Rothesay Bay, at anchor following convoy duties and on other occasions. My uncle and aunt had entertained quite a few of us at their large home, 'Arlington', in Rothesay, a busy wartime naval base, on two or three occasions. The place had many fond memories for me. It was where I'd joined my first ship, HMS *Alecto*, in early 1941.

I went up to Rothesay to see *Brilliant* for the last time. I crossed in the ferry from Wemyss Bay and was saddened to see her lying at anchor, rusty, derelict and deserted, off the Cowal Coast, which is across the bay from Rothesay.

After persuading my uncle Alistair Fisher to go with me in a row boat from Port Bannetyne, we set out across the bay. We had no lifebelts and I was worried when the water got a bit choppy. Eventually, we got alongside. My uncle held on to the Jacob's Ladder while I climbed on board for one last look and to say goodbye to HMS *Brilliant*.

I made for the ERA's Mess and stayed there for a minute or two. The silence was uncanny. Moving aft, I went down the steel ladder into the gloomy interior of the engine room. It was a really strange experience. Everything remained there as I'd known it, the controls, levers and wheels, still shiny, the pressure gauges, the engine revolution counters, the two great turbine engines capable of pushing 1,400 tons of steel ship through moderate seas at speeds sometimes exceeding 50 mph...

I hurriedly made my way back up on deck and then down the ladder to the waiting boat. I apologised to my uncle for the delay and for my somewhat foolish nostalgia, but he fully understood. My uncle was a real gentleman.

Many years ago I made brass models of HMS *Brilliant* and HMS *Alecto*. They are now both on the window sill of my office. Everything is solid – hull, superstructure, gun turrets, etc. Not quite strictly to scale, of course, just memory. I periodically dip the brass models in very hot water with washing-up liquid and they emerge nice, shiny and clean. As they sit in my office, I look at them and the memories come flooding back; the good, the bad, the glad and the sad.

In conclusion, I consider myself, and HMS *Brilliant*, very lucky to have survived all the hazards of a vicious, pitiless war. Friends I'd known in *Brilliant* who had gone to other ships hadn't been so fortunate and were lost. Jim Heather, ERA, had been the one lost when HMS *Manxman* was damaged in the Mediterranean. He'd just gone on watch... 'Monty' Montgomery, a Leading Stoker, had left us temporarily to replace an ill man and was lost in HMS *Isis*, off Cape de la Hague, north-western France...

I recall the good times with good friends, but I try to push the bad times behind me. I had to get on with my life. The great tragedy was that many thousands of young British sailors had gone down with their destroyers during the six long years of the Second World War.

I never had any contact with anyone after I was 'demobbed' in 1946. However, the American veterans of the 10th Battalion, Black Panther Regiment, US Army, must have heard about me being the ERA on watch during the rescue of many of their number by HMS *Brilliant* off Cherbourg that fateful night in December 1944. Many years ago, I'd made a tape-recording of the events of that night exactly as I'd seen them and sent a copy to America.

In 1996, my wife and I were invited to a reunion in Omaha, Nebraska. We travelled by air from our home in southern Scotland to Washington, were warmly welcomed by ex-Lieutenant Morton Peter Woods and his wife and entertained at their lovely home. We then went on the long car journey to Nebraska.

The welcome at the Annual General Meeting of the Black Panther Regiment's veterans for my wife and I was out of this world. It was almost overwhelming. I was asked to stand up in the large hall and introduce myself. The applause was almost deafening and I was nearly mobbed by ex-GIs who wanted to hug me and shake hands. A little later, I addressed over 600 people at the banquet during that quite magnificent, emotional and unforgettable evening.

A VIEW FROM THE MERCHANT NAVY 1944-2000

Sidney Davies, Merchant Navy

In May 1944, we were commissioned by the US Army and signed (voluntarily) the 'Liberation of Europe' articles. The *Freeman Hatch* steamed to Barry, Wales, to load US Army supplies which would then be unloaded into DUKWs off the 'Omaha' beachhead, following the invasion of France. It was during our second trip that we witnessed the tragic loss of HMS *Boadicea* [described elsewhere in events of 13 June 1944].

I paid off *Freeman Hatch* in October 1944, and the Federation asked me to take an eight week course as Wartime Watchkeeping Officer. After completing the course, I signed on the Standard Oil Tankers (Esso) for the next 12 months, from Aruba to Venezuela.

On VE Day, 8 May 1945, I was serving as Third Mate on the *Mosquito Fleet* in the sunny Caribbean, sailing to the Maracaibo Lakes for the 'Black Gold'. The oil tankers were manned by British officers and West Indian crews. They were very happy ships, the crews enjoyed good pay, good food and good conditions, but the appalling poverty which the local people endured in Venezuela was in stark contrast to that country's numerous cathedrals and churches with their ceilings adorned with gold leaf. It made me very cynical about those Latin countries.

In August 1945, the Japanese finally surrendered.

So that was my war... During those traumatic years I'd witnessed many heart-rending sights, often in mid-ocean, and being absolutely helpless to intervene. There were, of course, many humorous incidents when the very best of human nature showed through despite extreme adversity. But for most of the time it was trying to fight against the fear, stress and tension while under attack – and then the long hours of boredom.

In November 1945 I boarded the tanker *Adula* as a passenger for the UK, via Rotterdam, Holland, where there were desperate shortages of food and fuel. People were queueing up outside centres to be taken in temporarily for food and warmth. I worked in the UK as Port Relief Officer on Esso Tankers, at the Isle of Grain, Firth of Forth, Swansea, etc., for a few months and then was discharged from the Merchant Navy Pool on 4 March 1946.

Since 1935, at the age of 15, I'd been in the Merchant Navy on tramps, colliers, tankers, meat boats, mud dredgers and pilot cutters. I have no regrets – and I'm still healthy.

However, I'm astonished at the demise of the British Merchant Fleet. In my opinion, this regrettable and sad decline is due to the greed of successive governments, the greed of insurers and the greed of ship-owners. Safety standards at sea have declined dramatically with the overwhelming majority of the world's shipping now sailing under a 'flag of convenience'.[65]

The British Merchant Navy has been allowed to fade into the past. What now remains of a once-proud fleet, including cruise ships, are crewed by non-British ratings, and a few British officers. British tankers, bulk-ore carriers, with 150,000 tons of ore or coal, dock at the local harbour of Port Talbot, all with foreign crews.

During my worldwide wanderings, all British Merchant Navy ships were 'dry' until the post-war period. Then, lo and behold, the shipowners put alcohol aboard, at a very low price in bars located in the crews' accommodation. It was like giving sweets to children, resulting in the inevitable drunkeness and indiscipline.

The shipowners then had the excuse to justify themselves in 'manning' their ships with cheaper foreign ratings. This was one of the main causes of the sad demise of the Merchant Navy in the opinion of current Merchant Navy officers with whom I've spoken.

Other contributory factors are less insurance and grossly inadequate and inefficient surveys, resulting in disastrous oil spills and a truly scandalous loss of life.

The first official recognition of the British Merchant Navy's losses and sacrifices during the Second World War took place on 3 September 2000, over 50 years overdue. 3 September was also the 61st anniversary of the day Prime Minister Neville Chamberlain declared war on Nazi Germany in 1939. The

---

[65] Richard Woodman makes the point that merchant ships are not 'registered' at Lloyd's of London, they may be classified by that organization in its capacity as a regulatory classification society. A merchant vessel is registered under a national flag, whether it be that of her beneficial owners or an open register, otherwise known as a 'flag of convenience'.

feelings of us all who served in the Merchant Navy during that war were well put in a letter, dated 28 August, 2000 to the national press by Derek Bristow, of Huntingdon, Cambridgeshire, Chairman of the Merchant Navy Association:

'September 3, will be the first ever Merchant Navy Day, declared last year by the government to celebrate and revere the sacrifice and part played by the men and women of the Merchant Navy in the defence and development of this country and the 44,000 who died in that cause.

However, it seems that each time I open my newspaper yet another tribute is paid to those of the Armed Forces who have so many memorials already.

The Armed Forces deserve the recognition they get, indeed I can think of no one more deserving. After all, the Merchant Navy should know, having served alongside them in every conflict. It has taken so long for the Merchant Navy to be publicly recognised for its deeds; I believe that many people consider this tribute long overdue.'

> You cheered your sailor lads in
> Their mighty iron-clads.
> And you spared a cheer
> For Tommy Atkins too.
> You went into a funk
> When you heard of convoys sunk.
> But did you ever give a damn
> About the crew?

Derek Bristow
(Chairman, Merchant Navy Association)

POSTSCRIPT

Ron Blacker, ex-HMS *Boadicea*

On 13 June 1996, after the annual Remembrance Service at Chatham Royal Navy Memorial for those lost on board *Boadicea*, I checked through the names of her crew and AB Len Batty is indeed among those lost [see entry 'Victory in the Pacific' above]. The survivors of *Boadicea*'s sinking who were present at that time remembered him quite well, as a nice, pleasant individual.

In 1993, I received a letter from a Captain David Crawford, BEM, RA, enquiring about the St. Valery action that had happened in June 1940. Apparently, his father, a 51st Highlander, had been one of the Scottish soldiers manning the pumps on board HMS *Boadicea* as she was being towed to safety by HMS *Ambuscade*.

Captain Crawford also informed me that apart from the French soldiers and civilians we had rescued, there were over 60 soldiers of the 51st Highland Division rescued by our motor boat and whaler on that dramatic day. The majority of these men were part of the 202nd Anti-tank Battery, formed from the 50th Isle of Bute Mountain Battery, Territorial Army. There are still quite a few veterans living on the Isle at Rothesay who were with that group of Scottish soldiers who were rescued by *Boadicea*, *Bulldog* and the *Ambuscade*. As a matter of interest, HMS *Ambuscade* was the ship that took the United Kingdom's gold reserves to Canada when a German invasion of southern England appeared to be imminent in 1940.

In July 1996, a beautifully-made scale model of HMS *Boadicea*, constructed over many hours by Len Perry, a veteran of HMS *Beagle*, was presented by one of *Boadicea*'s few survivors, John Randall, to the mayor of Hyndburn Borough Council, Councillor Mirza Yousaf, for display in Accrington Town Hall. The two foot long model is now impressively displayed in a glass case immediately below the existing memorial plaque of HMS *Boadicea*.

The destroyer was 'adopted' by the people of Accrington and the surrounding area during the Second World War. When 'Warship Week' was held from 7 to 14 February 1942, the people of the district were set a target of raising £400,000 toward paying for the destroyer. But they managed to raise a phenomenal £557,092 in that one week for the war effort – an astonishing amount at that time.

The crew of HMS *Boadicea* were proud of their adopted town. During their shore leave, the ship's football team wore the colours of Accrington Stanley Football Club both in foreign and British ports. HMS *Boadicea* wasn't out of my life after I left her in 1940. The memories remain, even after 60 years.

'REQUIEM FOR A FLEET'

Can you recall 'ere memory fades,
From '39 through six decades.
The names of ships familiar that we knew,
Tragically famous names are few?
Though our fleet is now depleted,
At least some great names have been repeated.

First, let us think of ships that made
The supreme sacrifice and paid
The price of freedom, bought at such cost.
Every day we heard with sadness
Of more victims of that madness.
And every day we mourned a shipmate lost.

The mighty *Hood* – just three men saved,
Her name in history forever engraved,
But how could this have happened
To this titan of our ships?
We couldn't comprehend
How quickly she met her end,
Worried questions from worried lips.

In whispers seamen spoke
Of *Barham* and the *Royal Oak*
Of *Repulse* and *Prince of Wales*
And their catastrophic loss.
Hermes and *Courageous*
Eagle, Ark Royal and *Glorious*
Dorsetshire and *Cornwall*
All were nailed upon the cross.

Southampton, Fiji, Gloucester
All listed in the roster
There are many more whose names
We have to put down here,
Calypso, Curaçoa,
Coventry and *Cairo.*
Curlew and *Calcutta*
And the tragic *Galatea.*

The victor of the River Plate,
Brave *Exeter* who met her fate
Along with *Encounter* and USS *Pope.*
For these men there was not much hope.
And now they lie beneath the Java Seas,
As their spirits hover in the breeze.

York and *Neptune* in the Med.
Add their numbers to the dead;
Edinburgh, Trinidad,
Manchester and *Naiad,*
Hermione, Bonaventure
And *Charybdis* had to go,
The waters of a British harbour
Left so long ago.

Remember the destroyer and corvette,

Whirlwind, Wessex and the *Wren,*
the *Wryneck* and the *Waterhen.*
Convoys relied on this gallant lot
At least a few survived
With the brave *Westcott.*
Scores of small ships perished in the fight,
This tragic list with not an end in sight.
The names of these are remembered in our heart,
As we sadly had to part.
Surely, as these names unfold,
Many great stories can be told.

How can we pay our debts,
To the overworked Corvettes,
The Landing Craft, the Sweepers,
MTBs and smaller fry?
Some didn't have a name,
But they're on the Roll of Fame,
Recalled by their crews as the years roll by.

Begonia and *Bluebell,*
Snapdragon, Asphodel;
These vessels had no warlike names,
U-boat crews may mock,
But in their iron tomb,
As they sank to their doom,
Would they still be mocking ships
With names as *Rose* and *Hollyhock?*

We now turn to the *Blanche* and the 'B's
To the *Dainty, Daring* and the 'D's.
Fearless and the 'F's, gallant *Gipsy* and the 'G's
Exmouth, Hyperion,
Inglefield and *Imogen.*
Their names go on and on.

The tales of *Laforey*, *Lance* and the *Larne*,
Their stories make a good yarn,
In the Med. these ships did roam,
But only Lookout survived and came home
The loss went on. Would it never cease?
Only four 'Tribals' saw the peace.
There are still many more,
Who fell victim to the war.

As we travel through the list
Of ships it's hard to see,
How Britain could exist,
With this casualty list.
Yet still the list grew longer
In that fight for victory.

Warspite and *Malaya*,
Whose names always portray a
Vision of the mighty ships
And their heroic deeds.
Ajax and *Achilles*,
Resolution, *Ramillies*.
Ships that man has ceased to build,
And man no longer needs.

These ships have now all gone,
But their memory lingers on.
While ageing seamen swing the lamp,
And talk of days gone by,
Of happy days and runs ashore,
In Hong Kong and Singapore.
And the thoughts of far horizons
Bring a glisten to the eye.

In Nelson's day,

They used to say,
That men were made of iron and their ships
Were made of wood,
But in the days of which I speak,
Men and ships attained their peak.
Men of steel, ships of steel,
Not better but just as good.

Sailors of today,
Are more technical, they say.
Pressing buttons, turning valves
Flicking switches on a panel
But sailors never change,
And to landlubbers may seem strange,
His special sense of humour,
And his aptitude for flannel!

But should the call for men
Be sent out once again.
If our way of life is threatened
By mad, ambitious nations.
We've seen it all before,
But we've never wanted war.
They should know our skill's
Been passed down generations.

Nelson, Rodney, Anson, Howe.
All are just a memory now.
The *KG5* and *Duke of York*,
The *Valiant* and *Renown*.
Venerable, Theseus
Pioneer, Perseus.
Regal ships with regal names
All worthy of a crown.

And the gallant band
Of men who manned
Ships whose names have made their mark
And passed away
Will sometimes shed a little tear
As they gather every year
To pay homage at The Cenotaph
On each Remembrance Day.

And for a little while
Their lips will wear a smile
As they think of ships
Shipmates and days of fighting men.
Their deeds will not diminish,
Though this era had to finish,
And this land will never see
That Mighty Fleet again at sea!

Anon

BRINGING FORGOTTEN STORIES BACK TO LIFE

Lisa Sabbage

It is a clear morning as the SS *Lane Victory* leaves the safety of her American harbour, bound for the open seas and loaded down with much-needed food, munitions and medical supplies for the Allied war effort in Europe. Suddenly, the calm skies are pierced by the 'Battle Stations' alarm as an enemy aircraft appears on the horizon and swoops down on the merchant ship like a hawk homing in for the kill. The Merchant Marines leap into action, guns bark, the plane dives and swoops, lining up the ship in its sights. Then two more aircraft appear – American – and the ship's crew cheer and shout triumphantly as their attacker turns tail and flies away.

Fortunately, this is not 1945 and the German aircraft is not carrying real bombs. Nor is this the North Atlantic Ocean, teeming with U-boats, but the peaceful waters off the Californian coast. In fact, the whole battle zone scenario is a carefully staged re-enactment of the kind of drama the SS *Lane Victory* faced when she was part of the Merchant Marine convoys to Europe.

Now a national historic landmark, the SS *Lane Victory* is the last fully operational ship of the 534 'Victories' built during the war. Today the *Lane Victory* is not only a floating maritime museum and a Hollywood star (having appeared in movies such as *Titanic* and *The Thin Red Line*), but she is a tribute to the thousands of seamen who lost their lives in World War II.

Slow moving and laden with supplies, Merchant Marine ships like *Lane Victory* were an easy target for German planes and U-boats. During the war, 674 ships were sunk and a total of 6,795 merchant seamen lost their lives, yet the heavy casualties went unpublicised for reasons of morale and security, and America did not afford war veteran status to the Merchant Marines until 1988.

Joe Vernick wanted to see that injustice set right. The veteran American merchant seaman, who was captured and imprisoned in a Japanese prison camp, decided that if he survived his incarceration in the Philippines he would create a living memorial to merchant seamen lying in unmarked graves at the bottom of oceans around the world.

He did survive and, after years of campaigning and restoration work, the 10,000-ton SS *Lane Victory* is that living memorial. Built in March 1945, and named for Isaac Lane, a former slave who educated himself and went on to found Lane College in Jackson, Tennessee, the ship served with distinction in World War II, Korea and Vietnam.

"In one very dramatic moment of the Korean conflict, she rescued 7,010 people from the North and took them South, arriving with 7,011 passengers – a baby had been born during the voyage," says the *Lane Victory*'s Public Relations Officer John Clayton.

It was the perfect ship for Vernick's project. But first he and his friends had to persuade the authorities to give them the *Lane Victory*, which had long since been mothballed in the Ready Reserve Fleet in Susiun Bay, just inland from San Francisco. It had languished there, with dozens of other ships, from 1971 until 1988, when President Ronald Reagan deeded it to the

United States Merchant Marine Veterans of World War II, saving it from being sold for scrap.

The following year, a US Navy tug towed the *Lane Victory* down to its berth in Los Angeles harbour where restoration work began in earnest. Vernick and his team of some 400 volunteers rescued the ship's booms, winches, lifeboats and deck gear, and placed them in their original positions. The engine room, galley, and entire ship were reworked and its guns were located, overhauled and mounted. "These old salts overcame – literally – incredible odds," says Clayton, "by working for nothing, except for the love of the job."

Finally, on 14 December 1991, all their hard work paid off when the *Lane Victory* was designated as a National Historic Landmark. And, while it is no longer on active duty, its one-day 'battle cruises' and maritime museum attract thousands of visitors to Los Angeles harbor, some of whom have themselves contributed to the history of the Merchant Marine.

Hans Philipsen, one of the *Lane Victory*'s corps of volunteers, worked on merchant ships throughout the war and was torpedoed four times. Indeed, if you were a merchant seaman on a cargo vessel in the first year of the war [1942 for the USA], your chances of being killed were higher than if you served in any of the US Armed Services. According to Philipsen, the worst convoys of all were the ones on the Murmansk run to Russia. Anyone unlucky enough to fall into the freezing sea had only minutes to live.

New Zealander John Middleton certainly remembers his time as a 16-year-old on the *Ocean Freedom* in a 1942 convoy that negotiated the dangerous waters around Russia and Europe. On 4 July 1942, his ship encountered yet another of the countless attacks by aircraft. The attack sank three ships and the surviving vessels in Middleton's convoy received orders to disperse and make their way independently to Russian ports in a desperate attempt to elude the German submarines and aircraft.

As if the enemy U-boats and bombers were not enough, there were also perilous ice fields to contend with. On 10 July, with its compasses out of action and after damage following an attack by four German aircraft, the *Ocean Freedom* limped into safe anchorage at the Dvina pilot station.

Of the 37 ships that begun the convoy, 24 had been sunk. The *Ocean*

Freedom survived but was sunk in an attack on Murmansk on 13 March 1943, just eleven months after her launch.

"Such a proud ship, such a short life," said Middleton. "I know that the 16-year-old youth, now turned 74-year-old, is proud to have had the opportunity of being a member of her crew."

Recollections like Middleton's continue to make history on the SS *Lane Victory*, adding to the anecdotes and interviews in its archives. Like so many veterans who visit the SS *Lane Victory*, he sees the ship as a fitting tribute to the friends he lost so many years ago, bringing their forgotten stories so vividly to life.[66]

PILGRIMAGE TO PORTLAND

Anthologist's Note: On 20 May, 2000, thirty five British veterans of the Arctic convoys met with American, Canadian and other Allied veterans and attended a very moving dedication ceremony at Portland, Maine, a thriving port on the north-eastern coast of the United States.

The ceremony was admirably organized by Royal Navy veteran Ron Wren (ex-HMS *Kenya*), Honorary Secretary of the Arctic Campaign Memorial Trust (ACMT). The dedication ceremony, in quiet and pleasant parkland overlooking the waters from where the great convoys bound for northern Russia had once assembled, paid tribute to the 3,000 Allied seafarers who had lost their lives.

A suitably inscribed Russian granite memorial was presented as a gift from the citizens of Murmansk to the citizens of the American nation.

Despite the grievous cost in lives, the remarkable mass-produced 'Liberty' and 'Victory' ships, laden with the weapons and the equipment of modern warfare themselves manufactured in vast quantities in factories and huge assembly plants throughout the United States and Canada, together with bulk carriers and vital oil tankers, proved ultimately decisive.

---

[66] The SS *Lane Victory* is at Berth 94, Los Angeles Harbor, California, USA. Website: www.lanevictory-ship.com

Other functions attended by the elderly veterans during the following few days included a beautifully conducted Service of Remembrance in the Anglican Church where a plaque was blessed recording the occasion, while a lone Scottish piper played a fitting lament in memory of all those lost.

AN EXTRAORDINARY REUNION

Charles Savona, CPO, USN, Ret'd, *LST 812*

A flashback in time of 57 years occurred on the SS *Lane Victory* on Saturday 2 February 2002. Three US Navy veterans of World War II, Francis Eddy, Frank Lofiego and myself, former crew members of the USS *LST 812*, were reunited. A mini-reunion was held on board the *Lane Victory* with many sea stories about our experiences in the South Pacific Theatre of Operations. We were involved in the invasions of Iwo Jima and Okinawa, which was the last major battle that ended World War II in the Pacific.

The *LST 812* formed up at Camp Bradford, Virginia, in September 1944, with orders to proceed by train to a shipyard at Evansville, Indiana, where the LSTs were being built using mass production methods.

The LSTs had a shallow draft, which enabled them to sail the Ohio River out to the Mississippi River and down to New Orleans, Louisiana, on the Gulf of Mexico. While in New Orleans, much work was still being done by the shipyard to ready the vessel for the long voyage to the South Pacific.

The *LCT 1269* was placed on our main deck for the 'piggyback' ride all the way to Saipan, in the Mariana Islands. Since *LCT 1269* was only 130 feet long it was too small to make the voyage to the South Pacific on its own.

While in New Orleans, a naval officer, Ensign Francis Eddy, arrived aboard the *LST 812* with a crew of 15 men. They were all assigned as temporary crew members. Ensign Eddy was the Commanding Officer of the *LCT 1269* we'd lashed down on our deck. Frank Lofiego and several other men came aboard in New Orleans and were assigned to Ship's Company and the Deck Department.

The shipyard employees completed outfitting the *812* for sea duty. We were ordered to sail around the Gulf of Mexico and over to St. Andrews, Florida, for practice beach landings. All hands were now getting some practical experience and the feel of the ship.

Once all this training was completed we were given orders to sail through the Panama Canal and on to San Diego, California. Once through the Canal we headed for San Diego on various courses. Upon arrival in the outer harbour of San Diego we received a 'blinker' message to proceed to San Pedro, and the Los Angeles Harbor, California.

Sailing north along the coast on various courses *LST 812* arrived at Los Angeles breakwater. Ensign Francis Eddy was Officer of the Deck and navigating the ship into Berth 218. While in Los Angeles the *812* took on food, water, fuel and more gear. All hands were granted liberty with many of the crew boarding the Red Car for the Hollywood canteen.

We set sail again, this time for Port Hueneme, California, which was a huge Naval 'Sea Bee' base (Construction Battalions). On our arrival there in December 1944, we picked up two pontoons that are used for causeways placed forward of the bow ramp to off-load vehicles from the tank deck. The pontoons were placed along the exterior of the hull, port and starboard. Once secured to the vessel we sailed for Pearl Harbor. About halfway to Hawaii we experienced some rough seas one early morning. A large wave dislodged the starboard pontoon, tearing away most of our railing with it.

Captain Sullivan ordered the ship to change course and we circled around but due to the pre-dawn darkness, we failed to locate the missing pontoon. We then resumed our heading and course to Hawaii. With the loss of the pontoon the ship listed to port; the ship's engineers shifted ballast and the list was corrected. Ensign Francis Eddy stood watches and was Officer of the Deck at sea. We finally arrived in Hawaii and enjoyed the liberty ashore.

Our next stop was at Maui where we did some training and loading of Amtracs in addition to about 200 US Marines of the Fifth Division. Our next stop was Eniwetok, and the Marshall Islands. We stopped at Guam where at the Army PX you could wait in a very long line for about an hour to be given a paper cup of warm beer. Many more Marines came aboard the *812* while we picked up more food, water, fuel and supplies.

We set sail again, this time for Saipan and much closer to the war front.

Upon arrival in Saipan, the *LCT 1269* was off loaded from the deck of *812*. The cables were removed, the dunage greased and the *812* listed to port 11 degrees. The *1269* slid off the skids into the water with a big splash then settled down alongside the *812*, bow and stern lines secured the LCT to the LST. With the LCT now off the ship and into the water Ensign Eddy took command and ordered his 15-man crew aboard *LCT 1269*. They soon shoved off and we never saw them again.

About five years ago, I located Francis Eddy, living in Dana Point, California where he's lived for the past 40 years. We lived only 30 miles from each other all these years and didn't know it.

At the end of the war in 1945 Francis Eddy was released from the Navy as a full Lieutenant. He said his claim to fame in World War II came when an Admiral and several other high-ranking officers came over to his vessel, the *LCT 1269*, and ordered him to sail toward the island of Tinian, where the cruiser USS *Indianapolis* was at anchor, and collect two wooden crates from the warship. These two crates were then taken to a lighter moored off Tinian. However, the *Indianapolis*, while on her way to the Philippines, was torpedoed during the night of 29/30 July 1945. From her crew of 1,199 only 316 were rescued after five days in shark-infested waters.

Several weeks later, after the two atomic bombs had been dropped on the Japanese cities of Hiroshima and Nagasaki, Francis Eddy realised what those two crates from the ill-fated *Indianapolis* had contained.

In 1946, Frank Lofiego was discharged from the Navy. He went to Medical School and became a physician. As for myself? I'm still sailing, a *Lane Victory* volunteer and crew member for these past 12 years.

SAVE OUR SHIP – HMS *CAVALIER*, THE LAST OF THE SECOND WORLD WAR BRITISH DESTROYERS

Two ships still survive from that mighty fleet of the Royal Navy during the Second World War – HMS *Belfast*, a cruiser, now moored permanently on the River Thames in London – and the destroyer HMS *Cavalier*, on active service with the Royal Navy from 1944 until 1972.

HMS *Cavalier* is a 'C' class destroyer of 1,710 tons, launched on 7 April 1944.

From a 1995 circular of the HMS *Cavalier* Association:
HMS *Cavalier* is the last of the World War Two destroyers left in the United Kingdom. [In 1995 she was] being preserved at Hebburn, Tyne and Wear, by South Tyneside Metropolitan Borough Council for our nation's heritage.

HMS *Cavalier* represents a very long line of destroyers that were built to fight the German U-boat threat and also represents the gallant sailors who served on them.

Cavalier joined the 6th Destroyer Flotilla Home Fleet. In February 1945 she took part in three operations off Norway: 'Selenium', a strike against enemy shipping, 'Shred' to provide fighter cover for a mine-sweeping flotilla, and 'Ground Sheet', an aircraft mine-laying strike. She was one of three destroyers sent from Scapa Flow to reinforce the escort of Arctic convoy RA 64 which had left Kola Inlet on 17 February, been attacked by U-boats and enemy aircraft, and scattered during severe gales. She joined the convoy during the evening of 23 February. Thirty one of the thirty four ships arrived safely in the Clyde on 1 March 1945.

After the war *Cavalier* was laid up in reserve until 15 July 1957. She served continuously from then until 5 July 1972. When she returned to Chatham for the last time, in 1972, she had given 28 years of valued and loyal service to the nation in war and peace.

On 4 October 1977, the ship was sold to the HMS *Cavalier* Trust for £65,000. She was towed from Chatham to Southampton by Royal Navy tugs on 11-12 October, where it was intended for her to become a floating museum dedicated to the Second World War destroyers.

Since then she has been to Brighton and now South Shields. Even now her future is not secure, and the Council are hoping to obtain a grant from the National Lottery.

The *Cavalier* Association was formed in 1989, not just for the purpose of bringing old shipmates together, but primarily to fight to save this ship for this nation's heritage. We are therefore hoping to enrol as many ex-*Cavalier*s as possible to help the Association in its quest. At present we have over 400 members.

We would be grateful to you if you would kindly give not only this Association additional publicity, but also this very fine ship to whom this nation owes its gratitude. Please help us to save the last of the Second World War destroyers – HMS *Cavalier*.

PRESERVING HMS *CAVALIER*

Mrs Jane Sharman, CBE, Chairman, HMS *Cavalier* (Chatham) Trust Ltd, May 2001:

HMS *Cavalier*, the Royal Navy's last operational Second World War destroyer, has now been rescued from the redundant dry dock in which she has lain for several years in Hebburn, near Newcastle-on-Tyne, for permanent preservation at the Historic Dockyard, Chatham.

The HMS *Cavalier* (Chatham) Trust Ltd. was formed to lead the preservation programme and includes members of the HMS *Cavalier* Association, the Friends of HMS *Cavalier* Trust and the Chatham Historic Dockyard Trust. Thanks to the very generous support of the National Heritage Memorial Fund and the considerable kindness of a large number of private individuals and charitable trusts, the first stage of the project has now been completed and HMS *Cavalier*'s immediate future secured. Much however remains to be done to complete the preservation process and although this work is now underway it is likely to be several years before it will be finished.

One of the main reasons for preserving HMS *Cavalier* is to present her as a memorial to the thousands of sailors who lost their lives in destroyers of the Royal Navy during the Second World War. A Memorial Steering Group, under the chairmanship of the Very Reverend Edward Shotter, Dean of Rochester, has been formed to help guide this process. The Group includes representatives of the Royal Navy, the Royal Naval Association, the Royal British Legion and the Eighth Destroyer Association.

CAVALIER OPENED BELOW DECKS

From *Cavalier News*, Autumn 2001

H MS *Cavalier* was formally opened below decks on Wednesday 25 July
2001. With press on hand to record the event, the internal reopening
of part of the destroyer marks a significant milestone in the restoration of
HMS *Cavalier*.

During the 18-month-long project a small, dedicated crew of old sailors,
including some from the ship's own company, ex-servicemen and old
Chatham 'Dockyard Mateys', signed up once more to serve aboard the ageing vessel, helping to put right over ten years of neglect.

The Forward Mess Decks, Petty Officer's Mess, NAAFI and Bridge
Wireless Office are the first internal parts of the ship to be restored and
reopened. The next locations to be worked on are the Wardroom and the
Operations Room.

Ship Keeper Brian Sanders said, "When this ship was operational there
was a crew of over 200 men to look after her each day; it has taken our crew
about 18 months to reopen this part of the ship. Looking after a vessel of this
scale is a massive undertaking and will be an ongoing task. We hope to open
up more of the ship as time and money allow."

A brief ceremony consisting of 'Up Spirits' took place on board with
members of the ship's company, volunteers and dockyard staff in attendance
to show members of the press around ship and for interview.

Richard Holdsworth, Museum and Heritage Director, commented, "The
reopening of the ship below decks has only been made possible with the hard
work of volunteers. Tackling a job of this scale requires dedication and the
HMS *Cavalier* Chatham Trust is grateful to everyone who has helped;
Chatham Historic Dockyard Volunteer Service, Friends of HMS *Cavalier*
and others."

HMS *CAVALIER* – THE SHIP

H MS *Cavalier* was one of 96 War Emergency destroyers ordered
between 1940 and 1942. Built at Samuel White's Cowes yard,

Cavalier was launched on 7 April 1944, and was completed in November 1944 before joining the Home Fleet. During the early months of 1945 she undertook a number of operations off Norway and in the Arctic. She was subsequently awarded the Battle Honour 'Arctic 1945'. By the spring of 1945 *Cavalier* was operating in the Western Atlantic. After the war in Europe ended in May 1945, she was allocated to the British Pacific Fleet, arriving at Colombo in time to take part in the final clearing up operations in the East Indies.

Refitted following the war, HMS *Cavalier* returned to active service in 1957 as a unit of the 8th Destroyer Squadron, Far East Fleet. She remained in service until 1972 when she paid off for the last time at Chatham at the end of an eventful 28-year career. In that time she had steamed 564,140 miles, seen action in the Second World War and completed many years of strenuous Cold War and peacekeeping duties.

In 1983 HMS *Cavalier* became a museum ship, first at Southampton and then at Brighton. In December 1998, after a decade on the River Tyne (mostly closed to visitors), *Cavalier* was acquired by The HMS *Cavalier* (Chatham) Trust Ltd. established to preserve the ship at The Historic Dockyard, Chatham. The Trust is a Registered Charity and a subsidiary of Chatham Historic Dockyard Trust, the charitable organization established by government in 1984 to take stewardship of the 80-acre Historic Dockyard following the closure of Chatham Dockyard.

In 1999 the generous support of the National Heritage Memorial Fund enabled a major programme of hull repairs to be undertaken to allow HMS *Cavalier* to be towed south to her new berth at Chatham. Work to secure her long-term preservation continues.

HMS *Cavalier* is now displayed in the largest part of the Historic Dockyard's three dry docks as part of a major 'Three-ship Attraction' with HMS *Ocelot*, an 'O' class submarine, and HMS *Gannet*, a Royal Naval sloop in service during the reign of Queen Victoria.[67]

---

[67] Chatham Historic Dockyard Trust Ltd., The Historic Dockyard, Chatham, Kent, ME4 4TZ, England.

THE NAVAL HYMN

Eternal Father, strong to save,
Whose arm doth bind the restless wave,
Who bidst the mighty ocean deep
Its own appointed limits keep:
O hear us when we cry to Thee
For those in peril on the sea.

O Saviour, whose almighty word
The winds and waves submissive heard,
Who walkest on the foaming deep,
And calm amidst its rage didst sleep:
O hear us when we cry to Thee
For those in peril on the sea

O sacred Spirit, who didst brood
Upon the chaos dark and rude,
Who bad'st its angry tumult cease,
And gavest light and life and peace.
O hear us when we cry to Thee
For those in peril on the sea.

O Trinity of love and power,
Our brethren shield in danger's hour
From rock and tempest, fire and foe,
Protect them wheresoe'er they go:
Thus evermore shall rise to Thee
Glad hymns of praise from land and sea.

W. Whiting

Appendices

APPENDIX I: **SECOND WORLD WAR STATISTICS**

NAVAL LOSSES 1939-1945
Submarines, frigates and all larger ships
Germany 672
Japan 433
Italy 300
Britain 296
America 157
France 129
Russia* 102
Holland 40
Norway 40
Greece 22
Yugoslavia 13
Others 36

MERCHANT SHIP LOSSES
Ships over 200 tons
Britain 3,194
Japan 2,346
Neutral 902
America 866
Other Allied 1,467

*Unconfirmed statistic

Compiled by: The 50th Anniversary of World War II Commemoration Committee, HQDA, SACC; Room 3E524, Pentagon, Washington, DC, 20310, USA.

APPENDIX II: **HISTORIES OF THE 'B' CLASS DESTROYERS**

Keith, Blanche, Basilisk, Boreas, Brazen, Brilliant, Beagle, Boadicea, Bulldog
General class particulars (as built):

Displacement: 1360 tons

Dimensions: 323' x 32'3" x 12'

Machinery: 2-shaft Parsons IR reduction geared turbines; 3 Admiralty 3-drum boilers, with superheaters; 34,000 SHP giving 35+ knots

Fuel: Oil; 380 tons

Endurance: 5,000 miles at 15 knots and 1,050 miles at full speed

Armament: 4 x 4.7-inch quick-firing guns, with 190 rounds per gun

     2 x 2-pounder pom-pom anti-aircraft guns, with 500 rounds per gun

     4 x .303 Lewis machine guns with 2,000 rounds per gun

     2 x 21-inch quadruple torpedo tubes, 8 x 21-inch torpedoes (later: 2 x depth charge throwers, 1 x depth charge rail and 30 depth charges)

Complement: 138

Ian Nethercott elaborates on the armament: 'The guns of the pre-war destroyers were 4.7-inch QF (quick firing) guns which could be either Director-controlled or go by the Gunlayer's firing.

The Director actually controlled the firing of all four 4.7-inch guns together, once the interceptors on each gun were closed to complete the 20-volt earth return circuits to the Director. The Director was controlled by the information supplied by the TS (Transmitting Station) deep under the bridge. The TS had a constant stream of ranges and bearings being fed to it by the Barr & Stroud rangefinder mounted at the back of the bridge. The TS had a large Plot Table with the ship and other vessels moved electrically as the action developed. The TS was controlled by the Gunnery Officer and the Chief Gunner's Mate.

The guns could be fired in 'local' control as the trigger-grip was actuated by a spring-loaded striker pin, which exploded the detonator at the base of the charge, and set off the shell cartridge case.

Quadruple torpedo tubes: contained four 21-inch Whitehead torpedoes launched by impulse charges. Would train to 90 degrees each side.

The ships were fitted with two sets of depth charge rails on the quarterdeck with the retaining trap at the end overhanging the sea. These depth charges were slung onto the rails by a derrick and fitted with hydrostatic pistols. The depth setting was set on the base-plate of the pistol and the key to do that was pulled out and retained by the crew.

There were also two depth charge throwers mounted forward of the after screen, one each side. These consisted of a hollow tube and an impulse charge open to the closed end. The depth charge was lowered onto a steel stalk with a welded frame to hold the charge loosely. The thrower was fired by lanyard and the charge blew the depth charge about 100 feet clear of the ship's side. The idea was to form a 'diamond' pattern of depth charges underwater, two or three from the stern rails and two from the throwers, all at a set depth.

The 2-pounder quadruple pom-pom anti-aircraft guns were mounted on raised gun decks, one each side, between the two funnels, ideally situated to blow away the ship's wireless aerials... Along with the two .303 twin Lewis machine guns on the wings of the flag deck, that was our complete armament.'

HMS *KEITH* (D 06)

On 9 June 1931 *Keith* commissioned at Chatham as Leader of the 4th Destroyer Flotilla and was then stationed with the Flotilla in the Mediterranean between June 1931 and August 1936.

On 24 August 1936 whilst on passage between Gibraltar and Portsmouth to refit, she was in collision in thick fog in the English Channel with the Greek steamer *Antonis G. Lemos*. She arrived at Portsmouth the next day and her refit and collision repairs were completed there during December 1936. However, modifications to the ventilation arrangements to the petrol compartment meant she did not recommission until 13 February 1937. She then spent six months in Reserve at Sheerness.

On 14 August 1937 she temporarily commissioned as the Leader of the 6th Destroyer Flotilla, whilst their Leader *Faulknor* was under repair following collision damage. *Keith* spent between August and September 1937 off the Biscay ports and the next month she undertook patrols from Gibraltar. She returned to Sheerness on 4 November 1937 and commissioned for service in the Reserve Fleet at the Nore 15 days later. She remained in Reserve until 9 May 1938. She then commissioned for temporary service with the 4th Destroyer Flotilla in place of *Beagle* and served in home waters until January 1939.

On 17 January she paid off and recommissioned with the crew of *Electra* for temporary service with the 5th Destroyer Flotilla until April 1939. During this period she undertook patrols from Gibraltar covering the end of the Spanish Civil War. She refitted at Chatham between 11 May and 15 July 1939, recommissioning into the Reserve Fleet on 31 July 1939.

On 3 September 1939 *Keith* was serving with the 17th Destroyer Flotilla with the Home Fleet, but almost immediately joined the Western Approaches Command and undertook anti-submarine patrols, based at Milford Haven until 29 October 1939, when she made passage to Harwich.

On 3 November 1939 *Keith* became the leader of the 22nd Destroyer Flotilla with the Polish Destroyer Division; *Boadicea, Griffin, Greyhound* and *Gipsy*. However, she soon entered Devonport Dockyard for propeller repairs which were not completed until 10 January 1940. During February 1940, *Keith* relieved *Codrington* as Leader of the 19th Destroyer Flotilla and served with this Flotilla until her loss.

On 5 March 1940 she escorted *Boadicea* whilst the latter was towing the

damaged tanker *Charles F. Meyer* into Southampton. She then undertook patrol
and escort duties until the German invasion of the Low Countries on 10 May
1940, when she was immediately embroiled in evacuation duties. On that day,
with *Boreas*, she escorted the cruisers *Arethusa* and *Galatea* and two merchant
ships carrying gold bullion from IJmuiden, Holland, to the United Kingdom.
She then returned to the Hook of Holland for Operation 'Ordnance', to evacuate British and Dutch troops. *Keith* was heavily attacked from the air about five
miles from the Hook of Holland breakwater, but suffered no damage.

An intelligence report received at about this time indicated that the Germans
might attempt to sail three large troop transports westward along the English
Channel. *Keith* and two other destroyers were sent out to the Goodwin Sands
area to intercept. Though they remained in the area for two days the troop transports were not sighted; instead, on the afternoon of 18 May, they were attacked
by German aircraft which bombed the three destroyers, but *Keith* again escaped
without damage.

Keith was subsequently involved in the Dunkirk evacuation, Operation
'Dynamo', which began on 26 May 1940, after assisting the destroyer *Whitley*,
which was sinking off Nieuport after being bombed on 25 May. Five days later
Keith sailed from Dover to Dunkirk, where she arrived at 2000 hours, returning
to Dover five hours later with 1,200 troops on board. She then returned to the
beaches of La Panne, Braye and La Rosendal, passing orders and marshalling
small boats bringing troops out from the shore.

During 31 May 1940, Vice Admiral Sir Bertram Ramsay, Flag Officer Dover,
and Field Marshal Lord Gort, the Commander of the British Expeditionary
Force, came on board *Keith*, conferring as they observed the progress of operations as the destroyer passed along the coast.

Just after midnight on 1 June, the *Keith* anchored off La Panne. Repelling the
almost incessant air attacks had reduced the supply of ammunition to only two
rounds of 3-inch and 150 rounds of pom-pom per gun.

Lord Gort and his Chief Staff officer left *Keith* at 0300 hours on 1 June 1940
in an anti-submarine motor boat and set course for Dover. Almost immediately
the destroyer was attacked by aircraft and damaged by machine gun fire. By the
time she was damaged by near misses at 0730 hours, her anti-aircraft ammunition was almost expended and her steering gear damaged.

Further air attacks followed and the destroyer was straddled; No. 2 Boiler
Room was set on fire and its crew killed by a bomb going down the funnel. *Keith*
listed heavily to port, with her upper decks touchingd the water. Torpedoes and
depth charges were jettisoned. As no power was available, she was anchored.

The dive-bombing continued. *Keith* eventually went down to a salvo of
bombs from about 50 Ju 87 Stuka dive-bombers after she was abandoned, and
sank at 0945 hours on 1 June 1940. Some of *Keith*'s survivors swam to the nearby

wreck of a merchant ship and were taken off by a motor lighter. Others transferred to whatever craft were within reach.

Three officers and 33 ratings were killed but her Commanding Officer, seven other officers and 123 men reached home safely by various means.

Keith lies in position 51°04'46"N, 02°26'47"E. HMS *Keith* was awarded the following Battle Honours: Atlantic 1939-40, Dunkirk 1940.

HMS *BLANCHE* (H 47) (Deputy Leader)

On 9 June 1931 *Blanche* commissioned at Portsmouth for service with the 4th Destroyer Flotilla of the Mediterranean Fleet where she was to serve until August 1936. Between 22 April and 25 April 1935 she carried the Flag of the Rear Admiral, Destroyers, at Malta. After refitting, *Blanche* and the remainder of the Flotilla joined the Home Fleet until March 1938. She saw service in Spanish waters between 2 April 1937 and 1 March 1938, based at Gibraltar.

On 6 March 1938, in position 37°26'N, 00°05'E, she was bombed, without damage, by five Nationalist aircraft. She had been closing on the British SS *Shakespear* to investigate another bombing incident that had just taken place.

After a refit at Portsmouth between 1 April 1938 and 11 June 1938, *Blanche* joined the Anti-Submarine Flotilla at Portland until March 1939. However, during the Munich crisis *Blanche* was one of the four destroyers that escorted the *Aquitania* and the battleship *Revenge* in the Channel on 30 September 1938. *Blanche* again refitted at Sheerness between 1 April 1939 and 15 July 1939 before becoming the Emergency Destroyer at the Nore.

On the outbreak of war, *Blanche* joined the 19th Destroyer Flotilla and for the next two months undertook patrol and escort duties in the English Channel and North Sea.

On 13 November 1939, *Blanche* and *Basilisk* were escorting the minelayer *Adventure* when the latter was mined off the Tongue light vessel in the Thames Estuary. A mine also detonated under the after portion of the *Blanche*. The upper deck was split forward of the after superstructure and all power was lost. The engine room, tiller flat and spirit room were all making water and *Blanche* was taken in tow for Sheerness by the tug *Fabia*. However, at 0950 hours the same day she capsized in a position one mile north-east of the Spit Buoy. A rating was killed and 12 others injured. The mines had been laid, that same night, by the German destroyers *Karl Galster, Wilhelm Heidkamp, Herman Kunne* and *Hans Ludman. Blanche* was the first destroyer lost to enemy action during the war.

HMS *BASILISK* (H 11)

Built and engined by John Brown & Co. Ltd., Clydebank, she was laid down 19 August 1929, launched 6 August 1930 and completed 4 March 1931. In August 1931 *Basilisk* joined the 4th Destroyer Flotilla in the Mediterranean, remaining with them there until September 1936. During that month the 4th Flotilla returned to the UK to become part of the Home Fleet. *Basilisk* remained with the 4th Destroyer Flotilla until March 1939 when she was reallocated to the Plymouth Command for service with the Devonport Emergency Destroyers.

In August 1939 *Basilisk* was transferred to the 19th Destroyer Flotilla, part of the Channel Force based at Dover and in the Nore Command. On 6 April 1940 *Basilisk* left Dover for Scapa Flow on temporary detachment to the Home Fleet.

German forces had invaded Norway eight days prior to the *Basilisk*'s transfer to the Home Fleet, which was engaged in conveying and supporting troops to Norway in an effort to stem the invasion.

On 8 April 1940 *Basilisk* sailed to Narvik in company with the battleship HMS *Resolution*, and the destroyers HM Ships *Hesperus* and *Wren*. In Norwegian waters *Basilisk* carried out anti-shipping and anti-submarine sweeps. She gave support during the Second Battle of Narvik on 13 April.

On 14 May 1940 *Basilisk* returned to the United Kingdom. In the meantime German land forces had invaded Holland and Belgium. By 23 May it became apparent that the possibility of the evacuation of the British Expeditionary Force was arising. On 26 May Operation 'Dynamo' commenced. On 30 May *Basilisk* was ordered south to Dover to assist in the evacuation. On 31 May she made three trips to Dunkirk, evacuating a total of 1,115 troops back to Dover that day.

On 1 June *Basilisk* was off the beaches at La Panne to lift troops when she came under attack at 0815 hours by nine Ju 87 Stukas, which dive-bombed her, dropping about 45 bombs. *Basilisk* was hit by one bomb and there were six near misses. All engine room and boiler room personnel were killed in this attack, which severely damaged *Basilisk* and rendered her immobile. Efforts were made by the Belgian fishing vessel *La Jolie Mascotte* and the destroyer HMS *Whitehall* to tow *Basilisk* but without success. At 0945 came another attack by nine aircraft but no further damage was done. At 1200 came yet another attack by a squadron of Stuka dive-bombers and *Basilisk* was smothered by direct hits and near misses. The destroyer was abandoned. *La Jolie Mascotte* and *Whitehead* picked up survivors, eight officers and 123 men. At 1213 hours *Basilisk* sank in four fathoms of water, position 51°08'16"N, 02°35'06"E. HMS *Basilisk* Battle Honours: Norway 1940, Dunkirk 1940.

HMS *BOREAS* (H 77)

HMS *Boreas* was built by Palmer's Shipbuilding and Iron Co. Ltd., Hebburn-on-Tyne. Ordered on 22 March 1929 and laid down on 22 July 1929, she was launched on 11 June 1930 and completed on 20 February 1931.

On completion she joined the 4th Destroyer Flotilla, Mediterranean Fleet. In July 1935 she arrived at Spithead to take part in the Jubilee Naval Review. The Flotilla transferred to the Home Fleet in 1936. In September 1937, however, there was concern over submarine attacks on merchant shipping in the Mediterranean, destined for the Loyalist side in the Spanish Civil War. Britain and France protested about this 'piracy' and, following a multi-power conference at Nyon, Switzerland in September 1937, a system of patrol zones was established. The British contingent was provided by ships of the Home Fleet.

The 4th Destroyer Flotilla was scheduled for patrol duty in the Western Mediterranean Area between 5 March and 26 March 1938. On 6 March, in company with HMS *Kempenfelt*, she went to the assistance of the Spanish Nationalist cruiser *Baleares*, which had been torpedoed off Cartegena. In the subsequent transfer of survivors to other nationalist ships, a rating from HMS *Boreas* was killed by bomb splinters during an air attack.

On 1 April 1938 *Boreas* was taken in hand at Portsmouth for refit, completing on 11 June. On 26 July she sailed from Portsmouth escorting the Royal Yacht *Victoria and Albert*, flying the Royal Standard during the Royal Tour of Scotland, and arriving at Aberdeen on 4 August. During the Munich crisis, *Boreas* escorted the battleship *Revenge* which was protecting the liner *Aquitania* on 29 and 30 September 1938. *Boreas* was retained in the 4th Destroyer Flotilla between 16 November 1938 and April 1939 in place of *Ashanti*, which although commissioned in December 1938 did not complete work-up until April 1939.

Boreas was briefly employed as a plane guard destroyer tender to the aircraft carrier *Ark Royal* in place of *Wren*, but in August 1939 she was transferred to the 19th Destroyer Flotilla of the Nore Command. *Boreas* spent the first months of the war on convoy escort duties along the east coast and the English Channel.

On 13 October 1939, the German submarine *U-40* struck a mine in the deep Folkestone-Gris Nez minefield and was destroyed. *Boreas* was in the vicinity and picked up three ratings who survived from the U-boat's crew.

On 4 February 1940, whilst rendering assistance to the stricken minesweeper *Sphinx*, bombed by German aircraft in the Moray Firth, *Boreas*'s stern was damaged at the waterline and she was under repair for the next month.

On 29 March 1940, *Boreas* was attached to the 12th Destroyer Flotilla for the next six weeks, but on 15 May 1940 she was in collision with her sister ship HMS *Brilliant* and received hull damage above the waterline that required repair on the Thames until 19 June 1940.

Boreas immediately joined the 1st Destroyer Flotilla at Dover but didn't remain long. On 25 July 1940, just before 1500 hours, a westbound convoy CW 8 (Southend to St. Helen's Roads) was attacked off Dover by two waves of dive-bombers. After a brief respite the convoy was attacked again off Sandgate at 1620 hours. At 1645 hours E-boats could be seen clearly from the cliffs and seemed likely to be proceeding to attack the convoy in the vicinity of Dungeness. Accordingly, HM Ships *Boreas* and *Brilliant*, the only two destroyers available, were ordered to proceed out of harbour independently to engage the enemy.

Two Motor Torpedo Boats were also detailed to accompany the destroyers.

At 1726 hours HMS *Brilliant* reported that she had six E-boats in sight, following this at 1745 hours with a report that she was engaging the enemy. By this time both destroyers were getting dangerously close to the French coast and, in fact, the shore batteries opened fire at a range of approximately 10,000 yards. As the E-boats had turned eastwards under cover of a smoke screen the destroyers were ordered to withdraw, without knowing whether any damage had been caused to the enemy.

On the return journey only ten minutes had elapsed when a heavy dive-bombing attack was made by a large number of Ju 87 Stukas escorted by Me 109 fighters. There were no direct hits but *Boreas* sustained damage from near misses which disabled the boiler room fans and dynamos. The engine room was slowly flooding and her steering was affected which caused her to stop temporarily. *Brilliant* remained standing by until *Boreas* got under way, proceeding at 17 knots by hand steering. Both ships resumed progress towards Dover, *Boreas* steering somewhat erratically.

When the ships were two to three miles off the harbour a second attack was made with more serious results. *Boreas* received a direct hit on the wing of her bridge which penetrated until it exploded in the galley flat causing severe casualties, with one officer and 20 ratings killed and 29 injured. *Brilliant* also received two direct hits, both on the quarterdeck, which passed right through the ship and exploded underwater, causing no casualties. Apart from obvious structural damage *Boreas* sustained damage to all boiler room fans and main cooler castings, making her unable to raise steam. *Brilliant*, as far as could be ascertained, had her steering gear put out of action and her steering compartments, magazine, shell rooms and spirit room flooded. After the second attack, tugs were dispatched and both destroyers were towed into Dover Harbour.

HMS *Boreas* was out of action for some six months while under repair at Millwall Docks, London, from 30 July 1940 to 23 January 1941, sustaining superficial damage from bomb splinters on 19 January 1941. During the repairs, *Boreas* was fitted with depth charge throwers which enabled her to fire a ten depth charge pattern.

After working at Scapa Flow during February 1941, *Boreas* joined the Western Approaches Command as an unallocated vessel. *Boreas* and *Brilliant* were then assigned as replacements for *Duncan* and *Foxhound* with the 18th Destroyer Flotilla of the South Atlantic Command. She left the Clyde as escort for the Armed Merchant Cruiser *Comorin* and rendezvoused with the *Glenartney* and the Canadian Leader *Assiniboine*, the vessels arriving at Gibraltar on 11 April 1941. After attending to defects at Gibraltar for ten days, *Boreas* arrived at Freetown on 28 April 1941. She then operated in West African waters on escort duties until 10 August 1941, when she arrived at Gibraltar to join convoy HG 70.

Subsequently, *Boreas* rescued five survivors from the British steamer *Alva* (sunk 19 August 1941), 24 survivors from the Norwegian *Spind* (sunk 23 August 1941), four survivors from the British tug *Empire Oak* (sunk 23 August 1941) and four survivors from the British steamer *Aldergrove* (sunk 23 August 1941). *Boreas* then returned to Gibraltar with these survivors on 25 August 1941.

Boreas subsequently refitted at Middle Docks, South Shields, from 19 September to 4 January 1942. She then undertook full power trials whilst on passage to Greenock on 6 January 1942 before leaving as escort for a WS convoy to Freetown four days later. She arrived at Freetown on 25 January 1942 and rejoined the 18th Destroyer Flotilla for the next nine months.

After escorting convoys around the Cape, *Boreas* arrived at Alexandria on 11 November 1942 and immediately participated in Operation 'Stoneage' – the convoy from Alexandria that lifted the siege of Malta. She then remained in North African waters until January 1943, escorting another convoy to Alexandria before returning to Gibraltar and a brief period of service with the 13th Destroyer Flotilla. She then returned to West African waters between February and June 1943.

Boreas was one of the reinforcements for the Mediterranean Fleet in June 1943 and participated in Operation 'Husky' – the Sicily Landings. She then returned to the UK for an urgently needed refit as an anti-submarine destroyer by Harland & Wolff at Liverpool between September 1943 and February 1944. Loaned to the Greek Navy on 10 February 1944, she was commissioned on 25 March 1944 as *Salamis*. She then returned to Scapa Flow to work-up, but was damaged, which necessitated repairs at Hull by Amos & Smith between 28 April 1944 and 13 June 1944. After working-up she made passage to Gibraltar, where she operated until October 1944. She subsequently served with the Greeks in the Eastern Mediterranean and Greek waters until the end of the European war.

Returned to the Royal Navy at Malta on 9 October 1951, she was subsequently allocated to BISCO. She arrived at Rosyth in tow of the tug *Merchantman* on 15 April 1952 for demolition by Metal Industries (Salvage) Ltd. before transferring to Charleston where breaking up was completed. Battle Honours for HMS *Boreas*: English Channel, 1940; Atlantic, 1941-1942; North Africa, 1942-1943.

HMS *BRAZEN* (H 80)

HMS *Brazen* was built by Palmers Shipbuilding and Engineering Co. at Jarrow on Tyne; laid down on 22 July 1929, launched on 25 July 1930 and completed on 8 April 1931.

After running her full power trials, *Brazen* was attached to the 4th Destroyer Flotilla, Mediterranean Fleet. In February 1931 she docked for new anti-fouling composition to be applied. Three months later on being docked at Devonport severe corrosion was noted fore and aft on the outer bottom. A different type of anti-fouling compound was then applied, but when *Brazen* was docked in Malta in December 1931, pitting was still active. Later tests revealed no hull defects and the cause of this extraordinary corrosion was never established.

Brazen was with the Mediterranean Fleet until 1935 during which time she visited Syracuse, Argostoli, Corfu, Souda Bay, and other Mediterranean ports. In August 1933 she sailed to Devonport for a refit, completed on 21 October; an additional refit at Malta was completed on 5 January 1934. At the end of 1935 the 4th Destroyer Flotilla was attached to the Home Fleet, and on return to the United Kingdom, *Brazen* was docked at Devonport for repairs, completed on 12 June 1936. After operating in Scottish waters during 1937, *Brazen* again docked at Devonport for repairs which were completed on 12 June 1938, after which she returned to Scottish waters.

The end of her service with the 4th Destroyer Flotilla coincided with her attendance at the abortive rescue operations on the submarine HMS *Thetis* which had sunk during trials in Liverpool Bay on 1 June 1939.

In August 1939, *Brazen* formed part of the 19th Destroyer Flotilla, under the Dover Command; on 7 September 1939 she attacked an enemy submarine in position 50°53'N, 00°15'E, but contact was not established. On 13 October 1939, *Brazen* picked up three survivors of *U-40*, which had struck a mine in the early hours of that day. On the following day she picked up a body from the same U-boat, which was buried at sea. These were the first of many U-boat searches in which *Brazen* took part until February 1940 when she was placed at the temporary disposal of the Commander-in-Chief, Home Fleet.

By the second half of February 1940, *Brazen* was again hunting U-boats, and on 17 February, in company with HMS *Encounter*, she proceeded to 58°22'N, 01°40'W (35 miles north of Kinnaird Head) to investigate reports that a U-boat, possibly damaged, was in the vicinity of the British merchant ship SS *Asiatic*. On the following day HMS *Daring* was sunk by a U-boat and *Brazen*, with *Encounter*, both of which were in the vicinity following the *Asiatic*'s report, were ordered to take over the convoy HN 12 which *Daring* had been escorting. A few hours later HM Ships *Brazen* and *Diana* picked up the survivors, 28 crew and one passenger, from the Norwegian ship *Sangstad* which had been torpedoed about 115 miles east of Kirkwall.

On 21 February HM Ships *Brazen* and *Boreas* were detailed as escorts for the minelayer *Teviotbank* on a minelaying mission in connection with Operation 'FA 2', and on 29 March 1940 she was placed under FOCOS Command for anti-submarine work in the Moray Firth and Orkney areas.

On 13 April 1940, *Brazen* formed part of the large troop convoy NP 1, on passage to Vestfjord and Namsos, Norway. Whilst escorting through Andfjord on the forenoon of 15 April 1940, *Fearless* and *Brazen* were detached to proceed through Topsundet and search for a submarine reported at Vaagsfjord. On entering the fjord south of Kjotta, *Fearless* stationed *Brazen* 2,000 yards on her port beam and proceeded for the Enjenes Light. At 1048 hours contact was made with the U-boat almost dead ahead, 68°53'N, 16°59'E, and an attack was carried out at 1054 hours with five depth charges which literally blew the U-boat to the surface in the middle of the pattern. The crew abandoned the submarine, *U-49*, and "started screaming in the most dreadful fashion."

When rescuing the survivors (four officers and 37 ratings were taken prisoner) *Brazen* picked up some papers which gave the entire dispositions for the Norwegian invasion. Following this, *Brazen* was employed as part of the screening force for HM Ships *Renown*, *Rodney* and *Valiant*, which arrived at Scapa Flow on 18 April 1940.

On 23 April, with HM Ships *Wolverine* and *Kimberley*, *Brazen* sailed from Leith for Namsos to escort the troop transport *Gunvor Maersk* in connection with the build-up for Operation 'Maurice', the main landing at Namsos. On 28 April, *Brazen* was bombed by enemy aircraft but sustained no damage.

During the first week of May 1940, *Brazen* escorted convoy FP 3, with which the Commander-in-Chief Norwegian Navy and Staff were travelling, to Narvik, arriving on 5 May. The convoy was immediately distributed, *Brazen*, with *Amazon* and *Warwick* escorting three French transports carrying the Polish Brigade to Tromso. *Brazen* continued with escort duties in this area. On 30 May 1940 at 0345 hours, whilst on passage to Harwich, *Brazen* struck a submerged wreck off the mouth of The Wash. Her after boiler room flooded and she proceeded to the Humber for docking. Repairs to this damage kept *Brazen* out of action during June 1940, but by early July she was again operational and back to her task of escorting convoys.

On 8 July 1940 whilst escorting the Channel coastal convoy OA off Hythe, *Brazen* was attacked by about 14 enemy aircraft at 1500 hours. One small ship, SS *Corundum*, was hit but was able to reach Dover.

During the afternoon of 20 July 1940, the westbound Channel convoy CW 7 was severely attacked at 1815 hours by about 30 German aircraft between Dover and Folkestone. The two escorting destroyers and shore anti-aircraft guns engaged the enemy aircraft and Royal Air Force fighters were soon on the scene. The attack, however, was pressed home with some success, one merchant ship being sunk and two others damaged.

Brazen, which was on patrol in the vicinity, joined in the defence of the convoy. Her gunners shot down three Ju 87 Stukas, but she was so badly damaged by near misses and a hit in the engine room that she sank at 2040 hours in position 51°0'12"N, 01°17'30"E with the loss of just one of her crew. Battle Honours for HMS *Brazen*: Norway, 1940; English Channel, 1940.

HMS *BRILLIANT* (H 84)

HMS *Brilliant* was ordered on 22 March 1929 as a unit of the second flotilla of destroyers to be built since the end of the First World War. Laid down at the Tyneside yard of Swan Hunter, Wigham and Richardson on 8 July 1929 she was launched on 9 October 1930 and completed four months later on 21 February 1931. On trials she exceeded her designed speed, reaching 35.56 knots. The total cost of the ship was £221,638.

After working up with the Nore Command and at Portland, *Brilliant* left to join the 4th Destroyer Flotilla, Mediterranean Fleet, arriving at Malta on 3 August 1931. Her first commission ended on 1 September 1933, when she returned to Chatham for a refit and to recommission; by 31 October she was back in the Mediterranean again. The next recommissioning visit was even shorter, for she spent less than three weeks in Chatham between June and July 1935 before returning to Malta.

The Spanish Civil War broke out a year later and *Brilliant* was sent to Malaga in early August 1936 to act as a guardship for the protection and eventual evacuation of British citizens. The 4th Destroyer Flotilla was reallocated to the Home Fleet early in September and was employed on Non-Intervention Patrols in the Bay of Biscay until the fall of the Republican towns in north-west Spain in the spring of 1937. Thereafter, the Flotilla was engaged in normal peacetime Fleet activities up to the eve of the Second World War.

At the outbreak of war *Brilliant* was transferred to the 19th Destroyer Flotilla in the Nore Command based at Dover for patrols in the English Channel and also for cross-Channel Escort duties. A collision with the Dover Breakwater on 12 September 1939 required six weeks of repairs but she resumed patrols in November.

The German offensive in the Low Countries began on 10 May 1940, and on that day *Brilliant* sailed for Antwerp with a demolition team embarked, to ensure that British shipping and citizens were evacuated and, if necessary, to deny the port facilities to the Germans. Twenty six allied ocean-going merchant ships were dispatched from Antwerp before *Brilliant* left in the afternoon of 12 May with approximately 100 British evacuees embarked. The demolition team was left to make its way by road to Dunkirk.

Two days later, *Brilliant* left Dover with her sister-ship *Boreas* to take part in a similar operation at the Hook of Holland, but the two destroyers collided and had to proceed to Sheerness for repairs and refits. *Brilliant* returned to Dover on 17 June to join the 1st Destroyer Flotilla, formed during her absence to continue the activities of the 19th Destroyer Flotilla which had been dissolved following heavy losses at Dunkirk.

At 1705 hours on 25 July 1940 *Brilliant* and *Boreas* were sailed to intercept

E-boats sighted off the French coast. *Brilliant* engaged them with gunfire, closing to within five miles of Cap Gris Nez and coming under the fire of shore batteries before the E-boats withdrew under cover of smoke. Soon after, at 1800 hours, the two destroyers began their withdrawal to Dover. At 1810 hours they were dive-bombed by eight Ju 87 Stukas four miles off South Foreland in spite of the presence of British fighter aircraft. The first attack scored no hits but a second, just off Dover, scored hits on both ships: *Brilliant* received two bombs on her quarterdeck, both failing to explode as they passed right through the ship, causing flooding of the steering gear, engines and spirit room but no casualties. Two Ju 87s were shot down into the sea. Flooding rapidly, *Brilliant* was forced to stop and she settled by the stern. She was lightened aft by the jettisoning of all twenty depth charges; protective plating and 'X' and 'Y' guns also went over the side. The two destroyers were towed into Dover at 1950 hours by tugs. *Brilliant* was subsequently towed to Chatham on 27 July for repairs which lasted until mid-October.

By this time, the 1st Destroyer Flotilla had been withdrawn from Dover and was divided between Portsmouth and Scapa Flow, the 2nd Destroyer Flotilla being attached to the Home Fleet. *Brilliant* joined the latter, escorting the new battleship *King George V* from the Tyne to Rosyth en route to Scapa Flow. *Brilliant* remained with the Home Fleet until the end of February 1941, escorting convoys around the north of Scotland and screening Fleet movements.

In early March she proceeded to Southampton to refit for services with the Western Approaches Command, alterations, including the substitution of a 3-inch high-angle anti-aircraft gun for one set of torpedo tubes, an increase in depth charge stowage from 20 to 60, and the addition of surface warning radar (Type 286) and two 20mm Oerlikon anti-aircraft guns. By the time that she completed on 8 May, she had been reallocated to the South Atlantic Command and she sailed for Freetown on 12 May 1941, screening the aircraft carrier *Furious* and the cruiser *London* as far as Gibraltar. She left Gibraltar on 24 May with *London*, bound for Freetown, but was diverted to search for German raider supply ships.

On 4 June 1941, *London* and *Brilliant* sighted the German tanker *Esso Hamburg* in a position halfway between Sierra Leone and Brazil. The German ship immediately fired scuttling charges and a boarding party from *Brilliant* was unable to stop her sinking. On the following day the tanker *Egerland* was sighted in the same general area and she too was abandoned and scuttling charges were fired. Again, *Brilliant*'s boarding party stated she could not be saved. Seven depth charges and a torpedo were required to finish *Egerland* off, five hours after she had been sighted. The interceptions were made because of the breaking of the German Naval Enigma code.

After such an eventful beginning to her period on the South Atlantic Station,

Brilliant settled down to a routine of local escort duties in the Freetown area, becoming Leader of the 18th Destroyer Flotilla when the Flotilla was constituted in August 1941. She returned to Chatham in early April 1942 and left again for Freetown at the end of May following a refit which had included the removal of the quarterdeck 4.7-inch gun and the addition of two more 20mm Oerlikon anti-aircraft guns. *Brilliant* did not rejoin the 18th Destroyer Flotilla until mid-August as she first accompanied a troop convoy to Durban, and thereafter she spent only two months based on Freetown before being attached to another command, on this occasion Force 'H' for the invasion of North Africa.

Brilliant arrived at Gibraltar on 31 October and sailed to join the Centre Task Force on 6 November. The invasion took place two days later, *Brilliant*'s task being close support of the landing at 'Y' Beach, Oran, where she fired on Vichy French defences and observed the battleship *Rodney*'s fall of shot. During the morning the Vichy French sloop *La Surprise* broke out at Mers el Kebir and attempted to attack the invasion transports off 'Y' Beach but was prevented from doing so by *Brilliant* who sank the sloop after a 14-minute gun engagement and then rescued the 21 survivors.

On 14 November 1942, *Brilliant* was officially transferred to the Gibraltar Command, where she joined the Gibraltar Task Force, serving in Escort Group 61 until the end of January 1943, when she left for Portsmouth for a refit. This was *Brilliant*'s longest break from service during the war and during the four and a half months she was modified as an escort destroyer, being fitted with a 'Hedgehog' forward-throwing anti-submarine weapon, improved radar, and stowage for 125 depth charges. The 3-inch Oerlikon anti-aircraft gun was removed and the second set of torpedo tubes was restored. After working up in the Clyde, *Brilliant* returned to Gibraltar in late August 1943, joining the 13th Destroyer Flotilla with the Gibraltar Escort Force and remaining until September 1944. During this period she escorted convoys and took part in several 'Swamp' operations, in which U-boats were hunted to exhaustion by the combined employment of large numbers of escorts and aircraft.

After spending six weeks at Portsmouth during which a set of torpedo tubes was again removed, *Brilliant* rejoined the 1st Destroyer Flotilla after an absence of four years. From November 1944 she undertook patrols and escort duties in the English Channel, hunting for schnorkel-equipped U-boats inshore and escorting Allied reinforcement convoys to Le Havre and Cherbourg. December was a particularly active month, *Brilliant* attacking four contacts during the last two weeks, two after successful U-boat attacks on her consorts.

On 22 January 1945 *Brilliant* collided with the Canadian corvette HMCS *Lindsay* in thick fog in the English Channel. Both ships sustained considerable damage. After emergency repairs at Portsmouth had made her seaworthy for a short passage, *Brilliant* proceeded to Antwerp – the first British ship to be sent there for long-term repairs since the port was reopened.

She left Antwerp on 23 April 1945 and returned to Portsmouth where she was modified for use as a 'Submarine Target and Escort Vessel' and smoke-generating apparatus was added for trial purposes. Leaving the dockyard on 26 May 1945, she acted as escort to the cruiser HMS *Jamaica*, taking His Majesty King George VI to Jersey on 7 June; on the same day it was proposed to Flag Officer Submarines, to whom *Brilliant* had been allocated, that she should be prepared for reserve.

The smoke trials with the Portsmouth Escort Flotilla did not end until 18 June. However, when *Brilliant* came under Flag Officer Submarine's orders she was sent to Holy Loch to join in the work of collecting the many surrendered U-boats from the various ports around the United Kingdom and escorting them to Holy Loch. As the mass scuttling of U-boats began in November 1945, *Brilliant*'s reduction to Reserve was approved and, stripped of radar and communications equipment, she was laid up in the Holy Loch on 29 April 1946. Although on the Disposal List, she was not actually sold for scrapping at Troon to the West of Scotland Shipbreaking Company Ltd. until 21 February 1948. HMS *Brilliant* – Battle Honours: English Channel 1940-1943, Atlantic 1941-1943, North Africa 1942-1943.

Brilliant's changing armament:

1931: 4 x 4.7-inch quick-firing guns, 2 x 2-pounder anti-aircraft guns, 4 x .303 Lewis machine guns, 20 depth charges, 8 x 21-inch torpedo tubes.

1942: 3 x 4.7-inch guns, 1 x 3-inch anti-aircraft gun, 2 x 2-pounder anti-aircraft guns, 2 x 20mm anti-aircraft guns, 70 depth charges, 4 x 21-inch torpedo tubes, air and surface warning radar (metric).

1944: 3 x 4.7-inch guns, 6 x 20mm anti-aircraft guns, 125 depth charges, 1 x 'Hedgehog', 8 x 21-inch torpedo tubes, air warning (metric) and surface warning (centimetric) radars.

HMS *BEAGLE* (H 30)

Beagle returned to Devonport on 27 August 1936 following over five years' service with the 4th Destroyer Flotilla in the Mediterranean since first commissioning in Plymouth on 15 May 1931. Her cost when launched on 26 September 1930 was £220,342. Before returning to the United Kingdom she had been dispatched, at the request of the High Commissioner to Palestine, to Jaffa to aid the civil power during the communal unrest.

Beagle refitted at Devonport on 16 January 1937 when she returned to the 4th Destroyer Flotilla, now part of the Home Fleet, until April 1938. Another leisurely refit at Devonport followed from 4 April 1938 until 17 September 1938 when *Beagle* commissioned to replace HMS *Stronghold* as the attendant destroyer to the aircraft carrier HMS *Furious* and Captain (Destroyers) of the 15th Destroyer Flotilla of the Home Fleet.

She was to be on these duties barely two months before undergoing a further period in dockyard hands between 24 November 1938 and 3 January 1939, prior to becoming plane-guard for the training carrier HMS *Argus* for the next four months.

Between 12 April 1939 and 3 May 1939 *Beagle* was under repair at Devonport after minor collision damage with HMS *Basilisk*, before undertaking another two months of plane-guard duties with *Furious* at Rosyth. A period for repairs and docking at Devonport completed her peacetime service before she joined the 19th Destroyer Flotilla at Dover during September 1939. She served with the flotilla on routine duties until April 1940, refitting at Falmouth between 18 December 1939 and 22 January 1940.

Beagle was occupied on convoy duties between the Orkneys and Narvik between April and June 1940, and then participated in the evacuation of British nationals fron Bordeaux to Plymouth. She carried one 25-foot fast motor boat, one 27-foot whaler, seven flotanets, six Denton rafts and five life floats, which gave a life-saving capacity of 351.

On 3 July 1940 she was ordered to join the 1st Destroyer Flotilla at Dover and for the next sixteen days she undertook patrols by day and night. However, on 19 July 1940 *Beagle* was damaged outside Dover Harbour by German Air Force Ju 87 Stuka dive-bombers and sustained damage to her gyro compass and boiler room that required repairs at Devonport until 16 August 1940.

On completion of repairs *Beagle* was retained at Devonport as a unit of the 22nd Destroyer Flotilla, serving in the English Channel for the next two months.

On 14 October 1940, *Beagle* was attached to the Home Fleet for escort duties and four days later escorted the aircraft carrier HMS *Argus* as she conveyed naval aircraft to Iceland and immediately afterwards escorted a convoy to West Africa.

In February 1941, *Beagle* was transferred to Western Approaches Command with the 4th Escort Group on the Clyde-Iceland convoy run. During severe weather on 24 October 1941 *Beagle* sustained a broken foremast and other damage, which was repaired at Greenock. At the same time she was fitted with radar. However, she was to sustain more extensive weather damage in December 1941 and proceeded to the Tyne for repairs. During this refit she was converted into a short-range escort with an early 'Hedgehog' installation and with torpedo tubes modified to launch a one-ton depth charge.

Beagle sailed as part of the escorts for convoy PQ 14 in April 1942 and while returning with QP 11 on 1 May 1942, *Beagle*, *Bulldog*, *Amazon* and *Beverley* beat off five separate attacks by three large German destroyers armed with a total of ten 5.9-inch guns and five 5-inch guns compared with the six 4.7-inch and three 4-inch guns of the British escorts. *Beagle* sustained minor shell splinter damage.

Between May and October 1942, *Beagle* returned to the Greenock Escort Force and escorted troop convoys from the Clyde to the south of Iceland where the ocean escort took over.

During October and November 1942, *Beagle* was attached to Force 'H' in the Mediterranean for escort duties during Operation 'Torch', the North African landings. She then escorted convoys JW 1A, RA 51 and JW 52 to and from North Russia. After being refitted with improved radar, anti-submarine warfare equipment and improved insulation for Arctic duties, *Beagle*, in true navy fashion, was duly dispatched to Freetown, West Africa, where she operated as a local escort in the South Atlantic until she returned to the Home Fleet in November 1943.

Beagle then made five round trips to North Russia with the 8th Escort Group between November 1943 and May 1944. While escorting the convoy JW 58 she participated in the sinking of *U-355* with aircraft from the escort carrier HMS *Tracker* on 1 April 1944.

Beagle then participated in Operation 'Neptune' until 19 July 1944, escorting landing craft and ships between the south coast of England and the assault areas on the west coast of France. She destroyed two German Air Force Ju 88s when attacked on 22 and 23 June 1944. She was then under repair at Sheerness between 19 July 1944 and September 1944 before rejoining the 8th Escort Group for a few more weeks.

On 11 March 1945 *Beagle* was reassigned to Plymouth Command at Devonport for escort duties in the western English Channel. From 12 April until 1 May 1945 *Beagle* operated with the Biscay blockade and attended, with HMS *Bulldog*, the surrender of the German Garrison in the Channel Islands on 9 May 1945.

Two weeks later *Beagle* was taken in hand at Devonport for de-storing and reduction to Category 'C' Reserve. She was approved for scrapping on 22 December 1945 and on 15 January 1946 was handed over to BISCO at Rosyth. She was moved to the Metal Industries (Salvage) shipbreaking yard in the north-west corner of the dockyard two days later. She was one of the few destroyers to be on active service with the Royal Navy throughout the Second World War. Battle Honours of HMS *Beagle*: Norway, 1940; Atlantic, 1941-1943; North Africa, 1942; Arctic, 1942-1944; English Channel, 1943; Normandy, 1944.

HMS *BOADICEA* (H 65)
Authorised in the 1928 Programme, built and engined by Hawthorne Leslie & Company Ltd., Hebburn-on-Tyne, she was laid down on 11 July 1929, launched on 23 September 1930 at a cost of £225,325, and completed on 7 April 1931. Commissioned at Portsmouth on 2 June 1931, *Boadicea* joined the 4th Destroyer Flotilla and served in the Mediterranean between July 1931 and

August 1936. She was detached to aid the civil power at Haifa and Famagusta between November 1935 and January 1936 and again at Haifa during June 1936. Her final months in the Mediterranean were spent at Cartegena and Valencia, evacuating British and other nationals from the disturbances that signified the start of the Spanish Civil War. Earlier, on 15 March 1935 *Boadicea* had been damaged when practising refuelling at sea with the battleship *Revenge*; repairs at Gibraltar were completed between 15 March and 18 April 1935.

After a further refit at Portsmouth between 21 August and 26 September 1936, *Boadicea* rejoined the 4th Destroyer Flotilla of the Home Fleet until January 1939, when the 'B's were superseded by the newly-commissioned 'Tribal' class destroyers. The next two months were spent on plane-guard duties with the aircraft carriers of the Mediterranean Fleet, and then *Boadicea* acted as the Emergency Destroyer at the Nore until being attached to the Reserve Fleet at Portland in August 1939 for the Review.

Armament at the outbreak of war was four 4.7-inch QF guns and two 2-pounder pom-poms. By October 1940, one 3-inch High Angle gun had been added. By April 1943 two 20mm Oerlikon guns were added. By April 1943 one 4.7-inch gun had been removed and by October 1943 another 4.7-inch gun had been removed. By April 1944 the 2-pounder pom-poms had been removed and two 6-pounder guns had been added.

For anti-submarine warfare *Boadicea* was fitted with two depth charge throwers and one rail, for which she carried an outfit of 30 depth charges. By October 1941, the depth charge equipment had been increased to four throwers and two rails, with an outfit of 60 depth charges. The number of charges was progressively increased until, by April 1944, it was 125 depth charges. By April 1944 'Hedgehog' anti-submarine mortar had been fitted.

The *Boadicea* was also fitted with two 21-inch quadruple torpedo tubes for which she carried an outfit of eight torpedoes. At the outbreak of the war in September 1939, *Boadicea* was attached to the 19th Destroyer Flotilla based at Dover, Kent, her duties being to cover the movement of troopships to France and cover minelayers carrying out lays during September and October.

At the end of October 1940, she was transferred to the 22nd Destroyer Flotilla based at Harwich, Essex, as part of the East Coast Defence. She returned to the 19th Destroyer Flotilla at Dover in early December 1939 to resume her former duties. On 4 March 1940, she towed the tanker *Charles F. Meyer* (10,500 tons) into Southampton Water after the tanker had struck a mine south of Dungeness.

Boadicea was taken in hand on 2 May 1940, for a refit at Chatham, Kent, not completed until early June. While under refit, the German Army overran Holland, Belgium and northern France and the evacuation of the British Expeditionary Force from Dunkirk had taken place. The German Army was progressing along the French coast when *Boadicea* was again operational. In company with other ships, she went to Le Havre on 9 June 1940, to assist in the evacuation of the 51st Highland Division. Whilst off Le Havre, *Boadicea* received three direct hits from aircraft bombs and was disabled. She was towed to Portsmouth for repairs, which kept her out of action for the next seven and a half months.

Whilst under repair, which included the fitting of Type 286 radar, *Boadicea* was allocated to the Home Fleet. On 14 February 1941, she left Portsmouth to take up her new duties. She was part of the screen when it left Scapa Flow on 14 March 1941 to search for the German battlecruisers *Scharnhorst* and *Gneisenau*, which had broken out into the Atlantic.

On the return of the Fleet, *Boadicea* left for Greenock, Scotland, where she joined the 4th Escort Group based on that port. Here her duties were to escort outward convoys to the mid-Atlantic dispersal line and then to pick up an incoming convoy at the rendezvous to escort it to the United Kingdom. Although *Boadicea* carried out several attacks on submarine contacts she did not succeed in sinking any U-boats. *Boadicea* continued on these duties until February 1942 when the 4th Escort Group was disbanded.

On 25 April 1942, *Boadicea* left Greenock for Iceland where she joined the escort for convoy PQ 15 to Russia on 28 April. Three of the merchant ships were sunk on 3 May, but these were the only losses sustained in spite of many air attacks. Several U-boats shadowed the convoy but didn't succeed in penetrating the escort. The escort carried out several promising attacks on the U-boats but didn't manage to sink any. The convoy arrived at Kola Inlet on 5 May.

Boadicea sailed as one of the escorts for the returning convoy QP 12, which, although shadowed by German aircraft, did not come under attack and arrived intact at Reykjavik, Iceland.

Boadicea then returned to Greenock where she joined the Special Escort Division whose primary function was escorting troopships to and from the United Kingdom. After escorting the *Dominion Monarch* from Halifax, Nova Scotia, eastern Canada to Liverpool in early August 1942, *Boadicea* went to the shipyards on the Clyde for a refit.

On 19 October 1942, she left the Clyde as one of the escorts for convoy KX 2, one of the preparatory convoys for Operation 'Torch', the Allied landings in North Africa. The convoy arrived at Gibraltar on 29 October.

On 2 November 1942, *Boadicea* was one of the destroyers that took over screening duties with Force 'H' so that the relieved destroyers could refuel in readiness for the operation. On 8 November 1942, *Boadicea* was on anti-submarine patrol off Oran while the landings took place when she was struck in the forward shell room by a 5.1-inch shell from a French destroyer. A hole in the ship's side was immediately plugged and the shell room pumped out. *Boadicea* was able to continue with her patrol duties. On 11 November 1942 she was in company with the troopship *Viceroy of India* when the latter was torpedoed and sunk. *Boadicea* rescued 425 survivors and took them to Gibraltar.

On 12 November 1942, *Boadicea* left Gibraltar, escorting convoy MKF 1 to the United Kingdom, arriving at Greenock on 19 November. On 14 December she escorted convoy JW 51A from Loch Ewe to Kola Inlet, arriving there on Christmas Day.

Boadicea next escorted convoy JW 53, joining it north-east of Iceland as part of a strong force of thirteen destroyers to cover the most dangerous part of the convoy's passage to northern Russia. She then helped escort the returning convoy, RA 53, from Russia to Iceland. On 10 March 1943, *Boadicea* reported extensive damage forward due to ice, which prevented her from steering faster than 15 knots. On return to the Clyde, *Boadicea* was taken in hand on 17 March 1943 for repairs which took eight weeks to complete.

On becoming operational again, *Boadicea* was transferred to the West Africa Command and was based on Freetown. She remained on this station until October 1943, escorting convoys to and from Freetown, Takoradi and Lagos, and occasionally to Cape Town. On 19 July 1943, she rescued 220 survivors from the SS *Incomati* which had been sunk.

On 15 September, *Boadicea* sailed from Freetown escorting convoy WS 33 to the United Kingdom. On her arrival, she underwent a long refit, being fully converted into an escort destroyer, not completed until late January 1944.

After working up, she rejoined the 8th Escort Group and on 20 February 1944, *Boadicea* left Loch Ewe as one of the escorts for convoy JW 57. In spite of determined efforts by U-boats no merchant ships were lost, but two U-boats were sunk, one by HMS *Keppel* and one by a long-range Catalina aircraft from Sullam Voe. Aircraft from the carrier HMS *Chaser*, which accompanied the convoy, carried out many attacks on U-boats attempting to attack the convoy, compelling them to submerge before they could develop any attacks.

Boadicea was one of the escorts for the return convoy RA 57. In spite of determined efforts by the U-boats, the voyage from northern Russia to the United Kingdom was accomplished with the loss of only one ship for three U-boats sunk by Swordfish aircraft from *Chaser*.

On 27 March 1944, *Boadicea* sailed to overtake convoy JW 58 which reached northern Russia without loss – as did the return convoy RA 58. The Germans, however, lost four U-boats and six shadowing aircraft.

Boadicea left Skaalefjord , Iceland, on 19 April 1944 to escort convoy RA 59 from Russia to the United Kingdom. Only one ship was lost from this convoy, the SS *William S. Thayer*, which was carrying a number of Russian passengers, some of them en route to the United Kingdom to take over HMS *Royal Sovereign*. The *Boadicea* managed to rescue several survivors. German losses were three U-boats.

In late May 1944, *Boadicea* moved to Plymouth in readiness for Operation 'Neptune' – the Allied landings in Normandy. On 6 June, she escorted one of the assault convoys over to the landing area at 'Omaha' Beach and continued to escort follow-up convoys across the English Channel during the following week. On 13 June 1944, while escorting a resupply convoy to 'Omaha' Beach, *Boadicea* came under attack 20 miles off Portland Bill, Dorset from a missile-carrying Dornier Do 217 aircraft and was hit by an HS 293 missile, sinking in three minutes with only 12 survivors being rescued. Battle Honours of HMS *Boadicea*: Atlantic, 1941-1943; North Africa, 1942; Arctic, 1942-1944; Normandy, 1944.

HMS *BULLDOG* (H 91)

Bulldog's most important contribution to the war effort occurred on 9 May 1941 when escorting convoy OB 318 off Iceland. *Bulldog*, another destroyer HMS *Broadway* and the corvette HMS *Aubretia* drove *U-110* (Kapitänleutnant Julius Lemp) to the surface and forced her crew to abandon ship. Lemp was killed and the survivors were picked up by *Aubretia* and *Bulldog*.

Commander Baker-Cresswell, Commanding Officer of *Bulldog*, realised that the survivors thought that *U-110* had sunk and told them nothing while a party from *Bulldog* stripped the submarine of her Enigma coding machine and captured the day's setting, which proved to be an immense cryptoanalytical gain for the Allies. *U-110* sank while under tow some time later.

Previous to this, she was launched on 6 January 1930 at a cost of £221,408, and was commissioned at Chatham into the 4th Destroyer Flotilla on 9 June 1931. *Bulldog* served with this flotilla in the Mediterranean until August 1936. The highlights of this portion of her career were her attendance at the earthquake-stricken island of Erissos in the Aegean between 28 September and 1 October 1932, and spending the last month of her Mediterranean service off the south coast of Spain.

Bulldog then refitted at Gibraltar between 12 May and 11 June 1932 and had a restricted refit at Malta between 1 June and 20 June 1936. The 4th Destroyer Flotilla, including *Bulldog*, returned to the United Kingdom during August 1936 and she remained with the Home Fleet until replaced by the destroyer HMS *Eskimo* in December 1938.

Bulldog was under repair at Chatham between 28 August and 14 October 1936 before refitting between 18 November 1936 and 9 January 1937.

Although nominally a Home Fleet destroyer, *Bulldog* spent long periods in Spanish waters; January to March 1937 off southern Spain; June to August 1937 off the ports of the Bay of Biscay; September to November 1937 on patrol between Gibraltar and Oran; and finally, between January and March 1938, based at Gibraltar. *Bulldog* then refitted at Sheerness between 31 March and 4

June 1938. During the Munich crisis *Bulldog* escorted the battleship HMS *Resolution* to Scapa Flow on 26 September 1938.

On being replaced by the *Eskimo*, *Bulldog* joined the Gibraltar (Local) Flotilla until March 1939, when she replaced HMS *Wishart* on plane-guard duties for the aircraft carrier HMS *Glorious*, firstly in the Mediterranean until the outbreak of war in September 1939, and then in the Red Sea and Indian Ocean until December 1939.

After refitting at Malta between 18 January and 22 February 1940, *Bulldog* and the destroyer HMS *Westcott* undertook similar duties for the aircraft carrier HMS *Ark Royal* between February and April 1940.

At the beginning of the Norwegian Campaign, *Bulldog* was ordered to return to Britain where, after degaussing and repairs to her feed water-heater between 19 April and 3 May 1940 at Devonport, she began operations.

Six days later *Bulldog* stood by the destroyer HMS *Kelly* after it had been torpedoed by the German destroyer *S31* in the Skagerrak, between southern Norway and northern Denmark.

Bulldog then towed the severely damaged *Kelly* across the North Sea and home to the shipyards on the River Tyne for repairs by Hawthorn Leslie, her builders. During the long tow *Bulldog* damaged her stern and was repaired at Swan Hunter's between 13 and 21 May 1940.

Bulldog then participated in the early stages of the Dunkirk evacuation, but was withdrawn for repairs at Chatham lasting until 4 June 1940, after damaging her propellers off Dunkirk on 27 May 1940.

Bulldog had been with the 1st Destroyer Flotilla just six days when she received severe bomb damage on 10 June 1940 while operating off the French coast during the unsuccessful attempt to evacuate the 51st Highland Division from St. Valery. She was attacked by six Ju 87s and three bombs struck and penetrated the destroyer, putting her steering gear out of action. The first bomb hit *Bulldog*'s upper deck at Station 104, passed through the engine room and then through the ship's side. The second bomb hit the upper deck at Station 94, entered the top of No. 3 boiler and, after passing through the generator tubes, came to rest on the water reservoir without exploding. The third bomb pierced the foreside of the after funnel and then passed through the fore-end of the boiler room. It failed to explode on impact, but later, as a result of the heat from the boilers, it eventually detonated.

After sustaining this severe damage, very fortunately without casualties, *Bulldog* steamed in several uncontrollable circles, listing heavily to starboard. Sufficient steam was raised and she was able to make 15 knots after the steering gear was temporarily repaired at 1815 hours. *Bulldog* eventually arrived at Portsmouth at 0700 hours on 11 June 1940.

Repairs at Portsmouth were not completed until 2 September 1940 after she sustained further bomb splinter damage during a heavy bombing raid on Portsmouth by the German Air Force on 24 August 1940. She then rejoined the 1st Destroyer Flotilla. On 8 and 10 September 1940, *Bulldog, Beagle, Berkeley* and *Atherstone* made sweeps off the French coast, attempting to intercept German convoys.

After a refit at Cammell-Laird between 2 January and 18 February 1941, *Bulldog* worked up and joined the 3rd Escort Group; her days as a Fleet escort ended and she spent the next eight months on Icelandic convoy duty, damaging *U-94* west of the Faeroe Islands on 7 May 1941 with the destroyer HMS *Amazon* and the sloop HMS *Rochester*, two days before her successful action against and capture of *U-110*.

Bulldog's sides were strengthened during a refit at Fairfield's on the Clyde between 24 October 1941 and 10 February 1942. She then rejoined Western Approaches Command as an unattached vessel. She stood by the destroyer HMS *Richmond*, damaged in a collision with the American ship *Francis Scott Keys* on 31 March 1942 in position 63°37'N, 22°05'W, approximately 70 miles due south of Reykjavik, Iceland.

By May 1942 the Arctic convoys to northern Russia were in full operation and while escorting QP 11 from Murmansk, the destroyers *Bulldog, Amazon, Beverley* and the corvette HMS *Snowflake* fought off five attacks on the convoy by the heavier armed German destroyers *Herman Schoemann, Z24* and *Z25*. The Germans sank the Russian straggler *Tsiolkovsky, Bulldog* received shell splinter damage and *Amazon* a hit to her steering gear.

Bulldog was under repair on the Clyde between 2 June and 14 August 1942. She then formed part of the Greenock Special Escort Division and participated in Operation 'Torch', the North African landings, in early November 1942.

After further repair at Greenock between 23 November and 14 December 1942 she joined the escort for the Russian convoy JW 51B from Loch Ewe to Murmansk on 20 December 1942, but damaged by severe weather she was again under repair on the Clyde between 28 December 1942 and 16 January 1943.

Bulldog then escorted Icelandic convoys for the next two months before refitting at Greenock between 29 March and 22 April 1943, prior to transfer to West African Command during May 1943. She undertook escort duties between Freetown, Lagos and Gibraltar for the next five months.

On her return to Britain, *Bulldog* refitted and rearmed as an escort destroyer at Portsmouth between 8 November 1943 and 24 May 1944. She was working up at Tobermory on 6 June 1944, before undertaking local escort duties between the Faeroe Islands and the Clyde.

On 26 June 1944 *Bulldog* sank *U-719* after a long search in the North Channel. However, on 24 August 1944 she was in collision with the frigate HMS *Loch Dungevan* in Gourock Bay. *Bulldog* was cut four feet inboard from the upper deck to three feet below the waterline. She was repaired at Androssan between 17 August and 4 September 1944.

Bulldog then operated on local escort duties between the Faeroes, Scapa Flow and the Clyde until November 1944, when major machinery repairs were begun at Elderslie, Clyde, which were not completed until 30 January 1945. During the last months of the war *Bulldog* was on local escort duties between Plymouth and the Irish Sea ports.

On 13 May 1945 *Bulldog* and *Beagle* accepted the surrender of the German Army Garrison on the Channel Islands.

Almost immediately afterwards, on 27 May 1945, *Bulldog* entered the Reserve at Dartmouth and was declared as Category 'B' Reserve on 26 June 1945. On 13 December 1945, she entered Category 'C' Reserve at Rosyth and was approved for scrap nine days later.

On 17 January 1946, *Bulldog* was delivered to Metal Industries (Salvage) Ltd. at Rosyth for demolition. She was another of the few destroyers to be on active service with the Royal Navy throughout the Second World War. Battle Honours of HMS *Bulldog*: Atlantic, 1941-1945; Arctic, 1942-1944.

ULTIMATE FATE OF THE NINE 'B' CLASS DESTROYERS

Keith (Leader) was bombed and sunk by German aircraft off Dunkirk in June 1940.

Blanche (Deputy Leader), the first destroyer casualty, was mined in the Thames Estuary on 13 November 1939.

Basilisk was bombed and sunk by German aircraft off Dunkirk, 1 June 1940.

Boreas was loaned to Greece in 1944, renamed *Salamis* and returned in 1952, and scrapped.

Brazen was bombed off Dover on 20 July 1940, but she shot down three German bombers before sinking, while trying to make harbour.

Brilliant survived the war and was used for damage control tests before being scrapped in 1948.

Beagle survived the war and was scrapped in 1946.

Boadicea was sunk by an air-to-surface HS 293 missile off Portland, Dorset, 13 June 1944.

Bulldog survived the war and was scrapped in 1946.

APPENDIX III:
DERIVATION OF 'B' CLASS NAMES & SHIPS' BADGES

See Plate Section III for illustrated ships' badges

HMS *KEITH*
From the Arms of Viscount Keith, Admiral Elphinstone, KB (1746-1823), Admiral of the Red, who landed General Abercromby's army of 16,500 in Egypt in 1801. The badge has a silver field with a red boar's head. The crest motto is 'Fatis fortior virtus': Valour is stronger than fate.

HMS *BASILISK*
For the purpose of the badge design, it was assumed that the origin of this name was from Greek mythology. The basilisk was an awesome creature, reputed to possess the power of killing by means of its deadly glance and its burning, poisonous breath. According to Pliny, it was so called from the spot on its head that resembled a diadem. Medieval authors furnished it with a 'a certain Combe or Coronet'. It was believed that if this creature was speared by a horseman, its poison passed through the weapon, killing both horse and rider. Although it was reputed to be only six inches in height, this creature was referred to as 'the King of the Serpents'.

The badge shows a cockatrice (which is another mythical creature, synonymous with the basilisk), depicted in a traditional style. The basilisk is more frequently depicted in heraldry as in the design, but drawn with a tail terminating in the form of a dragon's head. Even taking this variation into account, the badge is a straightforward illustration of the name.

HMS *BEAGLE*
The beagle is the smallest species of dog used for hunting in Great Britain and they are normally used with foot beagle hunts, whose quarry is the hare. This breed can be traced back to the fifteenth century, when diminutive fox-beagles were kept. They possess an extraordinarily keen scent, an acute intelligence and great perseverance.

The use of green for the field of this badge is thought to denote the countryside, as green is often used in heraldry for this purpose; however the term 'beagle green' is common within hunting circles and is used to define the green colour of the uniform coat usually worn by beagle hunts. The dog is depicted in his natural colours and the complete design is an illustration of the name.

HMS *BLANCHE*

This is a prize name, formerly the French *Blanche*, captured on 21 December 1799 by HMS *Suffolk* and HMS *Magnificent* off St. Lucia.

This design perpetuates the memory of the tenth ship of the name. A light cruiser, she was present at the Battle of Jutland on 31 May 1916, under the command of Captain J. M. Casement, RN. Her role was to repeat signals between units of the Grand Fleet, and this vital task was well executed, Captain Casement being mentioned in the dispatches of Admiral Sir John Jellicoe. He later rose to Flag rank, retiring with the rank of Admiral. The complete design is part of his Arms. The use of white as the field colour in the design alludes to the name itself and also to its origin. The French word *blanche* is the feminine of *blanc* – both words meaning 'white'.

HMS *BOADICEA*

The history of Boadicea, Queen of the Iceni, did not come to light until the early sixteenth century, when the works of the Roman historian Tacitus were discovered and published in Italy. The name is mis-translated from 'Boudicca', a name of Gaelic origin meaning 'Victoria'. Her husband, King Prosutagus, a tenant king in what is now the county of Norfolk, died in 59 AD, and he stipulated in his will that his kingdom was to be divided up between the Emperor Nero and his two daughters. But, in collecting the Emperor's legacy, the Procurator confiscated the entire kingdom, dispossessed the Icenian nobles and carried off the able-bodied as slaves. The worst outrage occurred at the royal palace when Prosutagus' two daughters were raped and Boudicca stripped and flogged.

Under her leadership, the remnants of the Iceni, together with the Trinovantes, a neighbouring tribe, took up arms against the Romans and a short but bloody campaign began. The important Roman garrison towns of *Camulodunum* (Colchester), *Verulamium* (St. Albans) and *Londinium* (London) were laid to waste, and the elite Ninth Legion were slaughtered to a man, probably near Cambridge, before Boudicca's force was defeated in battle by seasoned Roman troops near Atherstone in 60 AD.

Boudicca escaped the final massacre and is presumed to have committed suicide rather than fall into the hands of the Romans.

The design closely follows that of an earlier unofficial badge for the third ship of the name, both inspired by the large bronze statue of Boadicea facing the House of Commons from the north-west corner of Westminster Bridge, London (sculpted by Thomas Thorneycroft and erected in 1902). The field colour, black, is used to signify the mourning and death of Boadicea, whilst the gold of the design indicates her royal status.

HMS *BOREAS*

Boreas, in Greek mythology, was the personification of the North wind, a son of the Titans Astraeus and Eos (the stars and the dawn), and brother of Eurus, Zephyrus and Notus. He dwelt in a cave on Mount Haemus in Thrace. He courted and forcibly carried off Otrithyia, a daughter of Erechheus, King of Attica. He sired three children, Zetes, Calais, and Cleopatra.

According to legend, during the first Persian war, Boreas aided the Athenians by destroying the ships of the Persians by storms; afterwards he was worshipped at Athens, where a festival called Boreasmi was celebrated in his honour.

This badge shows Boreas creating a storm of the North wind. A storm from the north is usually cold and bitter, very destructive and accompanied by dark skies. The design intimates this both by the use of a black field and the placing of the stream of wind.

HMS *BRAZEN*

The verb 'brazen' means 'to make bold', or 'to face impudently', most suitable for a 'small-ship' name! As an adjective it means 'made of brass'.

The alternative meaning of the name was chosen to inspire the design of this badge. The term 'brazen trumpets' is well known, and because a Latin motto was to be given to the ship a Latin trumpet (the Roman *cornua*) would be very appropriate. It has been placed on a red field to symbolise martialism.

HMS *BRILLIANT*

The name was introduced into the Royal Navy by the capture of the French sloop *Brilliant*, in 1696. The word 'brilliant' means shining brightly, glittering, sparkling or lustrous.

The design is derived from the badge of the seventh ship of this name, a second class cruiser which participated in the action at Ostend on 23 April 1918, when she was sunk as a blockship in an unsuccessful attempt to deny the harbour to the occupying German forces.

That badge had a letter 'B' within a ring surrounded by twelve rays. Mr Ffoulkes modified this design by removing the letter 'B', altering the shape of the twelve rays and leaving the centre of the ring a plain flat surface. This was to give an alternative meaning to the word 'brilliant', namely a diamond of the finest cut. In the diamond trade a brilliant has horizontal faces on its upper and lower side, which are surrounded and united by facets. Therefore, this design shows the 'table' of a diamond within its setting and surrounded by rays. The use of black as a field colour also has more than one meaning. Firstly, it may mourn the loss of life at Zeebrugge and Ostend in April 1918, but more importantly, it is also another reference to a diamond. In heraldry it was formerly a fashion to blazon the Arms of Royalty and nobles with jewels. Black, blazoned by jewels, is diamond.

HMS *BULLDOG*

This is a breed of dog, probably a sub-variety of the mastiff crossed with lesser breeds and, as its name indicates, it was originally employed for the baiting of bulls. In Elizabethan times, these dogs were perhaps the most sought-after English breed because of the prevalence of the sports of bull- and bear-baiting. Their ability to seize and cling to the larger animals they baited became proverbial, due in part to their innate courage, and partly to the fact that the 'underbite' or locked jaw peculiar to the breed made it difficult for them to release their hold.

During the eighteenth and nineteenth centuries the breed was in high favour because of its fighting abilities.

This design was suggested by the Director of Naval Equipment, Vice Admiral J. W. Henley, RN. The badge shows a 'standard' white English bulldog. The use of black is thought to indicate that the design was for a destroyer. This field colour was frequently used for early destroyer designs and where no other allusion was intended it is thought that it was in reference to the fact that destroyers were originally painted black.

APPENDIX IV: **DESTROYER SONGS**

These are 'Destroyer Songs' which were heard being sung by ship's crews during their runs ashore in pubs in Liverpool, Londonderry, Portsmouth, etc. All have additional verses of varying content. Contributed by Iain Nethercott, HMS *Keith*.

(To the tune of 'The Little Boy that Santa Claus Forgot')
We're the Little Ships that Churchill clean forgot
And goodness knows they didn't ask a lot
A few more whacks of leave would do us all the world of good.
We haven't got the comforts of the *Rodney* or the *Hood*
When it comes to weekend leave, there's none for us
We're always shoving off to do our stuff.
Now the bigger ships get swing-time
All we get is bloody sea-time
We're the Little Ships that Churchill clean forgot.

(To the tune of 'Loch Lomond')
Now you take the paint-pot
And I'll take the paint-brush
We'll both paint the ship's side together
And when Jimmy comes along
We'll sing the same old song
Thank God we never joined for ever.

(To the tune of 'Bring Back my Bonny to Me')
If the Skipper fell into the ocean
If the Skipper fell into the sea
If the Skipper fell into the ocean
He'd get no bloody lifebelt from me
Swim back, swim back, oh swim back you bastard to me
Swim back, swim back, swim back you bastard to me.

'Harwich Naval Force Song 1939'
Don't send away the *Sandhurst*
Don't send her out to sea
If you send away the *Sandhurst*
Then down comes Parkeston Quay.

'A Chinese Maiden's Lament'
(To the tune of 'Twinkle, Twinkle Little Star')
Me no likee English sailor
When Yankee sailor come ashore
English sailor plentee money
Yankee sailor plentee more
Yankee sailor call me "Ducky darling"
English sailor call me "Chinese whore"
Yankee sailor shag for short time
English sailor shag for evermore.

'Can A Dockyard Matey Run?'
(To the tune of 'Come, Ye Thankful People Come')
Can a Dockyard Matey run?
Yes, by God, I've seen it done
At five o'clock you'll hear the bell
He drops his tools and runs like hell
Over planks and by the dock
Exerting every ounce of strength he's got
Tearing past at a frantic rate
He's on his bike and out the Gate

'Ode To a Dying Anti-Aircraft Gunner'
Oh Mother, my mouth is full of stars
Like the cartridges in a tray
My blood flows in a forked stream
As it flows and flows all away

'Cooks to the Galley' has sounded off
And the lads are down in the Mess
But I lie done, by the Forward Gun
With a bullet in my breast

Farewell Aggie Weston's, the Barracks at Guzz
Hang my Tiddley suit back on the door
They'll sew me up neat in a canvas sheet
And I'll never be home no more.

'The Submariner's Song'
(To the tune of 'Underneath the Arches')
Big ships we never cared for,
Destroyers they can keep
There is only one place that we know,
That is deep down, deep
Underneath the surface
We dream our dreams away
Underneath the surface
On battery boards we lay
There you'll always find us
Tired out and worn.
Waiting for the Captain
To sound the klaxon horn
Then we'll all get busy
The Tiffies and the 'Swain
Shutting vents and blows
And both our hydroplanes
And when the panic's over
We'll take her down again
Underneath the surface
We'll dream our dreams away.

APPENDIX V:
TERMS AND EXPRESSIONS USED BY THE ROYAL NAVY

By The Corps of Guides, HMS *Victory*, HM Naval Base, Portsmouth. None of these terms described can be guaranteed as the true derivative of the term, but these seem to the most commonly accepted.

Ahoy: Used to attract the attention of the Coxswain of the boat as it approaches the ship. Two possible explanations:

1. A small boat is known as a 'hoy'.

2. The company that supplied stores to the Royal Navy was named A. Hoy. So when challenged as their boats approached a ship they would reply "A HOY".

Bedlam: A place of uproar. At the beginning of the nineteenth century, one in a thousand men were being discharged from the Royal Navy as insane. This figure, compared with one in 7,000 for the whole country, was probably due to several reasons: a regular half pint of rum per man per day, frequent floggings and continual knocks from heavy gear all contributed.

Such was the scale of the problem that the Navy had its own lunatic asylum, the Bethlehem Royal Hospital, in Moorfield, London, commonly known as 'Bedlam'. Today, this former hospital houses the Imperial War Museum.

Bitter End: The inboard of a ship's cable. From the centre-line bollards called 'bitts' to which the cables of ships were once attached, if the cable was veered to its end, this was 'the bitter end'.

Blazer: The name for a jacket. Before the days of uniform for ratings of the RN, a few ships' captains dressed some of their crews in special 'rigs' for prestige purposes. The Captain of HMS *Blazer*, Captain J. W. Washington, RN, had his boat's crew dressed in blue jackets with patch pockets and silver buttons.

By and Large: A nautical term now used to mean 'broadly speaking, all things considered'. In fact, it was an order to the men steering the ship to steer *by* the wind, keeping it *large*, i.e. in the quarter.

Clean Slate: Meaning that the past is forgotten and a new start may be made. The expression comes from the days when a slate was used in order to record the courses steered and distances run during a watch at sea. At the end of the watch, the details were transferred to the Deck Log and the slate wiped clean.

Cut and Run: The Spanish Armada 'cut and ran' when they were threatened by fireships in the Calais Roads, the narrowest part of the English Channel. The expression originated with the method used by square rigged ships to get under way speedily, which entailed stopping furled sails with rope yarns which could be cut quickly to let the sails fall.

Dog Watch: Two short two-hour periods, inserted in the ship's routine to equalize the duty roster. To say that someone has only been in half a dog watch implies that he or she has been in the Royal Navy for a comparatively short time. Probably derived from 'dodge watches' as they were incomplete in one sense; other sources suggest that these were normal watches that had become 'cur-tailed'.

Two additional possible explanations:

1. Known as a 'Dog Watch' because it has been shortened or 'dogged'. The 'Dog Watches' ('First Dog' 1600-1800 hours, 'Last Dog' 1800-2000 hours) were assigned so that you didn't have the same watch on two consecutive days. By this arrangement an uneven number of watches is made – seven instead of six watches in 24 hours; otherwise there would be a succession of the same watches at the same hours throughout the voyage.

2. It was at the time of the day when the Dog Star appeared in the evening sky.

Fanny: Mess pot. In 1867 the Royal Victualling Yard commenced issuing tinned mutton to Portsmouth warships on a trial basis but it did not find favour with the sailors. In the same year, Frederick Baker, a solicitor's clerk from Alton, Hampshire, enticed a nine-year-old girl named Fanny Adams away from her playmates and murdered her, dismembering her body. The new and unpopular meat issue was thereafter dubbed 'Fanny Adams'. With an opening handle wired to the top, the meat tin lent itself to various domestic uses on board ship such as drawing the daily rum ration for the mess.

Freeze the Balls off a Brass Monkey: Extremely cold. This is a corruption of the seventeenth century term 'freeze the balls *of* a brass monkey'. A 'monkey' was a brass cannon and in freezing temperatures the iron cannon balls and the brass cannon shrank at different rates, making the cannon inoperable. An alternative version is that the Brass Monkey, as used ashore and not on ships, was a triangular piece of brass made of three circles joined together that looked like the face of a monkey. Round shot was stored on these so that the cold ground would affect the brass rather than the iron of the shot. If it was that cold that the brass shrunk so much that the balls fell off the monkey, then it was 'cold enough to freeze the balls off a brass monkey'.

Get Your Finger Out! Hurry! This was once the order given to a gunner to remove his finger from the vent-hole of a muzzle-loading cannon whilst it was being loaded. The hole was sealed by this method while sponging to create a partial vacuum within the gun, so assisting in the extinguishing of residue from the previous cartridge.

Grog: In 1740, Admiral Vernon decreed that the men must mix their ration of spirit with four parts of water. The sailors referred to this drink as 'grog' because the Admiral was referred to as 'Old Grogram' because he always wore a weatherproof jacket made of material called 'grogram'. This was shortened to 'grog'.

Even today, we still use the term. If you have had too much to drink, or you don't feel well, you feel a bit 'groggy'.

Guzz: Devonport. The name comes from 'guzzle' as a reference to the good food associated with the West Country. Men returning from sea, following a long voyage on poor victuals, could always be assured of plenty to eat and drink when putting into Devonport (Plymouth).

Jack Dusty: A rating of the Stores Branch dealing with victualling. It comes from the old term for the Purser's Assistant who was known as "Jack-of-the-dust" because he was employed in the bread room from where the flour issue was made.

Killick: A term for a Leading Seaman. His badge is a small anchor which is known as a 'killick anchor'. In fact, the anchor was a 'fouled anchor' as the anchor cable is wound around the stock of the anchor.

Landlubber: A useless long-shorer; a vagrant stroller. The term 'landlubber' is derisively applied by seamen to the mass of landsmen who have never been to sea, or who have never learned seamanlike ways; hence a lubber or 'lubberly'.

Leathernecks: Royal Marines. The corruption 'boot neck' is more commonly used. Derived from the leather tongue they once wore at the junction of the collar of their tunics.

Letting the Cat out of the Bag: The secret is out, someone is in trouble. The 'Cat O'Nine Tails' was usually taken to the quarterdeck in a green or red baize bag. When the man was tried by the Captain, and the punishment of a flogging decreed, the 'cat' would be taken out of its bag.

Limeys: The Americans' nickname for the British. Scurvy (a disease caused by a lack of vitamin C) was a major problem in the RN, so when possible the men would be given fresh fruit to combat the disease. If this was not available, a raw onion would suffice. Another option was to give the men limejuice, hence the term 'Limeys'.

Mess: A space allocated to a number of men for the purpose of eating and sleeping. The name comes from the sixteenth century when the hands sat down in groups to 'mess from the common pot', derived from the Old French 'mes', a dish.

Nipper: Meaning a small boy. When raising the anchor and cable, the boys would be used to assist in binding the messenger cable and anchor cable together. This was referred to as 'nipping'.

Not Enough Room to Swing a Cat: The punishment of flogging with the 'Cat o' Nine Tails' was carried out on the quarterdeck so that all the crew could witness it. Because of the amount of space required to get a good swing of the cat, this was also used to indicate the lack of space in an area.

On the Fiddle: To ensure the food didn't roll off the square plates, an additional lip or rim was attached; this was referred to as a 'fiddle'. If you had so much food on your plate that it went over the fiddle, you were cheating – you were 'on the fiddle'.

Plain Sailing: Something is easy, no problem, 'from now on it will be "plain sailing"'. The basic set of sails used on the mast were known as 'plain sails' and were relatively easy to handle, hence 'plain sailing', 'easy'. However, in light winds, it became necessary to extend the yardarms with studding booms and attach studsails. If these were difficult to handle, it was no longer 'plain sailing'.

Poop: Any raised deck right aft, above the upper deck. In large square-rigged sailing ships this deck formed the roof of the 'coach' or 'roundhouse' where the master had his cabin; Middle English 'pupe' from the Latin 'puppis', also from the Spanish 'poapa' meaning 'opposite to the bow'.

Port: The left-hand side of the ship looking forward towards the bows. This side of the ship was originally called 'larboard' from the Middle English 'ladebord', the lading or loading side, as the steering oar projected from the 'steerbord' side making it difficult to lie alongside, starboard side-to. Sailing warships had entry 'ports' on this side and the term 'port' had been used for some time in order to avoid a confusion of 'larboard' with the similar sounding 'starboard'. The change was officially made by Admiralty order in 1844.

Show a Leg / Shake a Leg: Expression used to rouse someone in the morning. Derives from the fact that when in harbour men were allowed to have their 'wives' or 'girlfriends' onboard. In the morning, the Bosun would rouse the men by shouting, 'Show a leg'. If a shapely, stocking-clad leg appeared, the 'lady' was allowed to remain in the hammock for a further thirty minutes while the men cleared the area. 'Women Allowed Aboard in Harbour' was banned in 1840.

Show you the Ropes: The first day on a new job, someone will 'show you the ropes'. At sea, a new crewmember would have his allocated task explained by being shown what each rope in the rigging does.

Skylarking: Fooling around. In Victorian days 'skylarking' was a form of 'follow my leader' played up and about the rigging by junior officers, derived from the practice of young sailors who used to come down from the rigging by sliding down the stays. 'Lark' is a corruption of the Old English 'lac', to play. Up to the beginning of the twentieth century, on long voyages the pipe 'hands to dance and skylark' would be made to encourage dancing as a form of exercise.

Slush Fund: A fund for financing bribery and corruption. When the food was cooked in the galley the fat and scum from the food was collected. This was known as 'slush'. Part of this was used to grease the wheels of the guns and the running blocks in the rigging. However, the sailors liked to mix this with flour to make a sort of dumpling, so the cook would keep some of the 'slush' back to bribe the men for small favours.

Son of a Gun: Some women gave birth onboard ships in harbour, and even at sea. Some officers were allowed to take their wives to sea. The confinement area would be set up between the guns and it is said that on occasions, in cases of a difficult birth, a gun would be fired to shock the lady into giving birth. The name of the child would always be entered into the ship's log: "Born today, Charles, Son of a Gun". "Daughter of a Gun" could also be used but this is no longer in everyday use.

Speed in Knots: Before the electronic methods of measuring the speed of a ship, simple and ingenious methods were used. The 'Hand Log': it was from this method that the term 'knot' as a unit of speed was derived. The Hand Log was a long line of 150 fathoms (900 feet) in length, wound onto a hand reel. To its end was attached a piece of wood shaped like the sector of a circle. Its bottom edge was weighted to ensure that it floated upright and thereby 'gripped' the water. This, then, was the 'Log'. When thrown overboard from the stern of a ship, it pulled the line from the reel, which was left to run free. When the log was clear of the turbulence of the ship, the measuring would begin. The line was marked with a piece of white bunting to start the measuring line and thereafter with knots to represent the speed. The distance between the knots was 47 feet 3 inches. The line was let to run out for a given time, 28 seconds, the number of 'knots' counted and, as the line ran out in that time, it would give the speed of the vessel.

The time interval was measured by using sandglasses. When the reading was complete, the line was 'tugged' to release one of the logs. This flattened the log for recovery. This was not always successful, hence the need for the ship to carry 12 Log Lines.

Splice the Main Brace: "Every man is to be given an extra tot". The extra tot was given because splicing the Main Brace was a particularly hazardous and difficult task. The braces are the ropes that were attached to the ends of the yardarms, and were used to 'brace' round the yards in order to catch the wind. The largest of these, and the most important, was attached to the lower yard on the main mast. From then on, any hard job, Royal occasion, review, birthday, coronation, etc., was usually marked with the signal "Splice the Main Brace".

Sprog: General description of any novice, either to the Royal Navy or to some branch of the Senior Service, e.g. a 'sprog pilot'. Said to be derived from the term frog-spawn, or a combination of sprocket and cog.

Square Meal: The only plates supplied by the RN to the men were square, flat pieces of wood, these being the cheapest and easiest to produce, and the most space-efficient along mess tables.

Starboard: The right-hand side of the ship looking forward towards the bow (front of the ship); from the Old English 'steobord', steer-board, the steer side from which a large steering oar was operated until superseded by the rudder.

The Andrew: The Royal Navy. From Lieutenant Andrew Miller who was a legendary member of the 'Press Gang' in Portsmouth who was said to claim ownership of the Navy because of the hundreds of men he had 'pressed' into service during the late eighteenth century.

The Heads: In most English-speaking navies of the world, the toilets are referred to as 'the heads'. This is because on sailing vessels of the time the toilets were always located at the front or 'head' of the ship, in an area known as the Beakhead. They were simply boxes with a hole to sit over. The waste would drop into the sea around the bows of the ship.

To be Taken Aback: To be suddenly surprised. A term from the days of sail which meant, through a shift in the wind or bad steerage, the wind came in front of the square sails and laid them back against the masts. The ship's onward course would be instantly stayed and she would have sternway on, which was very dangerous in a gale.

To Take The Can Back or **To Carry The Can:** To take the blame. It was once the custom in some dockyards to employ a boy to fetch large cans of beer from a local public house. This boy was invariably blamed if accounts were unpaid or cans not returned.

To Take the Wind Out of One's Sails: To verbally deflate, to anticipate another or to gain advantage over a competitor. King Henry VIII issued an order that no junior captain should "take the wind out of his admiral", meaning to cross to windward and take the wind from his sails.

Watch: The name for a wrist or pocket clock. In 1758, James Harrison had perfected an accurate clock (later called a chronometer) as an aid to calculating longitude, by celestial observation in conjunction with the difference in time to that of Greenwich. Captain James Cook was one of the first users of such an instrument on his second voyage of exploration. He referred to the clock in his journal as a "watch machine", watches being the division of time aboard ship.

APPENDIX VI:
SOME CONVOY ESCORT TERMS AND PROCEDURES

Commander Ian Leitch, RN, Retd., HM Ships *Cygnet* & *Lapwing*, 'Black Swan' class sloops, Arctic convoys 1943–45

Zigzag 45: An Admiralty booklet issued to all ships in convoys gave instructions and diagrams for about 50 different types of zigzags to suit various conditions and to confuse hostile U-boats and aircraft during daylight. The Senior Escort Commander would decide which type of zigzag to order, no. 45 being one of them.

MLA: Mean Line of Advance – the true course of the convoy.

80-80 Relative: Asdic would be 'pinging' ahead over an arc of 160 degrees, i.e. 80 degrees each side of the bow, regardless of the course the ship was on.

Unifoxer: In 1944, Germany developed an acoustic homing torpedo which picked up the turbulence noise from ships' propellers and 'homed' on to the target. Unifoxer was a type of minesweeper's float with 'chattering' flukes, towed about 100 yards on either quarter, hopefully to attract the acoustic homing torpedo astern. Its operation could be checked occasionally by sweeping with Asdic sonar.

ARL Plot: Admiralty Research Laboratory plotting table, about 3' by 3', with a glass top, epicyclic gearing underneath from the gyro, adjustable scales and plotting instruments. By placing the current chart on top and a photoelectric cell underneath, the ship's position was pinpointed with a spot of light, moving coincident with the ship.

PPI: Plan Position Indicator, a kind of thin television screen with concentric range circles, ship's radar at centre, the same as any radar screen, but it *never* detected the periscopes of the U-boats!

APPENDIX VII: **THE ENIGMA MACHINE**
Royal Naval Museum Factsheet No. 100

The Enigma machine was invented by the Germans in 1918. It was first patented in 1919, and adopted by the German Navy in 1926, German Army in 1928 and German Air Force in 1935. It was also used by the railways and other government departments. From then until 1939, and throughout the war, successive refinements were made to the Enigma machine.

What is the Enigma machine? The Enigma is an electro-mechanical device which scrambles a plain text message into a ciphered text. It was used solely to encipher and decipher messages. It consisted of a keyboard of 26 letters in the pattern of a normal German typewriter, but with no keys for numerals or punctuation. Behind the keyboard was a lampboard made up of 26 small circular windows, each bearing a letter in the same pattern as the keyboard, which could light up one at a time. Behind the lampboard is the scrambler unit consisting of a fixed wheel at each end, and a central space for three rotating wheels. If a key was pressed on the keyboard any other letter could light up, and the sequence would only repeat itself after 16,900 (26 x 25 x 26) keyings, when the inner mechanism returned to the same position.

Messages were limited to a maximum of 250 letters to avoid this recurrence, which might otherwise have helped the British code-breakers. Thus potentially the number of ciphertext alphabets was vast – and this led German military authorities to believe in the absolute security of this cipher system.

The code-breakers of Hut 6 at Bletchley Park, a stately home 40 miles north of London, made a great breakthrough on 22 May 1940, when they broke the Luftwaffe cipher of the Enigma machine. The code-breakers were a group of scientists, mathematicians and chess-masters. They succeeded by using the first British-built 'Bombe', an electro-mechanical device which could do hundreds of computations every minute, to break the Luftwaffe's 'Red' key. This meant that all the Luftwaffe's operational and administrative traffic could be read, despite the added security devices built into the Enigmas in preparation for the assault on the west.

On 9 May 1941, HMS *Bulldog* forced *U-110* to surrender south of Greenland and a naval party was able to board the submarine and seize the Enigma cipher machine and codebooks. These would enable the British code-breakers at Bletchley Park to decipher signals sent between the U-boats and their Headquarters near Paris, so that convoys could avoid U-boat concentrations. However the Germans then developed a modified Enigma machine called M4, which baffled the code-breakers from the beginning of 1942, because of the additional rotor which it used.

On 30 October 1942, Lieutenant Tony Fasson, Able Seaman Colin Grazier and Canteen Assistant Tommy Brown from the destroyer HMS *Petard* seized an M4 Enigma machine and its key settings from the sinking *U-559*, after it had been scuttled by destroyers 70 miles off Egypt. The men passed the machine to safety, but Fasson and Grazier were unable to escape before the U-boat sank. For their actions Fasson and Grazier received the George Cross; Brown received the George Medal, the youngest recipient for this decoration, as it was then discovered that he had been under age when he'd first joined up. They did not receive the Victoria Cross as they had not acted in the face of the enemy.

It took three weeks for the machine to reach Bletchley Park, and on Sunday, 13 December 1942, Bletchley Park code-breakers finally cracked the Enigma cipher used by Admiral Dönitz to communicate with his U-boats in the Atlantic. By using the fourth rotor in the neutral position it made the M4 Enigma machine equivalent to the three rotor Enigma machine used by shore weather stations. The cryptanalysts (code-breakers) learned that the four-letter indicators for regular U-boat messages, were the same as the three-letter indicators for weather messages that same day, except for an extra letter. Therefore, once a daily key was found for a weather message, the fourth rotor had to be tested only in 26 positions (the number of keys the Enigma machine had), to find the full four letter key. This gave Hut Eight code-breakers at Bletchley Park little difficulty.

Later that same day solutions of the four-rotor Enigma U-boat key, called Shark, started to emerge. In the afternoon Hut Eight telephoned the Submarine Tracking Room to report the breakthrough. In an hour of this news the first intercept came through and revealed the position of fifteen U-boats in the Atlantic. Other intercepts arrived in an endless stream until the early hours of the next morning. The breaking of the code enabled the Admiralty's Submarine Tracking Room to once again route British convoys away from the German U-boat concentrations, and halved sinkings of British vessels in January/February 1943.

One naval officer who worked at the Admiralty wrote of how "we used to wait breathlessly for the electronic machines at Bletchley to get the answers and then we would get a phone call saying they had it out and in no time at all the new U-boat positions were plotted on the chart. We had every move and every order direct from Dönitz."

BLETCHLEY PARK –THE BEST KEPT SECRET OF WORLD WAR II
Captain R. J. Schlaff, USN, Ret'd

Winston Churchill called them "the geese that laid the golden eggs and never cackled." The geese were the code-breakers at Bletchley Park. The eggs were translated solutions of coded messages transmitted by the German High Command to Hitler's forces during World War II. They were received secretly by Allied commanders throughout the war. Declaring them "of priceless value," Dwight D. Eisenhower said after the D-Day invasion at Normandy that they had "saved thousands of British and American lives."

How did it happen? Operating from 'Room 40' of the Old Building of the Admiralty in London, British code-breakers had earned legendary fame for their efforts in the First World War. As far back as 1917, they had solved the most famous cryptogram of all time – the 'Zimmermann Telegram'. From that, President Woodrow Wilson, who had been working to keep America out of the war in Europe, learned from the words of the German Foreign Secretary Arthur Zimmermann that U-boats were about to begin unrestricted warfare against shipping in the Atlantic, and that the Germans were promising parts of Texas, Arizona and New Mexico to Mexico in exchange for help if the Americans entered the war.

On the eve of World War II the code-breakers had become the Government Code and Cipher School (GC&CS) and were expanding in anticipation of the coming conflict. They had been highly successful in reading important diplomatic codes, and had some success with the easier military ones.

But the tougher German military codes had eluded them. This was attributed to the fact that German messages were encoded by a machine called Enigma.

Code-breakers in Poland had duplicated the machine and, knowing that their own country was about to be invaded, had given one to the British. By studying its operation they determined that even the earliest models allowed some 17,000 permutations for every letter typed.

The Germans considered these machine codes unbreakable. In 1974, when German Admiral Karl Dönitz was told how the Allies had cracked his U-boat codes, he left the distinct impression he simply did not believe it. Many Britons also considered the machine codes unbreakable. But the Munich crisis in September 1938 had made it abundantly clear that a determined effort was going to be necessary. So, with only meager increases in funding and personnel, the code-breakers went searching for larger, safer, and more secure working spaces.

They settled on a 56-acre site near the little town of Bletchley, Buckinghamshire, some 47 miles north-west of London. First settled by the Romans it had passed through a series of Bishops, Lords and Dukes until eventually it was but a small part of the estate of a wealthy Etonian barrister. It was a decidedly country estate with its rolling meadows, lush pastures, green gardens, tall trees and a cricket field that had witnessed numerous country fairs. The property also lay beside the major north-south, east-west railways and was easily reached by the well-travelled road from London.

In addition, it was midway between Oxford and Cambridge universities, where the mathematicians so essential to code breaking could be recruited. A short tree-lined footpath from the railway station into the park can still be walked. There also remains evidence of a tunnel leading from the station to Bletchley Park. This would have allowed visiting VIPs to arrive and depart without attracting attention. Churchill, for example, is officially reported to have visited only once. Yet some former workers claim to have seen him there many times.

· In the grounds was a pseudo-Gothic manor house simply called 'The Mansion'. Constructed in the 1870s, it became code-breaker headquarters. Eventually, some 12,000 men and women were assigned eight-hour shifts, 24 hours a day, 7 days a week, throughout the war. Wooden huts, hastily erected to accommodate the overflow of code-breakers from the mansion, were shielded by brick walls added for bomb protection. The site was never actually attacked though a jettisoned bomb did move one building off its foundation. The next morning the building was lifted back into place, and work continued.

Most of those who worked at Bletchley were unaware of what was really going on. They were told nothing they did not 'need to know'. They performed their assigned tasks in their assigned huts with very little knowledge of what was happening even in the hut next door. In fact, in the autumn of 1992 at an 'Enigma Symposium', some 300 'Old Bletchleyites' listened spellbound as they were told for the first time just exactly what it was they had been doing and what they had achieved. They learned that the coded radio messages transmitted by the Germans had been intercepted by 'Y Service' listening posts located throughout Great Britain and around the globe. One former operator of a 'Y Service' intercept station explained, "To almost any frequency the operator tuned his receiver he heard a medley of Morse emanating from an uncountable variety of transmitters." The messages were then logged and forwarded to Bletchley. Some arrived by telegraph while others came in pouches carried by the hundreds of motorcycles that passed daily through the guarded rear gate. Some even arrived by carrier pigeon.

The process of decoding and translating was enormously complex and time-consuming. But it had to be performed quickly for the results to be of immediate value. This led to the design and development of machines to speed each process. One device called 'Colossus' was installed at Bletchley in 1943 and is now regarded as the world's first programmable, electronic computer.

Of course, it wasn't called a 'computer' as that word had not taken on its new meaning. It was thought of more as the 'universal machine' envisaged by Bletchley Park's very own Cambridge mathematician, Alan Turing, whose ideas eventually condensed exactly into what was to become the computer. So, in addition to being the site of some of the greatest code-breaking in modern history, Bletchley Park can also justly claim the title of 'Birthplace of the Modern Computer Industry'.

Once decrypted, messages code-named Ultra were delivered by hand in locked boxes to a select audience that included Prime Minister Winston Churchill and President Franklin Roosevelt. Messages for commanders were sent to Special Liaison Units located at the Headquarters of the major Allied staffs. But they went first by secure landlines to radio transmitters located away from Bletchley Park. This was to prevent the Germans from locating the transmitters with their direction finders and identifying the location of 'Britain's Best Kept Secret'.

Just how productive were they? In 1978, at a conference held in Bad Godesburg, Germany, it was reported that the British Public Records Office has 324,000 decrypted Navy messages that were intercepted between 25 June 1941 and 5 January 1945. Ultra messages sent to the Army and Air Force totalled 48,000 between 18 November 1943 and 24 March 1945.

Ultra intelligence supplied by Bletchley Park played an important role in virtually every major conflict in World War II including the evacuation of Dunkirk and the Battle of Britain in 1940; the defeat of General Erwin Rommel's Afrika Korps in North Africa and the sinking of the German battlecruiser *Scharnhorst* in 1943; and the Normandy invasion on D-Day in 1944. It was even used to warn Stalin that he was about to be invaded by the Germans in June 1941, a warning he did not believe and chose to ignore. But it was the Battle of the

Atlantic that kept the code-breakers challenged throughout the entire war. And it was there that casualties mounted so quickly when the code-breakers were unable to find keys to the codes.

For Churchill, this battle "was the dominating factor all through the war... and everything happening elsewhere depended ultimately on its outcome." The Allies knew that an Atlantic lifeline was vital to Britain's survival during the first years of the war, and as casualties mounted and ships were being destroyed faster than they could be built, code-breakers at Bletchley Park attempted to keep pace with decoding German messages. As Ultra became more advanced, code-breakers were able to read many of the instructions sent to many U-boats and to identify their locations. A lack of manpower and cipher machines made it difficult to achieve quick results in the Atlantic, but by mid-1943, Allied forces halted U-boat domination and prevented German attempts to block sea routes.

Although some Ultra intelligence had long been sent regularly to the United States, it was not until early in 1941 that there were any Americans at Bletchley Park. Their initial contribution was one of the six 'Purple' machines they had constructed after cracking the Japanese cipher – another success story of code breaking. Americans at Bletchley included William Bundy who went on to become Assistant Secretary of State and Editor of *Foreign Affairs*; Alfred Friendly, who became Managing Editor of *The Washington Post*; and Lewis Powell, who became a US Supreme Court Justice.

But the most lasting legacy of the earliest group of Americans to arrive is probably the tennis court which is still in use today. When Winston Churchill visited in the late summer of 1941 he noticed Americans playing baseball on the old croquet lawn. He thought they were playing the English game called 'rounders', which he considered a girls' game. He asked whether there weren't other forms of recreation available. Told there were no other sporting facilities, Churchill pointed to an old maze and instructed that tennis courts be built "there!" They were, and they are still there.

Next to the tennis courts and in front of the Mansion is a circular driveway. Throughout the war some 70 camouflaged trucks were parked there. Each morning their engines were started; they were fuelled, and left parked – empty. Although few knew it, they were to be used only in the event of an evacuation. They were to carry the code-breakers and their equipment to Liverpool where a ship was ready to take them to America. The vacant third floor of New York's Rockefeller Center was prepared to provide a safe haven.

The fact that Churchill's geese "never cackled" remains one of their most astonishing legacies. Secrecy was of the utmost importance because the slightest suspicion that codes were being broken would have caused the Germans to change them. The British took the matter most seriously. More than one British employee told the story of a recruiting interview ending with a security officer placing his revolver on the table beside them, saying, "If you ever speak a word of any of this, I personally shall shoot you..."

But it was the British Official Secrets Act that demanded continued silence even when the war was over. The Act dictates secrecy for some events for 30 years, 50 years or sometimes even forever. So it wasn't until 1974 that the former officer in charge of the security and dissemination of Ultra messages, Group Captain Winterbotham, RAF, wrote *The Ultra Secret* (HarperCollins, New York, 1974) and told the story of those things that could be revealed after 30 years. This book was the first to disclose to the world the secrets of Bletchley Park. It also revealed some of the secrets for the first time to many of the people who had worked there.

A walk in the grounds of Bletchley Park today enables you to see it as it was. Most of the buildings are still there. The Enigma cipher machine and a complete rebuild of the 'Colossus' are also on display. Two rooms of the mansion are dedicated to the life and work of Winston Churchill, who personally supported the efforts of code-breakers at Bletchley Park during the war. And although for fifty years following the end of the war there was absolutely no acknowledgment that anything at all ever happened there, visitors are now welcome, and Bletchley Park's history is now on proud display. The legacy of the code-breakers speaks foremost to the value of individual hard work. And while it highlights the utility of intellect, education, and training, it emphasizes the multiplied benefits of teamwork – by man, woman and machine. Perhaps 'The Few' of 1940 to whom so much is owed by so many, are not as few as we've thought.

The Bletchley Park Trust was established in 1992 to prevent demolition of the former code breaking buildings and establish them as museums of intelligence, cryptology, and computing in addition to radar, air traffic and telecommunications which also have ties to Bletchley Park. Trust members want to promote the national and international significance of 'Britain's Best Kept Secret' and preserve it as a tribute to the successes achieved by intellect and teamwork.

APPENDIX VIII:
SHIPS STRUCK BY GERMAN AIR-TO-SURFACE MISSILES

Losses and damage sustained by Allied shipping to German Air Force air-to-surface missiles, the HS 293 and Fritz-X, launched by Dornier 217s and Heinkel 111s:

25.8.1943	Sloop	*Bideford*	British	Damaged	HS 293
25.8.1943	Destroyer	*Waveney*	British	Damaged	HS 293
25.8.1943	Sloop	*Landguard*	British	Damaged	HS 293
27.8.1943	Sloop	*Egret*	British	Sunk	HS 293
27.8.1943	Destroyer	*Athabascan*	Canadian	Damaged	HS 293
9.9.1943	Battleship	*Roma*	Italian	Sunk	Fritz-X
9.9.1943	Battleship	*Italia*	Italian	Damaged	Fritz-X
9.9.1943	Destroyer	??	Italian	Damaged	Fritz-X
9.9.1943	Destroyer	??	Italian	Damaged	Fritz-X
11.9.1943	Cruiser	*Savannah*	American	Damaged	Fritz-X
11.9.1943	Cruiser	*Philadelphia*	American	Damaged	Fritz-X
13.9.1943	Cruiser	*Uganda*	British	Damaged	Fritz-X
13.9.1943	Destroyer	*Loyal*	British	Damaged	Fritz-X
13.9.1943	Destroyer	*Nubian*	British	Damaged	Fritz-X
14.9.1943	Cargo Ship	??	??	Sunk	Fritz-X
??	Cargo Ship	??	??	Sunk	Fritz-X
??	Battleship	*Warspite*	British	Damaged	Fritz-X
??	Battleship	*Valiant*	British	Damaged	Fritz-X
30.9.1943	Landing Craft	*LST 79*	British	Sunk	HS 293
??	Landing Craft	*LCT 2231*	British	Sunk	HS 293
4.10.1943	Cargo Ship	*Fort Fitzgerald*	British	Sunk	HS 293
4.10.1943	Cargo Ship	*Samite*	British	Damaged	HS 293
4.10.1943	Cargo Ship	??	??	Damaged	HS 293
4.10.1943	Cargo Ship	??	??	Damaged	HS 293
21.10.1943	Cargo Ship	*Saltwick*	British	Sunk	HS 293
11.11.1943	Cargo Ship	*Birchbank*	British	Sunk	HS 293
11.11.1943	Cargo Ship	*Indian Prince*	British	Sunk	HS 293
11.11.1943	Cargo Ship	*Carlier*	French	Sunk	HS 293
11.11.1943	Tanker	*Nivose*	French	Sunk	HS 293
11.11.1943	Destroyer	*Rockwood*	British	Damaged	HS 293

13.11.1943	Destroyer	*Dulverton*	British	Sunk	HS 293
23.1.1944	Destroyer	*Janus*	British	Sunk	HS 293
23.1.1944	Destroyer	*Jervis*	British	Damaged	HS 293
26.1.1944	Cargo Ship	*Sam. Hunt'don*	American	Sunk	HS 293
26.1.1944	Destroyer	*Plunkett*	British	Damaged	HS 293
29.1.1944	Cruiser	*Spartan*	British	Sunk	HS 293
29.1.1944	Cargo Ship	??	??	Sunk	HS 293
12.2.1944	Landing Craft	??	??	Sunk	HS 293
12.2.1944	Cargo Ship	??	??	Damaged	HS 293
15.2.1944	Destroyer	*Herb. C. Jones*	American	Damaged	HS 293
15.2.1944	Cargo Ship	??	??	Sunk	HS 293
15.2.1944	Cargo Ship	*Elihu Yale*	American	Sunk	HS 293
15.2.1944	Landing Craft	*LCT 32*	American	Sunk	HS 293
19.2.1944	Cargo Ship	??	??	Damaged	HS 293
19.2.1944	Cargo Ship	??	??	Damaged	HS 293
19.2.1944	Destroyer	??	??	Damaged	HS 293
25.2.1944	Destroyer	*Inglefield*	British	Sunk	HS 293
20.4.1944	Cargo Ship	*El Biar*	French	Sunk	HS 293
??	Cargo Ship	*Royal Star*	British	Sunk	HS 293
??	Destroyer	*Lansdale*	American	Sunk	HS 293
20.4.1944	Cargo Ship	*Samite*	British	Damaged	HS 293
20.4.1944	Cargo Ship	*Stephen Austin*	British	Damaged	HS 293
8.6.1944	Frigate	*Lawford*	British	Sunk	HS 293
13.6.1944	Destroyer	*Boadicea*	British	Sunk	HS 293
8.8.1944	Cargo Ship	??	??	Sunk	HS or FX
??	Destroyer	??	??	Damaged	HS or FX
11.8.1944	Cargo Ship	??	??	Damaged	HS or FX
15.8.1944	Cargo Ship	??	??	Sunk	HS or FX
15.8.1944	Landing Craft	*LST 282*	American	Sunk	HS or FX
15.8.1944	Destroyer	*Le Long*	American	Damaged	HS or FX
15.8.1944	Landing Craft	*LST 312*	American	Damaged	HS or FX
15.8.1944	Landing Craft	*LST 384*	American	Damaged	HS or FX

APPENDIX IX: STANDARD OIL/ROYAL DUTCH SHELL EXPORTS TO I. G. FARBEN GROUP

In 1992, while researching for his book *In the Footsteps of a Flying Boot*, concerning his escape and evasion, Arthur Horning, a former 91st Bombardment Group navigator, 8th USAAF (Bassingbourne, Cambridgeshire), came across the following excerpt which confirmed his report of gasoline being supplied to the Germans during wartime. The excerpt is from the book *Trading with the Enemy* (Delacourt Press, New York, 1983), written by Charles Higham (biographer and former *New York Times* writer):

In 1946, the young, very sharp lawyer James Stewart Martin, of the Department of Justice's investigative team, came to Europe from Washington.

At the I. G. Farben headquarters in Frankfurt, Martin discovered files that confirmed beliefs that Schmitz [Hermann Schmitz, president of Farben and director of Deutsche Landesbank] had laid out plans for a conquered world in which America would join in triumph. He began to understand why Schmitz and the others at I. G. Farben had turned against Hitler.

It was clear that Hitler wanted to attack the United States with Goering's bombers when sufficiently long-distance aircraft were developed. But Schmitz was loyal to his American colleagues, preferring to maintain the alliances in perpetuity. These alliances could be sustained if Himmler and/or the German Generals ran the Third Reich. They would be content with Schmitz's idea of a negotiated peace.

Further evidence came to light showing the continuing connection between Schmitz and the United States during the war. In 1943 a magazine article by R. T. Haslam of Standard Oil appeared in *The Petroleum Times*. It stated that the relationship with I. G. Farben had proved to be advantageous to the United States government. A special report of I. G. Farben emphatically denied this, pointing out the innumerable benefits that Germany had obtained from her American friends, including the use of tetraethyl, without which the war effort would have been impossible, and the supply of which had been approved by the United States War Department.

The report said: "At the outbreak of war we were completely prepared from a technical point of view. We obtained standards not only from our own experiences but also from those of General Motors and other big manufacturers of automobiles." The report also revealed that Standard Oil had sold $20 million worth of mineral oil products, including airplane benzene, to I. G. Farben (the huge chemical conglomerate whose products included Zyklon B gas pellets for the death camps).

The report concluded: "The fact that we actually succeeded in buying these quantities demanded by the German government from Standard Oil Company and the Royal Dutch Shell group and importing them into Germany was only because of the support of Standard Oil Company."

Even more damning, Martin found that I. G. Farben had placed a 50 million mark credit to Karl Lindemann's Standard subsidiary in Germany in the Deutsch Landesbank, wholly owned by I. G. Farben with Hermann Schmitz as chairman, in 1944.

Thus, it was clear that Standard's business in Nazi Germany was open as usual and that its German subsidiary was being paid handsomely for pre-war agreements.

Martin and his team were hampered at every turn. He wrote in his book *All Honourable Men*:

'We had not been stopped in Germany by German business. We had been stopped in Germany by American business. The forces that stopped us had operated from the United States but had not operated in the open. We were not stopped by a law in Congress, by an Executive Order of the President, or even by a change in policy approved by the President... in short, whatever it was that had stopped us was not 'the government.' But it clearly had command of channels through which the government normally operates.

The relative powerlessness of governments in the growing economic power is, of course, not new... national governments stood on the sidelines while bigger operators arranged the world's affairs.'

APPENDIX X: **NAVAL OBITUARIES**

CAPTAIN A. J. BAKER-CRESSWELL

From *The Times*, London, 6 March 1997

Captain A. J. Baker-Cresswell, DSO, wartime destroyer commander, died on 4 March aged 96. He was born on 2 February 1901.

Through his quick thinking during a U-boat attack on a convoy in the North Atlantic in May 1941, Joe Baker-Cresswell made an immeasurable contribution to the Royal Navy's victory in the Battle of the Atlantic. When the U-boat *U-110* was brought to the surface by Baker-Cresswell's ship *Bulldog* and abandoned by her crew, it was a natural instinct to sink her by gunfire or ramming, before picking up survivors.

But just as one of *Bulldog*'s escorting destroyers was getting up speed to accomplish the latter, Baker-Cresswell suddenly remembered his staff college lecture on the capture of valuable ciphers from the light cruiser *Magdeburg* in 1914. To the surprise of his fellow escort commanders, he ordered all offensive action to cease and instead had the German submarine boarded. Among the resulting haul of highly classified documents and equipment recovered was the German Enigma machine which enabled high-grade 'officer only' *Kriegsmarine* signal traffic to be read. It was one of the vital blows struck in the battle against the U-boats.

Addison Joe Baker-Cresswell was educated at Gresham's School, Holt, and joined the Royal Navy in 1918. Specialising in navigation, he was promoted to Commander in 1937 and the outbreak of war found him on General Wavell's staff in Cairo.

From 1940 he was on convoy escort duty and was to be involved, in one way or another, in anti-submarine warfare until the end of the war. On 9 May 1941 he was commanding the destroyer *Bulldog* as senior officer of the escort group covering convoy OB 318 in the North Atlantic south of Iceland. OB 318 had already been attacked by a number of U-boats, among which was *U-110*, commanded by Kapitänleutnant Fritz-Julius Lemp, whose sinking of the liner *Athenia* on 1 September 1939 had precipitated the U-boat war.

With Leutnant Kuppisch in *U-94* Lemp had already scored some striking success against OB 318, sinking two of its merchant ships. But in a momentary lapse of concentration he failed to perceive the danger from the convoy's escorts and was himself attacked by the destroyers *Bulldog, Broadway* and *Aubretia*, the last of which wreaked terminal damage on the submarine, with a well-placed pattern of depth charges. With hydroplanes and rudder wrecked, all power and lighting out and the water surging in, Lemp ordered all tanks to be blown and the stricken *U-110* lurched to the surface.

Baker-Cresswell ordered his gun crews to open fire and set course to ram, as did the captain of *Broadway*. Lemp, meanwhile, told his crew to abandon ship as 4.7-inch, 3-inch and pom-pom shells burst about his stricken craft.

It was at that point that Baker-Cresswell had the happy inspiration not to administer the *coup-de-grace*, but to board the hapless enemy. Ordering his own and *Broadway*'s gun crews to check their fire, he had *Bulldog*'s seaboat launched. But with foresight he had the German prisoners picked out of the water first, and hustled below so that they should not see what was happening.

Lemp, however, could see exactly what was intended and, in the confusion, swam back to *U-110* with one of his petty officers, perhaps with some idea of manning her gun, or of going below and destroying the top-secret material. Baker-Cresswell, who had no intention of allowing himself to come under fire from an enemy craft whose life he had already spared, ordered fire to be opened again with the Lewis gun, and the two men, who could be seen in the vicinity of the U-boat's deck gun, were hit and disappeared over the side. Lemp was never seen again.

Bulldog's whaler now closed with the submarine and Sub-Lieutenant Balme, who was in charge of the boat, went below and discovered unsuspected riches of codebooks, charts showing German minefields and, above all, the invaluable naval Enigma machine. The list of settings for it was found in Lemp's cabin, making this one of the most important naval intelligence breakthroughs of the war. This priceless acquisition was ferried back to HMS *Bulldog*.

From that moment until February 1942 high grade German naval signals traffic could be read without delay at the decoding facility at Bletchley Park. There was then a gap when the Germans introduced extra rotors to the Enigma. But when HMS *Petard* captured the new rotors from *U-559* in the Mediterranean in November 1942, the flow of signals could be decyphered once more.

Once the signals office of *U-110* had been cleared of valuable material, the U-boat was taken in tow by *Bulldog*. The aim was to tow her into Reykjavik, but during that night a gale sprang up and she suddenly started sinking by the stern. Reluctantly, Baker-Cresswell ordered the towline to be slipped. But the accident was perhaps a lucky one. The Germans heard that *U-110* had been sunk and throughout the war never realised that the Enigma she carried had been compromised.

In Britain, too, all records of the event were expunged, even from the official naval history. *The War at Sea* (1954), by Captain S. W. Roskill, made no mention of it. At the investiture for his DSO, Baker-Cresswell was told by King George VI that his feat was one of the most significant events of the war at sea, and but for the necessity for security, a higher award would have been made. It was only in the 1980s, when the secret of Ultra intelligence was allowed to be published, that Baker-Cresswell's exploit entered the public domain.

After *Bulldog*, Baker-Cresswell was put in charge of training the crews of escort vessels from the converted steam yacht *Philante*, and was subsequently Chief of Staff to Sir Max Horton, Commander-in-Chief Western Approaches. His last wartime appointment was as Senior Officer Far Eastern Escort Vessels. After the war he served as Deputy Director of Naval Intelligence, retiring from the Navy in 1947.

In retirement in Northumberland, he threw himself into local public service as a JP and as chairman of Alnwick Infirmary. He was appointed High Sheriff of Northumberland in 1963. He loved country sports, particularly fishing.

In 1926 he married Rona, from Auckland. She and a son and daughter survive him. Another daughter predeceased him.

CAPTAIN JOHN BOUTWOOD
From the *Daily Telegraph*, London, 10 August 1993

Captain John Boutwood, who has died aged 94, was Captain of the anti-aircraft cruiser HMS *Curaçoa*, which in October 1942 was run down and sunk by the liner *Queen Mary*.

The two giant 80,000-ton 'Queens' – the *Mary* and the *Elizabeth* – were being used as troop-ships, carrying more than 15,000 servicemen across from America on each voyage. They crossed the Atlantic alone, relying on their great speed of nearly 30 knots, constant zigzagging and evasive routing to keep them clear of U-boats. They were provided with escorts only for the last part of their voyages.

On the morning of 2 October 1942 *Queen Mary* was met off the north coast of Ireland by *Curaçoa* (which was to provide close anti-aircraft cover) and four destroyers as anti-submarine escorts. Boutwood had escorted *Queen Mary* before and knew from previous conversations with her Captain what zigzag pattern he would most likely be using. But he was not informed – nor did he inquire – which leg *Queen Mary* was on.

Queen Mary slowed by two or three knots to allow *Curaçoa*, whose full speed was about 25 knots, to keep up. *Curaçoa*'s proper station was close astern of *Queen Mary*, and Boutwood intended to reach it by first taking station ahead and then gradually dropping astern. *Queen Mary* was passing close to and fro across *Curaçoa*'s stern as she zigzagged, but Boutwood was still not sure of her exact movements. There was a dramatic near miss just after 1.30 p.m., when *Curaçoa* was so close she was almost out of sight under *Queen Mary*'s port bow, and *Queen Mary*'s Officer of the Watch ordered hard-a-starboard. On hearing the order *Queen Mary*'s Captain went on to the bridge; told that he was too close to the cruiser, he ordered the zigzag to be carried out, saying: "You needn't worry about that fellow... He'll keep out of your way."

Just after 2 p.m. *Curaçoa* was on *Queen Mary*'s starboard bow, and the next 'zig' was to starboard. But then the Officer of the Watch realised that *Curaçoa* was much too close and ordered hard-a-port. Boutwood, who had taken over his ship from his Officer of the Watch, did his best to avoid collision. But it was too late.

Queen Mary's giant bow caught *Curaçoa* about a third of her length from aft and sliced her clean in two. *Queen Mary* was badly damaged forward and slowed to ten knots, but it was forbidden to stop because of the risk of U-boats. The after-part of *Curaçoa* sank almost at once. The forward part righted itself for a short time before sinking. Destroyers picked up 72 of *Curaçoa*'s company of 410. Boutwood was one of two ship's officers and the only officer on the bridge to survive.

The Admiralty did not officially announce the loss until May 1945, when the European war was over. But in these matters the Navy is like a whispering gallery, and *Curaçoa*'s fate was soon common knowledge.

The Admiralty enquiry exonerated him, and he was appointed in command of the 'Algerine' class minesweeper HMS *Fantome*. On commissioning in December 1942 he cleared the lower deck and told the ship's company to forget whatever they might have heard about the *Curaçoa*. If the Admiralty had no confidence in him he would not be their captain. They had a job to do.

In 1943 Boutwood took *Fantome* out to the Mediterranean, where he commanded the 12th Minesweeping Flotilla. On 9 May the 12th and 14th Minesweeping Flotillas began Operation 'Antidote', to clear a passage of some 600 miles around Cape Bon and through the Sicilian Channel. Despite hundreds of enemy anti-sweeping devices, the minesweepers swept over 250 mines, clearing the Mediterranean for the Allies. *Fantome* herself had her stern blown off on 20 May 1943 and was towed to Bizerta, where she was declared a total loss. Boutwood was awarded the DSO.

Boutwood shifted his pennant to HMS *Fly* and then to HMS *Albacore*, and commanded the minesweeping forces for the landings in Sicily in July 1943 and Salerno in September. Later, as Senior Officer (Minesweeping) Mediterranean, he planned and organized minesweeping at Anzio and the south of France and the clearance of huge numbers of mines from the Adriatic, the Ionian Sea and the Dardenelles. He was Mentioned in Dispatches for his part at Salerno.

The official inquiry [into the *Curaçoa* loss] opened in June 1945. If blame fell on *Queen Mary* then her owners (Cunard) would have to compensate the families of those who had lost their lives. If *Curaçoa* was to blame the dead men's relatives would only receive naval widows' pensions. The inquiry found the liner blameless and the collision solely due to *Curaçoa*'s negligence. The Admiralty appealed to the Court of Appeal, which found *Curaçoa* two thirds to blame, *Queen Mary* one third. The House of Lords upheld that judgement.

John Wilfrid Boutwood was born on 31 March 1899 and joined the Navy in 1913, going to Osborne and Dartmouth. His first experience of minesweeping was as a Sub-Lieutenant in 1918 in HMS *Fraser Eaves*.

He specialised in gunnery in 1925 and served in the destroyers HMS *Broke*, HMS *Keith* and HMS *Whitby* and the cruisers HMS *Cambrian* and HMS *Berwick* on the China Station and in HMS *Emerald*. He was a qualified diver and while serving in HMS *Iron Duke* in Scapa Flow early in the war he dived on the wreck of the battleship HMS *Royal Oak*, sunk in October 1939.

In 1944 he went to Rosyth as Chief of Staff to Flag Officer Scotland and Northern Ireland. His last appointment before retirement in 1950 was Captain of HMS *Royal Arthur*, the Petty Officers' Leadership School.

Boutwood remained tight-lipped about *Curaçoa*, but certainly did not agree that he was two-thirds to blame. In a tape-recording made some 10 years ago he said he "could sleep at nights without any feeling of conscience or shame about it."

He was married, and had a son and a daughter.

COMMANDER FRANCIS BRODRICK

By Michael Back, Secretary, HM Ships *Beagle, Boadicea* & *Bulldog* Association.

From newsletter of 28 May 1983

Commander Francis Cumberland Brodrick, Royal Navy, the Commanding Officer of HMS *Boadicea* from 1942 to 1944, died peacefully at his home at Pladen, near Rye, Sussex, on 5 September 1982, aged 75.

When I joined the *Boadicea* in the summer of 1942, Lieutenant Commander (as he then was) Brodrick seemed to me the very personification of a Royal Navy destroyer captain. He was a man of impressive appearance and few words, and a superb seaman whose shiphandling earned him a reputation throughout our Escort Groups.

His ship's company had absolute trust in him, and in our different ways we all learnt from him. When he was on the bridge everyone felt safe, and everyone who was there will always remember his calm coolness in a brilliant surface action against two destroyers off Oran in November 1942.

He commanded destroyers from the first day of the war to the last, first in HMS *Brilliant* and then in the *Hurricane, Boadicea* and, lastly the *Nubian*. He took part in some of the first destroyer actions of the war in *Brilliant* in the English Channel, and one of the last when in the *Nubian* he sunk a Japanese warship off Sumatra in the summer of 1945.

Although he was awarded a Belgian Croix de Guerre after shooting down a German aircraft, saving a very considerable number of invaluable merchant ships, tugs and barges from German forces during a 'Cloak and Dagger' operation at Antwerp in May 1940, and was Mentioned in Dispatches while commanding *Brilliant*, it seems extraordinary that he never received a British decoration. Those most close to him believe that his exceptional modesty and reserve were largely accountable for this.

He was a Captain who was always fair and who always cared for his ship's company, and we always knew this. It was a source of great pleasure and pride to us that Commander Brodrick was one of the earliest supporters of this Association, and one of the twelve who attended our first reunion in December 1968, as well as many subsequently.

Early last summer, Lieutenant H. E. Howting, his Gunner (T) in *Boadicea*, had personally prepared an extremely attractive carved wood shield of the ship's badge which he presented to the Commander at his home. He was clearly very touched and pleased. It was a timely presentation as his final illness was then becoming apparent.

Five former crew members of *Boadicea* attended Commander Brodrick's funeral in the Parish Church at Pladen, where he was laid to rest in a peaceful corner of the churchyard. Our deep sympathy goes out to his widow, Mrs Betty Brodrick, daughter Frances, sons Tim and Peter, and to all his family.

CAPTAIN SAM LOMBARD-HOBSON
From the *Daily Telegraph*, London, 22 January 2000
Officer whose command of a wartime corvette inspired his First Lieutenant, Nicholas Monsarrat, to write *The Cruel Sea*.

Captain Sam Lombard-Hobson, who has died aged 86, commanded the corvette HMS *Guillemot* during the Second World War; the ship and her experiences escorting convoys shaped the books later written by her First Lieutenant, Nicholas Monsarrat, RNVR.

There could well have been friction between Monsarrat and his captain. Lombard-Hobson was a career officer, straight RN, with little experience of the RNVR although, he said, "I like a few amateurs about the place. It reminds you that there is an outside world after all." Monsarrat was three years older, a convinced pre-war pacifist, who had just come from another corvette whose captain he loathed.

In fact, the two got on very well together. Lombard-Hobson found Monsarrat a highly intelligent and able officer, thoughtful for the sailors' welfare. As for Monsarrat, in *Three Corvettes* (published in 1945) he described Lombard-Hobson as "R.N., almost the naval officer of fiction; correct, resourceful, unfoolable, his handling of the ship a perpetual delight to watch."

Almost their only disagreement was over the title of *The Cruel Sea* (1951). When Monsarrat sent drafts to Lombard-Hobson to comment on, the latter insisted that it was not the sea but the war which was cruel. Many incidents in *The Cruel Sea* actually happened to *Guillemot*, including the moment when a captain faced a terrible dilemma: whether to stop and rescue survivors in the water or to go after the enemy. On the night of 15 March 1942, the destroyer HMS *Vortigern* was torpedoed off Cromer, Norfolk by an E-boat which had been lurking on the landward side of the convoy. *Guillemot* picked up two men but then obtained a radar contact and broke off to attack. Two E-boats were sunk and a third damaged, while the convoy of 52 merchant ships escaped unscathed. Ten more from *Vortigern* were rescued. The rest of her company of 134 were lost. Lombard-Hobson was mentioned in dispatches.

Samuel Richard Le Hunte Lombard was born on 23 February 1913. Like his father, he later had to take the additional name of Hobson under Irish laws of inheritance, and dropped the Lombard.

Sam went to Dartmouth as a cadet in 1926. When his father then died he was persuaded by his Lombard relations to resume the name, but Irish legislation prevented him dropping the Hobson. "Since that day," he said, "I have endured the not inconsiderable inconvenience of a double-barrelled name, with very little material gain in compensation."

His first ship in 1930 was the battleship HMS *Queen Elizabeth*, flagship of the Mediterranean Fleet. In 1934, he was one of three officers who took the trawler *Barnet* from Yarmouth, Norfolk out to Hong Kong. He then served in the cruiser HMS *Kent*, flagship of the China Fleet, and in the river gunboat HMS *Bee*, flagship of the Senior Officer Yangtze Flotilla.

Lombard-Hobson was Officer of the Watch when the destroyer HMS *Isis* ran aground on the Turkish coast in 1937. He had no doubt he was entirely to blame, but the court martial case against him was dismissed. His Captain was severely reprimanded. From 1937 to 1939, he was ADC to the Governor-General of New Zealand. He was then appointed First Lieutenant of the 1919-vintage destroyer HMS *Whitshed*, escorting Atlantic convoys. On 30 January 1940, *Whitshed*, the sloop HMS *Fowey* and a Sunderland of No 228 Squadron RAF sank *U-55* in the Western Approaches.

In May 1940, *Whitshed* landed demolition parties at the Dutch port of IJmuiden and was damaged in an air attack. She then took part in the evacuation of troops from Boulogne, coming alongside a crowded jetty amid scenes of utter chaos. However, companies of the Welsh and the Irish Guards marched on board in perfect order and *Whitshed* put to sea despite enemy fire. *Whitshed* then went to Dunkirk and took off more than 1,000 troops of the British Expeditionary Force. For has service in *Whitshed*, Lombard-Hobson was Mentioned in Dispatches.

On 31 July 1940 while carrying out an anti-shipping sweep off the Dutch coast, *Whitshed* was mined and badly damaged. Nearly half her company were killed or wounded. Her survivors commissioned the new 'Hunt' class destroyer HMS *Southdown*.

In July 1942 Lombard-Hobson had another command, the new 'Hunt' class destroyer HMS *Rockwood*, which joined the 5th Destroyer Flotilla at Alexandria in 1943. She then took part in Operation 'Husky', the invasion of Sicily, in July, and in the disastrous campaign in the Aegean, which began in September. Lacking air cover, the Royal Navy lost a cruiser and five destroyers. When the cruiser HMS *Carlisle* was crippled by a direct hit in the Scarpanto Strait between Rhodes and Crete on 9 October, *Rockwood* towed her 300 miles to Alexandria. Lombard-Hobson was Mentioned in Dispatches for the third time.

On the night of 11 November 1943 *Rockwood* was hit by an HS 293 glider bomb. It did not explode, but caused so much damage that *Rockwood* had to be towed into Turkish waters for repairs. She came home on one shaft but was then sold for scrap. Her active life had been 53 weeks. Lombard-Hobson was her first and only captain. For the rest of the war, he was on the Staff at HMS *King Alfred*, the RNVR officers' training establishment at Hove, Sussex.

After the war, he served on the staff at Gibraltar, commanded the destroyer HMS *Jutland* from 1947 to 1949, had two appointments in Naval Intelligence, and was Executive Officer of the cruiser HMS *Newcastle* in the Korean War from 1952 to 1953, when he was promoted to Captain and appointed OBE.

His final sea command was the frigate HMS *Apollo*, from 1957 to 1958. He was Naval Attache in Rome from 1960 to 1962, was appointed CVO in 1961, and ADC to the Queen in 1963. He retired in 1964 to become General Secretary of the Institute of Brewing. He was High Sheriff of Sussex in 1983.

During the war, 'Hunt' class ships would write to their namesake fox hunts, who generally responded with football boots and other comforts for the sailors. Lombard-Hobson wrote from *Southdown* to the Southdown Hunt but due to an oversight had no reply; so he wrote to the Southdown Bus Company. They were thrilled to know that a ship had been named after them. A party from the company visited the ship and *Southdown* was showered with football boots. Lombard-Hobson published his war memoirs, *A Sailor's War*, in 1983. He married, in 1944, Rosemary Beale-Browne; they had two daughters.

CAPTAIN HAROLD CHESTERMAN
From the *Daily Telegraph*, London, 13 February 1997
Officer whose experiences with the Gibraltar convoy OG 71 inspired Nicholas Monsarrat's *The Cruel Sea*.

Captain Harold Chesterman, who has died aged 79, played a part in winning the Battle of the Atlantic as one of that company of young Australian sea officers who came to this country in 1939 to serve in the Naval Reserve.

In 1941 Chesterman was First Lieutenant of the 'Flower' class corvette *Zinnia*, commanded by Lieutenant Commander Charles Cuthbertson RNR, on whom Nicholas Monsarrat based Lieutenant Commander Ericson, one of the main characters in his novel *The Cruel Sea*.

On 5 August 1941, *Zinnia* was escorting convoy SL 81, homeward bound from Freetown, Sierra Leone, when SS *Cape Rodney* was torpedoed by *U-75* west of Ireland. Chesterman led a party on board to try and save her by taking her in tow, but was unable to prevent her sinking on 9 August. He was Mentioned in Dispatches.

Later that month, *Zinnia* sailed as part of the escort for convoy OG 71, outward bound for Gibraltar. It was perfect summer weather, and the convoy was soon found by long-range Focke-Wulf Condor aircraft, which summoned up the U-boats.

A four-day running fight began on 19 August with the loss of the destroyer

Bath from the escort and four ships, including SS *Aquila*, torpedoed some 450 miles south-west of Land's End. She had on board a party of 21 Wrens and a naval nursing sister, who were all lost.

In all, the convoy lost nine ships, and another escort, *Zinnia*, which was torpedoed by *U-564* as dawn was breaking on 23 August and blew up with an explosion which rang around the convoy. Her back was broken, and she sank within 20 seconds. Cuthbertson and Chesterman were both thrown into the sea as the ship turned over. Chesterman swam for some time through thick oil before he found and clung to one of *Zinnia*'s smoke floats. He had given up, and decided to let himself drown, when he had a memory of his wife Caroline, and what life could still hold for him.

He struggled back to the surface and hung onto the smoke float again until he was picked up by a boat from *Campion*, another 'Flower' class in the escort. He and Cuthbertson were among only 17 survivors from *Zinnia*'s company of eighty-five.

Monsarrat, who was serving in another of OG 71's escorts, said that the Gibraltar convoy was his worst experience of the war, and he incorporated many of its events into *The Cruel Sea*. The loss of the *Sorrel* in the novel was based on *Zinnia*.

After such an experience, when they were both hauled aboard *Campion*, "passing blood and oil from both ends", Cuthbertson and Chesterman might have had enough of the Atlantic. But the pair were irrepressible. Within months, Cuthbertson had another corvette command, *Snowflake*, and Chesterman was delighted and flattered to be asked to be his No. 1 again.

Escorting Atlantic and Arctic convoys in the winter of 1941-42, *Snowflake* proved herself to be a ship whom an escort group commander could always rely on. She never broke down, but was always available to take her place in the screen, or to run down a U-boat contact, or round up a straggler.

In June 1942, when Cuthbertson was given a destroyer command, the Admiralty took the unusual step of promoting Chesterman to command the same ship in which he had been First Lieutenant. Under Chesterman, *Snowflake* escorted many of the large Atlantic convoys of the winter and spring of 1942-43. Over the months Chesterman worked up a special rapport with *Snowflake*'s 'chummy' ship *Sunflower* and her Canadian captain Lieutenant Commander Plomer, so that *Snowflake-Sunflower* became a famous anti-submarine duo. Some convoy reports even referred to them as *Snowflower* and *Sunflake*.

Both ships served in Escort Group B7, under the celebrated Commander Peter Gretton, and both took part in the 10-day battle around convoy ONS 5 in May 1943, which proved to be the turning point in the Allies' favour in the Battle of the Atlantic. Chesterman and Plomer were both awarded the DSC.

On 19 May, defending convoy SC 10, homeward bound from Halifax, Nova

Scotia, *Snowflake* joined with the destroyer *Duncan* in sinking *U-381*. Chesterman was awarded a Bar to his DSC.

Harold Geeves Chesterman was born on 28 February 1917 in Melbourne and educated at the Church of England Grammar School, Malvern, near Melbourne, and at HMS *Worcester*, the cadet training ship on the Thames.

He served with the Dominion Line and joined the RNR as a Midshipman in 1934. In September 1939 he was serving in the cruiser *Devonshire* in the Home Fleet.

In 1940, Chesterman served as a Sub-Lieutenant in the anti-submarine trawler *Kingston Turquoise*, before joining the 'Flower' class corvette *Burdock*, and then *Zinnia*. Chesterman spent the entire war, except for survivor's leave, at sea. After *Snowflake*, he commanded the corvette *Hurst Castle* until she was sunk in September 1944. From her, he went on to the destroyer *Ambuscade*, and, after the war, the frigates *Loch Achray* and *Loch Killisport*. He was awarded the Reserve Decoration and two Bars.

Returning to Australia, he joined the Australian Lighthouse Service, commanding vessels which carried out 4,000-mile voyages, tending buoys, lights and light vessels along the Great Barrier Reef and in the Coral Sea.

He was appointed MBE in 1982, and then started a successful practice as a nautical consultant, advising barristers on nautical matters.

Early in the war, Western Approaches Command, which fought the Battle of the Atlantic, was very unfashionable in the regular RN, and as a result was sent many failures from Scapa Flow, retired officers, and incompetents. When Chesterman and Cuthbertson commissioned *Zinnia*, they had to work six hours watch to watch, because her junior officers were so green.

Chesterman was a professional seaman to his fingertips. He had tremendous physical stamina, and was able to keep on his bridge for days at a time in all weathers.

In 1993 he attended the 50th anniversary celebrations of the Battle of the Atlantic, had dinner on board *Britannia*, and enjoyed reminiscing on television.

Harold Chesterman is survived by his wife Caroline, and two sons.

COMMANDER CHARLES CUTHBERTSON
From the *Daily Telegraph*, London, 13 April 1994

Commander Charles Cuthbertson, who has died aged 87, was the corvette captain in the Battle of Atlantic on whom Nicholas Monsarrat based Lieutenant Commander Ericson, one of the main characters in his novel *The Cruel Sea*.

The two men first met after the tragic passage of convoy OG 71, which had been outward bound to Gibraltar in August 1941, when Cuthbertson commanded the 'Flower' class corvette *Zinnia* and Monsarrat was First Lieutenant of

Campanula. The convoy – which Monsarrat afterwards called "my personal nightmare" – was attacked by U-boats and lost several ships including the *Aguila*, torpedoed and sunk with great loss of life 470 miles west of Land's End on 19 August 1941.

In the early hours of 23 August *Zinnia* was hit amidships by a torpedo from *U-564*. She broke in two and sank in seconds. Cuthbertson remained in the water, "rapidly approaching complete exhaustion and ready to meet my Maker", until he was picked up, covered in oil, by a whaler from *Campion*, another 'Flower' class corvette.

He still had his binoculars round his neck, and heard a sailor say: "Corblimey, he must be an officer, he's got a pair of glasses round his bleeding neck!" When he later applied to keep his binoculars as a souvenir, the Admiralty accused him of trying to steal them.

On *Campion*'s deck Cuthbertson could not stop himself shaking, but took care to explain that this was not because he was frightened, "but because I was so bloody cold!" Later he was found collapsed on the deck of *Campion*'s bathroom "with blood and oil fuel coming out of me at both ends." He was one of only 17 survivors from *Zinnia*'s company of 85.

In Gibraltar, Cuthbertson called on *Campanula*, where Monsarrat gave him a gin and tonic ("the only stuff that would stay down") and questioned him closely on what it was like to be torpedoed. In his post-war memoirs Monsarrat wrote that Ericson's character "was based, so far as looks, achievement and reputation were concerned, on Lieutenant Commander Cuthbertson".

Charles George Cuthbertson was born on 3 September 1906 and went to HMS *Worcester*, the training ship at Greenhithe on the Thames. He joined the Royal Naval Reserve as a probationary midshipman in January 1923, and the Union Castle Line as a cadet in September. He served in Union Castle ships around the world, while continuing his annual naval training. In 1939 he was second officer on the liner *Carnarvon Castle*, with the rank of Lieutenant Commander, RNR.

For the first year of the war Cuthbertson commanded the flotilla of 70 anti-submarine trawlers on the east coast of Scotland. During the Norwegian campaign in the spring of 1940 he volunteered for special service in the 'Gubbins Flotilla'. This was a mixed force of trawlers and 'puffer' fishing boats which operated in the fjords, supplying General Gubbins' independent companies (fore-runners of the Commandos) with stores, personnel and equipment.

They came under frequent air attack, and Cuthbertson twice had his ship sunk under him.

In October 1940 he took command of the corvette *Hibiscus*, escorting Atlantic convoys, and was awarded the DSC for successfully attacking U-boats. Undeterred by his experience in *Zinnia*, he took command of *Snowflake*, another corvette, in October 1941, escorting Atlantic and Arctic convoys. He was Mentioned in Dispatches for *Snowflake*'s part in defending convoy QP 11 in May 1942.

Cuthbertson then commanded the destroyer *Scimitar* until July 1943, operating in the North Atlantic; promoted Commander, he took command of the new frigate *Helford* as Senior Officer of an Escort Flotilla.

In 1944 *Helford* went out to the Far East to join the British Pacific Fleet, and Cuthbertson was again Mentioned in Dispatches after escorting two floating docks under tow from Cochin in India to the fleet base at Manus in the Admiralty Islands. He was proud that when *Helford* came home after a two-and-a-half-year commission she still had the same ship's company with which she had sailed.

In 1946 Cuthbertson was commander of the Royal Naval Victory Parade Camp in Kensington Gardens and marched at the head of the Navy's column during the parade. He returned to Union Castle in 1946, and was elected a young brother of Trinity House and a member of the Honourable Company of Master Mariners. His last sea appointment was as Master of the *Sandown Castle* in 1948.

He then came ashore and set up as a nautical consultant and assessor. In 1953 he was appointed a nautical surveyor in the Marine Survey Service of the Ministry of Transport and Civil Aviation.

He was twice married and had a son by his first marriage.

CAPTAIN ROGER HICKS

From *The Times*, London, 27 October 1997

Captain Roger Hicks, DSO, wartime destroyer commander, died on 12 October aged 87. He was born on 27 December 1909.

In May 1940, in the desperate last hours before the Germans captured Boulogne, Roger Hicks, as captain of the destroyer HMS *Vimiera*, played a prominent role in evacuating several thousand men of the 20th Guards Brigade from the port. Of the group of destroyers sent in to try to rescue the Guards, *Vimiera* was the only one to return twice to Boulogne, which she did in the evening of 23 May 1940, and again in the small hours of 24 May. In doing so she took off 2,400 men of the Welsh and Irish Guards, who were brought back to Britain to fight another day.

There was something appropriate about *Vimiera* being employed in this hazardous work. She was one of the destroyers that had escorted two battalions of the brigade across to France in the first place. On 21 May, *Vimiera*, under Hicks's command, and the destroyer HMS *Whitshed*, had seen the 2nd Irish Guards and the 2nd Welsh Guards and their supporting anti-tank batteries safely ashore at Boulogne, whose defence was considered vital as a supply port for the British Expeditionary Force in the aftermath of the German breakthrough to the mouth of the Somme at Abbeville, the previous day.

It was already too late. Guderian's panzers had by now an irresistible momentum. Although the German XIX Corps war diary was to record "in and around Boulogne the enemy is fighting tenaciously for every inch of ground in order to prevent the important harbour falling into German hands," the Guards really had their backs to the wall from the moment of embarkation. In spite of this, both the Welsh and Irish battalions repulsed several tank attacks.

But at daybreak on 23 May, the Germans captured Fort de la Creche, on the heights to the north of Boulogne, from its French defenders. From that moment their artillery, mortars and machine guns were able to fire at will into the town and harbour. In addition, air attacks pounded British shipping anchored in the roads.

Against this unpromising backdrop the Royal Navy was ordered in to try to bring the Guards off. In addition to *Vimiera* and *Whitshed*, four other British destroyers and several French ships drew in towards the shore and shelled German artillery positions and machine gun nests. But a heavy toll was exacted by German guns and bombers. The captains of both HMS *Keith* and HMS *Vimy* were killed on their bridges and the French destroyer *Orage* was sunk.

It was obvious that an evacuation must be attempted immediately and Admiral Ramsay, as Flag Officer Dover, ordered Hicks and the captain of *Whitshed* to enter the harbour. By this time the enemy were swarming into the town and as the destroyers went alongside they were engaging German tanks over open sights. Amid a ferocious exchange of fire, each destroyer embarked 1,000 guardsmen and carried them to safety. As they withdrew, the other destroyers came alongside and although all sustained some damage hundreds more troops were brought off.

Darkness fell, and that appeared all that could be achieved. But Ramsay, at Dover, was aware that a substantial body of troops was still onshore. Although by this time the Germans were masters of the scene, he reluctantly gave the order that Hicks should return and attempt to rescue them. At 1.40 a.m. on 24 May, *Vimiera* steamed into Boulogne harbour which had, after the tumult of the previous day, fallen strangely silent. In a feverish hour, during which her officers and men fervently hopped that there would not be a repetition of the German assaults, 1,400 more guardsmen were surreptitiously re-embarked and Hicks thankfully gave the order to slip and proceed to sea. *Vimiera* was by this time dangerously overloaded and in addition was dive-bombed as she stole away from the French coast. But thanks to skilful shiphandling she reached Dover safely. For his part in the audacious rescue from under the noses of the enemy of so many valuable fighting troops, Hicks was awarded a well-earned DSO.

Roger Bertram Nettleton Hicks was born at St. Columb, Cornwall, the son of an Army officer. His father died in 1915 from wounds suffered on the Western Front. Hicks was educated at Winchester, where he was a War scholar, joining the Royal Navy in 1927. Thereafter, he served in the heavy cruiser HMS *Devonshire* on the China Station and in the light cruiser HMS *Danae* in the West Indies. During the pre-war crises of the Italian invasion of Abyssinia and the Spanish Civil War he was, first, standing by at Alexandria in the destroyer HMS *Firedrake* and later patrolling the Mediterranean.

In 1940 he took command of HMS *Vimiera*, in whose name hangs a small tale. The name first occurs in the Royal Navy in 1808, the year of the Peninsular War Battle of Vimiero, after which the ship was (incorrectly) christened. The mistake was perpetuated in her successor, Hicks's command. (Another curious such case is HMS *Curaçoa* of which no fewer than four have been thus incorrectly named after the Netherlands Antilles island of Curaçao, since 1809.)

Hicks next commanded the destroyer HMS *Antelope*, which was sent to search for survivors after the sinking of the battlecruiser HMS *Hood* by the German battleship *Bismarck*. He also helped to evacuate Norwegian and Russian coal-miners from Spitzbergen. In the autumn of 1941, Hicks was appointed to the staff of the Commander-in-Chief, East Indies, who had specifically requested a young destroyer officer with command experience. Unfortunately, the tide of Japanese victories in the Far East and the increasing importance of the Royal Navy's war against the U-boats in the Atlantic meant that Hicks was stranded in a comparative backwater at a vital stage of his career. He found himself in Colombo, latterly on the staff of Flag Officer Ceylon, until 1944.

Returning to England, Hicks commanded the destroyer HMS *Zest* on Murmansk convoys and helped to evacuate Norwegian civilians from the island of Soroy, then threatened by retreating German troops. For this, he was appointed an honorary Knight First Class of the Norwegian Order of St. Olav. On VE Day *Zest* was at Copenhagen for a jubilant welcome, and at the end of the war in the Far East Hicks was in Singapore, in charge of working parties of surrendered Japanese naval personnel.

After further sea and staff appointments, in 1956 he took command of the aircraft carrier HMS *Warrior*, which was to have taken the nuclear bombs to Christmas Island for the Pacific tests. In the event, the bombs were flown out, but *Warrior* acted as the general mother ship to the various naval units taking part. On arrival at Christmas Island in March 1957, Hicks was appointed Commodore of the Operation 'Grapple' naval task group, as its putative commander had fallen ill in Britain.

Three tests were carried out over Malden Island, and on completion of the third, Hicks flew down to New Zealand, to thank the authorities for the loan of two frigates which had taken part in the operation. His last appointment was as

Chief of Staff to the Commander-in-Chief, the Nore. He retired in 1960.

In 1964 Hicks returned to his native Cornwall, serving as a Bodmin JP and being active in a wide range of local affairs. Hicks's first wife, Iris died in 1941. He married, secondly, in 1946, Joan Say, and is survived by her, their daughter and son, and by the daughter and son of his first marriage.

PROFESSOR SIR HARRY HINSLEY
From the *Daily Telegraph*, London, 18 February 1998
Naval intelligence expert who helped to break the Enigma code and went on to become Master of St. John's College, Cambridge.

Professor Sir Harry Hinsley, who has died aged 79, played a leading part in breaking the German wartime Enigma code and assembling the Ultra intelligence from decoded messages; later he became Master of St. John's College, Cambridge, and Vice-Chancellor of the University of Cambridge.

When war broke out, Hinsley was a second-year undergraduate at St. John's, but within a few months he found himself pitch-forked into the Naval section at the Government Code and Cypher School at Bletchley Park. At Bletchley, Hinsley became the leading expert on the wireless organization of the German Navy, listening for clues that might be of value to the Admiralty's Operational Intelligence Centre (OIC).

Hinsley was one of the few channels of liaison between Bletchley and the OIC. "I used a direct telephone line which I had to activate by turning a handle energetically before speaking," Hinsley remembered. "On this I spoke, a disembodied voice, to people who had never met me."

At first the Admiralty showed little interest in his reports, for example ignoring his warnings "something unusual was taking place in the Baltic", shortly before Germany invaded Norway.

A breakthrough came in 1941 when Hinsley concluded that German trawlers stationed off Iceland were carrying the Enigma machines, although they were not using them. In May, the OIC arranged the capture of one of the trawlers; among the material seized were the Enigma settings for June. More cryptanalytical material was fortuitously secured from a captured U-boat, *U-110*. A second trawler was captured in June, and within a month the mastery by the Bletchley team of naval Enigma was complete.

Hinsley and his team were then able to analyse decodes of Admiral Dönitz's signals to his U-boats. This crucial intelligence helped to win the battle against the U-boats in the Atlantic.

As an interpreter of decrypts Hinsley was unrivalled. His ability to sense from tiny clues in the decrypts that something unusual was afoot was legendary. He was well versed in the ways of navies, having on more than one occasion spent time with the Home Fleet at Scapa Flow, where he was known as 'The Cardinal'.

He later recalled: "I knew Dönitz best of all. He ran the U-boats like a prep school. There was a time when I could tell you whether Dönitz was personally on duty. I could tell from the way he planned it. He was good. Mind you, he had a fairly rigid mind."

For 30 years after the war ended, Hinsley, like the other Bletchley Park staff, kept his knowledge to himself. He claimed he never found this difficult, partly because he had been able to discuss it with his wife, another Bletchley hand.

"It was a lovely life," Hinsley recalled, "Bletchley Park was like a university. We lived the anarchic lives of students. There was a tremendous social life, parties, amateur dramatics, lots of young ladies and lots of young men."

Francis Harry Hinsley was born at Walsall on 26 November 1918, the son of a wagoner who drove a horse and cart between the local ironworks and the railway station. He attended Queen Mary's Grammar School, Walsall, and in 1937, won a scholarship to St. John's College, Cambridge, to read history.

Following his wartime service, Hinsley returned to St. John's as a research fellow. He became a lecturer in history in 1949. In 1965 he was made a Reader in the History of International Relations, and in 1969, Professor. His publications include *Command of the Sea* (1950), *Hitler's Strategy* (1951), *Sovereignty* (1966), *Nationalism and the International System* (1973).

In 1979, Hinsley became Master of St. John's College, then in 1981, Vice-Chancellor of Cambridge University, a post he held for two years. He had the difficult task of implementing reductions in the numbers of academic staff at the University, a task he achieved through an early retirement scheme, helping to avoid redundancies.

Harry Hinsley was a slightly built, bespectacled figure known for his refreshing ability to bring the past to life. Unable to break the habit of his days at Bletchley Park, he would amuse his students by eavesdropping retrospectively on the intimate conversations of the great, irrigating the driest tracts of European history. Through clouds of pipe tobacco smoke, partially dispersed by the vigorous gestures of their mentor, undergraduates, seated in the odd clearing on his book-strewn floor, would be asked: "Imagine Charlemagne on the blower to the Pope. What do you think he is saying?"

In 1972, Hinsley had been appointed official historian of British Intelligence in the war, heading a team of four historians. Their study, *British Intelligence in the Second World War*, published in five volumes between 1979 and 1990, was a monumental survey of the influence of intelligence on strategy and operations. It described how British Intelligence which, at the beginning of the war, had been a backwater, starved of funds and hidebound by official turf wars, overcame these handicaps to make a vital contribution to the Allied war effort.

The triumph of Hinsley's narrative was the integration of his account of the intelligence picture with the decision of the commanders in the field and in Whitehall. He described the failures as well as the successes of this relationship. For example, when Bletchley warned Montgomery of Hitler's intention to hold the mouth of the Scheldt, after the whirlwind advance from Normandy, Montgomery chose to mount the Arnhem operation nonetheless. Not only was Arnhem a defeat, but the defence of the Scheldt robbed the Allies of the ability to build a strong base of supply close to the German border, so setting back the invasion of Germany by several months.

Hinsley's narrative concluded that the intelligence gleaned at Bletchley Park was not a war winner, but was a "war-shortener". As he put it: "Without it Rommel would have got to Alexandria. The U-boats would not have done us in. But they would have got us into serious shortages and put another year on the war."

Hinsley deliberately wrote his account "sans monstres, sans héros", but some found it altogether too dry. Sir Maurice Oldfield, the former Director General of MI6, described it as "remarkable that there are hardly any names in it. You get the impression that the intelligence war was won by committees in Whitehall."

But Hinsley was unrepentant: "It was meant to be bloodless," he said. Besides, he saw the achievement of the Bletchley code-breakers as a genuine collective effort.

Hinsley later provided a more colourful account of life at Bletchley Park when he edited a collection of memoirs by people who worked there. *Codebreakers: The Inside Story of Bletchley Park* (1993) was launched at a reception and reunion in the Imperial War Museum to which the old Bletchley Park hands were invited through a coded invitation placed in the 'Peterborough' column of the *Daily Telegraph*.

In 1988 Hinsley had been appointed to review the findings of a team appointed by the British Government to investigate the alleged involvement of President Kurt Waldheim of Austria in the execution of 13 British commandos who disappeared in 1944 after being captured in Greece. The team concluded that there was no proof that Waldheim was directly involved or that British authorities attempted a cover-up to protect him.

Harry Hinsley was knighted in 1985. He married, in 1946, Hilary Brett. They had one son and two daughters.

LIEUTENANT HERBERT 'GINGER' LE BRETON
From the *Daily Telegraph*, London, 15 October 1997

Ginger Le Breton, who has died aged 90, was the only sailor to take part in the mutiny of the Atlantic Fleet at Invergordon in September 1931 and then to go on to be commissioned as an officer. Le Breton was an Able Seaman

Torpedoman in the cruiser HMS *Dorsetshire* when, as a result of a financial crisis in 1931, drastic cuts were announced in public sector pay. In the Navy, one shilling (5p) a day was to be cut from everyone's pay.

A shilling meant very little to an Admiral. But to an Able Seaman on four shillings a day it was a cut of 25 per cent. Many sailors, who had wives and young families and rents to pay, faced ruin. An incompetent and insensitive Board of Admiralty, who had failed utterly to present the Navy's case to the Government, also bungled the announcement of the cuts. The first the sailors at Invergordon heard of them was through rumour and the newspapers, followed by bald statements on the ships' notice boards.

At that time, there was no effective means of airing lower-deck grievances. The so-called 'normal channels' were known to be useless. Le Breton and thousands of other sailors had to choose between patriotism and justice. They chose to stand against injustice.

Thus, as the sailors had decided the previous Sunday, early on the morning of Tuesday, 15 September 1931, when the fleet was due to put to sea for exercises, crowds of defiant sailors, in moods of mixed exhilaration and trepidation, mustered on the fo'c's'les of their ships and began to cheer. Echoing Spithead in 1797, the cheering swept down the lines of warships, as the signal for the mutiny to begin. It was a very polite affair, more a sit-in than a mutiny. There was no violence. The sailors bore their officers no ill-will. Their grievance was with the Government and the Admiralty.

In *Dorsetshire*, Le Breton was among 100 sailors who sat down on the mess deck and refused to fall in for work. "Eventually the Commander came forward to speak to us," he recalled. "He started talking about what we were doing wrong, and letting down the Navy and then eventually said: 'Right, everybody on deck.' He gave us an order. And we just sat there. Did nothing. Just looked at him. And he looked at us and his face went red. So angry. You could see the anger on his face. Then he said: 'All right then, if you won't go aft, then go down to the lower mess deck,' where we would have been battened down. We just laughed."

Dorsetshire's torpedomen chose Le Breton as their delegate to make their case to the Torpedo Officer who was, according to Le Breton, "understanding and sympathetic".

"There was then a pipe that the Captain (Arthur John Power, a much-loved and respected officer) would talk to us on the fo'c's'le. He strolled along, with no other officers, his cap under his arm. This was a great piece of leadership and psychology. He more or less staked his career. We liked him. We trusted him. After a few sensible words, saying the Admiral had gone down to London, there was nothing more we could do, and the situation was in hand, he said that he had work to do, and was going aft, and he hoped we would do the same. Putting his cap on, he walked aft. The bugler sounded 'Fall In'. And that is just what we did

– walked aft." The mutiny in *Dorsetshire* was over, but in some ships it lasted until the Friday, and eventually ended in a partial victory for the lower deck. The shilling a day was scrapped, and the sailors' pay cut by only 10 per cent.

Le Breton and his fellow mutineers had sent a seismic political and financial shock around the world, and forced Britain off the gold standard. The home naval ports were soon swarming with MI5 and Special Branch agents, looking for mutineers and evidence of communist influence in the Navy. About 100 'ringleaders' were rounded up. Some of them, on mere hearsay evidence provided by their own shipmates, were subjected to 'physical training' which was unpleasantly close to punishment and then, although most had character and conduct assessments of 'Very Good, Superior', summarily discharged from the Royal Navy as 'SNLR' – Services No Longer Required.

Two of *Dorsetshire*'s torpedomen, friends of Le Breton's, suffered this fate, on the word of another torpedoman whom the Commander had asked to watch out for 'ringleaders'. Le Breton himself was very fortunate not to be picked out as a prominent mutineer. Apart from his distinctive ginger hair, he was well known on board, playing football for the ship, and, as the only lower deck member of the ship's cricket team, being personally acquainted with many of the officers. So he was relieved to see that his next annual assessment was still 'Very Good, Superior'.

Meanwhile, a humiliated and vengeful Admiralty Board, who had themselves been entirely responsible for the debacle, searched for scapegoats and found them in the officers, many of whom had their careers permanently blighted, merely because they had been serving in ships which had mutinied. The Torpedo Officer who had been so sympathetic to Le Breton was promoted to Commander only years later, when he was on the Retired List.

Herbert William Le Breton, known from his earliest days as 'Ginger', was born on 22 June 1907 and joined the Training Ship *Impregnable* at Devonport as a Boy Seaman, Second Class, in 1922. His first ship was HMS *Resolution*, in which he gained accelerated advancement to Ordinary Seaman, aged 17. He qualified as a Torpedoman at HMS *Defiance*, the Devonport Torpedo School, in 1926 and gained a First-Class pass in the Higher Educational Test for warrant rank the next year.

After two and a half years in the destroyer HMS *Vanquisher*, he joined *Dorsetshire* for her first commission in 1930, and remained with her in South Africa (during which time he ran an illicit book-making business). In 1935 he became Chief Quartermaster in the aircraft carrier HMS *Glorious* in the Mediterranean, at the time of the Abyssinian crisis. He came home to undergo the course for Torpedo Gunner, qualifying and being promoted to Warrant Rank on 1 July 1937. "I was now Mister Le Breton," he said, "a very big day in my life."

He was the Gunner (T) in the destroyer HMS *Basilisk* from 1937 to 1939, and then joined the destroyer HMS *Hasty* for a hectic first 20 months of the war: capturing the German merchant ship *Morea* off the Portuguese coast in February 1940; taking part in the Norwegian campaign in April; in the sinking of the Italian cruiser *Bartolomeo Colleoni* off Crete in July; and joining with HMS *Havock* to sink the Italian submarine *Berillo* off Egypt in October.

By the time Le Breton left *Hasty* in May 1941, she had been engaged in the night action off Cape Matapan in March when three Italian heavy cruisers and two destroyers were sunk, and in the evacuation of the British Army from Greece in April.

Until June 1943 Le Breton commanded the trawler *Redwing*, *Defiance*'s torpedo target and recovery vessel in Looe Bay. He was then appointed to the fast minelayer HMS *Ariadne*, serving with the US 7th Fleet in the Pacific until 1945. His last appointment before retiring in 1948 with the War Service rank of Lieutenant was as *Defiance*'s Mining and Explosives Instructor.

After 26 years in the Royal Navy, Le Breton then spent 24 years in the licensed trade, becoming a well-known figure in Old Portsmouth as landlord of the Dolphin Hotel in the High Street. To the end of his life 'Ginger' Le Breton was unrepentant about his part in the mutiny. In the programme 'Mutiny' in the BBC series *The Call of The Sea*, he said: "I'm in no way sorry about Invergordon. I look on it with pride. Otherwise I wouldn't be telling you, if I felt I'd been a traitor. I wasn't. I was doing the right thing."

He and his wife Phyllis, whom he married in 1940, had a son.

CAPTAIN GRAHAM LUMSDEN
From the *Daily Telegraph*, London, 15 August 1995

Captain Graham Lumsden, who has died aged 81, could justifiably be described as one of the luckiest officers in the Royal Navy. In six years as a navigating officer in the Second World War, which he spent almost entirely at sea, he survived several bomb and torpedo attacks, twice had a ship sunk under him, and was unharmed when his Captain was killed next to him. His navigation also survived defective compasses, Officers of the Watch who misunderstood their course orders, and lighthouses falsely lit by the enemy to deceive Allied ships. On the day his ship ran aground, he happened to be ashore.

His war began quietly enough with a passage to Freetown, Sierra Leone, in the seaplane carrier HMS *Albatross*. The climate and the boredom of life in West Africa were enervating, and when Lumsden passed through Freetown two years later he was shocked to see the physical deterioration of his former mess-mates.

He himself was glad to be appointed to HMS *Keith*, leader of the 19th Destroyer Flotilla. In May 1940, after the German invasion of Holland, *Keith* helped to evacuate the Dutch royal family from IJmuiden, with a considerable amount of gold bullion. Later that month *Keith* and another destroyer, HMS *Vimy*, went to Boulogne to take off as many as possible of the 6,000 men surrounded in the town, including Coldstream Guards and Royal Marines.

Both ships were subjected to accurate dive-bombing attacks while alongside, and small arms fire made *Keith*'s bridge untenable. Lumsden was descending from the bridge when a sniper's bullet passed over his head and killed the Captain just behind him. The First Lieutenant, an RNR officer, asked Lumsden to take the ship to sea. "I had never conned a ship in a sternboard," Lumsden said, "and certainly not down a narrow and curving channel, peering through a small scuttle and with bullets hitting people between me and the men who would carry out my orders!

"I found myself replying, 'Of course I can, Number One!'"

Under a new captain, *Keith* took part in the Dunkirk evacuation and on 30 May embarked some 1,400 soldiers from the harbour mole. Once again she was subjected to fierce air attacks and by the evening of 31 May had expended all her anti-aircraft ammunition.

Early the next day *Keith* was dive-bombed and had to be abandoned. She was later hit again, and sank. Lumsden and the other survivors were taken off by the tug *St. Abbs*, which was herself soon bombed and sunk. Lumsden found himself swimming for his life: "Thinking of something that would powerfully reinforce my will to swim on," he said, "I found myself picturing my wife's small but beautiful backside." He reached the shore, where French sailors gave him some dry clothes.

Back at Dover, Lumsden went to the castle, where his wife, a WRNS Watchkeeper in the Cipher Room, had already seen the signal that *Keith* had been sunk and that there was no news of any survivors. She did not recognise her husband, with his oil-covered face, seaman's jersey and matelot's cap with pompom, and when she did she accused him of smelling of French perfume.

A grateful Queen Wilhelmina of the Netherlands awarded *Keith* the order of Oranje Nassau, with the rank of Chevalier. *Keith*'s officers voted that Lumsden should receive it. He was also Mentioned in Dispatches.

Lumsden was then appointed to the new light cruiser HMS *Phoebe* for two hectic years in the Mediterranean. She escorted convoys from Alexandria to Malta; covered the Army's withdrawal from Greece in April 1941 (for which Lumsden was again Mentioned in Dispatches); evacuated the Army from Crete in May (for which he was awarded the DSC); and took part in the Syrian campaign of June and July.

On a trip to Tobruk in August 1941 *Phoebe* was badly damaged by an aerial torpedo. Repaired in New York, she took part in the 'Pedestal' convoy to Malta in August 1942, one of the most spectacular naval operations of the war. In

October, when *Phoebe* was on her way to the 'Torch' landings in North Africa, she was torpedoed by a U-boat off Pointe Noire in the Congo, and again had to leave for repairs.

Lumsden was pleased by *Phoebe's* farewell signal from Admiral Cunningham, commanding the Allied Naval forces for 'Torch': "Romans Ch. 16 verses I & II". ("I commend unto you Phoebe our sister... for she hath been a succourer of many, and of myself also.")

After a few months at HMS *Dryad*, the Navigation School near Portsmouth, teaching "a course of young officers in the gentle art", Lumsden was appointed Navigating Officer of the cruiser HMS *Sheffield*. He took part in operations in the Bay of Biscay in the summer of 1943, and gave bombardment support to the Salerno landings in September. On 26 December 1943, *Sheffield* took part in the Battle of the North Cape of Norway, when ships of the Home Fleet, led by Admiral Sir Bruce Fraser, flying his flag in the battleship HMS *Duke of York*, pursued and sank the German battlecruiser *Scharnhorst*.

In a long and anxious day of manoeuvring in Arctic cold and darkness, *Scharnhorst* twice threatened convoy JW 55B on its way to Russia, and was twice driven off by the cruisers HMS *Belfast*, HMS *Norfolk* and *Sheffield*. The sharp eyesight of Lumsden and the Chief Yeoman of Signals enabled *Sheffield* to be the first to make the signal "Enemy in Sight" on both occasions. But during the pursuit *Sheffield* suffered a defect in one of her propeller shafts and had to drop back, thus missing *Scharnhorst's* final moments. Lumsden was awarded a bar to his DSC.

In 1944 Lumsden was appointed Navigating Officer of the light fleet carrier HMS *Venerable*, which joined the British Pacific Fleet and was present at the Japanese surrender of Hong Kong in August 1945.

Graham James Alexander Lumsden was born on 24 November 1913 and joined the Navy as a Cadet at Dartmouth in 1927. He served as a Midshipman in the cruiser HMS *Suffolk* on the China Station, and as a Lieutenant in the cruiser HMS *Ajax* and the aircraft carrier HMS *Courageous*, qualifying as a Navigating Officer in 1937.

Lumsden returned to *Dryad* on the Staff after the war and then served in the cruiser HMS *Superb*, and in the Admiralty Signal and Radar Establishment at Portsdown, near Portsmouth. In 1951 he relieved the Duke of Edinburgh in command of the frigate HMS *Magpie* in the Mediterranean. His last appointments before retiring in 1958 were in the Admiralty, in the Directorate of Navigation and Direction.

He married Daphne Sturrock in 1938.

CAPTAIN RALPH MEDLEY

From the *Daily Telegraph*, London, 31 August 1999

Naval officer who duelled with *Graf Spee* at the Battle of the River Plate and later helped to save an Arctic convoy from German raiders.

Captain Ralph Medley, who has died aged 92, was Operations and Intelligence Officer on the staff of Commodore Henry Harwood, who flew his broad pennant in the cruiser *Ajax* in the Battle of the River Plate in December 1939.

The German pocket battleship *Admiral Graf Spee* sailed from Wilhelmshaven on 21 August 1939 and sank the British merchant ship *Clement* off Brazil on 30 September. The Admiralty organized eight hunting groups to search worldwide for the raider. Harwood's Force 'G', of the cruiser *Exeter* and *Cumberland*, later joined by *Ajax* and *Achilles*, operated off the south-east coast of America.

By 7 December 1939, when *Graf Spee* had sunk eight ships in the Atlantic and one in the Indian Ocean, Harwood and his staff concluded that the raider would most likely head for the busy shipping routes off the River Plate. By 12 December, Harwood had concentrated his three cruisers, *Exeter*, *Ajax* and *Achilles* (*Cumberland* was in the Falklands), some 150 miles off the Plate estuary.

Early on the morning of 13 December, smoke was sighted on the north-west horizon. *Exeter* signalled: "I think it is a pocket battleship." *Graf Spee*'s shooting with her 11-inch guns was excellent, hitting and damaging *Exeter* so badly she had later to retire to the Falklands for repairs, and putting five of *Ajax*'s eight guns out of action. But *Graf Spee* also made fatal mistakes. "Her best tactic," as Medley himself summed up, "would have been to turn away from us, where the great range of her guns would have enabled her to engage only *Exeter* (with 8-inch guns) before *Ajax* and *Achilles* could get within range of her, and then attack our smaller ships with relative impunity.

"Instead, she apparently mistook these two for destroyers and allowed us all to engage her from different directions and thereby confuse her gunnery. In fact she took the only action that allowed us to defeat her."

Graf Spee took refuge in Montevideo, while Churchill and the BBC conjured up vast but entirely imaginary forces waiting outside to destroy her. *Graf Spee*'s commanding officer, Captain Hans Langsdorff, scuttled his ship then committed suicide. It was a great victory which, as Churchill said, "in a cold and dark winter warmed the cockles of our hearts." Commodore Harwood was promoted to Rear Admiral, and Medley was Mentioned in Dispatches.

Medley remained on the South American Station for another two years, serving in eight different cruisers, before coming home in December 1941 and taking command of the destroyer *Beagle* in the Greenock Escort Force early in 1942.

In April 1942, *Beagle* was part of the escort of the Arctic convoy QP 11, homeward bound from Murmansk. On 29 April, the cruiser *Edinburgh* was hit by two torpedoes from *U-456*. Her stern was blown off and she started back towards Murmansk at slow speed, escorted by two of the convoy's destroyers. She later had to be sunk by Allied forces.

Meanwhile, on the afternoon 1 May 1942, QP 11 was attacked by three large German destroyers. The convoy's four remaining destroyers, *Amazon*, *Beverley*, *Bulldog* and *Beagle*, had had their after guns removed to make more room for depth charges. They mounted six 4.7-inch and three 4-inch guns between them, with antiquated fire control systems, against the Germans' modern six 5.9-inch and five 5-inch guns.

In theory, it should have been a clear victory for the enemy, followed by the destruction of the convoy, but the four elderly destroyers, audaciously led by Commander Maxwell Richmond in *Bulldog*, defended with such vigour that they convinced their opponents that they were much stronger than they actually were.

Over a period of several hours the destroyers drove off five enemy lunges at the convoy; *Amazon* was hit and damaged and one convoy straggler was sunk, but QP 11 was otherwise unscathed. Medley and the other three destroyer captains were all awarded the DSO.

Ralph Cyril Medley was born on 2 October 1906 and joined the Navy as a cadet in 1920, going to Osborne and Dartmouth. His first ship as a Midshipman in 1924 was the old coal-burning battleship *Benbow* and he went on to serve as a Sub-Lieutenant in the cruiser *Cornwall* on the China Station. Between 1928 and 1936, he served as a Lieutenant in the sloop *Sandwich* and the cruiser *Devonshire* on the China Station, and in the destroyer *Crusader* in the Home Fleet.

His first commands, in 1938 and 1939, were the destroyers *Stronghold* and *Beagle* (for the first time). In 1943, Medley was loaned to the Royal Canadian Navy as Senior Officer of C3 Escort Group, commanding the destroyers *Saskatchewan* and *Burnham*, and later the frigate *Prince Rupert*. The largest Atlantic convoy C3 escorted was colossal: 150 ships, in 15 columns spread across a front of ten miles, with ten ships in each column, carrying a million tons of cargo. C3 at that time consisted of *Prince Rupert* and five corvettes, but the convoy crossed without loss. *Prince Rupert* assisted in the sinking of *U-575*, west of Cape Finisterre, on 13 March 1944.

In 1944, Medley was appointed Staff Officer (Operations) to the Commander-in-Chief Mediterranean, Admiral Sir John Cunningham in Italy, and then to Admiral Sir Algernon Willis in Malta. He was appointed OBE in 1946. He was disappointed to be sent to Portsmouth as Drafting Commander in 1946, which he thought was a dead-end job, but he was promoted Captain in 1947. A year later, he took command of the frigate *Cardigan Bay* in the

Mediterranean and then went out to China as Captain (F), 4th Frigate Flotilla.

Medley was appointed Deputy Director of the Operations Division in 1950, and Senior Naval Directing Staff Officer at the Joint Services Staff College, Latimer, in 1952. His last appointment, from 1955 until he retired in 1957, was as Chief of Staff to the French Admiral Jaujard at NATO Headquarters, Fontainebleau, with the rank of Commodore. From 1960 to 1971, Medley was Clerk to the Worshipful Company of Saddlers, and he was a Freeman of the City of London. He was one of the participants who advised on Powell and Pressburger's 1956 film *The Battle of the River Plate*, and he also assisted with Mike Powell's book on the battle. He himself published several books on the history of the Medley family.

In 1934, he married Letty Boyce. As a First Officer WRNS, she was appointed MBE in 1944 for her work as Senior Cypher Officer, Plymouth Command, during Operation 'Neptune'. They had two daughters.

Bibliography

The following list is a combination of sources for the previously-published pieces in this anthology and other secondary material. The anthologist and the publishers are very grateful for permission to reproduce this material. Every effort has been made to acknowledge all copyright owners prior to going to press. Conway Maritime Press deeply regrets any omissions or inaccuracies. These will be rectified at the earliest opportunity.

Brown, David, *Warship Losses of World War Two* (Arms and Armour Press, London, 1990)

Deighton, Len, *Blood, Tears and Folly* (Jonathan Cape: Reprinted by Random House, London, 1993)

Foynes, Julian, *The Battle of the East Coast* (Self-published, 1994)

Gallery, Rear Admiral Daniel V., USN, Ret'd, *We Captured a U-Boat* (Sidgwick & Jackson, London: Reprinted by Macmillan Publishers Ltd., London, 1958)

Hamilton, John, *The War At Sea 1939-1945* (Blandford Press, 1986)

Hawkins, Ian, *B-17s Over Berlin* (Batsford Brassey Inc., Washington DC, 1995)

Hawkins, Ian, *The Munster Raid: Before and After* (FNP Military Division, Connecticut, 1999)

Higham, Charles, *Trading with the Enemy* (Delacourte Press, New York, 1987)

Horning, Arthur, *In the Footsteps of a Flying Boat* (Carleton Press Inc., New York, 1994)

Lenton, H. T., & J. J. Colledge, *Warships of World War II, Part II: Destroyers and Submarines* (Ian Allan Publishing Ltd., 1962)

Lewin, Ronald, *Ultra Goes To War* (Hutchinson's, Reprinted by Random House, London, 1978)

Lombard-Hobson, Captain S., RN, Retd., *A Sailor's War* (Orbis Publishing: Little, Brown & Co., London, 1983)

March, Edgar J., *British Destroyers 1892-1953* (Seeley Service & Co., London, 1966)

Middlebrook, Martin, *Convoy* (Allen Lane, Penguin Books, London, 1978)

Monsarrat, Nicholas, *The Cruel Sea* (Cassell & Co. Ltd., London, 1951)

Rohwer, J., & G. Hummelchen, *Chronology of the War At Sea* (Ian Allan, 1972)

Roskill, Captain S. W., RN, *The Secret Capture* (HarperCollins, 1959)

Ruegg, Bob, & Arnold Hague, *Convoys To Russia* (World Ship Society, 1992)

Ruge, Vice Admiral Friedrich, *Sea Warfare 1939-1945: A German Viewpoint*, trans. Commander M. G. Saunders, RN (Cassell & Co. Ltd., London, 1957)

Smith, Peter C., *Hold the Narrow Sea* (Naval Institute Press, 1984)

Wilkinson, B. J., T. P. Stopford & D. Taylor (eds), *The A to Z of Royal Naval Ships' Badges 1919-1989* (Neptune Books, 1987)

Woodman, Richard, *Arctic Convoys* (John Murray, London, 1994)

Wynn, Kenneth, *U-Boat Operations of the Second World War* (Chatham Publishing, 1997)

Newspapers, Periodicals, Association Newsletters

Bulletin Air War 1939-1945 (Editor: Mr Henny Kwik), Studiegroep Luchtoorlog, Holland.

Cambridge Evening News, Cambridge, Cambs., UK.

Daily Express, London, UK.

Daily Telegraph, London, UK.

East Anglian Daily Times, Ipswich, Suffolk, UK.

Eastern Daily Press, Norwich, Norfolk, UK.

Evening Standard, London, UK.

HMS *Cavalier* Association.

HMS *Ganges* Association.

HM Ships *Beagle*, *Boadicea* & *Bulldog* Association.

LST Scuttlebutt, United States Navy LST Association, Toledo, Ohio, USA.

Mendlesham Memories, 34th Bombardment Group (H) Memorial Association (8th USAAF), Texas, USA.

Milwaukee Sentinel, Milwaukee, Wisconsin, USA.

Navy News, HMS *Victory*, Portsmouth Dockyard, Portsmouth, Hampshire, UK.

News, 392nd Bombardment Group (H) Memorial Association (8th USAAF), Frankfort, Indiana, USA.

Retired Officers Association, Alexandria, Virginia, USA.

Royal Air Force Bomber Command Association, RAF Museum, Hendon, London, UK.

Royal Air Force Aerospace Museum, Cosford, Shropshire, UK.

Royal Hospital School Association.

Sea Breezes Magazine, Braddan, Isle of Man.

South Western Star (1945), Battersea, London, UK.

Submariners' Old Comrades' Association.

The Corps Of Guides: HMS *Victory*, HM Naval Base, Portsmouth, Hampshire, UK. (Via Ron Bannister & Peter Green.)

The New Yorker, New York, USA.

The Times, London, UK.

'V & W' Class Destroyer Association.

Warship World Magazine, Liskeard, Cornwall, UK.

Yorkshire Post, Leeds, West Yorkshire, UK.

Index